W. H. AUDEN

PROSE

VOLUME I: 1926–1938

THE COMPLETE

WORKS OF

W. H. AUDEN

POEMS

PLAYS (WITH CHRISTOPHER ISHERWOOD)

LIBRETTI (WITH CHESTER KALLMAN)

PROSE

W. H. AUDEN

PROSE

AND
TRAVEL BOOKS IN
PROSE AND
VERSE

VOLUME I

□

1926–1938

EDITED BY

Edward Mendelson

PRINCETON UNIVERSITY
PRESS

Published by Princeton University Press, 41 William Street, Princeton, New Jersey 08540

ALL RIGHTS RESERVED

Library of Congress Cataloging-in-Publication Data
Auden, W. H. (Wystan Hugh), 1907–1973.
Prose and travel books in prose and verse   /   W. H. Auden ;
edited by Edward Mendelson.
p.   cm. — (The Complete works of W. H. Auden)
"This book (v. 1) contains all of Auden's prose from 1926 thru 1938,
and is the first of several projected vols. of his completed prose.
The book also includes the complete prose, verse, and photographs from
Auden's 2 travel books, Letters from Iceland, written in
collaboration with Louis MacNeice, and Journey to a War,
written in collaboration with Christopher Isherwood"—
Publisher's info.
Includes bibliographical references and index.
Contents: v. 1. Prose, 1926–1938.
ISBN 0-691-06803-8 (alk. paper   :   cl)
I. Mendelson, Edward. II. Title. III. Series: Auden, W. H.
(Wystan Hugh), 1907–1973. Works. 1996.
PR6001.U4A6   1996
818'.5208—dc20   95-38162

This book has been composed in Linotron Baskerville

Princeton University Press books are printed on
acid-free paper and meet the guidelines for permanence
and durability of the Committee on Production
Guidelines for Book Longevity of
the Council on Library Resources

Printed in the United States of America by
Princeton Academic Press

2   4   6   8   10   9   7   5   3   1

CONTENTS

.

JOURNEY TO A WAR

APPENDICES

TEXTUAL NOTES

PREFACE

THIS volume, the third to be published in a complete edition of Auden's works, includes the essays, reviews, and other prose that he published or prepared for publication from the start of his career until he left England for America in January 1939. It also includes the complete prose, verse, and illustrations in his two travel books, *Letters from Iceland*, written in collaboration with Louis MacNeice, and *Journey to a War*, written in collaboration with Christopher Isherwood. Further volumes of Auden's prose are projected. They will be followed by a complete edition of Auden's poems. The two volumes in the edition already published contain his complete plays, libretti, and other dramatic writings. The texts in this edition are, wherever possible, newly edited from Auden's manuscripts, and the notes report variant readings from all published versions.

ACKNOWLEDGEMENTS

EVERY detail of the text and notes in this volume has benefitted from the learning and intelligence of Nicholas Jenkins. The entire edition is based on years of research by B. C. Bloomfield, followed by many more years of his advice. Don Bachardy labored patiently and generously to make possible a detailed account of the composition of *Journey to a War*. Cheryl Mendelson's expert criticism was, as always, indistinguishable from warm encouragement.

For help with many difficulties, I am grateful to Jill Balcon, Kathleen Bell, Michael Black, John Bodley, Katherine Bucknell, Paul Day, Nicholas Dennys, Valerie Eliot, John Fuller, Sir Rupert Hart-Davis, Christopher Hawtree, Andrew Hewson, Samuel Hynes, Christopher Isherwood, John Johnson, Charles Madge, Magnus Magnusson, Naomi Mitchison, Joseph Needham, Charles Plumb, Peter H. Salus, Janet Adam Smith, Stan Smith, Arnold Snodgrass, Sir Stephen and Lady Spender, Julian Symons, Kathleen Tinkel, Robert Woof, T. C. Worsley, Michael Yates, and Chungchen Yeh.

The explanatory notes to "Auden and MacNeice: Their Last Will and Testament" in *Letters from Iceland* were written with Richard Davenport-Hines, without whose learning and ingenuity the task of annotation would scarcely have been imaginable. He and I were able to complete these notes only through the generous help of friends who responded to persistent requests with unabating kindness. Among those who deserve to be listed as collaborative authors of the notes are Walter Allen, Keith Brace, Sean Day-Lewis, Sir Frank Kermode, Dan MacNeice, Paul Morgan, Peter Parker, Christopher Phipps, Sir Christopher Pinsent, Bart., Janet Adam Smith, Sir Stephen and Lady Spender, and Jon Stallworthy. One of the more complex annotations derives from *Holman Hunt and "The Light of the World,"* by Jeremy Maas. For other information on the bequests in the poem, we are indebted to Lord Annan, Bernard Bergonzi, Sir Isaiah Berlin, Nancy Binyon, B. C. Bloomfield, L. A. Burton, Gabriel Carritt, Elsie Duncan-Jones, Gavin Ewart, Lord Hailsham, Marybelle B. Hanna, Alan Heuser, Arend Hubrecht, Marie-Jaqueline Lancaster, Sir Hugh Lloyd-Jones, Robert Medley, Charles Monteith, F. E. Pardoe, Dr A. D. B. Poole, Michael Rosenthal, Dr I. A. Shapiro, Maria Twist, Peter Vansittart, John Whitehead, Michael Yates, and William Zinsser.

The curators and staffs of many libraries helped make my work on this volume feel almost luxurious. I continue to be indebted above all to Francis O. Mattson, Stephen Crook, and Philip Milito at the Henry W.

and Albert A. Berg Collection of the New York Public Library, and to the curators of all the many departments of the Columbia University Library. I received assistance beyond all obligation from Patrick J. Stevens at the Fiske Icelandic Collection at the Cornell University Library. My warm thanks also go to Katie Sambrook at the Birmingham University Library; Robert Bertholf and Michael Basinski at the Poetry/Rare Books Collection at the State University of New York at Buffalo; Krista L. Ovist at the University of Chicago Library; Jean Archibald and John V. Howard at the Edinburgh University Library; Christopher Sheppard at the Leeds University Library; Michael Bott and David Sutton at the Reading University Library; Sigþrúður Jónasdóttir at the Borgarbókasafn Reykjavíkur; Cathy Henderson at the Harry Ransom Humanities Research Center at the University of Texas at Austin; Lori Curtis at the University of Tulsa Library; and, for much assistance over many years, the curators and staff at the School of Oriental and African Studies Library, the India Office Library, the Yale University Library, the Princeton University Library, and the Harvard University Library.

At the BBC Written Archives Centre at Caversham Park, I received assistance and courtesies from John Jordan, Jacqueline Kavanagh, Cedric Messina, J. P. Mullins, and Trevor White. At Oxford University Press, I was helped by Peter Foden, Peter Sutcliffe, and Kim Scott Walwyn. At the British Film Institute, Susan Woods and others found solutions to apparently intractable problems.

Jane Lincoln Taylor, who edited the manuscript for Princeton University Press with sympathy and attention, caught errors that had escaped all previous editors. Beth Gianfagna's extraordinary expertise and care immeasurably assisted in the production of this and earlier volumes of the edition. Auden's readers will share my continually deepening gratitude to Jan Lilly for the clarity and elegance of the design.

INTRODUCTION

IN his essays and reviews in the 1930s Auden tried to find arguments that could promote justice, and a vocabulary and style in which justice could be comprehended and praised. He wrote about biology, psychology, education, politics, literature, drama, religion, and love, but his constant theme was the condition he called duality: the separation of instinct and intellect, unconscious mind and deliberate will, collective action and individual thought, or, for an artist, the subject matter shared with his audience and the concealed technique of his workshop. Auden's poems and prose presupposed the personal and social costs of duality. But his poems, except for a few experiments in propaganda, explored the complexity of the problem, while his prose, except for a few experiments in parable, tried to recommend ways in which the problem could be solved. The division of the secret labyrinths of his poems from the lucid highways of his prose was itself one of the dualities he tried to overcome in the 1930s by learning a more public style for his poetry and a more personal style for his prose.

Auden's first published essays were the prefaces he wrote at the end of his first and second years at Oxford for the 1926 and 1927 volumes of the undergraduate annual *Oxford Poetry*. He wrote both prefaces in collaboration with coeditors, the first with his distant acquaintance Charles Plumb, the second with his close friend Cecil Day-Lewis. Both prefaces displayed the arch, nervous self-consciousness of undergraduate ambition. In the 1927 preface, which Auden half-seriously told his friends would be as important as the preface to *Lyrical Ballads*, he acknowledged that an intelligent reader might experience distaste when reading the poets of a generation to whom "no universalized system—political, religious or metaphysical—has been bequeathed", and he placed the blame on centuries of "acedia and unabashed glorification of the subjective". Even if the poems gave pleasure, they were "but an infinitesimal progression towards a new synthesis" that the preface made no effort to imagine or describe.

After he left Oxford in 1928 Auden spent ten months in Germany, and, as he recalled in "Letter to Lord Byron", "ceased to see the world in terms of verse." A few months before his allowance from his parents came to an end on his twenty-third birthday, in February 1930, he began to look for paying jobs. In the autumn of 1929 he worked in London for a few months as a tutor to the son of the sister of one of his friends, but he hoped for something more permanent. In November he wrote to Naomi Mitchison, whom he had met through his Oxford friend Richard Cross-

man: "Do you by any chance know of a job for me? Anything from nurs-
ing to burglary: Is it possible to get into a publishing firm in any capac-
ity?"* Early in 1930, he heard that Cecil Day-Lewis was leaving his
teaching job at Larchfield Academy near Glasgow, a down-at-heels pre-
paratory school for boys, and successfully applied to succeed him. He
arrived at Larchfield in April. Around the same time, T. S. Eliot accepted
Auden's first book of poems for publication by Faber & Faber, and Au-
den's first book review appeared in the April number of Eliot's quarterly,
The Criterion. In the January number Eliot had printed Auden's first pub-
lished work outside school and university magazines, "Paid on Both Sides:
A Charade". Auden's first review, of *Instinct and Intuition: A Study in Men-
tal Duality* by George Binney Dibblee, concerned itself with social and
psychological issues, with the distinction between an "instinctive intel-
ligent faculty" and the "intellect proper", and said nothing about litera-
ture. Its shifts in style from a schoolmasterly opening—"Duality is one of
the oldest of our concepts"—to a portentous ending—"That which de-
sires life to itself . . . casts itself, like Lucifer, out of heaven"—were signs
that the young reviewer had still to find his voice.

Auden next asked Eliot for reviewing work in October 1930, when he
sent Eliot a letter of thanks for the first copies of his *Poems:* "If you have
any books you would care to let me review for the *Criterion* I should be
grateful as I am very hard up." In reply, Eliot asked Auden to suggest
from time to time books that interested him, and Auden responded a few
days later with a note on Baudelaire's *Intimate Journals,* recently published,
with an introduction by Eliot himself, in a translation by Christopher Ish-
erwood. Eliot told Auden that he did not wish to publish a review of the
book in the *Criterion* but suggested that Auden transform his note into an
essay. A few days later Auden wrote to his brother John Bicknell Auden,
who was working as a geologist in India: "I have been trying to write an
article for the Criterion on Puritanism but I shall chuck it. I can't say
things that way. Context and contact are everything. Or else joking verse."

For about a year, until the autumn of 1931, Auden wrote no critical or
expository prose, but worked instead on the dramatic fictional prose that
made up much of his second book, *The Orators,* when it appeared in 1932.
As Auden implied in his letter to his brother, these prose monologues had
none of the detachment of a prose essay, and used the "context and con-
tact" of their fictional authors to make their parabolic social and psycho-
logical arguments. In the spring of 1931 he wrote "The Initiates", the
four dramatic monologues in prose that became the first of the three
parts of *The Orators;* during the summer he wrote the prose and interpo-
lated verse of "Journal of an Airman", which became the second part of

* Sources for quotations are listed on p. xxxiv.

the book. When an invitation arrived during the summer to review for the little magazine *Échanges,* published in Paris by an American editor, Auden volunteered to write about David Garnett's novel *The Grasshoppers Come.* The central incident of the novel is the crash landing of a small airplane among the locusts and alienations of a desert—an incident that almost certainly helped suggest to Auden the closing pages of "Journal of an Airman", in which the airman prepares for his flight of surrender into the desiccated impersonality that he had, before his surrender, identified as his enemy.

Auden's review protested against what he called the privacy and self-regard of Garnett's allegory, and in "Journal of an Airman" he dramatized a similar self-regard and its fatal consequence. His review was the first of many in which he conducted in prose an explicit version of the debate with other writers that he conducted implicitly in his poems. His next review, written at Eliot's invitation late in 1931, of a new edition of the poems of John Skelton, was the first of many in which he praised the work of an earlier poet as an exemplary justification of the kind of poetry he was writing at the time he wrote the review—in this instance, the satiric and flyting verse that he included in *The Orators* and that he continued to write early in 1932 in the long, satiric dream vision "A Happy New Year."*

All these satires were revolutionary, but, in a manner that was more plausible in the early 1930s than it was later, they expressed no loyalties to any party or any program of action. In writing them Auden explored his divided feelings about the healers, heroes, and leaders who seemed to offer the only alternative to social disintegration, yet who also threatened to resolve public chaos through personal tyranny. Thirty years later, Auden wrote of *The Orators:* "My name on the title-page seems a pseudonym for someone else, someone talented but near the border of sanity, who might well, in a year or two, become a Nazi. . . . My guess to-day is that my unconscious motive in writing it was therapeutic, to exorcise certain tendencies in myself by allowing them to run riot in phantasy."

Late in 1931, shortly after finishing *The Orators,* Auden wrote privately of his hope for a revolution that would scarcely be a proletarian one. Michael Roberts, a poet and schoolmaster who later edited anthologies that gave pride of place to Auden and his friends, asked Auden to work with him on a magazine designed to serve as a rallying point for their generation. When he replied on 11 December 1931, Auden characteristically treated the question of the purpose of the magazine as inseparable from the question of its style:

---

* He wrote his review of Skelton after Eliot refused or ignored a request Auden sent him on 2 August 1931 to review Lancelot Hogben's 1930 book *The Nature of Living Matter,* which Auden mistakenly referred to in his letter as *The Properties of Living Matter.*

About this magazine. What are [you] really out to do? Discuss Economics or cause a Revolution? If the former I'm not interested. If the latter, good, but have you the money. We want cyclostyled satires dropped by aeroplanes and all that. Secondly, if you are out for propaganda, who do you want to reach? I cannot state too clearly that no paper which does not set out to preach to the vicarages and golf-clubs and Badminton courts, is of the slightest interest to me.

I felt bitterly ashamed of having contributed to *Dope* when I saw it.* I [?dislike] that smart talk and [?purely nasty] humour. We must write like gentlemen; and with the gentleman's type of rudeness when necessary; not the Americanised whinney of the [Laura] Riding push.

In my opinion you have got to model your paper on Punch, being all that Punch could and ought to be if it wasn't directed from Hell.

At around the same time he wrote this letter Auden began work on his first commissioned essay, and finished it in January 1932. Naomi Mitchison was compiling a children's encyclopedia, *An Outline for Boys and Girls and Their Parents,* for the publisher Victor Gollancz, whose list specialized in left-wing politics. She asked Auden to contribute an essay on the nature of writing, as one of a group of essays on dance, architecture, and the other arts. Auden told Christopher Isherwood that he had to set aside his work on revising the play they were writing in collaboration, *The Enemies of a Bishop* (not published during their lifetimes), and, with the prospect of payment in mind, added: "It is impossible to be more wicked than this." (In the end, Gollancz never paid his editor or contributors.) Despite Auden's ironic detachment, and despite the obligation to write his essay in a style suitable for an audience of children, he made it into a comprehensive manifesto on the modern crisis of language. Because he was writing for an unsophisticated audience, he felt free to make large, direct statements about isolation and longing, statements he was unable to make in the self-conscious polysyllabic elaborations he wrote when the audience he wanted to convince was the editor of the *Criterion.*

Auden's essay, titled "Writing" (and printed in this edition without the cuts and palliations introduced by Mitchison), described all speech and writing as an attempt to cross a gulf that can never be bridged. The history, psychology, and anthropology of language in the essay derived from the work of Malinowski, W. H. R. Rivers, Freud, and others, many of them filtered through the scientific popularizer Gerald Heard, whom Auden had met through Mitchison. But Auden took a far more extreme

---

* *Dope* was a magazine in newspaper format edited by Bernard Causton, who had been at Oxford a few years before Auden. The first of its two issues, dated New Year 1932, was written almost entirely in a superior and cynical style; its lead story was a rhymed satire on Noël Coward, and Auden's poem "Watching in three planes" (later included in *The Orators*) appeared on the back page.

view of the isolation of language from its speakers and its subjects than anything he found in his sources. Modern linguistics emphasized that words do not imitate the objects they stand for; Auden made the difference between words and objects the source of language's emotional force. "In fact, most of the power of words comes from their *not* being like what they stand for." Language originated in group violence: ancient bands of hunters made noises in the excitement of the kill, and individual hunters in their isolation after the hunt repeated those noises in an attempt to recover the excitement of the united group.

Auden's essay described speech and writing as "two tributary streams, rising at different sources, flowing apart for a time until they unite to form a large river." But both spring from a similar wish: "The urge to write, like the urge to speak, came from man's growing sense of personal loneliness, of the need for group communication. But while speech begins with the feeling of separateness in space, of I-here-in-this-chair and You-there-in-that-chair, writing begins from the sense of separateness in time, of 'I'm here to-day, but I shall be dead to-morrow and you will be alive in my place and how can I speak to you'." In the same way in which speech seeks to recover a unity remembered from the moment of the kill, writing seeks to recover a unity broken in the anticipation of one's own death. As personal isolation deepens from one century to the next, the isolation and triviality of literature increases along with it. Auden's first draft pointed to a solution in a concluding passage that he cut before publication, probably at Mitchison's request. It was time, he wrote, to reverse the course of history and "let literature start again by oral tradition." This new beginning required a new psychological and social order: "One thing is quite certain. We shall do absolutely nothing without some sort of faith either religious like Catholicism or political like Communism." In his essays and reviews after 1932, although he practiced more discretion in his language and his suggestions than he did in this abandoned conclusion, Auden continued to give as much weight to religious solutions as he did to political ones.

Auden found Larchfield Academy increasingly uncongenial, and decided to leave in the spring of 1932. After failing to get a job at Winchester College or the experimental progressive school at Dartington Hall (and after fruitlessly asking his school friend John Pudney for help finding a job in business), he found a position at the Downs School, Colwall, and began teaching there in the autumn of 1932. His pupils at Larchfield had been puzzled by him; his pupils at the Downs delighted in his anarchistic energy and eccentricity, and he built a close circle of friends among the masters. At the time he arrived at the Downs, he published the first of many reviews and essays on education that he wrote during the 1930s. Writing in the second number of *Scrutiny* (where he reviewed regularly until 1935, when the editors declared him immature and irresponsible), Auden adopted D. H. Lawrence's style to make the Lawrentian argument that schooling will remain useless until society transforms itself, and that, in the meantime, teaching must remain a private indulgence. In his first review for the *New Statesman and Nation,* a few weeks later, he argued that education serves only society, not the individual, because individual growth is the product of passionate relations, while modern education fails because no one believes in the society into which children are educated.

Auden's revolutionary rhetoric had grown more intense and partisan as the economic crisis worsened in the later months of 1932. When Rupert Doone (who had recently founded the Group Theatre and commissioned Auden to write his first produced play, *The Dance of Death*) concluded from this review that Auden was ready to join the Communist Party, Auden replied "No. I am a bourgeois. I shall not join the C. P." Auden conducted his political arguments in different vocabularies when addressing different audiences. In the spring of 1933 he told the mass audience of the *Daily Herald* that to achieve freedom from the tyranny of the machine, "you must first establish a Socialist State in which everyone can feel secure, and, secondly, have enough self-knowledge and common sense to ensure that machines are employed by your needs, and not your needs by the machinery."

At almost the same moment, he adopted a more agnostic tone for the better-educated readers of the *Twentieth Century* ("one of those dreadful little papers with a priggish title and no money", he described it to T. S. Eliot), which was the organ of the Promethean Society, one of the many gathering places that opened in the 1930s for those who considered themselves progressive on personal and social issues without committing themselves to Communism. Here he wrote: "We live in an age in which the collapse of all previous standards coincides with the perfection in technique for the centralised distribution of ideas; some kind of revolution is inevitable, and will as inevitably be imposed from above by a minority; in consequence, if the result is not to depend on the loudest voice, if the majority is to have the slightest say in its future, it must be more critical than it is necessary for it to be in an epoch of straightforward development." And on the more theoretical and psychological heights of the *Criterion,* he had even slighter hopes about the democratic prospects of the new order: "If we want a decent sex life, happy human relations, if we want to be people at all, and not behaviorist automatons, we must see to it that our dictators can have no personal or class axe to grind and we must hurry or it will be too late."

Auden paid conscientious tribute in his prose to the books that most affected his poetry and thought. His earliest reviews and essays alluded to the psychoanalytic and anthropological studies he read in the late 1920s and early 1930s, and his prose after 1931 reflected his studies in Marxist and visionary politics. In June 1931 Gerald Heard published *Social Substance of Religion,* the second book in a trilogy that began in 1929 with *The Ascent of Humanity* and concluded in 1935 with *The Source of Civilization.* The passage in Heard's book that made the deepest impression on Auden was an account of the feast of agape in early Christianity, and the suppression of the feast by the Mass when Catholic Christianity became an organized institution. Heard argued, and Auden for a time believed, that the lost unity of the small group inspired by the agape was precisely what the isolated individual of the modern age most urgently needed. In Auden's essay "The Group Movement and the Middle Classes", written late in 1933 as a critique of Frank Buchman's Oxford Group (which had no connection with Oxford University, and was later renamed Moral Rearmament), he paraphrased Heard on the "formation of the cell or small group" in the Nazi and Communist movements as well as in the Oxford Group: "Only in a group of very moderate size, probably not larger than twelve, is it possible for the individual under normal circumstances to lose himself, for his death instincts to be neutralized in the same way as those of the separate cells of the metazoa neutralize each other in the body. What the individual is after has been well expressed by Mr Gerald Heard in *The Social Substance of Religion.*" Auden then quoted Heard on the early Christians who "found real salvation from the lust for self-salvation in complete devotion to the group, to the new, small, intensely beloved community of like believers."

In his essay for *An Outline for Boys and Girls and Their Parents* early in 1932, Auden had already begun to echo Heard on the importance of the small group, but in 1933, in "The Group Movement and the Middle Classes", he was writing from direct experience. In June 1933, sitting with three friends who taught with him at the Downs School, he experienced what he described thirty years later as a "vision of agape", when he felt himself

> invaded by a power which, though I consented to it, was irresistible and certainly not mine. For the first time in my life I knew exactly— because, thanks to the power, I was doing it—what it means to love one's neighbor as oneself. I was also certain, though the conversation continued to be perfectly ordinary, that my three colleagues were having the same experience.

Auden responded to the experience in a poem, "Out on the lawn I lie in bed". The poem never gave a name to the event that prompted it, but in its setting—"Equal with colleagues in a ring"—it alluded to Heard's description of the feast of agape: "The small group of about a dozen lent [*sic*] over the cushion of the pulvinus, or sigma, and so formed an inward-looking group—perhaps a ring". In Auden's prose, the immediate effect of the experience was the exalted tone he adopted for his review in the *Criterion* of *The Book of Talbot,* a worshipful biography of the explorer Talbot Clifton by his widow. Auden asked to review the book within a month after his experience, and produced a review unlike anything he wrote before or after:

> *The Book of Talbot* is a great book, not because he went to Ver-khoyansk, the coldest place in the world, but because Lady Clifton*
> would have been just as interested in his adventures if he had gone to
> Wigan.
>
> It shows more clearly than anything I have read for a long time
> that the first criterion of success in any human activity, the necessary
> preliminary, whether to scientific discovery or to artistic vision, is in-
> tensity of attention or, less pompously, love.
>
> Love has allowed Lady Clifton to constellate round Talbot the
> whole of her experience and to make it significant.

In Heard's account, the agape was supplanted by the Mass and the ecstatic charity of the small group was transformed into the ascetic hierarchy of the church. Auden, throughout the 1930s, insisted in public and private on his distaste for organized religion, yet he both recognized and resisted the connection between his vision of agape and the religion to which he returned seven years after it occurred. "One may be repelled by Roman Catholicism", he wrote in his review of *The Book of Talbot*; "one may regard the system of society which made Talbot's life and character possible as grossly unjust, but I cannot imagine that anyone who is fortunate enough to read this book, will not experience that sense of glory which it is the privilege of great art to give."

Until the end of 1934 Auden continued to write prose that shifted abruptly between dry analysis and apocalyptic prophecy, but he was grad-ually finding a mature voice that included neither extreme. Early in 1934, in a review of a biography of T. E. Lawrence, he described both T. E. Lawrence and D. H. Lawrence as prophets of the failure of personal inti-macy, and proposed that, in our state of isolation, sexual relations could only postpone our cure. The same review included Auden's only prose statement of praise for the solitary leader-principle that had rioted through *The Orators* in 1931: "I mentioned Lenin. He and Lawrence seem to me the two whose lives exemplify most completely what is best and significant in our time, our nearest approach to a synthesis of feeling and

---

* She had a title only in Auden's imagination.

reason, act and thought, the most potent agents of freedom and to us, egotistical underlings, the most relevant accusation and hope."*

At around the same time, early in 1934, Auden wrote about the schools as a political battleground on which pupils were trained to fight, on one side or the other, the political battles of adulthood. In a review of a life of Lord Baden-Powell, founder of the Boy Scout movement, he wrote: "One half of the educational battle, the defeat of the academic in the training of the physical machine, has been fought, and Lord Baden Powell is one of its generals. The other half, the attack on the psychological front, has only just begun"—an allusion to the institutionalized team spirit recommended by such writers on education as Cyril Norwood, whom Auden repeatedly denounced in the 1930s. "Educationalists must always be revolutionaries", he wrote in the same review, but his sense of revolution was different from Lenin's: "A state has to train its youth not only to be its good citizens, but to change it, i.e. to destroy its present existence." And in a memoir of his own public school commissioned by Graham Greene for the collection *The Old School* in 1934, Auden wrote: "The best reason I have for opposing Fascism is that at school I lived in a Fascist state."

By the end of the year, in a review for *Scrutiny* of E. M. Forster's *Goldsworthy Lowes Dickinson*, Auden made explicit his hope that political revolution could be achieved by psychological means. "People and civilizations are saved by a change of heart; whether physical violence, loathsome as it is, is necessary to secure it, or whether if we are concerned enough, it can be brought about by 'mental fight' alone, we cannot answer". He added that "it is particularly important that those capable of waging the latter should not lose patience: to such Lowes Dickinson and also, I think, E. M. Forster, are examples permanent and alert." Forster remained until the end of the decade Auden's model for private and inner resistance, and the essay Forster wrote in 1938 for the collection *I Believe* (to which Auden also contributed) gave him the image of the "points of light" flashed out by the just in "September 1, 1939." But in the later 1930s Auden increasingly questioned whether a point of light was an honorable and effective focus of resistance, or merely a self-satisfied center of isolation, and when he revised the typescript of "September 1, 1939" before its first publication he replaced "The little points of light"—an almost direct quotation of Forster's "the little lights"—with the more self-questioning "Ironic points of light".

* In January 1934, at the suggestion of the headmistress of the Crichel School (the sister school of Bryanston, the boys' school to which most of the best pupils at the Downs proceeded), Auden sent his books to the Russian literary critic Prince D. S. Mirsky, who had recently left London for Moscow after joining the Communist Party. Auden also drafted (and probably sent) a letter to Mirsky in which he asked "if there are any possibilities of a job in Russia teaching English; I know no Russian" (letter in a private collection).

By the beginning of 1935 Auden had already dropped his revolutionary rhetoric, and he had begun to write an extraordinary series of panoramic and assured essays that drew ambitious connections among psychology, literature, politics, and religion. "Psychology and Art To-day", Auden's opening essay in a collection of essays titled *The Arts To-day*, comprised a summary and critique of Freudian theory, a tabular history of Western society, and a concluding demonstration of the mutual ignorance and mutual need that now divided and must someday link the psychologist and the socialist. "The Good Life", Auden's opening essay in the collection titled *Christianity and the Social Revolution*, was an even more nuanced exploration of the shared teleologies and structural similarities that joined psychology, Communism, and religion, despite their apparent antagonisms. "Psychology and Art To-day" ends with a warning that the socialist, after his victory, would need to call in the psychologist to attend to matters for which, as Auden now acknowledged, politics has no cure. "The Good Life" ends with an ambiguous suggestion that Christianity may be tested by the illegality and oppression that it endures under twentieth-century Communism as it was tested and proved triumphant in first-century Rome.

In 1935 Auden's writings on education became concerned less with the revolution and more with the classroom. In collaboration with a schoolmaster friend, John Garrett, he compiled an anthology of poetry for schoolchildren, *The Poet's Tongue*. The book was a defense of poetry against both the psychologist, who "maintains that poetry is a neurotic symptom," and "the propagandist, whether moral or political," who "complains that the writer should use his powers over words to persuade people to a particular course of action, instead of fiddling while Rome burns." The book also had a political point to make, which Auden borrowed more from Eliot's essays than from political tracts:

> Artistic creations may be produced by individuals, and because their work is only appreciated by a few it does not necessarily follow that it is not good; but a universal art can only be the product of a community united in sympathy, sense of worth, and aspiration; and it is improbable that the artist can do his best except in such a society.

He immediately followed this half-revolutionary, half-nostalgic wish with a statement of its lethal contemporary danger:

> Something of this lies behind the suspicion of and attack upon the intellectual which is becoming more and more vocal. It is hardly possible to open a number of *Punch* without seeing him spectacled, round-shouldered, rabbit-toothed, a foil to a landscape of beautifully

unconscious cows, or a whipping-boy for a drawing-room of dashing young sahibs and elegant daughters of the chase. Cross the channel and this dislike, in more countries than one, has taken a practical form, to which the occasional ducking of an Oxford æsthete seems a nursery tiff.

Auden and Garrett, "after some thought," arranged the poems in the book in an anonymous alphabetical order by first lines, with the authors identified only in the index. By presenting all the poems as if they had been written by Anon., Auden and Garrett treated poetry as "a human activity, independent of period and unconfined in subject", and not to be judged by its role in history or its social recommendations.

A year later, in an essay on poetry that he wrote for a Workers' Educational Association magazine, Auden appropriated a slogan from *The Communist Manifesto* to defend the uniqueness of individual personalities: "The secret of good art is the same as the secret of a good life; to find out what you are interested in, however strange, or trivial, or ambitious, or shocking, or uplifting, and deal with that, for that is all you can deal with well. 'To each according to his needs; from each according to his powers', in fact."

Auden left the Downs School in the summer of 1935, and, except for a term filling in for a vacationing master at the Downs in the summer of 1937, he did not return to teaching until after he left England. At first he planned to move to Bryanston, but the school's offer of a job was withdrawn after the headmaster saw a letter from Auden to a Bryanston pupil who had been at the Downs, in which Auden jokingly told the pupil to "put an onion in the chalice for me" when the headmaster of the Downs was scheduled to preach at Bryanston. Auden told Michael Roberts: "I am very much in two minds as to what to do. Whether to go on teaching or not. If I do, I think a secondary school. What I *think* I should really like is a B.B.C. job connected with education."

During his last months at the Downs, in the summer of 1935, he began writing verse to be used in documentary films produced by the Film Unit, which John Grierson had organized under the financial umbrella of the General Post Office. Auden was commissioned by his Oxford friend Basil Wright, who understood that film work was an obvious next step for a poet who had been writing stage plays since 1928. The Group Theatre had produced Auden's play *The Dance of Death* and was now planning to produce Auden and Isherwood's *The Dog Beneath the Skin*, but Rupert Doone's stagings were chaotic and absurd, while Grierson's films were masterworks of economy and efficiency. In September 1935 Auden began full-time work at the Film Unit's offices in London, where his title was apprentice and his jobs included carrying film cans, taking the part of Father Christmas in a film called *Calendar of the Year,* and directing scenes in *Night Mail.*

Auden recognized quickly that the socialist sympathies of the Film Unit were compromised by the unit's financial dependence on the government and by the enormous cost of filmmaking itself. The documentaries produced at the Film Unit were rushed to completion before their middle-class directors had time to learn about their working-class subjects. When Auden stated these concerns in a review in the *Listener* of Paul Rotha's book about documentary film, he received a sharp rebuke, probably written by Grierson, in a film magazine. But by the time Grierson's rebuke appeared in print, Auden had already resigned from the Film Unit after only five months.

His experience there confirmed his skepticism about propaganda art, and the play he wrote with Christopher Isherwood immediately thereafter, *The Ascent of F 6,* was an allegory of the destruction of an artist by his own wish to rescue helpless humanity. (It was also an allegorical portrait of T. E. Lawrence, through which Auden renounced his earlier attempt to believe in Lawrence as an agent of freedom.) But Auden had made good use of his time at the Film Unit. He and his closest friend there, the painter William Coldstream, repeatedly slipped away for coffee and conversation. In the course of their talks, Auden articulated an aesthetic that rejected the abstract ambitions of many contemporary writers and artists, and, in the service of a humane politics, refused the generalizing claims of the psychologist and the propagandist. As he recalled in a verse letter to Coldstream in *Letters from Iceland* in 1936, "Upstairs in the Corner House . . . / We'd scrapped Significant Form, and voted for Subject". In his review on documentary film, early in 1936, he wrote: "The first, second and third thing in cinema, as in any art, is subject. Technique follows from and is governed by subject." A few weeks later, in a review of a book of essays by Herbert Read, he wrote:

> I cannot believe—and this incidentally is why I cannot sympathise with Mr Read in his admiration for abstract art (symbolic art is another matter)—that any artist can be good who is not more than a bit of a reporting journalist.
>
> To the journalist the first thing of importance is subject and, just as I would look at a painting of the Crucifixion before a painting of a still life, and cannot admit that "the pattern may have some more or less remote relation to objects, but such a relation is not necessary" . . . so in literature I expect plenty of news.

His example of interesting subject matter was less accidental than his tone implied.

Auden wrote his review of Read's book for *New Verse*, the little magazine edited with fierce critical authority by Geoffrey Grigson, who had also edited the book of essays *The Arts To-day*. Grigson began the magazine in 1933 largely to provide a setting for the kind of poetry in which a mass audience could take no interest, and partly, as he wrote when he closed the magazine in 1939, to promote Auden. Auden in turn favored *New Verse* as the forum in which he published his most skeptical and unfashionable prose. He pressed his campaign for human subject matter in a commentary headed "Honest Doubt" and pseudonymously signed J. B. (perhaps signifying John Bull), which he wrote for *New Verse* about the International Surrealist Exhibition that opened in London in 1936. He also arranged to write a book with plenty of news by obtaining a commission to visit Iceland and write about his travels.

"I've deserted the films and am more or less a simple literary crook", he wrote to a former pupil from the Downs in May 1936. He was being slightly unfair to himself in his role of freelancer, because almost all his essays and reviews dealt with issues that deeply engaged him. He had stopped writing for small-circulation quarterlies such as the *Criterion* and *Scrutiny* and now wrote mostly for weeklies such as the *Listener* and the *New Statesman and Nation*, but his only attempts to write solely for money were two unconvincing surveys of detective fiction for the *Daily Telegraph* late in 1936—and even these sprang from the personal interest that led him to write his poem "Detective Story" for *Letters from Iceland* earlier in the same year. He reduced his expenses by living with his parents in Birmingham, where his father was the city's school medical officer and a part-time professor of public health at the university, and although Auden needed to earn money from writing, he did not need much.

"Am off next week or so to Iceland to write a travel book thereon", he continued in his letter to his former pupil.

> Terrified at the prospect of those horses—I've never ridden one but I fell off a donkey when I was four. There's even a possibility that we may have to shoot with a real gun. My account of that will become a classic of English comic prose. Nothing of Hemingway about me.

A journey to the Carpathians in 1934 had already liberated Auden to become a writer of comic prose, but "In Search of Dracula", his diary of the trip, appeared only in the Downs School magazine, a deliberately risky setting for the diary's intimations of sexual irregularity.

Auden left Birmingham for Iceland in June 1936 and remained there until September. (While he was away Faber & Faber printed his second book of poems under the title *Look, Stranger!*—a title chosen by the publishers without Auden's consent; he titled the American edition *On This Island*.) During his last few weeks in Iceland he was joined by Louis Mac-

Neice, whom he had invited to collaborate with him on the travel book;
Auden had known MacNeice distantly at Oxford but became friendly
with him only in the early 1930s, when MacNeice began teaching at Bir-
mingham University. By prearrangement, Auden and MacNeice also
joined a party of four schoolboys and a master from Bryanston for an
eight-day journey across the Langjökull ice field, using tents and ponies.
Auden and MacNeice wrote some prose and verse during their travels,
but finished most of their travel book, which they titled *Letters from Iceland,*
after their return.

Auden wrote his share of the book—about two-thirds of the whole—
both as an argument for journalistic art and as an example of it. In his
review of Herbert Read's essays he had declared himself uninterested in
abstract art. Now he went further. He denounced the impulse toward
abstraction as the same impulse that produces oppressive and false politi-
cal generalizations, and that offers a tempting prospect of inaction and
despair. Abstraction was not, as the great tradition of modernist art had
assumed, the privileged superior of representation, but its distorted par-
ody. In a verse letter pointedly addressed to Richard Crossman, the only
one of Auden's friends with political ambition, Auden described "our vul-
gar error" of evading minute particulars by seeing abstractions in their
place:

> When we see nothing but the law and order,
> The formal interdiction from the garden,
> A legend of a sword, and quite forget
> The rusting apple core we're clutching still.

It is through formal abstraction, through a conviction that History or
Class is the cause of our unhappiness, that we avoid understanding our-
selves and others, and seek instead delusive healers like Lawrence or delu-
sive avengers like Lenin:

> It's that that makes us really selfish:
> When the whole fault's mechanical,
> A maladjustment in the circling stars,
> And goodness just an abstract principle
> Which by hypothesis some men must have,

> For whom we spend our idle lives in looking,
> And are so lazy that we quickly find them,
> Or rather, like a child that feels neglected,
> Our proof of goodness is the power to punish,
> We recognise them when they make us suffer.

Auden's letter acknowledged his own temptation to the abstractions of History:

> Until indeed the Markafljōt I see
> Wasting these fields, is no glacial flood
> But history, hostile, Time the destroyer
> Everywhere washing our will. . . .

The artist's prayer, earlier in the poem, was a prayer to overcome this temptation: "Let me find pure all that can happen. / Only uniqueness is success!"

In the opening lines of this letter Auden portrayed himself walking among his Icelandic settings "taking photographs". Whatever the scene might lack,

> Nevertheless let the camera's eye record it:
> Groups in confabulation on the grass,
> The shuffling couples in their heavy boots,
> The young men leaping, the accordion playing.
> Justice or not, it is a world.

He included in *Letters from Iceland* his photographs of groups, couples, accordions, and much else, and the photographs were an essential element of the book's journalistic ambition. They deliberately refused the picturesque, well-composed pictorial style typical of travel books. Instead, their baffling perspectives and unbalanced compositions gave them the same kind of ironically heightened vernacular style that Auden devised for his songs and ballads at around the same time.

Through both its epistolary form and its miscellaneous up-to-date content, *Letters from Iceland* emphasized that it was both personal and journalistic. Auden's two letters to Erika Mann (whom he married in 1935 in order to provide her with a British passport) mentioned the outbreak of the Spanish Civil War and reported on a visit to Iceland by a brother of Hermann Goering. The charts and tables that Auden gathered for the appendix at the back of the book stood at the farthest possible extreme from the poetic. In "Letter to Lord Byron" Auden casually remarked that he was writing for money, an unprecedented confession for a twentieth-century poet: "I love my publishers and they love me, / At least they paid a very handsome fee / To send me here." MacNeice's diary of the journey across the Langjökull, written in the guise of an English schoolmistress, was the counter-Hemingway classic of English comic prose that Auden, in his letter to his former pupil, anticipated writing himself.* The verse

---

* The code names Hetty and Nancy, as Jon Stallworthy first recognized, refer to the heterosexual MacNeice and to his (in the slang of the period) "nancy" friend Anthony Blunt. Mac-

"Last Will and Testament" that Auden and MacNeice jointly wrote for the book was in part, as Evelyn Waugh described it in a contemptuous review, a "gossip column".* The book was marked throughout by a journalist's combination of moral outrage and political skepticism, and refused to grant any special respect to the dignified. Among the sights that Auden recommended to visitors to Reykjavík were four persons widely known in Iceland: a painter, a professor of Icelandic history, and two dishevelled lunatics.

"Auden and MacNeice: Their Last Will and Testament" was an astonishing work of journalistic rudeness, whose authors and publishers risked wholesale libel through its coded revelations of the sexual preferences of famous contemporaries. The Last Will devoted as many lines to private jokes about the authors' friends as it did to public jokes about politicians and writers, and the private jokes were designed to be enjoyed by readers who knew nothing about the subjects but who understood the pleasure of private meanings shared among friends. The Last Will was written not for an audience of insiders—each of the authors' friends understood a different and minuscule portion of the private jokes—but for the unique personal audience of each of its readers.† A year later Auden celebrated the literary impulse of the poem in a broadcast, "In Defence of Gossip". Gossip, he said, when "played under the right rules," is "an act of friendliness, a release of the feelings, and a creative work of art."

The "Last Will and Testament" ended in a prayerful bequest that did not contradict but explained the personal impulse behind the anarchistic impertinence of the rest of the poem:

Neice briefly resumed the character of Hetty in his travel book *I Crossed the Minch* (1938), where he printed a letter from Hetty to Maisie, who had been Hetty's companion on their journey across the ice field. Among many other matters, Hetty alludes to the review of *Letters from Iceland* in the *New Statesman and Nation*, 7 August 1937, by Edward Sackville-West, who approved of everything in the book by Auden but dismissed MacNeice's couplets as "exceedingly slovenly" and described "Hetty to Nancy" as "overdone to the point of dullness":

I have just been perusing [Hetty wrote] a stack of reviews of our Memoirs from Greenland. They seem to think that poor Hetty is rather a passenger on it. Little do they know the time she had doing the proofs. And what cheek saying there is nothing in the book about Greenland. Let 'em go there, I say, and see what they can do with it. You might lend them your tent, my dear. If they come out of *that* without pneumonia, the higher English journalism has a great deal more stamina than I credit it with. *The New Parson and Parish*—bevy of second-rate sensitive minds!

* Waugh's review appeared in the short-lived weekly *Night and Day*, 12 August 1937. As Hetty wrote to Maisie in *I Crossed the Minch*,

Christine [Christopher Isherwood] gave me a copy of that new paper, *Dawn and Twilight*, with a review of Greenland in it. By Evelyn Priest the man who used to write novels. It was not awfully funny I thought, but then I couldn't very well think it funny as Priest had no use for our book. I think he must be jealous of you for writing *Not Suède but Kid*.

† The notes in this edition explain the less-familiar public references and virtually all the private references in the "Last Will and Testament".

> And to the good who know how wide the gulf, how deep
> Between Ideal and Real, who being good have felt
> The final temptation to withdraw, sit down and weep,
>
> We pray the power to take upon themselves the guilt
> Of human action, though still as ready to confess
> The imperfection of what can and must be built,
> The wish and power to act, forgive, and bless.

The earlier stanzas included at least three bequests of religious belief to nonbelievers: to Bertrand Russell a belief in God; to Herbert Read the "Dictatorship of the Holy Spirit"; and to Naomi Mitchison a "faith period" to follow her changing political enthusiasms.

Letters from Iceland had the air of a book written on holiday, in the knowledge that a time of fatal seriousness would follow. In December 1936, shortly before he and MacNeice finished the manuscript, Auden decided to join the International Brigades that were fighting to defend the Spanish Republic from the Nationalist invaders. He explained his decision to his friend E. R. Dodds, who had recently moved from Birmingham to Oxford to become Regius Professor of Greek, and whom Auden regarded as a voice of conscience in public matters: "I so dislike everyday political activities that I won't do them, but here is something I can do as a citizen and not as a writer." In a response to the letter that Dodds wrote him in reply, however, he justified his decision for its importance to him as a writer: "I feel I can speak with authority about the Condition Humaine of only a small class of English intellectuals and professional people and that the time has come to gamble on something bigger. I shall probably be a bloody bad soldier but how I can speak to/for them without becoming one?" A few weeks earlier, he had told Mitchison that he hoped to work as a teacher of adults in a different class from his own: "I'm looking for a W.E.A. [Workers' Educational Association] job in Yorkshire next year, so sow the seed."

By the time Auden left for Spain in January 1937 he had decided to volunteer as an ambulance driver instead of as a soldier, and he secured from a doctor friend a supply of opiates to give the wounded. When he arrived in Spain the Government refused to let him drive an ambulance and set him to work broadcasting propaganda from Valencia. In his first days there he wrote for the *New Statesman and Nation* the only work of pure propaganda that he ever published, but he wrote it in a tone that transparently betrayed his lack of political conviction. He stopped broadcasting after a week or less and spent the next few weeks travelling to the front. When he returned to England in March—two months sooner than he had originally planned—he said almost nothing about his experiences. He had been disillusioned by the murderousness of Stalin's agents and of some of the other groups that fought for the Spanish Republic, but he knew that anything he said about his disillusionment could only serve Franco and Franco's patrons in Berlin and Rome. A few months later, when asked for a statement in support of the Republic for a pamphlet, *Authors Take Sides on the Spanish War*, he wrote a paragraph that said nothing about the Republic's virtues or faults, but affirmed that its defeat by the forces of Fascism would contribute to an atmosphere "in which the creative artist and all who care for justice, liberty and culture would find it impossible to work or even exist." In the same dutiful and reticent manner, he reviewed Christopher Caudwell's *Illusion and Reality* in *New Verse* by writing a few emphatic sentences of praise for the book's Marxist argument and then quoting from the book at length, but he did not write a detailed personal response of the kind that he wrote in all his other reviews in *New Verse* and elsewhere of books that mattered to him.

Because, as he told A. E. Dodds, "livings must be earned", he wrote a pamphlet late in 1937 about education. His coauthor was T. C. Worsley, a former schoolmaster whom he knew through Stephen Spender; at a public meeting a few months earlier, Auden had burst into tears while reading aloud a description that Worsley had written of the sufferings of Spanish refugees. Auden and Worsley expected their pamphlet to be published as one of the numbers of the left-wing monthly *Fact*, but the editors rejected it as overly theoretical, and it did not appear until the Hogarth Press issued it in 1939. The first part of the pamphlet was a well-informed précis of current educational policy, the second a polemical theory of education, and the third a set of recommendations for change. The last two sections, both of them mostly written by Auden, were alternately rebellious and utopian. In the section on theory Auden observed, characteristically, that "loyalty and intelligence are mutually hostile. The intelligence is always disloyal." The list of recommendations began with the assumption that all ideas about reform must remain "highbrow and unreal" until society is transformed to the point where "equal social value is put upon all forms of employment" and "class distinctions are obliterated". But the recommendations themselves were less dependent on revolution than on the informed good will of teachers, and the pamphlet ended with a short-term program that could be carried out "in the event of a Socialist Government being returned to power without a radical change in the class system and the private ownership of capital".

Shortly thereafter, near the end of 1937, Auden wrote his introduction to *The Oxford Book of Light Verse*, the anthology that he had persuaded the press to commission from him during the summer. The book was Auden's most elaborate attempt to confront the problem of "how to find or form a genuine community, in which each has his valued place and can feel at home." Light verse, as Auden presented it in this anthology, need not be comic and need not be trivial; it comprised most of the work of Chaucer, Pope, and Byron. Light verse included all poetry that took "for its subject-matter the everyday social life of its period or the experiences of the poet as an ordinary human being". It also included poems written to be sung or spoken in performance before an audience and "such nonsense poetry as, through its properties and technique, has a general appeal". Poems written in all three categories performed one common and crucial task: they joined a poet with an audience in ways that bridged the gaps of enmity and time that Auden had mapped in his essay "Writing" in 1932. Poetry for children and nonsense poetry originated in the nineteenth century when "the breakdown of the old village or small-town community left the family as the only real social unit, and the parent-child relationship as the only real social bond. The writing of nonsense poetry which appeals to the Unconscious, and of poetry for children who live in a world before self-consciousness, was an attempt to find a world where the divisions of class, sex, occupation did not operate".

Today, if poetry is again to be, as it was before the nineteenth century, "at the same time light and adult", if poets are to write for an audience larger than a coterie without sacrificing their sensibility or their integrity, they must find a society that "is both integrated and free." The political vocabulary of Auden's introduction obliged it to suggest that such a society can only be "fostered by a deliberate effort of the will and the intelligence." But in a review that Auden wrote for *New Verse* within a few weeks of this introduction, he used a very different vocabulary. He devoted most of a review of Laurence Housman's memoir of his brother A. E. Housman to the division deep in the self that resists social unity, the same division between intellect and instinct that he had named in his first review in 1930:

> Heaven and Hell. Reason and Instinct. Conscious Mind and Unconscious. Is their hostility a temporary and curable neurosis, due to our particular pattern of culture, or intrinsic in the nature of these faculties? Can man only think when he is frustrated from acting and feeling? Is the intelligent person always the product of some childhood neurosis? Does Life only offer two alternatives. . . .

After describing the devastating effects of this division in Housman's life and work, he concluded:

> Yes, the two worlds. Perhaps the Socialist State will marry them; perhaps it won't. . . . Perhaps again the only thing which can bring them together is the exercise of what Christians call Charity. . .

In January 1938, soon after writing this review, Auden left England for a six-month journey to China. He and Isherwood had been commissioned by Random House, the American publisher of Auden's poems and the Auden-Isherwood plays, to write a travel book set in the East. Almost immediately after the commission arrived the Japanese campaigns in China began, and Auden and Isherwood chose to write about the Sino-Japanese War. During their four months in Hong Kong and China, and a few days in Japan, they lived and worked as foreign correspondents. They alternated in keeping a diary, which Isherwood transformed into dispatches that they sent to American and British weeklies. From Japan they crossed the Pacific and Canada, and then spent two weeks in New York. During their visit to New York they decided to return to America for an indefinite stay once they had finished their book about China and assisted at the production of their third and last play, *On the Frontier*. (They had begun the play in hopes of seeing it performed commercially in the West End or on Broadway, and saw it expire quietly in a Group Theatre production paid for by Maynard Keynes.)

While waiting to go back to America, Auden spent as little time as possible in England. After returning to England from New York in July 1938, he stayed only two weeks before leaving in August for two months in Brussels. At around the time he left for Brussels, he responded to a request for a contribution to a special "Commitments" number of *New Verse* by writing a distinctly uncommitted parable, "The Sportsmen". This piece repeated the historical argument of *The Oxford Book of Light Verse*, but in an entirely different tone.

The sportsmen are the poets, and their quarry is their poems. Long ago, the sportsmen sold in the open market the ducks they shot in the open country; more recently, when no one wanted birds any longer because everyone bought food in tins, the sportsmen, now isolated in a dense forest, practiced trick shots that they devised according to their own arbitrary rules, and quarrelled over their respective methods in the *Sporting Quarterly*. Then rumors arrived of a far country—evidently as far away as Russia—where ducks had become plentiful again and shooting parties were in fashion. Inspired by this distant example, a few villagers set out, in opposition to the local squire, to clear the forest, and invited the sportsmen to join them. Some refused out of fear. Of the rest, an older man, the finest sportsman of them all, wished the villagers every success but declined to join them because it was his vocation to study the rare and beautiful eagle—not unlike the poet whom Auden frequently called "the agèd eagle", after a phrase in *Ash-Wednesday*. A few others thought it would be grand to shoot a duck again but were so used to trick shots they missed the few ducks that came into range. So they decided to deceive the villagers by modelling ducks out of clay and old newspapers. "Some of the younger villagers who had never seen duck except in a museum were impressed, and praised the sportsmen highly for their skill; but the older and wiser among them fingered the models, and smelt them, and said: 'These are not duck; they are only clay and old newspapers.'"

Auden returned from Brussels on the last day of the Munich crisis in September 1938. He spent the next two months mostly in Birmingham, where he worked on *Journey to a War,* the book he and Isherwood were now writing about their visit to China. Isherwood wrote all the prose for the book, although he incorporated some passages from Auden's manuscript diaries; Auden wrote poems in his most solemn and elevated manner, and gathered his Chinese photographs into a "Picture Commentary" on the unique particulars that his poems treated in terms of allegory.

During these same two months, October and November 1938, Auden also travelled across England to lecture on China, wrote an introduction for an anthology, *Poems of Freedom,* published by Victor Gollancz, who once again contrived not to pay him for his work, and wrote weekly book reviews for the *Town Crier,* a Birmingham weekly newspaper recently bought by Frank Pakenham, transformed into a Labour paper, and put under the editorship of Philip Toynbee. During his month and a half as a regular reviewer Auden wrote about whatever books interested him, whether new or old. He covered poetry, novels, politics, and anthropology, and in his final review, before he returned to Brussels for another month at the end of the year, he surveyed books that teachers of English would find useful if they were sensible enough to teach "all the various kinds of prose needed by man" instead of force-feeding their pupils with great literature. The primary task of the teacher of English was to help pupils learn "to express their thoughts and feelings accurately and honestly", because democracy requires that "we must learn to know and to speak the truth ourselves, and recognise when we are being deceived by others, and it is the duty of the English teacher to begin to train us when we are young." He built his argument on a distinction between the vocational education required by a totalitarian state and the general education, based on the use of language, required by a democracy, in which every citizen is expected to take part in political life, "using 'political' in its widest sense". Democratic truth telling, the falsehoods of propagandists, and the ways in which poetry "makes us more difficult to deceive" were recurrent themes in Auden's prose after his return from Spain in 1937, when all he was willing to say to Stephen Spender about what he saw there was that political expedience was no justification for lies.

In August 1938, when he was first in Brussels, Auden had written for *Journey to a War* his complex and contemplative sonnet sequence "In Time of War". When he sent the sonnets to A. E. Dodds, whom he had recruited to serve as his literary conscience in the same way her husband served as his political conscience, he wrote: "When I look at the newspapers I wonder what the hell I'm doing". Back in England in October or November he followed the sonnets with a simplistic moralizing commentary in terza rima, which he sent to A. E. Dodds with the comment that he was "very uncertain whether this kind of thing is possible without becoming a prosy pompous old bore". As for his work outside literature, he added:

> I get very depressed running all over the place chatting about China. Does it do any good? Should I be better employed at my own work? If so am I being immoral? Or is this just selfish.

In public, however, he suppressed his doubts, and in consequence also suppressed his beliefs. At a conference on education in October 1938 he told an audience of schoolmasters "that their first job now is to take part in political action, for as long as society is unequal as it is, the whole idea of democratic education is a sham". In his contribution to *I Believe*, the volume of "personal philosophies" that also included an essay by Forster, he succumbed to precisely the temptation that he had rejected in his verse letter to Richard Crossman in *Letters from Iceland*, and wrote an overwhelmingly impersonal philosophy that traced all unhappiness and evil to external conditions. The essay had nothing whatever to say about the intractable inner disorder that he never forgot while writing his poems and most of his prose. This was the last extended essay Auden wrote before he sailed to America in January 1939, and one of his most compelling motives for leaving England was to stop himself from writing any more essays like it.

<h2 style="text-align:center">REFERENCES</h2>

Page xiv

> *Do you by any chance*   Letter to Naomi Mitchison, [November 1929] (Berg Collection, New York Public Library).

> *If you have any books*   Letter to T. S. Eliot, 6 October 1930 (Faber & Faber archives).

> *I have been trying to write*   Letter to John Bicknell Auden, 15 November 1930.

Page xv

> *My name on the title-page*   Foreword to the third edition of *The Orators* (1966), pp. 7–8.

Page xvi

> *About this magazine.*   Letter to Michael Roberts, 11 December 1931 (private collection).

Page xviii

> *No. I am a bourgeois.*   Letter to Rupert Doone, 19 October 1932 (Berg Collection).

one of those dreadful   Letter to T. S. Eliot, 23 October 1931 (Faber & Faber archives).

Page xix

found real salvation   Slightly misquoted from Heard's *Social Substance of Religion* (1931), p. 205.

invaded by a power   Introduction to *The Protestant Mystics*, ed. Anne Fremantle (1964), p. 26; reprinted in *Forewords and Afterwords* (1973), p. 69.

The small group of about   Heard, *Social Substance of Religion* (1931), p. 213.

Page xxiii

put an onion and *I am very much*   Letter to Michael Roberts, 22 April 1935 (Berg Collection).

Page xxv

I've deserted the films   Letter to Dermott Grubb, 25 May 1936.

Page xxvi

It's that that makes   See p. 242; for the sake of clarity this quotation substitutes a comma for the period at the end of the first stanza.

Page xxix

I so dislike   Letter to E. R. Dodds, 8 December 1936 (Bodleian Library).

I feel I can speak   Letter to E. R. Dodds, [December 1936] (Bodleian Library).

I'm looking for a W.E.A.   Letter to Naomi Mitchison, 5 November 1936 (Berg Collection).

Page xxx

livings must be earned   Letter to A. E. Dodds, [13 November 1937] (Bodleian Library).

Page xxxiii

When I look at the newspapers   Letter to A. E. Dodds, 5 September 1938 (Bodleian Library).

Page xxxiv

very uncertain whether   Letter to A. E. Dodds, [November 1938] (Bodleian Library).

THE TEXT OF THIS EDITION

SOME of Auden's prose works were printed exactly as he wrote them; others were cut and reshaped by editors; and it is often impossible to say how closely a printed text represents the text that Auden wrote. In the few instances where a manuscript exists, the text in this edition has been newly edited from it. In all other cases, the printed text has been reprinted with a minimum of regularization. All footnotes and square brackets in the main text (but not those in the titles, appendices, or notes) are the work of Auden or his collaborators.

The two travel books reprinted in this volume were written in collaboration, and each was prepared for the press largely by Auden's collaborator. The text of *Letters from Iceland* is a riot of inconsistencies and mistranscriptions, although the chapters written by MacNeice are slightly more careful than those written by Auden. The text of *Journey to a War*, in contrast, displays Isherwood's characteristic neatness and care. The text of that work in this edition restores for the first time some passages removed by the publisher, without the authors' knowledge, at the request of the journalist Peter Fleming, who read the manuscript for Faber & Faber after the authors had left for America. Some of the illustrations in both travel books are slightly reduced from the originals, and a few are laid out differently on the page, but the order of presentation is unchanged.

Essays signed with their full names jointly by Auden and a coauthor have the authors' names listed below the title; essays initialled jointly with a coauthor have the initials at the end, as in the originals. Pseudonymous and unsigned essays and reviews are identified as such at the end of each such work. The unsigned reviews in this volume were all written for the regular section of brief unsigned reviews in the *Listener,* and Auden may not have known in each instance whether his review would or would not appear over his signature. The reviews that appeared over initials, generally in the *Criterion,* were evidently not written specifically to be signed by initials rather than by name. The one pseudonymous essay in this volume, "Honest Doubt", was, however, clearly intended to appear over a pseudonym.

Most of the reviews and many of the essays in this volume were almost certainly given their titles by the editors of the magazines and books in which they appeared. Reviews that originally appeared without a title have been supplied with titles in the form "A Review of . . .". Other titles supplied by the editor of this volume are printed within square brackets. Where Auden's manuscript title was replaced by an editor, Auden's original title has been restored and the more familiar title has been printed below it within square brackets. Subtitles and breaks that were obviously inserted by newspaper subeditors have been omitted.

In all book reviews, the author, title, publisher, and price of the book reviewed are listed at the head of the review in a consistent format. The format of these headings in the original publications varied according to the style sheets of the magazines and newspapers in which the reviews appeared, and I have omitted such obvious editorial additions as references to the size of the book—for example, "Demy 8vo". Auden's errors in transcribing the author or title of the book reviewed have been retained in the text and in the heading that lists the title, publisher, and price of the book. The correct versions are given in the notes and in the titles supplied for this edition in the form "A Review of . . .".

The essays and reviews are arranged as closely as possible in chronological order of composition. In most cases, however, no direct evidence of the date of composition survives, and chronological order of publication has been used instead. The original date and place of publication is printed at the end of each work, together with the date of composition when this is known to have been much earlier than the date of publication. The dates in the running heads are dates of composition, if known, as are the bracketed dates on the title pages of the travel books.

Auden almost invariably made minor errors when copying extracts from other authors. The text in this volume corrects the obvious misspellings that the original editors could reasonably be expected to have caught, but in all other instances I have preferred to print the text Auden wrote, instead of the text that he perhaps ought to have written. The text Auden wrote includes the words he thought he found on the page from which he was copying, and not the text that was in fact printed there. The textual notes indicate all significant deviations from the originals. Where Auden so drastically misspelled a word when copying that the resulting word exists nowhere else or is not among common variant spellings of the original word, I have restored the original, as in his recurring mistranscription of "cyclothymic" as "cyclothermic" in his extracts from Christopher Caudwell's *Illusion and Reality*. I have also corrected errors that are clearly the work of a typist or compositor working from Auden's hand. A typical example is the misreading of "Beanlands" as "Beaulands" by the French compositor who set Auden's review of David Garnett's novel *The Grasshoppers Come*.

A relatively extreme but not entirely untypical example of Auden's treatment of quotations occurs in the essay "The Good Life" (page 113). The printed text of one of Auden's quotations has two obvious errors and many less-obvious ones:

"No intelligent question can be framed concerning causality unless there exist two co-isolates of a larger neutral isolate. The question "What is the cause of the changing universe? accepts the existence of a co-isolate of the universe" (Professor Levy).

Even without consulting the original, a reader can see that this requires, first, the substitution of a single quotation mark for the double one that precedes "What is", and, second, the addition of a closing single quotation mark after "changing universe?". But Auden's errors were more extensive than this. The essay he was misquoting was H. Levy's contribution to the collective volume *Aspects of Dialectical Materialism*, by H. Levy, John MacMurray, Ralph Fox, R. Page Arnot, J. D. Bernal, and E. F. Carritt (1934). Levy wrote:

If we adopt this approach to the problem of Causality, we recognize that no intelligible question can be framed concerning it unless there exist at least two co-isolates of a larger neutral isolate. From this point of view no meaning can be attached to the question: "What is the Cause of the Changing Universe?" To accept the question tacitly accepts the existence of a co-isolate of the universe, a partner in the process, and the celestial door is opened wide for mysticism to enter.

In emending Auden's version, I have corrected the errant quotation marks but have let stand his rearrangement of the original. Because Auden's manuscript is lost, it is impossible to know whether the change from "intelligible" in Levy's essay to "intelligent" in Auden's was made by Auden himself or by a typist or compositor unable to read his hand. But the misreading is comparable to others that occur in surviving manuscripts of Auden's early prose, so I have let it stand in the text while recording it in the textual notes.

Auden divided most of his essays by using subheadings and outline levels. The indents and spacing in this edition have been very slightly regularized. In some instances, the punctuation of outline numbers has been changed from a style evidently introduced by a publisher to a style that more closely represents the typical punctuation in Auden's prose manuscripts. Auden generally circled the numbers and letters of his outline headings; these circles are represented here by pairs of parentheses, thus: (1). Where a surviving typescript has only a closing parenthesis after a number in a heading, an opening parenthesis has been added. One convention has been added: where an open square (□) appears at the foot of a page, it indicates a break in the prose or between stanzas or verse paragraphs that might not otherwise be evident.

The textual notes provide brief histories of the magazines to which

Auden contributed; more detail is provided for lesser-known publications than for familiar ones. The notes also explain references otherwise accessible only to a small group of friends or to pupils and teachers at a school where Auden taught. In the case of "Auden and MacNeice: Their Last Will and Testament", where the poem consists largely of private references and contemporary allusions, a separate section of explanatory notes has been provided.

ESSAYS AND REVIEWS

1926–1936

Preface to *Oxford Poetry 1926*

Now that it has become obvious that *Oxford Poetry* can only "represent" the minority of Oxford with whom poetry has importance, the death of that controversy might seem to have robbed the present editors of any material for a preface. But we owe it to a brotherly feeling for our critics, since editors are, in so far as they are allowed to be, themselves critics, to provide them with some starting-point for their estimations.

In this selection we have endeavoured to pacify, if not to content, both the progressive and the reactionary. And to the latter, who will doubtless be in the majority, we would suggest that poetry which does not at least attempt to face the circumstances of its time may supply charming holiday-reading, but vital interest, anything strictly *poetic*, it certainly will not. If it is a natural preference to inhabit a room with casements opening upon Fairyland, one at least of them should open upon the Waste Land. At the same time the progressive would be unreasonable to expect confidence until he has proved that his destination justifies his speed.

While expressing our acknowledgement to the editors of *The Oxford Outlook, The Oxford University Magazine, The Cherwell* and *The Oxford University Review,* for permission to reprint poems from their pages, we should like to take the opportunity of congratulating Mr Blackwell upon the growing success of *Oxford Poetry,* if its sales and the number of contributors are any evidence, and of thanking those especially of the latter, whom we have not been able to include, for their expected forbearance towards our possible lack of discernment.

C.T.P.
W.H.A.

Oxford Poetry 1926, edited by Charles Plumb
and W. H. Auden

Preface to *Oxford Poetry 1927*

Did it serve no other purpose, this volume should at least offer a rebutment of the tendency, shared by many serious-minded and a few single-minded persons, contemptuously to credit Oxford with "the undergraduate mind." We confess ourselves able neither to comprehend such an abstraction nor to surmise what increment may result from the fitting of any intellectual caption to so many diverse heads. Our minds are sparse enough, in all

conscience: they must not also be held obnoxious to the charge of uni-
formity.

On the other hand, the chaos of values which is the substance of our
environment is not consistent with a standardization of thought, though,
on the political analogy, it may have to be superseded by one. All genuine
poetry is in a sense the formation of private spheres out of a public chaos:
and therefore we would remind those who annually criticize us for lack of
homogeneity, first, that on the whole it is environment which conditions
values, not values which form environment; second, that we must hold
partly responsible for our mental *sauve-qui-peut*, that acedia and un-
abashed glorification of the subjective so prominent in the world since the
Reformation.

> Im Winkel König Fahrenheit
> hat still sein Mus gegessen
> —„Ach Gott, sie war doch schön, die Zeit,
> die man nach mir gemessen!"*

A tripartite problem remains, and may be stated thus:

(*a*) The psychological conflict between self as subject and self as object,
which is patent in the self-consciousness and emotional stultification re-
sultant from the attempt to synchronise within the individual mind the
synthesis and the analysis of experience. Such appears to be the prime
development of this century, our experiment in the "emergent evolution
of mind." Emotion is no longer necessarily to be analysed by "recollection
in tranquillity": it is to be prehended emotionally and intellectually at
once. And this is of most importance to the poet; for it is his mind that
must bear the brunt of the conflict and may be the first to realize the new
harmony which would imply the success of this synchronization.

(*b*) The ethical conflict; a struggle to reconcile the notion of Pure Art,
"an art completely isolated from everything but its own laws of operation
and the object to be created as such,"† with those exigencies which its
conditions of existence as a product of a human mind and culture must
involve, where the one cannot be ignored nor the other enslaved.

(*c*) The logical conflict, between the denotatory and the connotatory
sense of words, which is the root-divergence of classic and romantic; be-
tween, that is to say, an asceticism tending to kill language by stripping
words of all association and a hedonism tending to kill language by dis-
sipating their sense under a multiplicity of associations.

In what degree this problem is realized and met in these pages, the
individual reader must decide. Those who believe that there is anything

* Christian Morgenstern, "Galgenlieder."
† Jacques Maritain, "Poetry and Religion"; *New Criterion*, V, 1.

valuable in our youth as such we have neither the patience to consider nor the power to condone: our youth should be a period of spiritual discipline, not a self-justifying dogma. As for the intelligent reader, we can only remind him, where he experiences distaste, that no universalized system—political, religious or metaphysical—has been bequeathed to us; where pleasure, that it is but an infinitesimal progression towards a new synthesis—one more of those efforts as yet so conspicuous in their paucity.

W.H.A.
C.D.-L.

Oxford Poetry 1927, edited by W. H. Auden and C. Day-Lewis

A Review of *Instinct and Intuition,* by George Binney Dibblee

Instinct and Intuition: A Study in Mental Duality. By George Binney Dibblee. Faber & Faber. 25s.

Duality is one of the oldest of our concepts; it appears and reappears in every religion, metaphysic, and code of ethics; it is reflected in (or perhaps reflects) the earliest social system of which we have knowledge—the Dual Organization in Ancient Egypt; one of its most important projections is war.

In Chapters XI to XVII of *Instinct and Intuition*, Mr Dibblee discusses various dualities, such as pleasure–pain, feeling–thought, conscious–unconscious, and decides, with good reason, that they are not fundamental. In their place he offers a thesis which may be summarised thus:—from introspection and from physiological evidence such as the Rivers-Head experiments on protopathic and epicritic sensibility—and the work on visual perception of Sir John Parsons, we may conclude that the mind is divided into two parts, an instinctive intelligent faculty on the one hand, acting both consciously and extra-consciously, the seat of which is the optic thalamus, and intellect proper on the other, resident in the cortex and cerebral hemispheres, termed reason when acting consciously, when extra-consciously intuition.

The argument is worked out with a caution, a wealth of detail, and a beauty of style that makes it difficult to criticise, nor is there space in a review to exhaust the many interesting questions it raises. We must confine ourselves to two—"What is human 'instinctive behaviour'?" and "Is there in any sense a Thalamo-cortical rivalry?"

Mr Dibblee points out the impossibility of arguing from the instinctive behaviour of animals and insects to that of man, but his conception of instinct seems more suitable to the former:

> It is the coincidence of three kinds of fitness which establishes instinct—the external network of circumstances in which the species can flourish and which is therefore fixed: the mediating corporeal mechanism whereby the necessary routine is made so easy as to be the readiest solution of a particular difficulty; and the deep traces of a neural path conducting unconscious intelligence, which has often presented before in the history of the species the same obvious and appropriate solution to the same regularly recurring problem. (p. 30) . . . It is the joint product of living afferent, central, and efferent mechanisms with the accent on the central link. (p. 45)

Such a definition will do in the case of animals, where, to our knowledge at least, all behaviour is instinctive, but in speaking of man it includes too much. Human instinct, if the term is to have meaning, must be limited to the subjective demands, proceeding from within outwards, existing independently of their objects (e.g. the instincts of creation and security). In so far as instinct may be gratified by the same behaviour towards the same objects, a habit is set up both of thought and action. (Is this Mr Dibblee's Advanced Instinct?) In so far as the behaviour or the object fail to satisfy, non-habitual reactions will tend to take place (emergency behaviour). Directed thinking is no less action than motor-activity, and is alike provoked by instinct. The sudden indiscretion of a middle-aged man is neither more nor less instinctive than his previous respectability, neither more nor less rational.

Mr Dibblee is hard to follow in his assumption of an "instinctive intelligence" of a different order from the rational and intuitional intelligence. The thalamus is phylogenetically older than the cortex, and there may well be division of labour, e.g. the thalamus may be the organ differentiating protopathic and epicritic sensations (Chap. XVIII); though here and elsewhere Mr Dibblee seems to rely too much on the Rivers-Head experiments which were too few not to admit of other interpretations. But that they are different in nature, or that one can act without the other, there is no evidence. The motor-control is cortical and the memory reserves of the hemispheres are dependent upon the sensory-receptor mechanism of the thalamus for their supply. The author is careful not to stress a rivalry between the two systems, but he does sometimes (p. 275, p. 307) suggest it.

The reason is an instrument, and cannot of itself control or inhibit anything; what it can do is to cause one desire to modify another. Reason alone can co-ordinate desires; reason alone can set them at each other's throats. Dual conceptions, of a higher and lower self, of instinct and reason, are only too apt to lead to the inhibition rather than the development of desires, to their underground survival in immature forms, the cause of disease, crime, and permanent fatigue. The only duality is that between the whole self at different stages of development—e.g. a man before and after a religious conversion. The old life must die in giving birth to the new. That which desires life to itself, be it individual, habit, or reason, casts itself, like Lucifer, out of heaven.

The Criterion, April 1930

A Review of *The Grasshoppers Come,* by David Garnett

The Grasshoppers Come. **By David Garnett. Chatto & Windus. 5s.**

Mr Garnett is well known; he has been highly praised; rightly so. A reader opening his latest book, expects to find a clean and careful prose, an ironic juxtaposition of circumstance, a faultless counterpoint; he does. The job is as perfectly turned out as ever. He reads to the end, interested, admiring and yet, when it is all over, a little unsatisfied; reminded perhaps of a sentence of Katherine Mansfield about E. M. Forster. "How beautifully he warms the pot. Yes, but there ain't going to be no tea." Why?

Take the plot. A rich middle-aged widow and an adventurer engage a professional pilot for a record long-distance flight. They make a forced landing somewhere in China. The couple set out to get help and disappear leaving the pilot alone with a sprained ankle. There is a swarm of locusts. He accidentally fires his machine and the glare attracts the attention of a Chinese pilot who rescues him.

Well, there's nothing the matter with that. The plot of the Odyssey is no more. But in the case of *The Grasshoppers Come* the final effect is very little more than the mere telling of the plot. Now I do not think that this is what Mr Garnett intends. If he were merely a good raconteur, there would be much more dialogue; as it is, the dialogue seems curiously clumsy, as if the author were uninterested in it. I think that Mr Garnett is not very interested in individuals or even their relations—nothing is made of the liaison between Lily Beanlands and Wilmot Shap, and very little of the "desperate" character of Wreaks—but that he is very interested in the human soul. I feel certain that the situations and incidents of this tale are profoundly significant to him, a revelation—call it an allegory if you will—of the nature of life. The reader is aware of this excitement but is not allowed to share it.

The reason for this failure in communication seems to me very important; it is characteristic of much of the best modern work—indeed it is a fault rarely found in inferior artists' understatement. Writers have been so afraid of saying what they don't mean, that what they do say, when not linked up by private associations, their own foreknowledge of their meaning, means very little. It is inadequate to say that this is merely a reaction against Victorian overstatement; they both have the same cause—fear. It is a commonplace of social observation that the blusterer and the mouse are both shy; the same is true in art. The non-committal manner is not a change of heart but only an advance in sophistication, a double bluff. The trouble is, not that these artists have no vision, but that they remain self-regarding; they are afraid of making fools of themselves over it.

This is not to say that *The Grasshoppers Come* is not worth reading; it is one of the most delightful books of this year. But its very charm gives the excited but baffled reader the right to expect more.

Échanges, December 1931

A Review of *The Complete Poems of John Skelton*

The Complete Poems of John Skelton. Edited by Philip Henderson. Dent. 10s. 6d.

First and foremost we should be all very grateful to Mr Henderson and Messrs Dent for making the whole of Skelton's work at last accessible to the general public in easily legible type and at a very reasonable price.

I must confess, however, that I do not clearly understand Mr Henderson's motives in modernizing the text, nor what he means exactly by a "popular" edition. Doubtless, there are extraordinary classes of readers—single-minded students of philology or prosody, American B. Litt. students, academies for young gentlemen—who demand special treatment, but the ordinary reader of poetry, I should have imagined, was someone like myself who, if he is prepared to read a fifteenth-century poet at all, likes to read what he wrote without bothering too much about occasional obscurities, and, if notes are necessary, prefers them relegated to the end to refer to on subsequent and more studied readings, and not to have his eye distracted by numbers in the middle of the line referring him to the bottom of the page and making him lose the place. If Skelton is obscure, which I doubt, it is not spelling which makes him so, but the vocabulary and allusions. If Mr Henderson, in the manner of Pound, had translated the language into that of Bowery or substituted the name of Bishop Barnes for that of Wolsey, his position would be perfectly clear. As it is, one never knows exactly how much of what one is reading is Skelton and how much Mr Henderson. Quotations are notoriously unfair, but in the following random extract, for example, I fail to see precisely what Mr Henderson's version gains in "popularity":

Some I make lyppars and lazars full horse	Some I make lepers and lazars full hoarse
And from that they love best some I devorse	And from that they love best some I divorse
Some with the marmoll to halte I them make	Some with the marmoll to halt I them make
And some to cry out of the boneake	And some to cry out of the boneache:
And some I vysyte with brennynge of fyre	And some I visit with burning of fire
Of some I wrynge of the neck lyke a wyre	Of some I wring the neck like a wire
And some I make in a rope to totter and walter	And some I make in a rope to totter and walter
And some for to hange themselfe in a halter	And some for to hang themself in a halter
And some I vysyte to batayle, warre and murther	And some I visit with battle war and murther
And make eche man to sle other	And make each man to slay the other

(*Magnificence* 1930–1939)

I should have thought that "brennynge" was no more the same word as "burning" than "marmoll" is the same as "ulcer", but that if it were a question of obscurity, a "popular" edition would first demand the emendation of the latter.

With these reservations, I hope every admirer of Skelton will buy this book: there is not likely to be another for a long time, and Skelton is a poet of whom, if you like any, you will like all.

Skelton's reputation is assured; the critics have made up their minds about him. I shall merely like to examine one or two critical judgments which do not seem to me to be quite as true as the frequency with which they are made would suggest.

Firstly, Skelton is generally regarded as an over-garrulous writer who did not know when to stop, and had no sense of proportion. Such a view overlooked an important factor in verse—that of tempo. By far the larger portion of English poetry is slow in movement and this has tended to fix the standard of criticism. In an interesting article in the *Criterion* Mr Sturge Moore recently criticized Hopkins' *Golden Echo* as redundant and offered a pruned version. This I think is a misunderstanding of the nature of rapid verse. Those interested in Gestalt psychology will be familiar with the problem of *real* wholes. The quicker the movement, the greater number of words which form a single apprehensible whole. If you try to analyse this whole into smaller parts the effect is destroyed. The smallest unit in slow verse (e.g. Milton), may be a line or half a line, in very rapid verse (a good modern example is Vachel Lindsay's *Bryan Bryan Bryan*), a whole paragraph. Read in this sort of way, Skelton, whose verse is perhaps the quickest of all the English poets, does not seem diffuse: the final effect is generally of a well-proportioned whole.

I am glad that Mr Henderson has called attention to the use of different kinds of verse for different characters in *Magnificence*. As far as I know Skelton is the only English poet who has done this. It is a commonplace that Shakespeare's characters are all rather like each other at emotional climaxes. Blank verse is a medium suitable to a certain type of character, the heroic: when the emotional tension is relaxed it tends to become flat. Skelton solves this problem of the verse-play successfully, and I believe *Magnificence* to be an excellent acting play. The subject is of topical interest to any age, the verse is easy to understand, an important advantage in poetry to be heard; a great deal of scope is left for action; and though the names of the characters may seem rather teasers to us, a sympathetic and intelligent producer could make them very significant.

Lastly, a sentence in Mr Henderson's introduction raises questions I cannot refrain from discussing:

> Had Skelton lived in almost any other age than his own, it is fairly certain that with a perfected instrument at his command, a regenerated language with a great tradition behind it, he would occupy a high and respected place in poetry, and his wit, applied to more modern problems, would most likely have won him the position of a Swift. . . .

As the greater part of Skelton's work is satirical, this involves deciding what we expect from a satirist.

In criticizing a satirical poem, I do not see how one can avoid reference to the abuses attacked. A satire, like an advertisement, should be a public service. More than in any other literary form, not only the magnitude and general interest of the subject, but also the size of the audience appealed to have to be considered. However brilliant his technical execution, if the satirist's subject be superficial or transitory, or his meaning obscure, the value of his work is lessened. I should be very sorry to see Skelton used as a convert's stick to beat the poor old Reformation with; but it is evident that there was less gap, both in language and interests, between the man-in-the-street and the intellectual in his time than in the age, say, of Pope; and that is the kind of society most favourable to good satire. Which is the major subject: that of *Why come ye not to court* or of the *Dunciad*, Wolsey or Grub Street? In addition, Skelton found an alliterative medium which had already proved its suitability for flyting, and which, depending, unlike the antithetical couplet and like swearing, on the emotiveness of certain words rather than on intellectual wit, was capable of reaching a wider and more unlettered audience.

The reader of *The Rape of the Lock* misses half the joke if he knows nothing of the eighteenth-century concept of the heroic poem; it presumes a high degree of literary sophistication. There is a similar kind of effect in *Philip Sparrow,* but there the only knowledge presupposed is an acquaintance with the Requiem Mass; which, to his contemporaries at any rate, was common knowledge.

In our own time it is even worse, partly because responsibility is now so diffused that the personal figure which satire demands is hard to find. A modern satirist in search of a subject would be far more likely to select a *Criterion* dinner than a Newspaper peer. Mr Wyndham Lewis, for example, even when he is attacking fundamental abuses attacks them *through* certain writers which the majority of people have never read: too often what promises to be really important degenerates into a private squabble between rival literary pushes.

How refreshing, then, to turn to the pages even of *John Bull* where, if one disagrees, one at least is clear what it is all about, or better to those of a poet like Skelton; who, using a language as direct as that of Burns, takes as his subjects matters of which the accidents may be peculiar to his times but the substance is common to all, and not least to our own.

The Criterion, January 1932

A Review of *Edda and Saga,*
by Bertha S. Phillpotts

Edda and Saga. By Dame Phillpotts. Thornton Butterworth:
Home University Library. 2s. 6d.

This little book is as good as Professor W. B. Ker's volume in the same series on *Mediæval English Literature;* that is, very good indeed. The chapters on the making of the Sagas and the technique of the Eddic poems are particularly excellent. Perhaps in a second edition, Dame Phillpotts will be able to include some original quotations from the Edda to set beside her own verse translations. The poems are not easy to procure (and Bray's Edda is disfigured by the most dreadful illustrations), and even the plainest reader would like to know what Old Norse looked and sounded like. There is a very complete glossary.

This book cannot fail to stimulate a greater interest in the sagas, and we can only hope that, as a result, we shall soon have new translations of all of them, less Wardour-Street in style than those of Morris and Dasent, and cheaper to buy.

The Criterion, January 1932

A Review of *The Prisoner's Soul—*
and Our Own, by Eivind Berggrav

The Prisoner's Soul and Our Own. By Eivind Berggrav. Translated
by Laura Gravely. Dent. 6s.

This book is the simply-written record of observations made by an able
and clear-sighted prison chaplain. That there is little in it which is star-
tlingly new to us, is a sign of how far the attitude of prison workers like
the author has already affected our attitude towards the criminal, though
our practice still rather lags behind. Over and over again he emphasizes
the paradox that the chief thing about the tough is that he is soft (see
particularly his chapters on the Mother-Martyr, and the Prisoner's reli-
gion); or rather it would be truer to say that we are all soft and that the
criminal is the one for whom softness is not enough. Most of us, lazy, just
manage to live our lives on the level of *Peg's Paper.* He can't: his anti-social
acts are a misdirected effort to grow up.

Bishop Berggrav has some interesting things to say about the treatment
of different kinds of prisoners (which seem to have been more carefully
considered in Scandinavia than in England). Whether solitary confine-
ment or a community prison is the better form of correction depends, as
he rightly says, on whether the criminals' trouble has been due to over- or
under-suggestibility to group influence. He also draws attention to the
difference between thieves and other classes of criminals which correlates
very well with the investigations of psychologists into the nature of theft,
that attempt to recover the lost or stolen treasure, love.

Miss Gravely's translation reads admirably.

The Criterion, July 1932

Writing

SPEECH

If an Australian aborigine were to sit down on a pin he would say "Ow".
Dogs with bones growl at the approach of other dogs. English, Russian,
Brazilian, all mothers "coo" to their babies. Sailors at any port, pulling
together on a hawser; watch them and listen—Heaving they grunt to-
gether "Ee-Ah".

This is the first language.

We generally think of language being words used to point to things, to say that something is *This* or *That,* but the earliest use of language was not this; it was used to express the feelings of the speaker; feelings about something happening to him (the prick of the pin) or attitudes towards other things in his world (the other hungry dog; the darling baby) or, again, as a help to doing something with others of his own kind (pulling the boat in). The first two uses are common to many animals but the last is peculiar to the most highly organized and contains more possibilities of development.

Life is one whole thing made up of smaller whole things which themselves are made up of smaller whole things and so on. The largest thing we can talk about is the universe, the smallest the negative electrons of the atom which run round its central positive nucleus, already a group. So too for us, nucleus and cell, cell and tissue or organ, organs or tissues and the human individual, individual and family, family and neighbours, neighbours and nation, nation and world, always groups linked up into larger groups, each group unique, an individual thing, different from every other thing, but without meaning except in its connection with other things. The whole cannot exist without the part, nor the part without the whole; and each whole is more than just the sum of its parts, it is a new thing (e.g. $2H_2 + O_2 = 2H_2O$, but the behaviour of water is not just the result of adding the behaviour of hydrogen to the behaviour of oxygen).

But suppose the part begins to work not only as if it were a whole (which it is) but as if there were no larger wholes; there is a breakdown (e.g. a cancer growth in the body). And this is what has happened to us. At sometime or other in human history, when and how is not known exactly, man became self-conscious; he began to feel, I am I, and You are Not-I; we are shut inside ourselves and apart from each other. There is no whole but the self.

The more this feeling grew, the more he felt the need to bridge over the gulf, to recover the sense of being as much part of life as the cells in his body are part of him. Before he had lost it, when he was doing things together in a group, such as hunting; when feeling was strongest, as when, say, the quarry was first sighted, the group had made noises, grunts, howls, grimaces. Noise and this feeling he had now lost had gone together; then, if he made the noise, could he not recover the feeling? In some way like this language began, but its development must have been very slow, like the development of full self-consciousness. Among savage tribes, for example, news travels much quicker than a messenger could carry it, by a sympathy which we, ignorant of its nature and incapable of practising, call telepathy. Dr Rivers tells a story somewhere of some natives in Melanesia getting into a rowing-boat. There was no discussion as to who should stroke or steer. All found their places as we should say by instinct.

Even among ourselves, two friends have to say very much less to understand each other's meaning than two strangers. Their conversation is often unintelligible to a third person. Even when we are listening to anyone, it is not only the words themselves which tell us what he means but his gestures (try listening with your eyes shut; it has been suggested that speech consists of movements of the larynx and other organs of speech which correspond to what were once movements of the hands), and also the extent to which he is talking to us personally (it is always difficult to understand what people are saying at another table in a restaurant; we are outside the group).

Self-conscious as we are, much of our speech is like a tunnel under which the currents of feelings can pass unseen. For example, take the kind of conversation one hears in railway carriages:

MAN. It's very cold for this time of year.
GIRL. Yes, it would be warmer if the sun were to come out.

What is really going on is something quite different, something like this:

MAN. What a nice looking girl you are. I hope you don't mind my speaking to you like this but I should like to know if your voice is as nice as your hat. Journeys are dull, aren't they, unless one finds somebody nice to talk to. I expect you have your difficulties too, like me. We all have. Let's be friends.
GIRL. You look nice but a girl has to be careful. You can never tell what men will be like if you encourage them too much. I hate trains too. Have you ever been in love? What was she like. Alright. We'll try and see how we get on.

MEANING

Words then are a bridge between a speaker and a listener. What the bridge carries, i.e. what the speaker gives and the listener receives, we call the *meaning* of the words.

In anything we say there are four different kinds of meaning; any one of them may be more important than the other three, but there is generally something of all four.

(1) *Sense* (typical case: fat stock prices on the wireless).
We say *something* or expect *something* to be said to us about something. "Stinker is a man". We now know that there is a thing called Stinker and that thing is a man and not a dog or anything else.

(2) *Feeling* (typical case: the conversation of lovers).

We generally have feelings about the things of which we are talking. "There's that horrible man Stinker". We now know that the speaker does not like Stinker.

(3) *Tone* (typical case: an after-dinner speech).

We generally have an attitude to the person we are talking to. We say the same thing in different ways to different people. "There's that swine Stinker", "There's Mr Stinker; of course I expect he's charming really, but I don't like him very much, I'm afraid."

(4) *Intention* (typical case: a speech at a General Election).

Apart from what we say or feel, we often want to make our listeners act or think in a particular way. "There's that man Stinker. I shouldn't have much to do with him if I were you". The speaker is trying to stop us seeing Mr Stinker.

LANGUAGE AND WORDS

Language as we know it consists of words, that is, a comparatively small number of different sounds (between forty and fifty in English) arranged in different orders or groups, each sound or group of sounds standing for something, an object, an action, a colour, an idea, etc.

To go back to our sketch of the origin of language: before language we have the people who feel something (the hunting group), the feeling (feeling of unity in the face of hunger or danger, etc.), the object which excites the feeling (the hunted bison), and the noise which expressed the feeling. If the noise was later used to recover the feeling, it would also present to the memory the idea or the image of the animal or whatever it was excited the feeling. Thus sounds would begin to have sense meaning, to stand for things, as well as having meaning as an expression of feeling.

It is unlikely therefore even at the first that language was entirely onomatopoeic, that is, that words were sounds imitating the sounds of things spoken about. Many words no doubt did, just as they still do (e.g. hissing, growling, splashing). It is only possible to imitate in this way actions or objects which make a noise. You could never for example imitate the sound of a chair. In fact, most of the power of words comes from their *not* being like what they stand for. If the word "ruin" for instance was only like a particular ruin, it could only serve to describe that one solitary building; as it is the word conjures up all the kinds of ruin which we know and our various feelings about them—ruined churches, ruined houses, ruined gasworks, loss of money, etc.

INFLECTION

All languages are originally inflected, that is to say, the sound standing for a particular object or action changes slightly according to how we are looking at it. E.g. the Roman said:

> Homo amat canem
> but   Canis amat hominem.

He felt that the man is a different man and the dog is a different dog if he is loving or being loved. But as people get more self-conscious, more aware of what they are feeling and thinking, they separate their feelings and thoughts from the things they are feeling or thinking about. They show the difference in attitude either by changing the word order or by using special words like prepositions. Thus in English, the least inflected language:

> The man loves the dog.
> The dog loves the man.
> The man gives a bone *to* the dog.

All languages show some inflection. (*I* love *him*. *He* love-*s me*.)

WRITING

Writing and speech are like two tributary streams, rising at different sources, flowing apart for a time until they unite to form a large river. Just as it is possible for sounds conveying their meaning by the ear to stand for things, pictures conveying their meaning through the eye can do the same.

The earliest kinds of writing, such as Egyptian hieroglyphs, or Mexican writings, are a series of pictures telling a story, as a sentence tells a story. The urge to write, like the urge to speak, came from man's growing sense of personal loneliness, of the need for group communication. But while speech begins with the feeling of separateness in space, of I-here-in-this-chair and You-there-in-that-chair, writing begins from the sense of separateness in time, of "I'm here to-day, but I shall be dead to-morrow and you will be alive in my place and how can I speak to you."

Primitive people, living in small groups, have very little idea of death, only a very strong sense of the life of the tribe which of course never dies. The moment man loses this sense of the continuously present group life, he becomes increasingly aware of the shortness and uncertainty of the life of the individual. He looks round desperately for some means of prolonging it, of living into the future, of uniting the past with the present. The earliest writings of which we know tell the exploits of dead kings. The writer is like the schoolboy who carves his initials on a desk; he wishes to live for ever.

How early speech joined up with writing it is impossible to say, but since sounds stood for things, they must also, as the sense or intellectual use of language developed, have stimulated visual images in the minds of the listeners, which would not have been very difficult to connect with real pictures. Just as sounds must soon have stopped imitating sounds of real objects, writing must soon have stopped being purely pictorial—drawings of each separate object. A language of this kind would have had to contain thousands of letters and would have been very difficult to learn and slow and clumsy to write. Chinese is still a language of this kind.

Further, abstract ideas would be impossible to represent by pictures (how, for example, could you draw a picture of "habit"?). Luckily, the fact that the number of different sounds which it is possible to make are comparatively few, presented a solution to this difficulty. By inventing an alphabet or code where one kind of mark stands for one kind of sound, any word could be written by arranging the marks or letters in the order in which the sounds were made. (Our own alphabet comes originally from Egypt through Phoenicia, Colchis and Italy.)

Spoken and Written Language

As long as people are living in small societies, and living generation after generation in one place, they have little need of writing. Poems, stories, moral advice, are learnt by heart and handed down by word of mouth from father to son. Oral tradition has certain advantages and certain disadvantages over writing. Generally speaking, the *feeling* meaning is transmitted with extraordinary accuracy, as the gestures and the tone of voice which go with the words are remembered also. With a statement in writing it is often impossible after a time to decide exactly what the author meant. (Think how easy it is to misunderstand a letter, or how many different interpretations have been made of Christ's saying, "Thou art Peter. Upon this rock will I build my church.") On the other hand, the sense meaning is apt to get strangely distorted. It is easy not to catch or to forget the exact words told to one, and to guess them wrongly; again we may be asked to explain something and add our own explanation which is passed on with the story. E.g. this message was once passed back from the front lines from mouth to mouth to the officer commanding the reserve: "Send reinforcements; the regiment is going to advance". What actually reached him was this: "Send three and fourpence; the regiment is going to a dance".

But as communities got larger and government became more centralised, writing became more and more important. Still, however, as long as copying of original manuscripts had to be done by hand, books were rare and too costly for any but the few. The invention of printing in the fifteenth century (it began with the printing of playing cards and religious pictures off wooden blocks) greatly increased the power of the written word, but the cost of books still limited their circulation. Popular printed literature during the sixteenth and seventeenth century, apart from some religious books, was confined to broadsheets and pamphlets peddled in the streets. The eighteenth century saw the rise of the magazine and the newspaper, and the introduction of steam power at the beginning of the nineteenth century, by cheapening the cost of production, put printed matter within the reach of anyone who could read or write. (N.B. also, the introduction of the penny post; and the effect of universal education. Strangely enough, the last five years, with the wireless and the talkies, have witnessed a revival in the use of the spoken word.)

The effect of this has been a mixed one. On the one hand it has made the language able to deal with a great many more subjects, particularly those which are abstract, like some of the sciences, to be more accurate, to draw finer distinctions of meaning. Words written down in one language can be translated into another. Thus the world's knowledge can be pooled, and words borrowed from another language for which the borrower has no word in his own with the exact shade of meaning which he wants (cf. clock—chronometer, stranger—alien, etc.). On the other hand increase in vocabulary makes a language more difficult to learn, not only just to learn the words, but to learn how to use them. When communities are small and their interests common to all their members, mere acquaintance with each other is enough to make people use their language well, but as communities increase and interests become specialised, as the past history of the language gets bigger and heavier, education in the use of language becomes more and more necessary. At present nobody gets such an education. The speech of a peasant is generally better, i.e. more vivid, better able to say what he wants to say, than the speech of the average University graduate. It's like juggling with balls. You may be able to juggle fairly well with three but if you try six, without careful practice you will probably drop them all. It is not the language that is to blame but our skill in using it.

VERSE FORM

Speech originated in noises made during group excitement. Excitement seems naturally to excite movement. When we are excited we want to dance about. Noise was thus in the beginning associated with movements of a group, perhaps dancing round food or advancing together to attack. The greater the excitement, the more in sympathy with each other each member of the group is, the more regular the movements; they keep time with each other; every foot comes down together.

Again, imagine a circle of people dancing; the circle revolves and comes back to its starting place; at each revolution the set of movements is repeated.

When words move in this kind of repeated pattern, we call the effect of the movement in our minds the metre. Words arranged in metre are verse.

Just as in a crowd we are much more easily carried away by feeling than when alone, so metre excites us, prepares us to listen readily to what is being said. We expect something to happen and therefore it does. When a poet is writing verse, the feeling as it were excites the words and makes them fall into a definite group going through definite dancing movements, just as feeling excites the different members of a crowd and makes them act together. Metre is group excitement among words, a series of repeated movements. The weaker the excitement, the less the words act together and upon each other. Rhythm is what is expected by one word of another. In scientific prose for example, what words do is only controlled by the sense of what is being said. They are like people in a street on an ordinary day. They can be or do anything they like as long as they keep to the left on the pavement, and don't annoy each other. But even here this much is expected. There is always some degree of rhythm in all language. The degree depends on the power of feeling.

Accents, long and short syllables, feet and all that, are really quite simple. You will always read a line of poetry rightly if you know its meaning (all four kinds). There are certain traditional rules in writing poetry, just as there are traditional steps in a dance, but every good poet, like every good dancer, uses them in his own way, which is generally quite distinct from that of any other poet. If you were describing a certain dance, you could do it in various ways—as consisting of ten steps, or of four long steps and six little steps, or of three heavy steps and six light ones; in the same way the motion or metre of a line of poetry can be described in different ways according as to how you choose to look at it. In English poetry, for example, we generally describe it by accents—light and heavy steps—because that is the most obvious feature about the movements of English speech. But remember always that such a description of movement is only a description; it isn't the movement itself.

Lastly, language may be ornamented in various ways. The two most familiar ornaments are alliteration (e.g. In a *s*ummer *s*eason when *s*oft was the *s*un) and rhyme (Old King *Cole* was a merry old *soul*).

Alliteration is found in the early verse of the teutonic people and rhyme, beginning perhaps in the marching songs of the Roman soldiers, was adopted by the early Christian hymn writers and so came into modern verse. Alliteration is the effect produced by an arrangement of words beginning with a similar sound, rhyme that produced by an arrangement of words ending in a similar sound. The sounds are similar but belong to different words and therefore have different meanings in each place. Through the likeness, thoughts and feelings hitherto distinct in the mind are joined together. They are in fact sound-metaphors.

Different Kinds of Writing

The difference between different kinds of writing lies not so much in the writing itself but in the way we look at it (and, of course, in the way the author wished us to look at it; but we often know very little about that). Literary forms do not exist outside our own minds. When we read any-thing, no matter what—a description of a scientific experiment, a history book, a ballad, or a novel—in so far as we pay attention only to what things are happening one after another to something or somebody, it is a story; in so far as we read it only to learn the way in which something or someone behaves in certain circumstances, it is science; in so far as we read it only to find out what has actually happened in the past, it is history.

People have often asked what is the difference between poetry and prose. The only difference is in the way the writer looks at things. (There is another difference between prose and *verse*; see above.) For instance, the novelist starts with a general idea in his mind; say, that people are always trying to escape from their responsibilities, and that escape only lands them in a worse mess. Then he writes a story about what happened to Mr and Mrs Smith. He may never say in so many words that they tried to escape, never mention his idea, but this idea is the force which drives the story along. The poet on the other hand hears people talking in his club about the sad story of Mr and Mrs Smith. He thinks: "There now. That's very interesting. They are just like everybody else; trying to get round life. It's like those sailors who tried to get to India by the North West passage. On they go, getting further and further into the ice, miles from home. Why, that's a good idea for a poem." He writes a poem about explorers; he may never mention Mr and Mrs Smith at all. The novelist then goes from the general to the particular, the poet from the particular to the general, and you can see this also in the way they use words. The novelist uses words with their general meaning and uses a whole lot of them to build up a particular effect, his character. The poet uses words with their particular meanings and puts them together to give a general effect, his idea. Actually, of course, nearly all novels and all poems, except very short ones, have both ways of looking at things in them (e.g. Chaucer's *Canterbury Tales* are more like novels in verse; Melville's *Moby Dick* is more like a poem in prose). All you can say is that one way is typical of the novelist and the other of the poet.

Another question. What is the difference between writing as a work of Art, what we call literature, and other kinds of writings. Again, it depends how you choose to look at it.

We are treating any piece of writing as a work of art when we regard our reading of it as a single act, confined to the reading and understanding of the writing itself, and not as one of a series of acts extending before and after our reading. I mean that, suppose I take up a bulb catalogue and just read it and do nothing more, I'm treating it as a work of art. If on the other hand, as is more likely, my reading of the catalogue is only one small part of a long process which began with my writing to the bulb grower for one, and will end only when the bulbs chosen from it, ordered from the grower, planted and watered in my garden, come to flower, I am not treating it as a work of art.

The absolutely pure work of art in this sense doesn't exist. The most we can say is that there are some kinds of writing which we know all the time we are reading them, why we are, and other kinds which we don't.

Why People Write Books

People write in order to be read. They would like to be read by everybody and for ever. They feel alone, cut off from each other in an indifferent world where they do not live for very long. How can they get in touch again; how can they prolong their lives? Children by their bodies live on in a life they will not live to see, meet friends they will never know, and will in their turn have children, some tiny part of them too living on all the time. These by their body; books by their minds.

But the satisfaction of any want is pleasant: we not only enjoy feeling full; we enjoy eating; so people write books because they enjoy it, as a carpenter enjoys making a cupboard. Books are written for money, to convert the world, to pass the time; but these reasons are always trivial beside the first two—company and creation.

How People Write Books

We know as much and no more about how books are made as we know about the making of babies or plants. Suddenly an idea, a feeling, germinates like a seed in the mind of the author and begins to grow. He has to look after it, manure and water the soil with his own experience, all that he knows and has felt, all that has happened to him in his life, straightening a shoot here, pruning a bit there, never quite certain what it is going to do next, whether it will just wither and die, come up in a single night like a mushroom, or thicken gradually into a great oak tree. The author is both soil and gardener, the soil part of him does not know what is going on, the gardener part of him has learnt the routine. He may be a careful gardener but poor soil; his books are then beautifully written but they seem to have nothing in them: we say he lacks inspiration. Or he may be excellent soil but a careless gardener. His books are exciting but badly arranged, out of proportion, harsh to the ear: we say he lacks technique. Good soil is more important than good gardening but the finest plants are the product of both.

Why People Read Books

When we read a book, it is as if we were with a person. A book is not only the meaning of the words inside it; it is the person who means them. In real life we treat people in all sorts of ways. Suppose we ask a policeman the way. As long as he is polite we do not bother whether he beats his wife or not, in fact if he started to tell us about his wife, we should get impatient: all we expect of him is that he should know the way and be able clearly to explain it. When we go to the music hall we want the comedian to amuse us; we don't want to go for a walking tour with him. But other people we treat differently; we want more from them than information or amusement; we want to live *with* them, to feel and think *with* them. When we say a book is good or bad we mean that we feel towards it as we feel towards what we call a good or bad person. (Remember though that a book about bad characters is not therefore bad, any more than a person is bad because he talks about bad people.)

Actually we know that we can't divide people into good and bad like that; everyone is a mixture; we like some people in some moods and some in others and as we grow older our taste in people changes. The same is true of books. People who say they only read good books are prigs. We all like some good books and some bad. The only silly thing to do is to pretend that bad books are good. The awful nonsense that most people utter when they are discussing or criticising a book, would be avoided if they would remember that they would never think of criticising a person in the same way. For example if a friend says "So and so is a swine" we don't say "That's absurd. He is a man so he can't be a pig." We know perfectly well he means that he has the same feelings of disgust towards So and so as he feels toward swine. Yet you often hear people criticising lines in poetry like

> The new horned moon
> With one bright star within the nether tip

for being untrue. Or they will say that they don't like a book because they don't agree with it. We think it rather silly when people can only be friends with those who hold the same views on everything. Or again they dislike it because they dislike the author, which is like saying you dislike a man because you disliked his father.

Reading is valuable just because books are like people and make the same demands on us to understand and like them. Our actual circle of friends is generally limited and all of us, I think, feel that our living, our relations with them are not as good as they might be, more muddled, difficult, unsatisfying than necessary. Just as a boxer exercises for a real fight with a punch ball or a sparring partner, so you can train yourself for relations with real people with a book. It's not easy, and you can't begin until you have some experience of real people first (any more than a boxer can practise with a punch ball until he has learnt a little about boxing), but books can't die or quarrel or go away as people can. Reading and living are not two watertight compartments. You must use your knowledge of people to guide you when reading books and your knowledge of books to guide you when living with people. The more you read the more you will realise what difficult and delicate things relations with people are but how worthwhile they can be when they really come off; and the more you know of other people, the more you will be able to get out of each kind of book, and the more you will realise how good a really good book can be, but that great books are as rare as great men.

Reading is valuable when it improves our technique of living, helps us to live fuller and more satisfactory lives. It fails when we can't understand or feel with what we read, either because of ignorance of our own, or obscurity in the writing.

It is a danger when we only read what encourages us in lazy and crude ways of feeling and thinking; like cheap company (too many people only read what flatters them; they like to be told they are fine fellows and all is for the best in the best of all possible worlds; or they only want to be excited, or to forget to-morrow's bills). It is also dangerous when it becomes a substitute for living; when we get frightened of real people and find books safer company: they are a rehearsal for living, not living itself. Swots and "bookish" people have stage fright.

BOOKS AND LIFE

A book is the product of somebody living in a particular place at a particular time. People have a nature they are born with, and they have a life which they lead and live through, which alters that original nature. They may be born with great talents but live in a society where they can't develop or use them; or they may be only averagely gifted but get the opportunity to make the most of them. Great men are a combination of talent and opportunity. Great books are as rare as great men, and, like them, they often come in batches. It is improbable that the men living in England in the sixteenth century were more naturally talented than those living in the eleventh, but they had a better chance, a more stimulating world. Take the greatest names in literature—Homer, Dante, Shakespeare. Homer is typical of a kind of writing called epic—long stories in verse about the exploits of a small group of young warriors under a leader, the pioneer or pirate band society, held together by their devotion to their leader, and by common interests in fighting and farming and wife-getting. Dante was a citizen of Florence, a small and ambitious city State (he was also a citizen of the universal religious State, the Catholic Church). Shakespeare was born in a small, young country, fighting for its existence as an independent nation. There is something common to all three: the small size of the society and the unity of interests. Whenever a society is united (and the larger the society the harder it is to unite and the cruder and more violent the only feelings which come) it has a great outburst of good writing; we don't only find one or two first-class writers, we find a whole mass of good small writers (think of Athens in the fifth century and the Elizabethan song-writers). Being made one, like the sailors pulling on the rope, it has all power.

But whenever society breaks up into classes, sects, townspeople and peasants, rich and poor, literature suffers. There is writing for the gentle and writing for the simple, for the highbrow and the lowbrow; the latter gets cruder and coarser, the former more and more refined. And so, today, writing gets shut up in a circle of clever people writing about themselves for themselves, or ekes out an underworld existence, cheap and nasty. Talent does not die out, but it can't make itself understood. Since the underlying reason for writing is to bridge the gulf between one person and another, as the sense of loneliness increases, more and more books are written by more and more people, most of them with little or no talent. Forests are cut down, rivers of ink absorbed, but the lust to write is still unsatisfied. What is going to happen? If it were only a question of writing it wouldn't matter; but it is an index of our health. It's not only books, but our lives, that are going to pot.

BOOKS TO READ

P. H. B. Lyon: *The Discovery of Poetry.*
T. Warner: *On the Writing of English.*
W. de la Mare: *Come Hither.*
A. Quiller-Couch: *The Art of Writing.*
L. A. G. Strong: *Common Sense about Poetry.*
I. A. Richards: *Science and Poetry.*

An Outline for Boys and Girls and Their Parents, edited by
Naomi Mitchison, 1932

Private Pleasure

The Year Book of Education 1932. Edited by Lord Eustace Percy.
Evans Brothers. 35s.
The Triumph of the Dalton Plan. By C. W. Kimmins and
Belle Rennie. Ivor Nicholson & Watson. 6s.
Reminiscences of a Public Schoolboy. By W. Nichols Marcy.
Elkin Mathews. 6s.

Here are three books—a bird's-eye view of the world of school—a puff of
a teaching method—a defence of a way of living. Here you may learn that
Monmouth demands a quarter of an hour longer for scripture than
Cornwall, that Ernie Todd aged twelve prefers the Dalton plan because
you can spend more time on the subjects in which you are weak, that louts
who accuse prefects of immoral relations with fags are, unless they
quickly apologise, justly and soundly thrashed. Data to support almost
any contention. Ratepayer, well-fed, daring his wife to contradict, may
thump the breakfast table, shout "Disgraceful. They're playing ducks and
drakes with our money. The nation can't afford it." Folk-dancer, remem-
bering a once-sore behind, thinks "Ah, had the masters loved me, I
should have expanded like a flower." Old boy in club, having another,
solemn as a clergyman declares "You can't get away from it. A good school
stamps a man."

It is going on. It is going to be like this to-morrow. Attendance-officer
will flit from slum to slum, educational agencies will be besieged by prom-
ising young men who have no inclination to business, examiners chuckle
over a novel setting of the problem of Achilles and the Tortoise, fathers
sell grand pianos or give up tobacco, that little Adrian or Derek may go to
Marlborough or Stowe.

Like everything else in our civilisation, the system we have made has
become too much for us; we can't stop the boat and we can't get out into
the cold sea. The snail is obeying its shell. All we can do is to become
specialists. Just as the soldier devises new methods of gas attack, or the
poet a new technique of verbal association, the teacher vigorously pursues
the logic of his tiny department. "How many pupils can I get?" "What is
the optimum method for getting the greatest number of them through
school certificate?" No one can afford to stop and ask what is the bearing
of his work on the rest of the world, its ultimate value. It's his job, his
bread and butter. Should he stop for one moment, there's his ego dinning
like a frightened woman "But what's going to happen to me? You'll be
sacked without a testimonial."

Education, all smoothly say, is the production of useful citizens. But, good God, what on earth is a useful citizen just now? If you are a police-man or a cabinet minister, it's a person who won't give you any trouble. Education is a dope to allay irritation. If he is poor, now that you no longer want him very much on the land but in mass-production plants, better give him something to think about lest he sense the absurd inade-quacy of the operations he is made to do, and start to smash. Better teach him enough to read the *News of the World*. Every worker shall attend an elementary school. If he's rich, your sort, then segregate him with the other young of your sort, let him year by year through his school-days feel all the excitement of a social climber, and make him so afraid of the opin-ions of your sort, that you may be sure he'll never do anything silly, like forgetting his class. Public school men will always lend each other money.

But there are some, who, though comfortably off, with no right to fear, have nightmares. "Of course, the world is really alright," they say, "it's only the way I look at it. If I'd been differently brought up, if men had understood me, life would be the jolly thing it ought to be. Besides, even if there is anything wrong with the world, if I do try to do anything about it, I shouldn't make any difference: I should only lose my money. It's all so very diffy. Let's go and ask the children. Perhaps they will know. Now remember; no slapping. The most wonderful thing in the world is love."

And off they go to live with the children, and splendid they are at it too. The children brighten up no end,—in their heads. Stupidity which is a natural defence against living beyond one's means collapses under the intense fire of their kindness. Girls of eleven paint like Picasso, boys of sixteen write pastiches of Joyce. Every child responds to the love smarm— for a bit. But emotionally it withers. Before a man wants to understand, he wants to command or obey instinctively, to live with others in a relation of power; but all power is anathema to the liberal. He hasn't any. He can only bully the spirit.

And so unconsciously the liberal becomes the secret service of the rul-ing class, its most powerful weapon against social revolution.

For the freedom they boast of is bogus, management by flattery, per-suading people that your suggestions are really their own. Its power lies in the inexhaustible vanity of the human heart. Don't think that you can behave as you like in a liberal school—a little recalcitrance, yes that is amusing, but a will of your own! Make no mistake about that.

The public schools are at least better than that. They offer an intense social field, the satisfactory nature of which can be seen in the fact that, their members, like bees taken from a colony, when they leave it, spiritu-ally die. They fail because they are only for the splendid people: they are economically parasitic. Those who leave them will not attempt to create a similar kind of society in the world because that would mean admitting the others, those who have frizzed hair, or eat peas with a knife.

But what can one do? Dearie, you can't do anything for the children till you've done something for the grown-ups. You've really got nothing to teach and you know it. When you have repapered the walls perhaps you will be allowed to tell your son how to hold the brush. In the meantime some of us will go on teaching what we can for a sum which even in its modesty we do not really deserve. Teaching will continue to be, not a public duty, but a private indulgence.

Scrutiny, September 1932

Problems of Education

Education and the Social Order. By Bertrand Russell.
George Allen & Unwin. 7s. 6d.

This book is excellent propaganda. Like most propagandists, Mr Russell is subtle to detect the psychological weakness of his opponents, but sometimes blind to his own. His book is full of valuable things.

> Conservatives and Imperialists lay stress on heredity because they belong to the white race but are rather uneducated. Radicals lay stress on education because it is potentially democratic . . .
>
> The town-dweller has, instead [of patriotism], a sentiment largely artificial, largely the product of his education and his newspapers.
>
> Progressive educators . . . have been inclined to generate self-importance in the child, and to let him feel himself a little aristocrat whom adults must serve.

And the whole of the chapter on class feeling in education shows Mr Russell as a brilliant critic, from an intellectual standpoint. For he is a propagandist for disinterested curiosity, the promotion of rational enquiry. One is tempted to feel that that is all he really does care about, that his only reason for disliking injustice is that it makes research difficult. "If a conquering dogmatic Marxism were to replace Christianity, it might be as great an obstacle to scientific progress as Christianity has been."

There is to be a ruling class, but it is to be a class of the clever boys who will be educated apart. As the cognitive part of man is the basis of his excellence, the only mortal sin is to be closed to argument, or to teach doctrines which cannot be intellectually proved.

It is curious that Mr Russell should be drawn to Communism, because he does not give the impression of liking community life very much. The physical presence of other people hinders thinking, and he would hate that. He says rightly that "science has so altered our technique as to make the world one economic unit" but omits to say that this has no connection with the psychological unit, to point out that Nationalism fails not because the nation is too small a group but because it is too large. It would be presumptuous of me to pretend to know what the proletariat think about Communism; but its increasing attraction for the bourgeois lies in its demand for self-surrender for those individuals who, isolated, feel themselves emotionally at sea. Does Mr Russell never contemplate the possibility that intellectual curiosity is neurotic, a compensation for those isolated from a social group, sexually starved, or physically weak?

In his treatment of sex and of religion he hates, not only the wrong kind of mystery, but any mystery, all that cannot be reduced to rational proportions or test tube knowledge. Knowledge will save the lover and the worshipper. All that is not understandable is "childish emotion." The trouble is that Mr Russell refuses to admit that man's nature is dual, and that each part of him has its own conception of justice and morality. In his passionate nature man wants lordship, to live in a relation of power with others, to obey and to command, to strut and to swagger. He desires mystery and glory. In his cerebral nature he cares for none of these things. He wants to know and be gentle; he feels his other passionate nature is frightening and cruel.

The liberal methods of education are far better for the latter; whether they are as satisfying to the former as the old methods, with all their grave faults, is more doubtful. Liberals like Mr Russell hate aristocracy and would substitute bureaucracy, since they hate personal power because of its frequent cruelty. The danger is, though, that, destroying it, man will grow dingy, society a collection of rentiers governed by an intellectual watch committee; instead of the terror, the spiritual bully.

Education, whatever it pretend, can do nothing for the individual; it is always social. The growth of an individual cannot be planned; it is the outcome of passionate relationships (hence the importance of the family. All the criticisms levelled at it are just and yet, as Mr Russell bravely admits, we cannot picture the world without it), and these exist under any society or system of education. Kropotkin owed as much to the *Corps des pages* as to anything else.

The failure of modern education lies not in its attention to individual needs, nor to methods, nor even to the moral ideals it preaches, but in the fact that nobody genuinely believes in our society, for which the children are being trained. All books—and this is one of them—which help to make people conscious of this lack of belief are valuable and should be read.

The New Statesman and Nation, 15 October 1932

A Review of *The Evolution of Sex,* by Dr Gregorio Marañón, and *The Biological Tragedy of Women,* by Anton Nemilov

The Evolution of Sex. By Dr Maranon. George Allen & Unwin. 15s.
The Biological Tragedy of Women. By Anton Nemilov.
George Allen & Unwin. 7s. 6d.

To assert that the female is an organism intermediate between the infantile or adolescent organism and the virile organism, and that the latter is a terminal phase of the former, is to pre-suppose one and the same root, sexually neuter or bi-valent, out of which springs the development of the two sexes, with a rhythm and intensity in each case. (p. 15)

Conditions of sexual confusion are so widely diffused that there is scarcely any human being whose sex is not tainted by a doubt. (p. 17)

The imposing mass of medical evidence with which Dr Maranon supports his argument, the layman must swallow whole, though casual remarks marks may startle. Why, for instance, is "enforced chastity in women not an 'organic' tragedy as it is in men . . . it may be a 'social' tragedy but nothing more" (p. 71)? I am not sure what is meant by "organic" and "social", but it seems a surprising statement for a biologist to make. Comrade Nemilov tells me that the tragedy of woman is that she is never set free from her physiological duties to the race as is man in whom sex is confined to the brief act of copulation after which he is free for world building. I should have concluded therefore that enforced chastity in women would have more serious psychological effects than in men. And why does an hermaphrodite who goes into the army show no inferiority-feeling (p. 128)? I should have thought it an obvious defence reaction.

These are minor points. We are to take it as settled, then, that we are none of us 100 per cent he-men or she-women. I must confess, however, that it is not as evident to me as it is to the professor that "the progress of humanity will be in the direction of greater differentiation and therefore of greater rigour in the normality of the relations between the sexes" (p. 233). Is it really true that the primitive human races show more inter-sexual states than a modern urban community? They may, but the professor doesn't give us the evidences of his faith. Hormonal influence, about which the doctor has a great deal to say (he mentions the interesting fact that hormones are unknown amongst the insects), which can modify even the original zygotic constitution of the organism, shows the increasing dependence in the superior animals of body growth and metabolism upon the higher nerve centres, the increasing centralization of control. Man, in fact, is perfectly capable, by taking thought, of adding cubits to his stature; he can become more or less virile as he chooses. In nomad tribes, for example, competition for grazing areas involves war, plunder and rapid movements. Tribal preservation depends on the male. Male beauty is exalted, female softness despised, and you get a patriarchal community where women are socially degraded, and the younger males form homosexual unions of the Achilles-Patroclus brotherhood-in-arms type. Capitalist industrial areas, on the other hand, exhibit the state of affairs analysed by Mr Wyndham Lewis in the *Doom of Youth*. To big business and for its trivial but exhausting tasks of mass production, an intermediate pert adolescent type is the most suitable; it is advertised for and obtained. The effect of mother on son, son on wife, so dear to the healers, is the process by which the valuable product is manufactured. There is a lot of schoolgirlish tittle-tattle about homosexuality among colonials and other ill-informed persons. The mere fact that A prefers girls and B boys is unimportant. The real cause for alarm lies in the large number of nervous and unhappy people who are incapable of any intimate faithful relationship at all, in whom sensation has remained at or regressed to the infantile level as an end in itself (Lawrence's Aphrodite of the Foam), and to whom, therefore, the object is really non-existent. It is true that nearly all homosexual relations are of this kind but so are a large proportion of heterosexual ones and there is nothing to choose between them. Big business encourages them because human relations are bad for trade. Vitality would not keep its eye on the conveyor-belt; neuters are cheaper and easier to handle.

"Everything will be all right if we get a proper education" is a favourite cry (the professor joins in it), but an evasion. What is the use of trying to remove complexes from individuals when the society into which they will go demands that they should have them? It is not time to talk of educating the young until you can guarantee them security of livelihood, interesting work, and a rational amount of leisure. Goodness knows these alone are not enough. Comrade Nemilov's excellently lucid little book proves that:

> I could mention thousands of cases of sexual licentiousness not only among the uninformed but among the most intelligent and advanced members of the working class. . . . One [of the reasons] is the absence of a distinct and healthy ideology in relation to sex problems. I insist upon ideology and advance it without fear of being considered an idealist or worse. (p. 203)

But education succeeds social revolution, not precedes. You cannot train children to be good citizens of a state which you despise.

Both these books plead for more sexual knowledge. That is necessary no doubt, but it must go far enough to know its own dangers. A schoolmaster said to me recently: "I want to make the boys able to talk about sex in an ordinary way, just as they would talk about the parts of a motor car." I could not help feeling that those who talk about sex in this way would be inclined to treat their wives like machines. Science which puts on airs with sex is bad science.

The last hundred years have seen an immense advance not only in knowledge, but also in the technique of spreading and instilling it: this means that Liberalism is gone for ever. Whoever possesses the instruments of knowledge, the Press, the Wireless, and the Ministry of Education, is the dictator of the country; and, my friends, it becomes increasingly difficult to overthrow a bad one because imitating our voice, he makes us believe that he does not exist. If we want a decent sex life, happy human relations, if we want to be people at all, and not behaviorist automatons, we must see to it that our dictators can have no personal or class axe to grind and we must hurry or it will be too late.

The Criterion, January 1933

Gentleman versus Player

Thoughts and Adventures. By the Rt Hon Winston S. Churchill, M.P.
Thornton Butterworth. 12s. 6d.

The English are a feminine race, the perfect spies and intriguers, with an illimitable capacity for not letting the right hand know what the left hand is doing, and believing so genuinely in their self-created legend of themselves as the straight-forward no-nonsense, stupid male that at first others are taken in. Afterwards they are not so sure; indeed to-day it would be difficult to find anyone in Europe, Africa, Asia or America who is. Mr Churchill has never really been trusted by the English because he is always letting the cat out of the bag. Honest Mr Baldwin is the ideal figure for the English fascist government, the professional posing as the amateur; Mr Churchill is the genuine article.

The amateur is always interested primarily in himself, in his ideas and deeds as a father in the career of his sons, as extensions of his own personality, hence his love of publicity. The professional, interested only in his job, knows that if you are to realise your wishes, the less other people know about them, the better.

No one reading this book or indeed any by Mr Churchill can credit him with having thought long or deeply about anything, but he is equally ready to write on any subject, the Quantum Theory, Cézanne, or the Old

Testament, and except for the title you will not be able to tell which is which:

(1) We may imagine a great ship of war steaming forward into battle. On the bridge there are only lay figures in splendid uniforms making gestures by clockwork and uttering gramophone speeches. The Engineer has taken charge of the vessel and, through the vessel, of the Fleet. He does not see a tithe of what is going on. How can he, locked in his engine-room far beneath the water-line and the armoured deck? He has stoked up all his boilers, he has screwed down all his safety-valves; he has jammed the rudder amidships. He utters nothing but the wild command, "Full speed ahead."

(2) No, we must take the loss with the gain. On the uplands there are no fine peaks. We must do without them while we stay there. Of course we could always if we wished go down again into the plains and valleys out of which we have climbed. We may even wander thither unwittingly. We may slide there. We may be pushed there. There are still many powerful nations dwelling at these lower levels—some contentedly—some even proudly. They often declare that life in the valleys is preferable. There is, they say, more variety, more beauty, more grace, more dignity—more true health and fertility than upon the arid highlands. They say this middle situation is better suited to human nature. The arts flourish there, and science need not be absent. Moreover it is pleasing to look back over the plains and morasses through which our path has lain in the past, and remember in tradition the great years of pilgrimage. Then they point to the frowning crag casting its majestic shadow in the evening light; and ask whether we have anything like that up there. We certainly have not.

(3) But it is in the use and withholding of their reserves that the great commanders have generally excelled. After all, when once the last reserve has been thrown in, the commander's part is played. If that does not win the battle, he has nothing else to give. The event must be left to luck and to the fighting troops. But these last, in the absence of high direction, are apt to get into sad confusion, all mixed together in a nasty mess, without order or plan—and consequently without effect. Mere masses count no more. The largest brush, the brightest colours cannot even make an impression. The battlefield becomes a sea of mud mercifully veiled by the fog of war. It is evident there has been a serious defeat. Even though the General plunges in himself and emerges bespattered, as he sometimes does, he will not retrieve the day.

I shall be surprised if the reader is able to detect that the first of these concerns Ludendorff, the second Democracy, the last the technique of painting.

Like all amateurs Mr Churchill is a hero-worshipper; first the pater, then the rest (can Lord Lloyd be the latest?). He has had the amateur's luck sometimes to have seen the wood where the professionals saw only the trees; he was one of the first in England to realize the weakness of *laissez-faire* and the necessity for State-planning but lacked the necessary patience and self-effacement to go further, the self-knowledge and moral courage to forgo the psychological satisfactions of home sweet home. Hence the sniffing round the dictators. He wants to have his cake and eat it. To enquire into the genuine nature of the State, to base his actions as the professional must upon a reasoned and deeply-felt philosophy, for that he has neither interest nor leisure: it was politics for him for the sake of the ride.

With the result that over Russia he exhibits all the hysteria of the invalid or of the unforgivably insulted; to discover that your coachman has not only thought of your schemes already, but is putting them into practice with a thoroughness and attention to detail of which you are incapable, must be galling, but Mr Churchill might make some pretence at rationalizing this annoyance. He appears to know no more about communism than our left boot. Nor was it wise to touch on anthropology if this is the best you can do:

> The story of the human race is War. Except for brief and precarious interludes, there has never been peace in the world; and before history began, murderous strife was universal and unending. But up to the present time the means of destruction at the disposal of man have not kept pace with his ferocity. Reciprocal extermination was impossible in the Stone Age. One cannot do much with a clumsy club. Besides, men were so scarce and hid so well that they were hard to find. They fled so fast that they were hard to catch. Human legs could only cover a certain distance each day. With the best will in the world to destroy his species, each man was restricted to a very limited area of activity. It was impossible to make any effective progress on these lines. Meanwhile one had to live and hunt and sleep. So on the balance the life-forces kept a steady lead over the forces of death, and gradually tribes, villages, and governments were evolved.

No, Mr Churchill cannot candidly be said to know anything, but he has his talent. He could have been, and indeed, to a certain extent he is, a great writer. His huge comic history of the war is in our opinion the best of all the war books. He has at times an extraordinary verbal sense, e.g. when describing the scene just before the German March offensive he says "It was an hour of intolerable majesty and *crisis*" or again at the meeting of Clemenceau and Foch in the volume before us, "But, thank God, at that moment the greatest Frenchmen of this *awful* age were supreme, and were friends." Indeed the whole article ("A day with Clemenceau") in which this paragraph occurs is Churchill at his very best.

We are unable to imagine any propaganda against Imperialist war more deadly than this account of senile homicidal maniacs:

> As we reached the road a shell burst among a group of led horses at no great distance. The group was scattered. A wounded and riderless horse came in a staggering trot along the road towards us. The poor animal was streaming with blood. The Tiger, aged seventy-four, advanced towards it and with great quickness seized its bridle, bringing it to a standstill. The blood accumulated in a pool upon the road. The French General expostulated with him, and he turned reluctantly towards his car. As he did so, he gave me a sidelong glance and observed in an undertone, "*Quel moment délicieux!*"

The old humbug can write. The contrast between artists and their creations is frequently startling, but we have never felt a more extraordinary one than this; to turn from the utterly humourless face which confronts us on the frontispiece to the savage vivid farce of the pages which follow.

Scrutiny, March 1933

A Review of *The Dark Places of Education,* by Dr Willi Schohaus

Dark Places in Education. By Dr Schohaus. Allen & Unwin. 12s. 6d.

"All power corrupts. Absolute power corrupts absolutely," said Lord Acton. If you do not believe it, take a look at these documents. And what is true in one field of human activity, is generally true in another. The recorded utterances and behaviour of politicians, generals, business wizards, newspaper magnates and headmasters, have a curious and unhappy resemblance to each other. People in authority very quickly become humour characters; all commanders are melodramatic.

Intending teachers would do well to read this book, not so much for the children's sake as for their own. An excessive interest in child welfare, like an obsession about cruelty to animals, is not a symptom of a healthy society; a preoccupation of those with small independent incomes, it is often a propitiation of the feelings of guilt at not attacking the fundamental abuses of a society, in which an unsatisfactory educational system is one of many results, not a cause.

Children have always to take pot luck; and a healthy child is more resilient than the experts would appear to believe. One's impression of the various contributions to Dr Schohaus's questionnaire is of workmen who are always complaining of their tools. One does not doubt the truth of their statements, but one feels that they are glad to find scapegoats for their own troubles. Those who "have never had a chance" rarely take them.

But to the teachers themselves, this book should be a terrible warning. As the author remarks: "To those who are not sure of themselves, the problem of discipline easily becomes a highly personal matter." It is typical of a topsy-turvy way of doing things, that while the pupils in our training colleges are taught child psychology, they learn nothing about their own, are given no sort of insight whatever into themselves, which, in a profession where adults are expected, perhaps inevitably, to profess official opinions on every subject of importance, to lead the private life of a clergyman, where a mask is essential, sets up a strain that only the long holidays of which other professions are often so jealous, safeguard from developing into a nervous breakdown.

The Dark Places in Education should help both the public and the teaching profession to realize the necessity of lightening these psychological burdens as much as possible, or at least of equipping masters and mistresses with the knowledge of how best to bear them.

The Criterion, April 1933

A Poet Tells Us How to Be Masters of the Machine

The machine is a mechanised tool; a tool in that it is a device for the economical use of power; mechanised in that the manipulation of the tool is transferred from a human being to a mechanism.

To the consumer then the machine is a means of obtaining an abundance of goods; to the producer a means of lightening his labour and increasing his leisure.

It sounds ideal: a four-hour working day; steam yachts and cigarette lighters all round. There aren't yet. Is it the fault of the capitalists? Not at all.

On the contrary, it is just what they might soon provide—except, of course, to the unemployed.

Imagine yourself in the near future a worker in some gigantic factory. For four hours every day you screw one nut on to each of a succession of chassis moving along a belt. By doing this you earn £6 a week.

You live in a villa, have your own car, a wireless in the sitting-room, an electrical refrigerator in the kitchen, everything that the advertisements tell you you need, much that in the nineteenth century could not be had for love or money.

You have the goods, and you have the leisure; goods, the material with which to satisfy your wants, and leisure, the time in which to satisfy them. Are you happy? If not, why not?

The question is, what do you really want? You want, I think, two things. First security, not to be afraid that you may lose your job, to be certain that other people like you and respect you, not only your friends, but the people you see in trams, or the policeman at the corner.

Secondly, you want to do something, to make things, to discover new facts, prove to yourself and others by your skill or brains that you are worth something, in fact, to give your existence a material meaning.

How does machinery help you? At present, not much. Security?—if you are a wage-earner, machinery means more unemployment; one person can look after many machines, and the work requires little skill but great intensity of labour, so that only the young are required.

The worker is too old at thirty. If you are a shareholder, the fierceness of competition and the constant trade booms and depressions keep you in a perpetual state of anxiety about your investments.

When people are anxious, leisure becomes a vacuum to be forcibly filled—never be alone, never stop to think. Half the machinery of the world is running to-day not to satisfy any real want, but to stop us remembering that we are afraid.

Does the machine help us to do or make things which make us proud of ourselves? Take the ordinary machine-minder. Most of the operations in a mass production plant are of such slight importance in themselves that no one could possibly feel that doing them made him a man.

They are only labour for wages, not work. The case of the machine-carter is different. Engine or crane drivers, for example, who have a powerful machine completely dependent on their judgment, or skilled electricians installing a lighting system, have a real job, needing all their faculties of body and mind.

But there are a limited number of such; there will always be required a mass of unskilled workers for whom their real life must lie outside their employment.

What of the machine, then, during leisure? Lack of security is attributable to a machined economic and social system, and the deluge of fancy luxury articles is largely an effect of capitalism, but in any kind of modern

State the abundance of goods which machinery makes possible will still raise the questions: Do I want all these things? What do I want them for?

If you are a mechanic, interested in the construction and technical working of machinery, the questions answer themselves.

If you are not, remember that while one machine can only do one thing, and do it all the time, human desire is intermittent, variable, and many-sided.

The machine therefore tends to dictate that the particular desire it satisfies is like it, unique and ever active, and to suppress those for which it is not constructed, unless you, its owner, are quite certain exactly what you want it for, e.g. I want this wireless set to listen to the concert next Wednesday, to hear the news at 9.20.

I do not want it to be turned on all day while I read.

Do not let the possession of a motorcycle oblige you to use it at times when you really want to go for a walk. Find out what you want first of all, and then if a machine will help you, use it.

In theory machines have made it possible for everyone to reach a standard of living formerly unattainable even by the very rich. In practice they have so far made a majority of mankind wretched and a minority unhappy, spoiled children.

If you are to make the theory fact, you must first establish a Socialist State in which everyone can feel secure, and, secondly, have enough self-knowledge and common sense to ensure that machines are employed by your needs, and not your needs by the machinery.

Daily Herald, 28 April 1933

A Review of *Culture and Environment,* by F. R. Leavis and Denys Thompson, and Other Books

Culture and Environment. By F. R. Leavis and Denys Thompson.
Chatto & Windus. 6s.
How to Teach Reading. By F. R. Leavis. Minority Press. 2s. 6d.
How Many Children Had Lady Macbeth? By L. C. Knights.
Minority Press. 2s. 6d.

What is a highbrow? Someone who is not passive to his experience but who tries to organise, explain and alter it, someone in fact, who tries to influence his history: a man struggling for life in the water is for the time being a highbrow. The decisive factor is a conflict between the person and his environment; most of the people who are usually called highbrows had either an unhappy childhood and adolescence or suffer from physical defects. Mr Leavis, Mr Thompson, Mr Knights, Mr Pound, the author and the reader of this review, are highbrows, and these books are a plea for the creation of more.

I think rightly. We live in an age in which the collapse of all previous standards coincides with the perfection in technique for the centralised distribution of ideas; some kind of revolution is inevitable, and will as inevitably be imposed from above by a minority; in consequence, if the result is not to depend on the loudest voice, if the majority is to have the slightest say in its future, it must be more critical than it is necessary for it to be in an epoch of straightforward development.

All these three books are concerned with school education. *How many children had Lady Macbeth?* is an attack on the bunk in most teaching of Shakespeare, with its concentration on the characters and plot, and its omission of the poetry. *How to teach Reading* is a demand for training in the technique of critical reading. *Culture and Environment* is a practical text book for assisting children to defeat propaganda of all kinds by making them aware of which buttons are being pressed.

All three books are good and will, I hope, be read seriously by all school teachers. *Culture and Environment* is particularly excellent because it sets the examination papers; teachers are usually hard-worked, and, while agreeing with the importance of this kind of instruction, are either too busy or too tired to prepare it themselves.

Also I am inclined to think that advertising is a better field than literature for such work, the aim of which, like that of psycho-analysis, is primarily destructive, to dissipate a reaction by becoming conscious of it. Advertising and machines are part of the environment of which literature is a reaction, those who are critically aware of their environment and of themselves will be critical of what they read, and not otherwise. I think it extremely doubtful whether any direct training of literary sensibility is possible.

Our education is far too bookish. To give children masterpieces to read, the reaction of exceptional adult minds to vast experiences, is fantastic. A boy in school remains divorced from the means of production, from livelihood; it is impossible to do much, but I believe that for the time being the most satisfactory method of teaching English to children is through their environment and their actions in it; e.g. if they are going to read or write about sawing wood, they should saw some themselves first: they should have plenty of acting, if possible, and under their English teacher movement classes as well, and very, very little talk.

These books all imply the more general question "What is to be done?" though, perhaps intentionally, they all avoid specifically stating or answering it. Mass production, advertising, the divorce between mental and manual labour, magazine stories, the abuse of leisure, all these are symptoms of an invalid society, and can only be finally cured by attending to the cause. You can suppress one symptom but only to create another, just as you can turn a burglar into an epileptic. Opinions differ both on cause and cure, but it is the duty of an investigator to state his own, and if possible the more important conflicting ones. Consciousness always appears to be uncontaminated by its object, and the danger of the methods advocated in these books is of making the invalid fascinated by his disease, of enabling the responsible minority to derive such intellectual satisfaction from contemplating the process of decay, from which by the nature of consciousness itself they feel insulated, that they lose the will and power to arrest it.

The Twentieth Century, May 1933

A Review of *The Poems of William Dunbar*

The Poems of William Dunbar. Edited by W. Mackay Mackenzie.
Porpoise Press. 7s. 6d.

Mr Mackenzie and the Porpoise Press are to be congratulated on giving us this edition of Dunbar which has long been overdue. The notes and vocabulary are wisely segregated from the text, and the introduction furnishes us with all the facts about the poet which we are likely to want, and disposes of the legend that he was directly influenced by Villon. Dunbar has suffered both from being inaccessible and from the extravagant praise of those who have a Scottish axe to grind; this edition at last makes it possible for the general poetry-reading public to judge him for themselves.

As the editor remarks in the preface, Dunbar is a "maker", not a seer. Those who search in his poetry for a message will find nothing, nor does he, like Villon or Burns, tell us much about the human heart.

Yet, on the other hand, if he is compared with other social poets such as Aristophanes, Juvenal, Dryden, or even Skelton, he is to be seen in a different class from them. All these poets are passionately interested in the movements, political, moral, or religious, of their time, and communicate to the reader a sense of their importance.

Dunbar does not. One is not tempted, as one would be if he were Dryden, to open a history book and read about sixteenth-century Scotland. His poetry is delightful but has no reverberations, it does not make us curious.

In fact, Dunbar is a drawing-room poet, the same kind of poet as Prior, and in a literature where prophets of large ideas and vague language are common, but such poets very rare, a good one, and Dunbar is very good indeed, is particularly welcome. Watch him at it and admire. Whatever subject you suggest, Women, Covetousness, Aberdeen, Dogs; whatever your taste, pious, gay, melancholy, bawdy; he will write a poem for you, apt and elegant. The first gift of such a poet is verse technique, and Dunbar is unfailingly brilliant. His poems never fail to do what he intends them to do. He knows exactly what kind of verse will suit any given subject, exactly what can be got out of a metre or a stanza form.

For horseplay:

> Lene larbar, loungeour, baith lowsy in lisk and lonye,
> Fy! skolderit skyn, thow art bot skyre and skrumple;

For moralizing:

> O wreche be war! this warld will wend the fro
>   Quhilk hes begylit mony greit estait;
> Turne to thy freynd, belief nocht in thy fo,
>   Sen thow mon go, be graithing to thy gait.

For gallantry:

> Sweit rois of vertew and of gentilnes
> Delytsum lyllie of everie lustynes
>   Richest in bontie and in bewtie cleir,
>   And everie vertew that is held most deir
> Except only that ye ar mercyles.

For hymns:

> The fo is chasit, the battel is done ceis
> The presone broken, the jevellouris fleit and flemit
> The weir is gon, confermit is the peis,
> The fetteris lowsit, and the dungeoun termit.

He is the master of any manner, but it remains only a manner. The *Lament of the Makaris* tempts one to wonder what poetry Dunbar would have written if he had been as consistently unfortunate and wretched as Villon, but apparently he was not. He remained the servant of a court society, of a class semi-civilized but anxious to catch up with other countries, cynical about the corruption of its Church but unable to imagine any other, and vaguely aware perhaps that its days were already numbered.

The Criterion, July 1933

What Is Wrong with Architecture?

Architecture in the Balance. By F. Towndrow. Chatto & Windus. 7s. 6d.
The Architecture of a New Era. By R. A. Duncan.
Denis Archer. 7s. 6d.

I'd better say at once that I know nothing more about architecture than any other member of the professional classes who has had a suburban home, been educated at boarding schools and universities, spent holidays in lodgings by the sea, and visited old churches on a bicycle. I can only hope that, as I found both these books interesting and provocative, they are intended for just such people, chiding them, not for their ignorance of technical facts which they never have the leisure to remedy, but for their lack of attention to make it truly their concern. For Architecture is willy-nilly everyman's business. He may be colour blind, stone deaf, decline absolutely to open even a newspaper, but a roof shelters him from the night, and the walls of public buildings circumscribe his hours of earning and sickness.

Civilizations are rightly judged by their architecture, not because buildings are more permanent than other artistic achievements, but because they represent a greater collective effort. They concern equally the drawing-room and the servants' hall.

Both these authors agree that there is something seriously defective with the architecture of to-day. Mr Duncan approaches his subject from the client's side. He analyses, very accurately I think, the changes in our world that the industrial revolution has effected, and reveals the discrepancy between our ideas which are a legacy of the Renaissance, and our methods of production to which they have no application, and concludes that progress in architecture will only be made by inquiring what exactly our machines are suited to make, and what social and economic organization will permit us so to use them.

Mr Towndrow's appeal is more directly to the architect himself, to conquer the pride of aestheticism. Beauty, like physical pleasure, is an indicator of rightness. It is not a need of the human heart, but a sign that its needs have been satisfied. The conscious aim of the architect should not be beauty, but *"to increase the efficiency of well-being,"* to enable the actions for which he designs to function as well as possible.

But, as he is careful to point out, these needs are not purely physical, though the physical is primary. "Functionalism" is not a purely engineering problem. Architectural faults (this is also Mr Duncan's thesis), like human failings, are functional in that they are propitiatory. They are an attempt to assuage needs which can never really be satisfied by architecture at all, just as an unpopular child will steal. The ornaments on a Victorian house were a compensation for the gracelessness of its occupants. If our pulses were not confused by the rush of our age, there would be no Ye Olde Tea Shoppes.

What today is called Functionalism is gaining ground because it professes to concern itself only with the physical scientifically verifiable world, and science is the only mode of the mind in which we believe, and in which, believing, we find the least opportunity to lie.

It is an over-simplification. The popular complaint that "modern" rooms look like operating theatres is quite just. "Functional" architects who succeed brilliantly with, say, the kitchen, where the problem is truly a scientific one, make the most amazing assumptions when they come to living-rooms, and the result is priggish, like a schoolmaster's lecture. "You shall behave in such and such a way. You shall only like such and such a kind of picture." Take one instance, the practice of building in. It is not uncommon to find a wireless set made an integral part of the wall. Heavens above, who is the architect to tell me that I am to want a wireless?

The problem for the architect is to know what wants he, and he alone, can satisfy, concentrate on doing so, and leave everything else well alone. And for us, his clients, it is the same, to bring to the study of the passions of our neighbours and ourselves the same kind of interest we take in the physical world, and to distinguish between those which are fulfilled in building and those which can only be satisfied in other spheres, social or personal, and by our own efforts.

The Architectural Review, August 1933

A Review of *The Book of Talbot,* by Violet Clifton

The Book of Talbot. By Violet Clifton. Faber & Faber. 15s.

Perhaps it is not the reviewer's business to criticize the dust-cover of a book, but I feel bound to say that in this case the remarks quoted very nearly made one reader throw the book straight in the fire. *The Book of Talbot* is too excellent to need a puff redolent of the worst features of Sunday journalism.

It is difficult to say more about it than to recommend everyone to read it and judge for themselves. It is the life of a husband written by a wife who loved him; of a man of old family whom fortune enables to realize every phantasy in action, by a woman who, I should imagine, read little but Homer, Dante, and Shakespeare. Both of them were devout Roman Catholics.

Henry James once said, reviewing a batch of novels: "Yes, the circumstances of the interest are there, but where is the interest itself?" How easily might that have been true of a book like this. The lives of explorers are not necessarily interesting: records of physical sensations can be as dull as any analysis of mental states. *The Book of Talbot* is a great book, not because he went to Verkhoyansk, the coldest place in the world, but because Lady Clifton would have been just as interested in his adventures if he had gone to Wigan.

It shows more clearly than anything I have read for a long time that the first criterion of success in any human activity, the necessary preliminary, whether to scientific discovery or to artistic vision, is intensity of attention or, less pompously, love.

Love has allowed Lady Clifton to constellate round Talbot the whole of her experience and to make it significant. One cannot conceive of her needing to write another line; one feels that she has put down everything. One is quite incurious to know whether Talbot was in actual life as magnificent a figure as he is in his book. Whatever his origins he is completely convincing. There is no trace of day dreaming.

Almost any passage will illustrate the writer's fixity of purpose.

A walk by the sea might bring an unforgettable experience, as on that summer day when Violet had thought "I must walk alone by the sea". She followed the causeway. She was exhilarated by her feeling of unity with nature, of unity with God. Like a breeze blowing among the marsh flowers, so God was the breath of common life. "We living creatures are all akin." She rounded a crag; a heron saw her, sent out a harsh warning and flapped away. A chough echoed the cry, gulls and curlews took up the chorus of fear; the sanderlings and the godwits sped off in silvery sweep. A red deer leapt up from the brake, a fallow bounded away. She had given out love, but fear had come back to her, and that so sharply that she was stunned. She saw herself cut off from the common breath, like a dead part in a living whole.

Talbot came upon her, past the flooded causeway, but he never quite understood why, at the moment, she seemed a being in ebb; nor why she caught hold of his hand and held it for the brief time he left it her. He but half heard her say something about his being her only friend.

It is this single-minded devotion that gives her her remarkable technical skill at combining the words of Talbot's diary and her own comments into a consistent texture of narrative. It also makes it possible for her to say things which in isolation look silly. For example, I doubt if many can read the following passage out of its context without embarrassment, yet few, I am certain, coming upon it in its proper place will feel it unjustified.

> Foreseeing the desolate time when he would no longer speak her name, she treasured his every call upon her. For the night, to prove love, she made a game. Every time that he woke or turned she would give a little cry to show her wakefulness, but if he had to say her name, then he had won. In those weeks he twice won the game. But every night she struck many matches, for he woke often.

One may be repelled by Roman Catholicism; one may regard the system of society which made Talbot's life and character possible as grossly unjust, but I cannot imagine that anyone who is fortunate enough to read this book, will not experience that sense of glory which it is the privilege of great art to give.

The Criterion, October 1933

The First Lord Melchett

Alfred Mond: First Lord Melchett. By Hector Bolitho. Secker. 12s. 6d.

This trashily-written and exceedingly readable biography leaves us with considerable respect for its subject and little for its author either as a man or as a literary gent. His style is cosmic gossip. Heads bow, bitter retorts fail to crystallize, a governor smooths out the wrinkles of a country's pain, something terrible comes out of the shadows of time. Here he is painting a word-picture:

> The symphony of marble circles was complete again, curve crossing curve, all leading to the central circle of clear water, water which was as still as the blue sky from which it took its colour; except when some Roman boy or girl rose up to the surface, naked and lissom, to rest wet brown hands upon the edge of the marble basin.

This would not matter much perhaps if it were not accompanied by an attitude of mind which, in view of recent developments not only on the Continent and in America but also here, seems to be more prevalent than one had supposed, and to present no common danger. I mean Mr Bolitho's conception of the admirable human being. A big strong man makes him swoon with pleasure. Mussolini, Mond, Beaverbrook, Goering, Al Capone, it's all the same. If you are large and able, rude though of course with a twinkle in the eye, ruthless though of course with a big heart, capable of working all night or putting a wench across your knee, you're alright with Mr Bolitho as you are with Mr Hemingway. What you do doesn't matter.

That Alfred Mond exalted industry; that he became Peer and Privy Councillor, and a Fellow of the Royal Society does not matter. What does matter in our estimate of him is his moral courage.

I regard this attitude as pernicious and reactionary, a symptom of a terrified refusal to face the contemporary situation. The post-war debunkers were tiresome enough, God knows; their motives were generally equally irrational, and they treated their subjects in the same way, as if they existed in a vacuum of personality, unaffected by their environment and unaffecting. But we want neither. We certainly want to hear about people's private lives, but only in order to understand their public ones. What matters to us about other people is what they do to us. If someone tells me that the man coming towards me with an axe has moral courage, I shall no doubt be pleased to hear it, but I should much rather know how he is going to show it. No biography is satisfactory that does not illuminate not only the motives but the results of the hero's actions, and estimate the latter consistently and rationally.

Mr Bolitho does not. For example:

Sir Alfred Mond stood up and had one fleeting glimpse of the Germans. His son pulled him down sharply, a few seconds before a bullet cracked past.

"What is that?" he asked.

"A German bullet," answered his son.

"Who are they shooting at?"

"You," he was told.

Suddenly a fine and primitive passion possessed him. "Where is a bloody rifle, I'm going to have just one shot back."

His son led him away. Sir Alfred Mond returned to Westminster inspired by terrible strength and ideas. He said in a speech to his electors, "I care not what views a man expressed before the War, or what views he is going to express when the War ceases. I say for God's sake let us join to win the War . . . We have to realize our enemy's cunning; there has been too much killing our opponent with the mouth instead of with the bullet."

This story may be true. It sounds only too probable. It is just the sort of way in which hatreds involving millions do originate. What is disquieting is Mr Bolitho's naïve narration of it as if it were something admirable, instead of a terrible parable of human folly.

Again Mr Bolitho introduces highly coloured scenes to explain Lord

Melchett's emotions about art, and tells us very little about the development of his emotions about property. Lord Melchett was not an artist and we don't care in the least why he came to like Renaissance statues. He was an industrialist and a politician, and we should like to know very much how a German Jew came to abandon Europe for Empire Free Trade. There are hints certainly but Mr Bolitho hardly seems to have recognized them as such or to have been much interested.

Alfred Mond's life history supports the contention that, of people who become remarkable in any way, few have a happy childhood and most pass through a critical period in early manhood when they appear to outsiders and anxious relatives as wasters. Ambition, it seems, is always the desire to overcome early emotional frustration, and there is a period when it is uncertain whether the frustration or the ambition will triumph, whether the latter will devise an adequate or a neurotic solution, freeze into sullen obscurity, liquefy into dissipated idleness, or assume a rational and living growth. The future peer might instead have become a cardsharper.

These reflections are of interest to us because the nature of the conflict dictates in some measure the nature of the solution. Man is neither completely free nor a mere puppet. There is freedom of choice, but within limits.

The conflict—a Jew and a foreigner—industry and cultured riches—a gruff authoritative father who prefers his elder brother—shame at his own clumsiness and physical ugliness.

The solution—the brilliant bureaucrat and industrialist—the anti-socialist—the Empire Crusader—the Zionist.

It is as a bureaucrat, as a practical administrator in the Office of Works and the Ministry of Health that he is most impressive:

> "The whole Book of Revelations occupies ten pages. I don't see why new wash-basins in the Revenue Office at Leeds should take a hundred pages. Take it away and bring us a short one, without details. It is for you to worry about those."

> "Our object in official life is not to get a minute written, pass the paper on to another individual or division and wash our hands of it, but to see that the person who writes to us actually gets his answer in decent time."

Under whom could he have had most opportunity? Under Mr Baldwin or the "foolish and mad" Stalin? The whole principle of bureaucracy is a socialist one. You do not possess—you administer. You are not a person, but a public servant; a conductor, not an owner of power. It implies interference and the end of *laissez-faire*. Yet this great official, who could make any companies merge he liked, could write of the land problem:

"The only real cure is to enable the cultivator of the soil to be the master of his own destiny, and to leave it to him to make a success or a failure of his venture, and to trust to the working of general economic laws that, in the long run, the efficient will displace the inefficient."

The truth is that all his talk about socialism levelling the clever to the level of the stupid is rationalizing poppycock. His reaction was emotional and irrational, a reaction against an unfamiliar world, without his art collections, without his papa. He still had to justify himself, remain personally a power. "In a small country," he once said, "one could be an influence and a power."

As a large-scale industrialist he knew the importance of internationalism, but—instead of a world union of republics, the British Empire, and finally Zion and the lights of home, the racial ideal. The boy who kicked the lonely football in Cheltenham for hours still limited his vision.

Had he lived longer, he would almost certainly have been a Fascist. Those who do not welcome Fascism, will be grateful to death for depriving it of a recruit of his talents and his calibre.

Scrutiny, December 1933

The Group Movement and the Middle Classes

Whether by accident or by design the Group Movement has appealed principally to the middle classes. Its success with the working class has so far been negligible. Nomenclature is never accidental, and terms like "Oxford," "House party," and "spiritual bath" indicate the kind of social world in which most of its members would prefer to dwell. It may not be unprofitable, therefore, to examine the present status and wants, both spiritual and material, of this class, and then to consider the Group Movement in relation to their satisfaction. The moment a religious movement has gathered more than a handful of converts, it becomes a body within the state with whose support or hostility politicians will have to reckon and, if possible, control. The moment it reaches the stage of having an organization, it needs money, and those who supply it will expect special considerations. There have been few assumptions less based on fact and more unedifying in their results than that of the divorce between the things of God and the things of Caesar. It may be compared in its effects to the psychological repression of an instinct. It has led, not to a purification of the religious life, but to its rationalization in the interests of material wishes, which, denied overt expression, have remained at a crude and infantile level. The speeches of bishops on the Factory Acts in the last century, and on the Great War at the beginning of our own, are only two examples; the history of the Church is strewn with its scandals. In the past there has been the excuse that unconscious hypocrisy was barely suspected. In private, at any rate, you knew what you believed. But to-day the light which has been shed by Freud and Marx on the motivation of thought makes it criminal to be uncritical, and no movement, secular or religious, which is afraid to examine dispassionately and to acknowledge openly what self-interest would make it want to believe, is worthy of anything but contempt.

How then does the middle class live? What has it been taught to believe and how has it been brought up to behave? What does it think it wants? Take first, religious upbringing. This will, of course, have varied from family to family; but it is not, I hope, too rash to say that for the vast majority it was liberal and individualistic, ethical rather than mystical, emotional rather than rational. The human side of Jesus was emphasized rather than the divine.

The child was not much terrified by hell fire* or perplexed by definitions of the Trinity; he was given, instead, many references to Truth, Goodness and Beauty. The good will was more important than the orthodox dogma. Further, religion was something you didn't talk about in public. It belonged to mother's bedroom; in some cases it was what father did. Its aim was to produce good individuals rather than a good society. You were all here on earth to help others; what on earth the others were here for you didn't know.

Of much greater importance to him, and—though often given a religious justification—capable of independent existence, was the conception of the good man as the man of character, character not personality—Mr Baldwin rather than Lloyd George.

Belief in character presupposes a belief in the superiority of the will over all other mental faculties, that is the conscious will, the will of the ego. It involves a doctrine of dualism, of the higher and the lower self, and a policy of actively resisting evil without too much thinking, for thinking by threatening the initial premises may bring the whole structure down in ruins.

Culturally, his training may have varied greatly in degree but not in kind, and in his complex of ideas, various strands may be distinguished.

---

* The sense of guilt under which every human being suffers was not, of course, lessened by the fading of hell. It was only transferred to medicine. The hospital and the asylum became the punishment for moral offences, particularly the sexual.

Firstly, those of the Renaissance, e.g. the importance of the individual, the ideal of scholarship (disinterested knowledge) itself a secular derivation of the medieval contemplative ideal, and of games (disinterested action) an adaptation of the more practical exercises of the feudal aristocracy to the new leisure of a more peaceful and numerous class. His hero is the Blue who takes a first in Greats. His idea of Greece and Rome is a Renaissance version, Plato the philosopher, not Plato the politician.

Secondly there are the ideas of Rousseau and the liberal humanitarians of the late eighteenth and nineteenth centuries with their belief in the fundamental goodness of man, in nature as the kind indulgent mother, in the superior virtues of children and animals, and with their dislike for political authority and reason. Peter Pan is a typical manifestation of the spirit on the negative side, child welfare and birth control on the positive.

Thirdly, there is the impression made on him by the success of the scientific method with its combination of theoretical reasoning and practical test. Though, as a class, he has resisted its advance in each successive field, he has in every case been forced to give way, and his rueful admiration or sad acquiescence conceals a deep and genuine hostility.

The very ease and rapidity of its success in applied technics, coupled with his divorce from the actual process of production, has made him take its material benefits, telephones, cars, and the like, for granted, and he is aware only of its threat to undermine his confidence in the rightness of his world, a threat which has recently become immeasurably more serious; for science, which in the last century was concerned with the visible material world, has now turned its attention to the inner world of subjective experience, that in which he has put all his trust. If he can't trust that decent feeling, where is he?

As a social animal he has depended on the family group for his satisfactions. During the last century the Victorian family was large enough to provide variety and lessen the intensity of parental relations, and small enough to provide emotional security. Its defects were that it was non-equalitarian (there was always economic and spiritual dependence on the parents), and that it recognized no larger units outside itself, which defect became worse as, under economic pressure, the family became smaller. Owing to this dwindling and to the increased ease of travel, the family is rapidly ceasing to be the natural social unit, but he is still looking for a group of the same kind. The Totalitarian state is a family image.

Lastly, there is his economic position. For a long time now the middle class has been the dominant one. Its material wants have been satisfied without difficulty. It seems to be generally true that physical or material needs have to reach a certain threshold value before they are recognized by the mind as such, as something that can only be satisfied by certain material objects outside the mind. Until they reach this intensity, their fluctuations are only experienced as fluctuations in subjective feeling of value.

Further, that we do not think until we are defeated, until the power of action is taken from us. The sustained comfort and power of the middle classes has led them to value things and ideas for the subjective benefits they confer, the feeling of rightness they give, rather than for the material gain or loss they represent: their criterion of truth that which allays the feeling of doubt, not necessarily that which is experimentally demonstrable.

This tendency to exalt feeling above reason has been stimulated, not weakened, by the growth of scientific knowledge, which on the one hand has forced the Protestant churches more and more to water down their dogmas, or to explain them in subjective terms, and on the other, by obliging its own students to become specialists—experts in one tiny corner taking the rest of the enormous building on trust—has deprived the individual of a coherent and intelligible world-picture to which he can relate all his behaviour and beliefs. The areas of truth which it is possible for him ever to explore experimentally have miserably shrunk.

And though still comfortable, the economic position of the middle class young man is deteriorating. Taxes and cost of living have reduced saving power. There must be many families like my own, whose members, two generations ago, had substantial incomes from investments, who are now entirely dependent on the salaries they earn.

Middle class unemployment has not become the terror it has in Germany, but it is there in the background like a bad smell. There is more competition than there was and the consequences of failure are more serious, though mental rather than physical. The unemployed young university graduate is unlikely to starve, but he will have to live at home, ask for his pocket-money, and endure the mutely resentful anxiety of his parents.* Thus insecurity threatens him from within and without: within, his belief in himself and his world, and without, his material situation.

Like every human being he desires security: security of belief, social security, to be surrounded by the faces of friends, to feel he is a valuable person, and material security, to be certain of his next meal. Peculiar to him, however, is his conception of such security. Long the dominant class, and still the most powerful, he puts his material claim last. He has been taught that material claims are selfish and bad, and that he should not question the motives behind idealistic claims or scrutinize their results.

---

* This decreasing sense of security manifests itself as a wish to spend more rather than save for the future, and in an expressed lack of ambition. I do not suppose there are more or less ambitious individuals now than forty years ago; but the attitude has changed. Then it was thought dreadful to have no ambition; now "Careerist" is a term of abuse.

He has not been taught intellectual discrimination, to distinguish between one ideal claim and another. To him all ideal claims are good, if accompanied by that subjective feeling of rightness which is the only test he knows. Socially, he can only think in terms of his own class, the only group he knows is the family or the school-team. Ethically, associations have been made between general moral concepts of the good character and quite peculiar attributes of the athletic gentleman, so that he cannot see them apart. In his economic, social, and ethical ideals, he has not changed. Trust in the intellect he never had. What his changed environment has, however, destroyed is his belief in the efficacy of the conscious will. It has failed to do its job, to make him a man of character. For character being a state of tension, though designed to make a man superior to circumstances, is sustained only by social pressure. Extremely successful when the environment is familiar or favourable, it becomes useless and dangerous when they are not. Just as a bee dies if removed from its hive, the character is lost in a changed world; he cannot adapt, or should he attempt adaptation, he has in reserve only those elements in his personality which he has repressed, and which have therefore remained infantile. The Spartans, as the ancient world knew, when they got away from home, could always be bribed.

Two courses are open to him, Liberalism* or Irrationalism, blind belief in the Unconscious. Liberalism involves faith in reason and he has never had that. His Liberalism has always been Utopian, emotional, feeling indulgent and full. It has always disappeared very rapidly when his position was threatened.

No, he can only exchange one dictatorship for another, that of the conscious for the unconscious.†

The Group Movement offers this. The ideal—to be perfectly loving,

* Modern Liberalism recognizes the power and importance of the Unconscious, but while admitting the weakness of reason, believes in its necessity and value. Metaphysically, it holds the doctrine of law as immanent, that "the order of nature expresses the characters of the real things which jointly compose the existences to be found in nature. When we understand the essences of these things, we thereby know their mutual relations to each other" (Whitehead: *Adventures of Ideas*). Ethically, it manifests itself as a reverence for life. Politically as socialism, scientific, not Utopian. As typical Liberals of this kind, I would mention Freud (see Thomas Mann's essay in *The Criterion*, June 1933) and Schweitzer in the world of thought, Nansen in the world of action.

† There have, of course, been other movements beside the Group Movement with this aim, but they have been confined to the intellectual *avant-garde*, those who have not fitted in with the mass of their class. Surrealism and D. H. Lawrence are two examples. The former, whose technique of writing bears striking resemblances to that of the groupers, is professedly communist, but communism is a rational movement. Lawrence's doctrines of the importance of the body and its instincts, throw the emphasis on the personal relations of individuals; as he himself admits in his letters, he had no political or social programme to offer. The Plumed Serpent is a day-dream. It is noteworthy that his hero, the gypsy or the gamekeeper, is dependent, even in a sense parasitic, on the middle class. As a specifically religious movement, there has been that of Barth in Germany, with its insistence on Grace.

perfectly honest, perfectly pure—the demands of the spirit to transcend the material, which always become insistent when the material needs are too easily satisfied—we have heard of before. The lack of rational criticism or a Weltanschauung is not new either. What is new is the emphasis on guidance, on the inner voice, the voice of the unconscious, and the technique, the quiet period of contemplation, the discharge in a small group. Neither of these, of course, is really new, but they are new for this class, and their results are one more witness to their importance.

Leaders of all mass movements are aware of the fact that they do not flourish unless the unconscious is tapped, unless the "heart" is touched. It is the author of good and evil alike.

> Not Creator, nor creature, was ever without love, either natural or rational; and this thou knowest. The natural is always without error; but the other may err through an evil object, or through too little or too much vigour. . . . Hence thou mayest understand that love must be the seed of every virtue in thee, and of every deed that deserves punishment.

To those brought up on repression the mere release of the unconscious is sufficient to give a sense of value and meaning to life. The sweeping away of "Hemmungen" is a vivid experience, but it is not guidance, which is an act of the intelligence. That the Group Movement succeeds in a number of cases in their release, there can be no doubt. The light in the eye, the sudden increase in energy, the missionary zeal, the intolerance of rivals; all the signs are there. To point to cases of hysteria as a proof of the worthlessness of the movement is silly; they are further evidence of its power, of a force strong enough to produce character mutations, all of which we cannot expect to have a positive survival value; there will always be throw-outs. If a movement is important, there will be scandals. What can, however, be said is that other movements are capable of producing the same effect. Anyone who has spoken to a young Nazi or Communist convert will know that they exhibit the same symptoms. He will tell you likewise that his movement has given him back his soul. As far as the feeling of the individual is concerned, ideology matters very little, except as a defence against hostile critics.

Further, it will be noticed that these movements use the same technique, the formation of the cell or small group, periodically visited by missionary officials, and the periodic gathering of cells for sudden public demonstration. This technique is the opposite of the individual preaching to large public crowds (one might call it the democratic method) employed, for example, in the Methodist revival or in the movement for the abolition of the slave trade. It is much more like the early Christian Church or the Quakers.

Its appearance and success in different and even contradictory move-ments suggests that the psychological importance of the small group is beginning to be realized. Only in a group of very moderate size, probably not larger than twelve,* is it possible for the individual under normal circumstances to lose himself, for his death instincts to be neutralized in the same way as those of the separate cells of the metazoa neutralize each other in the body. What the individual is after has been well expressed by Mr Gerald Heard in *The Social Substance of Religion*.

> The gospel is not salvationist. It is not a cautious, far-sighted calcula-tion of the individual's chances, a contemptible repetition of Noah's saving of himself and leaving the rest to drown. It is the opposite. It goes below any equal sharing between each, to the only possible set-tlement, the fusing in a cause of love of all separate selves into a common being. It is an overwhelming wish to be saved altogether, a determination to be saved by the very fact of being together. . . . Those who were swept by the gospel, were attempting nothing so cold, individual and intellectual, as the saving of their own souls after death. They threw aside personal salvation and, starting back, they found salvation in throwing away their concern for it for themselves. They found real salvation from the lust for self-salvation in complete devotion to the group, to the new, small, intensely beloved commu-nity of like believers.

Such a catharsis is threatened, on the one hand by competing loyal-ties to other groups such as the family, a rivalry which would seem, for example, to have injured the Quakers, and on the other, by mission-ary success tending to increase the size of the group beyond the propor-tions which provide the right psycho-physical field, until the more self-conscious remain unabsorbed. This difficulty has been met in the Churches, by the use of Ritual and a dogmatic framework of ideas, a rationalistic justification for behavior which was originally self-sustaining. There are signs, however, as we have seen, that this dogma is failing to be efficacious, partly under the assault of science, but much more because it has remained officially non-political; its dogmas have included no social doctrines other than relief-works, and therefore its politics, for a large body in society, have been those of its governors; it has been used as a class-weapon. It is permissible to doubt whether any large-scale organiza-tion which professes no political programme, is likely to command wide interest in the near future.

---

* The Middle Class are well aware of the satisfactions of this kind of group from team games. Those who have complained of athletics in schools as a religion, were right in their diagnosis, but have made no attempt to supply a better substitute.

The problem of all modern communities, where the size of the psycho-logical unit bears no relation to that of the economic, is of finding for the masses as a whole a suitable object on which to focus the life-hostile, de-structive death instincts, or rather of placing these at the disposal of the life instincts, as they are for the individual, for instance, in the sexual act.

So far mankind has only discovered one method, war. Given a suitable hate-object—the Kaiser, Marxists, Bourgeois—we can feel really loving towards the neighbours who share it. As André Gide has said, "A friend is someone with whom one does something discreditable." Those who are aware of the horrors of war will fail in their efforts if they do not recog-nize its enormous psychological benefits, and find a more efficient substitute.

The Group Movement is reaching the stage where it is imperative for it to recognize this. To talk as it does of being perfectly loving, is folly unless it is fully aware of the ambivalency of love. If to be perfectly loving means that hate is abolished, it is nonsense: it is only true if it means that hate is to be used constructively (as a sculptor hates the marble block), that death is to be swallowed up by life.

If the Movement fails to realize this, if on the one hand, it allows its groups to increase in size (a house party is already too large unless its members are all "classy"), and on the other, fails to find something useful for its members to do as one whole (and this means a definite material and political programme), something in which the small group can them-selves be lost, it will fail, and there are plenty of others waiting outside to provide a devil. Which devil its middle-class members are likely to choose it is not hard to guess. A grouper has said that Fascism is preferable to Communism because it appeals to ideals, to self-sacrifice rather than self-interest. This is a warning. Unless in immediate physical need, the psyche responds to ideals, whatever the motive, because they keep it in good conceit with itself. Schoolmasters and rulers depend on this. Ideals can very easily be only a method of persuasion. None of the accounts of group meetings (e.g. that of Margaret Roper in the *Church Times*) inclines one to believe that the Groupers realize the extent of human conceit.

The Movement has certainly succeeded in effecting a psychological revolution in many people. That is no test. So have many others. Idealist and non-political, it has reached a size where it is becoming of material and political importance. Irrational, it lays itself open to having its think-ing done for it by more intelligent and less scrupulous people. Middle class, given a crisis of real importance and a compulsory choice, it would seem likely to choose Fascism. At the recent London meeting there were several German Christians.

Oxford and the Groups, edited by R. H. S. Crossman, 1934

The Liberal Fascist

[HONOUR]

No account of school life ever appears disinterested to those who disagree with it: it will always appear the work of either a nest-fouler or a nest-whitewasher. I can only say that if, in my account of Gresham's School, Holt, I am sometimes critical, it is not, I hope, from personal motives. Of its fairness and accuracy I must leave those directly acquainted with the school in the first half of the last decade to judge.

As what one sees depends on what one is, I must begin with a description of myself at that time. The son of book-loving Anglo-Catholic parents of the professional class, the youngest of three brothers, I was—and in most respects still am—mentally precocious, physically backward, short-sighted, a rabbit at all games, very untidy and grubby, a nail-biter, a physical coward, dishonest, sentimental, with no community sense whatever, in fact a typical little highbrow and difficult child. It says much—or perhaps little—for Holt that I was never bullied or molested, I was allowed to make my friends where I chose, and was, taking everything into consideration, very happy throughout my time there.

The first condition for a successful school is a beautiful situation and in that respect we were at Holt very fortunate. The school authorities, with extraordinary good sense, set virtually no bounds, a liberty rarely, I believe, abused. Watching a snow storm come up from the sea over the marshes at Salthouse, and walking in a June dawn (not so legally) by Hempstead Mill are only the two most vivid of a hundred such experiences.

If the buildings were not lovely—their date precluded that—they were better than many, and comfortable. Class-rooms were warm and well-lit. In my own house we had dormitories with cubicles (smaller dormitories of four or six beds without cubicles would be better I think) and studies, shared with two or three others for the first two years, and single afterwards: so we cannot be said to have been unduly herded together. Fagging, during one's first year or so, was extremely light, hot-water was plentiful, and the cooking, if undistinguished—no one seems ever to have solved the problem of school maids who are invariably slatternly and inefficient—was quite adequate.

So much for the surroundings which were all that a parent could desire. What about the education?

On the academic side I can't say much because I remember so little, but I imagine it was pretty good. Holt is a modern school, i.e. it does not teach Greek and concentrates on science, history, etc. We had a magnificent library, perhaps the only requisite because most people who can learn, given that chance, will teach themselves; the labs were excellently equipped, all the staff were conscientious and some efficient, and our scholarship list was quite satisfactory.

As regards out-of-school activities the school was extremely sensible. Athletics were treated as they ought to be treated, as something to be enjoyed and not made a fetish of, every kind of hobby was encouraged (I remember with special pleasure the expeditions of the Sociological Society which did no more sociology than my foot, but had a grand time visiting factories in a charabanc). There was plenty of acting, house plays in the winter and a Shakespeare play in an open-air theatre in the summer. And if I think that all out-of-door plays are detestable, that is a personal prejudice.

I can't say that we were given any real sense of the problems of the world, or of how to attack them, other than in vague ideals of service, but then I have never heard of any school that did, and my own convictions are perhaps too extreme for me to expect to see them acted upon. Indeed it is impossible to see how any school, which is not directly attached in some way to an industrial or agricultural unit, and where boys and staff are both drawn from the monied classes, can hope to see the world picture of that class objectively.

The fact remains that the mass production of gentlemen is their *raison-d'être,* and one can hardly suggest that they should adopt principles which would destroy them. The public school boy's attitude to the working-class and to the not-quite-quite has altered very little since the war. He is taught to be fairly kind and polite, provided of course they return the compliment, but their lives and needs remain as remote to him as those of another species. And I doubt very much if the same isn't true of the staff as well. I do remember hearing however that a master was sacked for taking part in left-wing politics outside the school, which if true, and I cannot vouch for the accuracy of the story, seems to me a shameful thing.

The only concrete suggestion I have to make here is that the staff might give up wearing those ridiculous black clothes (if they still do) which made them look like unsuccessful insurance agents, and certainly did not increase our respect for them; if we were allowed—and rightly—to wear blazers and flannel trousers, the staff as well might surely be allowed a sensible costume.

I suppose no one ever remembers actually being taught anything, though one remembers clearly enough when one failed to learn. My efforts at engineering which must have been as distressing to the very nice military man who taught that subject as they were boring to me—the sum total of my achievement was two battered ash-trays and any number of ruined tools—are still vivid.

Where one was more successful, one remembers only the idiosyncrasies of the masters, that X shouted in class—a horrible habit—that Y would come up behind one on a bicycle ride and pinch one's seat, that Z wore his cap like a racing-tout, and so on. For, as people, those who at one time or another have taught me stand out in my memory very clearly, far more clearly in fact than my friends, and this seems a common experience.

It is perhaps as well that teachers can never realise how intensely aware of their personalities their charges are, because if they could they would be terrified to move or to open their mouths. A single act or remark is quite sufficient to queer the pitch. For example a certain master once caught me writing poetry in prep, writing a poem which I knew to be a bad one. He said "You shouldn't waste your sweetness on the desert air like this, Auden"; and even to-day I cannot think of him without wishing him evil.

It is pleasant to turn from such thoughts to remember two men to whom I owe an immense debt, the master who taught Classics and English, and the Music master. The former, who was never tired of showing us the shallowness of those who despised the classics, had the most magnificent bass reading voice I have ever heard, and from listening to him read the Bible or Shakespeare I learnt more about poetry and the humanities than from any course of University lectures.

To the latter I owe not only such knowledge of music as I possess, but my first friendship with a grown up person, with all that that means. As a musician he was in the first rank. I do not think it was partiality that made me feel, later when I heard Schweitzer play Bach on the organ, that he played no better.

As a person he was what the ideal schoolmaster should be, ready to be a friend and not a beak, to give the adolescent all the comfort and stimulus of a personal relation, without at the same time making any demands for himself in return, a temptation which must assail all those who are capable of attracting and influencing their juniors. He was in the best sense of the word indifferent, and if the whole of the rest of my schooldays had been hateful, which they weren't, his existence alone would make me recall them with pleasure.

Finally, no acknowledgments of mine would be complete without a reference to one—call him Wreath—who though not a member of the staff, yet as captain of my house when I was still a junior, stood to me in much the same relation. A really good prefect is as rare as a comet—authority makes most boys of eighteen or any other age into stuck-up little idiots—but he was a born leader and the only person, boy or master, who ever made the conventional house and school loyalties have any meaning for me.

It does not of course follow that what one remembers is necessarily the most significant, but I cannot help feeling that in education the staff themselves, their characters or personalities or what you will, are far more important than anything else.

I have no wish to belittle a profession to which I have the honour to belong. Its members are practically all extremely conscientious, hard working, keen on their job, and sometimes very intelligent. At the same time if one were invited to dine with a company representing all trades and professions, the schoolmaster is the last person one would want to sit next to. Being a schoolmaster is not like being a bank-clerk—it is not enough just to be efficient at teaching; one must be a remarkable person. Some schoolmasters are, but far, far too many are silted-up old maids, earnest young scoutmasters, or just generally dim.

Some of the reasons for this are clear; in the first place the profession has generally to be entered young, and those of university age who are attracted to it are rarely the most vital and adventurous spirits. On the contrary they are only too often those who are afraid of the mature world, either the athletic whose schooldays were the peak of their triumph from which they dread to recede, or else the timid academic whose qualifications or personal charm are insufficient to secure them a fellowship; in either case would-be children. It is not improbable that those who enter teaching as a *pis-aller,* as they might become stevedores or bootleggers, are often the best; which may be the reason why the staffs of preparatory schools seem so superior to those of public schools.

In the second place, partly because they have never had the chance, and sometimes I am ashamed to say as the result of a definite policy of the school authorities, they have no outside interests. This seems to me disastrous, leading inevitably to them becoming either lifeless prunes or else spiritual vampires, sucking their vitality from the children. Indeed if I were a headmaster—which heaven forbid—I would have no unmarried man on my staff who was not definitely engaged on some work outside the school. Better still, the number of professional teachers would be very small, the product of a very vigorous selection. The rest would be conscripted. Every citizen after some years in the world would be called up to serve his two or three years teaching for the state, after which he would return to his job again. However that is only a daydream and I must return to Holt and its education of our morals.

That side was run on what was called the Honour System, and for the benefit of those who do not know the school, some explanation of this is necessary.

About a week after arrival every new boy was interviewed separately by his housemaster and the headmaster—half-watt hypnotism we used to call it—and was asked—I need hardly say how difficult it would have been to refuse—to promise on his honour three things.

(1) Not to swear.
(2) Not to smoke.
(3) Not to say or do anything indecent.

Having done so, two consequences followed:

(1) If you broke any of these promises you should report the breakage to your housemaster.
(2) If you saw anyone else break them, you should endeavour to persuade him to report and if he refused, you should report him yourself.

Before I say anything in criticism, I must add that the system worked, in public at any rate. One almost never saw anyone smoke, heard anyone swear, or came across any smut. From the point of view of master and parent, it would seem ideal. Here at last was the clean and healthy school they had been looking for.

From the boys' point of view, on the other hand, I feel compelled to say that I believe no more potent engine for turning them into neurotic innocents, for perpetuating those very faults of character which it was intended to cure, was ever devised.

Everyone knows that the only emotion that is fully developed in a boy of fourteen is the emotion of loyalty and honour. For that very reason it is so dangerous. By appealing to it, you can do almost anything you choose; you can suppress the expression of all those emotions, particularly the sexual, which are still undeveloped; like a modern dictator you can defeat almost any opposition from other parts of the psyche, but if you do, if you deny these other emotions their expression and development, however silly or shocking they may seem to you, they will not only never grow up, but they will go backwards, for human nature cannot stay still; they will, like all things that are shut up, go bad on you.

Of the two consequences of our promises, the second, the obligation to interfere with one's neighbour, is of course much the most serious. It meant that the whole of our moral life was based on fear, on fear of the community, not to mention the temptation it offered to the natural informer, and fear is not a healthy basis. It makes one furtive, dishonest and unadventurous. The best reason I have for opposing Fascism is that at school I lived in a Fascist state. Of the effect of the system on the boys after they left school, I have little direct experience outside my own and those whom I knew personally, but all those with whom I have spoken, whether old boys or others who have come into contact with old boys, have borne out my conclusion that the effect is a serious one in many cases. I am fully aware that the first five years of life are more important than any others, and that those cases I am thinking of would have had a difficult time anyway, but I am convinced that their difficulties were enormously and unnecessarily increased by the Honour System.

Though the system was a peculiarity of Holt, it is only an extreme example of a tendency which can be seen in the running of every school, the tendency to identify the welfare of the school with the welfare of the boys in it, to judge school-life not by its own peculiar standards as a stage in the development towards maturity, but as an end in itself by adult standards. Every headmaster is inclined to think that so long as all's fair in his own little garden, he has succeeded. When later he sees what some of his old boys have turned into, he seldom realises that the very apparent perfection he was so proud of is partly responsible.

You can, I repeat, do almost anything by utilising the sense of community so long as the community is there, but as soon as the pressure is removed your unfortunate pupils are left defenceless. Either the print has taken so deeply that they remain frozen and undeveloped, or else, their infantilised instinct suddenly released, they plunge into foolish and damaging dissipation.

The first truth a schoolmaster has to learn is that "if the fool would persist in his folly he would become wise"; in other words, to leave well alone and not to give advice until it is asked for, remembering that nearly all his education is done by the boy himself with the help of other boys of his own age. There is far too much talk about ideals at all schools. Ideals are the conclusions drawn from a man of experience, not the data: they are essentially for the mature. Whether for good or ill dogmatic religion, that is to say a Christian world picture, has broken down among schoolmasters, and religion without dogma ends in nothing but vague uplift, which soon becomes, as it did at Holt, as flat as an old bottle of soda water. For the young without experience, ideals are as grave a danger in the moral sphere as book learning is in the intellectual, the danger of becoming a purely mental concept, mechanising the soul.

In the absence of an orthodoxy, and we shall have to reconcile ourselves to that for some time, education has to rely almost entirely upon the quality of the teacher. For a teacher to be of real value to his pupils, he must be a mature and above all a happy person, giving the young the feeling that adult life is infinitely more exciting and interesting than their own; he must be prepared to give them all his powers of affection and imaginative understanding when they want them, yet to forget them completely the moment they are gone, to be indifferent to them personally; and lastly he must have no moral bees-in-his-bonnet, no preconceptions of what the good child should be; he must be shocked or alarmed at nothing, only patient to understand the significance of any piece of behaviour from the child's point of view, not his own; to see in the perfect little ape his most promising charge, and watchful to remove as tactfully and unobtrusively as possible such obstacles to progress as he can. He must, to use a phrase of Mr Gerald Heard's, and I know no better, "be an anthropologist".

I have written about Holt because I was there and therefore have known it from the inside, but any other school would have done as well. If I have criticised certain things, it is not because I think Holt is worse than other schools—in many respects it is probably considerably in advance of them—but because at a time like the present when the world into which our young emerge is bound to be a very difficult one, it is particularly important that they should get the best start we can give them, and too many suggestions are better than none. I offer mine for what they are worth. More nonsense is talked about education than about anything else and I cannot hope to do better than my fellow amateurs, but if one of these should strike the readers of this book as sensible, I shall be content.

The Old School, edited by Graham Greene, 1934

"T. E. Lawrence"

"T. E. Lawrence". By Liddell Hart. Jonathan Cape. 15s.

If this article is very little about Captain Liddell Hart's book, it is because he has presented his matter so clearly and convincingly that the reader forgets all about him. Excepting the almost mythical *Seven Pillars* there is no better account of the Arabian campaign than this, and no more living portrait of Lawrence: nor is there likely to be.

Thinking of Lawrence, I am reminded of two stories; the first, Turgenev's *A Desperate Character,* particularly the incident of the hero found sitting in an inn with the notice in front of him "Anyone who wishes to flip a nobleman on the nose may do so for two roubles", and how he nearly killed one who tried to take two flips for his money. The second, which I read I believe in McDougall's *Abnormal Psychology,* was the statement made by a man after he had cut the throats of his wife and family. "No, I am not the truly strong man. The truly strong man lounges about in bars and does nothing at all."

To me Lawrence's life is an allegory of the transformation of The Truly Weak Man into the Truly Strong Man, an answer to the question "How shall the self-conscious man be saved"; and the moral seems to be this. "Self-consciousness is an asset, in fact the only friend of our progress. We can't go back on it. But its demands on our little person and his appetites are so great that most of us, terrified, try to escape or make terms with it, which is fatal. As a pursuer it is deadly." Only the continuous annihilation of the self by the Identity, to use Blake's terminology, will bring us to the freedom we wish for, or in Lawrence's own phrase "Happiness comes in absorption".

But a misinterpretation of absorption is one of the great heresies of our generation. To interpret it as blind action without consideration of meaning or ends, as an escape from reason and consciousness, that is indeed to become the truly weak man, to enlist in the Great Fascist Retreat which will land us finally in the ditch of despair, to cry like Elijah: "Lord take away my life for I am not better than my fathers."

From Lawrence's own account of himself, no one has found this temptation harder nor conquered it more resolutely, or better demonstrated the truth that action and reason are inseparable; it is only in action that reason can realize itself, and only through reason that action can become free. Consciousness necessitates more action not less, and vice versa.

To the problem of human relations he has an equally important contribution to make. Different as they appear on the surface, both he and his namesake, D. H. Lawrence, imply the same, that the Western-romantic conception of personal love is a neurotic symptom, only inflaming our loneliness, a bad answer to our real wish to be united to and rooted in life. They both say "Noli me tangere". It is at least doubtful, if in our convalescence sexual relations can do anything but postpone our cure. It is quite possible that the way back to real intimacy is through a kind of asceticism. The self must learn to be indifferent; as Lenin said "To go hungry, work illegally and be anonymous." Lawrence's enlistment in the Air Force and Rimbaud's adoption of a trading career are essentially similar. "One must be absolutely modern."

I mentioned Lenin. He and Lawrence seem to me the two whose lives exemplify most completely what is best and significant in our time, our nearest approach to a synthesis of feeling and reason, act and thought, the most potent agents of freedom and to us, egotistical underlings, the most relevant accusation and hope.

No one who is interested in anything at all should fail to read this book.

Now and Then, Spring 1934

Life's Old Boy

Lessons from the Varsity of Life. By Lord Baden Powell.
C. Arthur Pearson. 10s. 6d.

The status of academic education was never lower than it is to-day, even among its exponents. The corpus of knowledge is so great that one don is as ignorant as the man in the street, of the labour of the don on the next staircase. Now that an elementary school-boy can become a fellow of All

Souls, it is no longer even a social distinction. And there is an economic crisis; learning does not necessarily buy bread. Competition puts a further premium on charm and an alertness not always honest, the Hatry virtues. So the Lifers have a ready hearing. Come to Mr Hemingway's Academy for Bright Boys and learn about Life.

Lord Baden Powell, nice old gentleman as he must be, is a Lifer and a Happiness-addict, and in hard times a Lifer is as blind a guide as a don. Their thesis is roughly this—the schools give you word knowledge, theories, mental experience, but destroy in the process, or at least fail to develop, your senses, your capacity for physical experience. They produce

> estimable young men, able to read and write, well-behaved and amenable to discipline, and easily made into smart-looking parade soldiers—but without individuality or strength of character, utterly without resourcefulness, initiative or the guts for adventure. (p. 272)

We will take you back

> to nature and backwoodsmanship, by taking the men back as nearly as possible to the primitive, to learn tracking, eye for a country, observation by night as well as by day, to learn to stalk and to hide, to improvise shelter, and to feed and fend for themselves. (p. 273)

So far, so good. The criticism is perfectly just and the alternative both feasible and productive. Is it enough? I don't think so, and for this reason. It assumes that life, i.e. the material order of things outside yourself, will teach you how to act, or if you like, that action is its own teacher. It ignores the subjective world of feeling, thereby placing us in its power. It is fatally primitive. To say that the Backwoods life is natural and City life artificial is nonsense. The only possible meaning of "artificial" in this connection is "un-habitual." Camping is really a highly artificial training for a better town life, and, valuable as it is, town life demands much more. The closer people live together, the more complex and civilized life becomes, the more one individual affects another and the more knowledge he needs about himself. It is here, to my mind, that scouting fails. Instead of treating the subjective world of feeling and impulse in exactly the same way as it treats the world of fires and knots, it falls back on the academic method of ideals. Its training of the senses has produced efficient executives but has left them irrational and thus in their very efficiency all the more dangerous.

Take two examples. Clause One of the Scout Promise: "To do his duty to God and the King." The bracketing of the Civitas Dei and the existing social order indicates that the scout is not encouraged to understand social structure. The accident that I personally dislike the present order is beside the point; it is an equally dangerous principle under any. Reform is always disloyalty to King, President, or Commissar.

Again Clause Ten of the Scout Law. "To be clean in Thought, Word, and Deed." Purity as an ideal merely places the adolescent at the mercy of his sense of guilt. If you are always scrubbing children, they will walk in puddles as soon as your back is turned. Children are no more born pure in the adult sense, than they are born observant, and they must learn it in the same way as they learn observation. All the adult can do is to make the environment as favourable to success as he can. And the same applies to courtesy, kindliness and all other virtues. To educate values by ideals is as bad as educating for action by books; it makes the same mistake—living at second hand.

The autobiography of the Chief Scout strengthens this impression. Lord Baden Powell has had an interesting career with many honours which I am sure he has deserved. Theatricals, sports, rich friendships, a happy marriage, two wars, the organization of a great youth movement, how interesting. But one would feel easier in one's mind if he were just a little less complacent about it. His Life Varsity is such a very comfortable one, and its master such a very genial Old Boy.

Anyone a thousand years hence reading this book would never guess that its author lived in one of the most terrible historical periods. Looking at the jolly little drawings, he would think: "What enormous fun they all had. Such larks. Polo, cucumber sandwiches on the lawn, faithful retainers, kindly treated, who knew their station. Just one big family."

One can easily forgive his snobbery—whatever we think of ourselves for it, we should all like to be able to say we had spoken with the King— but less easily his complete unacknowledgment of the existence of agony, hunger, disease, madness and death. His Varsity has very high walls. He has the compensating coldness of the general, and at times even an unpleasant facetious strain of cruelty.

> I watched with interest from my tent his further procedure with the prisoners.
>
> He cut down a small tree so that it lay about a foot above the ground, and he made the whole lot of eight men sit on the ground and put their legs under the tree with their feet projecting on the far side; then each man had to lean over and touch his toes with his fingers; the Hausa then came along and tied every thumb to every great toe.
>
> This was his idea of a stocks and there he left them for the night. The prisoners, however, devised a method of obtaining release—or thought they did. One of them started to yowl in a miserable way at the top of his voice, and as soon as his breath ran out the yowl was

taken up by the next, and so it went on in succession. This they hoped would disturb me to such an extent that I should order their release.

But before I could suggest a remedy the Hausa himself had devised one. He cut a thin whippy cane and went to the singer and smote him across the back, and then stood by the next man ready to smite the moment he began his song.

The singing stopped like magic and was not resumed.

The moral effect of this little episode on the rest of my force was excellent. (p. 163)

There is no hint that he was ever troubled, for example, about the moral justification of the Boer War. His only suggestion for ensuring peace rivals the utterances of Mr MacDonald in its vagueness.

Yes, hog-hunting is a brutal sport—and yet I loved it, as I loved also the fine old fellow I fought against. I cannot pretend that I am not inconsistent. But are many of us entirely consistent? Do what we will and say what we like, although we have a veneer of civilization, the primitive man's instincts are still not far below the surface. Murder will out. Did we not see it in all its horridness in the War?

But apparently the Churches recognized the fact; at any rate one does not remember that they made any attempt to stop us killing our fellow-men, our fellow-Christians.

Until we get our education upon a more spiritual foundation instead of being content with mere academical scholarship, more of character training than standard of knowledge, we shall only have the veneer. (p. 86)

(On his ideas of peace and war there is an illuminating cartoon on page 286.) A charming man certainly; a great man perhaps, a civilized man, no. (For the civilized soldier see *T. E. Lawrence*, by Liddell Hart, Cape.)

His scout movement is not a military movement but, though I do not for a moment suggest that he consciously intended it to be, it is a class weapon. From his experience, partly as a sportsman, partly as a soldier, the experience of the leisured officer class, he learnt the educational value of contact with nature, and wished that all classes should profit by it. For that he deserves much honour. But on the emotional side, the side of values, in his conception of the material and political embodiments of the Good Life, he never became objective. Had he done so, he would have been branded as a dangerous Socialist, and the Scout movement would have failed, because the upper classes would not have given it their support, but he might have been remembered by later generations as a master. But he did not do so and scouts, as the General Strike demonstrated, in return for favours received, and mentally defenceless, can be mobilized by the Conservatives. I must repeat that this mistake, though perhaps unusually serious at this moment, is a mistake in any society. The progress of the realization of values is like that of scientific inventions; it renders obsolete its predecessors. A state has to train its youth not only to be its good citizens, but to change it, i.e. to destroy its present existence. Educationalists must always be revolutionaries.

One half of the educational battle, the defeat of the academic in the training of the physical machine, has been fought, and Lord Baden Powell is one of its generals. The other half, the attack on the psychological front, has only just begun.

Scrutiny, March 1934

A Review of *The Poetry of Gerard Manley Hopkins,* by Elsie Elizabeth Phare

Gerard Manley Hopkins. By E. E. Phare. Cambridge
University Press. 6s.

Miss Phare has written a book of 150 pages about a major poet. She is obviously not only very intelligent but has a deep appreciation of poetry in general and Hopkins's poetry in particular, and she has taken great pains. Presumably it was written as a University thesis and, as such, it is admirable; it would convince any examiner that she knew her subject. With her judgment of individual poems and her view of Hopkins there is little quarrel. If then it is difficult to imagine anyone reading this book for pleasure or deriving real profit from reading it, the fault is not with the author, who has done this kind of thing as well as it can be done, but with the whole academic system of literary criticism, with the University English school.

Critics have two duties, to arouse interest in others, and to make that interest self-supporting and self-developing; it is most emphatically not intended to force the critic's impression of poems on a second reader. To arouse interest the critic must advertise, i.e. he must quote with as little comment as possible, and the anthology, much as poets dislike it, is the best form of advertising. (I myself became interested in Hopkins through reading "Spring and Fall" in *The Spirit of Man.*) Comment defeats itself in the same way that "So and So's jam is the best" does. Public comment that is; private recommendation between friends is another matter.

The second and more important function of criticism, the fostering

and development of taste, has generally I think to be approached indi-
rectly. There are the following approaches.

(1) The Technical. Textual and Prosodical criticism.
(2) The Grammatical. Analysis of verbal meaning.
(3) (a) The Psychological. Study of the relation of the poet's life to his
    ideas and his poetry. (b) The Philosophical. Study of the relation of
    the poet's ideas to his poetry.
(4) The Social Historical. Study of the society to which the poet belongs
    and of his poetry as a product of that society.

The first of these needs no comment. The second was practically in-
vented by Dr Richards and is still largely unexplored (in fact Mr Empson
is the only other distinguished exponent known to me). A fascinating
game in itself, I wonder whether its educational use is other than to con-
vince readers that a poem must be read carefully and often to get its full
value. Miss Phare quotes Mr Richards's and Mr Empson's analysis of *The
Windhover*. Whether one gains by becoming conscious of what I am per-
fectly prepared to admit does go on when one reads the poem, I don't
know. Quite probably. At any rate it must be done thoroughly and scien-
tifically if it is done at all. A generalized prose gloss is useless.

The psychological approach is unfashionable with serious critics, be-
cause of the excesses of psychologists with no interest in literature other
than as clinical material, but no study of the creative process can afford to
neglect it. Anyone who reads poetry at all seriously is soon able to tell
whether a poem is good or bad, but of the ways in which it may be bad, of
the reasons why a poet should succeed at one time and fail at another, he
is generally quite ignorant. And such questions psychology can some-
times answer. We don't need a doctor to tell us a person is ill, but to tell us
what is the matter. The critic has the same function.

The philosophical and social approach are easy to grasp in theory. Sau-
rat's *Milton* is a good example of the former. I am unacquainted with first
rate work of the latter category. Literary criticisms tend to isolate litera-
ture as the relation of one writer to another from the rest of the historical
process; their treatment of the effect of the form of a society on art has, as
far as I know, only scratched the surface of this profoundly interesting
problem.

What Miss Phare in the main gives us, and in fairness to her, one must
add so do Lamb and Swinburne, is her reactions; more sophisticated than
theirs, but still reactions. I choose a page at random.

Take for example the lovely childlike poem which he calls *The Star-
light Night*. The ecstasy which takes possession of him as he looks up
at the starlight sky is not at first one in which the soul is concerned.

His mind and body thrill at the sight of the starry skies, as Words-worth's did when he looked over the vale of Grasmere in the early morning. Even when he has diverted the ecstasy into a religious channel he does not deny Nature her due. The sight which he has before him is so beautiful that he will not say that it is merely the type of the reward: it *is* the reward. However by making the starry sky the outermost wall of heaven he rationalizes his rapture. The skies are only lovely because Christ is lovely. Hopkins is never so happy as when he feels that the beauty of God and Nature are the same. (p. 129)

Now frankly Miss Phare's reactions, and mine, or anyone else's may be of interest to ourselves and to examiners, but they aren't to anyone else. As an analysis of the meaning they don't go far enough to qualify for approach 2. The phrase "rationalizes his rapture" is a use of psychological terms which demands far greater expansion to be intelligible. The next sentence raises a philosophical question we should like to learn much more about.

It seems to me that this kind of criticism is uncomfortably like the notes on Shakespeare that have to be dictated to candidates for the school cer-tificate examination. As an attempt to make one accept someone else's experience rather than one's own, it is either boring or dangerous, boring if one already has one's experience, dangerous if one hasn't. The book is an excellent record of what an intelligent and sensitive reader makes of Hopkins, of what we ought to do each for ourselves. What it does not do, and what I think it ought to do is, by giving the ordinary reader facts and ideas which no mere reading of the poems alone could give, to enable him to read Hopkins and through him all poetry with greater understanding (e.g. one of the most interesting parts of Miss Phare's book is the discus-sion of *inscape*, p. 81).

Perhaps it will make my meaning clearer if I venture some of the things I should like to know about Hopkins and his poetry, and therefore would look for in a book about him.

Prosody and meaning I should prefer to puzzle out for myself; that is essentially the readers' business. On the other hand there are many ques-tions of psychology, philosophy, and social history, of which I am igno-rant, and would like both information and interpretation.

For example take "The Bugler's First Communion" which Miss Phare discusses on pages 48 and 49. I do not have to be told it is a failure, but I do want to know how a poet of Hopkins's sensibility has such a dreadful lapse in this poem, and not in "Portrait of Two Beautiful Young People". Reading the poem suggests a conflict in Hopkins between homosexual feelings and a moral sense of guilt. Does "The Bugler" fail because the guilt is unacknowledged, and "The Portrait" succeed because it is transformed into the unspecified moral danger which he fears for the subjects of the poem? I don't know, but would like to, not, I hope, out of any unseemly curiosity about Hopkins's life, but because it would shed light on the ways in which the emotions of poets combine for success or failure.

Again Hopkins would be a good opportunity for discussing the extraordinary interest of the Victorians in accidents, particularly in shipwrecks.

Hopkins is one of the few English poets with a philosophical training; Miss Phare does say something about Duns Scotus, but it is short and not very illuminating. What was the relation between his religious ideas and his poetry? In one place (p. 142) she says: "I cannot think that Hopkins's despondency [*re* one of the sonnets] was a particularly religious one; the analogy is with Swift, not with Cowper . . . his religion, though it may supply material on which to exercise his disgust, is in no way the cause of it." As it stands, I don't understand it. What is a religious despondency as opposed to an irreligious? How does religion supply material for anything? I am sure Miss Phare does mean something, but it needs much expansion.

Of Hopkins as a social figure there is nothing here. Surely his idealization of the working class man shown in "Adam Ploughman", and many other poems, together with his hatred of radicalism, warrant elucidation by a competent authority.

I cannot end this review without repeating, that my quarrel is not with Miss Phare, who has succeeded under the conventions of this kind of criticism, but with the conventions themselves and with those who frame them.

The Criterion, April 1934

A Review of *Modern Poetic Drama,* by Priscilla Thouless

Modern Poetic Drama. By Priscilla Thouless. Blackwell. 15s.

This book is like an exhibition of perpetual motion models. Here they all are, labelled Phillips, Davidson, Yeats, some on the largest scale, some on the tiniest, some ingenious in design, some beautifully made, all suffering from only one defect—they won't go. Miss Thouless is an excellent showman and shows sound literary judgement. (One would have thought, though, that Davidson and Lawrence, despite certain similarities, were two very different cups of tea.) If she declines to offer an opinion on the future of poetic drama, there is no reason why she should be so rash, and she gives the reader the necessary material upon which to form his own.

Though their influence in this country has so far been slight, some account of the continental writers like Cocteau, Obey, and Bert Brecht would have been welcome.

As Miss Thouless points out, modern English poetic drama has been of three kinds: the romantic sham-Tudor which has occasionally succeeded for a short time on the strength of the spectacle; the cosmic-philosophical which theatrically has always been a complete flop; and the high-brow chamber-music drama, artistically much the best, but a somewhat etiolated blossom. Drama is so essentially a social art that it is difficult to believe that the poets are really satisfied with this solution. The truth is that those who would write poetic drama, refuse to start from the only place where they can start, from the dramatic forms actually in use. These are the variety-show, the pantomime, the musical comedy and revue (Miss Thouless rightly discerns the relation between the success of *Hassan* and *Chu Chin Chow*), the thriller, the drama of ideas, the comedy of manners, and, standing somewhat eccentrically to these, the ballet. Only one of these is definitely antipathetic to poetry, the comedy of manners or characters. The drama of ideas is very dangerous to touch, but not impossible. Poetry, the learned commentators on Shakespeare's characters notwithstanding, has very little to do with character. All characters who speak verse are as flat as playing-cards. So are they also in the popular dramatic forms today. Poetic drama should start with the stock musical comedy characters—the rich uncle, the vamp, the mother-in-law, the sheik, and so forth—and make them, as only poetry can, memorable. Acrobatics of all kinds are popular and are poetry's natural allies. It is the pure West-end drama that is talk without action. If the would-be poetic dramatist demands extremely high-brow music and unfamiliar traditions of dancing, he will, of course, fail; but if he is willing to be humble and sympathetic, to accept what he finds to his hand and develop its latent possibilities, he may be agreeably surprised to find that after all the public will stand, nay even enjoy, a good deal of poetry.

Unsigned. *The Listener*, 9 May 1934

A Review of *English Poetry for Children*, by R. L. Mégroz

English Poetry for Children. By R. L. Mégroz. (Fen series No. 7.) 2s.

Mr Mégroz's essay is presumably addressed to teachers, to those who, without much knowledge of poetry themselves, find that they are committed to giving poetic instruction to the young. It should give them many valuable hints. He deals with both poetry, the history of poetry written specially for children (his separation of the sheep from the goats is admirable), humour in poetry, and the childlike consciousness.

I am only uncertain firstly whether the appreciation of poetry can be taught, and secondly whether the average child of school age is as unsophisticated and imaginative as Mr Mégroz assumes.

Since English ceased to be the Cinderella of educational subjects, the introduction of the child to poetry has begun to be taken seriously, not to say solemnly. Anthologies and manuals for the prosaic teacher pour from the press. Never having taught girls, I cannot generalize about them, but as regards boys, I notice that not only are they expected to read more poetry, but poetry of a different kind.

It used to be assumed that boys would only take to martial and patriotic poems—Macaulay and Campbell were stand-bys. (The divinity hour when we learnt the collects and psalms was divinity not English.) Now all that is démodé, as poetry about nature and animals are held to be the natural boyish taste. I suspect that this is due to a change in the teacher rather than in the taught. That it should meet with a positive response from the children is not in the least surprising. The relation between a master or mistress and a class is a kind of hypnosis. An enthusiastic teacher can make his pupils like almost anything, as conversely, his disapproval can quench an incipient excitement. We may yet see Pope and Dryden elevated to academic honour with just as convincing results.

On the whole I am inclined to think that few boys between nine and fourteen care for poetry, though they can often recite very good poems themselves of a surréalist kind. They do not care for it, that is, unless combined with physical movements as in acting, at which they are excellent. Painting is much more the art of this period. Like painting, poetry cannot really be taught except by practitioners, and there are fewer poets than painters. To those who are not one can only suggest that they should get away from attempting to teach appreciation which means imposing their personal taste on the immature, a spiritual bullying. By all means set good poetry to be learnt by heart with an eye to the future, but let it be a taste of learning, nothing else. Do not enlarge on its beauties, but see that the vocabulary is understood. Devote more time to the technical side; set prosodical exercises on concrete subjects, with a list of banned commonplace words. They will learn more about the meaning of poetry by writing it, than by any explanation you can give. Concentrate as far as possible on dramatic literature, so that they may build up words and physical sensations, and remember that for better or worse, writing is the most intellectual and self-conscious of the arts.

The Criterion, July 1934

In Search of Dracula

Tuesday, 14th.—Arrived with Michael at 12.30 to find Peter rocking a cradle outside the Lodge. Lunch beautifully hot but missed Mr Pup's carving. Mr Booge, a good samaritan as usual, helped us to tie on our stores, tents, theodolites, sleighs, reindeer food, etc. Photographs of the doomed heroes were taken, babes and sucklings held up.

Raced a quartet of beauties in dinky scarves as far as the Watford by-pass. Dropped Peter to say good-bye to his parents—sneaking into his drive like an assassin. Found a bed at the Yids' Home in Regent Street. Dinner at Boulestin's. Must remember not to go there again unless invited by an elderly literary admirer. Still, it was worth an unemployed family's country holiday. "Your god is your belly" my aunt used to tell me.

Went to see *Men in White*. Good slick acting and quite a nice set, but the usual American wickedness about germs, the don't-kiss-your-baby-on-the-mouth lie. Dropped into the Café Royal to have coffee but were soon driven out by two art-bores.

Wednesday, 15th.—Breakfast in bed. Talked to toothless chambermaid about Brighton. P. arrives and we set off, throwing cigarettes to lorry drivers, exchanging hats and yelling like idiots. Lunch at the Falstaff at Canterbury. Loathsomely genteel. Arrived Dover about 2 and flirted with policeman till 4 when we managed to get on to the quay. New boat, the *Prince Baudouin*, very posh. Mutual photography. Went first-class out of bravado and to look at the splendid people in their soup plates. Sea calm unfortunately as I was looking forward to seeing Peter sick over a cocktail bar. St Anne of Cleves or someone was having a feast in Ostende so all hotels full. Drove out in the dark to Gistelle, Peter very excited about driving on the right, followed by a bore on a motor bike who continued his conversation in a thieves' kitchen. Food rotten; beds hard; sanitation none. Peter had nightmares about losing his passport.

Thursday, 16th.—Agree entirely with Baudelaire's opinion of the Belgians. A dingy race with too many large cars fitted with trumpets which they blow continuously. Michael is beginning to despise the Morris and call it a hearse, Peter hoots all the time. Ghent, Bruxelles, Louvain. Visited nothing. Thank goodness Peter only shows slight tendencies to be a tourist and Michael none at all. I once went to Yugoslavia with father and wished I was dead. German frontier at tea. Officials politer than the English but rather like Stainless to explain anything to. Pestered in Aachen by a German scoutmaster, probably a spy. Reached Cologne and went to a Christian boarding house. First row with Peter about money. Sat in the Café am Dom all evening delivering a message about the Good Life while Peter and Michael gorged themselves on sickly cake and ices.

Friday, 17th.—All rather subdued this morning and no wonder in this country which is being run by a mixture of gangsters and the sort of school prefect who is good at Corps. Voting for the Reichskanzler on Sunday. Every house waves a flag like a baby's rattle. Private yachts for the flagmakers. Each shop has pasted a notice, "We are all going to vote yes". Slogans hang screaming above the cobbled streets of tiny hamlets, "One Folk: One Leader: One Yes". Photographs of the circus manager followed by a multitude of men and women showing their uvulas are pasted on the walls of barns, together with the information, "The voting is absolutely free. Do YOUR DUTY." Tea near Marburg where there were hornets. In a furious temper for some reason or other (O, Mr Censor), skidding round corners on two wheels through pretty wooded hills. Reached Eisenach, Bach's birthplace, thinking of the Rector and Superbos. Talked to hotel proprietor who suddenly stopped and rushed to open the window. The Labour Corps were passing and one must be keen. After they had gone he closed it with a sigh of relief. Sat in a café in the market square listening to Hitler shouting from Hamburg. Sounded like a Latin lesson. Peter ate an ice out of his handkerchief.

Saturday, 18th.—Weimar, Leipsig, Dresden. Roadmending, that mask of bankruptcy, everywhere, but the roadmender's singlet or nothing a pleasant contrast to the English workman's waistcoat and stiff collar. Peter getting impatient for his mountains. Argument about the scenery cult. Personally give me a good hotel and a petrol pump or city streets in a fog. Reached Dresden for tea. Very beautiful Varogne buildings ruined by flags, and the only nice church bell I have ever heard. Michael went off to photograph and I took Peter to be inoculated by a stage German doctor who took half an hour to sterilize his instruments, peering over the top of his spectacles and grunting like a gas engine. Flicks after dinner. Film *A Man wants to Return to Germany,* about a German colonial officer who escapes from internment camp and the wiles of a non-Aryan temptress. Every time he said "I must do my duty", which was every 20 feet of film, he made a face as if he had swallowed the cap of his fountain pen. The old faithful retainer comic relief which shows how much Socialism we are to expect. Came home feeling rather sick.

Sunday, 19th.—Peter rather seedy after inoculation. Pleasant drive over Erzgebirge reaching a doll's house frontier village for lunch. Thank God we're out of the sight of flags at last. Waiter intrigued to see Peter drinking chlorodyne and water. A man with false teeth leant over from the next table to whisper in my ear a warning about the temptations of Prague and fell off his chair.

Stopped in Bruch to ask the way from two garage attendants looking, acting and dressed like Tweedledum and Tweedledee down to the school caps. Reached Schloss Eisenberg, a seventeenth century building the size of the Malvern Girls' School, armed with letters of introduction to Princess Lobkovics (provincial papers please copy). Albert the butler, flat-footed and terrifying, inspected my trousers and Peter's social credit shirt with his dolphin's eye but finally led us to our respective suites. Michael had left his rucksack in the car which I asked Albert to send for. The footman brought up the tents and the stove. Temperature low. A fine collection of pictures, including a magnificent Breughel. Michael caught opening a chest in the hall. Temperature arctic. Prince, Princess and American friend returned at last. Explored estate after tea. Lovely dinner. Albert apparently has a grudge against the greyhound which he keeps surreptitiously kicking. Played Battle, a game with billiard balls which excites the worst passions and smashes the Louis Quinze chairs. Peter, determined not to miss anything, had a whiskey and soda but didn't look as if he liked it. Talked about Hölderlin and the Prince gave a marvellous imitation of Hitler. Peter is getting off with Henny-Penny, the American.

Monday, 20th.—The Princess and Henny-Penny went to have their hair done, so off to Karlsbad where those who are afraid of weighing machines go. All pansied up in helmets, goggles and fur coats. Bought a new coat to placate Albert and inspected improper postcards, but forgot Mr Day until too late. Drove back through the Pilsner hop fields.

Partridges for dinner. Played Battle again which brings that dangerous light to Peter's eye which we all know so well. To bed, worrying about tips.

Tuesday, 21st.—Very hot. Settled tipping question, and arrived in Prague for lunch in the courtyard where the diplomats go incognito. Peter and Michael went off to bathe in the Elbe and I went to bed with a detective story. Dinner on a restaurant boat. Ordered Bubbly which didn't suit our clothes but made us feel very on-the-Continong.

Wednesday, 22nd.—Drove steadily all day through Brod and Jihlava but then lost the road and beached in a field. O Mummy. Started to sing "Now the Day is Over", until Peter suggested getting out of the car and we managed to get her off again, careering like Puck over hill and dale till we found a road and reached Ur Hradista in the dark. Good and cheap but camera stolen.

Thursday, 23rd.—Hills at last but Peter suffering from gardener's leg. Over the Bile Carpathians to Trencin and thence through Salvator Rosa gorges to Poprad near the Tatras. Gardener's leg very bad so magnanimously decided to give Dracula a miss and stay here for two days. Town full of peasants with their leathery everlasting faces. Went in the evening to see strong man run over by a motor car and stood upon by the local Fatty Arbuckle.

Friday, 24th.—To-day according to the others we are going to camp. I don't see why we can't make up that part. Bought a sausage as big as a Michelin tyre and a bottle of local wine tasting like sanitary fluid, and set off for the Tatras. Real tourist resort, full of Tyrolese hats and peaks. Poured with rain so returned to hotel and cooked eggs in our bedroom. Went to see Conrad Veidt in the *Wandering Jew,* a sad come-down from his Student-of-Prague days and then got off with the hotel band who by request played Hungarian music into the small hours, which always makes me feel like the exiled lover pulling on his snow boots in the middle of Siberia. To bed a little tiddley. "Why am I a Schoolmaster?" I asked Peter, but he was asleep so now I shall never know.

Saturday, 25th.—Through mist-hidden forests to the Dobsina Ice Caves. Guide's information and delivery a fit subject for a Sherlock Holmes monograph. Suppose people were once really interested in that kind of thing and it survives like mediæval Latin in prep. schools. Went our first and last walk after lunch and inspected the new railway they are building. Very pansy. Returned in violent hailstorm which the hood is designed to concentrate on the driver's neck. Band very inquisitive and thirsty. The school where I teach, I told them, is the most aristocratic in England. The headmaster never appears except in spurs and on an Arab stallion and the games master lives on the raw flesh of freshly killed stags.

Sunday, 26th.—Very wild country to Lucenec where we met a private detective who showed us his photograph. On reflection have decided it was Mr Telfer in disguise. Hungarian frontier doubted my Englishman's word and said we ought to have visas and must buy them in Budapest. Steering very peculiar since we met Mr Telfer. One skid and two punctures before we got to Budapest which we had to pay to enter. Found a garage run by a sinister old lady on a couch, and a codfish. Peter very suspicious indeed and for once rightly. Went to Café Hungaria in the evening to see and be seen by those who matter.

Monday, 27th.—BLACK MONDAY. Went to see Cod who was full of praises but no performance. After two hours of waiting, I tore off my pearls in the street and stamped on them. The Cod burst into tears but gave up the car after I had payed a king's ransom. Returned to hotel to find the Police Station closed till 4. Went to Bank which charged 20 per cent. for the privilege of having their beastly pengos.

Michael has bought himself a pair of brown and white shoes, which means I shall have to go to the bank again to-morrow. Walked in a blistering sun for miles with the local Deadly Nightshade to find the police station, only to be told that I was quite right and needn't have come. In the middle of the night Michael had an acute attack of indigestion. Am in no mood to be a member of the League of Nations Union.

Tuesday, 28th.—Shook the dust off our feet but lost our way. Much weeping but ran over a hen and felt better. Reached Vienna in a thunderstorm. Went to the theatre to see a Viennese light opera *The Princess on the Ladder;* good. Had to speak to Peter very severely for pulling feathers out of the wrap of the lady in front.

Wednesday, 29th.—Peter off to see museums. Michael and I on a charabanc tour of the city. Trip out improved by an English spinster with a face like a horse, a voice like a spoilt little girl in a hotel, and a flat enthusiasm like stale Vichy water. Michael's shoes put her off, but not enough. Free time after lunch so mooched about. Went to flicks in the evening to see Bela Lugosi in *The White Zombie.*

Thursday, 30th.—Wobbled to Salzburg. Too poor to make whoopee, so played Bogey Bogey in the lounge.

Friday, 31st.—Stopped at Kitzbuhel to see Hedwig but found she was lunching at a Schloss near by. Peter's trouser buttons missing so he had to change in the road. Owner of Schloss a real treasure. Very fat, quite buttonless, he lives on snails, keeps lions, and says things to the ladies at table in an Austrian dialect which I cannot possibly repeat here. Stopped for the night at a little gasthouse beyond Innsbruck, all beams and swallows. Caught after supper by a schoolmaster belonging to the Vaterland Front. The Pope has blessed our revolvers.

Saturday, September 1st.—Over the Arlberg which was covered in snow and through part of Switzerland to Pfäffikon on Lake Zurich. Hate Switzerland. Cooking rotten and architecture hideous. Tormented Peter by hiring a concertina player to play just behind him.

Sunday, 2nd.—Zurich, Basel, and here are the tichy little Frenchmen of the Première Année. Steering much worse and Peter driving like a fireman. Reached Bar-le-Duc and had an epic meal. Champagne very cheap. Peter eclipsed all previous efforts.

Monday, 3rd.—Started at 6 a.m. Peter started to sing but was dissuaded. He must have the worst repertoire of songs of any man in Europe. The coffee at Rheims exceeded even that at the Winter Gardens, Malvern, in rankness and horror. Contretemps at Frontier about the store and Peter very upset at having his clothes inspected. Through the battlefields which were full of girl guides to Ostend, the hood behaving like the baby in *Alice in Wonderland.* Pa has come up to scratch and sent a fiver. Spent the evening hating the other English guests.

Tuesday, 4th.—Having lost a document had to pay a tax which leaves us penniless. Only sandwiches for lunch, and situation not improved by forgetting to wait for eight bob's worth of change at Dover. Telephoned to friends but all were out. Very unhappy. Spent all but fourpence on dinner, and rang up again. Managed to raise £8 in return for promises of post-dated cheques. Sent Peter and Michael in a taxi for five of it, and went to the Fairy Ring in Piccadilly to collect the remaining three from the half-wit brother of a friend. Stayed at Hotel Russell. Too respectable.

Wednesday, 5th.—Called on Gerald to hear the latest news about the Dinosaurs. Apparently they suffered from arthritis. Then past the new factories on the Great West Road, past the Old College, to Colwall. Dropped Peter in the road and turned north.

The Badger, Downs School, Autumn 1934
and Spring 1935

To Unravel Unhappiness

A Life of One's Own. By Joanna Field. Chatto and Windus. 7s. 6d.

This is a remarkable and, I think, important book. It is best described as a record of auto-analysis, a detailed account of a series of experiments in minor psychotherapy. The first important thing about the book is that the author was not a "case"; she was a lecturer in academic psychology, had many friends, and early in the experiment became happily married; i.e. she is a perfectly ordinary example of the middle-class educated and intelligent woman who has to earn her living and is quite capable of looking after herself and getting on with other people of both sexes—no better and no worse than nine-tenths of the people one knows.

One day she realised that she was unhappy and decided to do something about it. That is the second important point. Nine-tenths of the people one knows either do not consciously realise that they are unhappy—and by unhappiness I do not mean sudden fits of acute misery or depression like the aftermath of 'flu, but that dull unrelenting pressure to which people, like those who live within earshot of a waterfall, grow so accustomed that they take it for granted—or if they do realise it for a moment, are afraid and thrust away the unpleasant idea, drugging themselves with work, parties or what not. Its presence in a neighbour even superficial observation will detect, but to admit it in oneself is so damaging to one's self-conceit, except to those to whom it is their sole luxury, that such admission is rare.

Miss Field set out first to discover the nature and objects of this unhappiness and then its remedy. The technique of discovery is nothing very new and exciting now: free association writing, either off the reel or on a set subject, automatic drawings, catching the wandering thought of the moment and putting it into words, transcribing dreams and so on. But the results were as startling to the subject as they would be to any of us who choose to apply them. She imagined herself intelligent, rational, civilised, believing in intellectual progress, and the experiments revealed her to herself as timid, desperately anxious about the effect she was having on other people, full of sly equivocations and tricks, hysterically violent and irrational in her judgments when her self was threatened, and at a deeper level terrified, terrified of the future and of the point of existence, of her instinctive self, and of God as the avenger and punisher.

I do not know if Miss Field is acquainted with the work of Homer Lane, but everything she says is a striking confirmation of his teaching. He used to say that the first question you should ask a patient is his opinion of God. Our way of bringing up children, by a combination of moral commands, forgiveness, penances and punishments—the Pharisaic law— implants in the unconscious a guilty hatred of God as he is consciously presented to us, and is responsible for those errors on which Blake so unerringly put his finger: "(1) That Man has two real existing principles— a Body and a Soul. (2) That Energy called evil is alone from the Body; and that Reason, called good, is alone from the Soul. (3) That God will torment Man in eternity for following his energies". The consequence of such beliefs is that man is divided against himself, and the energies or instincts are not allowed to develop beyond the infantile possessive level; i.e. that he can never be self-forgetful. Of this possessive personal unconsciousness dominated by automatic thinking, Miss Field gives a searching and devastating analysis. She does not say much about her childhood, perhaps wisely. She refused to undergo psychoanalysis, feeling it was not quite playing the game. Few people have the time or money for it, and one ought to be able to discover a method which one can work oneself, taking the forgotten incidents of childhood as given, and working from the present.

It would be unfair to her book, which is as exciting as a detective story, to give away all the methods she tried, but they included both physical and mental exercises, the former paralleling in an interesting way the work of Mr Matthias Alexander. She found that the first, hardest, and most essential task was to learn to relax that physical and mental rigidity to which we all become habituated.

What, then, was entirely under the control of my will? It seemed that the only thing that was even potentially so controlled was my attention. I could not control what I saw when I looked in a certain direction, but I could at least control what direction I should look in. . . .

It had also been one of my greatest discoveries that when I could not attend as I wished, then I must deliberately turn my attention loose and let it lead me to the distracting cause. . . . Selfishness is not usually a failure of will, it is not that one deliberately sees a selfish and an unselfish attitude and chooses the selfish. It is that one is selfish because one unwittingly indulges in a kind of thinking, which cannot, by its very nature, recognise the realness of other people's needs.

Secondly, that—unacceptable as it may be to those who earn their living by it—academic knowledge, logical comprehension of ideas in books were quite useless, indeed, more often than not, even a form of escape. Thirdly—and this throws some light on literature—that the expression of thought in words, becoming aware of it, was the beginning of a process of development and enrichment.

In perceiving the external world the effort to express what I saw invariably brought rich results. Often, when vaguely bored in a restaurant or the street, it would be enough to say, for instance: "That man looks like a pig", and at once I would find he had become alive. . . .

And, lastly, that the unconscious is not only the refuge of childish phantasies and fears, but a source of creative wisdom; there is an instinctive sense of living, if it is trusted; a trust, however, quite different from blind irrationalism.

One is tempted again and again to quote passages for their richness of insight, but quotation could not do justice to the sustained interest of Miss Field's story which culminates in a mystical experience.

The last chapter of interpretation is, inevitably, less interesting, but the author would be the last to claim it as important. I doubt whether speaking of male and female elements explains anything. If there are both elements in every individual, neither can be sacrificed without damage— the Gretchen is as unsatisfactory as the school teacher.

A Life of One's Own is an account of the unhappiness of the average person, and of methods to overcome it which could be employed by anyone, provided they have the patience and the courage of the experimenter. Such qualities, unfortunately, especially the first, are rare, but this book should do much to stimulate them.

The Listener, 28 November 1934

Lowes Dickinson

Goldsworthy Lowes Dickinson. By E. M. Forster.
Edward Arnold. 10s. 6d.

To write the biography of a teacher is not easy; for a teacher, like an actor, leaves little behind him; his life lacks the compulsive thrill of that of the man of action, the nervous excitement to know what happened next, and also the works of the artist, the tangible relics to be reverently examined and compared; what remains are other lives, and a life of Shakespeare by Hamlet would probably not be a good one.

> They don't mind dying much in China, do they? shouted Liebling to the Chinaman, hoping to introduce a story he had heard about how one could buy a substitute to be accepted for one. "Always dying" said the Larmah "millions by starvation flood plague at this moment so thick on the ground." That explains why they believe in metamorphosis don't you think said the clever student confidentially to the Larmah. "May be its true for all I know" said the Larmah shaking his hands towards the two remaining sausages reposing on their cold beds of mincemeat, and just for a moment Liebling was quite certain that in the whole world there was only this funny old man sitting in front of two cold sausages saying I don't know my dear boy, and feeding the starving.

Liebling describes perfectly the feeling that any great teacher inspires, but he could not for that very reason have written Lowes Dickinson's biography.

It requires a kind of love which is impossible to define but is easy to recognize when found, and nowhere, I think, is it more obvious and pervading than in this book of Mr E. M. Forster's.

Of course Mr Forster has many qualifications, the novelist's skill in presentation, e.g. his arrangement of the letters, verbal sensibility—

> But these amenities lay at the edge of his life. Its centre was covered with rubbish and worry. And at its opposite edge lay an imbecile boy whom he sometimes kicked in order to ingratiate himself with his school-fellows;

sense of humour—

> Nor was he even insensitive to the joys of Jingoism; there are some letters to R. C. Trevelyan during the Diamond Jubilee of 1897 which make painful reading for his steadier admirers; he explains how wonderful it is to see the Empire marching past, and he contemplates

bicycling down to Spithead to see the Naval Review. He never reached Spithead. It was too far;

and the necessary detachment—he did not share Dickinson's tastes for Plato, Shelley and Goethe; and further he has a thorough dislike and distrust for all professional influences:

One hesitates to call him "a popular don," for the words suggest some cheery empty creature.

But none of these explain his success. Perhaps the secret which he shares with Dickinson and which made them friends is a sense of the mystery of life, a hatred of all tabus and systems which would enforce a proscribed pattern, and a belief that what matters is that each should discover his unique treasure.

For that is the lasting impression which this biography makes: that Lowes Dickinson, every bit as much as Napoleon, was a man of destiny; he discovered his life and lived it; and what other success is there? Those who do not earn their living with their bodies should not fail to read this book; it will teach them to avoid their besetting sin, jealousy of the other world.

We do not know enough about either heredity or psychology to know exactly which conditions produce the intelligent and the sensitive: if the causes lie probably in the parental relations, if most intellectuals are psychically bound to their mothers, they are not thereby explained.

The effect on Lowes Dickinson of his mother's death, as described by himself (p. 33), the enhanced feeling for Cambridge, the release from dogmatic religion, is intensely interesting and illuminating, but Mr Forster wisely abstains from comment.

Whether intellectual curiosity, the wish to understand experience rather than be lived by it, is first caused by emotional frustration, or inability to feel and act as impulse directs, or whether the curiosity causes the isolation, the two are generally found together, and found early in life, and further the combination of intelligence and sensibility with physical grace and skill is rare, e.g. Dickinson's typing.

Lowes Dickinson's problem is the problem of everyone who finds himself committed before his choice to a life of understanding.

For such who seems to himself to stand and to be stood outside the world of action and passion with all its powers and awards, there are two temptations, either to take fright and retire into a private world of phantasy, religious or bookish, or denying his gift to adore uncritically blood and action, an invalid poet hoping with an ode to buy the society of an inarticulate boxer.

Except for the unsuccessful bicycle-ride to Spithead, Lowes Dickinson was never guilty of this treason of the clerks; his danger was the first rather than the second. The interest and example of his life to an outsider lies in his steady progress from himself to others, from a few to many, his persistent testing of ideas by things. It did not come easily to him; he made all kinds of false starts. Buddhism, Hegel, Medicine, an attempt to combine sensibility and action which was unsuited to him, but once he discovered political history he never looked back. More capable of intimate friendship than most, he came to write

> I cannot understand how I thought that this personal passion in transitory individuals could be the key to the universe.

The young extension lecturer who

> had no notion how to get into touch with ordinary people, and no desire to do so, for I thought I was the bearer of a message which transcended all actual life

became the Lowes Dickinson of the broadcast talk; the shy young don, the inspirer and the confidant of perky undergraduates.

People and civilizations are saved by a change of heart; whether physical violence, loathsome as it is, is necessary to secure it, or whether if we are concerned enough, it can be brought about by "mental fight" alone, we cannot answer, but at a time when intellectual is a term of abuse fit only for the Jews, it is particularly important that those capable of waging the latter should not lose patience: to such Lowes Dickinson and also, I think, E. M. Forster, are examples permanent and alert.

Scrutiny, December 1934

John Skelton

To write an essay on a poet who has no biography, no message, philosophical or moral, who has neither created characters, nor expressed critical ideas about the literary art, who was comparatively uninfluenced by his predecessors, and who exerted no influence upon his successors, is not easy. Skelton's work offers no convenient critical pegs. Until Mr Robert Graves drew attention to his work some years ago, he was virtually unknown outside University-honour students, and even now, though there have been two editions, in the last ten years, those of Mr Hughes and Mr Henderson, it is doubtful whether the number of his readers has very substantially increased. One has only to compare him with another modern discovery, Hopkins, to realise that he has remained a stock literary event rather than a vital influence.

My own interest dates from the day I heard a friend at Oxford, who had just bought the first Hughes edition, make two quotations:

> Also the mad coot
> With bald face to toot;

and

> Till Euphrates that flood driveth me into Ind,

and though I should not claim my own case as typical, yet I doubt if those to whom these lines make no appeal are likely to admire Skelton.

Though little that is authentic is known of Skelton's life, a fairly definite portrait emerges from his work: a conservative cleric with a stray sense of humour, devoted to the organisation to which he belonged and to the cultural tradition it represented, but critical of its abuses, possibly a scholar, but certainly neither an academic-dried boy or a fastidious high-brow; no more unprejudiced or well-informed about affairs outside his own province than the average modern reader of the newspapers, but shrewd enough within it, well read in the conventional good authors of his time, but by temperament more attracted to more popular and less respectable literature, a countryman in sensibility, not particularly vain, but liking to hold the floor, fond of feminine society, and with a quick and hostile eye for *pompositas* in all its forms.

Born in 1460, he probably took his degree at Cambridge in 1484, and was awarded a laureate degree by Cambridge, Oxford, and Louvain, which I suppose did not mean much more then than winning an essay prize or the Newdigate would to-day, became tutor to the future Henry VIII, was sufficiently well known socially to be mentioned by Erasmus and Caxton; took orders at the age of thirty-eight, became Rector of Diss, his probable birthplace, about 1500; began an open attack on Wolsey in 1519, and died in sanctuary at Westminster in 1529. Thus he was born just before Edward IV's accession, grew up during the Wars of the Roses, and died in the year of Wolsey's fall and the Reformation Parliament. In attempting to trace the relations between a poet's work and the age in which he lived, it is well to remember how arbitrary such deductions are. One is presented with a certain number of facts like a heap of pebbles, and the number of possible patterns which one can make from them are almost infinite. To prove the validity of the pattern one chooses, it would be necessary first to predict that if there were a poet in such and such a period he would have such and such poetical qualities, and then for the works of that poet to be discovered with just those qualities. The literary historian can do no more than suggest one out of many possible views.

Politically Skelton's period is one of important change. The Plantagenet line had split into two hostile branches, ending one in a lunatic and the other in a criminal. The barons turned their weapons upon each other and destroyed themselves; all the English Empire in France except Calais was gone; the feudal kind of representative government was discredited and the Church corrupt. The wealth of the country was beginning to accumulate in the hands of the trading classes, such as wool merchants, and to be concentrated in the cities of the traders. Traders want peace which gives them liberty to trade rather than political liberty, secular authority rather than a religious authority which challenges their right to usury and profit. They tend therefore to support an absolute monarchy, and unlike a feudal aristocracy with its international family loyalties, to be nationalist in sentiment. Absolute monarchies adopt *realpolitik* and though Machiavelli's *Prince* was not published till 1513, his principles were already European practice.

Skelton's political views are those of the average man of his time and class. A commoner, he had nothing to lose by the destruction of the old nobility; like the majority of his countrymen, he rejoices at royal weddings and national victories, and weeps at royal funerals and national defeats. With them also he criticises Henry VII's avarice.

Immensas sibi divitias cumulasse quid horres?

Like a good bourgeois he is horrified at the new fashions and worldliness at Henry VIII's court, but cannot attribute it to the monarch himself, only to his companions; and hates the arrogance and extravagance of Wolsey, who by social origin was no better than himself.

In religious matters he is naturally more intelligent and better informed. Though Wyclif died in 1384, his doctrines were not forgotten among the common people, and though Skelton did not live to see the English Reformation, before he was fifty Luther had pinned his protest to the church door at Wittenberg, and he lived through the period of criticism by the Intelligentsia (*The Praise of Folly* was written in 1503) which always precedes a mass political movement.

The society of Colet, Grocyn, Linacre, and More was an intellectual and international one, a society of scholars who, like all scholars, overestimated their capacity to control or direct events. Skelton's feelings towards them were mixed. Too honest not to see and indeed in *Colin Clout* unsparingly to attack the faults of the Church, he was like them and like the intelligent orthodox at any time, a reformer not a revolutionary, that is to say, he thought that the corruptions of the Church and its dogmatic system were in no way related; that you could by a "change of heart" cure the one without impairing the other; while the revolutionary, on the other hand, attributes the corruption directly to the dogmas, for which he proposes to substitute another set which he imagines to be fool-proof and devil-proof. Towards the extremists he was frightened and hostile.

> And some have a smack
> Of Luther's sack . . .
> And some of them bark
> Clatter and carp
> Of that heresiarch
> Called Wickleuista
> The devilish dogmatista.

His difference from the early reformers was mainly temperamental. He was not in the least donnish and, moving perhaps in less rarefied circles, saw that the effect of their researches on the man in the street, like the effect on our own time, for example of Freud, was different from what they intended.

He has been unjustly accused of opposing the study of Greek; what he actually attacked was the effect produced by the impact of new ideas upon the average man, never in any age an edifying spectacle.

> Let Parrot, I pray you, have liberty to prate
> For aurea lingua greca ought to be magnified
> If it were cond perfitely and after the rate
> As lingua Latina, in school matter occupied
> But our Grekis, their Greek so well have applied
> That they cannot say in Greek, riding by the way,
> "Ho, ostler, fetch my horse a bottel of hay."

As a literary artist, it is difficult to escape the conclusion that Skelton is an oddity, like Blake, who cannot be really fitted into literary history as an inevitable product of the late fifteenth century. There is every reason for the existence of Hawes or even Barclay as the moribund end of the Chaucerian tradition; it is comparatively easy to understand Elizabethan poetry as a fusion of the Italian Renaissance and native folk elements; but the vigour and character of Skelton's work remains unpredictable.

One may point out that the *Narrenschiff* influenced the *Bouge of Court*, that Skeltonics may be found in early literature like the Proverbs of Alfred,

> Ac if þu him lest welde
>   Werende on worlde.
> Lude and stille
>   His owene wille,

or that the style of his Latin verses occurs in Goliardic poetry or Abelard.

> Est in Rama
> Vox audita
> Rachel fluentes

Eiolantes
Super natos
Interfectos.

But that a writer should be found at that particular date who would not succumb to aureate diction, and without being a folk writer, should make this kind of rhythm the basis of work, would seem, if it had not occurred, exceedingly improbable.

Excluding *Magnificence*, Skelton's poetry falls naturally into four divisions: the imitations of the "aureate" poetry of Lydgate and similar fifteenth-century verses, such as the elegy on the duke of Northumberland and the prayers to the Trinity; the lyrics; the poems in rhyme royal such as the *Bouge of Court* and *Speke Parrot;* and those like *Elinor Rumming, Philip Sparrow,* and *Colin Clout,* written in skeltonics.

Of the first class we may be thankful that it is so small. The attempt to gain for English verse the sonority of Latin by the use of a Latinised vocabulary was a failure in any hands except Milton's, and Skelton was no Milton. It was dull and smelt of the study, and Skelton seems to have realised this, and in his typically ironical way expressed his opinion.

For, as I tofore have said
I am but a young maid
And cannot in effect
My style as yet direct
With English words elect. . . .

Chaucer that famous clerk
His terms were not dark
But pleasant, easy and plain
No word he wrote in vain.

Also John Lydgate
Writeth after a higher rate
It is diffuse to find
The sentence of his mind
Some men find a fault
And say he writeth too haut

(*Philip Sparrow*);

and in the *Duke of Albany* he rags the aureate vocabulary by giving the long words a line a piece:

Of his nobility
His magnaminity
His animosity
His frugality

His liberality
His affability, *etc. etc.*

As a writer of lyrics, on the other hand, had he chosen he could have ranked high enough. He can range from the barrack room "'Twas Xmas day in the workhouse" style of thing, to conventional religious poetry like the poem "Woefully arrayed" and the quite unfaked tenderness of the poem to Mistress Isabel Pennell, and always with an unfailing intuition of the right metrical form to employ in each case. Here is an example of his middle manner, Fancy's song about his hawk in *Magnificence*.

> Lo this is
> My fancy ywis
> Now Christ it blesse!
> It is, by Jesse.
>
> A bird full sweet
> For me full meet
> She is furred for the heat
> All to the feet:
>
> Her browès bent
> Her eyen glent
> From Tyne to Trent
> From Stroud to Kent. . . .
>
> Barbed like a nun
> For burning of the sun
> Her feathers dun
> Well favoured, bonne!

Skelton's use of Rhyme Royal is in some ways the best proof of his originality, because though employing a form used by all his predecessors and contemporaries and at a time when originality of expression was not demanded by the reading public, few stanzas of Skelton's could be confused with those of anyone else.

The most noticeable difference, attained partly by a greater number of patter or unaccented syllables (which relate it more to a teutonic accentual or sprung rhythm for verse) lies in the tempo of his poetry. Compare a stanza of Skelton's with one of Chaucer's:

> Suddenly as he departed me fro
>   Came pressing in one in a wonder array
> Ere I was ware, behind me he said "BO"
>   Then I, astonied of that sudden fray
> Start all at once, I liked nothing his play

> For, if I had not quickly fled the touch
> He had plucked out the nobles of my pouch.
>
> (Skelton.)

> But o word, lordlings, herkeneth ere I go:
> It were full hard to finde now a dayes
> In all a town Griseldes three or two
> For, if that they were put to such assayes,
> The gold of hem hath no so bad aloyes
> With brass, that though the coyne be fair at ye,
> It would rather breste a-two than plye.
>
> (Chaucer.)

In Chaucer there is a far greater number of iambic feet, and the prevailing number of accents per line is five; in the Skelton it is four.

Indeed, the tempo of Skelton's verse is consistently quicker than that of any other English poet; only the author of *Hudibras,* and in recent times Vachel Lindsay, come anywhere near him in this respect.

It seems to be a rough-and-ready generalisation that the more poetry concerns itself with subjective states, with the inner world of feeling, the slower it becomes, or in other words, that the verse of extrovert poets like Dryden is swift and that of introvert poets like Milton is slow, and that in those masters like Shakespeare who transcend these classifications, in the emotional crises which precede and follow the tragic act, the pace of the verse is retarded.

Thus the average pace of mediæval verse compared with that of later more self-conscious ages is greater, and no poetry is more "outer" than Skelton's.

His best poems, with the exception of *Speke Parrot,* are like triumphantly successful prize poems. The themes—the death of a girl's sparrow, a pub, Wolsey, have all the air of set subjects. They may be lucky choices, but one feels that others would have done almost equally well, not, as with Milton, that his themes were the only ones to which his genius would respond at that particular moment in his life; that, had they not occurred to him, he would have written nothing. They never read as personal experience, brooded upon, and transfigured.

Considering his date, this is largely to the good. Pre-Elizabethan verse, even Chaucer, when it deserts the outer world, and attempts the subjective, except in very simple emotional situations, as in the mystery plays, tends to sentiment and prosy moralising. Skelton avoids that, but at the same time his emotional range is limited. The world of "The soldier's pole is fallen" is not for him:

> We are but dust
> For die we must
> It is general
> To be mortal

is as near as he gets to the terrific. This is moralising, but the metre saves it from sententiousness.

The skeltonic is such a simple metre that it is surprising that more poets have not used it. The natural unit of speech rhythm seems to be one of four accents, dividing into two half verses of two accents. If one tries to write ordinary conversation in verse, it will fall more naturally into this scheme than into any other. Most dramatic blank verse, for example, has four accents rather than five, and it is possible that our habit of prefacing nouns and adjectives by quite pointless adjectives and adverbs as in "the *perfectly* priceless" is dictated by our ear, by our need to group accents in pairs. Skelton is said to have spoken as he wrote, and his skeltonics have the natural ease of speech rhythm. It is the metre of many nursery rhymes.

> Little Jack Horner
> Sat in a corner;

or extemporised verse like the *Clerihew:*

> Alfred de Musset
> Used to call his cat pusset;

and study of the Woolworth song books will show its attraction to writers of jazz lyrics:

> For life's a farce
> Sitting on the grass.

No other English poet to my knowledge has this extempore quality, is less "would-be," to use a happy phrase of D. H. Lawrence.

It makes much of his work, of course, quite unmemorable—it slips in at one ear and out at the other; but it is never false, and the lucky shots seem unique, of a kind which a more deliberate and self-conscious poet would never have thought of, or considered worthy of his singing robes:

> Your head would have ached
> To see her naked.

Though much of Skelton's work consists of attacks on people and things, he can scarcely be called a satirist. Satire is an art which can only flourish within a highly sophisticated culture. It aims at creating a new

attitude towards the persons or institutions satirised, or at least at crystal-
lising one previously vague and unconscious. It presupposes a society
whose prejudices and loyalties are sufficiently diffuse to be destroyed by
intellectual assault, or sufficiently economically and politically secure to
laugh at its own follies, and to admit that there is something to be said on
both sides.

In less secure epochs, such as Skelton's, when friend and foe are more
clearly defined, the place of satire is taken by abuse, as it always is taken in
personal contact. (If censorship prevents abuse, allegorical symbolism is
employed, e.g. *Speke Parrot*.) If two people are having a quarrel, they do
not stop to assess who is at fault or to convince the other of his error: they
express their feelings of anger by calling each other names. Similarly,
among friends, when we express our opinion of an enemy by saying "so
and so is a closet" we assume that the reasons are known:

> The Midwife put her hand on his thick skull
> With the prophetic blessing, "Be thou dull,"

is too much emotion recollected in tranquillity to be the language of a
quarrel. Abuse in general avoids intellectual tropes other than those of
exaggeration which intensify the expression of one's feelings such as,
"You're so narrow-minded your ears meet," or the genealogical trees
which bargees assign to one another.

Further, the effect on the victim is different. Abuse is an attack on the
victim's personal honour, satire on his social self-esteem; it affects him
not directly, but through his friends.

Skelton's work is abuse or flyting, not satire, and he is a master at it.
Much flyting poetry, like Dunbar's and Skelton's own poems against Gar-
nesche, suffer from the alliterative metre in which they were written,
which makes them too verbal; the effect is lost on later generations, to
whom the vocabulary is unfamiliar. The freedom and simplicity of the
skeltonic was an ideal medium.

> Dundas, drunken and drowsy
> Scabbed, scurvy and lousy
> Of unhappy generation
> And most ungracious nation!
> Dundas
> That drunk ass
> That rates and ranks
> That prates and pranks
> Of Huntly banks
> Take this our thanks:—
> Dundee, Dunbar

> Walk, Scot,
> Walk, sott
> Rail not too far!

Later literary attempts at abuse, such as Browning's lines on Fitzgerald or Belloc's on a don, are too self-conscious and hearty. Blake is the only other poet known to me who has been equally successful.

> You think Fuseli is not a great painter; I'm glad
> This is one of the best compliments he ever had.

With his capacity for abuse Skelton combines a capacity for caricature. His age appears to have been one which has a penchant for the exaggerated and macabre, and he is no exception. His description of a character is as accurate in detail as one of Chaucer's, but as exaggerated as one of Dickens's. Compared with Chaucer he is more violent and dramatic; a favourite device of his is to interpolate the description with remarks by the character itself.

> With that came Riot, rushing all at once
> A rusty gallant, to-ragged and to-rent
> As on the board he whirled a pair of bones
> Quater trey dews he clattered as he went
> Now have at all, by Saint Thomas of Kent!
> And ever he threw and cast I wote n'ere what
> His hair was growen through out his hat. . . .
>
> Counter he could O lux upon a pot,
> An ostrich feather of a capon's tail
> He set up freshly upon his hat aloft:
> "What revel rout!" quod he, and gan to rail
> How oft he had hit Jenet on the tail,
> Of Phillis featuous, and little pretty Kate
> How oft he had knocked at her clicket gate.

This has much more in common with the Gothic gargoyle than with the classicism of Chaucer; *Elinor Rumming* is one of the few poems comparable to Breughel or Rowlandson in painting. The effect is like looking at the human skin through a magnifying glass.

> Then Margery Milkduck
> Her kirtle she did uptuck
> An inch above her knee
> Her legs that ye might see
> But they were sturdy and stubbed
> Mighty pestles and clubbed

> As fair and as white
> As the foot of a kite
> She was somewhat foul
> Crooked-necked like an owl;
> And yet she brought her fees,
> A cantel of Essex cheese,
> Was well a foot thick
> Full of maggots quick:
> It was huge and great
> And mighty strong meat
> For the devil to eat
> It was tart and pungate.

All Skelton's work has this physical appeal. Other poets, such as Spenser and Swinburne, have been no more dependent upon ideas, but they have touched only one sense, the auditory. The Catherine-wheel motion of Skelton's verse is exciting in itself, but his language is never vaguely emotive. Indeed, it is deficient in overtones, but is always precise, both visually and tactually. He uses place-names, not scientifically like Dante, or musically like Milton, but as country proverbs use them, with natural vividness:

> And Syllogisari was drowned at Sturbridge Fair.

Naturally enough the figures of classical mythology which appear in all mediæval work (just as the Sahara or Ohio appears in modern popular verses) occur in Skelton also, but he is never sorry to leave Lycaon or Etna for the Tilbury Ferry and the Plains of Salisbury. The same applies to the Latin quotations in *Philip Sparrow;* not only have they dramatic point, but being mainly quotations from the Psalter, they make no demands upon the erudition of his audience, any more than would "Abide with me" upon a modern reader.

Of Skelton's one excursion into dramatic form, *Magnificence,* not much need be said. It is interesting, because he is one of the few dramatists who have attempted, and with success, to differentiate his characters by making them speak in different metres, thus escaping the tendency of blank verse to make all the characters speak like the author; which obliged the Elizabethans to make their comic characters speak in prose; for the future of poetic comedy it may prove important. Its fault, a fatal one in drama, is its prolixity, but cut by at least two-thirds it might act very much better than one imagines.

Skelton's reputation has suffered in the past from his supposed indecency. This charge is no longer maintained, but there are other misunderstandings of poetry which still prevent appreciation of his work. On the one hand, there are those who read poetry for its message, for great thoughts which can be inscribed on Christmas calendars; on the other, there are admirers of "pure" poetry, which generally means emotive poetry with a minimum of objective reference. Skelton satisfies neither of these: he is too carefree for the one, and too interested in the outer world for the second.

If we accept, and I think we must, a distinction between the visionary and the entertainer, the first being one who extends our knowledge of, insight into, and power of control over human conduct and emotion, without whom our understanding would be so much the poorer, Skelton is definitely among the entertainers. He is not one of the indispensables, but among entertainers—and how few are the indispensables—he takes a high place. Nor is entertainment an unworthy art: it demands a higher standard of technique and a greater lack of self-regard than the average man is prepared to attempt. There have been, and are, many writers of excellent sensibility whose work is spoilt by a bogus vision which deprives it of the entertainment value which it would otherwise have had; in that kind of pride Skelton is entirely lacking.

The Great Tudors, edited by Katherine Garvin, 1935

Psychology and Art To-day

> Neither in my youth nor later was I able to detect in myself any particular fondness for the position or work of a doctor. I was, rather, spurred on by a sort of itch for knowledge which concerned human relationships far more than the data of natural science.—Freud

> Mutual forgiveness of each vice
> Such are the gates of paradise.—Blake

To trace, in the manner of the textual critic, the influence of Freud upon modern art, as one might trace the influence of Plutarch upon Shakespeare, would not only demand an erudition which few if any possess, but would be of very doubtful utility. Certain writers, notably Thomas Mann and D. H. Lawrence, have actually written about Freud, certain critics, Robert Graves in *Poetic Unreason* and Herbert Read in *Form in Modern Poetry*, for example, have made use of Freudian terminology, surrealism has adopted a technique resembling the procedure in the analyst's consulting room;* but the importance of Freud to art is greater than his

---

* But not the first. The Elizabethans used madness, not as a subject for clinical description but an opportunity for a particular kind of free associational writing (e.g. *Lear* or *The Duchess of Malfi*). Something of the kind occurs even earlier in the nonsense passages in the mummer's play.

language, technique or the truth of theoretical details. He is the most typical but not the only representative of a certain attitude to life and living relationships, and to define that attitude and its importance to creative art must be the purpose of this essay.

THE ARTIST IN HISTORY

Of the earliest artists, the paleolithic rock-drawers, we can of course know nothing for certain, but it is generally agreed that their aim was a practical one, to gain power over objects by representing them, and it has been suggested that they were probably bachelors, i.e. those who, isolated from the social group, had leisure to objectify the phantasies of the group, and were tolerated for their power to do so. Be that as it may, the popular idea of the artist as socially ill adapted has been a constant one, and not unjustified. Homer may have been blind, Milton certainly was, Beethoven deaf, Villon a crook, Dante very difficult, Pope deformed, Swift impotent, Proust asthmatic, Van Gogh mental, and so on. Yet parallel with this has gone a belief in their social value. From the chiefs who kept a bard, down to the Shell-Mex exhibition, patronage, however undiscriminating, has never been wanting as a sign that art provided society with something for which it was worth paying. On both of these beliefs, in the artist as neurotic, and in the social value of art, psychology has thrown a good deal of light.

THE ARTIST AS NEUROTIC

There is a famous passage in Freud's introductory lectures which has infuriated artists, not altogether unjustly:

> Before you leave to-day I should like to direct your attention for a moment to a side of phantasy-life of very general interest. There is, in fact, a path from phantasy back again to reality, and that is—art. The artist has also an introverted disposition and has not far to go to become neurotic. He is one who is urged on by instinctive needs which are too clamorous; he longs to attain to honour, power, riches, fame, and the love of women; but he lacks the means of achieving these gratifications. So, like any other with an unsatisfied longing, he turns away from reality and transfers all his interest, and all his Libido, too, on to the creation of his wishes in life. There must be many factors in combination to prevent this becoming the whole outcome of his development; it is well known how often artists in particular suffer from partial inhibition of their capacities through neurosis. Probably their constitution is endowed with a powerful capacity for

sublimation and with a certain flexibility in the repressions determin-
ing the conflict. But the way back to reality is found by the artist thus:
He is not the only one who has a life of phantasy; the intermediate
world of phantasy is sanctioned by general human consent, and ev-
ery hungry soul looks to it for comfort and consolation. But to those
who are not artists the gratification that can be drawn from the
springs of phantasy is very limited; their inexorable repressions pre-
vent the enjoyment of all but the meagre day-dreams which can be-
come conscious. A true artist has more at his disposal. First of all he
understands how to elaborate his day-dreams, so that they lose that
personal note which grates upon strange ears and become enjoyable
to others; he knows too how to modify them sufficiently so that their
origin in prohibited sources is not easily detected. Further, he pos-
sesses the mysterious ability to mould his particular material until it
expresses the idea of his phantasy faithfully; and then he knows how
to attach to this reflection of his phantasy-life so strong a stream of
pleasure that, for a time at least, the repressions are out-balanced
and dispelled by it. When he can do all this, he opens out to others
the way back to the comfort and consolation of their own uncon-
scious sources of pleasure, and so reaps their gratitude and admira-
tion; then he has won—through his phantasy—what before he could
only win in phantasy, honour, power, and the love of women.

Misleading though this may be, it draws attention to two facts, firstly
that no artist however "pure" is disinterested: he expects certain rewards
from his activity, however much his opinion of their nature may change as
he develops; and he starts from the same point as the neurotic and the
day-dreamer, from emotional frustration in early childhood.

The artist like every other kind of "highbrow" is self-conscious, i.e. he is
all of the time what everyone is some of the time, a man who is active
rather than passive to his experience. A man struggling for life in the
water, a schoolboy evading an imposition, or a cook getting her mistress
out of the house is in the widest sense a highbrow. We only think when we
are prevented from feeling and acting as we should like. Perfect satisfac-
tion would be complete unconsciousness. Most people however fit into
society sufficiently too neatly for the stimulus to arise except in a crisis
such as falling in love or losing their money.*

The possible family situations which may produce the artist or intellec-
tual are of course innumerable, but those in which one of the parents,
usually the mother, seeks a conscious spiritual, in a sense, adult relation-
ship with the child, are probably the commonest, e.g.,

* e.g. the sale of popular text-books on economics since 1929.

(1) When the parents are not physically in love with each other. There are several varieties of this: the complete fiasco; the brother-sister relationship on a basis of common mental interests; the invalid-nurse relationship where one parent is a child to be maternally cared for; and the unpassionate relation of old parents.

(2) The only child. This alone is most likely to produce early life confidence which on meeting disappointment, turns like the unwanted child, to illness or anti-social behaviour to secure attention.

(3) The youngest child. Not only are the parents old but the whole family field is one of mental stimulation.*

Early mental stimulation can interfere with physical development and intensify the conflict. It is a true intuition that makes the caricaturist provide the highbrow with a pair of spectacles. Myopia, deafness, delayed puberty, asthma—breathing is the first independent act of the child—are some of the attempts of the mentally awakened child to resist the demands of life.

To a situation of danger and difficulty there are five solutions:

(1) To sham dead. The idiot.
(2) To retire into a life of phantasy. The schyzophrene.
(3) To panic, i.e. to wreak one's grudge upon society. The criminal.
(4) To excite pity. To become ill. The invalid.
(5) To understand the mechanism of the trap. The scientist and the artist.

ART AND PHANTASY

In the passage of Freud quoted above, no distinction was drawn between art and phantasy, between, as Mr Roger Fry once pointed out, *Madame Bovary* and a *Daily Mirror* serial about Earls and Housemaids. The distinction is one which may perhaps be best illustrated by the differences between two kinds of dream.

A child has in the afternoon passed the window of a sweetshop, and would have liked to buy some chocolate it saw there, but its parents have refused the gift—so the child dreams of chocolate.

Here is a simple wish fulfilment dream of the *Daily Mirror* kind, and all art, and the juvenile work of artists, starts from this level. But it does not

* The success of the youngest son in folk tales is instructive. He is generally his mother's favourite as physically weaker and less assertive than his brothers. If he is often called stupid, his stupidity is physical. He is clumsy and lazy rather than dull. (Clumsiness being due to the interference of fancies with sense data.) He succeeds partly out of good nature and partly because confronted with a problem he overcomes it by understanding rather than brute force.

remain there. For the following dream and its analysis I am indebted to Mr Maurice Nicoll's *Dream Psychology:*

A young man who had begun to take morphia, but was not an addict, had the following dream:

> "I was hanging by a rope a short way down a precipice. Above me on the top of the cliff was a small boy who held the rope. I was not alarmed because I knew I had only to tell the boy to pull and I would get to the top safely." The patient could give no associations.

The dream shows that the morphinist has gone a certain way from the top of the cliff—the position of normal safety—down the side of the precipice, but he is still in contact with that which remains on the top. That which remains on the top is now relatively small, but is not inanimate like a fort, but alive; it is a force operating from the level of normal safety. This force is holding the dreamer back from the gulf, but that is all. It is for the dreamer himself to say the word if he wants to be pulled up (i.e. the morphinist is *deliberately* a morphinist).

When the common phrase is used that a man's will is weakening as he goes along some path of self-indulgence, it implies that something is strengthening. What is strengthening is the attractive power of the vice. But in the dream, the attractive power of morphia is represented by the force of gravitation, and the force of gravitation is constant.

But there are certain variable elements in the dream. The position of the figure over the cliff can vary and with it the length of the rope. The size of the figure at the top of the cliff might also vary without in any way violating the spirit of the dream. If then, we examine the length of the rope and the size of the figure on the cliff top in the light of relatively variable factors, the explanation of the *smallness* of the figure on the cliff top may be found to lie in the length of the rope, as if the rope drew itself out of the figure, and so caused it to shrink.

Now the figure at the top of the cliff is on firm ground and may there symbolise the forces of some habit and custom that exist in the morphinist and from which he has departed over the edge of the cliff, but which still hold him back from disaster although they are now shrunken. The attractive power of the morphia is not increasing, but *the interest the morphinist takes in morphia* is increasing.

A picture of the balance of interest in the morphinist is thus given, and the dream shows that the part of interest situated in the cliff top is now being drawn increasingly over the precipice.

In this dream, we have something which resembles art much more closely. Not only has the censor transformed the latent content of the dream into symbols but the dream itself is no longer a simple wish fulfilment, it has become constructive, and if you like moral. "A picture of the balance of interest"—that is a good description of a work of art. To use a phrase of Blake's "It's like a lawyer serving a writ."

Craftsmanship

There have always been two views of the poetic process, as an inspiration and as a craft, of the poet as the Possessed and as the Maker, e.g.,

> All good poets, epic as well as lyric, compose their beautiful poems not by art, but because they are inspired and possessed.—*Socrates.*

> That talk of inspiration is sheer nonsense: there is no such thing; it is a matter of craftsmanship.—*William Morris*

and corresponding to this, two theories of imagination:

> Natural objects always weaken, deaden, and obliterate imagination in me.—*Blake.*

> Time and education beget experience: experience begets memory; memory begets judgment and fancy. . . . Imagination is nothing else but sense decaying or weakened by the absence of the object.—*Hobbes.*

The public, fond of marvels and envious of success without trouble, has favoured the first (see any film of artists at work), but the poets themselves, painfully aware of the labour involved, on the whole have inclined towards the second. Psychoanalysis, naturally enough, first turned its attention to those works where the workings of the unconscious were easiest to follow—Romantic literature like *Peer Gynt,* "queer" plays like *Hamlet,* or fairy tales like *Alice in Wonderland.* I should doubt if Pope's name occurs in any text-book. The poet is inclined to retort that a great deal of literature is not of this kind, that even in a short lyric, let alone a sustained work, the material immediately "given" to consciousness, the automatic element, is very small, that, in his own experience, what he is most aware of are technical problems, the management of consonants and vowels, the counter-pointing of scenes, or how to get the husband off the stage before the lover's arrival, and that psychology, concentrating on the symbols, ignores words, or treatment of symbols, and fails to explain why of two works dealing with the same unconscious material, one is aesthetically good and the other bad; indeed that few psychoanalysts in their published work show any signs of knowing that aesthetic standards exist.

Psychoanalysis, he would agree, has increased the artist's interest in dreams, mnemonic fragments, child-art and graphiti, etc., but that the interest is a *conscious* one. Even the most surrealist writing or Mr James Joyce's latest prose shows every sign of being non-automatic and extremely carefully worked over.

THE CONSCIOUS ELEMENT

Creation, like psychoanalysis, is a process of re-living in a new situation. There are three chief elements:

(1) The artist himself, a certain person at a certain time with his own limited conflicts, phantasies and interests.

(2) The data from the outer world which his senses bring him, and which, under the influence of his instincts, he selects, stores, enlarges upon, and by which he sets value and significance.

(3) The artistic medium, the new situation, which because it is not a personal, but a racial property (and psychological research into the universality of certain symbols confirms this), makes communication possible, and art more than an autobiographical record. Just as modern physics teaches that every physical object is the centre of a field of force which radiating outwards occupies all space and time, so psychology states that every word through fainter and fainter associations is ultimately a sign for the universe. The associations are always greater than those of an individual. A medium complicates and distorts the creative impulse behind it. It is, in fact, largely the medium, and thorough familiarity with the medium, with its unexpected results, that enables the artist to develop from elementary uncontrolled phantasy, to deliberate phantasy directed towards understanding.

WHAT WOULD BE A FREUDIAN LITERATURE

Freudianism cannot be considered apart from other features of the contemporary environment, apart from modern physics with its conception of transformable energy, modern technics, and modern politics. The chart here given makes no attempt to be complete, or accurate; it ignores the perpetual overlap of one historical period with another, and highly important transition periods, like the Renaissance. It is only meant to be suggestive, to see if we agree to divide the Christian era into three periods, the first ending with the fifteenth century, the second with the nineteenth, and the third just beginning, what would seem the typical characteristics of such periods.

MISCONCEPTIONS

Freud belongs to the third of those phases, which, in the sphere of psychology may be said to have begun with Nietzsche (though the whole of Freud's teaching may be found in *The Marriage of Heaven and Hell*). Such psychology is historically derived from the Romantic Reaction, in particular from Rousseau, and this connection has obscured in the minds of the

	1st Period.	2nd Period.	3rd Period.
First Cause	God immanent and trancendent.	Official: God transcendent. The universal mechanic. Opposition: God immanent. Romantic Pantheism.	Energy appearing in many measurable forms. Fundamental nature unknown.
World view	The visible world as symbol of the eternal.	Official: The material world as a mechanism. Opposition: The spiritual world as a private concern.	The interdependence o observed and observe
The end of life	The City of God.	Official: Power over material. Opposition: Personal salvation.	The good life on earth.
Means of realisation	Faith and work. The rule of the Church.	Official: Works without moral values. Opposition: Faith.	Self understanding.
Personal driving forces	Love of God. Submission of private will to will of God.	Official: Conscious will. Rationalised. Mechanised. Opposition: Emotion. Irrational.	The unconscious directed by reason.
The sign of sucess	The mystical union.	Wealth and power.	Joy.
The worst sinner	The heretic.	The idle poor. (Opposition view—the respectable bourgeois.)	The deliberate irrationalist.
Scientific method	Reasoning without experiment.	Experiment and reason: the experimenter considered impartial. Pure truth. Specialisation.	Experiment directed by conscious human needs.
Sources of power	Animal. Wind. Water.	Water. Steam.	Electricity.
Technical materials	Wood. Stone.	Iron. Steel.	Light alloys.
Way of living	Agricultural and trading. Small towns. Balance of town and country.	Valley towns. Industrialism. Balance of town and country upset.	Dispersed units connecte by electrical wires. Restored balance of tow and country.
Economic system	Regional units. Production for use. Usury discouraged.	Laissez faire capitalism. Scramble for markets.	Planned socialism.
Political system	Feudal hierarchy.	National democracy. Power in hands of capitalists.	International Democrac Government by an Order.

general public, and others, its essential nature. To the man in the street, "Freudian" literature would embody the following beliefs.

(1) Sexual pleasure is the only real satisfaction. All other activities are an inadequate and neurotic substitute.
(2) All reasoning is rationalisation.
(3) All men are equal before instinct. It is my parents' fault in the way they brought me up if I am not a Napoleon or a Shakespeare.
(4) The good life is to do as you like.
(5) The cure for all ills is (*a*) indiscriminate sexual intercourse; (*b*) autobiography.

THE IMPLICATIONS OF FREUD

I do not intend to take writers one by one and examine the influence of Freud upon them. I wish merely to show what the essence of Freud's teaching is, that the reader may judge for himself. I will enumerate the chief points as quickly as possible:

(1) The driving force in all forms of life is instinctive; a libido which of itself is undifferentiated and unmoral. Of itself it is the "seed of every virtue and of every act which deserves punishment".
(2) Its first forms of creative activity are in the ordinary sense of the word physical. It binds cells together and separates them. The first bond observable between individuals is a sexual bond.
(3) With the growth in importance of the central nervous system with central rather than peripheral control, the number of modes of satisfaction to which the libido can adapt itself become immeasurably increased.
(4) Man differs from the rest of the organic world in that his development is unfinished.
(5) The introduction of self-consciousness was a complete break in development, and all that we recognize as evil or sin is its consequence. Freud differs both from Rousseau who denied the Fall, attributing evil to purely local conditions ("Rousseau thought all men good by nature. He found them evil and made no friend"), and also from the theological doctrine which makes the Fall the result of a deliberate choice, man being therefore morally responsible.
(6) The result of this Fall was a divided consciousness in place of the single animal consciousness, consisting of at least three parts: a conscious mind governed by ideas and ideals; the impersonal unconscious from which all the power of the living creature is derived but to which it was now largely denied access; and a personal uncon-

scious, all that morality or society demanded should be forgotten and unexpressed.*

(7) The nineteenth century doctrine of evolutionary progress, of man working out the beast and letting the ape and tiger die, was largely false. Man's phylogenetic ancestors are meek and sociable, and cruelty, violence, war, all the so-called primitive instincts, do not appear until civilisation has reached a high level. A golden age, comparatively speaking (and anthropological research tends to confirm this), is an historical fact.

(8) What we call evil was once good but has been outgrown, and refused development by the conscious mind with its moral ideas. This is the point in Freud which D. H. Lawrence seized and to which he devoted his life.

> Man is immoral because he has got a mind
> And can't get used to the fact.

The danger of Lawrence's writing is the ease with which his teaching, "trust the unconscious", by which he means the impersonal unconscious, may be read as meaning, "let your personal unconscious have its fling", i.e. the *acte gratuit* of André Gide. In practice, and particularly in personal relations, this itself may have a liberating effect for the individual. "If the fool would persist in his folly he would become wise." But folly is folly all the same and a piece of advice like "Anger is just. Justice is never just", which in private life is a plea for emotional honesty, is rotten political advice, where it means "beat up those who disagree with you". Also Lawrence's concentration on the fact that if you want to know what a man is, you must look at his sexual life, is apt to lead many to believe that pursuit of a sexual goal is the only necessary activity.

(9) Not only what we recognize as sin or crime, but all illness, is purposive. It is an attempt at cure.

(10) All change, either progressive or regressive, is caused by frustration or tension. Had sexual satisfaction been completely adequate human development could never have occurred. Illness and intellectual activity are both reactions to the same thing, but not of equal value.

(11) The nature of our moral ideas depends on the nature of our relations with our parents.

(12) At the root of all disease and sin is a sense of guilt.

(13) Cure consists in taking away the guilt feeling, in the forgiveness of

---

* The difference between the two unconscious minds is expressed symbolically in dreams. E.g. motor cars and manufactured things express the personal unconscious, horses, etc., the impersonal.

sins, by confession, the re-living of the experience, and absolution, understanding its significance.

(14) The task of psychology, or art for that matter, is not to tell people how to behave, but by drawing their attention to what the impersonal unconscious is trying to tell them, and by increasing their knowledge of good and evil, to render them better able to choose, to become increasingly morally responsible for their destiny.

(15) For this reason psychology is opposed to all generalisations. Force people to hold a generalisation, and there will come a time when a situation will arise to which it does not apply. Either they will force the generalisation in the situation (repression), where it will haunt them, or they will embrace the opposite. The value of advice depends entirely upon context. You cannot tell people what to do, you can only tell them parables; and that is what art really is, particular stories of particular people and experiences, from which each according to his immediate and peculiar needs may draw his own conclusions.

(16) Like Marx, Freud starts from the failures of civilisation, one from the poor, one from the ill. Both see human behaviour determined, not consciously, but by instinctual needs, hunger or love. Both desire a world where rational choice and self-determination are possible.

The difference between them is the inevitable difference between the man who studies crowds in the street, and the man who sees the patient, or at most his family, in the consulting room. Marx sees the direction of the relation between outer and inner world from without inwards, Freud vice versa. Both are therefore suspicious of each other. The socialist accuses the psychologist of caving in to the status quo, trying to adapt the neurotic to the system, thus depriving him of a potential revolutionary: the psychologist retorts that the socialist is trying to lift himself by his own boot tags, that he fails to understand himself, or the fact that the lust for money is only one form of the lust for power; and so that after he has won his power by revolution he will recreate the same conditions.

Both are right. As long as civilisation remains as it is, the number of patients the psychologist can cure are very few, and as soon as socialism attains power, it must learn to direct its own interior energy and needs the psychologist.

CONCLUSION

Freud has had certain obvious technical influences on literature, particularly in its treatment of space and time, and the use of words in associational rather than logical sequence. He has directed the attention of the writer to material such as dreams and nervous tics hitherto disregarded;

to relations as hitherto unconsidered as the relations between people playing tennis. He has revised hero-worship.

He has been misappropriated by irrationalists eager to escape their conscience. But with these we have not, in this essay, been concerned. We have tried to show what light Freud has thrown on the genesis of the artist and his place and function in society, and what demands he would make upon the serious writer. There must always be two kinds of art, escape-art, for man needs escape as he needs food and deep sleep, and parable-art, that art which shall teach man to unlearn hatred and learn love, which can enable Freud to say with greater conviction:

> We may insist as often as we please that the human intellect is power-less when compared with the impulses of man, and we may be right in what we say. All the same there is something peculiar about this weakness. The voice of the intellect is soft and low, but it is persistent and continues until it has secured a hearing. After what may be countless repetitions, it does get a hearing. This is one of the few facts which may help to make us rather more hopeful about the future of mankind.

BIBLIOGRAPHY

Freud. *Collected Works.* International Library of Psychoanalysis. Hogarth Press.

Jung. *Psychology of the Unconscious.* Allen and Unwin. *Two Essays on Analytical Psychology.* Baillière, Tindall and Cox.

Klages. *The Science of Character.* Allen and Unwin.

Prinzhorn. *Psychotherapy.* Jonathan Cape.

Rivers. *Conflict and Dream.* Kegan Paul.

Nicoll. *Dream Psychology.* Oxford University Press.

Trigant Burrow. *The Social Basis of Consciousness.* Kegan Paul.

Heard. *Social Substance of Religion.* Allen and Unwin.

Thomas Mann. *Essays.*

Blake. *Collected Works.* Nonesuch Press.

D. H. Lawrence. *Psychoanalysis and the Unconscious. Fantasia of the Unconscious. Studies in Classical American Literature.* Secker.

Homer Lane. *Talks to Parents and Teachers.*

Lord Lytton. *New Treasure.* Allen and Unwin.

Matthias Alexander. *The Use of the Self.* Methuen.

Groddeck. *Exploring the Unconscious. The World of Man.*

Herbert Read. *Form in Modern Poetry.* Sheed and Ward. *Art Now.* Faber and Faber.

I. A. Richards. *Principles of Literary Criticism,* etc. Kegan Paul.

Bodkin. *Archetypal Patterns in Poetry.*
Robert Graves. *Poetic Unreason.*
Bergson. *The Two Sources of Morality and Religion.*
Benedict. *Patterns of Culture.*

The Arts To-day, edited by Geoffrey Grigson, 1935

Introduction to *The Poet's Tongue*

BY W. H. AUDEN AND JOHN GARRETT

Of the many definitions of poetry, the simplest is still the best: "memorable speech." That is to say, it must move our emotions, or excite our intellect, for only that which is moving or exciting is memorable, and the stimulus is the audible spoken word and cadence, to which in all its power of suggestion and incantation we must surrender, as we do when talking to an intimate friend. We must, in fact, make exactly the opposite kind of mental effort to that we make in grasping other verbal uses, for in the case of the latter the aura of suggestion round every word through which, like the atom radiating lines of force through the whole of space and time, it becomes ultimately a sign for the sum of all possible meanings, must be rigorously suppressed and its meaning confined to a single dictionary one. For this reason the exposition of a scientific theory is easier to read than to hear. No poetry, on the other hand, which when mastered is not better heard than read is good poetry.

All speech has rhythm, which is the result of the combination of the alternating periods of effort and rest necessary to all living things, and the laying of emphasis on what we consider important; and in all poetry there is a tension between the rhythm due to the poet's personal values, and those due to the experiences of generations crystallised into habits of language such as the English tendency to alternate weak and accented syllables, and conventional verse forms like the hexameter, the heroic pentameter, or the French Alexandrine. Similes, metaphors of image or idea, and auditory metaphors such as rhyme, assonance, and alliteration help further to clarify and strengthen the pattern and internal relations of the experience described.

Poetry, in fact, bears the same kind of relation to Prose, using prose simply in the sense of all those uses of words that are not poetry, that algebra bears to arithmetic. The poet writes of personal or fictitious experiences, but these are not important in themselves until the reader has realised them in his own consciousness.

> Soldier from the war returning,
> Spoiler of the taken town.

It is quite unimportant, though it is the kind of question not infrequently asked, who the soldier is, what regiment he belongs to, what war he had been fighting in, etc. The soldier is you or me, or the man next door. Only when it throws light on our own experience, when these lines occur to us as we see, say, the unhappy face of a stockbroker in the suburban train, does poetry convince us of its significance. The test of a poet is the frequency and diversity of the occasions on which we remember his poetry.

Memorable speech then. About what? Birth, death, the Beatific Vision, the abysses of hatred and fear, the awards and miseries of desire, the unjust walking the earth and the just scratching miserably for food like hens, triumphs, earthquakes, deserts of boredom and featureless anxiety, the Golden Age promised or irrevocably past, the gratifications and terrors of childhood, the impact of nature on the adolescent, the despairs and wisdoms of the mature, the sacrificial victim, the descent into Hell, the devouring and the benign mother? Yes, all of these, but not these only. Everything that we remember no matter how trivial: the mark on the wall, the joke at luncheon, word games, these, like the dance of a stoat or the raven's gamble, are equally the subject of poetry.

We shall do poetry a great disservice if we confine it only to the major experiences of life:

> The soldier's pole is fallen,
> Boys and girls are level now with men,
> And there is nothing left remarkable
> Beneath the visiting moon.
>
> They had a royal wedding.
> All his courtiers wished them well.
> The horses pranced and the dancers danced.
> O Mister it was swell.
>
> And masculine is found to be
> Hadria the Adriatic Sea,

have all their rightful place, and full appreciation of one depends on full appreciation of the others.

A great many people dislike the idea of poetry as they dislike over-earnest people, because they imagine it is always worrying about the eternal verities.

Those, in Mr Spender's words, who try to put poetry on a pedestal only succeed in putting it on the shelf. Poetry is no better and no worse than human nature; it is profound and shallow, sophisticated and naïve, dull and witty, bawdy and chaste in turn.

In spite of the spread of education and the accessibility of printed matter, there is a gap between what is commonly called "highbrow" and "lowbrow" taste, wider perhaps than it has ever been.

The industrial revolution broke up the agricultural communities, with their local conservative cultures, and divided the growing population into two classes: those whether employers or employees who worked and had little leisure, and a small class of shareholders who did no work, had leisure but no responsibilities or roots, and were therefore preoccupied with themselves. Literature has tended therefore to divide into two streams, one providing the first with a compensation and escape, the other the second with a religion and a drug. The Art for Art's sake of the London drawing-rooms of the '90's, and towns like Burnley and Rochdale, are complementary.

Nor has the situation been much improved by the increased leisure and educational opportunities which the population to-day as a whole possess. Were leisure all, the unemployed would have created a second Athens.

Artistic creations may be produced by individuals, and because their work is only appreciated by a few it does not necessarily follow that it is not good; but a universal art can only be the product of a community united in sympathy, sense of worth, and aspiration; and it is improbable that the artist can do his best except in such a society.

Something of this lies behind the suspicion of and attack upon the intellectual which is becoming more and more vocal. It is hardly possible to open a number of *Punch* without seeing him spectacled, round-shouldered, rabbit-toothed, a foil to a landscape of beautifully unconscious cows, or a whipping-boy for a drawing-room of dashing young sahibs and elegant daughters of the chase. Cross the channel and this dislike, in more countries than one, has taken a practical form, to which the occasional ducking of an Oxford æsthete seems a nursery tiff.

If we are still of the opinion that poetry is worth writing and reading— and if we are not we should banish it at once from the classroom—we must be able to answer such objections satisfactorily at least to ourselves.

The "average" man says: "When I get home I want to spend my time with my wife or in the nursery; I want to get out on to the links or go for a spin in the car, not to read poetry. Why should I? I'm quite happy without it." We must be able to point out to him that whenever, for example, he makes a good joke he is creating poetry, that one of the motives behind poetry is curiosity, the wish to know what we feel and think, and how, as E. M. Forster says, can I know what I think till I see what I say, and that curiosity is the only human passion that can be indulged in for twenty-four hours a day without satiety.

The psychologist maintains that poetry is a neurotic symptom, an attempt to compensate by phantasy for a failure to meet reality. We must tell him that phantasy is only the beginning of writing; that, on the contrary, like psychology, poetry is a struggle to reconcile the unwilling subject and object; in fact, that since psychological truth depends so largely on context, poetry, the parabolic approach, is the only adequate medium for psychology.

The propagandist, whether moral or political, complains that the writer should use his powers over words to persuade people to a particular course of action, instead of fiddling while Rome burns. But Poetry is not concerned with telling people what to do, but with extending our knowledge of good and evil, perhaps making the necessity for action more urgent and its nature more clear, but only leading us to the point where it is possible for us to make a rational and moral choice.

In compiling an anthology such considerations must be borne in mind. First, one must overcome the prejudice that poetry is uplift and show that poetry can appeal to every level of consciousness. We do not want to read "great" poetry all the time, and a good anthology should contain poems for every mood. Secondly, one must disabuse people of the idea that poetry is primarily an escape from reality. We all need escape at times, just as we need food and sleep, and some escape poetry there must always be. One must not let people think either that poetry never enjoys itself, or that it ignores the grimmer aspects of existence. Lastly, one must show those who come to poetry for a message, for calendar thoughts, that they have come to the wrong door, that poetry may illuminate but it will not dictate.

In an anthology primarily intended for schools certain further provisions must be made. The selection must be limited to poems which, though they may deal with adult experiences, do not demand for their comprehension the experiences themselves. It would be foolish to include, for example, the love poems of Donne, or the mystical poetry of Hopkins.

At the same time it must be remembered that individual children vary enormously, and provision should be made for the exceptional or quickly maturing child as well as for the backward; and further, that though a child's experience on reading a poem may be quite different from that of an adult, it may be none the less genuine and valuable.

Again, now that the study of the classics is diminishing, much of the training in the discipline of language which used to fall to Latin and Greek devolves on the English teacher, and works which make serious demands on understanding or afford material for the study of prosody should be included.

As regards arrangement we have, after some thought, adopted an alphabetical, anonymous order. It seems best to us, if the idea of poetry as something dead and suitable for a tourist-ridden museum—a cultural tradition to be preserved and imitated rather than a spontaneous living product—is to be avoided, that the first approach should be with an open mind, free from the bias of great names and literary influences, the first impression that of a human activity, independent of period and unconfined in subject. Historical study is of course valuable and essential for examinations, and we hope that the indexes will make it easy for teacher and pupil to find the poems relevant to the poet, period, or subject he wishes to investigate.

Verse-speaking choruses and theatricals have developed greatly in schools in recent years, and suitable examples for both have been included, but only such as may be unfamiliar or difficult to obtain. Every teacher will have his own list. Similarly, the list of books given at the end of the *Second Part* is intended to be suggestive, not comprehensive.

> *The Poet's Tongue*, an anthology chosen by
> W. H. Auden and John Garrett, 1935

The Good Life

Man is an organism with certain desires existing in an environment which fails to satisfy them fully. His theories about the universe are attempts, whether religious, scientific, philosophical, or political, to explain or overcome this tension. If we regard the environment as static, then the problem is one of modifying our desires; if we take the organism as static, one of modifying the environment. Religion and psychology begin with the first; science and politics with the second.

If we choose the first, we have to answer three questions:

(1) What are our desires? Why do we do what we do do?
(2) If our desires are mutually incompatible, which are we to choose? i.e. what ought we to desire and do, and what ought we not to desire and do?
(3) How are we to desire what we ought to desire?

If we choose the second, the questions are:

(1) In what respects does our environment fail to satisfy us?
(2) How can we change it?

Further, whichever side we approach the problem from, there are three possible kinds of resolution:

(1) Those which assert that what is, must be, and that progress of any kind is a vain delusion. This defeatist view appears in Stoicism and in Fascist ideology, and is in general associated with a ruling class which is losing ground. Oppressed classes, without hope, desire vengeance, and may easily adopt a blind eschatology.

(2) The contradiction between what is, and what ought to be, is an illusion arising from the finite nature of human knowledge. In reality there is no Good and Bad.

(3) What is, is a necessary stage in the realisation of what ought to be. This realisation may be:

(*a*) Sudden and catastrophic.

(*b*) A slow evolution.

(*x*) Voluntary—depending on the determination of the majority of individuals, i.e. it is possible for the consummation to be rejected.

(*y*) Determined—though the individual can accept or reject it; if he rejects it he joins the losing side.

Christianity is undecided about (*a*) and (*b*), but holds (*y*) not (*x*).

Social Democracy holds (*b*), and is undecided about (*x*) and (*y*).

Psychology, on the whole, holds (*b*) and (*x*).

Communism holds (*a*) and (*y*).

I. THE POLITICS OF THE GOSPELS

(1) *God or Cæsar?* To extract a political theory from the teaching of Jesus requires the ingenuity of a Seventh-Day Adventist. The suggestion that the cleansing of the Temple is a watered-down version of a revolutionary act—that the disciples were to form the corps of a militant International, that Jesus was really a Communist, can only be maintained by entirely unjustifiable manipulation of the evidence, which on the contrary, as in the account of the Temptation, Cæsar's coin, or the Trial, states that He decisively rejected the political solution. The whole of His direct teaching is concerned with the relation of the individual to God and to his neighbour, irrespective of the political system under which he may happen to live—though, as in the parables of the Pharisee and the publican, and the Good Samaritan, or the story of the healing of the centurion's daughter, He demonstrates the evil and absurdity of class and racial prejudice; but the emphasis is laid, not on the necessity for consciously setting out to abolish these, but on behaving as if class and race did not exist, on the supposition that if we so live, they will automatically disappear.

In this sense the teaching of Jesus is fundamentally non-political in that it regards all institutions as a product of the heart, the form of which can be changed, and only changed by a change in the latter. The parable of the house swept and garnished emphasises this.

(2) *Economic inequality.* The cause of inequality is Greed. The cure is the abandonment of money-getting as a motive.

(3) *Eschatology.* It is possible for the historian to say that, even supposing Jesus to have believed the ideal society to be a Communist one, the circumstances and date of His birth would have made revolutionary advice to His disciples both foolish and immoral. A militant Communist movement at such a period of technological advance would have been destroyed as quickly and brutally as the Anabaptists were later, but the eschatological teaching of Jesus makes such reflections irrelevant. E.g. Mark ix.1, xiii.26, xiv.62, despite the efforts of Jerome, Origen, and others to explain them away, making a distinction, for example, between "tasting" and "seeing" death, cannot mean anything except that Jesus Himself believed: (i) That the Parousia was imminent, an event to take place within the disciples' lifetime. (ii) That even before the final consummation the Kingdom of God is present on earth in the remnant of which He Himself is the head, the *saving* remnant of Deutero-Isaiah, that is, rather than the saved remnant of earlier prophecies. (iii) That it is not a compensation for the sufferings of the remnant, but the result of them. (iv) That it will come suddenly and not by a slow evolution. (Parable of the robbed householder in Luke xii.) (v) It will be a judgment at which the principal criterion will be the attitude taken up by men to Jesus Himself, or, in a general sense, each individual is judged on his merits as determined by the disposition of his will towards the Kingdom of God, as manifest in his day and generation. (vi) It will be a moral, not a political, victory. The world powers are not to be overthrown by earthly or supernatural weapons. (vii) It marks the division between the past age and the age to come. It ushers in a universe purged of evil.

To such beliefs politics can have no meaning. All through history men have attempted to prove that Christianity stood for Feudalism, Absolute Monarchy, Democracy, and what not, and the political activities of the Church remain obscure until we see them as those of an organised and therefore political society professing an a-political faith.

Christianity, then, like most religions, is one which accepts the environment as given and concerns itself with controlling man's behaviour towards it.

What our desires are. Since the cause and sustainer of the universe is God, who is good, our real desire is to be at one with Him. When human the relationship between ourselves and Him is one of father to son. Ultimately that is the purpose of our actions.

What we ought to desire. In practice we desire all sorts of other things. Some of these may be explained as being modes of desiring God—immature stages in development, good in so far as they lead us to God. Others are evil—evil being anything that is self-centred. To them must be attributed the overt symptoms of suffering that we experience. Their existence in us is to be explained by the Fall—an inherited defect in our nature, which, since God is good, must be attributed to a volitional act of rebellion at some period of human development. Further, there is in the universe an evil principle—Satan—hostile to good—but finally inevitably to be vanquished.

II. THE MEANS OF REALISATION

The teaching of Jesus is unique in that it is absolutely non-moralistic. It contains little dogmatic teaching about the nature of evil, but, as regards the methods of overcoming it, He is very definite. His repeated attacks on the scribes and Pharisees, not as individuals, but as a class (except your righteousness exceed the righteousness of the scribes and Pharisees, ye shall in no wise enter the Kingdom of Heaven), His verdict on John the Baptist (nevertheless I say unto you, the least in the Kingdom of God is greater than he), and the sayings about resisting evil, and those who take the sword, condemn as useless—and, more than that, as provoking those very evils it is designed to cure—the whole intellectual system of moral imperatives which had governed human life up to this time and has continued to govern it. The two commandments of loving God and thy neighbour imply that the good life is a product, and only a product, of an attitude of complete love and faith toward both. On repeated occasions He indicated that the term neighbour admits of no distinction or qualification whatever. Every individual is of equal value.

"If a man love not his brothers whom he hath seen, how shall he love God whom he hath not seen?"

"Not everyone that saith unto Me, 'Lord, Lord,' shall enter into the Kingdom of Heaven; but he that doeth the will of My Father which is in heaven."

"Inasmuch as ye did it unto the least of these My brethren, ye did it unto Me."

"Every good tree bringeth forth good fruit, but a corrupt tree bringeth forth a corrupt fruit."

Christianity is not a quietist religion—it does not in fact really take the environment as given and static, but states that a change of heart can, and must, bring about a change in the environment. The test of the former, indeed, is the latter. Behaviour—and behaviour is always material action—is the only criterion. Whatever creed or social code men profess, if the results are evil, either the creed or code, or men's interpretation of it, is condemned. Faith and works—which last cannot possibly be construed to mean "works" in the district-visitor sense—are not independent. A faith stands or falls by its results.

"Except ye be born again, ye cannot enter into the Kingdom of Heaven."

"Be ye perfect—even as your Father in Heaven is perfect."

Christianity is a twice-born catastrophic religion. Jesus teaches that a real conversion is required, not a slow amelioration. Further, that the good life is possible here and now. The call to enter the Kingdom is an immediate one, not a reference to something which may take place after death. A theology which stresses an absolute gulf between God and man, and the *inevitable* corruption of the world, is not really consonant with his teaching.

PSYCHOLOGY

Psychology is principally an investigation into the nature of evil. Its essential problem is to discern what it is that prevents people having the good will. It holds:

(1) The driving force in living things is a *libido* which is unconscious and creative—Dante's "Amor Naturalis" which is always without error. Beyond that psychology does not go—that is to say, it is a naturalistic theory which refuses to raise the question of the Unmoved Mover, which it would say is not a real question at all. "No intelligent question can be framed concerning causality unless there exist two co-isolates of a larger neutral isolate. The question, 'What is the cause of the changing universe?' accepts the existence of a co-isolate of the universe" (Professor Levy). When we ask the question, "Who made the world?" we are really asking, "Why isn't it made as we should like it?"

It does not conceive of this *libido* apart from matter or having a personality other than that it acquires in individual consciousness. The psychologist's unconscious could only be equated with a God of Blake's kind "which only acts and is in existing beings and men".

(2) The development of self-consciousness in man marked a break with the rest of the organic world. Henceforward the conscious image or idea could interfere and govern* the unconscious impulse which had hitherto governed it. What we call evil is a consequence of this. Man

---

* See *The Science of Character*, by Klages: Allen & Unwin.

developed a personal unconscious. As D. H. Lawrence wrote, in *Psycho-Analysis and the Unconscious,* Adam and Eve fell, not because they had sex or even because they committed the sexual act, but because they became aware of their sex and of the possibility of the act. When sex became to them a mental object—that is, when they discovered that they could deliberately enter upon and enjoy and even provoke sexual activity in themselves—then they were cursed and cast out of Eden. Then man became self-responsible; he entered on his own career. When the analyst discovers the incest motive in the unconscious, surely he is only discovering a term of humanity's repressed *idea* of sex. It is not even suppressed sex-consciousness, but *repressed*—that is, it is nothing pristine and anterior to mentality. It is in itself the mind's ulterior motive—that is, the incest motive is propagated in the pristine unconscious by the mind itself, and in its origin is not a pristine impulse but a logical extension of the existent idea of sex and love. Or more succinctly: "Man is immoral because he has got a mind and can't get used to the fact." Such a theory differs sharply from the nineteenth-century evolutionary doctrine of man moving

> Upward, working out the beast,
> And let the ape and tiger die.

On the contrary it suggests that most of what we call evil is not primitive at all. The "cave man"—and recent anthropology confirms this—is a product of a relatively high civilisation. The Garden of Eden has more historical justification than is usually believed.

Again, it is opposed to Rousseau in that it regards evil as being due to more than immediate environmental conditions, and differs from the theological doctrine, at least in its Augustinian form, in that it does not make the Fall the result of a conscious moral choice, but regards it as inevitable. It denies original guilt.

(3) What we call evil is something that was once good but has been outgrown. Ignorance begets the moralistic censor as the only means of control. Impulses which are denied expression remain undeveloped in the personal unconscious. From this it follows that the impulse behind all acts which we term evil is good. Psychology will have nothing to do with dualistic theories of Satan or the higher and lower self.

(4) What can be loved can be cured. The two chief barriers are ignorance and fear. Ignorance must be overcome by confession—i.e. drawing attention to unnoticed parts of the field of experience; fear by the exercise of *caritas* or *eros paidogogos*.

Psychology, like Christianity, is pacifist, with a pacifism that enjoins abstention not only from physical violence, but also from all kinds of dogmatic generalisation and propaganda—from spiritual coercion. The only method of teaching it recognises is parabolic. You cannot convince anyone of anything until they have reached the stage in development when they can relate it to their personal experience— i.e. until they can convince themselves. You must never tell people what to do—only tell them particular stories of particular people with whom they may voluntarily identify themselves, and from which they voluntarily draw conclusions. A dogmatic intellectual expression of a truth can be accepted consciously by those who have not related it to their experience, but this always results either in their holding it in a simplified view, which, when it is met by facts they had not envisaged, is rejected (the parable of the man who built on sand), or its meaning is twisted to suit the personal unconscious (Satan in the Temptation). People are not cured by reading psychological textbooks. The mistake of liberalism was imagining that free discussion was all that was needed to let truth triumph, whereas, unless people have substantially the same experience, logical controversy is nothing more than systemised misunderstanding.* The task of revealing the hidden field of experience, of understanding and curing by love, is a very slow, but ultimately the only satisfactory, one. "The chief sin", wrote Kafka, in one of his aphorisms, "is impatience. Through impatience man lost Eden, and it is impatience that prevents him from regaining it." People take to violence because they haven't the strength and nerve to be absorbent.

(5) Psychology is fundamentally a rationalist movement. It does not say, as some, like Lawrence, have been inclined to say, "Trust your instincts blindly". Just because it believes that the exercise of the reason is the only way through, its first task is to show how little the reason is able to effect directly. Nor does it deny the possibility of free will, except in a sense which is also true of Christian theology. Just as the theologian says that every man is fallen and in bondage to Satan, so the psychologist says that everyone is neurotic, at the mercy therefore of his repressed impulses, and unable to escape from his image. At the same time his aim is to release his patient through increased self-knowledge, so that he may really exercise his reason and make a genuine choice. The ideally "cured" patient would be one in whom the unconscious and the conscious were at one, and who would obey his impulses—which is only deterministic in the sense of "in his will is

* See *Mencius on the Mind*, by I. A. Richards.

our peace". No more than Communism rejects Capitalism does psychology reject self-consciousness and reason. Both theories believe in the law of the negation of the negation, and that attempts to put the clock back, either in economic or physical life, are reactionary and disastrous.

(6) Lastly, psychology does not wish, as both it and Communism have been accused of wishing, to make everyone the same. It has no conception of normality. Like both Communism and Christianity, it believes in the equal value of every individual—i.e. potential value. It does not claim to turn all the geese into swans. It aims at making each discover for himself his unique treasure. What you lose on the swings you gain on the roundabouts, and, further, you can *only* gain on the roundabouts if you lose on the swings.

THE CHURCH

As long as Christianity remained the religion of small "converted" groups, expecting an imminent second coming, in an empire to which it was conscientiously bound to refuse allegiance, it could preserve its enthusiastic, non-economic, anarchic character. But as it grew in numbers and importance, as it became the recognised State religion, as whole countries became converted *en bloc*—sometimes, as in Norway, extremely forcibly—this became impossible. Augustine's *communio sanctorum*, whose minds and lives were directed towards God instead of self, could no longer be identified with the baptised, or even with the Church. Dante was not unorthodox in placing a pope in Hell. It became organised, wealthy, and powerful, and no society which is these, however unworldly its final ends, can be anything but worldly in its immediate ends (which, as the hope of an immediate Parousia faded, became more important); it will favour those forces and persons who favour its organisation, wealth, and power, and oppose those which oppose it, without considering too closely their individual moral value. However much it seeks to define in theory what belongs to God and what to Cæsar,* in practice it is obliged not only to make generous terms with Cæsar, but itself to make Cæsar's claims. Offering a socially honourable career, it offers worldly inducement. And, as the standard religion, it ceases to demand conversion as a condition of membership. Men are Christian, not necessarily because of a revelation, but because their parents were. As Professor Powicke says, "What we call abuses or superstition in the medieval Church, were part of the price paid for, not obstacles to, its universality. They were due to the attempt of pagans to appropriate a mystery. If the people paid, so did the

---

* e.g. the modification of the strict theological condemnation of usury.

church. We distort the facts if we try to separate clergy and laity too sharply, for paganism was common to both. By paganism, I mean a state of acquiescence, a merely professional activity unaccompanied by sustained religious experience or inward discipline. It is not a state of vacancy and scepticism. It is confined to no class of persons, and is not hostile to, though it is easily wearied by, religious observance. It accepts what is offered without any sense of responsibility, and easily recovers from twinges of conscience. At the same time it is full of curiosity, and is easily moved by what is now called the group-mind. It is sensitive to the activities of the crowd, is often emotional, and can be raised to those moods of passion, superstition, and love of persecution into which religion, on its side, can degenerate. A medieval remained a Christian because he was born a Christian and most medieval Christians were probably men of this kind. In the eleventh century Cardinal Peter Damiani pointed out, in his lurid way, that it was no use to try to keep the clergy apart from the laity unless strict evangelical poverty were insisted upon for all clergy alike. But Damiani and all the preachers of evangelical poverty who came after him were entangled on the horns of a dilemma. If it is the function of the Church to drive out sin, it must separate itself from sin; if the Church separates itself from sin it becomes a 'clique.'" (*Legacy of the Middle Ages.*)

The task of the Church became to act for the mass of more or less pagan and ignorant people as a spiritual pacifier; to protect them from their terrors, and to provide the opportunities for those who wished to live a genuinely Christian life, to do so.

Hence the problem of dogma and the liberty of the private conscience. Divergent theoretical views, whether religious or political, result in divergent actions. What at first seems to be a merely academic difference of opinion may finally land the disputants on opposite sides of the barricade. "The records of the Holy Inquisition are full of histories which we dare not give to the world, because they are beyond the belief of honest men and innocent women; yet they all began with saintly simpletons. Mark what I say: the woman who quarrels with her clothes and puts on the dress of a man, is like the man who throws off his fur gown and dresses like John the Baptist; they are followed, as surely as the night follows the day, by bands of wild women and men, who refuse to wear any clothes at all." (*St Joan.*)

So the Catholic. The Protestant can retort, and with equal truth, that orthodoxy does not necessarily result in goodness, that many of the orthodox are more wicked than those whom they persecute. In fact, such an orthodoxy is extremely rare; the intellectual acceptance of an idea, without its experience, is no guarantee of its effectiveness. There is little doubt, for example, that, whatever the correct theological attitude, a great many people regard Heaven as a good time, and a reward for not having a good time in this world (i.e. you mustn't enjoy yourself in this world; i.e. the working classes should congratulate themselves); and infer from the doctrine of the Virgin Birth that sexual intercourse is wicked.

III. THE POLITICAL MIND

No politician can really be a liberal in practice, for no society can be liberal unless membership is voluntary; we become members of a State by birth, and we do not choose to be born. Similarly the governor cannot choose the governed; he must accept them all—the just and the unjust, the rich and the poor, the selfless and the self-seeking—and the bias of his own mind, for he himself is within the State.

Many political theories are vitiated, either:

(1) By confusing what the State is with what it ought to be. Few people, for example, consciously desire Dante's *vita felice*, the actualising of the potential intellect, or, with Aristotle, to live virtuously. The majority want security, to be free from material and psychological anxiety, to be liked, and to feel of some importance.

(2) By assuming that there is in fact a community of will. The social contract is a grotesque simplification. In animal herds, or Dr Rivers' boat crew, the unconscious formation of a group pattern, a united will, may be an adequate description of what happens, but in any more conscious and specialised community the social order is accepted;

(a) Because it is customary;

(b) Because one is fortunately placed;

(c) Because, though unfortunately placed, one lacks the knowledge and power to change it.

There is no such thing as a community of will, nor has the will of the majority any effectiveness apart from the material power it is able to wield. A successful change depends on the support of the armed forces.

(3) By using false analogies, e.g. the biological theory of the State (the story of the belly and the members), a theory which could only be invented by a cell in the central nervous system. Every unit in the State is a conscious one and capable of different functions. Since the governor has always immediate ends to consider, and since the unity of will is a fiction, he cannot afford to wait until this unity is voluntarily reached—i.e. he must coerce either physically, or by the propagandist organisation of public opinion. He may believe, and most of the experimental evidence in the treatment of individuals, either in

education, medicine,* or the training of animals, will confirm this belief, that violence is inefficient; but he will point to history to refute the view that violence has never accomplished anything, and he knows that he is compelled to use it, to bring about that organisation of society which can make a real unity of will possible.

Ruling a mass, and knowing that you cannot convert a mass as a mass, because they are individually at different stages and in different positions, he must accept the actual rather than the potential character of the governed, and attempt to modify them by modifying those things which are alone in his power to modify—material conditions and social structure. His view of morality must be one of social utility. For him, that is immoral, and that only, which causes a conflict of will—e.g. theft or ownership relations are rightly a matter of legal regulation, but sexual behaviour, which is by mutual consent, is not. The authoritative exercise of what we usually call moral judgment is only justifiable in a society where membership is entirely voluntary.

IV. PSYCHOLOGY AND RELIGION

Psychology does not deny the fact of religious experience, the usefulness of religious theory, in the past, to assist men to live well. In offering an explanation of the idea of God as a projection of parental images, or as what is left over of the sense of group identity after the individual has taken his lion's share, or of the mystical experience as an eruption from the subconscious, and in condemning the religious explanation as one which the world has outgrown, it asks to be tested by results. It believes that it has a more scientific theory—i.e. one which will work better—and claims that, given a free hand, and time, more people will lead better lives than they would with the help of religion. The Christian will retort that the findings of psychology do not necessarily invalidate a belief in God— that, for example, there is no reason why the parental relation should not be a symbol of the divine relation, instead of vice versa, and can point to a weak spot in psychology, the problem of transference. In order to free the patient from himself, the psychologist must make his claims in the name of something greater. What is it to be?

Every confession, within whatever framework it may be made, passes through two phases of a curative effect. First: that one opens oneself to another person, breaks through those walls of loneliness wherein all guilt, whether in the sense of sacrilege or sin, whether it was due to rebellion, oversight, error, weakness, the lust of destruction, or what-

---

* See a very interesting essay on Constipation, in Dr Groddeck's *Exploring the Unconscious*, on the evils of forcible purgative treatment.

ever other incitement, at first imprisons every upright man. Confession, simply as openly answering for oneself, and one's conduct, puts an end to the danger of all self-deception by taking this first step towards a fellow man, and sets foot on the slender ladder of trust in humanity by choosing another as humanity's representative. This step of voluntary surrender, this renunciation of cowardly cunning, and of lying on behalf of one's imposing public façade, as does the man of the world, is like a deep expiration of air. Secondly: into the lungs thus freed there follows, with the second step, a deep inspiration; the father confessor gives what he has to give. If the answer of the private person with difficulty conceals his lower thoughts of tricks and power policy even to active intrigue, so that the sensitive person is stricken with horror, like the bird before the snake—then surely we must introduce poison-gas into the parable. If the private person answers with the fascination of his own ripe and broad humanity, so that the lonely one, suddenly freed, feels, whether he represses it or shows it: "Thou, my redeemer!"—then we must speak of intoxicating gas. But when one who knows, answers so that he, with all his private humanity, is as a speaking-tube for something which is not his, but in whose service he is, and in whose name he acts—only then can we say that he pours forth the free strong breath of life, which so fills the lungs of the other, that at one stroke the poison-air is overcome. (Prinzhorn—*Psychotherapy.*)

V. COMMUNISM AND PSYCHOLOGY

Psychology and Communism have certain points in common:

(1) They are both concerned with unmasking hidden conflicts.

(2) Both regard these conflicts as inevitable stages which must be made to negate themselves.

(3) Both regard thought and knowledge not as something spontaneous and self-sufficient, but as purposive and determined by the conflict between instinctive needs and a limited environment. Communism stresses hunger and the larger social mass affected by it; psychology, love and the small family unit. (Biologically nutrition is anterior to reproduction, so that the Communist approach would seem from this angle the more basic one.) E.g. the psychologist explains the clinging child by the doting mother. Communism explains the doting mother by the social conditions which drive her to be doting.

A discovery, like that of Malinowski, that the typical Œdipus dream of murdering the father and committing incest with the mother, occurs only in patriarchal communities, while in matriarchal communities it is one of murdering the mother's brother and committing incest with the sister, shows the importance of social structure in influencing character formation.

(4) Both desire and believe in the possibility of freedom of action and choice, which can only be obtained by unmasking and making conscious the hidden conflict.

The hostility of Communism to psychology is that it accuses the latter of failing to draw correct conclusions from its data. Finding the neurotic a product of society, it attempts to adjust him to that society, i.e. it ignores the fact that the neurotic has a real grievance. It should say to him, "Your phantasies are just, but powerless, and a distorted version of something which, if you choose to act, you can alter." The failure to say this has reduced psychology to a quack religion for the idle rich.

VI. COMMUNISM AND RELIGION

The hostility of Communism to religion has two sides:

(1) The religious approach, it says, is the method of those who see no hope of understanding and altering the environment. As long as in one human lifetime no material progress is visible, man is bound to rely upon individual moral progress. The more power he obtains over material objects, the more he finds he is able to make changes which seemed previously to depend solely on moral attitudes—e.g. the influence of the ductless glands on character.

(2) When a religious body becomes an organised Church it becomes a political movement, and the historical evidence can point to no occasion on which the Church has been able to avert either war or economic changes, however contrary to their theories. On the contrary, it has always made the maintenance of its official position its criterion of conduct, accepted the political *status quo*, shut its eyes to the violence and mad character of its supporters, persistently lent its strength to crush proletarian movements, and whilst preaching the necessity for settlement by agreement, whenever the violent crisis has occurred, has stood by the forces of reaction. A tree must be judged by its fruits.

The contrary objections of the church to Communism are:

(1) That, without the Christian transcendental beliefs, the Communist will fail to secure the results, in so far as they are good, which he intends. Further, that there is a wretchedness in man's condition without God, that is independent of material conditions.

(2) The Communist use of violence is indefensible.

(3) He wishes to destroy the individual and make a slave State.

(4) That private property is necessary to develop human personality and responsibility.

(5) That he wishes to destroy the family.

(2) *The use of violence.* Unless the Christian denies the value of any Government whatsoever, he must admit, as Schweitzer did when destroying trypanosomes, the necessity for violence, and judge the means by its end. He cannot deny, if he is honest, the reality of the class conflict, and, unless he can offer a better method of surpassing it (supposing that he is not stupid enough to be taken in by the fiction of the corporative State, which is the word and not the thing) than the Communists, he must accept it.

(3) *The individual.* A theory which culminates in the words, "To each according to his needs, from each according to his powers", cannot be accused of denying the individual in intention. In fact Communism is the only political theory that really holds the Christian position of the absolute equality in value of every individual, and the evil of all State restraint. It is hardly necessary to add that this doctrine of equality does not assert that everyone has the same talents—i.e. that the individual has no uniqueness and is interchangeable with another—nor does it necessarily imply absolute equality of social reward. Communism looks on coercion, the dictatorship of the proletariat, neither as the redemption which it is to the Fascist, nor as an inevitable and perpetual punishment of original sin, but solely as a transitory means to an end.

(4) *Property* has been the subject of subtle and obscure study, particularly by French Catholic writers. Their arguments would be more convincing if they condemned monastic orders, in which the individual's sense of responsibility is developed by the administration of community property. Further, Communism has never suggested that no one should have private belongings; it only condemns that possession which gives its owner power over the personality of others.

(5) *The family.* Communism has been subjected to the most fantastic attacks, by ignorant and interested persons, on this score. It has no quarrel whatever with the family, as such—only with the narrowing of loyalties to a single one. In depriving the family of economic power, it leaves it free to be what it should be—an emotional bond—instead of what, as psychologists or common-sense observation can testify, it, at present, so often is—a strangling prison, whose walls are not love, but money.

VII. THE CHRISTIAN DILEMMA

In that the Christian is a member of society he must have an attitude towards political movements, and increasingly so as he discovers that many things which he recognised as evil, but believed were unchangeable, the consequences of sin, to be endured, can be changed. The behaviour and utterances of indiscreet Fascists should be enough to disillusion him of that solution, which would otherwise, by its bogus idealist appeal, and its attempt to return to pre-industrial conditions, be a temptation to a religion founded on a pre-industrial event. Social Democracy claims to achieve the same end as the Communist, by non-violent means and with religious tolerance; it is questionable, however, whether its behaviour in Europe, its pretence that it uses no violence, or its assumption that the possessing classes, however ready to make concessions, will ever voluntarily abdicate, can much longer convince.

At the same time it would be foolish to gloss over the antagonism of Communism to religion, or to suppose that, if Communism were to triumph in England, the Church would not be persecuted. The question for the Christian, however, is not whether Communism is hostile to Christianity, but whether Christianity is less hostile to Communism than to any other political movement—for no political movement is Christian. If it is, then this very persecution is his chance of proving, if he can, that religion is not the opium of the people, not something that has long been outgrown, but a vital truth. Deprived of all economic and social support, with no axe to grind, he can make no illegitimate appeal. The Christian will have to see if what occurred in the first century can occur again in the twentieth. A truth is not tested until, oppressed and illegal, it still shows irresistible signs of growth.

Christianity and the Social Revolution, edited by
John Lewis, Karl Polanyi, and Donald K. Kitchin, 1935

Everyman's Freedom

Plain Ordinary Man. By Arthur Radford. Routledge. 5s.
Education and the Citizen. By Colonel Loftus. Routledge. 5s.

Knowledge of an evil is the first step towards its eradication, and an age, like our own, which lacks economic stability and in consequence standards of conduct or settled beliefs, has at least the virtue of curiosity. The private diary and the social document are saleable. Both these books are excellent examples of their kind. The style is clear and simple, the matter informative, and the treatment objective. Both, I imagine, are intended to be read primarily by the more fortunate social classes. On reading the title of Mr Radford's book, I saw instantly Mr Punch's Everyman, the bowler-hatted suburban father with an income of some £500 a year. It was salutary to have this reflex inhibited and to realise once and for all that the "plain ordinary man" is a poor man, and a wage earner. Similarly those educated or teaching in expensive schools know nothing whatever about the grades and costs of State schools, of the difference for example between a Secondary and a Central school. Colonel Loftus makes it easy to know. Mr Radford's book being largely a statement of facts which I am not competent to check, and with a minimum of personal comment (except the rather surprising opinion that a surgeon does not find his work intrinsically pleasant) is the more difficult to review. The thing that remains most vividly in my mind is his account of the marriage age in different classes.

> When population is classified occupationally it is found that the unskilled workers marry at the youngest average age, semi-skilled at the next higher age, then skilled and so on to the professions of medicine and the Bar. This fact would suggest that the tendency of most people is to marry young but that they wait until they can marry and maintain their status or the status of their group. The unskilled on this account have not long to wait; they soon reach their maximum rates. Society and pictorial newspapers seem to show that in the ranks of those who are born into maximum incomes or incomes at least adequate to their social requirements the age of marriage approximates to that of the poor.

And his moving description of the average day of a working class wife and mother should make the well-off male upholders of the Gretchen theory feel thoroughly uncomfortable. And if there are still people who believe in the freedom of labour contracts, they should read the chapter called "The Cog and the Wheel".

Colonel Loftus is more deliberate and direct in his attack on the privileged school and the classical-academic, culture snob, monastic kind of education derived from it. While little that he says of them is unjustified, in the present state of society, it is possible that the privileged school has its value. It can make, rarely though it does so, educational experiments which a State school cannot justifiably do because the parents cannot choose the school, and in a good school of this kind, if for no other reason than the size of the classes—twelve is quite large enough—the education may be better. Again under present conditions, when the only child is common in professional families, there may be more to be said for the boarding school as a means of psychological weaning, than Colonel Loftus admits.

The examination racket is puzzling because it is impossible to trace its authors. No don or teacher has a good word for it, yet it persists. Can the answer be simply that employers want to save themselves trouble in filling posts. Perhaps Colonel Loftus' next book will enlighten us.

Lastly three details: Colonel Loftus rightly condemns the untrained teacher (it is a pleasure to find the infant teacher properly appreciated), but says too little about the quality of the training given at training colleges, which is lamentably deficient; at what college, to mention only one example, does the student learn anything about his own psychology as distinct from child psychology. He recommends scouting as a remedy for class consciousness, but as long as the movement is run by the upper class, it will succeed no better in this respect than the Duke of York's camp—it smacks too much of slumming; and he favours the supervision of hobbies by teachers—surely the essence of a hobby is that it is an interest chosen by the child for himself and preferably perhaps in opposition to the wishes of adults.

Mr Radford and Colonel Loftus have much in common. They are intelligent, experienced and humane. Both expose faults in our society which no rational person can either deny or ignore. It would be unfair to say that both are disappointingly vague about remedies, because they are primarily concerned with the evidence, but, being humane and intelligent, they are, I think, unduly optimistic about the possibility of a humane and an intelligent change.

The difficulty about the class war is that few on either side know what they are fighting for or even that they are fighting at all. Do not these writers underestimate the power of their opponents? Does Mr Radford think that a Bill, say, to make all property on death go to the Crown except an annuity for the first generation, or Colonel Loftus one to confiscate the endowments of Public Schools, would have the smallest chance of success? One would like to think so.

The New Statesman and Nation, 23 March 1935

The Bond and the Free

Growing Opinions. Edited by Alan Campbell Johnson. Methuen. 6s.
I Was a Prisoner. By William Holt. John Miles. 5s.
Means Test Man. By W. Brierley. Methuen. 5s.
Caliban Shrieks. By Jack Hilton. Cobden-Sanderson. 6s.

If the business of a reviewer is to describe the contents of the books he reviews and to appraise their value, this is not going to be a review.

Growing Opinions is a collection of articles by members of the rising generation who, like the readers of this magazine, have had luck. They can and do read difficult books, they have no reason to con the road in order to avoid meeting a policeman. If their ideas are not startling, they are cogently reasoned and well expressed. Mr Stovin and Mr Lovelock's articles on Education and Sport respectively seem to me particularly good.

Anyone who does not know what the intelligent young man or woman with a university education is thinking about Life may learn it here. As a whole they seem well-informed and well-intentioned, sensible and serious, unrhetorical and a trifle dull. Perhaps, though here I may be doing them an injustice, they are a little self-satisfied, a little too conscious of their good sense, and their status as the Free.

The writers of the other three books, on the other hand, are all below the salt. Two of them have done time. The third is technically at liberty to walk out of his front door but as he cannot afford to go anywhere else, he may also be included among the Bond.

Those who cannot imagine for themselves what a modern prison is like, a fairly easy task, may learn to do so from Mr Holt. Those who cannot imagine for themselves what the Means Test is like, a very difficult task, may learn to do so from Mr Brierley. Those who for whatever reason feel a bitterness and hatred against life will find such a feeling expressed in magnificent Moby Dick rhetoric by Mr Hilton, the finest writer of them all.

And then.

What is to be done?

"What we need is a new faith" say the growing opinions, but wait for a leader to provide one.

"Make up your minds. Act", shouts the politician to the eight-year-old, knowing that the latter will be only too delighted to hear that he hasn't got to learn any more.

"The whole bloody chute is going to bust soon, and a damn good job too", shrieks Caliban, but shrinks from wielding the crowbar because he doesn't like the sight of a bloody crown.

Every sensitive and intelligent person knows that the Means Test and the Prison are as these books describe them, and that a social system under which they are possible is grotesque. Then why does it endure a second longer?

It does so in the first place because of the quiet unostentatious courage, honesty, intelligence, kindliness and good-will of millions of individuals in their own small circle. Those therefore like the Communist, who see most clearly the defects of the system, are inclined to distrust and even dislike the considerate employer or the unembittered wage-earner. If things have got to grow worse before they can improve, then the bigger the bully chosen as Means Test inspector, the greater martinet the Prison governor, the better.

And in the second place, to those who feel that perhaps the Communist does not hold all the cards, the most disquieting fact is that the armament firms, the yellow and gutter press, the advertising agencies are staffed, not by monsters, but by extremely intelligent young men of liberal opinions.

Is the economic argument then unanswerable, or have we got to be even more pessimistic about the future of the human race?

For there are two things that every educated middle-class man (or woman) really knows to be true:

(1) That violence is always and unequivocally bad. No personal experience, no scientific knowledge, gives any other verdict than that what you can self-forgetfully love, you can cure.

> As I fall sometime in the dark,
> Do not shout as dogs do bark.
> Give me sympathy and example
> So that in your steps I will surely trample.
> Spare the rod and save the child,
> Imprisonment is bleak and punishment wild.

We know this perfectly well, but we are only prepared to act on it as long as it's no trouble and there's no difficult problem. When there is we send for the hangman and the bombing plane and shut our eyes and ears.

Bernard Shaw remarks somewhere that in a really civilised community flogging would be impossible because no man could be persuaded to flog another. But as it is, any decent warder will do it for half-a-crown, not probably because he likes it or even thinks it desirable on penal grounds, but because it is expected of him. "There! you see", says the economist, "the economic reason again."

(2) That he is spending more on himself than he need, and is doing less for others than he could. But he doesn't want to seem a prig. We ought to move in such and such a direction, towards, say, a moral life or universal disarmament but let's move all together.

In other words, "I don't want the responsibility, let a revolution do it for me."

The difficulty is that we all know, the Communist himself is a splendid example, that if we choose, we can reject self-interest, and that only when we do so, do we achieve anything worth while.

"But I can't do that, without a faith." But in these words we reject one. And hope that an easier one will be forced on us.

Bernard Shaw's speech in *Too True to be Good,* quoted in *Growing Opinions,* is a warning:

"I must have affirmations to preach" [We have but we don't]. "Without them the young will not listen to me; for even the young grow tired of denials. The negative-monger falls before the soldiers, the men of action, the fighters, strong in the old uncompromising affirmations which give them status, duties, certainty of consequences; so that the pugnacious spirit of man in them can reach out and strike deathblows with steadfastly closed minds. Their way is straight and sure but it is the way of death."

Scrutiny, September 1935

[From the Series "I Want the Theatre to Be . . ."]

Drama began as the act of a whole community. Ideally there would be no spectators. In practice every member of the audience should feel like an understudy.

Drama is essentially an art of the body. The basis of acting is acrobatics, dancing, and all forms of physical skill. The Music Hall, the Christmas Pantomime, and the country house charade are the most living drama of to-day.

The development of the film has deprived drama of any excuse for being documentary. It is not in its nature to provide an ignorant and passive spectator with exciting news.

The subject of Drama on the other hand, is the Commonly Known, the universally familiar stories of the society or generation in which it is written. The audience, like the child listening to the fairy tale, ought to know what is going to happen next.

Similarly the drama is not suited to the analysis of character, which is the province of the novel. Dramatic characters are simplified; easily recognizable, and over-life size.

Dramatic speech should have the same compressed, significant, and un-documentary character, as dramatic movement.

Drama in fact deals with the general and universal, not with the particular and local, but it is probable that drama can only deal, directly at any rate, with the relations of human beings with each other, not with the relations of Man to the rest of nature.

Group Theatre program for *Sweeney Agonistes* and
The Dance of Death, 1 October 1935

A Review of *Documentary Film,* by Paul Rotha

Documentary Film. By Paul Rotha. Faber. 12s. 6d.

Mr Rotha has written a very interesting book, and an opportune one too. It is particularly encouraging that the author, who is himself one of our best known documentary directors, should criticise so acutely his own movement. "One of the most serious shortcomings of the documentary film has been its continued evasion of the human being". The so-called documentary film began in reaction to the commercial cinema, and has suffered, like all reaction movements, from its negative qualities. Disgusted, and rightly, with the standardisation of theme and the star system of personality exploitation, it began by saying: "The private life is unimportant. We must abandon the story and report facts, i.e. we must show you people at their daily work, show you how modern industry is organised, show you what people do for their living, not what they feel". But the private life and the emotions are facts like any others, and one cannot understand the public life of action without them. This puritanical attitude of "reality" and entertainment to what even Mr Rotha can call *"mere fiction"* resulted in films which had many excellent qualities, but to the ordinary film-goer were finally and fatally dull. It was valuable, however, in two ways. Firstly a film is expensive to make, and it was this attitude of the British documentary directors in the early days to work and industry that brought them the support of public bodies like the E.M.B. and the G.P.O., without which they could have made no films at all, nor learnt from their mistakes. Secondly, the intractability of the subject matter incited the directors to experiments in technical problems, which would not otherwise have been undertaken and which have proved of permanent importance.

The only genuine meaning of the word "documentary" is true-to-life. Any gesture, any expression, any dialogue or sound effect, any scenery that strikes the audience as true-to-life is documentary, whether obtained in the studio or on location. Because of the irreversibility and continuous unvaried movement of the film, it is not the best medium for factual information. It is impossible to remember the plot of the simplest commercial film, let alone the intricacies of, say, the sugar beet industry. The effect of a film is to create a powerful emotional attitude towards the material presented.

Because of the mass of realistic detail which the camera records, no medium has ever been invented which is so well suited to portray individual character, and so badly suited to the portrayal of types. On the screen you never see *a* man digging in *a* field, but always Mr Macgregor digging in a ten acre meadow. It goes far beyond the novel in this.

Every good story is what Mr Flaherty calls "the theme of the location". A story is the device by which the public and private life are related to each other for the purposes of presentation, and no film which ignores either completely can be good. The first, second and third thing in cinema, as in any art, is subject. Technique follows from and is governed by subject.

Mr Rotha is alive to all this, but does not point out quite clearly enough the exact nature of the obstacles. The first and most important of these is the time factor. No reputable novelist would dare write his novel before he has spent years acquiring and digesting his material, and no first-class documentary will be made until the director does not begin shooting before he has the same degree of familiarity with his. Inanimate objects, like machines, or facts of organisation, can be understood in a few weeks, but not human beings, and if documentary films have hitherto concentrated on the former, it is not entirely the fault of the directors, but is also due to the compulsion on them to turn out a film in a ridiculously short period. It is a misfortune that the art which is the slowest to create, should at the same time be the most expensive. The second obstacle is class. It is doubtful whether an artist can ever deal more than superficially (and cinema is not a superficial art) with characters outside his own class, and most British documentary directors are upper middle.

Lastly, there is the question of financial support. A documentary film is a film that tells the truth, and truth rarely has advertisement value. One remains extremely sceptical about the disinterestedness of large-scale industry and government departments, or about the possibility that they will ever willingly pay for an exact picture of the human life within their enormous buildings.

Unsigned. *The Listener*, 19 February 1936

Psychology and Criticism

In Defence of Shelley. By Herbert Read. Heinemann. 10s. 6d.

It is probable that the only method of attacking or defending a poet is to quote him. Other kinds of criticism whether strictly literary, or psychological or social, serve only to sharpen our appreciation or our abhorrence by making us intellectually conscious of what was previously but vaguely felt; it cannot change one into the other.

In his title essay Mr Read takes his stand upon what he calls ontogenetic criticism.

> . . . Mr Eliot's objection to Shelley's poetry is irrelevant prejudice; . . . and such I would suggest is the kind of poetic approach of all who believe, with Mr Eliot, that "literary criticism should be completed by criticism from a definite ethical and theological standpoint". I do not deny that such criticism may have its interest; but the only kind of criticism which is basic, and therefore complementary not only to literary but also to ethical, theological and every other kind of ideological criticism, is ontogenetic criticism, by which I mean criticism which traces the origins of the work of art in the psychology of the individual and in the economic structure of society. (p. 71)

He dissects lucidly though perhaps not fully enough,—in a psychological analysis one expects to hear something about the parents—certain traits in Shelley's character, "his liability to hallucinations, his interest in incest, and his lack of objectivity in his modes of self-expression", and demonstrates their emergence in his poetry. This is interesting but does not explain why Mr Read admires Shelley, and Mr Eliot does not.

He continues, with the help of Dr Burrow's *Social Basis of Consciousness,* by showing that Shelley, like every neurotic, had a just grievance, and that his very neurosis was the source of his insight.

> "It is the distinction of the neurotic personality that he is at least consciously and confessedly nervous", so the special value of Shelley is that he was conscious of his direction; he had, in the modern sense, but without expressing himself in modern terminology, analysed his own neurosis. He did not define his autosexuality; but he allowed the reaction full scope. That is to say, he allowed his feelings and ideas to develop integrally with his neurotic personality; and the élan of that evolution inevitably led to the formulation of a "clearer, more conscious social order." (p. 60)

This is extremely interesting but still I am no clearer why I cannot read Shelley with pleasure.

Is it then a difference of moral opinion? I would disagree with Mr Read when he implies that ontogenetic criticism makes no moral judgements. Every psychology, certainly Dr Burrow's, every economic analysis contains therapeutic intentions, i.e. they presuppose an idea of what the individual or society could and should become, and Mr Read himself comes down heavily in favour of "sympathy and infinitude"; but still we are no nearer the nature of our difference. I find, and I imagine Mr Read does too, the

Weltanschauung of Prometheus more to my taste than that of Coriolanus, but I would rather read the latter. It is not a question of expressed belief.

No, the crucial difference between us is reached. I think, in Section VII.

There are always these two types of originality: originality that responds like the Aeolian harp to every gust of contemporary feeling, pleasing by its anticipation of what is half formed in the public consciousness; and *originality that is not influenced by anything outside the poet's own consciousness, but is the direct product of his individual mind and individual feeling.* (p. 80)

What does Mr Read mean by not influenced by *anything*? Consciousness is filled by outside impressions and could not exist without them. If he means other men's intellectual ideas, it certainly does not apply to Shelley. Rilke in a fine passage which Mr Read has himself quoted in *Form in Modern Poetry* enumerates the enormous mass of sensory experiences that should go to the making of a single poem. That is precisely my objection to Shelley. Reading him, I feel that he never looked at or listened to anything, except ideas. There are some poets, Housman for example, whose poetic world contains very few properties, but the few are objectively presented; others again, like Edward Lear, construe them according to laws other than those of socialised life, but the owl and the pussy cat are real. I cannot believe—and this incidentally is why I cannot sympathise with Mr Read in his admiration for abstract art (symbolic art is another matter)—that any artist can be good who is not more than a bit of a reporting journalist.

To the journalist the first thing of importance is subject and, just as I would look at a painting of the Crucifixion before a painting of a still life, and cannot admit that "the pattern may have some more or less remote relation to objects, but such a relation is not necessary" (p. 218), so in literature I expect plenty of news.

Admittedly the journalistic side of the artist can easily and frequently does kill his sensibility; there must always be a tension between them (allied perhaps to the tension Mr Read describes in the essay on Hopkins, the conflict between "sensibility and belief") but a lack of interest in objects in the outside world, the complete triumph of the wish to be "a man without passions—party passions, national passions, religious passions" (p. 181) is equally destructive.

Abstractions which are not the latest flowering of a richly experienced and mature mind are empty and their expression devoid of poetic value. The very nature of Shelley's intellectual interests demanded a far wider range of experiences than most poets require (the more "autosexual" a poet, the more necessary it is for him to be engaged in material action), and his inability to have or to record them makes, for me, the bulk of his work, with the exception of a few short pieces, empty and unsympathetic.

New Verse, April–May 1936

A Review of *Questions of Our Day,* by Havelock Ellis

Questions of Our Day. By Havelock Ellis. Bodley Head. 8s. 6d.

Mr Havelock Ellis is a great man, and the least of his writings commands our serious attention. There are newspapers which run a column where Aunt Martha receives letters from correspondents perplexed about their private life or the world around them, and gives them public advice to the best of her ability, and, in *Questions of Our Day* the author acts this role to perfection.

These columns of advice cover almost every sphere of human life, politics, sex, religion, art. The problems set are general, not particular, and the answers, backed by the varied experience of a long and active life, equally so. A reviewer is tempted to linger over individual passages such as: "My friend is too one-sided in her contempt for cults. There may be something to say for the elderly group in the Chelsea cellar" or, "There may be hope for our planet even as a Mental Hospital," but it is his duty to indicate what general attitude is common to them all.

Mr Havelock Ellis, like Freud and Einstein, is one of the finest flowers of a liberal tradition that, while acknowledging to the full the power of unconscious forces, has not lost its faith in the voice of reason which, though "low and weak, rests not till it finds a hearing". Outside the Communists, there are very few people today who do not, in their heart of hearts, believe that the world is going smash, that human nature is deteriorating, and that they are powerless to arrest it. Mr Havelock Ellis does not believe this. "If way to the better there be, it exacts a full look at the worst", and it is often dangerous to offer people any comfort, but at the present day when the worst is so importunate, when courage is failing, and many cry for the old self-confident past, it is important to draw men's attention to features of the present which are not altogether unworthy, and this *Questions of Our Day* nobly does. To those who are immediately engaged in action and decision, Mr Havelock Ellis stresses, perhaps, the psychological at the expense of the economic; the reflections on politics are the least interesting. But if these pages offer little advice as to what we should do here and now, at least they make no pretence of such an offer.

Patience, toleration, beauty, have sometimes to be deliberately put by, but never the recognition that a worthy civilisation depends on these qualities, nor the belief that in the long run human nature will respond to them. To such a faith and such a recognition Mr Havelock Ellis is an inspired witness. He is, in our time, one of the greatest of those—there are never, perhaps, very many, but always more than we think—who towards the really better world have turned their faces.

Unsigned. The Listener, 22 April 1936

Selling the Group Theatre

Art is of secondary importance compared with the basic needs of Hunger and Love, but it is not therefore necessarily a dispensable luxury. Its power to deepen understanding, to enlarge sympathy, to strengthen the will to action and, last but not least, to entertain, give it an honourable function in any proper community.

The content and structure of social life affect the content and structure of art, and art only becomes decadent and a luxury article when there is no living relation between the two. But because of natural laziness and the friction of opposing and vested interests, development in art, as in society, is not a purely unconscious process that happens automatically. It has to be willed; it has to be fought for. Experiments have to be made, and truth and error discovered in their making. An experimental theatre ought to be regarded as as normal and useful a feature of modern life as an experimental laboratory. In both cases not every experiment will be a success; that should neither be expected nor desired, for much is learned from failure; but, in its successes important avenues of development may be opened out, which would not otherwise have been noticed.

Research scientists know how difficult it is to get support for their work, unless immediate results of commercial or military advantage are forthcoming.

And if scientists find it difficult, how much worse is it for artists, since most have faith in science, and very few in art.

It is all the more necessary then to remind those who recognize the value of an experimental theatre like the Group Theatre that such a theatre depends on their support, that their numbers are small, and that they cannot leave the support to the other man.

During the last year, the Group Theatre has produced three experimental plays, *The Dance of Death, The Dog Beneath the Skin,* and *Fulgens and Lucrece*—plays which would not have been handled by the West End or Repertory Theatres; and the interest, even passion, aroused by these productions, not only in England, but in America and elsewhere, have more than justified them.

So much for the past. In addition to our other activities we are embarking on some new ones. In order to keep our members in touch not only with our own productions but also with any others of special interest, in England or elsewhere, we intend to issue a periodical Bulletin. In addition to news and articles on theatrical matters, we hope to publish extracts from members' plays.

Similarly, with a view to broadening our outlook and contacts, we have joined the New Theatre League, an association of Dramatic Societies, which will attempt to pool experiences, and co-operate in the organisation of audiences.

Finally we are forming a Film Group, under the direction of Mr Basil Wright of the G.P.O. Film Unit, for showing films of particular interest, and ultimately, we hope, with a view to making them.

Such then are our activities, and we do not think that there is another theatrical organisation of this kind in England, which offers ones so many and so various.

Naturally we think them worth while or we shouldn't do them. If you don't, come and see our next production. If you do, then remember that, like everything else in this world, they cost money, and that money does not fall out of heaven, but can only come out of the pockets of those who think as you do.

Therefore please support the Group Theatre yourself, both financially by subscription and actively by patronising its performances, and get others to do the same. Thank you.

Group Theatre Paper, June 1936

Honest Doubt

My only knowledge of Surrealism is derived from Mr Gascoyne's books, a few French writers like Breton and Aragon, some paintings of Dali, Ernst, and others, and from the pages of The Minotaur. I have never met a surrealist, so my ideas of the movement may be completely misconceived. I hope therefore that surrealists will forgive my asking some very elementary questions, in the hope that they will answer them for me. Surrealism claims to have both aesthetic and political implications, so I shall divide my inquiry into two parts.

A. Aesthetic.

(1) Is genuine surrealist writing always and absolutely automatic, and never consciously worked over? If, as I imagine, this is not always the case, at what point does it cease to be surrealist? Obviously all poets make a great use of unconscious imagery; indeed in all verbal thinking of any kind, the words and images are given from the unconscious and it is impossible to decide how much of the activity is conscious and how much unconscious.

(2) Has all repressed material an equal aesthetic value? What are the aesthetic standards and how are they applied? Are all subjects of equal importance?

(3) The work which seems to me, perhaps wrongly, the best kind of surrealist writing e.g. that of Lewis Carroll, Edward Lear, and Rimbaud in *Les Illuminations* is the work of highly repressed individuals in a society with very strong taboos. I should have thought it probable that surrealism could only flourish

either (a) where people know nothing about their unconscious, i.e. where psychoanalysis is unheard of

or (b) in a society with a strong sexual or political censorship, e.g. under Fascism (cf. political satire like *Little Jack Horner*)

and that the moment you are allowed either by yourself or society to say exactly what you like, the lack of pressure leaves you material without form. Am I quite wrong?

(4) There is a passage in Jacobsen's novel *Niels Lyhne*, (quoted by Mr Leishmann in the introduction to his translation of Rilke) which seems to me true, and a warning to surrealism.

. . . nothing is more uniform, more monotonous than fantasy; in the apparently infinite and eternally changing country of dreams there are in reality certain short, given roads which everyone travels and no one gets beyond. People can be very different, but their dreams are not; for there they get themselves presented, more or less quickly, more or less completely, but nevertheless constantly and conjointly, with the three or four things they desire; there is no one who really sees himself with empty hands in his dream; therefore no one discovers himself in his dream, never becomes conscious of his peculiarity; for his dream knows nothing of the satisfaction one finds in winning the treasure, how one lets it go when it is lost, how one is sated when one enjoys, what path one sticks into when one does without.

B. Political.

(1) As far as I understand him, the surrealist writer says "The conscious mind, its reason and its judgement, are so conditioned to-day by the Bourgeois world, that to the revolutionary writer it is artistically valueless." If this is correct,

(*a*) Does this apply to all individuals, proletarian as well as Bourgeois?

(*b*) Why does not it also apply to the repressed unconscious, which always contains material which has been worked over by the conscious mind, elaborated and rejected?

(2) What is the peculiar revolutionary value in the automatic presentation of this repressed material? Is it

(*a*) A socially moral one; holding the mirror up to the face of the bourgeois? If it is, is it not then only the task of the revolutionary bourgeois writer, i.e. the writer with the bourgeois unconscious, with the genuine copy?

or is it (*b*) A personally moral one; autoanalysis? If it is, is it not then only the preliminary task of the would-be revolutionary writer before he can see clearly to create genuine revolutionary art?

(3) Is it true to say that the surrealist rejects absolutely the use of reason and the conscious faculties in creative work, not only at the beginning of work but throughout all the stages of creation? If it is, how does this square with Communism and Psycho-analysis, both of which are profoundly rational, believing, certainly, in unconscious forces, economic or instinctive, as the driving forces in life, but also in the necessity for their conscious recognition and rational understanding and guidance? There is a rough and ready parallelism between the Conscious and the Unconscious, and the Masses and the Communist Party.

J.B.

New Verse, June–July 1936

[Robert Frost]

The term "Nature poetry" could not have been used as a critical label before the development of an industrial economy, that is to say, before the social life of the town and that of the country had become so specialized and so divergent in their interests as to seem separate fields of experience.

Before such a point is reached, there may be other divisions—there may be poetry by the learned, and popular poetry, the court poet and the ballad vendor—but not between the town and the country. There is no lack of reference in Homer or Dante or Shakespeare to natural objects and natural scenery, but these are not introduced as something special, but as a proper background to normal human activities. Man is naturally anthropocentric and interested in his kind and in things or animals only in so far as they contribute to his life and sustain him; he does not interest himself in things to the exclusion of people till his relations with the latter have become difficult or have broken down.

Nature poetry is a sign of social specialization and social strain:

> The world is too much with us, late and soon
> Getting and spending we lay waste our powers
>
> If men were as much men as lizards are lizards
> They'd be worth looking at.

Corresponding to these two tendencies are two kinds of nature poets, the man who lives in the country because he has to, because he works there; and the sensitive who lives in the country because he can afford to and because he dislikes the city. Wordsworth and Lawrence belong to the latter. The former can be again subdivided into two classes, the landed gentleman who is responsible for his land but does not work it with his own hands, such as the Virgil of the Georgics, and the small farmer who works it himself. Of this last Robert Frost is almost the only representative. His qualities of irony and understatement, his mistrust of fine writing, are those of the practical man:

> For them there was really nothing sad.
> But though they rejoiced in the nest they kept,
> One had to be versed in country things
> Not to believe the phoebes wept.

His poems on natural objects, such as "Birches", "Mending Wall", or "The Grindstone", are always concerned with them not as foci for mystical meditation or starting points for fantasy, but as things with which and on which man acts in the course of the daily work of gaining a livelihood. Hence also the slow pace of his verse, so unlike the energetic and violent insight of Lawrence. Nor is he, like Wordsworth, a poet who has had a vision in youth which he can spend the rest of his life in interpreting. His material is not given him in a rush at the beginning. What de la Mare wrote of Frost's friend, and to some extent pupil, Edward Thomas, applies equally to him. "These poems tell us, not so much of rare exalted chosen moments, of fleeting inexplicable intuitions, but of his daily and, one might say, common experience." There is very little poetry about the country which one can feel confident would be immediately understood and appreciated by countrymen, but of these poems one is certain. They are not written for townees.

Frost speaks as a farmer on a small scale, and the civilization in which he feels most at home is one in which each man can own a small holding. Competition is mild, and personal eccentricities are possible and tolerated. He is a liberal.

> I wouldn't be a prude afraid of nature . . .
> . . . Nothing not built with hands of course is sacred.
> But here is not a question of what's sacred;
> Rather of what to face or run away from.
> I'd hate to be a runaway from nature.
> And neither would I choose to be a puke
> Who cares not what he does in company,
> And, when he can't do anything, falls back
> On words, and tries his worst to make words speak
> Louder than actions, and sometimes achieves it.
> It seems a narrow choice the age insists on.
> How about being a good Greek, for instance?
> That course, they tell me, isn't offered this year . . .
> . . . Well, if I have to choose one or the other,
> I choose to be a plain New Hampshire farmer
> With an income in cash of say a thousand
> (From say a publisher in New York City).
> It's restful to arrive at a decision,
> And restful just to think about New Hampshire.
> At present I am living in Vermont.
>
> ("New Hampshire")

The places of which Frost writes, New Hampshire and Vermont, belong to such a world, but he is under no illusions as to its permanence. Further, if, in consequence, the tone of his work is melancholy and stoical, it is completely free from anger or self-pity. He describes what he knows without comment.

The bulk of his work consists of monologues or dialogues written in an even colloquial blank verse. The effect is cumulative, the poem as a whole, rather than any one line; which makes him a difficult poet to quote from. Detached from their context the lines seem pedestrian and monotonous, but few writers have managed naturalistic conversation in verse with so little self-consciousness and fuss.

> I'd seen about enough of his bulling tricks
> (We call that bulling). I'd been watching him.
> So when he paired off with me in the hayfield
> To load the load, thinks I, Look out for trouble.
> I built the load and topped it off; old Sanders
> Combed it down with a rake and says, "O.K."
> Everything went well till we reached the barn
> With a big catch to empty in a bay.
> You understand that meant the easy job
> For the man up on top of throwing *down*
> The hay and rolling it off wholesale,
> Where on a mow it would have been slow lifting.
> You wouldn't think a fellow'd need much urging
> Under these circumstances, would you now?
> But the old fool seizes his fork in both hands,
> And looking up bewhiskered out of the pit,
> Shouts like an army captain, "Let her come!"
> Thinks I, D'ye mean it? "What was that you said?"
>
> ("The Code")

Only a mature and disciplined poet could keep every line so deliberately flat, and yet achieve a poetic effect. His characters are people in whom "poetic" language would be out of place, and on the rare occasions when he introduces it, it strikes a false note, e.g.:

> I'll sit and see if that small sailing cloud
> Will hit or miss the moon.
>
> ("The Death of the Hired Man")

Similarly his descriptions of his characters keep the same texture. They read like good village gossip, not a physician's report, or an historian's brilliant *mot*.

> Lancaster bore him—such a little town,
> Such a great man. It doesn't see him often
> Of late years, though he keeps the old homestead
> And sends the children down there with their mother
> To run wild in the summer—a little wild.
> Sometimes he joins them for a day or two
> And sees old friends he somehow can't get near,
> They meet him in the general store at night,
> Preoccupied with formidable mail,
> Rifling a printed letter as he talks.
> They seem afraid. He wouldn't have it so:

> Though a great scholar, he's a democrat,
> If not at heart, at least on principle.

Frost's longer poems have many themes, but there is something common to them all. Just as Browning was excited by the conflict in the minds of men and women of the world between spiritual values and those of high society and success, so Frost returns again and again to the odd country character, to the deranged ("A Servant to Servants", "Snow"), to the unsuccessful ("The Death of the Hired Man"), to those who do not live by the ordinary standards of material profit ("The Self-Seeker", "The Axe-Helve").

It is noteworthy, however, that he never draws a universal moral from these. He never says, "It is better to be mad, or unsuccessful," or "No one should bother about money". He merely says, "There are such people and they manage to live and you must take account of them. The values of any civilization are never complete".

He knows that, however much we may resent it, our life depends on material things, and when he writes:

> Ah, when to the heart of man
>   Was it ever less than a treason
> To go with the drift of things,
>   To yield with a grace to reason,
> And bow and accept the end
>   Of a love or a season?

one feels that it is not merely the exigency of the rhyme that places the emphasis on "season" rather than "love", and that though reason is an uncertain guide, it is the light by which man must live.

Selected Poems, by Robert Frost, 1936

Pope

About 1705 Wycherley's visitors began to "meet a little Aesopic sort of animal in his own cropt hair, and dress agreeable to the forest he came from—probably some tenant's son of Wycherley's making court for continuance in his lease on the decease of his rustic parent—and were surprised to learn that he was poetically inclined and writ tolerably smooth verses." As is so often the case, just as Proust was a Jew, and Hitler is an Austrian, the man who was to epitomise Augustan culture was not of it by birth. The invalid self-educated son of a Roman Catholic linen merchant, it was not a very promising beginning for the man who was to become the friend of dukes, the gardener and gourmet, the poet to whom a mayor was to offer £4,000 for a single couplet.

If Pope's social advantages were few his physical charms were even less. Only four feet six in height, he was already a sufferer from Pott's disease, "the little Alexander whom the women laugh at", and in middle age was to become really repulsive. ". . . So weak as to stand in perpetual need of female attendance; extremely sensible of cold, so that he wore a kind of fur doublet, under a shirt of a very coarse warm linen with fine sleeves. When he rose, he was invested in a bodice made of stiff canvas, being scarce able to hold himself erect till they were laced, and he then put on a flannel waistcoat. One side was contracted. His legs were so slender, that he enlarged their bulk with three pairs of stockings, which were drawn on and off by the maid; for he was not able to dress or undress himself, and neither went to bed nor rose without help. His weakness made it very difficult for him to be clean. His hair had fallen almost all away. . . ."

Nor, it must be admitted, even if not as sublimely odious as Addison, was he a prepossessing character. He was a snob and a social climber, who lied about his ancestry and cooked his correspondence; he was fretful and demanded constant attention, he was sly, he was mean, he was greedy, he was vain, touchy, and worldly while posing as being indifferent to the world and to criticism; he was not even a good conversationalist.

As a poet, he was limited to a single verse form, the end-stopped couplet; his rare attempts at other forms were failures. To limitation of form was added limitation of interest. He had no interest in nature as we understand the term, no interest in love, no interest in abstract ideas, and none in Tom, Dick and Harry. Yet his recognition was immediate, and his reputation never wavered during his lifetime.

If we are to understand his contemporary success, if we are to appreciate the nature of his poetry and its value, we must understand the age in which he lived.

At the beginning of the eighteenth century, although one quarter of the population was in receipt of occasional parish relief, England was the most prosperous country in Europe. According to Gregory King, out of a population of about five million, the two largest classes were cottagers and paupers, and the labouring people and outservants, both of which the Act of Settlement of the Poor prevented from leaving the parishes in which they were born; about a quarter were tenant farmers or freeholders; an eighty-seventh small landed gentry with an income of from £250–450 a year; and the remainder the large landowners. One tenth of the population lived in London which was more than fifteen times larger than her nearest rival, Bristol. The relative prosperity of the country was due, partly to colonies and Britain's favourable position on the Atlantic sea-board, partly to her export of cloth to Europe, partly to her free internal trade and partly to the comparative lack of friction, compared, for example, with France, between the landed aristocracy and business. Though the former professed to look down on the latter, they were ready to profit from them; the younger sons of the poorer gentry were frequently apprentices to business houses, and successful business men could and did become landed gentry. The Act of Toleration prevented religious difference from interfering with trade; and the establishment of the Bank of England and the National Debt drew financial and political interests close together.

The dependence on air and water for motive power preserved the balance between town and country; indeed, through the wish to escape obsolete borough restrictions, industry was less urban than in earlier times. There was therefore no emotional demand for "nature" poetry.

If a large number of the population were illiterate; if, by our modern liberal standards, their amusements of drinking, gambling, and cock-fighting were crude, their sanitation primitive, their politics virulent and corrupt, there had nevertheless been an improvement. There were more educated people than ever before, a greater interest in education—charity schools were being built everywhere—and England's increasing importance in, and ties with, Europe, gave her culture a breadth and balance hitherto unknown. The arts have hitherto flourished best where cultured society was large enough to provide variety and small enough to be homogeneous in taste. The eighteenth century in England fulfilled both these conditions. There was a growing consciousness of the value of refinement and good manners—a society for the Reformation of Manners is a symptom of a social rather than a puritan conscience—and the age saw the development of these typical modern amusements—smoking—tea- and coffee-drinking—shooting birds on the wing instead of sitting—horse-racing—and cricket. Whether intentional or not, the wearing of wigs helped to delouse the upper classes, and in politics bribery may not be desirable but it is an improvement upon imprisonment and political murder.

You have, then, a society which, in spite of very wide variations in income and culture varying from the cottager with his bible and peddler's ballads, through the small squire with his *Hudibras* and Foxe's *Book of Martyrs*, through the Squire Westerns and the Sir Roger de Coverleys, up to the Duke with his classical library, his panelled room, his landscape garden, his china and mahogany furniture, and his round of London, Bath, and his country estate, was at no point fundamentally divided in outlook and feeling. Owing to the fusing of landed and trade interests, owing to the fact that England was still rural, was a genuine economic unit, and rising in power, there was little clash between politics and economics, no apparent class conflict.

In studying the ideas and art of this period, therefore, we are studying firstly those of any rising class which has recently won power and security for itself—(perhaps the surest sign of victory in a political struggle is the removal of the Censorship; this happened in 1695)—and secondly those of a particular example of such a class in a small European island shortly before the Industrial Revolution. In consequence we may find certain characteristics which seem likely to recur through history, and others which are peculiar to the particular circumstance of the time, and can never happen again.

To take the more universal characteristics first; what should we expect to find? Those who have risen from a subordinate to a dominant position are, firstly, pleased with themselves, and, secondly, anxious to preserve the status quo. No one is so ready to cry Pax and All's well as he who has just got what he wants. They are optimistic, full of vitality, pacific within their circle, and conservative.

> All Nature is but Art, unknown to thee;
> All Chance, Direction, which thou canst not see;
> All Discord, Harmony not understood;
> All partial Evil, universal Good;
> And, spite of Pride, in erring Reason's spite,
> One truth is clear, WHATEVER IS, IS RIGHT.

Secondly, they bring with them a sense of social inferiority; they are anxious to possess and develop the culture and social refinements of the class they have replaced. Contempt for art and manners is a symptom of a rising class that has not yet won power. When they have, they will welcome and reward handsomely art which teaches them refinement, and proves them refined. Because they have been successful, they are interested in themselves. The art of their choice will celebrate their activities, flatter their virtues, and poke fun at their foibles.

Certain qualities of Augustan poetry, then, its air of well being, its gusto, its social reference,

> Correct with spirit, eloquent with ease.

are those which might occur after any social revolution. Others are more unique.

The Reformation split the conception of a God who was both imma-nent and transcendental, a God of faith and works, into two, into the Inner light to be approached only through the private conscience, and the Divine Architect and Engineer of the Physical Universe and the laws of Economics, whose operations could be understood but not interfered with. The religious life tended to become individualized, and the social life secularized. The evil effects of what a Catholic writer has described as

> Sundering the believer from his laicised body
> Sundering heaven from an earth evermore hireling, secularised,
>   enslaved,
> Tied down to the manufacture of the useful.

are more apparent now than then, but of the importance of such an attitude to nature and historical law in the development of the physical sciences, there can be no doubt, and the secularization of education hastened the growth of culture among others than those in orders, and the creation of a general reading public.

At first the emphasis was all on the liberty of the individual conscience, and the Renaissance glorification of the individual, on anti-authoritarianism and anti-popery. But when those who believed in private illumination gained political and public power, they became, as they were bound to become, tyrants. After the Restoration, therefore, there was a swing over to the other pole, to a belief, equally one-sided, in reason against inspiration, in the laws of nature against enthusiastic private illumination, in society against the individual fanatic.

> For Forms of Government let fools contest;
> Whate'er is best administered is best:
> For Modes of Faith let graceless zealots fight;
> His can't be wrong whose life is in the right:
> In Faith and Hope the world will disagree,
> But All Mankind's concern is Charity:
> All must be false that thwart this one great end;
> And all of God, that bless Mankind or mend.

Anti-popery remained, reinforced by the events of 1688, Louis XIV's power in Europe, and his persecution of the Huguenots, but to it was added Anti-Dissent. Neither were violent enough to lead to real persecution or to prevent social intercourse; they were the natural distrust that people who are doing very nicely as they are, have for those who might interfere with them, with their social order, their pleasures, and their cash, but are in point of fact powerless.

The appreciation of law extended itself naturally enough to literature, and literary criticism became for the first time a serious study. Suspicious of enthusiasm and inspiration, Dryden and his successors based their psychology of creative work on Hobbes.

Time and education beget experience.

Experience begets Memory.

Memory begets Judgement and fancy.

Memory is the world in which the Judgement, the severer sister, busieth herself in a grave and rigid examination of all the parts of Nature, and in registering by letters their order, causes, uses, differences, and resemblances; whereby the Fancy, when any work of Art is to be performed, finding her materials at hand and prepared for her use, needs no more than a swift motion over them.

Imagination is nothing else but sense decaying or weakened by the absence of the object.

Such a theory reduces imagination to a recording device, and makes creative work a purely conscious activity. It has no place for the solar plexus or the Unconscious of modern writers, nor for the divine inspiration of the Ancients. Poetry becomes a matter of word-painting of the objective world.

The difference is apparent if we compare Pope's invocation at the beginning of his philosophical poem with those of a Catholic like Dante, or a puritan like Milton.

O good Apollo. . . .
Into my bosom enter thou, and so breathe as when thou drewest
Marsyas from out what sheathed his limbs.

And chiefly thou, O spirit, that dost prefer
Before all temples the upright heart and pure,
Instruct me, for thou knowest . . .
. . . What in me is dark
Illumine; what is low, raise and support.

Awake, my St John! leave all meaner things
To low ambition and the pride of Kings.
Let us (since life can little more supply
Than just to look about us and to die)
Expatiate free o'er all this scene of Man;
A mighty maze! but not without a plan.

But it would be a mistake to say that the best poetry of Dryden or Pope or any of the Augustans was deliberately written to their theories. The writing of poetry is always a more complex thing than any theory we may have about it. We write first and use the theory afterwards to justify the particular kind of poetry we like and the particular things about poetry in general which we think we like. Further, like most theories, it has its points. We, who have been brought up in the Romantic tradition, are inclined to think that whenever the Augustans wrote bad poetry, they were using their own recipe, and whenever they wrote good poetry they were using the Romantic recipe by mistake. This is false. Without their ideas on nature and the Heroic poem, we should miss *The Rape of the Lock* and the *Dunciad* just as much as we should be spared *Eloisa to Abelard* or Darwin's *Loves of the Plants*. The gusto, objectivity, and perfection of texture of the one, owe quite as much to their theories, as does the bogus classicalism of the other.

All theories are one-sided generalizations; and are replaced by their opposite half-truths. When society has become too big to manage, when there is a class of persons whose incomes are drawn from investments without the responsibilities of landowners or employers, when the towns are congested, we shall hear other voices. Instead of Hobbes's psychology, we shall have Blake's "Natural objects deaden and weaken imagination in me". Instead of Pope's modest intention to please, the poets will proclaim themselves, and be believed in so far as they are listened to at all, as the Divine legislators of the world.

We, again, fancy we know better now; that the writing of poetry is a matter of neither a purely unconscious inspiration, not purely conscious application, but a mixture of the two, in proportions which vary with different kinds of verse; that it is rarely the tortured madness which some of the Romantics pretended it was, and certainly never the effortless and thoughtless excitement the cinema public imagines it to be.

If the Augustans had the defects of their qualities, so did the Romantics. If the former sometimes came down, according to the late Professor Housman, to "singing hymns in the prison chapel", the latter sometimes went off into extempore prayers in the county asylum.

And on the whole, yes, on the whole, I think we agree with Byron "Thou shalt believe in Milton, Dryden and Pope. Thou shalt not set up Wordsworth, Coleridge and Southey". But then we know better now.

During the two centuries preceding Pope, the literary language had undergone considerable change. We cannot tell how far Shakespeare's conversation in *The Merry Wives of Windsor* is a realistic transcript, but it is remote from us in a way that the dialogue of the Restoration dramatists is not. In Dryden's essay on *The Dramatic Poesy of The Last Age* he gives as the reason, "the greatest advantage of our century, which proceeds from *conversation*. In the age wherein these poets lived, there was less of gallantry than in ours; neither did they keep the best company of theirs."

The change in social status is important. It is doubtful if the Elizabethan dramatists would have been received in the best drawing-rooms. The poets of a later age certainly were, and if poetry lost that complete unity of language and sensation which the Elizabethans at their best achieved,

> In her strong toil of grace

the rise of the writer into society was at least partly responsible. A classical education and the company of ladies and gentlemen may have advantages, but they make an instinctive vocabulary very difficult.

But it is the mark of a great writer to know his limitations. Had Dryden attempted to continue the Elizabethan traditions, he would have been no greater than Massinger. Instead, he did what Nature has usually done in evolutionary changes, he turned to a form which, though it had once been important, during the last age had played second fiddle to blank verse.

The couplet had nevertheless had a continuous history, parallel to and influenced by blank verse. The couplet of Chaucer's time degenerated with the dropping of the final "e", and with the exception of Dunbar's *Freiris of Berwik,* is hardly seen, till it turns up again in Spenser's *Mother Hubbard's Tale.*

> To such delight the noble wits he led
> Which him relieved as their vain humours fed
> With fruitless follies and unsound delights.

Its principal use was for narrative, as in Marlowe and Chapman's *Hero and Leander,* with enjambement and spreading of sentences over several couplets, a feature which developed in Donne and Cowley to a point where the feeling of the couplet is almost lost.

> Seek true religion, O where? Mirreus,
> Thinking her unhoused here and fled from us,
> Seeks her at Rome, there, because he doth know
> That she was there a thousand years ago;
> And loves her rags so, as we here obey
> The state-cloth where the prince sate yesterday,
> Crants to such brave loves will not be enthrall'd,
> But loves her only who at Geneva's call'd
> Religion, plain, simple, sullen, young,
> Contemptuous yet unhandsome; as among
> Lecherous humours, there is one that judges
> No wenches wholesome, but coarse country drudges,
> Graius stays still at home here, and because
> Some preachers, vile ambitious bawds, and laws,
> Still new, like fashions, bid him think that she
> Which dwells with us, is only perfect, he
> Embraceth her, whom his godfathers will
> Tender to him, being tender; as wards still
> Take such wives as their guardians offer, or

> Pay values. Careless Phrygius doth abhor
> All, because all cannot be good; as one,
> Knowing some women whores, dares marry none.

But side by side with this, through the use of rhyming tags to round off dramatic scenes, through the conclusions of the sonnets, and occasional addresses, there is a development of the end-stopped epigrammatical couplet. Lytton Strachey in his essay on Pope has drawn attention to a series of couplets in *Othello,* ending,

> She was a wight if ever such wight were
> To suckle fools and chronicle small beer.

And there are plenty of other instances. Fairfax's Tasso and Sandys's Metamorphoses are no sudden new developments. The evolution of the end-stopped couplet from Spenser through Drayton to them and Waller and Denham, and on to Dryden and Pope is continuous. It is only the pace of the development that alters.

The choice of a verse form is only half conscious. No form will express everything, as each form is particularly good at expressing something. Forms are chosen by poets because the most important part of what they have to say seems to go better with that form than any other; there is generally a margin which remains unsaid, and then, in its turn, the form develops and shapes the poet's imagination so that he says things which he did not know he was capable of saying, and at the same time those parts of his imagination which once had other things to say, dry up from lack of use.

The couplet was not Dryden's only instrument—the *Ode on St Cecilia's Day, Annus Mirabilis,* the *Threnodia Augustalis* succeed in expressing things that the couplet could not have expressed—but it was Pope's.

Nor is the heroic couplet the only tune of the eighteenth century. There are the octosyllabics of Swift, the blank verse of Thomson, the odes of Gray and Collins. There is Prior:

> Now let us look for Louis' feather
> That used to shine so bright a star
> The generals could not get together
> Wanting that influence, great in war.

There is Gay, forestalling Byron.

> See generous Burlington with Goodly Bruce
>   (But Bruce comes wafted in a soft sedan)
> Dan Prior next, beloved by every Muse;
>   And friendly Congreve, unreproachful man!

> (Oxford by Cunningham hath sent excuse;)
> See hearty Watkins come with cap and can,
> And Lewis who has never friend forsaken;
> And Laughton whispering asks "Is Troytown Taken?"

or Dr Johnson, forestalling Housman,

> All that prey on vice and folly
> Joy to see their quarry fly;
> There the gamester light and jolly
> There the lender grave and sly.

and a host of popular songs and hymns.

> Come cheer up, my lads, 'tis to glory we steer
> To add something more to this wonderful year.

No, the poetry of the eighteenth century is at least as varied as that of any other, but Pope is labelled as the representative Augustan poet, and as he confined himself to the couplet, the couplet is labelled as the medium of Augustan poetry. As far as Pope personally was concerned, his limitation of form—he even denied himself the variety of an occasional Alexandrine—had its advantages. "Of this uniformity the certain consequence was readiness and dexterity. By perpetual practice, language had in his mind a systematical arrangement, having always the same use for words, he had words so selected and combined as to be ready at his call."

With this limit of form went a limit of interest. Pope was interested in three things, himself and what other people thought of him, his art, and the manners and characters of society. Not even Flaubert or Mallarmé was more devoted to his craft. "What his nature was unfitted to do, circumstance excused him from doing"; and he was never compelled to write to order, or to hurry over his work. He missed nothing. If he thought of something in the midst of the night, he rang for the servant to bring paper; if something struck him during a conversation, he would immediately write it down for future use. He constantly altered and rewrote, and always for the better. The introduction of sylphs and gnomes into the *Rape of the Lock*, and the conclusion of the *Dunciad* were not first thoughts.

> Let there be Darkness (the dread power shall say)
> All shall be Darkness, as it ne'er were day:
> To their first chaos Wit's vain works shall fall
> And universal Dullness cover all.
> No more the Monarch could such raptures bear;
> He waked, and all the Vision mixed with air.

(1728)

Lo! the great Anarch's ancient reign restored
Light dies before her uncreating word. . . .
Thy hand, great Dullness! lets the curtain fall
And universal Darkness covers all.
Enough! enough! the raptured Monarch cries;
And through the ivory gate the Vision flies.

(1729)

and finally,

Lo! thy Dread Empire, Chaos! is restored
Light dies before thy uncreating word.
Thy hand, great Anarch! lets the curtain fall
And universal darkness buries all.

The beauties and variety of his verse have been so brilliantly displayed
by others, notably Miss Sitwell, that I shall confine myself to considering
two popular ideas about Pope. That his language is either falsely poetic,
or "a classic of our prose" and that his poetry is cold and unemotional.
The question of poetic diction was the gravamen of the Romantics'
charge. The answer is that Pope and his contemporaries were interested
in different fields of experience, in a different "nature". If their descrip-
tions of cows and cottages and birds are vague, it is because their focus of
interest is sharp elsewhere, and equal definition over the whole picture
would spoil its proportion and obscure its design. They are conventional,
not because the poets thought that "the waterpudge, the pilewort, the
petty chap, and the pooty" were unpoetic in their naked nature and must
be suitably dressed, but because they are intended to be conventional, a
backcloth to the more important human stage figures. When Pope writes
in his preface to the *Odyssey*, "There is a real beauty in an easy, pure,
perspicuous description even of a low action," he is saying something
which he both believes and practises.

To compass this, his building is a Town,
His pond an Ocean, his parterre a Down:
Who but must laugh, the Master when he sees,
A puny insect, shivering at a breeze!
Lo! what huge heaps of littleness around!
The whole, a laboured Quarry above ground;
Two Cupids squirt before; a Lake behind
Improves the keenness of the Northern wind.
His Gardens next your admiration call,
On every side you look, behold the Wall!
No pleasing Intricacies intervene,

No artful wildness to perplex the scene;
Grove nods at grove, each Alley has a brother,
And half the platform just reflects the other.
The suff'ring eye inverted Nature sees,
Trees cut to Statues, Statues thick as trees;
With here a Fountain, never to be played;
And there a Summer-house, that knows no shade;
Here Amphitrite sails through myrtle bowers;
There Gladiators fight, or die in flowers;
Un-watered see the drooping sea-horse mourn,
And swallows roost in Nilus' dusty Urn.

Now lap-dogs give themselves the rousing shake,
And sleepless lovers, just at twelve, awake:
Thrice rung the bell, the slipper knocked the ground,
And the pressed watch returned a silver sound.

There is no vagueness here. There are the images of contemporary life. This poetry, not Wordsworth's, is the ancestor of "the patient etherized on the table", of Baudelaire's

On entend ça et là les cuisines siffler,
Les théâtres glapir, les orchestres ronfler;
Les tables d'hôte, dont le jeu fait les délices,
S'emplissent de catins et d'escrocs, leur complices,
Et les voleurs, qui n'ont ni trêve ni merci
Vont bientôt commencer leur travail, eux aussi,
Et forcer doucement les portes et les caisses
Pour vivre quelques jours et vêtir leurs maîtresses.

Those who complain of Pope's use of periphrasis, of his refusal to call a spade a spade, cannot have read him carefully. When he chooses he is as direct as you please.

So morning insects that in muck begun
Shine, buzz, and flyblow in the setting sun.

And when he does use a periphrasis, in his best work at least, it is because an effect is to be gained by doing so.

While China's earth receives the smoking tide.

To say that Pope was afraid to write, as Wordsworth might have written,

While boiling water on the tea was poured

is nonsense. To the microscopic image of tea-making is added the macroscopic image of a flood, a favourite device of Pope's, and the opposite kind of synthesis to Dante's, "A single moment maketh a deeper lethargy for me than twenty and five centuries have wrought on the emprise that erst threw Neptune in amaze at Argo's shadow."

There are places in Pope, as in all poets, where his imagination is forced, where one feels a division between the object and the word, but at his best there are few poets who can rival his fusion of vision and language.

> Chicane in furs, and casuistry in lawn
>
> Bare the mean heart that lurks beneath a star.
>
> How hints, like spawn, scarce quick in embryo lie,
> How new-born nonsense first is taught to cry,
> Maggots half-formed in rhyme exactly meet,
> And learn to crawl upon poetic feet.
> Here one poor word an hundred clenches makes,
> And ductile Dulness new maeanders takes;
> There motley images her fancy strike,
> Figures ill paired, and Similes unlike.
> She sees a Mob of Metaphors advance,
> Pleased with the madness of the mazy dance;
> How Tragedy and Comedy embrace;
> How Farce and Epic get a jumbled race;
> How Time himself stands still at her command,
> Realms shift their place, and Ocean turns to land.
> Here gay Description Egypt glads with showers,
> Or gives to Zembla fruits, to Barca flowers;
> Glitt'ring with ice here hoary hills are seen,
> There painted valleys of eternal green;
> In cold December fragrant chaplets blow,
> And heavy harvests nod beneath the snow.

You will call this Fancy and Judgment if you are an Augustan, and the Imagination if you are a Romantic, but there is no doubt about it.

Like Dante, Pope had a passionate and quite undonnish interest in classical literature. The transformation of the heroic epic into *The Rape of the Lock* and the *Dunciad,* is not cheap parody; it is the vision of a man who can see in Homer, in eighteenth century society, in Grub Street, similarities of motive, character, and conduct whereby an understanding of all is deepened. Rams and young bullocks are changed to folios and Birthday odes, and

> Could all our care elude the gloomy grave
> Which claims no less the fearful than the brave
> For lust of fame I should not vainly dare
> In fighting fields, nor urge thy soul to war

becomes

> O if to dance all night and dress all day,
> Charmed the small pox, or chased old age away;
> Who would not scorn what housewife's cares produce,
> Or who would learn one earthly thing of use?

Literature and life are once more happily married. We laugh and we love. Unlike Dryden, Pope is not a dramatic poet. He is at his best only when he is writing directly out of his own experience. I cannot feel that his Homer is anything but a set task, honourably executed: the diction gives it away. But show him the drawing-rooms where he longed to be received as a real gentleman, let him hear a disparaging remark about himself, and his poetry is beyond praise. The *Essay on Man* is smug and jaunty to a degree, until we come to Happiness and Fame

> All that we feel of it begins and ends
> In the small circle of our foes and friends.
> To all beside as much an empty shade
> An England living, as a Cæsar dead.

Pope knew what it was to be flattered and libelled, to be ambitious, to be snubbed, to have enemies, to be short, and ugly, and ill, and unhappy, and out of his knowledge he made his poetry, succeeded, as Rilke puts it, in

> Transmuting himself into the words.
> Doggedly, as the carver of a cathedral
> Transfers himself to the stone's constancy.

and won his reward as he perceived

> . . . how fate may enter into a verse
> And not come back, how, once in, it turns image
> And nothing but image, nothing but ancestor,
> Who sometimes, when you look at him in his frame
> Seems to be like you and again not like you.

From Anne to Victoria, edited by Bonamy Dobrée, 1937

A Review of *The Book of Margery Kempe*

The Book of Margery Kempe. A Modern Version by
W. Butler-Bowdon. Cape. 10s. 6d.

The literature of the Middle Ages is a specialised taste, and it is rarely that one can confidently recommend a mediæval book to the general reader. *The Book of Margery Kempe,* however, is one of the exceptions. In the first place it is very easy to read in Mr Butler-Bowdon's excellent version; in the second it appeals to a variety of interests; to the historian of manners as a graphic picture of everyday life in the Middle Ages, to the travel lover, to the psychologist as a remarkably detailed case-history, and to the student of human nature as a picture of a great comic character.

Born of a prosperous middle-class family at the beginning of the fifteenth century, Margery Kempe went off her head after childbirth, was haunted by an unconfessed sin—the psychologist's only complaint about this book will be that its nature is not stated—recovered, and after two false starts at being a brewer and a miller, found her real vocation as a religious eccentric.

From now on her relations with the Trinity were continuous and intimate, but her inability to keep them to herself made her extremely embarrassing to her worldly friends, and highly suspicious to the ecclesiastical authorities. After persuading her husband to chastity—in return she paid his debts—she went on a pilgrimage to the Holy Land where the sight of the Holy Places set her "crying and roaring though she would have died of it". The roaring became an uncontrollable habit and the rest of her life is a history of the scrapes she got into over it. She roared in church during the sermon, she roared if she saw a male baby, she roared if she saw a beggar. She tried to stifle the roars so as not to annoy the neighbours, but it was no use, and when she had a brief interval she wasn't happy either.

> She might neither weep loud nor still but when God would send it, for she was sometimes thus barren of tears a day or half a day, and had such great pain for the desire she had of them, that she would have given all this world if it had been hers, for a few tears, or have suffered right great bodily pain to have got them with.

The common people disliked the noise but were rather impressed and:

> The said creature was desired by many people to be with them at their dying, and to pray for them for, though they loved not her weeping or crying in their lifetime, they desired that she should both weep and cry when they should die, and so she did.

The Church was put in the same quandary as it was with Joan of Arc, or any individual professing private visions. Where did they come from, God or the Devil? If the former she was a saint, if the latter a heretic. There was Lollardry about, and Lollardry had dangerous political implications. Margery had a narrow escape from the stake. Luckily for her, her visions had no reference to the crucial articles of the Faith, such as the influence of the priest's private life or the validity of the Sacrament, and she had the confidence and backing of her confessor in details like wearing white clothes. Perhaps also she was so exasperating that the strongest wish of her examiners was never to see her again:

Then anon the Archbishop said:

"Where shall I get me a man who might lead this woman away from me?"

Immediately there started up many young men, and every one of them said:

"My Lord, I will go with her".

The Archbishop answered: "Ye be too young. I will not have you".

Then a good man of the Archbishop's household asked his Lord what he would give him if he should lead her. The Archbishop proffered him five shillings, and the man asked a noble. The Archbishop answering said:

"I will not spend so much on her body".

"Yes! Good sir", said the said creature (Margery). "Our Lord shall reward you right well in return".

Then the Archbishop said to the man:

"See, here is five shillings, and lead her fast out of this country".

If she were alive today, one fears she would probably be locked up (perhaps not in America) or at least sent to a psychoanalyst who would explain to her her dread of winds and rape, her relations with the Manhood and Godhead of the Trinity, her dream of the three cushions, and her desire to kiss lepers, and we should be deprived of a character who, if embarrassing to live with, would be wonderful to meet on a 'bus.

In addition to Mr Butler-Bowdon, a word is due to Professor Chambers who contributes a model introduction.

Unsigned. *The Listener,* 28 October 1936

A Modern Use of Masks
An Apologia

Everything we do, everything we think or feel modifies our bodies. Starting as babies with almost unlimited potential characters, with every choice we make, the future possibilities become more limited until the individual is more or less fixed and more or less unique. This uniqueness of character is reflected in a physical uniqueness, and because we wear clothes, we judge people by their faces.

Furthermore, we all possess, to a greater or less degree, the power of posing, the power of adopting another character, and the greater the power to do this, the more power we have to change our faces.

It is on the recognition of this relation of the psychical and the physical that the use of the mask in the theatre depends.

Taken for granted in the theatre of classical times and the modern circus, it has disappeared in the realistic prose drama, because in the latter almost the whole of the effects are confined to the conversation. The physical attractions and repulsions of the star actors are only their own. They have nothing to do with the play as a play—(farcical characters, of course, by violent make-up, extraordinary clothes, and a comedian's particular talent for distorting his face have always retained physical methods of expression.)

The mask then is an attempt on the part of the painter to reinforce and parallel the intellectual effects of the writer, by physical effects which are independent of the particular actors.

In the cinema, close-ups, angle shots, and special lighting can do the same thing with the faces of the actors themselves, but in the theatre the great distance between the audience and the actor makes the mask necessary.

All art implies selection. Just as the dramatist limits the behaviour and conversation of his characters to the particular end in view, so the mask-maker selects from many facial characteristics the one to which he wishes to draw attention. A mask can be realistic but only in a limited way. Owing to its immobility it must be exaggerated or satirised. Even if the mask is a three quarter mask, as used by the Group Theatre in its productions of *Sweeney Agonistes* and *The Dog Beneath the Skin*, the same is true, because of the use which the actor normally makes of his forehead.

Incidentally, the masks in these two plays illustrate two opposite uses. In *The Dog* they were used to exaggerate the obvious, to make the hotel inmates, for example, look more like Hotel Inmates, to emphasize the normal vision. In *Sweeney*, on the other hand, they were used to reveal the real character behind the actual face, the contrast between inner reality and what we show the world, the hidden terrors behind the normal every-day expression, mask if you like, which meets us as we walk about the streets.

Fantastic masks, like those of a Christmas party, or the animal masks in the Group Theatre's production of the *Agamemnon*, are used for decoration and strangeness; like posing in real life they are play and fancy.

Lastly, the chorus masks in *Agamemnon* show the use of masks for special effects. In presenting a Greek play to a modern audience without a classical education, one of the difficulties of the producer is to prevent the audience regarding it as a quaint costume piece of purely archaeological interest. Just as the Greek has to be translated into modern English, so the visual effects have similarly to be translated. The chorus masks in combination with the modern jackets are intended to give an effect of timeless formality, the masking resembling a leaded head in a stained glass window.

Unsigned. *Group Theatre Paper*, November 1936

Are You Dissatisfied with This Performance?

Quite possibly. The chorus have rehearsed altogether about three times. Why? Because the actors have had to go to paid engagements. However keen an actor may be on a part, he must live. Seven men participate in the chorus. Seventeen different actors have rehearsed in it.

The Group Theatre has certain initial advantages. It has playwrights who wish to write plays for it, painters who wish to design for it, composers who wish to compose for it. But it suffers under an overwhelming disadvantage. It has too little cash. There are actors who would like to play for it, IF they could afford it.

There are all the possibilities here for a vital theatre, neither drawing-room drama, nor something private and arty, but a social force. We have a lot to learn, but are willing, we think, to do so if we get the right support. Unfortunately the art of the theatre differs from literature or painting or music, in that it can not be created by one or two people in a room. It is extremely expensive.

It can go a certain way on membership of a club principle, but only a certain way, and the Group Theatre has gone as far as it can along these lines. Of course the greater the membership the better. Get everyone you can to join. But we need something more than that. The Group Theatre personnel can not work any longer without money.

We appeal for a patron or patrons, for a person or persons, who care about the theatre and feel that what we are trying to do is worth doing, and feel that sufficiently strongly, to make it, by their personal help, possible for us to do it, and make a permanent theatre.

Group Theatre program for *Agamemnon*,
1 November 1936

The Average Man

Portrait of an Unknown Victorian. By R. H. Mottram. Hale. 12s. 6d.

Self-love must always make us peculiarly interested in the lives of the obscure of another historical period. The historian tells us of the monuments of the exalted, the average laws of behaviour, the civic triumphs and catastrophes, but pays little attention to our first question, which is: "What should I have done if I'd been there?" We want to know what kind of a job we should have had, how much money we should have made, what we should have eaten, what hobbies we should have taken up, what sort of things would have irritated or amused us. Only when these questions have been answered is our curiosity really free to consider the distinguished and the eccentric. Because Mr Mottram does really answer them, his *Portrait of an Unknown Victorian*, in spite of the fact that he sometimes writes like a Cabinet Minister, is a fascinating book.

He has been lucky in finding a subject who was not only perfectly fitted by career to his needs but who also had an excellent memory. He really was the average man. The average man must feel perfectly at home in the life and standards of his class, he must be successful but not too successful, he must have some unspectacular triumphs and reverses, a slight peculiarity or two, and at least one high moment of exceptional behaviour. The subject of this portrait was a dissenter who just remembered Queen Victoria's coronation and died, apparently, during the Great War; he worked for fifty years in a private bank in Norwich, and rose to be chief cashier; his triumphs were becoming organiser of the orchestra at the musical festival and Counter at the reformed elections; his reverses, the loss of his first wife and becoming too old for his work; his heroic moments, when he sent for the military during a fire and when in his old age he took matters out of the hands of a feeble chairman; his peculiarities, his musical talent and above all his absolute but quite unambitious devotion to his work.

Mr Mottram has painted his portrait with exemplary care, so that we watch it growing and ageing like a living person and even the most trivial detail seems significant. We learn, for example, how an attempt to interest the boy in Wordsworth somehow failed, how the young man of the 'fifties took to the Volunteer movement and the cold bath, but the middle-aged man of the 'seventies could not take to the bicycle, that the Devil's Walk amused him, but not the chapter in *Poor Jack* about spontaneous combustion, that the new atmosphere of the 'sixties, typified in political life by the abolition of public executions, the Education Bill and the Ballot Act, was reflected in one private life by the development of an interest in the microscope. Like most average men he met some distinguished ones. In his case they were mostly musicians; but he saw Dickens and disliked his tie, he met Wilde at lunch and foretold his end; he met Galsworthy on business and was impressed, and his second wife gave Mr Gladstone a cup of tea.

As we finish the book with the memory of this hard-working man, just and merciful in all his dealings, we are tempted to forget that the average man is always the average man of a class, in this case of the lower middle-class, a man living in an agricultural part of the country, where, when disasters occurred, they were small enough to be dealt with by the local subscriptions of a few public-spirited rich men. Mr Mottram himself does not seem to have escaped this temptation. It may be enough for the private individual only "always to try to do what is right," but the historian is required to think. Mr Mottram gives way to machine-hating—"the shadow of a machine fell across the path of human progress"—and to the specious view that the present state of Europe is simply due to naughtiness, to not being Victorian.

When the earth rattled on his coffin it was Peace and Prosperity that were being buried. When they cut his name on the stone that stood in line with his father's and grandfather's, they might just as well have inscribed: "Here lies twenty shillings in the pound." For, by then, most of the nations of Europe were fatally and finally bankrupt, and the curious process of governing people by forcing them to do what they do not want, was inevitable because well-being had been blown to pieces by intricate devices . . . he represented the achievement of a great time and was content to merge in it. Something like it will certainly return. The day will come again when people prefer to be honest, sane and tolerant—in a word, scrupulous.

They will, but only when, not only our political leaders, but the average man have learned to combine this unknown Victorian's devotion to work and integrity of life with a capacity for "abstract thought and impersonal consideration" of the society in which of necessity they live, but which it is in their power consciously to change.

The New Statesman and Nation, 7 November 1936

Four Stories of Crime

Cards on the Table. By Agatha Christie. Collins. 7s. 6d.
Death Meets the Coroner. By John Knox Ryland. Stanley Paul. 7s. 6d.
Thirteen Guests. By J. Jefferson Farjeon. Collins. 7s. 6d.
The Clue of the Bricklayer's Aunt. By Nigel Morland. Cassell. 7s. 6d.

One of the chief difficulties before the writer of detective novels is the victim. A good story must sound credible, but a good plot demands a number of suspects, and in real life a private individual whom several people have strong motives for murdering is hard to find. That is why the blackmailer is such a popular figure, though I imagine that in fact the blackmailer with a number of different kinds of victims at the same time is a rare bird, because obtaining the necessary scandalous information is so much a matter of luck.

Anyway out of the three pure detective stories before us, two have a blackmailer to be murdered, while the third, Mrs Agatha Christie's, chooses someone very near it in *Cards on the Table*.

Mr Shaitana does not want money, but enjoys the feeling of power. Among other things he collects successful murderers, those who have done it and got away with it. His hold over them is based less on knowledge than on the suggestion that he knows, and, as a matter of fact, in one case he was mistaken. To amuse himself he gives a party for eight people; four probable murderers: a popular doctor, an explorer, a distinguished middle-aged lady, and a quiet young girl; and four investigators of crime: a police superintendent, a clever lady writer of detective stories, a secret service official, and, of course, Hercule Poirot.

At the end of the evening the host is found stabbed with one of his own ornamental daggers. The murderer or murderess must have been one of four people, and must have been dummy. The four representatives of detection set out to solve the problem in their different ways.

Mrs Agatha Christie's powers are too well known to need praise from me; I can only say that I think *Cards on the Table* her best so far.

Jonathan Cravé, the coroner in Mr Ryland's *Death Meets the Coroner*, combines philandering with blackmailing; indeed, I find his unpleasantness a little too much to be credible, but as he swallows poison in the first chapter, perhaps it doesn't matter much.

The scene is the modern English countryside, with its contrast of sleepy market towns and flashy roadhouses, a world where parents have to make sacrifices to give their children a good education. The Chief Constable of Chipping Wykewood with his interest in roses and little domestic inventions and his sense of humour, is a charming character and so is his daughter; but his undergraduate son is spoilt and when Investigator Rodway comes down to investigate the murder, he feels that all is not right in their home.

Both the police and the suspects are living characters, the descriptions of scenery are good, and the faint hint of a romance growing up between the inspector and the Chief Constable's daughter adds an extra flavour to this excellent book, *Death Meets the Coroner*.

In Mr Farjeon's *Thirteen Guests* we rise to the world of the country house, stag-hunting, political magnates and beautifully gowned women. A handsome young man sprains his ankle jumping out of a train. A beautiful widow witnesses the accident and, finding that he has no plans, brings him, uninvited, to Bragley Court, where he overhears conversations which he was not meant to hear.

Next day there is trouble, and an efficient and cynical policeman, helped by an even more efficient and cynical gossip writer, is faced with the awkward task of deciding which of a number of well-known people murdered an unpleasant fellow guest and defaced the canvas of a merciless portrait painter.

Mr Farjeon is as skilful as ever at drawing character and evoking atmosphere.

The interest of *The Clue of the Bricklayer's Aunt* lies less in the problem itself than in the incidents that follow on a woman's effort to solve it. Mr Morland's detective, Mrs Pym, has the distinction of being probably the most unpleasant detective in modern fiction.

Those who prefer car chases, street fights and violent action to credibility, logical reasoning and style, and who believe in treating the criminal rough, will find *The Clue of the Bricklayer's Aunt* to their taste.

The Daily Telegraph, 17 November 1936

Poetry, Poets, and Taste

One hundred per cent he-men, very grown-up doctors, and a certain kind of social reformer have no use for poetry. The first thinks it a cissy occupation, the second an infantile and neurotic method of escape, and the third fiddling while Rome burns. As a poet I am naturally interested in persuading people to buy poetry, so I shall try to answer these objections.

The first gentleman is easy. I shall only ask him if he knows the one about the Lady of Gloucester. His objection is largely the result of bad education. School teachers, and, I'm afraid, a lot of other people who ought to know better, think of Poetry with a P, as something which concerns itself only with the Higher Life, or what some snob with a genius for nauseating titles has called "Higher-grade living". This is, of course, quite untrue. Poetry has as varied a subject matter and treatment as human character. It deals with the mysteries of the universe certainly—well even the most hard-headed business man sometimes thinks if only convalescent after influenza, "Why am I here?"—but it deals just as much with the joke at lunch or the face of the lady opposite.

> Cover her face, mine eyes dazzle. She died young

is poetry. So is—

> Early in the morning at half-past three
> They were all lit up like a Christmas tree.
> Lil got up and started for bed,
> Took another sniff and then she fell down dead.

And so is—

> And masculine is found to be
> Hadria, the Adriatic sea.

There is solemn poetry and light poetry, comic poetry and serious poetry, pure poetry and obscene poetry, and to say that you only like one kind, is like saying "I only like Archdeacons" or "The only people I have any use for are barmaids." Really to appreciate archdeacons, you must know some barmaids and vice versa. The same applies to poetry.

The doctor and the social reformer are tougher opponents. I lump them together because both their criticisms raise the question of the nature of artistic activity. The doctor's argument is something like this: "I've had plenty of these artists in my consulting-room and I know what I'm talking about. Their health's generally rotten, they're mentally completely unstable, their private lives are a disgrace and they never pay my bills. Look at Homer, blind as a bat. Look at Villon, a common or garden crook. Look at Proust, asthmatic, a typical case of mother fixation, etc., etc."

And he's quite right. As a matter of fact, I think we shall find that all intelligent people, even the great doctor himself, are the product of psychological conflict in childhood, and generally share some neurotic traits. I rather suspect that if the world consisted solely of the psychologically perfect, we should still be eating roots in the jungle. But I'll leave that and concentrate on the artist. When we are confronted with an emotional difficulty or danger, there are three things we can do. We can pretend that *we* are not there, i.e. we can become feeble-minded or ill; we can pretend that *it* isn't there, i.e. we can daydream; or we can look at it carefully and try to understand it, understand the mechanism of the trap. Art is a combination of these last two; there is an element of escape in it, and an element of science, which only differs from what we generally call by that name, in that its subject is a different order of data.

The first half of art, then, is perceiving. The artist is the person who stands outside and looks, stands even outside himself and looks at his daydreams.

The second half of art is telling. If you asked any artist why he works, I think he would say "To make money and to amuse my friends."

He is a mixture of spy and gossip, a cross between the slavey, with her eye glued to the keyhole of the hotel bedroom, and the wife of a minor canon; he is the little boy who comes into the drawing-room and says, "I saw St Peter in the hall" or "I saw Aunt Emma in the bath without her wig."

So the doctor is wrong. If the artists sometimes give us escape, let us be grateful, for we all need a certain amount of escape, just as we need sleep; but he also tells us the truths which we are too busy or too ashamed to see.

And the social reformer is wrong, too. When an artist writes about the slums or disease or Hell, it is quite true that he wants them to be there because they are his material, just as dentists want people to have decaying teeth. You can rarely expect him to be a good politician, but you can use what he gives you, the truths he tells, to strengthen your will, and amuse you in your hours of relaxation. Aunt Emma may buy some hair restorer after all.

There are two more points I should like to touch on, one trivial, the other more important. Firstly, what is poetry as distinct from the other arts, and secondly, how do you distinguish good poetry from bad. I think there is no absolute division between poetry and prose. "Pure" poetry would, I think, be words used with only emotional significance and without any logical significance, and prose be the reverse. In practice pure poetry and prose do not exist, any more than pure substances do in nature, and if they did would be unreadable, just as pure chemicals do not react. All you can say is that

> Sing a song of sixpence,
> A pocket full of rye,

is near the pure poetry end of the scale, and

> This table is six feet long,

is near the pure prose end, and there is every possible shade between them.

As for taste, it ultimately rests with the individual reader. Every reader and every age think naturally enough that they have the key to absolute taste, but history should make us humble. There is only one general rule and that is sincerity, which is easy to say, but impossible to obey perfectly. Admit to yourself that you like quite different kinds of poetry in different moods, and if you find you really prefer Ella Wheeler Wilcox to Shake-speare, for heaven's sake admit it. Some people can never be poets be-cause they don't happen to have any genuine interest in words, in the telling side of the art; i.e. they are not really interested in poetry. Others fail because they are not interested in their subject, in the perceiving side. But the commonest cause of badness in any of the arts is being really interested in one subject while pretending to be interested in another. The secret of good art is the same as the secret of a good life; to find out what you are interested in, however strange, or trivial, or ambitious, or shocking, or uplifting, and deal with that, for that is all you can deal with well.

"To each according to his needs; from each according to his powers", in fact. Personally the kind of poetry I should like to write but can't is "the thoughts of a wise man in the speech of the common people".

The Highway, December 1936

Adventures in the Air

High Failure. By John Grierson. Hodge. 12s. 6d.

Perhaps we should say at once that the author of *High Failure* is neither the film producer nor the murderer. If talent consists in knowing that you prefer doing A to B, and happiness in doing A, then Mr Grierson is a very talented and happy young man. A Christmas present of 10,000 things a Bright Boy can do decided his career at the age of 15, and since then nothing has been able to stop it. Not even the Army machine: sent to India to learn aerial photography, he simply flew away. His first trip to the Arctic got no further than Iceland, and all the cash was spent. In order to raise money and to learn more about flying he spent a winter flying round Europe giving demonstrations of the Marconi homing apparatus. Luckily for adventurers there is always the Press, so finally he was able to start again with a new but still comparatively diminutive machine. Again he smashed a float at Reykjavik, but came back to England and got another: then he got lost on the Ice Cap, then he turned off the petrol by mistake and got a scare when the engine suddenly failed and so on. Narrow es-capes every five pages, but he gets to Ottawa in the end. The last chapter is a discussion of the possibilities of a civil North Atlantic air route *via* Iceland, Greenland and Baffinland. Mr Grierson argues, very convinc-ingly, that it is quite feasible.

To all students of flying or heroic travel, *High Failure* will scarcely need recommendation, but it has a wider interest than that. It is a portrait of a well-marked and attractive type of human character. It goes without saying that Mr Grierson is a very brave man; he is also the complete high-brow in the real sense of the word, i.e. he sees the whole world in terms of his particular interests of aeroplanes and, like most Scotsmen perhaps, of "the invincible power of nature". Everything else is undersize. He was in Vienna just after the suppression of the Socialists.

> After driving past the commune houses, freshly spattered by bullets and even shell holes, by the recent rioting, I was ushered into a hotel and went straight to bed. . . . Unless I was a jolly sight better next day, in bed I should remain with flying out of the question.

Commander von Grönau contributes a foreword and gives way, we are sorry to see, to a sneer against the "highbrow" who dislikes deserted country, which is as cheap as the latter's sneer against those who do.

The Listener, 2 December 1936

A Novelist's Poems

Visiting the Caves. By William Plomer. Jonathan Cape. 5s.

Mr Plomer is one of the most important novelists of our time. It is difficult therefore for a poet not to be jealous of his incursion into the poetic field, or to betray his jealousy by being patronizing. The truth is that a good novelist must also be a potential poet, but a good poet need not also be a potential novelist. It is possible to write a novel without any feeling for language, but not a good one; but good poetry can be written without any feeling for character.

Mr Plomer's poetry shows all the characteristics of a good novelist. In the first place, a first-class visual imagination. I don't think visual imagery is essential to all poetry, but it is a very valuable poetic gift:

> Fissures appeared in football fields
> And houses in the night collapsed.
> The Thames flowed backward to its source,
> The last trickle seen to disappear
> Swiftly, like an adder to its hole,
> And here and there along the river-bed
> The stranded fish gaped among empty tins;
> Face downward lay the huddled suicides
> Like litter that a riot leaves.

In the second place, a good but not a hypersensitive ear. It is easy to speak, but the difference between speaking and reading is not conspicuous. Thirdly, he has an acute sense of character. The best poems in this book, and they are very good, seem to me "Captain Maru", "John Drew", and "Murder on the Downs", all of which are delineations of character. All of them might have been written as short stories. The imagery of "Murder on the Downs", for example, gains its effects from its close relation to the characters of the lovers:

> . . . she turned
> Dissolving in his frank blue eyes
> All her hope, like aspirin.

He is less successful in the more personal lyrics, like "Visiting the Caves" or "In the Night", by reason of his very virtues as a novelist. A novelist must be painstaking, cautious, objective, non-committal, or he makes an utter fool of himself. Good lyric poetry depends on the opposite qualities, on throwing caution to the winds, accepting the subjective as God-given, wildly taking sides, becoming in fact what Mr Yeats has described as "a foolish passionate man". This is not to say that Mr Plomer's lyrics are bad; they are not. But I don't think they are his kind of country.

There is far too little modern poetry with a sense of character, and from a writer who can write with the power of the conclusion of "Captain Maru", we can only hope that we shall hear more and often:

> And now he has appeared to someone in a dream
> Or rather a nightmare, menacing, a giant,
> With no back to his head, uttering a taunt—
> It is the challenge of his race, the short man scorned
> Not satisfied with power, but mad for more.

Poetry, January 1937

Crime Tales and Puzzles

Murder in the Family. By James Ronald. Bodley Head. 7s. 6d.
A Puzzle for Fools. By Patrick Quentin. Gollancz. 7s. 6d.

I have forgotten how many possible plots there are said to be, but they are few. Under the stimulus of competition the detective story has developed many mutations, of which at least two are now as important as the original parental stock. These are, to borrow a terminology from the film studio, the "Documentary Murder" and the "Murder on Location". A characteristic feature of both is that the main interest of the story does not lie in the detection of the murderer.

The Documentary Murder, of which Mr Francis Iles is the recognised master, is the realistic study of the characters involved in a murder, frequently of the murderer himself, the actual murder being only the crisis which reveals the characters of the actors. In the Murder on Location, which most people will associate at once with Miss Dorothy Sayers, the murder provides an excuse for the investigation of some unusual and interesting activity or form of social life.

Murder in the Family, for instance, is a documentary murder. The Osborne family is the kind of suburban family we all know and like. The self-sacrificing parents, the one ugly but devoted rough diamond of a maid, the charming children with their various interests in motor-bikes, or clothes, or books. Their Uncle Simon, a lovable waster who drinks and writes penny dreadfuls, and their detestable Aunt Octavia, mean, rich and domineering, are equally familiar, and all too common also the situation in which Stephen Osborne finds himself when he is sacked from his office during the slump after 25 years' service.

In despair he turns for help to Octavia, who has come down with her companion on one of her periodical and dreaded visits, but she, who has always hated his marriage, refuses to help. The unusual and terrifying thing now happens, for Aunt Octavia is found strangled in the drawing-room, and the deed must have been done while the 19-year-old Anne was actually sitting there reading *Henry V*.

The rest of the book is a study of what ordinary decent people who get involved in a murder case must suffer from neighbours, schoolmates and newspapers. The story ends happily but Mr Ronald describes their sufferings so convincingly that I found myself several times deeply moved. With the exception of Aunt Octavia and a man in the train, there is not a single unpleasant character in the book, and to those who appreciate a careful portrait of a very charming family, *Murder in the Family* may be confidently recommended.

The interest of *A Puzzle for Fools* is just the opposite. Instead of taking the people we meet every day, Mr Quentin selects the most abnormal characters he can find; the scene is laid in a high-class sanatorium in America. Instead of feeling "surely none of these people could be murderers," we feel, "Well, any one of them might have done it."

The story is told by one of the inmates, a young theatrical producer called Duluth, who is being cured of dipsomania, a reaction to seeing his girl burnt in a theatre fire. All is not well in the sanatorium. Mysterious voices are heard, patients are not getting on as well as they should, and matters come to a head when one of the masseurs is found strangled in a strait jacket, and a little later Mr Lavibee, a steel magnate, who has entrusted the remnants of his fortune to Dr Lenz, the head of the sanatorium, is stabbed during a cinema show.

The mental condition of the patients makes police interrogation almost impossible, and Dr Lenz, partly perhaps for therapeutic reasons, asks Duluth to keep his eyes and ears open, a task in which he is assisted by the elegant Geddes, another patient suffering from narcolepsy, or sleeping attacks.

I do not think the dénouement is as unexpected as the jacket claims, but all the characters, whether of the patients like the Bostonian kleptomaniac, Miss Powell, or of staff like the slightly sinister Dr Moreno, are excellently drawn, and *A Puzzle for Fools* gives a vivid picture of what life must be like in such an institute.

The Daily Telegraph, 5 January 1937

LETTERS FROM ICELAND

Leaving Hraensnef

Letters from Iceland

BY W. H. AUDEN
AND LOUIS MACNEICE

[1936]

TO
GEORGE AUGUSTUS AUDEN

PREFACE

A travel book owes so little to the writers, and so much to the people they meet, that a full and fair acknowledgment on the part of the former is impossible.

We must beg those hundreds of anonymous Icelanders, farmers, fishermen, busmen, children, etc., who are the real authors of this book to accept collectively our gratitude. In particular we should like to thank The Icelandic Shipping Co., The Stat-Tourist Bureau, Mr and Mrs Erikur Benedictzon, Mr Olafur Briem, Mr Ragnar Jonasson, Professor Sigardur Nordal and Professor Arni Pāllsson of Reykjavik University, Dr Jonas Lárusson and Dr Gislisson of the Studentagardur, Mr and Mrs Kristian Andreirsson, Mr Stefan Stefansson, Mr Snaebjorn Jonsson, Mr and Mrs Little, Mr Atli Olafson, Mr Halldor Laxness, Mr Tomas Gudmundsson, Dr Sorenson, Mr Thorbjorn Thordarson, Dr Kristiansson of Saudakrökur, Mr Bjarkans of Akureyri, Mr Gerry Pāllsson, our two guides Stengrimur and Ari (we never found out their other name), Mr Joachimsson of Isafjordur, Mr Gudmundur Hagalin, and Dr Sveinsson and family, to whom we must also apologise for entirely destroying a bed.

Lastly we must express our gratitude to Professor E. V. Gordon for invaluable introductions and advice, to Mr Frazer Hoyland for three photographs and much else, and to Mr Michael Yates for his company and the use of his diary.

W.H.A.
L.M.

CONTENTS

ILLUSTRATIONS

            Photograph by W. F. Hoyland

Diagrams

CHAPTER I
Letter to Lord Byron
Part I

Excuse, my lord, the liberty I take
    In thus addressing you. I know that you
Will pay the price of authorship and make
    The allowances an author has to do.
    A poet's fan-mail will be nothing new.
And then a lord—Good Lord, you must be peppered,
Like Gary Cooper, Coughlin, or Dick Sheppard,

With notes from perfect strangers starting, "Sir,
    I liked your lyrics, but *Childe Harold*'s trash",
"My daughter writes, should I encourage her?"
    Sometimes containing frank demands for cash,
    Sometimes sly hints at a platonic pash,
And sometimes, though I think this rather crude,
The correspondent's photo in the rude.

And as for manuscripts—by every post . . .
    I can't improve on Pope's shrill indignation,
But hope that it will please his spiteful ghost
    To learn the use in culture's propagation
    Of modern methods of communication;
New roads, new rails, new contacts, as we know
From documentaries by the G.P.O.

For since the British Isles went Protestant
    A church confession is too high for most.
But still confession is a human want,
    So Englishmen must make theirs now by post
    And authors hear them over breakfast toast.
For, failing them, there's nothing but the wall
Of public lavatories on which to scrawl.

So if ostensibly I write to you
    To chat about your poetry or mine,
There're many other reasons; though it's true
    That I have, at the age of twenty-nine
    Just read *Don Juan* and I found it fine.

I read it on the boat to Reykjavik
Except when eating or asleep or sick.

The fact is, I'm in Iceland all alone
   —MacKenzie's prints are not unlike the scene—
Ich hab' zu Haus, ein Gra, ein Gramophone.
      Les gosses anglais aiment beaucoup les machines.
     Το καλον. glubit. che . . . what this may mean
I do not know, but rather like the sound
Of foreign languages like Ezra Pound.

And home is miles away, and miles away
    No matter who, and I am quite alone
And cannot understand what people say,
    But like a dog must guess it by the tone;
    At any language other than my own
I'm no great shakes, and here I've found no tutor
Nor sleeping lexicon to make me cuter.

The thought of writing came to me to-day
    (I like to give these facts of time and space);
The bus was in the desert on its way
    From Mothrudalur to some other place:
    The tears were streaming down my burning face;
I'd caught a heavy cold in Akureyri,
And lunch was late and life looked very dreary.

Professor Housman was I think the first
    To say in print how very stimulating
The little ills by which mankind is cursed,
    The colds, the aches, the pains are to creating;
    Indeed one hardly goes too far in stating
That many a flawless lyric may be due
Not to a lover's broken heart, but 'flu.

But still a proper explanation's lacking;
    Why write to you? I see I must begin
Right at the start when I was at my packing.
    The extra pair of socks, the airtight tin
    Of China tea, the anti-fly were in;
I asked myself what sort of books I'd read
In Iceland, if I ever felt the need.

I can't read Jefferies on the Wiltshire Downs,
    Nor browse on limericks in a smoking-room;

Who would try Trollope in cathedral towns,
    Or Marie Stopes inside his mother's womb?
    Perhaps you feel the same beyond the tomb.
Do the celestial highbrows only care
For works on Clydeside, Fascists, or Mayfair?

In certain quarters I had heard a rumour
    (For all I know the rumour's only silly)
That Icelanders have little sense of humour.
    I knew the country was extremely hilly,
    The climate unreliable and chilly;
So looking round for something light and easy
I pounced on you as warm and civilisé.

There is one other author in my pack:
    For some time I debated which to write to.
Which would least likely send my letter back?
    But I decided that I'd give a fright to
    Jane Austen if I wrote when I'd no right to,
And share in her contempt the dreadful fates
Of Crawford, Musgrove, and of Mr Yates.

Then she's a novelist. I don't know whether
    You will agree, but novel writing is
A higher art than poetry altogether
    In my opinion, and success implies
    Both finer character and faculties.
Perhaps that's why real novels are as rare
As winter thunder or a polar bear.

The average poet by comparison
    Is unobservant, immature, and lazy.
You must admit, when all is said and done,
    His sense of other people's very hazy,
    His moral judgments are too often crazy,
A slick and easy generalisation
Appeals too well to his imagination.

I must remember, though, that you were dead
    Before the four great Russians lived, who brought
The art of novel writing to a head;
    The help of Boots had not been sought.
    But now the art for which Jane Austen fought,

Under the right persuasion bravely warms
And is the most prodigious of the forms.

She was not an unshockable blue-stocking;
        If shades remain the characters they were,
No doubt she still considers you as shocking.
        But tell Jane Austen, that is, if you dare,
        How much her novels are beloved down here.
She wrote them for posterity, she said;
'Twas rash, but by posterity she's read.

You could not shock her more than she shocks me;
        Beside her Joyce seems innocent as grass.
It makes me most uncomfortable to see
        An English spinster of the middle-class
        Describe the amorous effects of "brass",
Reveal so frankly and with such sobriety
The economic basis of society.

So it is you who is to get this letter.
        The experiment may not be a success.
There're many others who could do it better,
        But I shall not enjoy myself the less.
        Shaw of the Air Force said that happiness
Comes in absorption: he was right, I know it;
Even in scribbling to a long-dead poet.

Every exciting letter has enclosures,
        And so shall this—a bunch of photographs,
Some out of focus, some with wrong exposures,
        Press cuttings, gossip, maps, statistics, graphs;
        I don't intend to do the thing by halves.
I'm going to be very up to date indeed.
It is a collage that you're going to read.

I want a form that's large enough to swim in,
        And talk on any subject that I choose,
From natural scenery to men and women,
        Myself, the arts, the European news:
        And since she's on a holiday, my Muse
Is out to please, find everything delightful
And only now and then be mildly spiteful.

Ottava Rima would, I know, be proper,
        The proper instrument on which to pay

My compliments, but I should come a cropper;
        Rhyme-royal's difficult enough to play.
    But if no classics as in Chaucer's day,
At least my modern pieces shall be cheery
Like English bishops on the Quantum Theory.

Light verse, poor girl, is under a sad weather;
        Except by Milne and persons of that kind
She's treated as démodé altogether.
        It's strange and very unjust to my mind
        Her brief appearances should be confined,
Apart from Belloc's *Cautionary Tales*,
To the more bourgeois periodicals.

"The fascination of what's difficult,"
        The wish to do what one's not done before,
Is, I hope, proper to Quicunque Vult,
        The proper card to show at Heaven's door.
        "Gerettet" not "Gerichtet" be the Law,
Et cetera, et cetera. O curse,
That is the flattest line in English verse.

Parnassus after all is not a mountain,
        Reserved for A.1. climbers such as you;
It's got a park, it's got a public fountain.
        The most I ask is leave to share a pew
        With Bradford or with Cottam, that will do:
To pasture my few silly sheep with Dyer
And picnic on the lower slopes with Prior.

A publisher's an author's greatest friend,
        A generous uncle, or he ought to be.
(I'm sure we hope it pays him in the end.)
        I love my publishers and they love me,
        At least they paid a very handsome fee
To send me here. I've never heard a grouse
Either from Russell Square or Random House.

But now I've got uncomfortable suspicions,
        I'm going to put their patience out of joint.
Though it's in keeping with the best traditions
        For Travel Books to wander from the point
        (There is no other rhyme except anoint),
They well may charge me with—I've no defences—
Obtaining money under false pretences.

I know I've not the least chance of survival
        Beside the major travellers of the day.
I am no Lawrence who, on his arrival,
        Sat down and typed out all he had to say;
        I am not even Ernest Hemingway.
I shall not run to a two-bob edition,
So just won't enter for the competition.

And even here the steps I flounder in
        Were worn by most distinguished boots of old.
Dasent and Morris and Lord Dufferin,
        Hooker and men of that heroic mould
        Welcome me icily into the fold;
I'm not like Peter Fleming an Etonian,
But, if I'm Judas, I'm an old Oxonian.

The Haig Thomases are at Myvatn now,
        At Hvitavatn and at Vatnajökull
Cambridge research goes on, I don't know how:
        The shades of Asquith and of Auden Skökull
        Turn in their coffins a three-quarter circle
To see their son, upon whose help they reckoned,
Being as frivolous as Charles the Second.

So this, my opening chapter, has to stop
        With humbly begging everybody's pardon.
From Faber first in case the book's a flop,
        Then from the critics lest they should be hard on
        The author when he leads them up the garden,
Last from the general public he must beg
Permission now and then to pull their leg.

END OF PART I

CHAPTER II

Journey to Iceland

A letter to Christopher Isherwood, Esq.

And the traveller hopes: "Let me be far from any
Physician"; And the ports have names for the sea;
    The citiless, the corroding, the sorrow;
    And North means to all: "Reject!"

And the great plains are for ever where the cold fish is hunted,
And everywhere; the light birds flicker and flaunt;
    Under the scolding flag the lover
    Of islands may see at last,

Faintly, his limited hope; and he nears the glitter
Of glaciers, the sterile immature mountains intense
    In the abnormal day of this world, a river's
    Fan-like polyp of sand.

Then let the good citizen here find natural marvels:
The horse-shoe ravine, the issue of steam from a cleft
    In the rock, and rocks, and waterfalls brushing the
    Rocks, and among the rocks birds.

And the student of prose and conduct, places to visit;
The site of a church where a bishop was put in a bag,
    The bath of a great historian, the rock where
    An outlaw dreaded the dark.

Remember the doomed man thrown by his horse and crying;
"Beautiful is the hillside, I will not go";
    The old woman confessing: "He that I loved the
    Best, to him I was worst",

For Europe is absent. This is an island and therefore
Unreal. And the steadfast affections of its dead may be bought
    By those whose dreams accuse them of being
    Spitefully alive, and the pale

From too much passion of kissing feel pure in its deserts.
Can they? For the world is, and the present, and the lie.
    And the narrow bridge over the torrent,
    And the small farm under the crag

Are the natural setting for the jealousies of a province;
And the weak vow of fidelity is formed by the cairn;
   And within the indigenous figure on horseback
   On the bridle path down by the lake

The blood moves also by crooked and furtive inches,
Asks all your questions: "Where is the homage? When
   Shall justice be done? O who is against me?
   Why am I always alone?"

Present then the world to the world with its mendicant shadow;
Let the suits be flash, the Minister of Commerce insane;
   Let jazz be bestowed on the huts, and the beauty's
   Set cosmopolitan smile.

For our time has no favourite suburb; no local features
Are those of the young for whom all wish to care;
   The promise is only a promise, the fabulous
   Country impartially far.

Tears fall in all the rivers. Again the driver
Pulls on his gloves and in a blinding snowstorm starts
   Upon his deadly journey; and again the writer
   Runs howling to his art.

Dear Christopher,

Thank you for your letter. No, you were wrong. I did not write: "the *ports* have names for the sea" but "the *poets* have names for the sea". However, as so often before, the mistake seems better than the original idea, so I'll leave it. Now, as to your questions:

1. "I can't quite picture your arrival. What was your impression of Reykjavik harbour? Is there any attempt to make the visitor feel that he is arriving at a capital city?"

Not much. There is nothing by the pier but warehouses and piles of agricultural implements under tarpaulin. Most of the town is built of corrugated iron. When we arrived, it was only half-past seven and we had to wait outside the harbour, because the Icelandic dockhands won't get up early. The town was hidden in low-lying mist, with the tops of the mountains showing above it. My first impression of the town was Lutheran, drab and remote. The quay was crowded with loungers, passively interested, in caps. They seemed to have been there a long time. There were no screaming hawkers or touts. Even the children didn't speak.

2. "What does R. look like?"

There is no good building stone. The new suburban houses are built of concrete in sombre colours. The three chief buildings are the Roman

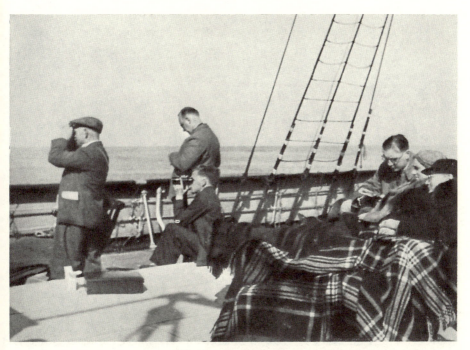

The Lover of Islands

Then let the good Citizen here find natural Marvels

And the weak Vow of Fidelity is formed by the Cairn

Catholic church, the (unfinished) theatre and the students' hostel, which looks like waiting-rooms of an airport. There is a sports ground, with a running-track and tennis courts, where the young men play most of the night. In the middle of the town there is a shallow artificial lake full of terns and wild duck. The town peters out into flat rusty-brown lava-fields, scattered shacks surrounded by wire-fencing, stockfish drying on washing-lines and a few white hens. Further down the coast, the lava is dotted with what look like huge laundry-baskets; these are really compact heaps of drying fish covered with tarpaulin. The weather changes with extraordinary rapidity: one moment the rain blots out everything, the next, the sun is shining behind clouds, filling the air with an intense lumi-nous light in which you can see for miles, so that every detail of the cone-shaped mountains stands out needle-sharp against an orange sky. There is one peak which is always bright pink.

3. "What do the Icelandic authors write about?"

Mainly about their own country, the emotional lives of the farmers and fishermen and their struggle with nature.

4. "I suppose the originals of the fiction-characters are generally well-known?"

Yes, often. I sometimes heard complaints; for example, that Halldor Laxness makes the farmers more unpleasant than they really are. But, as far as I could gather, there are no laws of libel.

5. "Isn't the audience of the Icelandic novelist very small?"

Relatively to the size of the population, it is larger than in most coun-tries. Most of the novels of any standing are translated into German and the other Scandinavian languages.

6. "Can he make a living?"

The best-known authors and painters receive support from the state, without any obligations as to output. People (in all cases, right wing) occa-sionally complained to me that politics influenced the awards; but I couldn't discover any authors of merit who had been neglected.

7. "Tell me about the young Icelander. What does he think about? What are his ambitions?"

As a race, I don't think the Icelanders are very ambitious. A few of the professional classes would like to get to Europe; most would prefer to stay where they are and make a certain amount of money. Compared with most countries, there is little unemployment in Iceland. My general im-pression of the Icelander is that he is realistic, in a petit bourgeois sort of way, unromantic and unidealistic. Unlike the German, he shows no ro-mantic longing for the south, and I can't picture him in a uniform. The attitude to the sagas is like that of the average Englishman to Shake-speare; but I only found one man, a painter, who dared to say he thought they were "rather rough". The difficulty of getting any job at all in many

European countries tends to make the inhabitants irresponsible and therefore ready for fanatical patriotism; but the Icelander is seldom irresponsible, because irresponsibility in a farmer or fisherman would mean ruin.

8. "What about the sex-life?"

Uninhibited. There is little stigma attached to illegitimacy. Bastards are brought up on an equal footing with legitimate children of the family. Before communications became better, there was a good deal of inbreeding. A farmer was pointed out to me who had married his niece, by special permission of the King of Denmark. Homosexuality is said to be rare. There is a good deal of venereal disease in the coastal towns, which has lately begun to spread inland. I know nothing about birth-control propaganda: there seems to be no particular drive to increase the population of the island. Emigration to America, which was common at the beginning of the century, has now stopped.

9. "Is there a typical kind of Icelandic humour?"

They are very fond of satirical lampoons. As you would expect on a small island, most of the jokes are about prominent personalities and difficult to understand without inside knowledge. There is a weekly comic paper called the *Spegelin,* which is more like *Simplicissimus* than like *Punch.* I saw no evidence of the kind of brutal practical joke practised in the sagas.

10. "What feelings did your visit give you about life on small islands?"

If you have no particular intellectual interests or ambitions and are content with the company of your family and friends, then life on Iceland must be very pleasant, because the inhabitants are friendly, tolerant and sane. They are genuinely proud of their country and its history, but without the least trace of hysterical nationalism. I always found that they welcomed criticism. But I had the feeling, also, that for myself it was already too late. We are all too deeply involved with Europe to be able, or even to wish to escape. Though I am sure you would enjoy a visit as much as I did, I think that, in the long run, the Scandinavian sanity would be too much for you, as it is for me. The truth is, we are both only really happy living among lunatics.

W.

CHAPTER III

Letter to Graham and Anne Shepard

Reykjavik.
August 16th, 1936.

To Graham and Anna: from the Arctic Gate
I send this letter to N.W.8,
Hoping that Town is not the usual mess,
That Pauli is rid of worms, the new cook a success.
I have got here, you see, without being sick
On a boat of eight hundred tons to Reykjavik.
Came second-class—no air but many men;
Having seen the first-class crowd would do the same again.
Food was good, mutton and bits of fishes,
A smart line-up of Scandinavian dishes—
Beet, cheese, ham, jam, smoked salmon, gaffalbitar,
Sweet cucumber, German sausage, and Rye-Vita.
So I came here to the land the Romans missed,
Left for the Irish saint and the Viking colonist.
But what am I doing here? Qu'allais-je faire
Among these volcanic rocks and this grey air?
Why go north when Cyprus and Madeira
De jure if not de facto are much nearer?
The reason for hereness seems beyond conjecture,
There are no trees or trains or architecture,
Fruits and greens are insufficient for health
And culture is limited by lack of wealth,
The tourist sights have nothing like Stonehenge,
The literature is all about revenge.
And yet I like it if only because this nation
Enjoys a scarcity of population
And cannot rise to many bores or hacks
Or paupers or poor men paying Super-Tax.
Yet further, if you can stand it, I will set forth
The obscure but powerful ethics of Going North.
Morris did it before, dropping the frills and fuss,
Harps and arbours, Tristram and Theseus,
For a land of rocks and sagas. And certain unknown
Old Irish hermits, holy skin and bone,
Camped on these crags in order to forget
Their blue-black cows in the Kerry pastures wet.

Those Latin-chattering margin-illuminating monks
Fled here from home without kit-bags or trunks
To mortify their flesh—but we must mortify
Our blowsy intellects before we die,
Who feed our brains on backchat and self-pity
And always need a noise, the radio or the city,
Traffic and changing lights, crashing the amber,
Always on the move and so do not remember
The necessity of the silence of the islands,
The glacier floating in the distance out of existence,
The need to grip and grapple the adversary,
Knuckle on stony knuckle, to dot and carry
One and carry one and not give up the hunt
Till we have pinned the Boyg down to a point.
In England one forgets—in each performing troupe
Forgets what one has lost, there is no room to stoop
And look along the ground, one cannot see the ground
For the feet of the crowd, and the lost is never found.
I dropped something, I think, but I am not sure what
And cannot say if it mattered much or not,
So let us get on or we shall be late, for soon
The shops will close and the rush-hour be on.
This is the fret that makes us cat-like stretch
And then contract the fingers, gives the itch
To open the French window into the rain,
Walk out and never be seen at home again.
But where to go? No oracle for us,
Bible or Baedeker, can tell the terminus.
The songs of jazz have told us of a moon country
And we like to dream of a heat which is never sultry,
Melons to eat, champagne to drink, and a lazy
Music hour by hour depetalling the daisy.
Then Medici manuscripts have told of places
Where common sense was wedded to the graces,
Doric temples and olive-trees and such,
But broken marble no longer goes for much.
And there are some who scorn this poésie de départs
And say "Escape by staying where you are;
A man is what he thinks he is and can
Find happiness within." How nice to be born a man.
The tourist in space or time, emotion or sensation,
Meets many guides but none have the proper orientation.
We are not changing ground to escape from facts

The Student of Prose
and Conduct

Fifteenth-century
Screen in Museum

But rather to find them. This complex world exacts
Hard work of simplifying; to get its focus
You have to stand outside the crowd and caucus.
This all sounds somewhat priggish. You and I
Know very well the immediate reason why
I am in Iceland. Three months ago or so
Wystan said that he was planning to go
To Iceland to write a book and would I come too;
And I said yes, having nothing better to do.
But all the same we never make any choice
On such a merely mechanical stimulus.
The match is not the cause of fire, so pause
And look for the formal as well as the efficient cause.
Aristotle's pedantic phraseology
Serves better than common sense or hand to mouth psychology.
"ἔσχε τὴν φύσιν" —"found its nature"; the crude
Embryo rummages every latitude
Looking for itself, its nature, its final pattern,
Till the fairy godmother's wand touches the slattern
And turns her to a princess for a moment
Beyond definition or professorial comment.
We find our nature daily or try to find it,
The old flame gutters, leaves red flames behind it.
An interval of tuning and screwing and then
The symphony restarts, the creature lives again—
Blake's arabesques of fire; the subtle creature
Swings on Ezekiel's wheels, finding its nature.
In short we must keep moving to keep pace
Or else drop into Limbo, the dead place.
I have come north, gaily running away
From the grinding gears, the change from day to day,
The creaks of the familiar room, the smile
Of the cruel clock, the bills upon the file,
The excess of books and cushions, the high heels
That walk the street, the news, the newsboys' yells,
The flag-days and the cripple's flapping sleeve,
The ambushes of sex, the passion to retrieve
Significance from the river of passing people,
The attempt to climb the ever-climbing steeple
And no one knows what is at the top of it,
All is a raffle for caps which may not fit,
But all take tickets, keep moving; still we may
Move off from movement or change it for a day;

Here is a different rhythm, the juggled balls
Hang in the air—the pause before the soufflé falls.
Here we can take a breath, sit back, admire
Stills from the film of life, the frozen fire;
Among these rocks can roll upon the tongue
Morsels of thought, not jostled by the throng,
Or morsels of un-thought, which is still better,
(Thinking these days makes a suburban clatter).
Here we can practise forgetfulness without
A sense of guilt, fear of the tout and lout,
And here—but Wystan has butted in again
To say we must go out in the frightful rain
To see a man about a horse and so
I shall have to stop. For we soon intend to go
Around the Langjökull, a ten days' ride,
Gumboots and stockfish. Probably you'll deride
This sissy onslaught on the open spaces.
I can see the joke myself; however the case is
Not to be altered, but please remember us
So high up here in this vertiginous
Crow's-nest of the earth. Perhaps you'll let us know
If anything happens in the world below?

L.M.

CHAPTER IV

For Tourists

Passports, Customs, etc.

No passports are required for Iceland. There are duties on most of the customary articles but the customs examination on board is courteous and not vigorous.

Currency

Icelandic currency is reckoned in kronur and öre, 100 öre to the kronur. The official rate of exchange in Iceland in summer 1936 was 22.15 kr. to the pound. But in Hull you could get 24.50. It is better therefore not to change money officially. Owing to the adverse trade balance it is extremely difficult for individual Icelanders to get English currency, and English people who have friends or acquaintances in Iceland will be doing them a great service if they change their money with them.

Travellers' cheques can of course be used, but in my experience, it is wiser to take cash and change it as you want it, so that you are not landed at the end of your visit with a lot of Icelandic currency which is difficult to dispose of.

Clothes and Equipment

(1) The most essential article is a pair of stout gumboots, but with smooth soles or they get caught in the stirrups. Riding-boots will be ruined and will not keep you dry. At least two pairs of socks should be worn inside the gumboots. A pair of walking shoes and a pair of slippers or gym-shoes will complete the foot-gear.

(2) For riding, either riding-breeches or plus-fours let down to the ankle.

(3) Oilskin trousers in one piece reaching to the waist.

(4) A long oilskin coat coming down well below the knees. A cape is useless.

(5) An oilskin sou'-wester as well as any other head-gear.

(6) A pair of warm but flexible gloves.

(7) As far as general clothing is concerned, the danger is of putting on too little rather than too much. On expeditions I always wore flannel trousers and pyjamas under my riding breeches, and two shirts and a golf-jacket and a coat under my oilskin. (So W.H.A. I did not wear nearly as much as this. L.M.)

(8) For expeditions into the interior, a tent, of course, is required. Make sure that your sleeping-bag is warm enough. It is wise perhaps to take a compass, but the mountains are sometimes magnetic and derange them. Air-tight tins for perishable food should be taken, and make sure that your stove is strong enough to stand up to the jolting it will get on a pack horse. Mine fell to pieces. In dry weather the lava dust can be very tiresome to the eyes, and it is a good thing to take a pair of tinted glasses. Finally, whether camping or not, a roll of toilet paper is invaluable.

(9) Everyone has their pet medicines, but from personal experience I would recommend chlorodyne as the best stuff to take in cases of internal disorder. Before I went, I heard a lot about mosquitoes, and went prepared. This is unnecessary. There are, I believe, mosquitoes at Myvatn, but elsewhere one need have no anxiety. In cases of emergency there are reliable doctors and dentists.

Maps, etc.

The best general map of the whole island is Daniel Bruun's, which gives all roads and footpaths and also camping sites. The whole island is being mapped in 8 sheets on a scale of a little over four miles to the inch. So far four sheets have appeared: South-West, Mid-West, North-West, and Mid-

North. There are also special larger-scale sheets of special areas, like Thingvellir and Myvatn. All the inhabited part of the island is to be done on a scale of 1–100,000 but only some have appeared. All these maps can be bought in Reykjavik. The best guide book is *Iceland for Tourists* by Stefan Stefansson.

Boats to Iceland

The Icelandic Steam Shipping Company run two boats, the *Gullfoss* and the *Bruarfoss*, from Leith, and two, the *Godafoss* and the *Dettifoss*, from Hull. As far as the second-class accommodation goes, it is better on the Hull boats and best on the *Dettifoss*. Fare from Hull to anywhere in Iceland, £4 10s. plus 5 kr. a day for food. The latter is nothing to write home about but eatable. The voyage should last 4½ days, but delays in starting and on the way are quite probable. In addition, of course, there are cruise boats like the Danish *Primula*, with first-class accommodation only, which also call at the Faroes. *Primula* fare: £8, plus 8s. a day for food. An alternative route, for those who like the sea, is to go to Bergen and take a Norwegian boat from there, either the *Lyra* which goes to the Faroes and Reykjavik, or the *Nova* which goes direct to Eskifjördur and then slowly northward round the coast to Reykjavik. During the season it is wise to book both the outward and the return journey some time beforehand as accommodation is limited.

The Icelandic boats go on from Reykjavik west and north via Isafjördur to Akureyri and then back to Reykjavik.

Reykjavik

There is not much to be said for Reykjavik. The six hotels are The Borg, The Island, The Skjalbreid, the Vik, the Hekla, and the Studentagardur. The Borg is called a first-class hotel but is not the kind of thing you like if you like that kind of thing; still it is the only place where you can get a drink. As far as rooms, price, and general comfort go, unquestionably the best place to stay is the Studentagardur, though I think the food there could be better. Price 10 kr. a day inclusive (except for laundry) plus 10% for service. Single meals (lunch or dinner) cost from 2.50 kr. to 6 kr. There is a café in the Ausserstraeti where you can get decent cream cakes. The Borg has a jazz band and dancing every evening. There are two cinemas and two quite decent bookshops. Arrangements for expeditions, guides, horses, etc., are made through the Stat-Tourist bureau near the harbour, but you should certainly visit as well, Stefan Stefansson, c/o Landsbanki, who speaks excellent English and is a mine of information. In the museum (open Wednesdays and Sundays) there is a remarkable painting on wood of the Last Supper which is worth seeing, and there is a collection of Icelandic paintings in the Parliament house. The

Einar Jonsson museum is not for the fastidious. The only other sights are Olli Maggadon at the harbour, Oddur Sigurgeirsson anywhere, Kjarval the painter, and Arni Pállsson the professor of Icelandic history.

Board and Lodging

Nearly every farm will put you up, and though the standard of comfort of course varies, they will all do their best to make you comfortable. Prices from 4 to 6 kr. a day inclusive. In the N.W. it is a little cheaper. At a farm in the Isafjördardjup, for example, I paid 10 kr. for three days including riding. Single meals (lunch and dinner), 2 kr. In the summer many of the schools in the country are turned into hotels, e.g. Laugarvatn, Reykholt, Holar, Hallorastadur. These are generally comfortable with good food. Prices from 10 kr. a day at Laugarvatn, the Gleneagles of Iceland, to 5 kr. inclusive. At Laugarvatn and Reykholt there are hot baths. There are also inns at Thingvellir and Geysir, and various other places, which are marked on the 4 miles to the inch maps. In the interior there are several saelihus or mountain huts, which again vary greatly in size and standard. These and camping sites are marked on Bruun's map. With regard to the other towns besides Reykjavik, there are three hotels in Akureyri, the nicest of which is the Gullfoss. In Isafjördur you can stay at the Salvation Army Hostel. Elsewhere difficulty and discomfort is to be expected. I recommend any single tourist who finds himself in Seydisfjördur to go to the old women's almshouses, where I was myself extremely comfortable.

Buses

There are excellent bus services to all parts of the island, except the North-West and the South-East, and the fares are very reasonable. There are, for example, four buses a week to Akureyri, a distance of about 300 kilometres, taking two days if you go by bus all the way, and one day if you take the motor ship *Laxfoss* to Borgarnes or Akranes. Single fare 30 kr. It is wise to book seats a day or two beforehand, and if staying on a bus route to telephone through to a previous stop. Where there are no official buses, there are often milk-cars which will take you very slowly but cheaply. Those who are car-sick will have, I'm afraid, a rough time. (The drivers are excellent.)

Horses and Guides

There are very few places in Iceland where it is pleasant to walk, and for long expeditions guides are absolutely necessary if you don't want to lose your horses or get drowned in a river. Besides, the farmers won't lend their horses without one. The price of a pony for a day varies from 3 kr. to 6 kr. in the fashionable places. The best ponies come from Skargafjördur in the North. For long journeys with a large party the price works out something like this:

An old Farm

A new School

The natural setting
for the Jealousies of
a Province

Grylla

Riding pony, 4 kr. per day—1 kr. for riding saddle		5 kr.
Pack pony, 3 kr. per day—2 kr. for pack saddle		5 kr.
Spare ponies, 3 kr. per day each		3 kr.
1st Guide per day		15 kr.
2nd Guide per day		10 kr.

For a party of seven plus two guides we needed seventeen horses, nine riding, five pack, and three spare.

I am told that some guides object to hobbling the horses at night. Ours hobbled them, but another party which did not take this precaution lost a whole day and one pony. On some expeditions fodder has to be carried.

Language

It is not to be expected that all the farmers will speak English, but a great many do speak a little, and an English-speaking guide can always be found, if you want one. German is also useful. There is a phrase-book for those who find that kind of thing any use, and for the conscientious there is Zoëga's *English-Icelandic Dictionary* (expensive and full of non-existent English words), and Snaebjorn Jonsson's *Primer of Modern Icelandic.*

Food

In the larger hotels in Reykjavik you will of course get ordinary European food, but in the farms you will only get what there is, which is on the whole rather peculiar.

Breakfast: (9.0 a.m.). If you stay in a farm this will be brought to you in bed. Coffee, bread and cheese, and small cakes. Coffee, which is drunk all through the day—I must have drunk about 1,500 cups in three months—is generally good. There is white bread, brown bread, rock-hard but quite edible, and unleavened rye bread like cake. The ordinary cheese is like a strong Dutch and good. There is also a brown sweet cheese, like the Norwegian. I don't like cakes so I never ate any, but other people say they are good.

Lunch and Dinner: (12 noon and 7 p.m.). If you are staying anywhere, lunch is the chief meal, but farmers are always willing to give you a chief meal at any time of the day or night that you care. (I once had supper at 11 p.m.)

Soups: Many of these are sweet and very unfortunate. I remember three with particular horror, one of sweet milk and hard macaroni, one tasting of hot marzipan, and one of scented hair oil. (But there is a good sweet soup, raspberry coloured, made of bilberry. L.M.)

Fish: Dried fish is a staple food in Iceland. This should be shredded with the fingers and eaten with butter. It varies in toughness. The tougher kind tastes like toe-nails, and the softer kind like the skin off the soles of one's feet.

In districts where salmon are caught, or round the coast, you get excellent fish, the grilled salmon particularly.

Meat: This is practically confined to mutton in various forms. The Danes have influenced Icelandic cooking, and to no advantage. Meat is liable to be served up in glutinous and half-cold lumps, covered with tasteless gravy. At the poorer farms you will only get Hángikyrl, i.e. smoked mutton. This is comparatively harmless when cold as it only tastes like soot, but it would take a very hungry man indeed to eat it hot.

Vegetables: Apart from potatoes, these, in the earlier part of the summer are conspicuous by their absence. Later, however, there are radishes, turnips, carrots, and lettuce in sweet milk. Newish potatoes begin to appear about the end of August. Boiled potatoes are eaten with melted butter, but beware of the browned potatoes, as they are coated in sugar, another Danish barbarism.

Fruit: None, except rhubarb and in the late summer excellent bilberries.

Cold Food: Following the Scandinavian custom, in the hotels, following the hot dish there are a number of dishes of cold meats and fishes eaten with bread and butter. Most of these are good, particularly the pickled herring. Smoked salmon in my opinion is an overrated dish, but it is common for those who appreciate it.

Sweets: The standard sweet is skyr, a cross between Devonshire cream and a cream cheese, which is eaten with sugar and cream. It is very filling but most people like it very much. It is not advisable, however, to take coffee and skyr together just before riding, as it gives you diarrhoea.

Tea: (4 p.m.). Coffee, cakes, and if you are lucky, pancakes with cream. These are wafer-thick and extremely good. Coffee and cake are also often brought you in the evening, about 10 p.m. Those who like tea or cocoa should bring it with them and supervise the making of it themselves.

Food for Expeditions

Bread, butter, cheese and coffee are safe to buy in Iceland. Those who can eat them will find the smoked mutton and dried fish travel well. There is also an excellent tinned and cooked mutton to be bought which is very useful. All chocolate or sweets should be bought in England.

Drink

Apart from coffee and milk and water, there is little to be said for the drink in Iceland, which is just recovering from Prohibition. In Reykjavik you can get drinks at the Borg if you can pay for them. A whisky and soda (Irish whisky is unobtainable) costs 2.25 kr.; and a glass of respectable sherry 1.45 kr. There are also government shops in various places where you can buy bottles furtively over the counter. They close at noon. A bottle of brown sherry cost me 9.50 kr. and a bottle of Spanish brandy

Café North Pole

Farm in the Desert

New Communications

New Contacts

(the only brandy they had) 6.50 kr. The beer is weak and nasty, and the lemonade unspeakable.

Illicit brandy can sometimes be got, and is sometimes insistently offered by friendly farmers, but it is deadly.

Oddities

For the curious there are two Icelandic foods which should certainly be tried. One is Hákarl, which is half-dry, half-rotten shark. This is white inside with a prickly horn rind outside, as tough as an old boot. Owing to the smell it has to be eaten out of doors. It is shaved off with a knife and eaten with brandy. It tastes more like boot-polish than anything else I can think of. The other is Reyngi. This is the tail of the whale, which is pickled in sour milk for a year or so. If you intend to try it, do not visit a whaling station first. Incidentally, talking about pickling in sour milk, the Icelanders also do this to sheeps' udders, and the result is surprisingly very nice.

Tobacco

There is a fairly wide range of choice both of cigarettes and pipe tobaccos in Reykjavik, but in the country nothing is obtainable but Commanders, an English cigarette which seems to be manufactured solely for export to Iceland.

Photography

Agfa and Kodak films can be got in Reykjavik, and sometimes in other towns, but it is not worth risking getting them elsewhere. You can get films developed in Reykjavik, but if you are particular about the results it is better to bring them home. As a complete tyro, it is presumptuous of me to give advice, but from my experience and that of others more competent than I, I think that in Iceland, even if you are using a meter, there is a tendency to over-expose.

Where to go

This of course depends on the individual. Those with special tastes like fishing, ornithology, or geology will know for themselves. Most tourists will presumably want to see Thingvellir and Geysir, but they should not miss Grylla, a small geyser in the South which spouts every two hours. The hearty will want to go to the interior, and a journey round the Langjökull is probably as good as any. Time from 7 to 9 days. Inclusive price for a largish party, a little over £12 a head. For the tough there is Vatnajökull or Askja. For those who like riding for its own sake, it is a little difficult to find large stretches of open flat country. Perhaps the delta of the Markaflot and the Thorsá in the South is the best, though they may find difficulty in getting really good horses there. For those who want to stay quietly in one place there are a number of places. Personally I should recommend either Reykholt in the West or Egilsstadur or Hallorastadur in the East.

If I had a fortnight to spend myself I should go to the North-West, as I think it both the most beautiful and the least visited part of Iceland. You come to Isafjördur by the Icelandic boats from Reykjavik, and move about either by horses or motor-boat. Anyone who does think of going there should get in touch with the British Vice-consul at Isafjördur, Mr Joachimsson, who is extremely kind and efficient.

For Motorists

Those who regard motoring as a convenient means of seeing places and not as an end in itself, and who like a holiday off the beaten track, might do worse than turn their attention towards Iceland. There has been a great deal of road-building since the war and from the map at the end of this book it will be seen that most of the island, except the north-west peninsula, the tract of glacier rivers south-east of the Vatnajökull, and the desert in the centre, can be now reached by car, and indeed along most of the roads there are already bus services. I travelled about largely by bus and am convinced that it is one of the best ways of seeing the country, though I should have preferred being able to stop when and where I liked, and the hire of private cars is very expensive. A road in Iceland, of course, is not always what one knows in England by that name. The roads to Thingvellir and Laugarvatn, those in Borgafirth, and indeed most of the road from Borgarnes to Akureyri, are fairly good third-class English roads.

The road from Husavik to Grimsstadur, on the other hand, consists of two ruts, along which the maximum speed is about 8 kilometres per hour, and the Thingvellir hill on the Thingvellir–Laugarvatn road is barely negotiable. Still cars do go along all these roads without mishap. I am told that they very rarely break a back-axle as they cannot go fast enough to do that, but that spare springs should always be carried. The commonest cars in Iceland are large American ones, mainly Chevrolets, but smaller-powered cars if strongly built are quite adequate, as the majority of the gradients, other than short dips over streams, are less than you would expect in a mountainous country. A high ground clearance is, however, essential. On the better roads the wheel tracks are sunk in loose grit, leaving a raised middle section for horses, and care is needed at higher speeds to avoid skidding. All bridges and nearly all roads are single, and passing another car means stopping.

The Icelanders are all sick in the buses, but a driver told me he had never known an Englishman to be. Practically every farm will put tourists up, and, though of course the accommodation is often limited and primitive, the farmers make every effort to do their best for one. Cars can always be left without anxiety as to their safety or the safety of things left in them, so that it is perfectly possible to combine motoring expeditions with trips on horses to places where motors cannot go. I had no personal experiences of garages, but I am told that there are good ones in Reykjavik and Akureyri. Elsewhere, of course, the driver must do his own repairs. It is unnecessary to carry spare petrol as the maximum distance between pumps is 58 kilometres, but running out of petrol means probably a long walk to the next station and a long ride back. The petrol is B.P. or Shell, price 32 öre per litre (about 1s. 5d. a gallon).

The Icelandic Shipping Company is prepared to ship cars from Hull or Leith. If there are five passengers, the fifth travels free. If there are four, there is no extra charge and so on. On arrival in Iceland, particulars about roads and regulations can be obtained from the Stat-Tourist bureau in Reykjavik, near the harbour. An international driving license is sufficient, and there is no car tax. Outside the towns there is no speed limit, but an average of 30 kilometres an hour is about as much as one can generally manage. Drive on the left.

BIBLIOGRAPHY

General Information
Icelandic Year-Book, *Iceland,* 1930.
Stefan Stefansson: *Iceland for Tourists.*

Language
Snaebjorn Jonsson: *A Primer of Modern Icelandic.*
Zoëga: *Ensk-Islenzk Ordabok; Islenzk-Ensk Ordabok.*

History and Literature
Knut Gjerset: *History of Iceland.*
W. P. Ker: *Epic and Romance; The Dark Ages; Collected Essays.*
Dame Philpot: *Edda and Saga.*
W. G. Craigie: *The Icelandic Sagas.*
Professor G. V. Gordon: *An Introduction to Old Norse; Romance in Iceland.*
F. L. Lucas: *Decline and Fall of the Romantic Tradition.*

Travel
See Bibliography to Chapter VI.

CHAPTER V

Letter to Lord Byron

Part II

I'm writing this in pencil on my knee,
    Using my other hand to stop me yawning,
Upon a primitive, unsheltered quay
    In the small hours of a Wednesday morning.
    I cannot add the summer day is dawning;
In Seythisfjördur every schoolboy knows
That daylight in the summer never goes.

To get to sleep in latitudes called upper
    Is difficult at first for Englishmen.
It's like being sent to bed before your supper
    For playing darts with father's fountain-pen,
    Or like returning after orgies, when
Your breath's like luggage and you realise
You've been more confidential than was wise.

I've done my duty, taken many notes
    Upon the almost total lack of greenery,
The roads, the illegitimates, the goats:
    To use a rhyme of yours, there's handsome scenery
    But little agricultural machinery;
And with the help of Sunlight Soap the Geysir
Affords to visitors le plus grand plaisir.

The North, though, never was your cup of tea;
    "Moral" you thought it so you kept away.
And what I'm sure you're wanting now from me
    Is news about the England of the day,
    What sort of things La Jeunesse do and say.
Is Brighton still as proud of her pavilion,
And is it safe for girls to travel pillion?

I'll clear my throat and take a Rover's breath
    And skip a century of hope and sin—
For far too much has happened since your death.
    Crying went out and the cold bath came in,
    With drains, bananas, bicycles, and tin,

And Europe saw from Ireland to Albania
The Gothic revival and the Railway Mania.

We're entering now the Eotechnic Phase
    Thanks to the Grid and all those new alloys;
That is, at least, what Lewis Mumford says.
    A world of Aertex underwear for boys,
    Huge plate-glass windows, walls absorbing noise,
Where the smoke nuisance is utterly abated
And all the furniture is chromium-plated.

Well, you might think so if you went to Surrey
    And stayed for week-ends with the well to do,
Your car too fast, too personal your worry
    To look too closely at the wheeling view.
    But in the north it simply isn't true.
To those who live in Warrington or Wigan,
It's not a white lie, it's a whacking big 'un.

There on the old historic battlefield,
    The cold ferocity of human wills,
The scars of struggle are as yet unhealed;
    Slattern the tenements on sombre hills,
    And gaunt in valleys the square-windowed mills
That, since the Georgian house, in my conjecture
Remain our finest native architecture.

On economic, health, or moral grounds
    It hasn't got the least excuse to show;
No more than chamber pots or otter hounds:
    But let me say before it has to go,
    It's the most lovely country that I know;
Clearer than Scafell Pike, my heart has stamped on
The view from Birmingham to Wolverhampton.

Long, long ago, when I was only four,
    Going towards my grandmother, the line
Passed through a coal-field. From the corridor
    I watched it pass with envy, thought "How fine!
    Oh how I wish that situation mine."
Tramlines and slagheaps, pieces of machinery,
That was, and still is, my ideal scenery.

Hail to the New World! Hail to those who'll love
    Its antiseptic objects, feel at home.

Lovers will gaze at an electric stove,
    Another poésie de départ come
    Centred round bus-stops or the aerodrome.
But give me still, to stir imagination
The chiaroscuro of the railway station.

Preserve me from the Shape of Things to Be;
    The high-grade posters at the public meeting,
The influence of Art on Industry,
    The cinemas with perfect taste in seating;
    Preserve me, above all, from central heating.
It may be D. H. Lawrence hocus-pocus,
But I prefer a room that's got a focus.

But you want facts, not sighs. I'll do my best
    To give a few; you can't expect them all.
To start with, on the whole we're better dressed;
    For chic the difference to-day is small
    Of barmaid from my lady at the Hall.
It's sad to spoil this democratic vision
With millions suffering from malnutrition.

Again, our age is highly educated;
    There is no lie our children cannot read,
And as MacDonald might so well have stated
    We're growing up and up and up indeed.
    Advertisements can teach us all we need;
And death is better, as the millions know,
Than dandruff, night-starvation, or B.O.

We've always had a penchant for field sports,
    But what do you think has grown up in our towns?
A passion for the open air and shorts;
    The sun is one of our emotive nouns.
    Go down by chara' to the Sussex Downs,
Watch the manœuvres of the week-end hikers
Massed on parade with Kodaks or with Leicas.

These movements signify our age-long rule
    Of insularity has lost its powers;
The cult of salads and the swimming pool
    Comes from a climate sunnier than ours,
    And lands which never heard of licensed hours.
The south of England before very long
Will look no different from the Continong.

You lived and moved among the best society
    And so could introduce your hero to it
Without the slightest tremor of anxiety;
    Because he was your hero and you knew it,
    He'd know instinctively what's done, and do it.
He'd find our day more difficult than yours
For Industry has mixed the social drawers.

We've grown, you see, a lot more democratic,
    And Fortune's ladder is for all to climb;
Carnegie on this point was most emphatic.
    A humble grandfather is not a crime,
    At least, if father made enough in time!
To-day, thank God, we've got no snobbish feeling
Against the more efficient modes of stealing.

The porter at the Carlton is my brother,
    He'll wish me a good evening if I pay,
For tips and men are equal to each other.
    I'm sure that *Vogue* would be the first to say
    Que le Beau Monde is socialist to-day;
And many a bandit, not so gently born
Kills vermin every winter with the Quorn.

Adventurers, though, must take things as they find them
    And look for pickings where the pickings are.
The drives of love and hunger are behind them,
    They can't afford to be particular:
    And those who like good cooking and a car,
A certain kind of costume or of face,
Must seek them in a certain kind of place.

Don Juan was a mixer and no doubt
    Would find this century as good as any
For getting hostesses to ask him out,
    And mistresses that need not cost a penny.
    Indeed our ways to waste time are so many,
Thanks to technology, a list of these
Would make a longer book than *Ulysses*.

Yes, in the smart set he would know his way
    By second nature with no tips from me.
Tennis and Golf have come in since your day;
    But those who are as good at games as he
    Acquire the back-hand quite instinctively,

Take to the steel-shaft and hole out in one,
Master the books of Ely Culbertson.

I see his face in every magazine.
    "Don Juan at lunch with one of Cochran's ladies."
"Don Juan with his red setter May MacQueen."
    "Don Juan, who's just been wintering in Cadiz,
    Caught at the wheel of his maroon Mercedes."
"Don Juan at Croydon Aerodrome." "Don Juan
Snapped in the paddock with the Agha Khan."

But if in highbrow circles he would sally
    It's just as well to warn him there's no stain on
Picasso, all-in-wrestling, or the Ballet.
    Sibelius is the man. To get a pain on
    Listening to Elgar is a sine qua non.
A second-hand acquaintance of Pareto's
Ranks higher than an intimate of Plato's.

The vogue for Black Mass and the cult of devils
    Has sunk. The Good, the Beautiful, the True
Still fluctuate about the lower levels.
    Joyces are firm and there there's nothing new.
    Eliots have hardened just a point or two.
Hopkins are brisk, thanks to some recent boosts.
There's been some further weakening in Prousts.

I'm saying this to tell you who's the rage,
    And not to loose a sneer from my interior.
Because there's snobbery in every age,
    Because some names are loved by the superior,
    It does not follow they're the least inferior:
For all I know the Beatific Vision's
On view at all Surrealist Exhibitions.

Now for the spirit of the people. Here
    I know I'm treading on more dangerous ground:
I know they're many changes in the air,
    But know my data too slight to be sound.
    I know, too, I'm inviting the renowned
Retort of all who love the Status Quo:
"You can't change human nature, don't you know!"

We've still, it's true, the same shape and appearance,
    We haven't changed the way that kissing's done;
The average man still hates all interference,

Is just as proud still of his new-born son:
Still, like a hen, he likes his private run,
Scratches for self-esteem, and slyly pecks
A good deal in the neighbourhood of sex.

But he's another man in many ways:
Ask the cartoonist first, for he knows best.
Where is the John Bull of the good old days,
The swaggering bully with the clumsy jest?
His meaty neck has long been laid to rest,
His acres of self-confidence for sale;
He passed away at Ypres and Passchendaele.

Turn to the work of Disney or of Strube;
There stands our hero in his threadbare seams;
The bowler hat who straphangs in the tube,
And kicks the tyrant only in his dreams,
Trading on pathos, dreading all extremes;
The little Mickey with the hidden grudge;
Which is the better, I leave you to judge.

Begot on Hire-Purchase by Insurance,
Forms at his christening worshipped and adored;
A season ticket schooled him in endurance,
A tax collector and a waterboard
Admonished him. In boyhood he was awed
By a matric, and complex apparatuses
Keep his heart conscious of Divine Afflatuses.

"I am like you", he says, "and you, and you,
I love my life, I love the home-fires, have
To keep them burning. Heroes never do.
Heroes are sent by ogres to the grave.
I may not be courageous, but I save.
I am the one who somehow turns the corner,
I may perhaps be fortunate Jack Horner.

I am the ogre's private secretary;
I've felt his stature and his powers, learned
To give his ogreship the raspberry
Only when his gigantic back is turned.
One day, who knows, I'll do as I have yearned.
The short man, all his fingers on the door,
With repartee shall send him to the floor."

One day, which day? O any other day,
       But not to-day. The ogre knows his man.
To kill the ogre—that would take away
       The fear in which his happy dreams began,
       And with his life he'll guard dreams while he can.
Those who would really kill his dream's contentment
He hates with real implacable resentment.

He dreads the ogre, but he dreads yet more
       Those who conceivably might set him free,
Those the cartoonist has no time to draw.
       Without his bondage he'd be all at sea;
       The ogre need but shout "Security",
To make this man, so loveable, so mild,
As madly cruel as a frightened child.

Byron, thou should'st be living at this hour!
       What would you do, I wonder, if you were?
Britannia's lost prestige and cash and power,
       Her middle classes show some wear and tear,
       We've learned to bomb each other from the air;
I can't imagine what the Duke of Wellington
Would say about the music of Duke Ellington.

Suggestions have been made that the Teutonic
       Führer-Prinzip would have appealed to you
As being the true heir to the Byronic—
       In keeping with your social status too
       (It has its English converts, fit and few),
That you would, hearing honest Oswald's call,
Be gleichgeschaltet in the Albert Hall.

"Lord Byron at the head of his storm-troopers!"
       Nothing, says science, is impossible:
The Pope may quit to join the Oxford Groupers,
       Nuffield may leave one farthing in his Will,
       There may be someone who trusts Baldwin still,
Someone may think that Empire wines are nice,
There may be people who hear Tauber twice.

You liked to be the centre of attention,
       The gay Prince Charming of the fairy story,
Who tamed the Dragon by his intervention.
       In modern warfare though it's just as gory,
       There isn't any individual glory;

The Prince must be anonymous, observant,
A kind of lab-boy, or a civil servant.

You never were an Isolationist;
        Injustice you had always hatred for,
And we can hardly blame you, if you missed
        Injustice just outside your lordship's door:
        Nearer than Greece were cotton and the poor.
To-day you might have seen them, might indeed
Have walked in the United Front with Gide,

Against the ogre, dragon, what you will;
        His many shapes and names all turn us pale,
For he's immortal, and to-day he still
        Swinges the horror of his scaly tail.
        Sometimes he seems to sleep, but will not fail
In every age to rear up to defend
Each dying force of history to the end.

Milton beheld him on the English throne,
        And Bunyan sitting in the Papal chair;
The hermits fought him in their caves alone,
        At the first Empire he was also there,
        Dangling his Pax Romana in the air:
He comes in dreams at puberty to man,
To scare him back to childhood if he can.

Banker or landlord, booking-clerk or Pope,
        Whenever he's lost faith in choice and thought,
When a man sees the future without hope,
        Whenever he endorses Hobbes' report
        "The life of man is nasty, brutish, short",
The dragon rises from his garden border
And promises to set up law and order.

He that in Athens murdered Socrates,
        And Plato then seduced, prepares to make
A desolation and to call it peace
        To-day for dying magnates, for the sake
        Of generals who can scarcely keep awake,
And for that doughy mass in great and small
That doesn't want to stir itself at all.

Forgive me for inflicting all this on you,
        For asking you to hold the baby for us;

It's easy to forget that where you've gone, you
> May only want to chat with Set and Horus,
> Bored to extinction with our earthly chorus:
Perhaps it sounds to you like a trunk-call,
Urgent, it seems, but quite inaudible.

Yet though the choice of what is to be done
> Remains with the alive, the rigid nation
Is supple still within the breathing one;
> Its sentinels yet keep their sleepless station,
> And every man in every generation,
Tossing in his dilemma on his bed,
Cries to the shadows of the noble dead.

We're out at sea now, and I wish we weren't;
> The sea is rough, I don't care if it's blue;
I'd like to have a quick one, but I daren't.
> And I must interrupt this screed to you,
> For I've some other little jobs to do;
I must write home or mother will be vexed,
So this must be continued in our next.

END OF PART II

CHAPTER VI

Sheaves from Sagaland

*An Anthology of Icelandic Travel addressed
to John Betjeman, Esq.*

PART I.—THE COUNTRY

Iceland is real

"Iceland is not a myth; it is a solid portion of the earth's surface."—
Pliny Miles.

Where is Iceland?

"I made several observations with an excellent Paris Quadrant, and as-
certained the elevation of the pole by means of a lunar eclipse which
happened in December, 1750. By a telescope accurately furnished with a
micrometer, I took the exact latitude of the island, and having deter-
mined it in a nicer manner than it ever was before, found that Iceland

lies almost four degrees more to the east than it has hitherto been computed."—Horrebow.

What does Iceland look like?

"The map of Iceland has been sometimes drawn by schoolboys as an eider duck, quacking with wide-opened beak."—Collingwood.

Impressions of a Viking

"To that place of fish may I never come in my old age."—Ketil Flatnose.

Impressions of a Poet

"A gallows of slush."—A Tenth Century Scald.

Impressions of the Middle Ages

> "To speak of Iceland is little need;
> Save of stockfish."—Hakluyt.

Impressions of an Archbishop

"On our arrival in Iceland we directly saw a prospect before us which, though not pleasing, was uncommon and surprising, and our eyes, accustomed to behold the pleasing coasts of England, now saw nothing but the vestiges of the operation of a fire, Heaven knows how ancient."—Van Troil.

Iceland is German

"Für uns Island ist das Land."—An unknown Nazi.

Concerning the Scenery

"Alone in Iceland you are alone indeed and the homeless, undisturbed wilderness gives something of its awful calm to the spirit. It was like listening to noble music, yet perplexed and difficult to follow. If the Italian landscape is like Mozart; if in Switzerland the sublimity and sweetness correspond in art to Beethoven; then we may take Iceland as the type in nature of the music of the moderns—say Schumann at his oddest and wildest."—Miss Oswald.

Concerning the Mountains

"This author says that the mountains are nothing but sand and stone."—Horrebow.

Concerning the uses of Volcanoes

"Surely were it possible for those thoughtless and insensible beings whose minds seem impervious to every finer feeling to be suddenly transported to this burning region and placed within view of the tremendous operations of the vomiting pool, the sight could not but arouse them from their lethargic stupor, and by superinducing habits of serious reflection might be attended with the happiest consequences, both to themselves and all within the sphere of their influence."—Henderson.

Concerning the Vegetation

"Nowhere a single tree appears which might afford shelter to friendship and innocence."—Van Troil.

Concerning the Climate

"Those who gave an account that it was so hot that they were obliged to go almost naked, had that day, I suppose, great quantities of fish to weigh out, and send aboard their respective ships."—Horrebow.

Concerning the Wild Life

"It is commonly reported that the noise and bellowing of these seabulls and seacows makes the cows ashore run mad. But none here ever saw any of these supposed animals, or noticed the bad effects of their bellowing."—*Ibid.*

Concerning the Insect Life

"McKenzie found a coccinella near the Geysir: and Madame Ida Pfeiffer secured two wild bees which she carried off in spirits of wine."—Burton.

Concerning the Capital

"Reykjavik is, unquestionably, the worst place in which to spend the winter in Iceland. The tone of society is the lowest that can well be imagined. . . . It not only presents a lamentable blank to the view of the religious observer, but is totally devoid of every source of intellectual gratification."—Henderson.

The Immortal Bard proves that nothing escapes him

"Pish for thee, Iceland dog. Thou prick-eared cur of Iceland."—Shakespeare: *Henry IV.*

PART II.—THE NATIVES

The Icelanders are human

"They are not so robust and hardy that nothing can hurt them; for they are human beings and experience the sensations common to mankind."—Horrebow.

Concerning their hair

"The hair which belongs to the class Lissotriches, subdivision Euplokomoi, seldom shows the darker shades of brown. The colour ranges from carroty red to turnip yellow, from barley-sugar to the blond-cendré so expensive in the civilised markets. We find all the gradations of Parisian art here natural; the corn golden, the blonde fulvide, the incandescent (carroty), the flavescent or sulphur-hued, the beurre frais, the fulvastre or lion's mane, and the rubide or mahogany, Raphael's favourite tint."—Burton.

Concerning their eyes

"A very characteristic feature of the race is the eye, dure and cold as a pebble—the mesmerist would despair at the first sight."—*Ibid.*

Concerning their mouths

"The oral region is often coarse and unpleasant."—*Ibid.*

Concerning their temperament

"The Icelander's temperament is nervoso-lymphatic and at best nervoso-sanguineous."—*Ibid.*

Concerning their appearance

"The Icelanders are of a good, honest disposition, but they are at the same time so serious and sullen that I hardly remember to have seen any of them laugh."—Van Troil.

Concerning their character

"This poor but highly respectable people."—McKenzie.

Concerning their sensibility

"The Icelanders in general are civil and well-disposed, but they are said not to feel strongly."—Barrow.

No nonsense about the Icelanders

"Practical men in Iceland vigorously deny the existence of the Gulf Stream."—Burton.

Disadvantages of the North Pole

"It is possible the Icelanders are not now as barbarous as formerly though it may rationally be supposed that a nation living so near the North Pole may not be so refined and polished as some others, especially among the vulgar sort, for people of fashion ought to be exempted from this rule (less or more) in most places."—Tremarec.

Concerning their courage

"They are far from being a dastardly race as some authors have represented them; for it is well-known that they made some figure in a military life, and have been raised to the command of a fortress."—Horrebow.

Concerning their morals

"'Happy the nations of the moral North' wrote Byron some years since. Without imagining that they are worse than their neighbours I fancy it is very much like the ideal morality of the so-termed middle-classes, which has been of late so ruthlessly shattered by Sir Cresswell Cresswell."—Forbes.

Concerning their food

"It cannot afford any great pleasure to examine the manner in which the Icelanders prepare their food."—Van Troil.

Concerning their butter

"Their butter looks very well and I could have ate it for the looks, if my nose did not tell me that it could not taste well. Mr Anderson says their butter looks green, black and of all colours."—Horrebow.

Concerning Hákarl

"This had so disagreeable a taste that the small quantity we took of it drove us from the table long before our intention."—Van Troil.

Eat more fish

"Ichthyophagy and idleness must do much to counter-balance the sun-clad power of chastity."—Burton.

Concerning their habits

"If I attempted to describe some of their nauseous habits, I might fill volumes."—Pfeiffer.

A young lady's opinion

"The Icelanders have no idea of out-of-doors amenity."—Miss Oswald.

Concerning their dress

"The dress of the women is not calculated to show the person to advantage."—McKenzie.

Concerning their baths

"The inhabitants do not bathe in them here merely for their health, but they are likewise the occasion for a scene of gallantry. Poverty prevents here the lover from making presents to his fair one, and Nature presents no flowers of which elsewhere garlands are made: 'tis therefore customary that instead of all this the swain perfectly cleanses one of these baths which is afterwards honoured by the visit of his bride."—Van Troil.

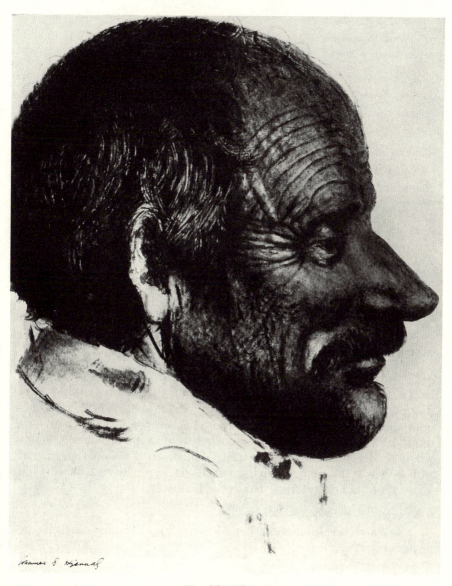

Head by Kjarval

Concerning their kissing

"I have sometimes fancied, when they took their faces apart, that I could hear a slight clicking sound; but this might be imagination."—Howell.

Concerning their laundry

"They wash their things tolerably well, though I must suppose, not to the liking of all persons."—Horrebow.

Concerning their music

"I heard a voice in the farm singing an Icelandic song. At a distance it resembled the humming of bees."—Pfeiffer.

Concerning their dancing

"They have no idea of dancing, though sometimes the merchants at the factories for their diversion will get a fiddle and make them dance, in which they succeed no better than by hopping and jumping about."—Horrebow.

Concerning their sculpture

"Thorwaldson, the son of an Icelander, dwelling on the classic ground of Rome, is at the present moment second only to Canova among the statuaries of Europe."—McKenzie.

Concerning their chessmen

"There is not a peasant in the country but what has a set, which they make out of fishbones. The whole difference betwixt theirs and ours being that our fools stand for their bishops because they say the clergyman ought to be near the King's person. Their rooks represent little captains whom the Icelandic scholars call their Centuriones. They are represented with swords at their sides, with bloated cheeks, as if they were blowing the horns they hold in both their hands."—Tremarec.

Good news for the Geography Mistress

"The search for this useful lichen forms the annual holiday of Icelandic girlhood."—Howell.

Bad news for the Watch Committee

"The Elder Edda may be searched through and through and there will not be found a single nude myth, not an impersonation of any kind that can be considered an outrage upon virtue or a violation of the laws of propriety."—Anderson.

Concerning their literary criticism

"In all departments of literature, there is a strong disposition among the Icelanders to critical severity. A curious instance of this kind occurred about a hundred years ago when an unfortunate man was publicly whipped as a punishment for the errors he had committed in a translation of the book of Genesis."—McKenzie.

Concerning their lack of education

"It is not uncommon in Iceland for people of all ranks, ages and sexes to sleep in the same apartment. Their notions of decency are unavoidably not very refined; but we had sufficient proof that the instances of this which we witnessed proceeded from ignorance, and expressed nothing but perfect innocence."—*Ibid.*

Concerning their high-grade living

"Publications connected with practical morality are very common in Iceland, and several excellent books of this kind have lately appeared in the island, adapted chiefly to the use of farmers or those of the middle-classes; in which moral instruction is judiciously blended with amusing information in various branches of knowledge. The most valuable of these writings is a work called *Evening Hours*."—*Ibid.*

Concerning their religion

"The influence of the Lutheran Church is practically universal, the Nonconformists of the island numbering probably but one or two of the Brethren, and a single Swedenborgian."—Howell.

Plato in the North

"Some of the clergy of the new school, instead of drawing the matter of their sermons from the Scriptures, gather it from the writings of heathen philosophers, and the morality found in these authors, which at the best is but dry and insipid, absolutely freezes when transported to Iceland."—Henderson.

The Scarlet Woman in Iceland

"An American organ leads the singing, which is slow but none the less devotional, and thoroughly Congregational. A gaudy red and yellow robe which the pastor wears during a portion of the liturgy is evidently a survival of the Romanist days. His black gown and white ruff are less obtrusive and more in keeping with a Christian service."—Howell.

Concerning their behaviour in Church

"Most of the congregation sat with their faces turned towards the altar, but the rule had its exceptions."—Pfeiffer.

Concerning the literary taste of the Clergy

"Assessor Grondal also composed several poetical satires in which, according to the information of the Bishop, there is much successful ridicule."—McKenzie.

Concerning the isolation of real Christians in Iceland

"The greater number of these individuals are, in all probability, known only to God, having little intercourse with each other, and the situation may, not unfitly, be compared to that of the generality of real Christians in Scotland about thirty or forty years ago."—Henderson.

A Problem for Missionaries

"A church was built in 984 by Thorvald Bodvarter and some persons received baptism, but others, though they had no objection to the Christian religion, could not be prevailed upon to suffer themselves to be baptised, as they pretended it would be indecent to go naked into the water, like little boys."—Van Troil.

A use for Icelandic women

"As wives they would be efficient correctives to the fine drawn framework and the over-nervous diathesis of southern nations."—Burton.

Tiddley om pom pom

"Die geistige Aufgeschlossenheit und rasche Aufnahmefähigkeit der Isländischen Frau hat in der Stadt in den letzen zehn Jahren einer Typus hervorgebracht, der die Eleganz und das künstliche Modespiel der Städtischen Festländerinnen noch zu überbieten trachtet. Das alles verfleucht jedoch wie ein dünner Spuk, wenn eine Isländische Frau einher schreitet in der Königlichen Festtracht ihres Landes und in Gewand und Haltung einer einzigen solchen Gestalt Tausendjähriges Isländertum in seiner menschlichen Stärke enthüllt."—Prinz.

The longest word in Icelandic

Haestarjettarmalaflutunesmanskifstofustulkonutidyralykill—a latch-key belonging to a girl working in the office of a barrister.

PART III.—THE TOURIST

Iceland is safe

"An eruption very seldom happens, and even when it does, it occupies but a small tract of time. Travellers cannot therefore be much obstructed by it."—Horrebow.

Reassurance to Girl Guides

"What! says someone, can ladies travel in Iceland? Certainly, as witness the expeditions of Miss Oswald and Miss Adelia Gates."—Howell.

A warning

"To be well received here it is necessary either to be rich or else to travel as a naturalist."—Pfeiffer.

Why go there? A reason

"Well, Rector, you are partly right. I do like getting out of the regions of respectability—pardon me—once in a way. Hard fare, too, for a time is a fine alternative. Persicos odi apparatus."—Metcalfe.

Another reason

"The traveller enjoys for himself the most absolute immunity; he may be offered a seat in the Cabinet, or accused of forgery, or portrayed in Vanity Fair,—he will know nothing about it till his return."—Viscount Bryce.

The Voyage Out. A cautious simile

"Whales ahead—their spoky back fins revolving close after each other in regular succession like the wheel of the *Great Eastern,* if it has one."— Metcalfe.

First sight of Iceland

"So I have seen Iceland at last. I awoke from a dream of the Grange, which, by the way, was like some house at Queen's Gate."—William Morris.

Ditto

"We were delighted at seeing some new faces, in spite of their nastiness and stench; and their grotesque appearance afforded us much amusement."—Hooker.

Character of a traveller

"Next I will introduce Mr Darwin, a really celebrated personage. He had written a learned book on Northern Antiquities in recompense of which a Scandinavian potentate created him a Knight of the second class of the Order of the Walrus, the riband of which illustrious Order was suspended across his brawny shoulders."—Umbra.

Character of a light blue

"A man taking delight in museums and houses of assembly, given to chemistry and the variations of European politics, fond of statistics and well instructed in stuffed vermin."—Anthony Trollope.

I was at B.N.C.

"It is very hard for a European, and perhaps especially hard for a graduate of one of the older English Universities to appreciate the squalid culture of these northern peoples."—Annandale.

A French humanitarian

"Que les agranomes et les membres du club des Jockeys vantent les belles races de mérinos et les familles pur sang de chevaux anglais. Pour moi dussé-je faire rire ceux qui n'ont jamais compati aux souffrances des animaux, j'avouerai que, dans mes excursions en Islande, j'ai souvent pressé entre mes mains, avec attendrissement, la tête de mon cheval."— Marmier.

An unfavourable comparison

"The French author gives a life-like sketch of the difference between the sailors who man these ships. The Frenchman, working for the owner, landing at times, listless, idle, with a pocket as lean as his poor cadaverous face, hopeless, miserable to a degree. The Yankee, paddling his own canoe, pocketing all the gains, dashing ashore in his civilian dress, and flinging his dollars everywhere, drinking, roystering, catching the ponies, and scampering off, frightening the Icelander out of his wits."— Howell.

Mr X.

"I discovered a curious fact about Mr X. which accounted for that gentleman's occasional readiness in making a quotation. Every night he wrapped himself in a large grey plaid of which he was very proud; it had been, he said, his companion in the mountains of Mexico. I now happened to examine some scarlet letters on the plaid and, to my amazement, discovered whole passages from Shakespeare and other poets embroidered in red silk. In fact Mr X. slept in a book and could always refresh his memory by studying when he woke."—Umbra.

A poet's athletic feat

"Had that celebrated Pope whose Christian name was Alexander believed that his immortal essay would have been translated into Icelandic verse, by a native Icelander, he would not have vaulted clear over the volcanic isle."—Miles.

Influence of the Gothic revival

"There was not one in our company who did not wish to have his clothes a little singed for the sake of seeing Hekla in a blaze."—Van Troil.

An inarticulate Wordsworthian

"I wish it were in my power, Sir, to give you such a description of this place as it deserves, but I fear mine will always remain inferior in point of expression. So much is certain, at least, Nature never drew from anyone a more cheerful homage to her Great Creator than I here paid Him."—Ibid.

Trials of a geologist

"Some of the pieces I handed to Arni to carry, who took them very reluctantly; the bulk, however, were by degrees thrown away, each succeeding rest seeing one or more of the specimens abandoned which at the rest preceding I had determined to preserve; greatly to the amusement of H., who is not disposed to subject himself to the least inconvenience for the cause of science."—W. G. Locke.

Trials of an author

"For a few minutes they remained quiet; then they began to whisper one to another, 'She writes. She writes.'"—Pfeiffer.

A fast Victorian

"There was no alternative; I must either turn back or mount as a man. Keeping my brother at my side, and bidding the rest ride forward, I made him shorten the stirrups and hold the saddle, and after sundry attempts succeeded in landing myself man fashion on the animal's back. The position felt very odd at first, and I was also somewhat uncomfortable at my attitude, but on Vaughan's assuring me there was no cause for my uneasiness, and arranging my dress so that it fell in folds on either side, I decided to give the experiment a fair trial. Perhaps my boldness may rather surprise my readers."—Mrs Alice Tweedie.

Acumen of a religious observer

"Having gained some knowledge of the Icelandic beforehand, I could easily collect the scope and substance of his discourse, and, from its general tenor, do not hesitate to pronounce it strictly Evangelical."—Henderson.

Inability of a Bishop to draw the line

"Here we saw the bishop himself countenancing vice in its worst shape, and appearing perfectly familiar with persons who, he must have known, bore the worst characters."—McKenzie.

Privations of a traveller

"As long as I remained in Iceland I was compelled to give up my German system of diet."—Pfeiffer.

An exchange of courtesies

"I plucked a flower, and speedily they brought a bunch. I touched a stone and half a dozen were at once forthcoming. However, I let them see that this was quite unnecessary."—Howell.

The translator of the Arabian Nights get the raspberry

"Among the gentler sex a soft look is uncommonly rare, and the aspect ranges from a stony stare to a sharp glance rendered fiercer by the habitual frown."—Burton.

A psychological observation

"A certain feeling of discomfort always attached to the fact of sleeping in a church alone in the midst of a graveyard."—Pfeiffer.

Curious behaviour of a Scotch baronet

"We instantly left our guides and the horses to manage matters as they could; and rushing over slags, lava, and mud, fell upon the snow like wild beasts upon their prey. My enjoyment was excessive; and the very recollection of it is so gratifying that I must be excused for recording a circumstance of so little importance."—McKenzie.

Art without malice

"The clergyman had a large family and McDiarmed good-naturedly took a blooming little maiden of six or seven years a ride on his pony; while Lord Lodbrog drew a very accurate sketch of his home and church. It was really very well done and when pinned up against the wall of the sitting-room had a smart appearance."—Umbra.

Hear, Hear!

"Let's go home. We can't camp in this beastly place.
—What is he saying?
—I'm not going to camp here.
—You must. All Englishmen do.
—Blast all Englishmen."—William Morris.

Moral drawn from a Geysir

"While the jets were rushing up towards Heaven with the velocity of an arrow my mind was forcibly borne along with them to the contemplation of the Great and Omnipotent JEHOVAH in comparison with whom these and all the wonders scattered over the whole immensity of existence dwindle into absolute insignificance; whose almighty commands spake the universe into being; and at whose sovereign fiat the whole fabric might be reduced, in an instant, to its original nothing."—Henderson.

Rudeness shown to the same Geysir

"Darwin profanely called the Geysir an old brute."—Umbra.

Spread of Nazi Doctrines among the Icelandic ponies

"Famous scientists, doctors, politicians, and writers, mounted her and rode for a wonderful week's tour. Richer in experience, strengthened and refreshed by Nature, ready for a new struggle with the arch-fiend culture, they went home and gave lectures."—Fleuron.

PART IV.—HOME AGAIN

Liar: or Miles on Pfeiffer

"Where she does not knowingly tell direct falsehoods, the guesses she makes about those regions that she does not visit—while stating that she does—show her to be bad at guesswork."—Miles.

Cissy: or Locke on Locke

"What a vacillating set! I would have gone on alone had I been of the party; and therefore it is pleasing to be able to disclaim relationship with one so wanting in firmness of purpose as the author of the Home of the Eddas appears to be from this and other incidents."—W. G. Locke.

THE 1809 REVOLUTION

(Mainly from Hooker and Mackenzie)

In the year 1808, when Great Britain was at war with Denmark, an eminent and honourable merchant of London, Mr Samuel Phelps, learned from a young Dane of twenty-seven, Mr Jörgen Jörgensen, that there was a large quantity of goods, chiefly tallow, for sale in Iceland. Jörgensen, though born of respectable parents, had been apprenticed on a British collier, served in the British navy, where, in his own words, he had imbibed the maxims, the principles, and the prejudices of Englishmen, and on his return to Copenhagen in 1806 had made himself unpopular by his pro-British sentiments. On the outbreak of war he had been put in command of a Danish privateer, but had been taken prisoner after an engagement off Flamborough Head with the *Sappho* and the *Clio,* landed at Yarmouth, and set free on parole.

As Iceland was wholly dependent on Denmark for necessary imports, the war was a serious matter for her, but the British, at the instigation of that exalted philanthropist Sir Joseph Banks, had given an undertaking to allow Danish merchantmen to trade unmolested with the island. These excellent intentions of His Majesty's Government were somewhat frustrated, however, by the behaviour of one of His subjects, for in 1808 a Captain Gilpin arrived in Reykjavik and made off with some 36,000 rix dollars apportioned for the relief of the poor. To return to Mr Phelps: acting on Jörgensen's information, he commissioned a Liverpool ship, the *Clarence,* commanded by Mr Jackson, to sail to Iceland with a cargo which, according to himself, consisted largely of necessaries, barley meal, potatoes, and salt, and according to Count Tramp, the Danish Governor of the Island, consisted largely of luxuries. Mr Jackson undertook to molest no Danish ships under a penalty of an £8,000 fine. The *Clarence,* with Jörgensen, who omitted to mention his departure to the authorities, and an English super-cargo, Mr Savigniac, set sail in December and landed in Reykjavik at the beginning of January 1809.

Here they discreetly showed an American flag and American papers, but were refused permission to trade, whereupon they hoisted the British flag, but with no greater success. As Icelandic trade was a legal Danish monopoly, this refusal on the part of the Danish officials was, perhaps, not unnatural. Mr Savigniac, however, was determined to bring the Government to a sense of its duty and interest, and ordered Captain Jackson to capture a Danish brig which had just arrived. The officials capitulated, and apparently gave some sort of permission, but the Icelanders, either because they were frightened, or because they did not want the goods—it was a bad time of the year for business—showed no inclination to buy or sell. So matters continued till June, when Count Tramp returned from Copenhagen on the *Orion*. A proclamation forbidding the Icelanders to trade with the English under point of death which had been previously composed but kept in a chest till his arrival was now published. Shortly afterwards, a British man-of-war, the *Rover*, commanded by Captain Nott, arrived, "with the object of which in these parts", says Count Tramp, "I was unacquainted, and the peaceable proceedings of which no convention secured." On June 16th it appears that a convention was arrived at between Count Tramp and Captain Nott permitting trade, but this agreement, though sent to the press, was somehow never published and the existing prohibition remained in force. The *Rover* departed, but on June 21st Mr Phelps arrived in person, with the *Flora* and the *Margaret and Anne*, a ship of ten guns under Captain Liston.

By June 25th Mr Phelps had decided that "longer delay would be materially prejudicial to his interests, and he must consequently be under the necessity of having recourse to measures no more consonant to his inclinations than to his feelings". He seized the *Orion*, and marching with an armed crew of twelve to the Governor's house, on Sunday afternoon after Divine Service, arrested Count Tramp in the middle of a conversation with a Mr Kofoed. According to his own account there were a number of Icelanders loitering about with long poles shod with iron spikes who made no attempt to resist them, in spite of the fact that "it is sufficiently known that in times of war the crews of merchant ships consist of such men only as are unfit for the service of His Majesty." He then asked Jörgensen to take over the government of the Island, a prospect which seems to have been highly agreeable to that young gentleman for, on the next morning, he issued a proclamation dissolving all Danish authority, confiscating all Danish property, confining all Danes to their houses, threatening all offenders against these decrees with being shot within two hours, and promising all native Icelanders "undisturbed tranquility and a felicity hitherto unknown". On the evening of the same day (June 26th) he issued a second proclamation by which Iceland was declared an independent republic, all debts to Denmark were repudiated, and the island was to be put in a state of defence. This last provision proved more difficult than was anticipated. A house-to-house search in Reykjavik only produced twenty to thirty old fowling pieces, most of them useless, and a few swords and pistols, so that the Icelandic army was necessarily restricted to "eight men who, dressed in green uniforms, armed with swords and pis-

tols, and mounted on good ponies, scoured the country in various direc-
tions, intimidating the Danes, and making themselves highly useful to the
new Governor, in securing the goods and property that were to be confis-
cated". (The value of these varies in different accounts from 16,000 to
19,000 rix dollars.) As a further act of authority, and to show the clem-
ency intended to be pursued, four prisoners confined in the Tught-hus
were released and the place itself converted into barracks for the soldiers.

The greater part of the army was soon employed in seizing the persons
of two of the civil officers, Mr Frydensburg and Mr Einersen, who were
kept in confinement, the former for one night, the latter for eight or ten
days. Hooker, who was an eye-witness of Einersen's arrest, says that "a
horse was taken for him upon which he was placed and, guarded by Jör-
gensen and his cavalry, was marched, or rather galloped, into the town."
Meanwhile Mr Samuel Phelps had not been idle, but, to protect the town,
"an office which he readily undertook for the security of the very consid-
erable property he now had there", was building Fort Phelps, which he
equipped with six guns that had lain buried in the sand on the shore for
over 140 years.

On July 11th Jörgensen issued yet another proclamation assuming the
title of his Excellency the Protector of Iceland, Commander-in-Chief by
sea and land, decreeing his private seal J.J. as the official seal, and forbid-
ding all irreverence to his person. A new flag, three split stockfish upon a
dark blue ground, was hoisted for the first time on the top of a warehouse
under a salute of eleven guns from the *Margaret and Anne,* and was after-
wards hoisted on Sundays. Having done this, his Excellency set out on
foot for the North with five of his army, and later returned with one.

All this time Count Tramp was a prisoner on board the *Margaret and
Anne,* where he does not appear to have been satisfied with his treatment.
"Bent down", he says, "under the weight of so much grief and affliction
united, it now became my lot to be kept confined in a narrow and dirty
cabin, and sometimes, when Captain Liston took it into his head, even
shut up in a small room, or rather closet, where I was deprived of the light
of the day. Constantly I was obliged to put up with the society of drunken
and noisy mates, and, with them for my companions, I was reduced to
exist on fare which even the men complained of as being more than com-
monly indifferent; in short, I was deprived for the space of nine weeks, of
every convenience and comfort of life to which I had been used, and
subjected to all the sufferings which the oppressor had it in his power to
inflict."

These sufferings, however, were not destined to last. On August 8th
occurred an event "as unforeseen as it was unfavourable to the present
state of political and commercial affairs." The *Talbot,* commanded by the
Honourable Alexander Jones, arrived in Hafnafjördur, and, after hear-

ing both sides and deciding that "owing to his former situation in life"
Mr Jörgensen was unwelcome to the inhabitants, arrested him for having
broken his parole, restored the Danish authority, destroyed Fort Phelps,
and, after a delay due to some Danes setting fire to the *Margaret and Anne*,
left Iceland at the end of August with Phelps, Count Tramp, Jörgensen,
and a congratulatory ode to himself composed in Icelandic and Latin by a
certain Magnus Finnursson, or Finnur Magnusson, from which the fol-
lowing is a translated extract:

> He pretended that he served the English King: that he depended
> on the protection of his armies.
> He armed brothers against each other: terror seized the remainder
> of the people,
> Who had never before beheld the sword or blood: and unwillingly
> submitted to the insolent yoke.
> He, more powerful, raised fortifications: and erected his standard
> black as hell.
> He took a lordly title: having dared to assume possession of the
> supreme power.
> He pretended that our people wished for these things: and that
> they all demanded these tumults.

The Revolution had lasted fifty-eight days, twelve men had been em-
ployed, but not a shot fired (except in salutes) nor a sabre unsheathed.

The subsequent history of Samuel Phelps, "who was in part to blame",
is unknown, but the unfortunate Jörgensen was sent to the hulks at
Chatham for a year, and was afterwards released on parole at Reading. In
prison, however, it seems that he had become a confirmed gambler, and
after sundry adventures was finally deported to Tasmania, where he be-
came an explorer and a policeman. He died at Hobartstown in 1844. On
February 7th, 1810, the British Government issued a decree guaranteeing
the immunity of Iceland, the Faroes, and Greenland, from British attack,
and encouraging British trade with these places. Count Tramp declared
that "the peculiar favour which Iceland and its concerns have met with
here and the manner in which His Majesty's ministers have interested
themselves in its welfare, and above all the security obtained for the fu-
ture, has entirely obliterated all bitterness from my heart", but good Im-
perialists, like Hooker, still grumbled a little. "England should no longer
hesitate," he wrote, "about the adoption of a step to which every native
Icelander looks forward as the greatest blessing that can befall his coun-
try, and which to England herself would, I am persuaded, be productive
of various signal advantages, the taking possession of Iceland and holding
it among her dependencies. Iceland, thus freed from the yoke of an inef-
ficient but presumptuous tyrant, might then, guarded by the protection

Mount Hekla from Odde

The Geysirs, as seen July 30, 1814

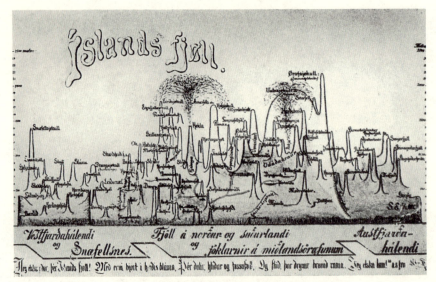

The Mountains of Iceland

Reykjavik 1735

of our fleets and fostered by the liberal policy of our Commercial Laws, look forward to a security that Denmark could never afford, and to a prosperity that the selfishness of the Danes has always prevented; while England would find herself repaid for her generous conduct by the extension of her fisheries, the surest source of her prosperity, and by the safety which the numerous harbours of the Island afford for her merchantmen against the storms and perils of the Arctic Ocean."

An Icelandic Supper in 1809

(Hooker)

"On the cloth was nothing but a plate, a knife and fork, a wine glass, and a bottle of claret, for each guest, except that in the middle stood a large and handsome glass-castor of sugar, with a magnificent silver top. The dishes are brought in singly; our first was a large tureen of soup, which is a favourite addition to the dinners of the richer people, and is made of sago, claret, and raisins, boiled so as to become almost a mucilage. We were helped to two soup plates full of this, which we ate without knowing if anything was to come. No sooner, however, was the soup removed, than two large salmon, boiled and cut in slices, were brought on and, with them, melted butter looking like oil, mixed with vinegar and pepper; this, likewise, was very good and when we had with some difficulty cleared our plates, we hoped we had finished our dinners. No so, for there was then introduced a tureen full of eggs of the Cree, a great tern, boiled hard, of which a dozen were put upon each of our plates; and for sauce, we had a large basin of cream, mixed with sugar, in which were four spoons, so that we all ate out of the same bowl, placed in the middle of the table. We devoured with difficulty our eggs and cream, but had no sooner dismissed our plates, than half a sheep, well roasted, came on with a mess of sorrel called by the Danes, scurvy-grass, boiled, mashed and sweetened with sugar. However, even this was not all; for a large dish of waffels as they are here called, that is to say, a sort of pancake made of wheat flour, flat, and roasted in a mould, which forms a number of squares on the top, succeeded the mutton. This was not more than half an inch thick and about the size of an octavo book. Then bread, Norway biscuit and loaves made of rye were served up: for our drink we had nothing but claret, of which we were all compelled to empty the bottle that stood by us, and this too out of tumblers rather than wine-glasses. The coffee was extremely good and we trusted it would terminate the feast; but all was not yet over; for a large bowl of rum punch was brought in and handed round in glasses pretty freely, and to every glass a toast was given. Another bowl actually came which we were with difficulty allowed to refuse to empty entirely; nor could this be done but by ordering our people to get the boat ready for our departure, when, having concluded this extraordinary feast by three cups of tea each, we took our leave and reached Reykjavik about ten o'clock, but did not for some time recover from the effects of this most involuntary intemperance."

ERUPTION OF THE ÖRAEFAJÖKULL, 1727

*(Jon. Thorlaksson, Minister of Sandfell,
quoted in Mackenzie)*

"In the year 1727, on the 7th August, which was the tenth Sunday after Trinity, after the commencement of divine service in the church of Sand-fell, as I stood before the altar, I was sensible of a gentle concussion under my feet, which I did not mind at first; but, during the delivery of the sermon, the rocking continued to increase, so as to alarm the whole congregation; yet they remarked that the like had often happened before. One of them, a very aged man, repaired to a spring, a little below the house, where he prostrated himself on the ground, and was laughed at by the rest for his pains; but, on his return, I asked him what it was he wished to ascertain, to which he replied, 'Be on your guard, Sir; the earth is on fire!' Turning, at the same moment, towards the church door, it appeared to me, and all who were present, as if the house contracted and drew itself together. I now left the church, necessarily ruminating on what the old man had said; and as I came opposite to Mount Flega, and looked up towards the summit, it appeared alternately to expand and be heaved up, and fall again to its former state. Nor was I mistaken in this, as the event shewed; for on the morning of the 8th, we not only felt frequent and violent earthquakes, but also heard dreadful reports, in no respect inferior to thunder. Everything that was standing in the houses was thrown down by these shocks; and there was reason to apprehend, that mountains as well as houses would be overturned in the catastrophe. What most augmented the terror of the people was, that nobody could divine in what place the disaster would originate, or where it would end.

"After nine o'clock, three particularly loud reports were heard, which were almost instantaneously followed by several eruptions of water that gushed out, the last of which was the greatest, and completely carried away the horses and other animals that it overtook in its course. When these exudations were over, the ice mountain itself ran down into the plain, just like melted metal poured out of a crucible; and on settling, filled it to such a height, that I could not discover more of the well-known mountain Lomagnupr than about the size of a bird. The water now rushed down the east side without intermission, and totally destroyed what little of the pasture-grounds remained. It was a most pitiable sight to behold the females crying, and my neighbours destitute both of counsel and courage: however, as I observed that the current directed its course towards my house, I removed my family up to the top of a high rock, on the side of the mountain, called Dalskardstorfa, where I caused a tent to be pitched, and all the church utensils, together with our food, clothes and other things that were most necessary, to be conveyed thither; drawing the conclusion, that should the eruption break forth at some other place, this height would escape the longest, if it were the will of God, to whom we committed ourselves, and remained there.

"Things now assumed quite a different appearance. The Jökull itself exploded, and precipitated masses of ice, many of which were hurled out to the sea; but the thickest remained on the plain, at a short distance from the foot of the mountain. The noise and reports continuing, the atmosphere was so completely filled with fire and ashes, that day could scarcely be distinguished from night, by reason of the darkness which followed, and which was barely rendered visible by the light of the fire that had broken through five or six cracks in the mountain. In this manner the parish of Oraefa was tormented for three days together; yet it is not easy to describe the disaster as it was in reality; for the surface of the ground was entirely covered with pumice-sand, and it was impossible to go out in the open air with safety, on account of the red-hot stones that fell from the atmosphere. Any who did venture out, had to cover their heads with buckets, and such other wooden utensils as could afford them some protection.

"On the 11th it cleared up a little in the neighbourhood; but the ice-mountain still continued to send forth smoke and flames. The same day I rode, in company with three others, to see how matters stood with the parsonage, as it was most exposed, but we could only proceed with the utmost danger, as there was no other way except between the ice-mountain and the Jökull which had been precipitated into the plain, where the water was so hot that the horses almost got unmanageable: and, just as we entertained the hope of getting through by this passage, I happened to look behind me, when I descried a fresh deluge of hot water directly above me, which, had it reached us, must inevitably have swept us before it. Contriving, of a sudden, to get on the ice, I called to my companions to make the utmost expedition in following me; and by this means, we reached Sandfell in safety. The whole of the farm, together with the cottages of two tenants, had been destroyed; only the dwelling houses remained, and a few spots of the tuns. The people stood crying in the church. The cows which, contrary to all expectation, both here and elsewhere, had escaped the disaster, were lowing beside a few hay-stacks that had been damaged during the eruption. At the time the exudation of the Jökull broke forth, the half of the people belonging to the parsonage were in four newly-constructed sheep-cotes, where two women and a boy took refuge on the roof of the highest; but they had hardly reached it when, being unable to resist the force of the thick mud that was borne against it, it was carried away by the deluge of hot water and, as far as the eye could reach, the three unfortunate persons were seen clinging to the roof. One of the women was afterwards found among the substances that had proceeded from the Jökull, but burnt and, as it were, parboiled; her body was so soft that it could scarcely be touched. Everything was in the most deplorable condition. The sheep were lost; some of which were washed up dead from the sea in the third parish from Oraefa. The hay that was saved was found insufficient for the cows so that a fifth part of them had to be killed; and most of the horses which had not been swept into the ocean were afterwards found completely mangled. The eastern part of the parish of Sida was also destroyed by the pumice and sand; and the inhabitants were on that account obliged to kill many of their cattle.

"The mountain continued to burn night and day from the 8th of August, as already mentioned, till the beginning of Summer in the month of April the following year, at which time the stones were still so hot that they could not be touched; and it did not cease to emit smoke till near the end of the Summer. Some of them had been completely calcined; some were black and full of holes; and others were so loose in their contexture that one could blow through them. On the first day of Summer 1728, I went in company with a person of quality to examine the cracks in the mountain, most of which were so large that we could creep into them. I found here a quantity of saltpetre and could have collected it, but did not choose to stay long in the excessive heat. At one place a heavy calcined stone lay across a large aperture; and as it rested on a small basis, we easily dislodged it into the chasm but could not observe the least sign of its having reached the bottom. These are the more remarkable particulars that have occurred to me with respect to this mountain; and thus God hath led me through fire and water, and brought me through much trouble and adversity to my eightieth year. To Him be the honour, the praise, and the glory for ever."

(For an account of the 1783 eruption see Magnus Stefansson's account, quoted in Hooker, pp. 405–426.)

Bibliography

Arngrimur Jonsson: *Brevis Commentarius*, 1592; *Anatome Blefkeniana*, 1612; *Epistola Defensoria*, 1618; *Apotribe Calumniae*, 1622; *Chrymogea*, 1609–1630; *Specimen Islandiae*, 1643.
Blefkenius: *Islandia*, 1607.

EXTRACT FROM SUARBAR PARISH REGISTER, 1805

Name of Farm	Name	Occupation	Age	Confirmed	Communicant	Able to Read	Conduct	General Abilities
Thyrill	Jorundur Gislasson	Constable	41	Yes	Yes	Yes	Well disposed and clean	Moderate abilities
	Margaret Thorstendottir	His wife	53	Yes	Yes	Yes	Good character	Piously disposed
	Gudrun Eireksdottir	Her daughter by a former husband	19	Yes	Yes	Yes	A hopeful girl	Well informed
	Gudrun Grimsson	Servant man	25	Yes	Yes	Yes	A faithful labourer	He has neglected his improvement and is therefore admonished
	Thorsdys Saensdottir	Maid-servant	42	Yes	Yes	Yes	Neat and faithful	Well informed
	Jarudur Stefansdottir	Her child	3	—	—	—	—	—
	Hristin Jonsdottir	A female orphan	8	—	—	—	A tractable child	Has finished her catechism. To be confirmed
	Waldi Sterindersson	A male orphan	6	—	—	—	Tractable and obedient	Is learning his catechism

Ionr Boty: *Treatise of the land from Iceland to Greenland* (Purchas III), 1608.

La Peyrère: *Account of Iceland* (Churchill II), 1644.

John Andersson: *Nachrichten von Island,* 1746.

*Niels Horrebow: *Nachrichten von Island,* 1750.

Tremarec: *Relation d'un voyage dans la Mer du Nord,* 1772.

*Joseph Banks and Van Troil: *Letters from Iceland,* 1772.

*Hooker: *Journal of a tour in Iceland,* 1811.

*Sir George MacKenzie: *Travels in Iceland,* 1812.

*Ebenezer Henderson: *Iceland,* 1818.

John Barrow: *A Visit to Iceland,* 1835.

Arthur Dillon: *A Winter (1834) in Iceland and Lapland,* 1840.

Marmier: *Lettres sur l'Islande,* 1837.

Paul Gaimard: *Voyage en Islande et au Groenland* (8 vols), 1838–1852.

Madam Ida Pfeiffer: *A Visit to Iceland,* 1854.

Pliny Miles: *Rambles in Iceland,* 1854.

Robert Chambers: *Tracings of Iceland and the Faroe Islands,* 1856.

Charles Edmund: *Voyage dans les Mers du Nord,* 1857.

*Lord Dufferin: *Letters from High Latitudes,* 1858.

Captain Forbes: *Iceland,* 1860.

Metcalfe: *The Oxonian in Iceland,* 1861.

Symington: *Pen and Pencil Sketches,* 1862.

Baring-Gould: *Iceland, its Scenes and Sagas,* 1863.

Umbra (Clifford): *Travels,* 1865.

Shepherd: *The N.W. Peninsula of Iceland,* 1867.

Paykull: *A Summer in Iceland,* 1868.

*William Morris: *Journal,* 1871–1873.

*Viscount Bryce: *Impressions of Iceland,* 1872 (pub. 1923).

Taylor: *Egypt and Iceland,* 1874 (pub. 1902).

Richard Burton: *Ultima Thule,* 1875.

Lord Watts: *Across the Vatnajökull,* 1876.

Anthony Trollope: *How the Mastiffs went to Iceland,* 1878.

C.W. Locke: *The Home of the Eddas,* 1879.

W.G. Locke: *Askja,* 1881.

Coles: *Summer-Travel in Iceland,* 1882.

Miss Oswald: *By Fell and Fjord,* 1882.

Mrs Alec Tweedie: *A Girl's Tour in Iceland,* 1882.

Eugène de Groote: *Island,* 1889.

Howell: *Icelandic Pictures,* 1893.

*Collingwood and Stefansson: *A Pilgrimage to the Saga-steads of Iceland,* 1899.

* Specially recommended.

William Bischer: *Across Iceland,* 1902.
Annandale: *The Faroes and Iceland,* 1905.
Daniel Bruun: *Iceland. Routes over the Highlands,* 1907.
W. Russell: *Iceland. Horseback Tours in Sagaland,* 1914.
Paul Hermann: *Island. Das Land und das Volk,* 1914.
Prinz: *Das Unbekannte Island,* 1932.
Mrs Chapman: *Across Iceland,* 1934.

CHAPTER VII

Letter to R. H. S. Crossman, Esq.

Mulakot, July 8th

A glacier brilliant in the heights of summer
Feeding a putty-coloured river: a field,
A countryside collected in a field
To appreciate or try its strength;
The two flags twitter at the entrance gates.

I walk among them taking photographs;
The children stare and follow, think of questions
To prove the stranger real. Beyond the wire
The ponies graze who never will grow up to question
The justice of their permanent discipline.

Nevertheless let the camera's eye record it:
Groups in confabulation on the grass,
The shuffling couples in their heavy boots,
The young men leaping, the accordion playing.
Justice or not, it is a world.

Isn't it true however far we've wandered
Into our provinces of persecution
Where our regrets accuse, we keep returning
Back to the common faith from which we've all dissented,
Back to the hands, the feet, the faces?

Children are always there and take the hands
Even when they're most terrified; those in love
Cannot make up their minds to go or stay;
Artist and doctor return most often;
Only the mad will never never come back.

For doctors keep on worrying while away
In case their skill is suffering and deserted;
Lovers have lived so long with giants and elves
They want belief again in their own size;
And the artist prays ever so gently—

"Let me find pure all that can happen.
Only uniqueness is success! For instance,
Let me perceive the images of history,
All that I push away with doubt and travel,
To-day's and yesterday's, alike like bodies."

Yes, just like that. See Gunnar killed
At Hlitharendi white across the river,
And Flosi waiting on Three Corner Ridge,
And as the dancing turns me round
The servants fighting up on Little Daimon.

But not these only, just as clearly
As them, as clearly as at the moment
The wraps of cellophane torn off
From cigarettes flit through the glass
Like glittering butterflies, I must see all.

The service yesterday among the copse of ashes,
The old men dragging hymns, the woman weeping
Leaning against her husband as he yawned;
And two days back the townee from the gasworks
Riding to Thorsmörk, highly-strung,

Loud-voiced, consumed with passion to excel
His slower-witted red-faced friend.
And see there if I can the growth, the wonder,
Not symbols of an end, not cold extremities
Of a tradition sick at heart.

For that's our vulgar error, isn't it,
When we see nothing but the law and order,
The formal interdiction from the garden,
A legend of a sword, and quite forget
The rusting apple core we're clutching still.

It's that that makes us really selfish:
When the whole fault's mechanical,
A maladjustment in the circling stars,

The shuffling Couples in their heavy Boots

Back to the Hands, the Feet, the Faces

The Accordion playing

And goodness just an abstract principle
Which by hypothesis some men must have.

For whom we spend our idle lives in looking,
And are so lazy that we quickly find them,
Or rather, like a child that feels neglected,
Our proof of goodness is the power to punish,
We recognise them when they make us suffer.

Until indeed the Markafljōt I see
Wasting these fields, is no glacial flood
But history, hostile, Time the destroyer
Everywhere washing our will, winding through Europe
An attack, a division, shifting its fords.

Flowing through Oxford too, past dons of good will,
Stroking their truths away like a headache
Till only the unicorn and the fabulous bogey
Are real, and distinctly human only
The anarchist's loony refusing cry:—

"Harden the heart as the might lessens.
Fame shall be ours of a noble defence
In a narrow place. No choices are good.
And the word of fate can never be altered
Though it be spoken to our own destruction."

Dear Dick,

I have just been staying in the Njàl country. I gather the Nazis look on that sort of life as the cradle of all the virtues. The enclosed laws and regulations seem so dotty, I thought they might interest you.

W.

Formula of Peace-Making

1. There was feud between N. N. and M. M. but now they are set at one and many:

As the meter meted
And the teller told
And the doomsman deemed
And the givers gave
And the receivers received
And carried it away
With full fee as paid ounce
Handselled to them that ought to have it.

2. Ye two shall be made men:
> At one and in agreement
> At feast and food
> At moot and meeting of the people
> At church-soken and in the king's house.
> And wheresoever men meet

Ye shall be so reconciled together as that it shall hold for ever between you.

3. Ye two shall share knife and carven steak
> And all things between you
> As friends and not as foes.

4. If case of quarrel or feud arise between you other than is well

It shall be booted or paid for with money and not be reddening the dart or arrow.

5. And he of ye twain that shall go against the settlement or atonement made
> Or break the bidden troth,
> He shall be wolf hunted, and to be hunted
> As far as men hunt wolves;
> Christian men seek churches;
> Heathen men sacrifice in temples;
> Fire burneth; earth groweth;
> Son calleth mother, and mother heareth son;
> Folk kindle fire;
> Ship saileth; snow lieth;
> The Fin skateth; the fir groweth;
> The hawk flieth the long Spring day,
> With a fair wind behind him and wings outspread;
> Heaven turneth; earth is dwelt on;
> Wind bloweth; waters fall to the sea;
> Churl soweth corn.

6. He shall be out-cast
> From Church and Christian men;
> From houses of Gods and from men,
> From every world save hell-woe or torment.

7. Now do ye two both hold one book and place the money on the book that N. N. payeth for himself and his heirs
> Born and unborn
> Begotten and unbegotten
> Named and unnamed.

8. N. N. taketh troth and truce as M. M. giveth it.

> Dear troth and strong troth
> An everlasting peace that shall hold for ever
> While the world is and men live.

9. Now are N. N. and M. M. at peace or atonement and accord wher-
ever they meet

> On land or water
> On sea or on horseback
> To share oar and bilge scoop
> Bench and bulwark if need be
> Even set with each other
> As father with son or son with father
> In all dealings together.

Now they lay hands together, N. N. and M. M. Hold well these troths,
by the will of Christ and of all those men that have now heard this form of
peace:

> May he have God's grace that holdeth these troths or truce
> And he His wrath that breaketh these troths or truce
> And he have grace that holdeth them.
> Hail, ye that are set at one
> And we that are set as witnesses thereto.

Codex Regius

LAW OF WAGER OF BATTLE

1. There should be a cloak of five ells in the skirt and loops at the
corners. They must put down pegs with heads on one end that were
called Tiosnos. He that was performing must go to the Tiosnos so that the
sky could be seen between his legs, holding the lobes of his ears, with this
form of words (words lost); and afterwards was performed the sacrifice
that is called the Tiosno-sacrifice.

2. There must be three lines about the cloak of a foot breadth; outside
the lines there must be four posts, and they are called hazels, and the field
is hazelled when this is done.

3. A man shall have three shields, and when they are gone, then he shall
step on to the skin though he have left it before, and then he must defend
himself with weapon henceforth.

4. He shall strike first that is challenged.

5. If one of them be wounded so that blood come on the cloak, they
shall not fight any longer.

6. If a man step with one foot outside the hazels, he is said to flinch; but
if he step outside with both feet, he is said to run.

7. His own man shall hold the shield for each of them that fight.

8. He shall pay ransom that is the more wounded, three marks of silver as ransom.

THE VIKING LAW

1. No man should enter that was older than fifty and none younger than eighteen winters. All must be between these ages.

2. Never should kinship be taken into account of when they wished to enter that were not in the league.

3. No man there should run before a man of like power or like arms.

4. Every man there should avenge the other as he would his brother.

5. None then should there speak a word of fear or dread of anything, however perilous things might be.

6. All that they took in warfare should be brought to the stang or pole, little or big, that was of any value; and if a man had not done this, he must be driven out.

7. None there should kindle discussion or waken quarrel.

8. And if tidings came no man should be so rash as to tell it to anyone, but all tidings should be told to the Captain.

9. No man should bring a woman into the fort.

10. And none should be abroad three nights together.

11. And though one had been taken into fellowship that had slain father or brother of a man that was there before, or any near kinsman, and it was found out after he was received, the Captain should judge the whole case and whatever quarrel might arise between them.

12. No man should have a sword longer than an ell, so close were they to go.

13. They never took prisoners, women nor children.

14. No man should bind a wound till the same hour next day.

15. No man of them had less strength than two ordinary men.

16. It was their custom to lie ever outside the nesses.

17. It was another custom of theirs never to put awnings on their ships and never to furl the sail for the wind.

CHAPTER VIII

Letter to Lord Byron

Part III

My last remarks were sent you from a boat.
　　I'm back on shore now in a warm bed-sitter,
And several friends have joined me since I wrote;
　　So though the weather out of doors is bitter,
　　I feel a great deal cheerier and fitter.
A party from a public school, a poet,
Have set a rapid pace, and make me go it.

We're starting soon on a big expedition
　　Into the desert, which I'm sure is corking:
Many would like to be in my position.
　　I only hope there won't be too much walking.
　　Now let me see, where was I? We were talking
Of Social Questions when I had to stop;
I think it's time now for a little shop.

In setting up my brass-plate as a critic,
　　I make no claim to certain diagnosis,
I'm more intuitive than analytic,
　　I offer thought in homoeopathic doses
　　(But someone may get better in the process).
I don't pretend to reasoning like Pritchard's
Or the logomachy of I. A. Richards.

I like your muse because she's gay and witty,
　　Because she's neither prostitute nor frump,
The daughter of a European city,
　　And country houses long before the slump;
　　I like her voice that does not make me jump:
And you I find sympatisch, a good townee,
Neither a preacher, ninny, bore, nor Brownie.

A poet, swimmer, peer, and man of action,
　　—It beats Roy Campbell's record by a mile—
You offer every possible attraction.
　　By looking into your poetic style,
　　And love-life on the chance that both were vile,

Several have earned a decent livelihood,
Whose lives were uncreative but were good.

You've had your packet from the critics, though:
　　They grant you warmth of heart, but at your head
Their moral and aesthetic brickbats throw.
　　A "vulgar genius" so George Eliot said,
　　Which doesn't matter as George Eliot's dead,
But T. S. Eliot, I am sad to find,
Damns you with: "an uninteresting mind".

A statement which I must say I'm ashamed at;
　　A poet must be judged by his intention,
And serious thought you never said you aimed at.
　　I think a serious critic ought to mention
　　That one verse style was really your invention,
A style whose meaning does not need a spanner,
You are the master of the airy manner.

By all means let us touch our humble caps to
　　La poésie pure, the epic narrative;
But comedy shall get its round of claps, too.
　　According to his powers, each may give;
　　Only on varied diet can we live.
The pious fable and the dirty story
Share in the total literary glory.

There's every mode of singing robe in stock,
　　From Shakespeare's gorgeous fur coat, Spenser's muff,
Or Dryden's lounge suit to my cotton frock,
　　And Wordsworth's Harris tweed with leathern cuff.
　　Firbank, I think, wore just a just-enough;
I fancy Whitman in a reach-me-down,
But you, like Sherlock, in a dressing-gown.

I'm also glad to find I've your authority
　　For finding Wordsworth a most bleak old bore,
Though I'm afraid we're in a sad minority
　　For every year his followers get more,
　　Their number must have doubled since the war.
They come in train-loads to the Lakes, and swarms
Of pupil-teachers study him in *Storm's*.

"I hate a pupil-teacher" Milton said,
　　Who also hated bureaucratic fools;
Milton may thank his stars that he is dead,

Although he's learnt by heart in public schools,
   Along with Wordsworth and the list of rules;
For many a don while looking down his nose
Calls Pope and Dryden classics of our prose.

And new plants flower from that old potato.
   They thrive best in a poor industrial soil,
Are hardier crossed with Rousseaus or a Plato;
   Their cultivation is an easy toil.
   William, to change the metaphor, struck oil;
His well seems inexhaustible, a gusher
That saves old England from the fate of Russia.

The mountain-snob is a Wordsworthian fruit;
   He tears his clothes and doesn't shave his chin,
He wears a very pretty little boot,
   He chooses the least comfortable inn;
   A mountain railway is a deadly sin;
His strength, of course, is as the strength of ten men,
He calls all those who live in cities wen-men.

I'm not a spoil-sport, I would never wish
   To interfere with anybody's pleasures;
By all means climb, or hunt, or even fish,
   All human hearts have ugly little treasures;
   But think it time to take repressive measures
When someone says, adopting the "I know" line,
The Good Life is confined above the snow-line.

Besides, I'm very fond of mountains, too;
   I like to travel through them in a car;
I like a house that's got a sweeping view;
   I like to walk, but not to walk too far.
   I also like green plains where cattle are,
And trees and rivers, and shall always quarrel
With those who think that rivers are immoral.

Not that my private quarrel gives quietus to
   The interesting question that it raises;
Impartial thought will give a proper status to
   This interest in waterfalls and daisies,
   Excessive love for the non-human faces,
That lives in hearts from Golders Green to Teddington;
It's all bound up with Einstein, Jeans, and Eddington.

It is a commonplace that's hardly worth
    A poet's while to make profound or terse,
That now the sun does not go round the earth,
      That man's no centre of the universe;
      And working in an office makes it worse.
The humblest is acquiring with facility
A Universal-Complex sensibility.

For now we've learnt we mustn't be so bumptious
    We find the stars are one big family,
And send out invitations for a scrumptious
      Simple, old-fashioned, jolly romp with tea
      To any natural objects we can see.
We can't, of course, invite a Jew or Red
But birds and nebulae will do instead.

The Higher Mind's outgrowing the Barbarian,
    It's hardly thought hygienic now to kiss;
The world is surely turning vegetarian;
      And as it grows too sensitive for this,
      It won't be long before we find there is
A Society of Everybody's Aunts
For the Prevention of Cruelty to Plants.

I dread this like the dentist, rather more so:
    To me Art's subject is the human clay,
And landscape but a background to a torso;
      All Cézanne's apples I would give away
      For one small Goya or a Daumier.
I'll never grant a more than minor beauty
To pudge or pilewort, petty-chap or pooty.

Art, if it doesn't start there, at least ends,
    Whether aesthetics like the thought or not,
In an attempt to entertain our friends;
      And our first problem is to realise what
      Peculiar friends the modern artist's got;
It's possible a little dose of history
May help us in unravelling this mystery.

At the Beginning I shall *not* begin,
    Not with the scratches in the ancient caves;
Heard only knows the latest bulletin
      About the finds in the Egyptian graves;
      I'll skip the war-dance of the Indian braves;

Since, for the purposes I have in view,
The English eighteenth century will do.

We find two arts in the Augustan age:
    One quick and graceful, and by no means holy,
Relying on his lordship's patronage;
    The other pious, sober, moving slowly,
    Appealing mainly to the poor and lowly.
So Isaac Watts and Pope, each forced his entry
To lower middle class and landed gentry.

Two arts as different as Jews and Turks,
    Each serving aspects of the Reformation,
Luther's division into faith and works:
    The God of the unique imagination,
    A friend of those who have to know their station;
And the Great Architect, the Engineer
Who keeps the mighty in their higher sphere.

The important point to notice, though, is this:
    Each poet knew for whom he had to write,
Because their life was still the same as his.
    As long as art remains a parasite,
    On any class of persons it's alright;
The only thing it must be is attendant,
The only thing it mustn't, independent.

But artists, though, are human; and for man
    To be a scivvy is not nice at all:
So everyone will do the best he can
    To get a patch of ground which he can call
    His own. He doesn't really care how small,
So long as he can style himself the master:
Unluckily for art, it's a disaster.

To be a highbrow is the natural state:
    To have a special interest of one's own,
Rock gardens, marrows, pigeons, silver plate,
    Collecting butterflies or bits of stone;
    And then to have a circle where one's known
Of hobbyists and rivals to discuss
With expert knowledge what appeals to us.

But to the artist this is quite forbidden:
    On this point he must differ from the crowd,

And, like a secret agent, must keep hidden
    His passion for his shop. However proud,
    And rightly, of his trade, he's not allowed
To etch his face with his professional creases,
Or die from occupational diseases.

Until the great Industrial Revolution
    The artist had to earn his livelihood:
However much he hated the intrusion
    Of patron's taste or public's fickle mood,
    He had to please or go without his food;
He had to keep his technique to himself
Or find no joint upon his larder shelf.

But Savoury and Newcomen and Watt
    And all those names that I was told to get up
In history preparation and forgot,
    A new class of creative artist set up,
    On whom the pressure of demand was let up:
He sang and painted and drew dividends,
But lost responsibilities and friends.

Those most affected were the very best:
    Those with originality of vision,
Those whose technique was better than the rest,
    Jumped at the chance of a secure position
    With freedom from the bad old hack tradition,
Leave to be sole judges of the artist's brandy,
Be Shelley, or Childe Harold, or the Dandy.

So started what I'll call the Poet's Party:
    (Most of the guests were painters, never mind)—
The first few hours the atmosphere was hearty,
    With fireworks, fun, and games of every kind;
    All were enjoying it, no one was blind;
Brilliant the speeches improvised, the dances,
And brilliant, too, the technical advances.

How nice at first to watch the passers-by
    Out of the upper window, and to say
"How glad I am that though I have to die
    Like all those cattle, I'm less base than they!"
    How we all roared when Baudelaire went fey.
"See this cigar", he said, "it's Baudelaire's.
What happens to perception? Ah, who cares?"

To-day, alas, that happy crowded floor
        Looks very different: many are in tears:
Some have retired to bed and locked the door;
        And some swing madly from the chandeliers;
        Some have passed out entirely in the rears;
Some have been sick in corners; the sobering few
Are trying hard to think of something new.

I've made it seem the artist's silly fault,
        In which case why these sentimental sobs?
In fact, of course, the whole tureen was salt.
        The soup was full of little bits of snobs.
        The common clay and the uncommon nobs
Were far too busy making piles or starving
To look at pictures, poetry, or carving.

I've simplified the facts to be emphatic,
        Playing Macaulay's favourite little trick
Of lighting that's contrasted and dramatic;
        Because it's true Art feels a trifle sick,
        You mustn't think the old girl's lost her kick.
And those, besides, who feel most like a sewer
Belong to Painting not to Literature.

You know the terror that for poets lurks
        Beyond the ferry when to Minos brought.
Poets must utter their Collected Works,
        Including Juvenilia. So I thought
        That you might warn him. Yes, I think you ought,
In case, when my turn comes, he shall cry "Atta boys,
Off with his bags, he's crazy as a hatter, boys!"

The clock is striking and it's time for lunch;
        We start at four. The weather's none too bright.
Some of the party look as pleased as Punch.
        We shall be travelling, as they call it, light;
        We shall be sleeping in a tent to-night.
You know what Baden-Powell's taught us, don't you,
Ora pro nobis, please, this evening, won't you?

END OF PART III

CHAPTER IX

W.H.A. to E.M.A.—No. 1

Studentagarthurinn
Reykjavik.

July 12th

As you see, I've really got here. I didn't go to Finland after all. I felt another country would only be muddling. Finland has not the slightest connection with Iceland, and a travel book about unconnected places becomes simply a record of a journey, which is boring. I dare say it's all right if you're a neo-Elizabethan young man who has a hair-breadth escape or meets a very eccentric clergyman every five minutes, but I'm not. As it is, I've been here a month and haven't the slightest idea how to begin to write the book. Gollancz told me before I left that it couldn't be done, and he's probably right. Still the contracts are signed and my expenses paid, so I suppose it will get done. At present I am just amusing myself, with occasional twinges of uneasiness, like a small boy who knows he's got an exam to-morrow, for which he has done no work whatsoever.

I spent a very miserable first week here, for all the people I had introductions to were away. Reykjavik is the worst possible sort of provincial town as far as amusing oneself is concerned, and there was nothing to do but soak in the only hotel with a license; at ruinous expense. There is a would-be English band there with a leader looking like a stage gigolo, and real revolving coloured lights in the ballroom after ten. But as it is broad daylight all night the effect is rather depressing. Gradually I began to meet people, so that my head is reeling with gossip that I know is libellous, and information that I suspect of being unreliable.

I hear, for instance, that such and such a politician is either the first gentleman in Iceland or is suffering from persecution mania since he was laughed at by some children at the ski-club, that such and such a professor pawned his marriage lines the day before the wedding, that such and such a girl is a "levis avis", that the German consul has smuggled in arms in preparation for a Putsch, that the Icelanders cannot discipline their children, that England is the true home of spiritualism, and that the only good drinks are whisky and vermouth.

My own personal impressions don't go far yet. There is no architecture here and the public statues are mostly romanticised Galahad-Vikings. The King of Denmark has paid a visit and I watched him come out of the prime minister's house accompanied by distinguished citizens. I know top-hats and frock coats don't make people look their best, but on their appearance alone I wouldn't have trusted one of them with the spoons.

He went to see the Great Geysir, which refused to oblige, and the current rumour gives as the reason that out of national pride they fed it with local soap instead of the Sunlight brand to which it is accustomed.

The other excitement has been a Swedish students' week. They gave a concert, to which I went. They sang well enough, but the songs were dull—none of the polyphonic kind which I like. The concert opened oddly. One of the students on the platform put on white gloves and a yachting cap, and took hold of an enormous flag. As they began to sing what I presume was the Swedish National Anthem as everyone stood up, he brought the flag smartly to the present. I'm sure it was much too heavy for him. The song over he took off his gloves and his hat, stood the flag in the corner, and joined the rest of the choir. It all looked very pompous and silly, more what one would expect from the Nazis than from a sensible Scandinavian democracy.

After the second song a bouquet was brought in for the conductor; I hoped that this was just to encourage him, and that they would bring in a new and better one after each song till the platform was like a greenhouse, but I was disappointed.

I've been to Thingvellir, the stock beauty spot, which is certainly very pretty, but the hotel is full of drunks every evening. A very beautiful one called Toppy asked me to ring her up when I got back.

Last week I went down into the country and had a nice time riding, but I can't tell you about that now as I must pack ready to set off to-morrow for the North. How I wish you were here to help me, as you know how I hate it. This hotel is all right, but not up to your standard of course. It's a hostel for university students in the winter. The furniture is of that cosmopolitan modern sort you find in the waiting-rooms of all European airports. Snags—the food which is often cold and the bath which won't work. The proprietor is a nice man who tells me that he is a practical idealist and that his children have perfect characters. I'll try and go on with this to-morrow.

Hraensnef. July 15th

A game of rummy prevented me writing last night, but now there is an hour or so before the bus is due and I am tired of helping with the hay, which I have been doing since breakfast.

One of the nice things about Iceland is its small size, so that everything is personal. A steam roller is called a Briett after a well-known feminist with deformed feet. I had a proof of this on Monday morning when I was going to catch the bus. A man I had never seen before stopped me in the street and said "There are some letters for you", took me along and unlocked the post office specially for my benefit. How he knew I was leaving town I don't know. Among them were the proofs of my poems, so I can

occupy odd moments by trying to put in logical punctuation, which is
something I don't understand. I can only think of them as breathing indi-
cations. I hope you will approve of the dedication. They are due out in
October, which is a pity, as they will be eclipsed by the posthumous vol-
ume of Housman which is due for then.

I wonder very much what there'll be in it. There was a nice quatrain
going about the Oxford Senior Common Rooms before I left England
which he is said to have woken up reciting to himself:

> When the bells jussle in the tower
>   The hollow night amid
> Then on my tongue the taste is sour
>   Of all I ever did.

I've been trying to find out something about modern Icelandic poetry. As
far as I can make out there has been no break since the Romantic Revival,
which got here via Denmark and Germany, i.e. no "modernist" poetry to
puzzle the old ladies. Technically it is of a very high standard, rhyme,
assonance, and alliteration are all expected. As a Latin example of an
Icelandic verse structure I was given the following, which you can recite to
any dirty-minded don you meet.

> Theodorus tardavit
> Tempore non surrexit
> Violare voluit
> Virginem non potuit.

They seem to have preserved a passion for ingenuity helped by their
damnably inflected language, since the days of the Scalds, whose verse
would have broken St John Ervine right up. Even now they write pal-
indrome verses which can be read forwards or backwards, like this:

Falla tímans voldug verk	Daga alla stendur sterk
Varla falleg saga.	Studla ríman snjalla
Snjalla ríman studla sterk	Saga falleg varla verk
Stendur alla daga.	Voldug tímans falla.

Sentiment: Art is long and life is short or life is short and art is long. Or
verses like this in which the second half is made up of the beheaded words
of the first:

Snuddar margur trassin traudur	Many a lazy idler lounges
Treinist slangur daginn	And finds the day long;
Nudda argur rassin raudur	The wicked one rubs his red
Reinist langur aginn.	bottom
	And finds discipline irksome

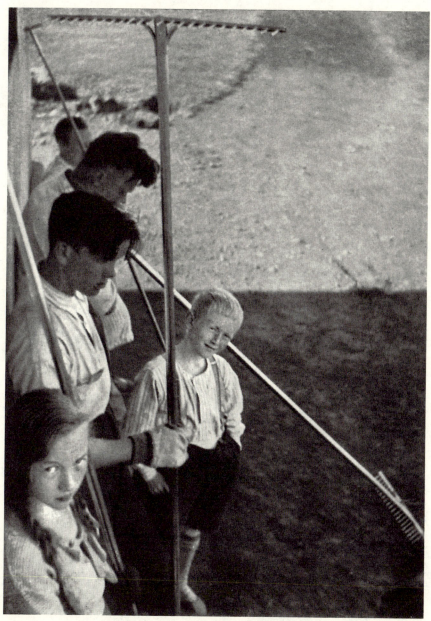

Haymakers resting

Herring-gutting

Lake shore

Another peculiar thing about Icelandic verse is the persistence of a genuine poetic language. In the following, for instance, which is the equivalent of a double entendre limerick like "The young people who frequent picture palaces", the first word for girl is as "poetic" as demoiselle.

> Yngissveinar fara á fjöll
>   Finna sprund i leynum
> Stúlkur elska atlaf böll
>   Ast fangnar í sveinum.

The proper version is:

> Young men go to embrace girls in secret
> Girls love to go to the ball
> In love with the young men.

But what has struck me most is that any average educated person one meets can turn out competent verse. When I was down in the South, I had an Icelandic student as companion; I gave him one of the ruthless rhymes:

> When baby's cries grew hard to bear
> I popped him in the Frigidaire.
> I never would have done so if
> I'd known that he'd be frozen stiff.
> My wife said "George, I'm so unhappé,
> Our darling's now completely frappé."

In twenty minutes he came back with this, which as far as I can make out is pretty literal.

> E grenjar kenja krakkinnmin
> Eg kasta honum i snjóskaflin
> Eg petta medal fljótast finn
> Thé frys á honum kjafturinn
> En sidan kveinar kerligin
> Ad króknad hafi ánginn sinn.

He also translated a serious poem of mine which I'm sorry to say I've lost but it sounded grand. I in return have been trying to teach them the Clerihew, and there are now, I hope, many little boys going about saying

> Jonathan Swift
> Never went up in a lift,
> Neither did Robinson Crusoe
> Do so.

I recited to my present companion, Ragnar, who is a mine of information about songs and proverbs, a touching little cri du coeur made by a friend:

> I think that I would rather like
> To be the saddle of a bike

only to find that the Icelandic equivalent in terms of horses already exists.

We are staying at a little farm under a cliff, called Hraensnef or Lava Nose, in Nordura, which is one of the great salmon fishing rivers, bought up of course and let to Harley Street surgeons and popular novelists. We started at eight o'clock yesterday morning. The buses are comfortable but the roads are not, and we hadn't gone ten miles before some of the passengers started to be sick. The driver tells me that the Icelanders always are. We stumbled along round a spectacular fjord called Hvalfjordur over a track that would have been rough going on foot, passing historical sites like the island from which a pirate's wife escaped her enemies by swimming to shore with her two children on her back, and the farm where a seventeenth-century clergyman called Peterssen wrote some famous passion hymns and died of leprosy, until we stopped for coffee at a little inn full of bad oil paintings and surrounded by bedraggled hens. In the last fifteen years or so there has grown up quite a school of Icelandic painters, and their work is to be found in all inns, schools, and public buildings. I've seen some heads by a man called Kjarval which I liked, one or two other landscapes by various people, and a farmer's own portrait of his mother; but Cézanne has done them no good. I suppose I should also say that we saw a pair of eagles. They looked far too heavy to fly.

We got to Hredavatn—a little lake about a mile and a half away, where we intended to stop—about half-past two, but the inn was full so we came on here, which is much better situated. Behind is a great escarpment of rock and to the left a cone-shaped mountain called Baula which looks fine from this distance, but I am glad I haven't got to climb it. To the right are some small craters which look as if they had been made the day before yesterday, as they are as destitute of vegetation as the slag heap of an iron foundry, and are surrounded by a tiny lava field which stops suddenly in the middle of the morass, like jam spilt out of a bowl.

The sitting-rooms of Icelandic farms are all rather alike. Like English cottages they are crammed with furniture and knick-knacks; there are pictures on the walls, and a bowl of picture postcards and snapshots of the family on the table, and there is always a harmonium. Unfortunately the music is nearly always the same, a book of psalm tunes and a book of songs something like Gaudeamus, all rather pom po pom pom. Here, however, I've found "Moonlight in the Sahara" but, alas, the vox humana won't work. The family consist of the farmer and his wife, an unmarried and rather spoilt daughter, a very independent son of eleven in a fetching red shirt, a little boy of four, the child of a relation, and a boy who is helping with the harvest and looks seventeen but is only fourteen. They are very hospitable and friendly.

Yesterday morning we spent riding, and to my great joy I got a really frisky horse who bucked and galloped as hard as one could wish. I got a scare once when we were going up the steep side of a valley and he started to slip.

In the afternoon we rode to Hredavatn and took a boat on the lake. It turned out a wonderful evening and we sat on an island and threw stones and waved at a girl in a bungalow on the shore. It took us about an hour to catch Ragnar's horse again, which tried to kick or bite when you came anywhere near it, but got home at last and spent the evening playing rummy, which I like because you can talk while you play. Svava, the daughter, had all the luck, and I discover that I am a very bad loser.

Ragnar is bothering me to come and pack, as the bus should be here any minute.

Saudakrökur

We caught the Icelandic Train Bleu all right. Two coaches crammed to capacity. How embarrassing it is to get into an already crowded bus when the passengers have got to know each other. We felt like the Germans invading Belgium. But the atmosphere soon thawed; I got my travelling rug well over my knees, found that my cigarettes had come out of their packet into my pocket, and settled down as an accepted citizen of a temporary regime.

In the front where the bunches of canvas flowers were, sat the élite, including an immense woman in a tiger skin coat. At the back where the bumps were at a maximum sat ourselves. In front of me a man with a convict's face looking very green, and next to me a man looking like Thomas Hardy. Presently the singing began. Two of the commonest tunes in Iceland are ones we know to Integer Vitae, and God save the King. Ragnar turned out to have a nice baritone, to know more songs, and to have more self-confidence than the others, so he led the singing while I fumbled for bass parts and occasionally got them. There was one long song about a person called Melakoff who I gather drank brandy and revived when the doctor began to dissect him.

I've got some gramophone records of more primitive local music, including an amazing one of a farmer and two children who yell as if they were at a football match. These are much more interesting; some of the music reminds me of the sort of intoning you get at a Jewish service, and with a curious prolonging of the final note.

The hills are all covered in mist. Road menders peered out of wayside tents, bridge sides suddenly shaved the bus. Loud cries of excitement told that someone had hit his head very hard on the roof at a bump. Thomas Hardy offered me some snuff and the bus roared when I sneezed. Now we were passing through a district of terminal moraines which looked too like the illustrations in a geography text book to be real. Here the last public execution took place in the early nineteenth century. Sweets were passed round. Sick streamed past the windows.

At four o'clock we reached Blonduos, a one-horse sort of place, where we were to have lunch. Everyone clattered off to their respective lavatories and then down to the dining-room, where I was lucky to arrive early enough to get a real chair instead of a bench. The first course was rice and raisins and ginger. I could have wept, I was so hungry. And the rest was scarcely better, enormous hunks of meat that might have been carved with a chopper smeared with half-cold gravy. No one can accuse the Icelander of being dainty. I watched a large man opposite leisurely stuffing down large pieces of tepid fat like the hero of a Sunday-school story.

On again, grinding over a watershed, up test gradients. The view from the top is said to be one of the best in the island, but it wasn't to-day. We came down to Vidamyri, where stands the oldest church in Iceland. Unfortunately we didn't stop, and I only caught a glimpse of it, squat and turf covered, like a shaggy old sheep with a bell round its neck. Shortly afterwards we reached the crossroads where we were to change horses. There was a hurricane blowing and the temperature outside wasn't far off freezing. As I paid the driver a ten krónur note blew away and I had to chase it for a hundred yards. The bus from Akureyri had also arrived, and Ragnar was talking to one of his old schoolmasters. I got into the primitive local bus and tried to get warm. Luckily it was only forty minutes or so to Saudakrökur, and we got there at eight. It might have been built by Seventh Day Adventists who expected to go to heaven in a few months, so why bother anyway. I have no wish to see it again. The inn is dirty, and smells like a chicken run. The proprietor has a wen on his face and charges 6 kr. a day. In my room are two embroidered samplers—*Blessed be the Lord* and *Blest are the pure in heart*—and an inferior print of Iceland's first fishing ship, dated 1876.

After supper I went to call on the local doctor, to whom I had an introduction. A very nice man with a face like a lizard, and a very keen diet crank. He has a hospital here and is very interested in cancer, the recent increase of which in Iceland he attributes to imported foods and too much sugar. He says the annual consumption of sugar per head is 80 lb. Came back to an early bed. The fishing ship creaked all night.

Decided to get out of this place as soon as possible, but it was not as easy as it sounded. A milk cart was due to leave for Holar at 2. It left at 5.30. There were three of us on a seat made for two, Ragnar, myself, and a gigantic red-faced consumptive boy. We stopped every five minutes to dump empty cans by the road side. Both my feet were sound asleep by the time we reached Holar: a church, a farm, and a large white agricultural school in the depths of a spectacular valley. The young Danish headmaster of the school welcomed us, and we sat and listened to the wireless while supper was prepared. Someone apparently has tried to assassinate Kind Edward VIII. Nobody looked very interested. Supper was poor, and we played rummy till bedtime with the consumptive and another boy with a bandaged finger. I scored 270 in one hand and was very pleased with myself.

Holar was the seat of a bishopric, and I spent the next morning in the church, which is as ugly as most protestant places of worship. The only relic of the past is the carved altar piece. I strummed on the harmonium, and balanced books and hassocks on the altar candlesticks, and stood on the altar in my socks and struck matches trying to photograph the carving. Mysterious violent figures rise out of the background slashing at prisoners without looking at them. Impassive horses survey another world than theirs. One of the thieves has his head thrown right back and on his forehead dances a bear holding a child. Serried figures, the Queen of Heaven with a tower, St Peter with no back to his head etc., rise like a Greek Chorus, right and left of the main panel. After lunch we got a couple of rather obstinate horses and started up the valley intending to visit the glacier at its head. It was a brilliant sunny day and we didn't get half way, but lay on the grass dozing and teasing a couple of bell spiders with a straw.

Great excitement here because Goering's brother and a party are expected this evening. Rosenberg is coming too. The Nazis have a theory that Iceland is the cradle of the Germanic culture. Well, if they want a community like that of the sagas they are welcome to it. I love the sagas, but what a rotten society they describe, a society with only the gangster virtues.

I saw Goering for a moment at breakfast next morning, and we exchanged politenesses. He didn't look in the least like his brother, but rather academic.

The milk cart back to Saudakrökur was worse than the first because we had to collect full cans. It took us four hours to go forty-two kilometres, and I had run out of cigarettes so just sulked into my waistcoat.

We didn't get away again till eight in the evening, but got through the afternoon somehow. We looked over the cheese works, a friendly place, not too efficient nor too clean, thank God. Two workmen were ragging about spinning each other round on a turntable. An old woman came in with a basket on her arm and begged for some cream. The doctor took me over his hospital and showed me the apple of his eye, his new X-ray apparatus. Most of the patients were very old women. A younger one who had had a cancerous breast removed the week before sat in a rocking chair and said she felt better. A surgeon's fees are not princely. 100 kr. for the removal of a breast, 50 kr. for an appendectomy, 18 kr. for amputating a finger. General practitioners get a small allowance from the state, but as they have to pay for their own dispensing, it must be hard to make ends meet. Chloroform is little used, and in the country districts the midwife has to act as anaesthetist.

The commonest complaints are T.B., cancer, and gastric ulcer.

We went back to the doctor for dinner. He may be a food crank but he has a very good table. He made us try two Icelandic specialities, old shark and whale pickled in sour milk, eccentric but not absolutely inedible. I smoked, but a little guiltily, as on his shelves were a number of books on the evils of tobacco. Time passed quickly enough as I got down some of his surgical books to read.

We got to our little farm Ulfstadur at last, about 11 p.m., to find a hot meal waiting for us, and went straight to bed.

Owing to some breakdown in the telephone system, the bus next morning had not been warned and was too full to take us, so we had to wait till the evening. Went riding in the morning, and pottered about in the afternoon. There was a lovely view from the lavatory. The bus came along about five and we didn't get to Akureyri till half-past eleven. Some of the passengers had bottles and were tight. Once we stopped for coffee and once we all had to get out, to cross a bridge the piles of which had sunk, making it unsafe. Ragnar was at school in Akureyri and was besieged by acquaintances the moment we arrived. It would be nice to be greeted like that at Victoria or Paddington. All the hotels were full and I was in rather a quandary, but a fair-haired artist friend of Ragnar's, one of a family of sixteen, had a butcher brother-in-law who was away, and we went off to his house, one of the new concrete ones, and made ourselves a meal of eggs and tea at one o'clock in the morning, feeling excited like sham burglars.

Monday

Went down to the Hotel Gullfoss for breakfast and looked round Akureyri, which is a much nicer town than Reykjavik. Unfortunately there is a fish factory to the north and to-day the wind is blowing from the north. There is a boat in the harbour going to Greenland on a geological expedition, loading up horses and fodder. With its single narrow funnel, its tall masts, and its crow's nest, it looks like an illustration out of a nineteenth-century adventure story. I went up to the school to see its collection of Icelandic paintings. They may not be very wonderful, but at least they are of interest to the Icelanders.

The artists are trying to amuse their friends, and their friends are not only artists. The pictures are not canned art from a Paris store which the locals must take because there is no other.

In the afternoon I had my hair cut and called on a lawyer, who gave me a whisky and cigar. We talked about capital punishment, beating, and boarding-schools. In the evening I went with a party of students to the only dance hall. The Blue Boy Band were deafening and never stopped playing for a second. Sweat poured off our faces. "A pity about Berg's death," I roared. But the band assured us all that the music goes round and round. A few tables off were the Greenland expedition, some of them half-caste Danish Eskimos. The eskimo features seem dominant. I stood it for about an hour and then went to bed.

Tuesday

I worked all this morning and finished a poem on Iceland at last, or rather it's about the voyage out and better, I hope, than William Morris's effort.

The only other one I've done is about why people read detective stories. Here it is.

DETECTIVE STORY

For who is ever quite without his landscape,
The straggling village street, the house in trees,
All near the church, or else the gloomy town house,
The one with the Corinthian pillars, or
The tiny workmanlike flat: in any case
A home, the centre where the three or four things
That happen to a man do happen? Yes,
Who cannot draw the map of his life, shade in
The little station where he meets his loves
And says good-bye continually, and mark the spot
Where the body of his happiness was first discovered?

An unknown tramp? A rich man? An enigma always
And with a buried past—but when the truth,
The truth about our happiness comes out
How much it owed to blackmail and philandering.

The rest's traditional. All goes to plan:
The feud between the local common sense
And that exasperating brilliant intuition
That's always on the spot by chance before us;
All goes to plan, both lying and confession,
Down to the thrilling final chase, the kill.

Yet on the last page just a lingering doubt
That verdict, was it just? The judge's nerves,

That clue, that protestation from the gallows,
And our own smile . . . why yes . . .

But time is always killed. Someone must pay for
Our loss of happiness, our happiness itself.

After lunch I went to bathe in what must be one of the most northerly
open-air swimming baths in the world. It is fed from a hot spring and as
the day was sunny and windless most attractive. The standard of swim-
ming here is high and there was one first-class diver. I cannot conceive of
anything else I would rather be able to do well. It's such a marvellous way
of showing off.

Have just heard for the first time of the civil war in Spain. Borrowed
two volumes of caricatures, which are really my favourite kind of picture,
and spent a very happy evening with Goya and Daumier and Max Beer-
bohm, only slightly marred by the consciousness of a sore throat, which
means one of my foul colds to-morrow.

I'll get this off in the post to-morrow morning, as I shan't be able to get
another one posted for several days, I expect, but I'll write something
every day and get it posted when I can.

W.

CHAPTER X

Eclogue from Iceland

Scene: The Arnarvatn Heath. Craven, Ryan,
and the ghost of Grettir. Voice from Europe.

R.   This is the place, Craven, the end of our way;
     Hobble the horses, we have had a long day.
C.   The lake is said to be full of trout;
     A pity the mist shuts the glacier out.
R.   There used to be swans but the frost last year
     Has brought their numbers down round here.
C.   I like this place. My personal choice
     Is always to avoid the public voice.
R.   You are quite right, Craven. For people like us
     This is an enviable terminus.
C.   To stay here a week like a placid brute

To explore the country, to fish and shoot.
R. That would be life, not having to shave,
    Clocking in as a wage-slave.
C. That would be life, Ryan, that would be life,
    Without kowtowing to boss or wife.
R. And beside this cold and silicate stream
    To sleep in sheepskin, never dream,
C. Never dream of the empty church,
R. Nor of waiting in a familiar porch
    With the broken bellpull, but the name
    Above the door is not the same.
C. And never wake to the maid's knock
R. Nor to the sour alarum clock,
C. Miss the faces fed at eight
    And the daily paper on your plate,
R. And miss the pile of letters from
    Forgotten Bill and ailing Tom.
C. Stop a moment. I think I hear
    Someone walking over there.
R. Hell, Craven. Who could it be?
    Except the echo of you and me.
C. There is someone there just out of sight—
    Will probably camp here to-night.
R. It is a damn bore anyhow.
    Look. There he is coming now.
    The mist makes him look so big
    And he is limping in one leg.
G. Good evening, strangers. So you too
    Are on the run? I welcome you.
    I am Grettir Asmundson,
    Dead many years. My day is done.
    But you whose day is sputtering yet—
    I forget. . . . What did I say?
    We forget when we are dead
    The blue and red, the grey and gay.
    Your day spits with a damp wick,
    Will fizzle out if you're not quick.
    Men have been chilled to death who kissed
    Wives of mist, forgetting their own
    Kind who live out of the wind.
    My memory goes, goes— Tell me
    Are there men now whose compass leads

Them always down forbidden roads?
Greedy young men who take their pick
Of what they want but have no luck;
Who leap the toothed and dour crevasse
Of death on a sardonic phrase?
You with crowsfeet round your eyes,
How are things where you come from?

C. Things are bad. There is no room
   To move at ease, to stretch or breed—

G. And you with the burglar's underlip,
   In your land do things stand well?

R. In my land nothing stands at all
   But some fly high and some lie low.

G. Too many people. My memory will go,
   Lose itself in the hordes of modern people.
   Memory is words; we remember what others
   Say and record of ourselves—stones with the runes.
   Too many people—sandstorm over the words.
   Is your land also an island?
   There is only hope for people who live upon islands
   Where the Lowest Common labels will not stick
   And the unpolluted hills will hold your echo.

R. I come from an island, Ireland, a nation
   Built upon violence and morose vendettas.
   My diehard countrymen, like drayhorses,
   Drag their ruin behind them.
   Shooting straight in the cause of crooked thinking
   Their greed is sugared with pretence of public spirit.
   From all which I am an exile.

C. Yes, we are exiles,
   Gad the world for comfort.
   This Easter I was in Spain, before the Civil War,
   Gobbling the tripper's treats, the local colour,
   Storks over Avila, the coffee-coloured waters of Ronda,
   The comedy of the bootblacks in the cafés,
   The legless beggars in the corridors of the trains,
   Dominoes on marble tables, the architecture
   Moorish mudejar churriguerresque,
   The bullfight—the banderillas like Christmas candles,
   And the scrawled hammer and sickle:
   It was all copy—impenetrable surface.
   I did not look for the sneer beneath the surface.
   Why should I trouble, an addict to oblivion,

Running away from the gods of my own hearth
With no intention of finding gods elsewhere?
R. And so we came to Iceland—
C. Our latest joyride.
G. And what have you found in Iceland?
C. What have we found? More copy, more surface,
   Vignettes as they call them, dead flowers in an album—
   The harmoniums in the farms, the fine-bread and pancakes
   The pot of ivy trained across the window,
   Children in gumboots, girls in black berets.
R. And dead craters and angled crags.
G. The crags which saw me jockey doom for twenty
   Years from one cold hide-out to another;
   The last of the saga heroes
   Who had not the wisdom of Njàl or the beauty of Gunnar,
   I was the doomed tough, disaster kept me witty;
   Being born the surly jack, the ne'er-do-well, the loiterer,
   Hard blows exalted me.
   When the man of will and muscle achieves the curule chair
   He turns to a bully; better is his lot as outlaw,
   A wad of dried fish in his belt, a snatch of bilberries
   And riding the sullen landscape far from friends
   Through the jungle of lava, dales of frozen fancy,
   Fording the gletcher, ducking the hard hail,
   And across the easy pastures, never stopping
   To rest among the celandines and bogcotton.
   Under a curse I would see eyes in the night,
   Always had to move on; craving company
   In the end I lived on an island with two others.
   To fetch fire I swam the crinkled fjord,
   The crags were alive with ravens whose low croak
   Told my ears what filtered in my veins—
   The sense of doom. I wore it gracefully,
   The fatal clarity that would not budge
   But without false pride in martyrdom. For I,
   Joker and dressy, held no mystic's pose,
   Not wishing to die preferred the daily goods
   The horse-fight, women's thighs, a joint of meat.
C. But this dyspeptic age of ingrown cynics
   Wakes in the morning with a coated tongue
   And whets itself laboriously to labour
   And wears a blasé face in the face of death.
   Who risk their lives neither to fill their bellies

Nor to avenge an affront nor grab a prize,
But out of bravado or to divert ennui
Driving fast cars and climbing foreign mountains.
Outside the delicatessen shop the hero
With his ribbons and his empty pinned-up sleeve
Cadges for money while with turned-up collars
His comrades blow through brass the Londonderry Air
And silken legs and swinging buttocks advertise
The sale of little cardboard flags on pins.

G. Us too they sold
The women and the men with many sheep.
Graft and aggression, legal prevarication
Drove out the best of us,
Secured long life to only the sly and the dumb
To those who would not say what they really thought
But got their ends through pretended indifference
And through the sweat and blood of thralls and hacks,
Cheating the poor men of their share of drift
The whale on Kaldbak in the starving winter.

R. And so to-day at Grimsby men whose lives
Are warped in Arctic trawlers load and unload
The shining tons of fish to keep the lords
Of the market happy with cigars and cars.

C. What is that music in the air—
Organ-music coming from far?

R. Honeyed music—it sounds to me
Like the Wurlitzer in the Gaiety.

G. I do not hear anything at all.

C. Imagine the purple light on the stage,

R. The melting moment of a stinted age,

C. The pause before the film again
Bursts in a shower of golden rain.

G. I do not hear anything at all.

C. We shall be back there soon, to stand in queues
For entertainment and to work at desks,
To browse round counters of dead books, to pore
On picture catalogues and Soho menus,
To preen ourselves on the reinterpretation
Of the words of obsolete interpreters,
Collate, delete, their faded lives like texts,
Admire Flaubert, Cézanne—the tortured artists—
And leaning forward to knock out our pipes
Into the fire protest that art is good
And gives a meaning and a slant to life.

G.   The dark is falling. Soon the air
     Will stare with eyes, the stubborn ghost
     Who cursed me when I threw him. Must
     The ban go on forever? I,
     A ghost myself, have no claim now to die.
R.   Now I hear the music again—
     Strauss and roses—hear it plain.
     The sweet confetti of music falls
     From the high Corinthian capitals.
C.   Her head upon his shoulder lies. . . .
     Blend to the marrow as the music dies.
G.   Brought up to the rough-house we took offence quickly
     Were sticklers for pride, paid for it as outlaws—
C.   Like Cavalcanti, whose hot blood lost him Florence
R.   Or the Wild Geese of Ireland in Mid-Europe.
     Let us thank God for valour in abstraction
     For those who go their own way, will not kiss
     The arse of law and order nor compound
     For physical comfort at the price of pride:
     Soldiers of fortune, renegade artists, rebels and sharpers
     Whose speech not cramped to Yea and Nay explodes
     In crimson oaths like peonies, who brag
     Because they prefer to taunt the mask of God,
     Bid him unmask and die in the living lighting.
     What is that voice maundering, meandering?
VOICE. Blues . . . blues . . . high heels and manicured hands
     Always self-conscious of the vanity bag
     And puritan painted lips that abnegate desire
     And say "we do not care" . . . "we do not care"—
     I don't care always in the air
     Give my hips a shake always on the make
     Always on the mend coming around the bend
     Always on the dance with an eye to the main
     Chance, always taking the floor again—
C.   There was Tchekov,
     His haemorrhages drove him out of Moscow,
     The life he loved, not born to it, who thought
     That when the windows blurred with smoke and talk
     So that no one could see out, then conversely
     The giants of frost and satans of the peasant
     Could not look in, impose the evil eye.
R.   There was MacKenna
     Spent twenty years translating Greek philosophy,
     Ill and tormented, unwilling to break contract,

      A brilliant talker who left
      The salon for the solo flight of Mind.
G.   There was Onund Treefoot
      Came late and lame to Iceland, made his way
      Even though the land was bad and the neighbours jealous.
C.   There was that dancer
      Who danced the war, then falling into coma
      Went with hunched shoulders through the ivory gate.
R.   There was Connolly,
      Vilified now by the gangs of Catholic Action.
G.   There was Egil,
      Hero and miser, who when dying blind
      Would have thrown his money among the crowd to hear
      The whole world scuffle for his hoarded gold.
C.   And there were many
      Whose common sense or sense of humour or mere
      Desire for self assertion won them through
R.   But not to happiness. Though at intervals
      They paused in sunlight for a moment's fusion
      With friends or nature till the cynical wind
      Blew the trees pale—
VOICE.   Blues, blues, sit back, relax,
      Let your self-pity swell with the music and clutch
      Your tiny lavendered fetishes. Who cares
      If floods depopulate China? I don't care
      Always in the air sitting among the stars
      Among the electric signs among the imported wines
      Always on the spree climbing the forbidden tree
      Tossing the peel of the apple over my shoulder
      To see it form the initials of a new intrigue,
G.   Runes and runes which no one could decode,
R.   Wrong numbers on the 'phone—she never answered.
C.   And from the romantic grill (Spanish baroque)
      Only the eyes looked out which I see now.
G.   You see them now?
C.   But seen before as well.
G.   And many times to come, be sure of that.
R.   I know them too
      These eyes which hang in the northern mist, the brute
      Stare of stupidity and hate, the most
      Primitive and false of oracles.
C.   The eyes
      That glide like snakes behind a thousand masks—
      All human faces fit them, here or here:

       Dictator, bullying schoolboy, or common lout,
       Acquisitive women, financiers, invalids,
       Are capable of all of that compelling stare,
       Stare which betrays the cosmic purposelessness
       The nightmare noise of the scythe upon the hone,
       Time sharpening his blade among high rocks alone.

R.   The face that fate hangs as a figurehead
       Above the truncheon or the nickelled death.

G.   I won the fall. Though cursed for it, I won.

C.   Which is why we honour you who working from
       The common premises did not end with many
       In the blind alley where the trek began.

G.   Though the open road is hard with frost and dark.

VOICE. Hot towels for the men, mud packs for the women
       Will smooth the puckered minutes of your lives.
       I offer you each a private window, a view
    (The leper window reveals a church of lepers).

R.   Do you believe him?

C.   I don't know.
       Do you believe him?

G.   No.
       You cannot argue with the eyes or voice;
       Argument will frustrate you till you die
       But go your own way, give the voice the lie,
       Outstare the inhuman eyes. That is the way.
       Go back to where you came from and do not keep
       Crossing the road to escape them, do not avoid the ambush,
       Take sly detours, but ride the pass direct.

C.   But the points of axes shine from the scrub, the odds
       Are dead against us. There are the lures of women
       Who, half alive, invite to a fuller life
       And never loving would be loved by others.

R.   Who fortify themselves in pasteboard castles
       And plant their beds with the cast-out toys of children,
       Dead pines with tinsel fruits, nursery beliefs,
       And South Sea Island trinkets. Watch their years
       The permutations of lapels and gussets,
       Of stuffs—georgette or velvet or corduroy—
       Of hats and eye-veils, of shoes, lizard or suède,
       Of bracelets, milk or coral, of zip bags,
       Of compacts, lipstick, eyeshade, and coiffures
       All tributary to the wished ensemble,
       The carriage of body that belies the soul.

C.   And there are the men who appear to be men of sense,

    Good company and dependable in a crisis,
    Who yet are ready to plug you as you drink
    Like dogs who bite from fear; for fear of germs
    Putting on stamps by licking the second finger,
    For fear of opinion overtipping in bars,
    For fear of thought studying stupefaction.
    It is the world which these have made where dead
    Greek words sprout out in tin on sallow walls—
    Clinic or polytechnic—a world of slums
    Where any day now may see the Gadarene swine
    Rush down the gullets of the London tubes
    When the enemy, x or y, let loose their gas.

G. My friends, hounded like me, I tell you still
    Go back to where you belong. I could have fled
    To the Hebrides or Orkney, been rich and famous,
    Preferred to assert my rights in my own country,
    Mine which were hers for every country stands
    By the sanctity of the individual will.

R. Yes, he is right.
C.   But we have not his strength,
R. Could only abase ourselves before the wall
    Of shouting flesh,
C.   Could only offer our humble
    Deaths to the unknown god, unknown but worshipped,
    Whose voice calls in the sirens of destroyers.

G. Minute your gesture but it must be made—
    Your hazard, your act of defiance and hymn of hate,
    Hatred of hatred, assertion of human values,
    Which is now your only duty.

C. Is it our only duty?
G.   Yes, my friends.
    What did you say? The night falls now and I
    Must beat the dales to chase my remembered acts.
    Yes, my friends, it is your only duty.
    And, it may be added, it is your only chance.

                                            L.M.

CHAPTER XI

W.H.A. to E.M.A.—No. 2

Akureyri.

Wednesday

I was right. My throat is much worse, like a lime kiln. I don't know whether this stage is the most unpleasant or the next, when I shall cry for two days. Most disfiguring and embarrassing and I've only got one hand-kerchief. I suppose my It is really repenting its sins, which it apparently has to do about every six months, but I wish it wouldn't. I caught the nine o'clock bus to Myvatn, full of Nazis who talked incessantly about Die Schönheit des Islands, and the Aryan qualities of the stock. "Die Kinder sind so reizend: schöne blonde Haare und blaue Augen. Ein echt Germanischer Typus." I expect this isn't grammatical, but that's what it sounded like. I'm glad to say that as they made this last remark we passed a pair of kids on the road who were as black as night. In the corner was a Danish ornithologist with a pursed little mouth, like a bank clerk who does a little local preaching in his spare time, who answered a Danish girl next to him in explosive monosyllables as if he were unused to talking and couldn't moderate his voice. Two more hikers got in, Austrians this time, and then a German ornithologist with a guide who looked a cross between Freud and Bernard Shaw. For the first time I have struck a dud bus. It developed a choke in the petrol feed and got slower and slower. We got to the Godafoss and I had some coffee while the Germans went to admire. One waterfall is extraordinarily like another. We didn't get to Myvatn till three o'clock and I was hungry and seedy and cross. The lake is surrounded by little craters like candle snuffers and most attractive. Hay was being made everywhere and the haymakers were using aluminum rakes, which I have never seen before. I had to make arrangements for an old German and his beautiful daughter who knew no English or Icelandic, who wanted to go to Dettifoss but didn't know if they dare. Papa was afraid it was too much for daughter, and daughter that it was too much for Papa, especially the horses. As he can't have weighed a pound under 16 stone, it is the horses who should worry. Afterwards I lay in the sun watching the hay being made and taking photographs. If I can get them developed in time, and any of them come out, I'll send you some. It's a pity I am so impatient and careless, as any ordinary person could learn all the technique of photography in a week. It is *the* democratic art, i.e. technical skill is practically eliminated—the more fool-proof cameras become with focusing and exposure gadgets the better—and artistic quality depends only on choice of subject. There is no place for the professional still photographer, and his work is always awful. The only decent photographs are scientific ones and amateur snapshots, only you want a lot of the latter to make an effect. A single still is never very interesting by itself. We started back about five, more crowded than ever, and the petrol stoppage much worse. We stopped to fill up and I was very annoyed because I was the wrong side of the bus to take the farmer's girl working the pump, which would have made a beautiful Eisenstein sort of shot. The bus got weaker and weaker and I thought we were going to run backwards down a hill. A lot of passengers got off at a school, thank goodness, and we tottered home, back-firing all the way, with a magnificent sunset over the mountains, and got in about ten. I went to eat and then ran into some drunk Norwegian sailors. An Icelandic acquaintance of theirs passed and greeted one by slapping him on the bottom, which started a furious argument conducted entirely in English, something like this.

—Why did you do that?

—Why shouldn't I?

—Don't you know it's an insult to slap a man on his arse?

—No, it isn't.

—Yes, it is.

—No it isn't. It's an Icelandic custom.

—Oh no, it isn't.

—How do you know?

—How do I know. Everybody knows.

—No, they don't.

—I tell you it's an insult to slap a chap's arse.

—How can you tell me when you don't know about Iceland?

—If you don't know that, you're goddam uneducated.

—How should I know that when I know it isn't.

(Two officers stroll up and stand by. The crowd begins to disperse.)

—Well, be more careful, next time, Mister, see.

—Same to you.

Thursday

Left at 8 a.m. for the east. The first part of the way was the same as yesterday. A couple were drawing nets out of a lake like a scene in the New Testament. At Godafoss one of the real professional English travellers got in, something I shall never be, handsome, sunburnt, reserved, speaking fluent Icelandic. Got to Husavik for lunch. A beautiful bay and much sun. On the pier herring gutting was in full swing; great beefy women standing up to their ankles in blood and slime, giving free demonstrations of manual dexterity. My cold has rolled over into the next stage and I am beginning to weep. After Husavik the road branched off into the desert and there were still large patches of snow on the stones, the remains of a particularly severe winter, looking as if a small boy had got loose with the whitewash. I amused myself by identifying the pictures. There was Australia, and there was Italy, and that one surely was meant to be Arthur Balfour. We crossed an estuary plain and stopped to look at Asbyrgi, a vaulted horseshoe-shaped ravine about two miles long, said to have been made by Odin's horse Sleipnir when he slipped. Ragnar pointed out a house to me where lived a painter who has a platonic passion for the Dettifoss and spends his days painting it.

After Asbyrgi the condition of the road defies description. Two ruts full of stones. Thank God there are only four of us in the bus. We can just manage about 5 m.p.h., first through a sort of scrub like the horrible country where O.T.C. field days are always held, then through absolute desert, sand and rocks, like the uninteresting and useless débris of an orgy. My cold keeps boiling over like a geysir. Hours pass. The lights are lovely. Now we are worming like a beetle through sandhills, sandhills of every shape, the pincushion, the carrot, the breaking wave. We sit swaying like sacks. Nobody speaks. About ten we get to Grimstadur, the farm where we are stopping the night. A bag of lime has burst in the luggage compartment and percolated into my pack. I watched the farmer's family crowding round him as he stood against a wall in the dusk and read the newspaper we had brought him. We had supper and tumbled into bed.

Friday

Lovely weather still, but my cold is still streaming so that I can't look anybody in the face. The country is a wide flat plain spotted with steep little hills and ridges. Herdubreid, looking with its glacier on the top like a large iced cake, stands up ahead of us, and far in the distance you can catch a glimpse of the Vatnajökull, the big icefield in the south. The road is better now and we get along quite quickly. We stop for a moment at the next large farm, Morduradalur, which is renowned for its home-made ale and a drunken clergyman. The country clergy here are all farmers as well, which brings them in touch with their parishioners, but perhaps rather secularises them. But I fancy that religion has never been very enthusiastic in Iceland. The church organisation certainly must have been the one thing which civilised the social structure of the settlers, but I can't picture Iceland producing St Francis or St Theresa.

I found a nice little story in the Faroe saga.

"Thora asked him what teaching his foster-father had given him on Holy Writ. Sigmund said he had learnt his paternoster and creed. Thora said—I would like to hear it! On which he sang his paternoster, as she thought, pretty well. But Sigmund's creed ran thus—

> Given to us are angels good,
> Without them go I ne'er a foot;

Where'er I am, where'er I fare
Five angels follow everywhere.
Paltering prayer, if so I be,
To Christ they bear them presently:
Psalms, too, seven can I sing—
Have mercy on me, God my King.

"At this moment Thrand comes into the room and asks what they are talking about. Thora answers and says her son has been rehearsing the Christian knowledge he had taught him. But the creed seems to be wrong! 'Ah!' said Thrand, 'Christ, you know, had twelve disciples or more, and each of them had his own credo. Now I have my credo, and you have the credo you have been taught; there are many credos, and they may be right without being exactly the same.' And with that the conversation ended."

We crossed the watershed and came down to Skjoldolfsstadur for a not very good lunch. Sweet soup, which I will not eat, and hot smoked mutton, which I can only just get down. Then on to Egilsstadur for tea where I say good-bye to Ragnar and get off. Egilsstadur is one of the largest farms in Iceland and the first place where I have got really good food. It has a private cemetery on a little hill, surrounded by birch trees, but private cemeteries aren't allowed any more. I went and looked at a fine bull, which looked absurdly like a film director I know called Arthur Elton, and then found the lavatory, which opens into a lower barn, giving such an updraught that the paper flies up instead of down and I had to chase it like a moth.

In the bus to-day I had a bright idea about this travel book. I brought a Byron with me to Iceland, and I suddenly thought I might write him a chatty letter in light verse about anything I could think of, Europe, literature, myself. He's the right person I think, because he was a townee, a European, and disliked Wordsworth and that kind of approach to nature, and I find that very sympathetic. This letter in itself will have very little to do with Iceland, but will be rather a description of an effect of travelling in distant places which is to make one reflect on one's past and one's culture from the outside. But it will form a central thread on which I shall hang other letters to different people more directly about Iceland. Who the people will be I haven't the slightest idea yet, but I must choose them, so that each letter deals with its subject in a different and significant way. The trouble about travel books as a rule, even the most exciting ones, is that the actual events are all extremely like each other—meals—sleeping accommodation—fleas—dangers, etc., and the repetition becomes boring. The usual alternative, which is essays on life prompted by something seen, the kind of thing Lawrence and Aldous Huxley do, I am neither clever enough nor sensitive enough to manage.

I hope my idea will work, for at the moment I am rather pleased with it. I attribute it entirely to my cold. It is a curious fact how often pain or slight illness stimulates the imagination. The best poem I have written this year was written immediately after having a wisdom tooth out.

Saturday

The weather has broken at last and it is cold and pouring wet. I consoled myself with the harmonium. There is more music here than usual, and my rendering of the Air on the G string was very moving, but I came to grief on a gavotte or a trumpet suite. One of the more curious jobs in this world must be inventing attractive names for harmonium stops, particularly for the tremolo. In this country I have seen it called: Vox humana—Aeolean harp—Vox seraphicum—Vox celeste and Cor angelicus.

Went for a short walk in the afternoon to the bridge over the half-lake, half-river which fills this valley. I was thinking about a picture of the seven ages of man I saw in some book or other. A girl playing a flute to a young man, two infants wrestling in a meadow, and an old man staggering to a grave, you know the kind of thing. After tea the thoughts developed into a poem.

> O who can ever praise enough
> The world of his belief?
> Harum-scarum childhood plays
> In the meadows near his home;
> In his woods love knows no wrong;
> Travellers ride their placid ways;
> In the cool shade of the tomb
> Age's trusting footfalls ring.
> O who can paint the vivid tree
> And grass of phantasy?
>
> But to create it and to guard
> Shall be his whole reward.
> He shall watch and he shall weep,
> All his father's love deny,
> To his mother's womb be lost.
> Eight nights with a wanton sleep,
> But upon the ninth shall be
> Bride and victim to a ghost,
> And in the pit of terror thrown
> Shall bear the wrath alone.

A rich tradesman and family from Reykjavik have arrived. Unpleasant. Smug with money and no manners. The children keep whispering.

Sunday

Still wet, but my cold is much better. Worked at the Byron letter in the morning and after lunch, thank goodness, the rich people went away. I asked for a horse and did I get one! The farmer gave me his own, which is the prize race horse of East Iceland. He came with me and we had a marvellous ride. I didn't start too well, as when I mounted in a confined courtyard with a lot of other horses near, I clucked reassuringly at him, which sent him prancing round, scattering people and horses in all directions. I was rather frightened, but got on all right after that. The moment we got on the road, we set off at full gallop, and on the last stretch home I gave him his head and it was more exciting than a really fast car. The farmer said, "You've ridden a lot in England, I expect." I thought of my first experience at Laugavatn a month ago, and how I shocked an English girl by yelling for help, I thought of the day at Thingvellir when I fell right over the horse's neck when getting on in full view of a party of picnickers. This was my triumph. I was a real he-man after all. Still, Ronald Firbank was a good horseman. And what about those Scythians.

Spent the evening playing rummy with the farmer's children, a girl of fourteen with an extravagant squint, and two boys of twelve and eight, all charming. I hope to go up to the valley to Hallormastadur to-morrow.

Monday

Arrived here safely this afternoon. This place is a school in the winter to teach girls weaving and cooking. The headmistress is the image of Queen Victoria and rather formidable, but I think she will thaw.

Staying here is a Scotch girl, an English lecturer at one of our provincial universities, and a great Icelandophil. She thinks them like the Greeks. Terribly enthusiastic, rushing at life like a terrier. I wonder if she really enjoys herself as much as she protests. I can imagine her in a siege saying at dinner, "What? Fried rats? Goody. How awfully exciting." But she is intelligent and extremely good-hearted.

Tuesday

I found an excellent collection of German songs and spent the morning playing them. Really, they choose funny things to cheer themselves up with. How about this for a soldier's song?

> Die bange Nacht ist nun herum
> Wir reiten still, wir reiten stumm
> Wir reiten ins Verderben.

Christian and
Mr Worldly Wiseman

The Arctic Stare

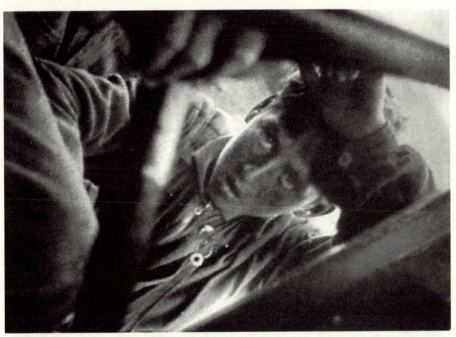

Local swimming
Sports

I found a nice nursery song from Saxony:

> Hermann, fla larman
> Fla pipen, fla trummen
> Der Kaiser will kummen
> Mit Hammer und Stangen
> Will Hermann uphangen.

It's a great pleasure to think that all the best nursery poetry shocks the Neo-Hygienic-child-lover. There's an Icelandic lullaby for instance:

> Sofúr thu svind thitt
> Svartur i áugum
> Far i fulan pytt
> Fullan af dráugum

which means, I think:

> Sleep, you black-eyed pig.
> Fall into a deep pit full of ghosts.

I also found a magnificent Dance of Death, which I expect you know, but I had never seen before, and which seems very topical. I like the grammar lesson in the last line:

> Der Tod reit' oft als General
> Beim Trommel und Kanonschall.
> Er gibt Parol, du musst ihm nach
> Ins Bivouac bis zum letzen Tag.
>
> Als klapperdürrer Musikant
> Zieht er durch Deutschland und welsche Land
> Und wenn er geigt, tanzt alles geschwind,
> Der Mann, das Weib, der Bursch, das Kind.

The book belongs to a German lady who married an Icelander, solely, as far as I can see, in order to have a child, as she left him immediately after, and now won't go back to Germany. She had a magazine from the Race Bureau of the N.S.D.P. which was very funny. Boy-scout young Aryans striding along with arms swinging past fairy-story negroes and Jews.

In the afternoon we rode over the lake to Brekka, where the local doctor lives, and had tea. A romantic evening sky over the lake but unfortunately no romance.

Wednesday

Still fine but beginning to cloud over, and we shall have rain before nightfall. I have just blistered both my hands by helping the busman to pump up a tyre with a dud pump, which is annoying, as I shan't be able to ride for several days. The only other people staying here are a couple of Dutch schoolmarms, intelligent, well dressed, and attractive, a great contrast to the English variety. They have seen the Pfeffermühle, I'm glad to say, and were very impressed. By the way, I've finished that sketch with the goose for Thérèse. I haven't got a copy as it's appearing in the next volume of *New Writing*, but I'll send you a proof copy as soon as it comes. I hope it will suit her.

Reykjavik, Sunday, August 9th

It's a very long time since I added anything to this letter, but I have been absorbed in the Byron letter. I've finished a draft of the first canto and bits of the second and third. My trouble is that the excitement of doing a kind of thing I've never tried to do before keeps making me think it's better and funnier than it is, which is the reverse of what I usually find.

I drove over last Sunday from Egilsstadur in the farmer's car to Seydisfjordur, where there was a sport-fest. The farmer and his wife have been very good to me. He is a power in the new farmers' party, which represents the richer ones, who want to lower wages and increase the price of meat. For the first time in my life I have become a wireless fan. I suppose it is due to being alone in a foreign country. I listen to everything from England, even the cricket matches and the Stock Exchange quotations. I wish I knew how things were really going in Spain. Do write and tell me if you know anything authentic.

There was still a lot of snow on the hills round Seydisfjordur, really deep drifts in places and snow bridges over the streams. The sport-fest was a primitive affair. Some part singing by middle-aged men in blue suits with brass buttons which was barely audible, male and female high jumping, and a swimming race in a shallow and very dirty-looking pond. I decided to stay in the town till Wednesday, when the *Nova* was due to arrive—by which I've come round the north back to Reykjavik—and put up at the home for decayed old ladies. The landlady had travelled a little and was snobbishly pleased to see me; but snobbish or not, she was kindness itself, and kept making dishes that she thought I should like—pies and French salads. Among her collection of post-cards was a remarkable diagram of the Icelandic mountains, which I stole, as I want to reproduce it in the book. Half the inmates were in bed dying, but those that were up were odd enough. An old postman and his wife crippled with arthritis, a lady who has fits of violent mania and paper tearing, but unfortunately not while I was there, a dipsomaniac, and an old man with the face of a saint who has a month to live (cancer). He has been a servant all his life to a farmer's widow who never paid his wages, made him sleep on the floor, and whenever he had any new clothes said "Those are too good for you. What do you want with fine things like that?" and gave them away.

The only comedian in Iceland arrived and gave a performance in a tent, patter songs and the Ruth Draper kind of imitations. As far as I could judge he was rather good. The audience howled with pleasure. While I was wandering about in the early hours of the morning waiting for the *Nova*, I ran into him. He was rather tight. He gave me a copy of his book of songs and told me many times how wonderful he was.

The boat was almost empty. There was a young American who had just taken his law finals and was having his last fling in Europe, one of those Americans who read everything, from poetry to anthropology and economics, with apparently no preferences; and a Norwegian fish merchant of twenty-four (looking nineteen) who runs his own business, and tells me you can't trust the Icelandic business man a yard.

I find voyages so boring that I can hardly remember a thing. The discipline was not aggressive and we could wander on to the bridge whenever we liked. The captain was charming and told us all about his children and their illnesses. He has only once got off the boat to go on shore in Iceland and that was to have a bath. He has a stock phrase: "I mustn't spoil my girlish figure." There was a selfish little English gentleman of independent means at Akureyri who said, apropos of Spain, "Why can't these foreigners behave themselves. It's sickening. You can't travel anywhere nowadays without running into trouble," and told me the French had no sense of discipline.

There were delicious pickled pigs' trotters to eat at dinner. And that's about all I remember except the whaling station at Talknafjördur. O no it isn't. I had a nightmare after reading a silly book on spiritualism. I woke up sweating and wrote it down there and then in the middle of the night, but now I can hardly decipher what I wrote. I was in hospital for an appendix. There was somebody there with green eyes and a terrifying affection for me. He cut off the arm of an old lady who was going to do me an injury. I explained to the doctors about him but they were inattentive, though presently I realized that they were very concerned about his bad influence over me. I decide to escape from the hospital, and do so after looking in a cupboard for something, I don't know what. I get to a station, squeeze between the carriages of a train, down a corkscrew staircase and out under the legs of some boys and girls. Now my companion has turned up with his three brothers (it may have been two). One, a smooth-faced, fine fingernailed blonde, is more reassuring. They tell me that they never leave anyone they like and that they often choose the timid. The name of the frightening one is Giga (in Icelandic *Gigur* is a crater) which I associate with the name Marigold and have a vision of pursuit like a book illustration and I think related to the long red-legged scissor man in *Shockheaded Peter*. The scene changes to a derelict factory by moonlight. The brothers are there, and my father. There is a great banging going on which they tell me is caused by the ghost of an old aunt who lives in a tin in the factory. Sure enough the tin, which resembles my mess tin, comes bouncing along, and stops at our feet, falling open. It is full of hard-boiled eggs. The brothers are very selfish and seize them, and only my father gives me half his.

I wish I could describe things well, for a whale is the most beautiful animal I have ever seen. It combines the fascination of something alive, enormous, and gentle, with the functional beauties of modern machinery. A seventy-ton one was lying on the slip-way like a large and very dignified duchess being got ready for the ball by beetles. To see it torn to pieces with steam winches and cranes is enough to make one a vegetarian for life.

In the lounge the wireless was playing "I want to be bad" and "Eat an apple every day". Downstairs the steward's canary chirped incessantly. The sun was out; in the bay, surrounded by buoys and gulls, were the semi-submerged bodies of five dead whales: and down the slip-way ran a constant stream of blood, staining the water a deep red for a distance of fifty yards. Someone whistled a tune. A bell suddenly clanged and every-one stuck their spades in the carcase and went off for lunch. The body remained alone in the sun, the flesh still steaming a little. It gave one an extraordinary vision of the cold controlled ferocity of the human species.

I got back here this afternoon about tea-time, and have been trying to read through my enormous pile of correspondence. I hope to get back to England about the middle of September. Louis has arrived but is still out seeing the Great Geysir. Now I have to make arrangements for this Bryanston party who arrive at the end of the week. Michael is coming with them and I hope he will stay on with Louis and me. It will be nice having some company for a change. To-morrow I have to give an interview to the press. I'm enclosing some oddments which may interest you; the fairy story which I came across again here used to be my favourite when I was small and my father used to read it to me. If it hadn't been for this story I don't suppose I should be here now.

W.

PROVERBS

A step-child will never get so well into the bosom but the feet will hang out.
Ale is another man.
Better drink from a beaker than from bent palms.
Better turn back while the car can run.
Between friends a narrow creek; between relations a wide fjord.
Bridals for young, barrows for old.
Dull edge and point should only carve soft meat.

Herring Factory

Whaling Station during the Lunch-hour

Flensing by Steam-winch

The Corpse

Every man likes the smell of his own farts.
Fear not raven at rest, nor ragged old man.
Folk are found even over the fells.
Gifts should be handed, not hurled.
He that falls will seldom fatten.
If mending will do, why cut off.
It's hard to bring many heads under one hat.
It is merely a transition, said the fox, when they flayed him alive.
Land is ruled by lip, sea by hand.
Love your neighbour but let his gate stand still.
Many a person thinks me like himself.
Many meet who made no tryst.
Many secrets are hidden in a fog.
Many tell of St Olaf who never saw him.
Men fight by day, devils by night.
No one becomes a bishop without a beating.
One must cultivate the oak under which one has to live.
Only those who have it can splash the skyr about.
Pissing in his shoe keeps no man warm for long.
Shameless is the robber that first seeks a settlement.
Tend the sapling; cut down the old oak.
The best muck is the mould that falls from the master's shoes.
The child brought up at home who has been nowhere, knows nothing.
The haddock never wanders wide, but it has the same spot by its side.
The meanest guest has keenest eye.
The oak gets what another tree loses.
The water is deep indeed for the old mare when the young foal has to swim.
The wolf has made friends before now of fighting swine.
They can't all have the bishop for their uncle.
Too bland is a blemish; too bluff greater.

GELLIVÖR

Near the end of the Roman Catholic times a certain married couple lived at a farm named Hvoll, situated on a firth in the east part of the country. The farmer was well to do, and wealthy in sheep and cattle. It was commonly reported that a female troll lived on the south side of the firth, who was supposed to be mild and not given to mischief.

One Christmas Eve, after dark, the farmer went out and never returned again, and all search for him was in vain. After the man's disappearance one of the servants took the management of the farm, but was lost in the same manner, after dark on the Christmas Eve following. After this the widow of the farmer determined to remove all her goods from the house and live elsewhere for the winter, leaving only the sheep and herds under the charge of shepherds, and returning to pass the summer there. As soon as the winter approached she made preparations for leaving Hvoll, until the next spring, and set the herdsmen to take care of the sheep and cattle, and feed them during the cold season.

For home use she always kept four cows, one of which had just had a calf.

Two days before her intended departure, a woman came to her in her dreams, who was dressed in an old-fashioned dress of poor appearance. The stranger addressed her with these words: "Your cow has just calved, and I have no hope of getting nourishment for my children, unless you will every day, when you deal out the rations, put a share for me in a jug in the dairy. I know that your intention is to move to another farm in two days, as you dare not live here over Christmas, for you know not what has become of your husband and of the servant, on the last two Christmas Eves. But I must tell you that a female troll lives in the opposite mountains, herself of mild temper, but who, two years ago, had a child of such curious appetite and disposition that she was forced to provide fresh human flesh for it each Christmas. If, however, you will do willingly for me what I have asked you to do, I will give you good advice as to how you may get rid of the troll from this neighbourhood."

With these words the woman vanished. When the widow awoke she remembered her dream, and getting up, went to the dairy, where she filled a wooden jug with new milk and placed it on the appointed spot. No sooner had she done so than it disappeared. The next evening the jug stood again in the same place, and so matters went on till Christmas.

On Christmas Eve she dreamt again that the woman came to her with a friendly salutation, and said, "Surely you are not inquisitive, for you have not yet asked to whom you give milk every day. I will tell you. I am an elf-woman, and live in the little hill near your house. You have treated me well all through the winter, but henceforth I will ask you no more for milk, as my cow had yesterday a calf. And now you must accept the little gift which you will find on the shelf where you have been accustomed to place the jug for me; and I intend, also, to deliver you from the danger which awaits you to-morrow night. At midnight you will awake and feel yourself irresistibly urged to go out, as if something attracted you; do not struggle against it, but get up and leave the house. Outside the door you will find a giantess standing, who will seize you and carry you in her arms across your grass-field, stride over the river, and make off with you in the direction of the mountains in which she lives. When she has carried you a little way from the river, you must cry, 'What did I hear then?' and she will immediately ask you, 'What did you hear?' You must answer, 'I heard someone cry, "Mamma Gellivör, Mamma Gellivör!"' which she will think very extraordinary, for she knows that no mortal ever yet heard her name. She will say, 'Oh, I suppose it is that naughty child of mine,' and will put you down and run to the mountains. But in the meantime, while she is engaged with you, I will be in the mountain and will thump and pinch her child without mercy. Directly she has left you, turn your back upon the mountain and run as fast as you possibly can towards the nearest farm along the river banks. When the troll comes back and overtakes you, she will say, 'Why did you not stand still, you wretch?' and will take you again in her arms and stride away with you. As soon as you have gone a little way you must cry again, 'What did I hear then?' She will ask as at first, 'What did you hear?' Then you shall reply again, 'I thought I heard someone calling "Mamma Gellivör, Mamma Gellivör!"' on which she will fling you down as before, and run towards the mountain. And now you must make all speed to reach the nearest church before she can catch you again, for if she succeed in doing so she will treat you horribly in her fury at finding that I have pinched and thumped her child to death. If, however, you fail in getting to the church in time, I will help you."

When, after this dream, the widow awoke, the day had dawned, so she got up and went to the shelf upon which the jug was wont to stand. Here she found a large bundle, which contained a handsome dress and girdle and cap, all beautifully embroidered.

About midnight on Christmas Day, when all the rest of the farm people at Hvoll were asleep, the widow felt an irresistible desire to go out, as the elf woman had warned her, and she did-so. Directly she had passed the threshold, she felt herself seized and lifted high in the air by the arms of the gigantic troll, who stalked off with her over the river and towards the mountain. Everything turned out exactly as the elf had foretold, until the giantess flung down her burden for the second time, and the widow made speed to reach the church. On the way, it seemed to her as if someone took hold of her arms and helped her along. Suddenly she heard the sound of a tremendous land-slip on the troll's mountain, and turning round saw in the clear moonlight the giantess striding furiously towards her over the morasses. At this sight she would have fainted with fear had she not felt herself lifted from the ground and hurried through the air into the church, the door of which closed immediately behind her. It happened that the priests were about to celebrate early mass, and all the people were assembled. Directly after she came into the church the bells began to ring, and the congregation heard the sound of some heavy fall outside. Looking from one of the windows they saw the troll hurry away from the noise of the bells, and, in her flight, stumble over the wall of the churchyard, part of which fell. Then the troll said to it, "Never stand again," and hurrying away took up her abode in another mountain beyond the confines of the parish of Hvoll.

CHAPTER XII

Hetty to Nancy

Gullfoss.

August 17th (Monday I think, but you can't be sure in these parts.)

Dearest Nancy,

How are you and I hope you are liking the Dolomites—it was the Dolomites, wasn't it—and what about your new girl-friend? I thought she sounded sweet but that may be just by contrast. With the last I mean; I warned you about her all along and what can one expect of someone who reads botany? You keep to the Arts, darling, though in Cambridge I suppose even the Arts are just a teeny bit marked with the beast—all this psychology and politics. Now don't *you* go and get political, because that would be the last straw. The hammer and sickle are all right where they belong but they don't suit lady dons. Oh dear, I am writing under such difficulties—that was Maisie gave me a kick then. Not intentional; it's the size of them you know. Maisie Reynolds, in case you think I mean Maisie Goldstein. Well, I am writing in a frightful tent made by Maisie's sister-in-law when she was convalescent. She must have been very ill, I think. We are going round a thing called the Langjökull; if you want to pronounce it you must move your mouth both ways at once, draw your tongue through your uvula, and pray to St David of Wales. Lang means long and jökull means glacier; depressing don't you think? Why we are doing this I can't imagine and if we had to do it, *why, oh why* like this? Here am I with Maisie in a tent and on our left side is another tent and on our right side is another tent. And what do you think are in those tents? SCHOOLGIRLS! Would you believe it? Robin will think I am returning to my vomit. He already holds it a great blot on my character, my having been a school-marm. Well, Maisie said it would be much cheaper to have these girls along. They were all fixed up with guides, you see. So I in a moment of weakness agreed to it. Four girls—Ruth, Anne, Mary, and Stella—and a marm called Margery Greenhalge. They are really quite possible, poor dears, but I mean, *I mean, darling,* does one come to Iceland for this? It's all very well for Maisie; it's copy for her, she's writing a new book about a schoolmistress who hanged herself, but when this pack of girls gets in The Great Open Spaces goodness knows what is going to happen. Sprained ankles is the least I should think (they've none of them ever ridden horses; nor have I for that matter). Talking of the G.O. Spaces Maisie says they are a closed book. I have been wondering if this would be considered an epigram because I couldn't see that it was very funny and Maisie is supposed to be witty, but then it is different in London, where

Stella's Boot

Shoeing

Horses on Lava

people have always been drinking sherry before you say anything to them. It is a pity you don't know Maisie though or you would see the joke of all this. Which brings me back to this tent. M. says it is my own fault for not bringing a tent of my own. Hers is a minute conical affair stuck up on a collapsible, not to say collapsing, umbrella-handle which comes (very much so) to pieces, three of them, and one of them we lost of course, it being already getting dark (Heavens what grammar!) so when you get it up in the end it is not more than five foot across but that gives you quite a wrong impression of amplitude because, as I said, it is a cone and it narrows so quickly that even when Maisie and I are on our hands and knees we can only talk to each other round the back of each other's heads—do you see what I mean—and goodness knows how we are going to sleep in it. M. says it would be all right if she were by herself as she always sleeps in the foetal position but sleeping in the foetal position means curling herself round the axle-tree (that *is* the word, isn't it) and I am just not going to have Maisie encroaching on my half of ground-sheet, it's not as if she were petite after all, still I have to try and be nice about it as Maisie has been rather vexed with me. You see, she never made it clear that she expected me to turn up for this expedition equipped with one of everything—one fork, one knife, one spoon, one cup, one plate—so naturally I came with none of everything because I thought they were provided by the company. But it seems not. I must try and become more like Miss Greenhalge, who has organised her little flock beautifully, they all have cups and knives and their tents look just like tents, which is more than Maisie's does. I don't mind the shape or the colour so much though Maisie's scores a blob on both but what really galls me is that the girls' tents have doors which lace up all snug and comfy whereas this thing has a large triangular hole in it open to the breeze and nothing to cover it. Maisie has brought a very flashy pneumatic mattress with her, yellow on one side and blue on the other, she looked like something out of Brueghel blowing it up but it does look definitely comfortable; I have only got a second-hand sleeping-bag, Miss Greenhalge calls it a flea-bag (Miss Greenhalge is one of those people who when in Rome insist on talking Roman) *my* bag was left behind by an explorer—doesn't that make one feel the real thing—and it had a corkscrew in it which seemed odd but Maisie says nothing need surprise you from an explorer and she is going to write a book about explorers some time called The Pole of Solitude. I am writing this by a candle. Maisie is holding it. The night outside is damp. Doubly damp in fact, (*a*) because there is a Scotch mist, (*b*) because in our efforts to do the right thing from the start we have pitched camp on the edge of a ravine and in the spray of a large waterfall. This waterfall is called Gullfoss. I am told that foss is also the Icelandic for bicycle because when they introduced the bicycle the natives could think of nothing

except a waterfall sufficiently velocitous to compare it with. Anyhow it is a
very fine waterfall as waterfalls go but, as Maisie says, they don't go far.
One of the girls, Mary, has a ciné-camera and took some photos of it in
the twilight. Maisie is getting tired of holding the candle but I must just
get down the events of the day for you. This morning we met our girls in
Reykjavik and took them buying oilskins. Miss G. wanted also to do the
sights but we dissuaded her. There is only one real sight in Reykjavik and
that is a museum of sculpture by a man called Einar Jonsson. The worst
sculpture I have ever seen in my life, and that is saying a lot. First of all all
the pieces are in plaster and you know how filthy plaster gets, secondly
they are all, or nearly all, *enormous,* thirdly they are symbolic. And the
symbolism, darling, is the sort they used to have in the Academy before
someone put their foot down or was it the effect of the war? You know—
Time pulling off the boots of Eternity with one hand while keeping the
wolf from the door with the other. The only one which didn't seem to be
symbolic was Queen Victoria on an elephant; a welcome piece of natural-
ism as Maisie remarked. So we didn't take the girls to this corrupting
spectacle but they had a look round the shops of the great city Reykjavik
and most of the things are imported from England, raspberry-coloured
baths and mauve lavabos, but there was one window of home-made Ice-
landic pottery which for some odd reason (or perhaps influenced by Einar
Jonsson's Victoria) consists mainly of mantelpiece figures of elephants.
This reminds me that we asked someone why Beatrix Potter shouldn't be
done in Icelandic and they said, "But the children wouldn't know any of
the animals." Which is true—frogs, squirrels, rabbits—you just don't find
those things here. Well, all the time we were looking at these novelties of
civilisation (comparative novelties here though I even saw some Elizabeth
Arden preparations and also heard some children singing The Music
Goes Round and Around in Icelandic which also no doubt is culture pace
Hitler who wants to reclaim this island and will no doubt substitute the
Eddas for the Lutheran prayerbook) Maisie, who is an indefatigable inter-
viewer, was interviewing a Social Democrat whom I saw at parting, a lost
soul M. says—was the first socialist here and is ending in sorry compro-
mise. All I noticed was the colour scheme of his hands—dark brown to
deep orange, strong black hair on them, and very light pink fingernails.
So we shook off the dust of that city and took our bus for Gullfoss. What
giggling, my dear! The bus was a combination bus and lorry. In the bus-
part sat ourselves—a *merry* little company—and in the lorry-part sat our
packs and food. The food is much but odd—10 kilograms of smoked
mutton (Hāngikýll in Icelandic, you'd never guess how that's pro-
nounced), Miss Greenhalge by the way doesn't use the word Icelandic, she
calls it the local lingo, 10 long loaves of brown bread, brick-hard, the sort
of thing you find in Egyptian tombs, a vast dried mat of Hardfiskur (dried

Head

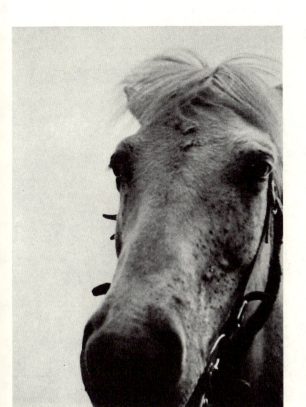

Tail

Free hot Water

With Paucity that never was Simplicity

fish), two enormous slabs of cheese (4 kilos each I think), 10 large tins of mutton. It seems a lot but we have to feed the guides as well—two guides, nice men but they have no English. Well, as we bussed it, we turned aside to look at a small geysir called Grylla which spouts of itself every two hours through a small round hole in a flat stone. Of course we didn't know when the two hours were due so we had to wait. There were sundry hot springs steaming away in the valley and Maisie who likes to play at being Every Girl Her Own Billican, insisted on making tea in one of them. Needless to say it was unspeakable as the springs are full of sulphur. The geysir was better value, it went off just as we were beginning to despair of it, a sweet little thing so slim and girlish, the girls devised a game of throwing a tin cup on to it, the jet stream works like a catapult and you should have heard how Miss Greenhalge laughed. She laughs conscientiously and seismically. She is very large, very red, and bespectacled (lenses as thick as beer-bottles). The girls among themselves call her La Paloma, you know how romantic they are in these schools. In Reykjavik I found a letter from a little girl called Elsie comparing me to a whole string of heroines, the first being Lucrezia Borgia and the last being Elizabeth Barrett Browning. So it looks like a week of pussy-talk in the lava-fields. Not that Miss Greenhalge would encourage that sort of thing. On the contrary she believes in making her girls behave like public schoolboys—I mean as public schoolboys behave in Ian Hay or in the Mind of God. She wants to see their stuffing, has been reading the latest Peter Fleming. They are all rather in trepidation about their horses. The guides tell us that the last ladies they took this way fell off their horses and all but refused to get on again. Which is a bad lookout when there is no human habitation for thirty miles or so and no possible means of transport and no food except an occasional bilberry. We met our horses for the first time in the gloaming, real little ducks, 17 in all—7 for us, 2 for the guides, 3 reserves, 5 pack-horses. Maisie fancies herself quite Melton Mowbray now as she rode her first pony several weeks ago. One of the girls, however, Stella, apparently rides at school and even knows how to jump. She is a flashy little girl and is the only one with real leather riding-boots, not that they will do her any good as in Iceland you keep riding through rivers and you need a good honest Dunlop. I am sorry to say that I come last in point of attire because whereas everyone else has riding-breeches I have only got a pair of hopcloth beach-trousers I bought in the South of France. They are somewhat baggy to squeeze into one's gumboots apart from being claret-coloured but why buy new clothes just for a week's Baden-Powelling? Maisie by the way is sleeping in this tent in pyjamas and was very shocked because I got into my sleeping-bag without undressing. To see Maisie struggling out of her undies in two square foot of space makes you realize what built the British Empire. She has been reproving me incidentally for mine—not my Empire, my undies—she says that to wear crêpe-de-chine panties may be all right for Metro-Goldwyn-Mayer but it won't do round the Langjökull. But then Maisie, who is a shirt-and-tie girl herself, is all for the approximation of the sexes; she says that to emphasise one's femaleness is a relic of barbarism like men wearing beards, and that if I do nothing else on this trip it is essential that I shall reduce my bust measurement. Which reminds me that the landscape to-day was rather nice from our bus, at one point there was a perfectly lovely vista all in stratas—first brilliant green grass, almost emerald, then a bank of pink clouds I suppose of dust, then blue serrated crags, and last but not least a glacier floating in the distance, milky-blue—you could hardly believe it was real. But what worries me is that they have no goats. Plenty of fine fat sheep and very clean compared with English ones, but ne'er a goat not even of the littlest. It is like the Irish over cheese. I firmly believe that if the I.F.S. would only (a) make cheese and (b) eat it, they would (a) improve their budget and (b) modify their characters—become more pacific like the Dutch. Q.E.D. and what was all the fuss about? M. says she is tired of holding the candle so will write you more to-morrow, darling, provided I've not broken my collar-bone. Sweet dreams in the Dolomites.

August 18th

Darling, *darling*, DARLING, it is very lucky your poor friend Hetty is alive. The worst night I have had since Aunt Evelyn walked in her sleep—you remember, the fire-extinguisher business. I had great difficulty to start with getting to sleep. For why? (1) Because we had pitched the tent with our heads running downhill, (2) because we had pitched it on bilberry bushes, which kept prickling me through the groundsheet, (3) because Maisie *would* get more and more foetal, so that in the end her feet were playing an absolute barrage on my tummy. All things, however, are possible and I did get to sleep in the end only to be woken by a clammy thing on my face like some very unpleasant beauty treatment—you know when they plaster you with eggs and whey and things—which turned out to be the tent or more precisely the inner cover of the tent because there are two. There was a frightful noise of rain outside and the whole tent was caving in under it, Maisie was swearing and saying she was going down with all hands. I took the ostrich's course and hid my head in my sleeping-bag. Not that that was unduly dry and the foot-end of it was sopping because that was where the door of the tent came. When I popped out my head again, the tent had become very much smaller (Heaven knows it was small enough to start with) and was closing in on us like something in Edgar Allan Poe. So I cowered round the pole in the middle and Maisie and I got entangled like a pair of wet tennis-shoes when one packs them in a hurry. And the rain fell 40 days and 40 nights. Or so it seemed. And the tent got smaller and smaller. For once in my life I was glad to get up at six—that's what you do on these expeditions. The rain had stopped but the air was full of waterfall. M. and I were very angry to learn that all the others had had a dry night and we made a surly breakfast in our oilskins, M. precariously cooking some coffee on her rather undependable stove. By the time breakfast was over there was actually some sun, in fact the day looked promising. There was much complication over the packing of the food panniers because when a pony carries a pannier each side they have to be exactly the same weight. It sounds easy but it isn't—who knows the relative weights of cheese and hardfiskur? While the others were taking a morning look at the rainbow spray of Gullfoss Maisie and I had our first lapse from esprit de corps and sneaked into the little tin house which caters for trippers where we had some very good coffee. After all there won't be anywhere to buy anything for a week. Then we sorted our horses, Maisie taking the best, a sturdy white beast with solid pillar-like legs (Ranelagh standards don't go here) and off we started. Off we started indeed, bang up the side of the valley; if you have never been on a horse before it does seem a little hard to start on the perpendicular. *I was scared stiff.* And when we got to the top they started trotting—simply terrifying and very very painful—I think my horse must do what is called a brock which even the professionals don't like. In any case their trot is too short for one to do any rising in one's saddle so we had to ride like the cavalry (*sic*) and I fully sympathised with Mary who kept telling the barren plateau that her legs were on fire in tones of bravado mingled with abject panic. We had a respite however when the pack-horses got lost. There is one very naughty white pack-horse who thought he would go home to Geysir where he came from and turning to the left at a fork went flat out for home before anyone realised what was happening. So the two guides and Maisie and Ruth and Anne followed him while the rest of us loitered along the right road at a walk and comparatively painlessly. In single file most of the time, the road being a mere track through stony deserts rather reminiscent of Hollywood. The day opened out and there were highly spectacular views on the left, intense blue amethyst mountains castellating the glacier. There ought to be another glacier on the right but we couldn't see it. Eventually the others came back with the pack-horses and about 1.0 we stopped for a rest at one of the rare patches of grass, taking off the horses' saddles and packs and I expected some food but it seems that that isn't done. Stella showed off a little by quite superfluously adjusting her horse's bit while the rest of us creakingly lowered ourselves on to the welcome turf. But very very shortly we started again and this time we did some cantering. Cantering is even more perilous but not so painful as trotting. Miss Greenhalge was riding a heavy black pony look-ing rather like something in a pantomime; you felt that *she* might just as well do the walking and the pony trot between her legs. She (Miss G.) is really very large indeed. (Maisie says that it is psychological being so tall and that tall people are running away from life. Hence, at the other end, Napoleon.) Well, gradually we came up to the hills on the left which flank the glacier and having passed a snappy little picture-postcard gorge we encamped about 5.0 on a spongy piece of grass where we hobbled our horses according to the guides' instructions (the guides are exceedingly nice not to say long-suffering), turned them adrift and began putting up our tents. It was then that Maisie and I made a scientific discovery. This tent of Maisie's has an outside cover and an inside cover. Well it seems that if you don't want to get wet you mustn't let these two touch. Now last night we went out of our way to peg them down absolutely flush. It seemed so much neater but that was why we got so wet. The tent is still pretty clammy by the way. Having put up the tents we ate a large meal. The girls are getting hungry and were quite willing to try the despised smoked mutton. Smoked, not cooked mind you; you put your teeth in a hunk and then haul away the hunk in both fists. After that Greenhalge took some of the girls up Bláfell, which is a craggy mountain on the left, while M. and I diverted ourselves more according to our years, stumping through a marsh on the right of our camp in order to inspect the gorge of the river Hvitá. The gorge like all Icelandic gorges is perpendicular and composed of that beastly breaking stone. The Hvitá was turbulent and a most peculiar colour. "The putty-coloured gletcher," Maisie said appreciatively. We amused ourselves rolling down stones into it while Maisie told me that her next novel is to deal with the English colony in Fréjus. As we picked our way back through the marsh we kept hearing a single desolate creaking sound—like a creaking gate as M. said—which it turns out is a plover. This land would really make a very good setting for Hell, it reminds me of Gustave Doré's illustrations to the Inferno. The sphagnum moss everywhere gives the effect of ruins and you can imagine the souls of wicked philosophers sitting here and there on the sharp stones, their beards covered with lichen repenting their false premises. We got back before the others, so had to make the coffee or rather the coffee and cocoa as Ruth can't drink coffee. M.'s petrol stove is not all it might be and has to be pumped all the time. Greenhalge and the girls came back from Bláfell, they hadn't reached the top of course and what they had was very hard going, all loose shale and stuff—every three foot forward they slipped two foot back. We opened another tin of mutton and found it much better than last night's; we think it has benefited from its jolting on horseback. After dinner Greenhalge opened a little case and, to Maisie's horror began to offer the girls quinine pills and vegetable laxatives. Maisie has a bee in her bonnet about laxatives; she thinks her inside knows best. I was thirsty after all the mutton and went to the stream for water—it is so cold that it seems to lacerate your gums. Greenhalge is a good sort really, always ready to lend you a knife or a cup and she does all the washing up. The girls don't do anything much in that line excepting possibly Anne who is going to be house-prefect next term. Anne is the best-looking though she will be better looking when she has learned not to pout. She probably has a nice little temper on occasions and does a power of grumbling. Her intonation and vowel sounds are just what you expect from a nice British schoolgirl. Ruth, I should say, is the most intelligent. She says hardly anything but is obviously terribly noticing and puts herself out for nobody. She has just got five credits in the School Certificate and ought to go far. Stella, who as I said is the horsewoman of the party, is conceited but perhaps a little pathetic. She talks a great deal with a lot of wasted emphasis, wears a vulgar but no doubt expensive bracelet, and altogether gives the effect of a cheeky terrier pup that has not been quite properly trained. Mary is an odd girl, neurotic, and capable of quite astonishing ineptitude. She puts questions to Greenhalge like an irrepressible child— "Why are the mountains that shape, Miss Greenhalge?" "How many kilometres are there in a mile, Miss Greenhalge?" and so on and so on indefinitely. She has a tight little mouth, at least she makes it tight through nervousness, which is rather incongruous with her figure, for she is a strapping wench and would look all right if she could stop putting her hands to her face and get the doleful expression out of her eyes. She has a nice nature and thanks one even superfluously when one does anything for her. She seems to enjoy herself in spite of her fear of the horses and gives vent to her enjoyment with a quaint mouse-like heartiness. She shares the large tent with Greenhalge and Anne while Stella and Ruth have the little tent. Talking of tents Maisie and I are much more comfortable this evening and I have invented a scheme for the candle which would do credit to a Girl Guide. Perfectly simple: you take an ordinary country shoe which laces up, insert the candle in the laced part, and fasten it there tightly. The shoe is Maisie's. Maisie says that this tent inside by candlelight looks like a Stratford-on-Avon set for Julius Caesar. Maisie is smoking like a tramp-steamer. I tell her she is one of those people like Midas; everything she touches turns to cigarettes. I have been explaining to her that she will feel the effects of it in ten years' time when she is forty. She in her turn has been lecturing me on marriage. She is afraid that I will become servile. I tell her that Robin is much too vague for anyone to be servile to him but she maintains that that makes him all the more dangerous and that I shall have to spend my time running after him with his season ticket. M. says only unintelligent women ought to get married. She would prefer me to have a career like yours, darling, but she forgets I am not qualified. Not that personally I could breathe if I lived in Cambridge. All those coffee-parties you have with people talking about Marx. *And the intrigues, darling, the intrigues!* No, it's marriage for me unless Robin thinks better of it. I shouldn't blame him, poor dear, but I don't think he will. It's curious one should attract people when one isn't really very attractive. How do you explain it? I really must go to sleep now, I feel a heroic stiffness in my joints and it seems highly doubtful whether I shall be able to mount a horse to-morrow. Maisie seems to be asleep with a cigarette in her mouth. Her pneumatic bed is sighing like something out of A. E. Housman. I shouldn't be surprised if it's flat by to-morrow. Good-night, darling.

August 19th

To-day started rottenly but was a good day afterwards. We had to pull down our tents and breakfast in icy rain. I had brought no gloves and felt my fingers were going to fall off. The girls looked none too happy though we didn't actually have any tears. We decided that we should all change horses from yesterday and that each day we should take them in rotation in order of age. This meant that I got the one Maisie had yesterday, which is the star horse and goes like the wind. It is pure white all over though Stella says it is technically a grey. But if you call a white horse grey, what do you call a grey horse? Anyhow this horse was a goer and for the first time I felt the joys of horsemanship, though to start with I was very much alarmed especially when it opened its throttle on the edge of a precipice. We had one terrific gallop (canter actually) down a long hill and across a plain of ashes, a dust-storm whipping our faces so that we were riding blind. I turned my face to the left to avoid the grit in my eyes and there saw suddenly a shining sea tilted obliquely upwards, catching the sun. Like something in the Ancient and Modern hymnbook. First I thought it was water and could not understand why it stayed put. It was the icefield. I liked it exceedingly. About mid-day we stopped for a rest and Greenhalge doled out chocolate—four tiny squares per head. I could hardly prevent myself asking for more; it is most instructive to note one's mental unadaptability, one just can't imagine there won't be a shop further on where one can buy all the chocolate one wants. As a matter of fact the next place we came to, Hvitanes, *was* very civilised. It is where I am writing now—in a very swish hut of corrugated iron buttressed all along the sides with growing turf and the walls lined inside with matchboarding. Near by is a little tin house with a man in it whom you pay one króna for your night's lodging and he sells you cigarettes. We arrived at this blissful spot about 2.0 and after a cold meal were marshalled once more on horses to go and see the glacier which runs down the mountain opposite into an attractive lake called Hvitavatn. Unfortunately I did not have the white horse again but one of the reserves or pack-horses and a very dim beast he was and needed a deal of slapping. We had an amazing trek across the flat grassland to the north of the lake which is nothing but a delta of broad, rapid, and ice-cold rivers. We had to ford them one after another and how the horses stand it I can't imagine. Anne and I had the worst horses and were left a long way behind floundering ignominiously and hoping the horses wouldn't fall down with us. Following a devious route we crossed our last river (about the ninety-ninth) and left the horses on the further bank under a steep cliff of shale. Which same we began to climb and clambering up that sort of thing in gumboots is, I may tell you, no Sunday-school treat. What was more, we had no idea why we were going up it. The guide can't talk English, you see. Well, why we were going up it was in order to have a close-up of the glacier but glaciers have very bad complexions, and for myself I would much rather see them from a distance. Greenhalge, Ruth, and I occupied ourselves by climbing a little conical hill to get a wider view of the countryside which was certainly very beautiful. We also saw a bit of ice fall off the edge of the glacier. On our ride home we saw about thirty young horses running through the grassland at their pleasure. Where ignorance is bliss . . . Little do they know that in a future season they will have to carry people like us about. On arriving at our hut Maisie at once began to cook dinner. She said it was quite time we had a hot meal so she poked about the hut and our luck was in, for what did she find but a primus stove and a large pan. So Maisie put the whole contents of one of the tins of mutton in the pan and mixed it (against my advice) with water and boiled it on the stove. Oddly enough the result was very good. I bought some more cigarettes from the man in the hut who seemed a little amused by us all. Perhaps they don't know their Angela Brazil round here. I notice that the Icelanders in spite of their tough existence have a certain whimsicality not common among the other Scandinavians. Perhaps the explanation is that given by an Icelander in Reykjavik—that it's the Irish in them which accounts for this. After dinner every girl washed her own dish but I not having a dish merely rinsed the grease from my hands in the broad and serene river that flows between the hut and the mountains. I should mention that a little further down this river is the most exquisite convenience, a kind of wooden sentry-box which projects over the water; I have already visited it twice; in this barren country such comfort is really lyrical. After washing up we wrote our names in the Visitors' Book and all of us except the guides played rummy by the light of an oil-lamp (unheard-of luxury!) in which Ruth had all the luck, sitting there saying nothing, with a pale quiet smile, time after time laying down her cards and going out. Irritating little girl! Not so irritating as Stella though, who talked without ceasing. The room got in the most awful fug as Greenhalge had allowed the girls to smoke (give a pawn and take a queen, you know; Greenhalge is all for making men of them) which is all right for them because they are sleeping upstairs (fancy having an upstairs!) but not so good for Maisie and me who are having this room to ourselves. I have just been outside for a breath of fresh air and saw the huge mountain opposite floating on nothing—the nothing was of course ice. There is some talk of another party whom we may meet on this route—N.U.S. I think—gloomy how educational the place seems to be becoming. I am not sure that I like the English in Iceland. The ones coming over on my boat were a very odd lot. The second class much nicer than the first. There was a little cockney confectioner who did tricks with his false teeth and was reading a book on how to be a successful writer. Then there were two Welsh Jews from Birkenhead who had a great many odd bits of curious knowledge and one of them used to sing The Rose of Tralee and Die Lorelei; fruity wasn't the word for it. There was a young tax-collector from Preston who carried the Oxford Book of English Verse in his pocket. And there were half a dozen old schoolmistresses (but they travelled first) from Manchester who had already gone the pace in Finland and Russia and Brussels. I wonder what they all want out of Iceland. Or just to say they have been there? My bed to-night is on a wooden bench with a mattress under my sleeping-bag. It being comparatively warm, I am sleeping in my panties and vest. I will now try if I can blow out the oil-lamp without getting up for it.

August 20th

Darling, I am nearly dead. Up at six again to-day and my horse was a demon. And that wicked Maisie who had it yesterday, never let on about it. It has the brock all right. When we started this morning the trouble began with its saddle slithering down under its tummy. These horses have a deplorable habit of inflating themselves when you fasten their girths. Well by the time I had tightened its girth I had to catch up the others, so first I trotted and then I cantered and really I don't know which was the more uncomfortable. Well, when we did catch up the others, my malicious beast charged straight in among the pack-horses and gored my leg against one of the wooden panniers. And after that it ran away with me, tossing me sky-high in its cantering so that I had to hang on by the mane and my eyes were streaming with the wind in them. "If I don't fall off this horse," I said, "I shall be very proud of myself." That finished it. We were then riding along a narrow track sunk in the ground to a depth of three feet or more—the sort of place you ought to proceed at a walk but where my horse suddenly decided to go full speed ahead so that my right foot caught in the right bank of the track and I fell gracefully over its tail with my foot still in the stirrup. I will say that the horse stood still till I disintricated myself. After that we got among rocks and there we all just had to walk. On our left was a river in a very narrow gorge, the sort you could jump over if you were a fool, and the sides moulded into all sorts of elegant concaves. The mountains beyond it licked down great tongues of ice and it would all have been very romantic if I had not felt so sore. We stopped for our midday snack in a pleasant meadow encircled by mountains and sitting in the shelter of a bank by a little stream ate smoked mutton and raisins. Maisie, who fancies herself with a camera, went round taking art shots of people through each other's legs. I must say we were well worth photographing. The cold weather makes us all look much funnier in our various defences against it. Maisie herself has taken to wearing a sou'-wester with an old felt hat fastened on over it with a safety-pin. Her sou'-wester is bright yellow, her oilskin coat is black, and her enormous gumboots are brown. Wisps of hair straggle down over her forehead and when she walks she moves like something that is more at home in the water. Margery Greenhalge also looks pretty odd. She wears an amazing woollen helmet with earflaps which combined with her goggles and general outsizeness makes her look like a piece of Archaic Greek sculptuary. Stella, goodness knows why, appears to be wearing a blue and white bathing-cap. Anne has a kind of a Cossack hat which would suit her as an equestrienne for Bertram Mills. After our snack, we took our horses by the reins and led them up over a very steep and stony ridge; it is the first time we have done this for as far as they are concerned they would carry us over a tightrope. At the top I let the others ride ahead and proceeded at a walk beside the guides and pack-horses. It was on this occasion that I thought I saw Greenhalge in the distance and it turned out to be a cairn. We caught up the advance-guard in a frightful state of emotion. Anne had cut her finger and two of the girls were in tears. Greenhalge, redder than ever, rushed round the pack-horses tearing open all the panniers for iodine; anyone would have thought the girl was going to die. Maisie was explaining that you usually cut your finger because you wanted to—like making Spoonerisms she said. Anne did her best to be a lovely martyr but she did not have the whole house with her as both the guides and little Hetty were definitely bored. These queens of the schoolroom begin to think that anything will go. The day was now getting misty and the ride dreary. I held in my beast and trailed along humbly with the jingling pack-horses, losing the sense of time. I thought the ride would never come to an end. But it did. Suddenly we came over a rise and there was a long and shallow valley, desolate enough for anyone and smoking away like the dumping-ground of a great city. I thought the whole valley was on fire but coming closer I saw that the smoke was trails of steam, dozens of ribbons of steam blowing from left to right. This was our destination—the hot springs of Hveravellir. It would now be about teatime, the others had already left their horses by the hut and were walking back to look at the springs. "You *must* see the hut," Maisie shouted to me, "it is just like a henhouse." And it *was*, my dear, but only the sort of henhouse you would find in a depressed area. The walls are of rough stone banked outside with turf, the corrugated iron roof is also covered with turf; the stone walls inside are unlined and the whole place is incredibly damp. There is a nasty platform to sleep on three foot up from the floor and another platform higher up under the roof which you reach by a ladder. After surveying these apartments I went to have a look at the springs. A real witches' laundry with the horizontal trailers of steam blowing through the mist, some from little pop-holes in the ground and others from quite large pools, most of them circular. Some of these latter were lovely, might have been invented by Arthur Rackham—stone basins of highly coloured water varying from Reckitt's blue to green, and round the edge yellowish growths of sulphur. The crust of stone around them seems only about four inches thick and you expect any moment to go down like Dathan and Abiram. The water is practically boiling and the whole valley smells of bad eggs. Hveravellir was where an eighteenth-century robber made his hide-out for a year; he must have got dreadfully tired of his sulphuretted drinking-water. We made our coffee with it and I cannot say I would fancy it every day. But it does seem a waste that all this hot water should be bubbling away here for nothing. When you think of all the trouble housewives are having this very minute with boilers and how people who still use ranges forget to put in or pull out the dampers and how every other lodging-house has a geyser over the bath which won't work properly. Why didn't Nature put Hveravellir in Bayswater? Greenhalge, Maisie, Anne, and I (being the elect) are sleeping on the upper platform close to the iron roof. The roof drips water and spiders. This evening was not a great success. When we opened the food panniers it was found that the cheese was thickly coated with coffee. Greenhalge, noble as ever, set to work to decarbonise it (her own phrase) but we were all discouraged as the cheese is the one food which anyone would think of eating in England. After supper we played rummy on the lower platform by the light of candles in shoes (my little patent, you remember) and a very odd scene we made like a Victorian engraving of a meeting of Old Covenanters. One good mot on this occasion: Greenhalge suddenly said "O here's a knave with such a sympathetic expression" to which Ruth replied quietly "Then it must be a queen". Maisie was frightfully pleased. The Icelandic cards all have different faces, you see, and there's no doubt that our present company see little need for a world of two sexes. They will grow out of that of course. I've seen 'em do it before. Incidentally I haven't noticed much galanterie on the part of the guides. Maisie says it's because the North is ascetic but I think it's just because we're dowdy. The Icelandic girl is never without her lipstick. Your poor Hetty has lost hers in her sleeping-bag. I said to Maisie "Haven't you got anything of the sort?" and she said "The only thing that ever goes on *my* face is good honest Lifebuoy Soap". She has a tablet with her which she takes down to the gletcher. Personally I'm giving up ablutions; when I get home I shall go to Elizabeth Arden's. Good-night, darling. Perhaps you're sleeping in a hut too. Mountaineers always do, don't they? Maisie has been telling me terrible things about mountaineers and I think you had better be careful with your new friend. What a life you have, don't you! But with all that choice you ought to hit it off some day. Good-night.

August 21st

I had to get up in the night—I think it was the sulphuretted coffee. Or rather I should say get down because there I was up on the platform absolutely wedged in with corpses. So instead of going down by the ladder I did a little exhibition of gym and swung myself down by my hands, nearly falling over a guide. It *was* unpleasant outside, a thick Scotch mist and the ground very cold under my stockinged feet. Of course I oughtn't really to be wearing my six-and-elevens from Marshall and Snelgrove out here but I never thought of bringing anything woollen. One can't think of everything after all. Maisie says she is going to write to Robin about me. Robin wouldn't know though; it is the sort of thing he does himself. I felt definitely ill when I got back to bed and kept wondering whether I had caught a disease from my sleeping-bag or whether it was just that nasty horse yesterday. But I will spare you the details of my symptoms. I woke up at 6.0 with a dream-couplet running in my head. Until I was properly awake I thought it was terribly good. It went like this:

> "We write not ethics down the cabin walls,
> There are no ethics at home at all."

I wonder would the Surrealists pay me anything for that. To-day we did our longest trek—70 kilometres. You work that out in miles and take off your hat to us! And what was more, we walked half of it on our own feet. Because to-day we were doing undiscovered country. Doesn't that excite you, darling? We had to get across, you see, from Hveravellir to Arnarvatn. Well, people don't do that direct. They go up much farther north and then down again. But we hadn't time for that because the girls have to catch a boat. The guides themselves were quite excited and amused themselves by building cairns—a game to which the country is admirably adapted. In the centre of Iceland there are only three kinds of scenery—Stones, More Stones, and All Stones. The third type predominated to-day. The stones are the wrong size, the wrong shape, the wrong colour, and too many of them. They are not big enough to impress and not small enough to negotiate. Absolutely unpicturesque and absolutely non-utilitarian. We stumbled over their points in gumboots, dragging the wretched horses behind us. And at the same time we were climbing. Maisie was disgusted. She said it was like after a party which no one had tidied up. It's certainly hard to think how a country gets in a mess like this. A geologist would know, I suppose. The glacier was now to our south and looking distinctly jaded. There were peaky mountains on our right, dull and sullen in the mist. About 1.0 we found a fallen-in cave, a thing like a subway and no more beautiful, and stopped there to eat chocolate. Ruth too seems to be suffering from the sulphur. Then we went on again over the stones. Next time we ford a river I shall be very surprised if our boots do not turn out to be punctured. I tried to remember my T. S. Eliot and said something to Maisie about stony rubbish and dry bones but Maisie said anyone would be an optimist who expected to find anything as human as a dry bone in these parts. Then we came to the dry bed of a river which seemed even more desolate still and was also a litter of stones. And then at long last we came to a miracle—a small patch of grass with sheep on it. Not that I would be those sheep all the same. Still they seem to thrive on it. In fact, the sheep in Iceland all look the size of horses. Once we had seen the sheep things went better. The sun even came out. We came to a clear stream where the horses could drink and not long after that we reached our destination—a very beautiful lake lined with long gleams of silver in the low sun. Here we found our third hut—far more primitive than even the last one and a great deal smaller. Maisie and I commandeered it on the ground that we are the least well equipped in the way of tents. I think we made a mistake. Not that it hasn't an admirable situation. It stands over a little river which falls in a cascade to the lake; it is called the Skammá or Short River and is rapturously cold to drink. Away to the south-east stands the Eiríksjökull, a dark, square, upstanding mass of mountain with white flaps of ice coming down over its walls. But it is built of turf and stone—the hut, I mean—and the turf is falling out of the walls and roof and the sleeping-platform was thick with earth and cobwebs and Maisie began by putting her foot through it. There is also a very peculiar smell. We prepared for a meal outside the hut and Maisie on opening the pack which contains her stove found that it had fallen irrevocably to pieces. The fruit of our long trek. Well, that was that—no coffee or cocoa and we had to drink the Skammá. So then we tried to think of something original to do and we played rummy in the hut. There was so little room when the girls all got on the platform that we had to stick the candles on the crossbeam. Every now and again a sod of turf would fall on us from the roof and tempers were none too good. The girls said they were jolly glad they were sleeping in their tents. Various people have written their names on the beams of this hut, including one F. J. Smith, who adds sympathetically "Very cold". The hut boasts one teacup with a design of pink roses and tied up with string. Maisie and I have been discussing what can cause the smell under our bed. Maisie was very pleased this evening because Stella broke her bracelet. She broke it in a typical manner by snapping it backwards and forwards. Maisie says all those ornaments are relics of barbarism and that both men and women nowadays should aim at dressing in uniforms. No frills and no bright colours. That is civilisation, Maisie says. A sweet-tooth is a bad sign too, she thinks, like the Icelanders sugaring their potatoes. I tend to agree here. I think I had now better put out the remaining candle as it is leaning sideways and plastering Maisie's shoe with wax. Her shoes are having a hard time as they are also used for ashtrays. This black hole of a hut has rather a roué appearance at the moment as Maisie has hung her brassière from the crossbeam. It is deplorably cold and the wooden platform is hard under my sleeping-bag. I thought very hard and managed to remember a Latin quotation—probitas laudatus et alget—which means roughly that it is a fine thing to be a Girl Guide but that you can't keep warm in kudos. How only too true, darling. "Never again" Maisie and I have been saying to each other. Well, here goes the light.

August 22nd

I woke at 6.0 feeling half frozen. Maisie in spite of her pneumatic mattress, sleeping-bag and extra blankets maintained that she was even colder. Rain came on at breakfast time blown by a cold wind off the Langjökull. After breakfast walking fifty yards up the Skammá I came upon a rock adorned with a hammer and sickle in red paint. It was like Robinson Crusoe seeing a human footprint. The rain became definitely vehement so we prepared ourselves for a bad day. I put on puttees over my beach-trousers and borrowed some gloves from Anne. Then we clambered into our already sopping saddles and set off leaning into the wind and trying to cover our knees with our oilskins. What a morning! As we moved south and drew level with the Eiriksjökull the wind increased, whipping straight across the glacier and nearly blowing us off our horses. The rain became hail. When we dismounted to give our horses a rest we realised how wet we were about the knees. Greenhalge remarked that when roughing it in this way it is always a good thing to think of the discomforts of the people climbing Everest. Maisie says she would rather think about the people dining at the Ritz. Maisie was looking odder than ever to-day as she had for the first time put on her yellow oilskin leggings. She began by wearing them inside her gumboots but after half-an-hour or so realised that the water was collecting round her feet so she put them on over her boots which no doubt served a purpose but no one could call it very chic. She looked as if she had webbed feet. Well, on and on we rode through the stinging rain; it was so nasty it was really rather enjoyable. And we all felt rather heroic, I think. I heard two of the girls telling each other what a lot of grit La Paloma has. La Paloma, you remember, is Miss Greenhalge. We came to a very nice round pool lying flat in the rocks which the wind was whipping up into ostrich feathers. What really kept us going however was the knowledge that to-night we should spend for the first time in a human habitation, an outpost farm at a place called Kalmanstunga. You have no idea what a difference it makes knowing that you won't have to bother with tents. As for huts the less said about last night's hut the better. In the afternoon the rain gradually subsided and stopping our horses on the brink of a yawning cave we climbed down into the shelter of its mouth and there ate our four portions of chocolate. It then transpired that the chief guide was for some unknown reason very anxious to do us the honours of the cave and lead us underground to another opening goodness knows how far distant. Wishing to be polite we agreed to this and our first impetus had carried us well into the darkness before we realised that to play this game with any success whatsoever you need a candle per head. Greenhalge, reliable as ever, produced a candle but one candle is inadequate for eight persons, and I thought we were due for a serious accident for in all directions you could hear people and rocks falling over each other. It was not a very handsome cave, what one could see of it, and the floor was entirely covered with a jumble of large rocks so that you could only make a yard of progress by climbing say six foot up and four foot down again. And one should not do these things in long oilskin coats. Our one candle did not promise to last and the girls, Anne in particular, became a trifle agitated so we explained to the guide, rather to his chagrin, that we would now go back again. The one attractive thing about this cave was the ice which grew in it, sprouting upwards in shapes like empty champagne bottles, each with a nice round hole in the top of the neck. I broke one of these bottle-necks off and sucked it on our return journey. It was deliciously refreshing. Poor Maisie had a rough passage, she kept falling over the flaps of her leggings and I was afraid she would break something. We all, however, emerged to the light without injury. The rain had now stopped and our clothes were again comparatively dry. After an hour or so we came to an unwonted sight—a gate. The first gate we had seen since Gullfoss. Admittedly it was a rather tenuous gate precariously suspended in a barely-existent fence. All the same it was a gate and a symbol of civilisation. The going was better now and we trotted happily for Kalmanstunga. We got there about 6.0, coming to it down a steep hill. Maisie had ridden ahead, announced our arrival and ordered coffee. The farmhouse is a large respectable building of corrugated iron standing in the middle of an emerald green tún. Tún (pronounced toon) is the specially cultivated meadow attached to an Icelandic farm. Kalmanstunga has many stone outhouses roofed with nice green sods; this kind of roof always has a Beatrix Potter look about it. Having got off my horse and splashed through the little stream separating the stables from the house I arrived in time to hear Greenhalge make the following remark—that it was a really astonishing thing in such a position to find a farmhouse of corrugated iron where one would expect a thatched cottage covered with wisteria. Personally I didn't care what it was covered with provided I got my hot coffee. Yesterday, remember, we had nothing but cold water. The house was already full of people, being the only house for miles and in a strategic position for travellers. We were waited on, in fact, by a fellow-guest, an Icelandic lady who had spent most of her life in Denmark, Scotland, and London. She was a non-stop talker but an efficient waitress, put two tables together for us and laid them with a wonderful meal of coffee and cakes. Marie Antoinette's economic suggestion, "If they have no bread, give them cake", would be a perfectly sound one in Iceland for the Icelanders are the world's greatest cake-eaters. In many of the farms they eat them at every meal starting with breakfast. When we had put down all we could the talkative lady cleared away and in the course of an enthusiastic statement of her love for Britain told us that dinner would be ready in half-an-hour. So for half an hour Maisie played the piano—it is very unusual to have a piano and not a harmonium—and then dinner arrived and our fears of a sweet soup were not fulfilled. The Icelanders when they want to give you a special treat put brilliantine in their soup or else flavour it perniciously with almond. Hot almond is not a good taste. The only thing to do with these soups is to drown them in stewed rhubarb which they tend to give you at the same time. Maisie says that Icelandic cooking makes her think of a little boy who has got loose with Mother's medicine-chest. After dinner we were shown our rooms—two rooms leading out of each other, very cosy and hospitable but with rather a shortage of beds. The four girls are sharing two small beds in the first room and in the second room are two beds which have been run together. Greenhalge naturally has one and Maisie and I are sharing the other. All the beds here are furnished with deckers, if you spell it like that, and as a decker can't be tucked in it is not ideal for covering two well-grown females such as Maisie and myself. Maisie is elbowing me inconsiderately so you must forgive my writing. I can quite clearly hear the girls whispering next door. Presumably they don't realise we can hear them. The two nearest to us are talking about La Paloma (La P. herself can't hear, I think, as she is the far side of us and seems to be already asleep). One of the two girls says that La Paloma has a very beautiful smile but the other says that it is not such a spiritual smile as one Miss Robinson's. Now they have got on to me. They do not think my smile is nice; one of them says it is cynical and the other says I use make-up (this is not at the moment true as I have lost my lipstick). Now they have reverted to La Paloma and are wondering if she meant either of them when she said to-day, "Some girls grow up much quicker than others." One of them says that Miss Robinson gave her a brooch at the end of last term—one of those too sweet little brooches with fox-terriers on them. The other refuses to believe this; they are both getting piqued. Now the other—I mean the one—has got out of bed to look for the brooch in her rucksack. She has found it and is showing it off in triumph. The other is distinctly huffy, she will not believe that it came from Miss Robinson but says that the one bought it herself in Wool-worth's. The one answers indignantly that you can see brooches like that in Bond Street. Now the other starts a hare; she says that *she* had a Christmas card from Miss Robinson last Christmas. The one is rather stumped over this but rallies and says in a sinister tone, "Last Christmas was last Christmas." Now there is going to be a scrap. No, there was no scrap; they merely had a general post and everyone changed beds. Maisie says there is nothing new under the sun. Good-night, darling.

August 23rd

To-day began in comfort and ended in misery. We got up for once at a rational hour and even had a little hot water to sponge our faces with. While we were dressing that extraordinary girl Mary had an attack of music. She gave a quite remarkably tuneless rendering of "O God our help in ages past". And when someone ironically congratulated her she said, "Yes and I'm also very fond of Jerusalem the Golden." Breakfast was at 9.0 and lunch at 10.0. We said, "Isn't that a little soon for lunch?" but they explained that it was quite all right because they kept their clocks two hours ahead of Reykjavik. Anyway lunch was a thundering meal—mutton drowned in gravy followed by a mix-up of fruit and sago. Over-night our clothes had been considerably dried and we now put on our numerous extras although the morning looked fine and mild. Our cau-tion was justified. The guides kept us waiting while they went over the horses' shoes and we stood outside the farm looking over to the Lang-jökull. They say that to cross the Langjökull here from Hvitavatn takes 13—or is it 16—hours. That is one thing we will *not* do though I am sure Greenhalge would have great fun rescuing the girls from crevasses. Greenhalge once went on a visit to a mission school in India where she heroically killed a scorpion. There was such a nice dog who talked to us while we were waiting, a sort of little sheepdog, black and white with a thick but not very long coat, a broad forehead and a spitzy foreface. Nearly all Icelandic dogs are of this type except that the colour varies. They are amazingly friendly creatures; it is considered a bad trait in an Icelandic dog if he barks at strangers. They tend to be called Gosi which is the name of the knave in an Icelandic pack of cards. I must bring you home some Icelandic cards; the kings and queens are figures from the sagas and the aces are waterfalls. Badly drawn but a less expensive souvenir than a sheepskin or a silver fox. Iceland is a barren land for souvenirs. Of course one can always bring home little bits of lava for one's friends—I saw the Manchester school-teachers doing this at the Great Geysir—but I am afraid I have the wrong sort of friends. Maisie and I had a conversation this morning about the foreignness of Iceland. We decided that not counting the scenery, which is of course unthinkable, there are only two really foreign things in the place—(1) the system of nomenclature and (2), as already mentioned, the food. The former is just lunatic; in order to use a telephone directory you have to know everyone's christian names and then you are not much farther because all their christian names are the same. The people themselves are not nearly so foreign as the Irish or the yokels of Somerset. You can't imagine any of them behaving like the people in the sagas, saying "That was an ill word" and shooting the other man dead. Disappointing, still one needn't travel if one wants to see odd behaviour. You are wonderfully situated, of course, in Cambridge. Talking of local colour did I tell you about the ship's electrician I met on the Flying Scot? He told me that Abyssinia was largely inhabited by black Jews with ginger hair. But to get on with my record. The guides finished tinkering with the horses and we set off gaily in the brisk and lively morning. They all waved us off from the farm. It would be rather nice to spend the winter at one of these farms—a terrific fug, constant jabber on the radio, ivy growing in pots and the family reading Hall Caine. It was sad to think there would be no farm to-night. But the reality was worse than our expectations. We began by fording a turbulent river, the water came over the tops of our boots—at least of our left boots—the girls thought it was a scream. It's not such a scream though to have water in your boots for hours afterwards. The Icelandic pony is of course an amphibian. He can even swim a river with someone in the saddle but it has to be the right someone. There is a legend of an Icelander who in the early days of tobacco used to swim his horse two miles out to sea to meet the tobacco boat. After fording the river the rain started, a drizzle but very unpleasant. One could not decide whether to fasten up the collar of one's oilskin or not. And then we went through a so-called birch forest—a scrubby little affair about four foot high but it does seem quite companionable after the miles and miles and miles of no vegetation but moss. A little later we reached a very nice piece of grassland where Ruth contrived to be thrown when her pony put its foot in a hole. From Kalmanstunga south we had been following a track which is used by cars—one of those thick red lines which look so impressive on the map. Nowhere else in the world I suppose would this be called a road but it is used as such for we met two buses on it. And as a matter of fact whoever constructed these roads is a public benefactor even though constructing consists merely in moving aside the stones, that is the bigger stones. Our progress to-day was again stony once we had left the short stretch of grassland. We got in between Langjökull on the left and a mountain with the charming name of Ok on the right and once we had done that all we could think of was getting somewhere else. But we didn't. We went on and on and the landscape remained the same. It was like walking the wrong way on a moving stair-case. We were close in under the Langjökull but it was covered with mist. Maisie was in a frightful temper. This valley is called Kaldidalur which means Cold Dale—apt but inadequate. The Icelanders are rather proud of it as a show-piece of scenery and no doubt on a clear day it may be quite beautiful if one drives through it quickly in a car. But all we could see was a thirty-foot radius of stones. The stones were too much for my horse and it took to stumbling. We came across the ancient wreck of a very primitive touring car—more desolate than the bones of a camel in a film about the Foreign Legion. The rain never came on very properly but it was contin-uously damp and we began to think we preferred yesterday's weather which at least made us feel heroic. About supper-time we got down into lower country and riding on ahead of the guides stopped our horses on a marshy piece of pasture ground on the edge of a dreary lake. We hoped this wasn't our destination but it was. It is called Brunnar. We set up our tents on squelchy ground in the drizzle and owing to the direction of the wind and the lie of the ground M. and I have to sleep with our heads out of the door to-night. However, we have erected across it a barrier of kit-bags, gumboots, and canvas panniers. The guides think we are funny because we all look so gloomy. The guides deserve high marks to-night for, after we had eaten a melancholy meal in the rain and were all moan-ing because, owing to the breakdown of Maisie's stove there was no hot drink to wash it down with, the guides came along rather shyly and asked (mainly by dumb show) if we would like the loan of their stove. We didn't know they had a stove but sure enough they brought along a minute rudi-mentary object like a small canister which we welcomed with open arms and it actually worked though I must admit it took some time. While we were waiting patiently for our coffee Maisie made a sudden scene and said she would *not* have highly scented foods in her bed. This referred to some cheese and smoked mutton which I had left there. When the coffee arrived we had to drink it not only, as always, without milk but also with-out sugar. The sugar is kept in an old tobacco tin, and when we opened it to-night every single lump had turned a deep puce colour. Quite inexpli-cable and rather sinister. No one, even the guides, had the nerve to try any of it. Maisie and I are now lying wedged in our tent hoping for the best. The Icelandic year has passed its prime and the guides are taking no more expeditions after this one. I feel I should mention that we saw some ptarmigan on arriving at Brunnar. You won't know any more about ptar-migan than I do but it is quite time I gave you a nature note (there is *awfully* little nature around here). Maisie and I, clammy and rheumatic, are listening to the schoolgirls chattering in their tents next door and are asking each other whose fault this is. We have told the guides that we want to start early to-morrow. To-morrow brings us to civilisation and there is no point in staying in this particular little swamp a minute longer than we need.

August 24th

Well, here we are in Valhalla—that really is what it is called—the hotel at Thingvellir. Thingvellir is where they used to have the Thing, which was the Icelandic name for parliament and a very good name too, don't you think. It is *the* historic showplace. Not that there is anything to see except geology but it is amusing geology—rifts and such. It would have been nicer if we had had better weather but the day has been damp and misty and Ruth quarrelled with Stella because Stella intrigued with Anne to prevent Mary riding beside Greenhalge. Mary was in tears (she admires Greenhalge intensely across a great gulf of incompatibility) and Ruth demanded back from Stella an Eversharp pencil which she had given her and which Stella refused to return. We were up this morning at 6.0 with no appetite whatsoever and intending to leave Brunnar as quickly as possible. Naturally the ponies chose just this one morning to get lost, the guides disappeared over the horizon in search of them and the rest of us waited in our marsh among our bags and chattels like people in a country railway station in the West of Ireland where the train has stopped on the way to talk to the cows. The tents were packed up, the food panniers strapped down, ourselves muffled in scarves, and Maisie running round taking photos. They will not come out of course but Maisie does not like to waste her time. At long last the horses returned quite unpenitent and off we started. I had an excellent horse to-day, a large black one with a white star on its forehead, and we got our best gallop yet across a long expanse of grey sand by a lake called Sandurvatn. In our heart of hearts I think we were all playing sheikhs. It is very nice when the sand flies up in your face and you plop up and down in the saddle to a perfectly regular rhythm—chichibu, chichibu, chichibu. It is not really galloping of course, only cantering. Our stampede across the sands went to the head of that old malefactor, the white pack-horse, who broke loose and galloped after us, throwing off Maisie's bed en route. Anne, who has a habit of mock indignation (at least it starts mock and ends serious) was very cross indeed with the white pack-horse and said it should be thoroughly well thrashed; she is soon, as I said, going to be house prefect. Maisie's bed was re-established (we had to gather up various very odd articles which had fallen out of it on the sands, it is by way of also being a hold-all) and we went up slowly over the water-shed, from the top of which we had a fine

view of the plain that reaches to Thingvellir, a fine plain that looks a lot
more livable than anything we have seen lately. We pastured our horses at
the foot of the descent and then went all out for our Mecca, reaching it
about 2.0 in the afternoon—a good deal earlier than we had expected.
We went straight to the hotel and ordered coffee. The hotel is about the
only building here but there is also a minute church. While we were wait-
ing for the guides and pack-horses who had been left a very long way
behind, we nearly had a serious mishap thanks to the incredible stupidity
of Mary and Stella. Stella, as you remember, is supposed to know about
horses. Well those two infant geniuses finding their horses had no hobbles
tied them to the two ends of a ladder belonging to the hotel. Inevitable
result: the horses ran amok and the ladder suffered from schism. Maisie
and I from the breakfast room looked out over the landscape and sud-
denly saw these two horses catapult across it with the ladders (or half a
ladder each I should say) clattering behind them. By some miracle they
escaped injury and we said nothing about the ladder at the hotel. After
our coffee Maisie and I, with the unanimous support of the girls (sloppy
little things!) began to work upon Greenhalge to induce her not to camp
out to-night; she had her eye upon a peculiarly unprepossessing site be-
tween two low-grade ditches. After all what is a tent? A tent is a make-
believe house; when there is a real house about why go on making a belief
one? Greenhalge lowered her standards to a compromise. We had sug-
gested, out of the cunning of our hearts, that we should all sleep in
sleeping-bags in the dance-hall. This sounded enough like a barracks to
appeal to Greenhalge's passion for hardship so she cried off the tents and
said we would all rough it in the dance-hall. But when we asked the hotel
people if we could rough it in the dance-hall they said unfortunately no
because it was wanted for 250 Frenchmen who are coming to breakfast to-
morrow. So (the virtuous are rewarded in the end) they have supplied us
instead with little cabins on the ground floor, six foot square, two beds in
each, walls of matchboarding, one krona a night. That is what I call good
value but poor Greenhalge felt she had been tricked. In the afternoon we
walked up the gorge. Everyone has to walk up the gorge here. Just like
when you go to Tintern Abbey you have to see the moon through an arch.
The gorge is an odd phenomenon and would be nice for a picnic. The
spirit of the sagas descended upon me and I walked through the river in
my gumboots. This was just above the fall and I liked to think it was
dangerous; whether it was dangerous or not I got a lot of water in my
boots and had to hurry home. Maisie, Ruth, and Mary remained behind
and in a spirit of emulation climbed down the waterfall itself; or so they
told me afterwards. I doubted it because they seemed to be quite dry.
When we were all together again in the hotel it was suggested we should
go a nice row on the lake in the mist. No one showed great enthusiasm for

this and we ordered some coffee instead. M. and I went to our cabin to change and I quite innocently did a perfect turn à la Brothers Bronett— you remember, the clowns at Olympia—by pulling off my boots and thereby flooding out our bedroom. Not only our bedroom because it flowed along the passage and we could hear it lapping on unknown doors in the distance. No one would believe so much water could come out of one pair of gumboots. Maisie was rather cross about it. We took our clothes to the kitchen to be dried and sat down to our coffee and cigarettes; we have been hard up for cigarettes since Kalmanstunga. Here as everywhere else you can only buy Commanders. There are several oil paintings in this hotel, notably a rather lunatic picture of the Thingvellir gorge by that curious painter Kjarval. Kjarval's gorge was not at all as we saw it but then most of the Icelandic painters seem to see with the eyes of chameleons. Cascades of paint, a drunk pink sky, a whole lot of things looking like sunflowers and wheels flying about over the rocks, a total effect of perfectly tropical luxuriance. I am not sure however that I do not prefer this mania for colour to the kind of fake Cézanne landscape which a few of their painters go in for. There is also here a very sombre lava-scape by one Johann Briem which only demonstrates that the Icelandic cubist has no call to distort as Nature has done that for him. I have also in this hotel been observing the Icelandic girls. Fine strapping wenches on the whole, with tilted noses, figures rather tight and slightly assertive bosoms. Their expression of face tends to be self-possessed. I should think there is no fluff in their relationships. We had hardly finished coffee when we had our evening meal in Greenhalge's cabin. We chose her room because she has it to herself but all the same I am sorry for her. It is not so nice to sleep in a room which is stuccoed with food. I haven't noticed if it applies to myself but I must say the others have become rather untidy eaters on this expedition. Greenhalge was wonderfully good-humoured about it; perhaps she felt it made up for not sleeping in a tent. After dinner we played a little desultory rummy and when the girls had gone to bed Greenhalge and Maisie had a long and very serious conversation about adolescence, education, and psychology. It all began when Greenhalge said that one of the "difficult" girls at her school had been sent to a psycho-analyst. This set Maisie off on her hobby-horse. No one, according to M., ought to go to an analyst except of their own free will, i.e. if they are so unhappy that analysis is the only hope for them. Now your "difficult" girls, as Maisie quite rightly maintains, are probably no more unhappy than anyone else; it is only that they get in the way of the headmistress. The headmistress wants everything to be right and tight in her own little hive and doesn't care a hang for the girls' lives as individuals. So off they go to the analyst who removes their difficulties and from then on they are as clean and harmless about the house as a neuter cat. (Maisie's comparison, not mine.)

All very well for the house but what about the cat, says Maisie. Maisie says it is a bad thing in Freud that he always suggests that neurosis is something to be got rid of. On the contrary, says M., all the progress in this world is due to neurosis. If Sylvia Pankhurst had been analysed in her 'teens, we shouldn't have women's suffrage. Let us have as much neurosis as we can stand. This reminded me of an argument I had with Robin, which I now repeated to Maisie. M. says I must tell Robin I refuse to have children if he is going to Truby King them. I must only have them on condition that they are to be exposed to germs, allowed to retain their neuroses and never on any account given purges. From purges we got on to religion and we all agreed that poor old Freud is sadly off the rails in *The Future of an Illusion*. All that stuff about the pure and scintillating mind of the child being blunted and crippled by its early religious instruction. Not that *I* am any advocate for religious instruction, which is one of the reasons I like Iceland. Iceland is one of the few places where you don't feel it in the air when it's Sunday. I dare say though that the introduction of Christianity did indirectly promote the amelioration of social conditions (just to show you I can write like a don too) for the life of the sagas was not quite what we call civilised. Talking of civilisation it is comfortable in this bed and I very much hope to-morrow night Greenhalge doesn't force us to camp out at Laugarvatn. She was saying sadly to-night that the expedition had really been very easy. No really gruelling tests of the girls' endurance. Judging by the girls' behaviour at Kaldidalur I should say this was just as well. How do you find your endurance in the Dolomites? Good-night, darling. To-morrow is our last trek.

August 25th

We had our last ride this morning and our first bath this evening. The baths at Laugarvatn are heated from the hot springs; with great good sense they do not use the actual water of the springs (sulphur again!) but with much ingenuity run some ordinary water through the springs in pipes. This morning we saw the 250 Frenchmen—the ones who were coming to breakfast. Many of them were Germans but even so there were a lot more French than one expects to see anywhere out of France. They were mostly middle-aged but included a few miserable girls in their 'teens whom Greenhalge was able to compare unfavourably with our ones. They had all motored out the 50 kilometres or so from Reykjavik and had the time of their lives taking cine-photos of four or five unhappy little native children togged up in pseudo-national dress and standing in awkward dumbcrambo attitudes against a blank wall. The invasion, needless to say, also included a few middle-aged Englishwomen, the sort with ankles lapping down over their shoes and a puglike expression of factitious enthusiasm combined with the determination to be in at the death, whoever

or whatever is dying. Maisie had a field-day with her Zeiss. And so to
Laugarvatn. I had the little brown pony which I had the first day, and,
strange to say, I now found it extremely comfortable. Greenhalge fell off
twice to-day but the really bad feature of the day was that the guides
produced another cave (they ought to be psycho-analysed). We entered it
by a small burrow and it took us three-quarters of an hour to reach the
other end of it. It was just as clammy, rugged, incoherent, dangerous, and
dark as the one near Kalmanstunga and once again we had only one can-
dle. There is nothing to be said for this type of cave. We saw more caves
later however; we went out of our way to see them in fact, branching up a
grassy slope to the left. These ones were rounded openings in a very soft
cinder-coloured stone which I maintain to be a kind of volcanic sand-
stone. Maisie says that a volcanic sandstone is a contradiction in terms; it
is a sad reflection on female education that none of us knows any geology.
One thing we do know however is that you can't find fossils in Iceland. A
pity; a fossil or two would make the place more homey. Well, till a few
years ago these sandstone or whatever-they-are caves were lived in by a
couple with a cow. The rock is very easy to cut and you could see where
they had cut slots for the door-bars, also where the cow had spent long
nights munching away the wall. The rock outside, which is of a very odd
formation—quite Barbara Hepworth—is covered with carved names,
names of people and ships and the registration numbers of cars. Some-
one has also carefully cut out the word SILLY and cut a square round it.
The road from here to Laugarvatn was mainly downhill and Maisie and
Anne rode ahead in a spirit of competition; Maisie likes to show she is not
as old as she was. Various signs of civilisation began to appear such as
stray agricultural implements. My little pony began to shy; I suppose it
thought they were monsters. I was not at all surprised when we reached
Laugarvatn to hear that Maisie had been thrown by her horse a hundred
yards from home. While galloping up the straight it suddenly turned at
right angles to itself, leaving Maisie in the air, from which in due time she
descended but, being Maisie, did not break anything or appear apprecia-
bly altered except for a little mud on the face. The hotel at Laugarvatn is a
school in the winter and an hotel in the summer. It is a very pleasant place
but we are not sleeping in it. The others have put up their own tents and
Maisie and I have hired one of the large tents which the hotel lets out in
the summer to surplus visitors. This is much more what a tent ought to
be. There is a camp-bed on either side of it plus mattresses plus bolsters,
and there is room to move about in the middle. There are of course spi-
ders. It is sad to think that they never have anything but grass and hay to
eat. Oh sorry—I must have left out a sentence. I meant to say that we had
said good-bye to our horses. Not the spiders, you see. Not but what the
spiders must have rather a thin time because there are very few flies in

this country. Perhaps they are Bernard Shaw spiders. We stood ourselves
a dinner in the hotel instead of making a last inroad on the smoked mut-
ton (by now rather sordid) and our dried fish who is so tattered he looks
like a scarecrow; he was a fine animal once. Dinner began with asparagus
soup—aren't we getting civilised—but I was very sorry we had no skyr.
Skyr is very good; it is a near relation of cream cheese and a distant rela-
tion of yaghourt. There were about fifty old women also having dinner—
a kind of mother's union for they were wearing their national costume
which with its gold medallions in front and long loops of hair behind
makes a lady, from my own point of view, look rather too much like a
horse. We treated ourselves to some citron and Maisie had an attack of
General Knowledge. She told us—what we all knew already—that the
population of Iceland is 110,000 of which 30,000 live in Reykjavik. Mary
wanted to know how they knew this. I am getting just a *teeny* bit tired of
communing with the budding mind of youth. The conversation of the
young has no doubt a certain artless charm which pleases for the length of
a tea-party but when prolonged all the way round the Langjökull it suf-
fers from the two minor flaws of being (a) invariably platitudinous and (b)
infinitely repetitive. They are all getting terribly excited about their train-
connections at Hull; to-morrow, you see, they are sailing for home. I think
they are banking too much on their boat running to schedule. No doubt
as far as *place* goes it will be reasonably accurate and land them in Hull
and not in Fishguard but I should allow a good 36 hours' margin for time.
They are only *little* boats after all. I can hear the young now; they are lying
in their tents next door, writing up their diaries. Two of them are talking
about Miss Robinson. Anne is going to stay behind to-morrow. She and
Maisie and I have an invitation to stay in the lunatic asylum. I shall send
this letter with Miss Greenhalge on the *Godafoss*. Good-night, liebchen.

August 27th

"And so the game is ended that should not have begun." We are now on
the *Godafoss* seeing off our party. You will notice that the boat is leaving a
day late; it probably stopped round the coast to pick up some fish-heads
(Icelandic boats have the courage of their caprices). I am writing this
with a blunt pencil leaning against the taffrail (?). Yesterday morning we
bussed back from Laugarvatn to Reykjavik and heard the sad news about
the boat. Greenhalge and the girls spent the night in the students' hos-
tel, Maisie and Anne and I accepted our invitation to the asylum, where
Maisie fell through her bed; it was a camp-bed and no doubt took against
Maisie for being a pacifist. The Lunatic Asylum is charmingly situated at
Kleppur and is quite fittingly the place where Marshal Balbo landed on
his flight across the Atlantic. The Reykjavik–Kleppur bus is designed like
a cathedral; there are a few seats scattered here and there down the side-
aisles and a vast empty space down the middle for people to stand in. The

road to Kleppur suffers from ribbon development and nothing, my dear, can look worse than a corrugated iron suburb if it is not kept tidy. The lunatics here are not much in evidence though they can be heard faintly cooing in the distance. They have a very fine bathroom. Our host, the doctor in charge, is a charming old man and so are all his family. He has whitish-grey hair, gold-rimmed spectacles, fiery blue eyes, a bad leg, and a black velvet smoking-jacket. M. thinks he looks rather like W. B. Yeats. That perhaps is because he also is said to be clairvoyant. Spiritualism, you know, has a great vogue in Iceland though they only have their séances in the winter—like the hunting season in England. There is a famous mystic called Dr Helgi Pjeturrs who has written a book about life on the other planets. Icelanders, he says, are the most spiritual people in the world, but, spiritual or not, we all go to the planets when we die and there we all have a very good time. Dr Sveinsson however (our asylum doctor) did not talk to us much about spiritualism but indulged his other passion, which is Latin. He has a habit of breaking into Latin in conversation which is a little embarrassing for Maisie and me whose classics are distinctly what you might call rusty. As for that poor girl Anne, she merely goes red in the face and says, "I'm awfully sorry, I'm afraid I'm jolly bad at it." It is very impressive however the way Dr S. will suddenly turn to you over his coffee and remark with terrific gusto, "Juppiter iratus buccas inflat" or "Multae sunt viae ingeni humani." His pronunciation, I may remark, is Icelandic. He showed us his English-Latin grammar, a mid-nineteenth century book by one Roby, which he says is a poem to him. When Dr S. was a young man he used to act as a guide and take visitors round the country on ponies. He had some very good stories about an old English eccentric he was guide to every summer—a hot-tempered gentleman who used to hit people with hunting-whips but he was so short-sighted he always hit the wrong ones. Mrs S. was very charming and hospitable and we had bilberries and cream and coffee before going to bed. Then came Maisie's episode with the bed. This morning we came in to Reykjavik and spent the whole morning drinking coffee in the Tea-Rooms, which is their actual name, and eating cream-cakes. We hear that last night two men in Reykjavik got drunk, one betted the other he would swim 100 metres in the harbour, jumped in, swam 50 and was drowned. . . . I must finish this off as the boat has begun to groan. (I don't blame it.) The girls are being seen off by a schoolmate who dropped on them out of the blue in Reykjavik and apparently is staying with friends here—a boring little girl who poses as rather fast and has begun using lipstick, needless to say very badly. Well, darling, goodbye—I don't suppose you will ever read all this stuff—give my love to Cicely. I hope to see you anon in Cambridge or Gordon Square, all my love till then,

HETTY

CHAPTER XIII

Letter to Lord Byron

Part IV

A ship again; this time the *Dettifoss.*
　　Grierson can buy it; all the sea I mean,
All this Atlantic that we've now to cross
　　Heading for England's pleasant pastures green.
　　Pro tem I've done with the Icelandic scene;
I watch the hills receding in the distance,
I hear the thudding of an engine's pistons.

I hope I'm better, wiser for the trip:
　　I've had the benefit of northern breezes,
The open road and good companionship,
　　I've seen some very pretty little pieces;
　　And though the luck was almost all MacNeice's,
I've spent some jolly evenings playing rummy—
No one can talk at Bridge, unless it's Dummy.

I've learnt to ride, at least to ride a pony,
　　Taken a lot of healthy exercise,
On barren mountains and in valleys stony,
　　I've tasted a hot spring (a taste was wise),
　　And foods a man remembers till he dies.
All things considered, I consider Iceland,
Apart from Reykjavik, a very nice land.

The part can stand as symbol for the whole:
　　So ruminating in these last few weeks,
I see the map of all my youth unroll,
　　The mental mountains and the psychic creeks,
　　The towns of which the master never speaks,
The various parishes and what they voted for,
The colonies, their size, and what they're noted for.

A child may ask when our strange epoch passes,
　　During a history lesson, "Please, sir, what's
An intellectual of the middle classes?
　　Is he a maker of ceramic pots
　　Or does he choose his king by drawing lots?"

What follows now may set him on the rail,
A plain, perhaps a cautionary, tale.

My passport says I'm five feet and eleven,
    With hazel eyes and fair (it's tow-like) hair,
That I was born in York in 1907,
    With no distinctive markings anywhere.
    Which isn't quite correct. Conspicuous there
On my right cheek appears a large brown mole,
I think I don't dislike it on the whole.

My name occurs in several of the sagas,
    Is common over Iceland still. Down under
Where Das Volk order sausages and lagers
    I ought to be the prize, the living wonder,
    The really pure from any Rassenschander,
In fact I am the great big white barbarian,
The Nordic type, the too too truly Aryan.

In games which mark for beauty out of twenty,
    I'm doing well if my friends give me eight
(When played historically you still score plenty);
    My head looks like an egg upon a plate;
    My nose is not too bad, but isn't straight;
I have no proper eyebrows, and my eyes
Are far too close together to look nice.

Beauty, we're told, is but a painted show,
    But still the public really likes that best;
Beauty of soul should be enough, I know,
    The golden ingot in the plain deal chest.
    But mine's a rattle in a flannel vest;
I can't think what my It had on It's mind,
To give me flat feet and a big behind.

Apart from lyrics and poetic dramma,
    Which Ervine seems more angered by than sad at,
While Sparrow fails to understand their grammar,
    I have some harmless hobbies; I'm not bad at
    Reading the slower movements, and may add that
Out of my hours of strumming most of them
Pass playing hymn tunes out of A. and M.

Read character from taste. Who seem to me
    The great? I know that one as well as you.
"Why, Daunty, Gouty, Shopkeeper, the three

Supreme Old Masters." You must ask me who
Have written just as I'd have liked to do.
I stop to listen and the names I hear
Are those of Firbank, Potter, Carroll, Lear.

Then phantasies? My anima, poor thing,
Must take the dreams my Alter Ego sends her,
And he's a marvellous diver, not a king.
But when I'm sickening for influenza,
I play concertos with my own cadenza;
And as the fever rises find it properer
To sing the love duet from a grand opera.

My vices? I've no wish to go to prison.
I am no Grouper, I will never share
With any prig who thinks he'd like to listen.
At answering letters I am well aware
I'm very slack; I ought to take more care
Over my clothes; my promise always fails
To smoke much less, and not to bite my nails.

I hate pompositas and all authority;
Its air of injured rightness also sends
Me shuddering from the cultured smug minority.
"Perpetual revolution", left-wing friends
Tell me, "in counter-revolution ends.
Your fate will be to linger on outcast
A selfish pink old Liberal to the last."

"No, I am that I am, and those that level
At my abuses reckon up their own.
I may be straight though they, themselves, are bevel."
So Shakespeare said, but Shakespeare must have known.
I daren't say that except when I'm alone,
Must hear in silence till I turn my toes up,
"It's such a pity Wystan never grows up."

So I sit down this fine September morning
To tell my story. I've another reason.
I've lately had a confidential warning
That Isherwood is publishing next season
A book about us all. I call that treason.
I must be quick if I'm to get my oar in
Before his revelations bring the law in.

My father's forbears were all Midland yeomen
    Till royalties from coal mines did them good;
I think they must have been phlegmatic slowmen.
    My mother's ancestors had Norman blood,
    From Somerset I've always understood;
My grandfathers on either side agree
In being clergymen and C. of E.

Father and Mother each was one of seven,
    Though one died young and one was not all there;
Their fathers both went suddenly to Heaven
    While they were still quite small and left them here
    To work on earth with little cash to spare;
A nurse, a rising medico, at Bart's
Both felt the pangs of Cupid's naughty darts.

My home then was professional and "high".
    No gentler father ever lived, I'll lay
All Lombard Street against a shepherd's pie.
    We imitate our loves: well, neighbours say
    I grow more like my mother every day.
I don't like business men. I know a Prot
Will never really kneel, but only squat.

In pleasures of the mind they both delighted;
    The library in the study was enough
To make a better boy than me short-sighted;
    Our old cook Ada surely knew her stuff;
    My elder brothers did not treat me rough;
We lived at Solihull, a village then;
Those at the gasworks were my favourite men.

My earliest recollection to stay put
    Is of a white stone doorstep and a spot
Of pus where father lanced the terrier's foot;
    Next, stuffing shag into the coffee pot
    Which nearly killed my mother, but did not;
Both psycho-analyst and Christian minister,
Will think these incidents extremely sinister.

With northern myths my little brain was laden,
    With deeds of Thor and Loki and such scenes;
My favourite tale was Andersen's *Ice Maiden*;
    But better far than any kings or queens
    I liked to see and know about machines:

And from my sixth until my sixteenth year
I thought myself a mining engineer.

The mine I always pictured was for lead,
      Though copper mines might, faute de mieux, be sound.
To-day I like a weight upon my bed;
      I always travel by the Underground;
      For concentration I have always found
A small room best, the curtains drawn, the light on;
Then I can work from nine till tea-time, right on.

I must admit that I was most precocious
      (Precocious children rarely grow up good).
My aunts and uncles thought me quite atrocious
      For using words more adult than I should;
      My first remark at school did all it could
To shake a matron's monumental poise;
"I like to see the various types of boys."

The Great War had begun: but masters' scrutiny
      And fists of big boys were the war to us;
It was as harmless as the Indian Mutiny,
      A beating from the Head was dangerous.
      But once when half the form put down *Bellus*,
We were accused of that most deadly sin,
Wanting the Kaiser and the Huns to win.

The way in which we really were affected
      Was having such a varied lot to teach us.
The best were fighting, as the King expected,
      The remnant either elderly grey creatures,
      Or characters with most peculiar features.
Many were raggable, a few were waxy,
One had to leave abruptly in a taxi.

Surnames I must not write—O Reginald,
      You at least taught us that which fadeth not,
Our earliest visions of the great wide world;
      The beer and biscuits that your favourites got,
      Your tales revealing you a first-class shot,
Your riding breeks, your drama called *The Waves*,
A few of us will carry to our graves.

"Half a lunatic, half a knave". No doubt
      A holy terror to the staff at tea;
A good headmaster must have soon found out

Your moral character was all at sea;
   I question if you'd got a pass degree:
But little children bless your kind that knocks
Away the edifying stumbling blocks.

How can I thank you? For it only shows
   (Let me ride just this once my hobby-horse),
There're things a good headmaster never knows.
     There must be sober schoolmasters, of course,
     But what a prep school really puts across
Is knowledge of the world we'll soon be lost in:
To-day it's more like Dickens than Jane Austen.

I hate the modern trick, to tell the truth,
   Of straightening out the kinks in the young mind,
Our passion for the tender plant of youth,
     Our hatred for all weeds of any kind.
     Slogans are bad: the best that I can find
Is this: "Let each child have that's in our care
As much neurosis as the child can bear."

In this respect, at least, my bad old Adam is
   Pigheadedly against the general trend;
And has no use for all these new academies
     Where readers of the better weeklies send
     The child they probably did not intend,
To paint a lampshade, marry, or keep pigeons,
Or make a study of the world religions.

Goddess of bossy underlings, Normality!
   What murders are committed in thy name!
Totalitarian is thy state Reality,
     Reeking of antiseptics and the shame
     Of faces that all look and feel the same.
Thy Muse is one unknown to classic histories,
The topping figure of the hockey mistress.

From thy dread Empire not a soul's exempted:
   More than the nursemaids pushing prams in parks,
By thee the intellectuals are tempted,
     O, to commit the treason of the clerks,
     Bewitched by thee to literary sharks.
But I must leave thee to thy office stool,
I must get on now to my public school.

Men had stopped throwing stones at one another,
    Butter and Father had come back again;
Gone were the holidays we spent with Mother
      In furnished rooms on mountain, moor, and fen;
      And gone those summer Sunday evenings, when
Along the seafronts fled a curious noise,
"Eternal Father", sung by three young boys.

Nation spoke Peace, or said she did, with nation;
    The sexes tried their best to look the same;
Morals lost value during the inflation,
      The great Victorians kindly took the blame;
      Visions of Dada to the Post-War came,
Sitting in cafés, nostrils stuffed with bread,
Above the recent and the straight-laced dead.

I've said my say on public schools elsewhere:
    Romantic friendship, prefects, bullying,
I shall not deal with, c'est une autre affaire.
      Those who expect them, will get no such thing,
      It is the strictly relevant I sing.
Why should they grumble? They've the Greek Anthology,
And all the spicier bits of Anthropology.

We all grow up the same way, more or less;
    Life is not known to give away her presents;
She only swops. The unself-consciousness
      That children share with animals and peasants
      Sinks in the "sturm und drang" of Adolescence.
Like other boys I lost my taste for sweets,
Discovered sunsets, passion, God, and Keats.

I shall recall a single incident
    No more. I spoke of mining engineering
As the career on which my mind was bent,
      But for some time my fancies had been veering;
      Mirages of the future kept appearing;
Crazes had come and gone in short, sharp gales,
For motor-bikes, photography, and whales.

But indecision broke off with a clean-cut end
    One afternoon in March at half-past three
When walking in a ploughed field with a friend;
      Kicking a little stone, he turned to me
      And said, "Tell me, do you write poetry?"

I never had, and said so, but I knew
That very moment what I wished to do.

Without a bridge passage this leads me straight
    Into the theme marked "Oxford" on my score
From pages twenty-five to twenty-eight.
    Aesthetic trills I'd never heard before
    Rose from the strings, shrill poses from the cor;
The woodwind chattered like a pre-war Russian,
"Art" boomed the brass, and "Life" thumped the percussion.

A raw provincial, my good taste was tardy,
    And Edward Thomas I as yet preferred;
I was still listening to Thomas Hardy
    Putting divinity about a bird;
    But Eliot spoke the still unspoken word;
For gasworks and dried tubers I forsook
The clock at Grantchester, the English rook.

All youth's intolerant certainty was mine as
    I faced life in a double-breasted suit;
I bought and praised but did not read Aquinas,
    At the *Criterion*'s verdict I was mute,
    Though Arnold's I was ready to refute;
And through the quads dogmatic words rang clear,
"Good poetry is classic and austere."

So much for Art. Of course Life had its passions too;
    The student's flesh like his imagination
Makes facts fit theories and has fashions too.
    We were the tail, a sort of poor relation
    To that debauched, eccentric generation
That grew up with their fathers at the War,
And made new glosses on the noun Amor.

Three years passed quickly while the Isis went
    Down to the sea for better or for worse;
Then to Berlin, not Carthage, I was sent
    With money from my parents in my purse,
    And ceased to see the world in terms of verse.
I met a chap called Layard and he fed
New doctrines into my receptive head.

Part came from Lane, and part from D. H. Lawrence;
    Gide, though I didn't know it then, gave part.
They taught me to express my deep abhorrence

If I caught anyone preferring Art
To Life and Love and being Pure-in-Heart.
I lived with crooks but seldom was molested;
The Pure-in-Heart can never be arrested.

He's gay; no bludgeonings of chance can spoil it,
    The Pure-in-Heart loves all men on a par,
And has no trouble with his private toilet;
    The Pure-in-Heart is never ill; catarrh
    Would be the yellow streak, the brush of tar;
Determined to be loving and forgiving,
I came back home to try and earn my living.

The only thing you never turned your hand to
    Was teaching English in a boarding school.
To-day it's a profession that seems grand to
    Those whose alternative's an office stool;
    For budding authors it's become the rule.
To many an unknown genius postmen bring
Typed notices from Rabbitarse and String.

The Head's M.A., a bishop is a patron,
    The assistant staff is highly qualified;
Health is the care of an experienced matron,
    The arts are taught by ladies from outside;
    The food is wholesome and the grounds are wide;
The aim is training character and poise,
With special coaching for the backward boys.

I found the pay good and had time to spend it,
    Though others may not have the good luck I did:
For you I'd hesitate to recommend it;
    Several have told me that they can't abide it.
    Still, if one tends to get a bit one-sided,
It's pleasant as it's easy to secure
The hero worship of the immature.

More, it's a job, and jobs to-day are rare:
    All the ideals in the world won't feed us
Although they give our crimes a certain air.
    So barons of the press who know their readers
    Employ to write their more appalling leaders,
Instead of Satan's horned and hideous minions,
Clever young men of liberal opinions.

Which brings me up to nineteen-thirty-five;
    Six months of film work is another story
I can't tell now. But, here I am, alive
      Knowing the true source of that sense of glory
      That still surrounds the England of the Tory,
Come only to the rather tame conclusion
That no man by himself has life's solution.

I know—the fact is really not unnerving—
    That what is done is done, that no past dies,
That what we see depends on who's observing,
    And what we think on our activities.
    That envy warps the virgin as she dries
But "Post coitum, homo tristis" means
The lover must go carefully with the greens.

The boat has brought me to the landing-stage,
    Up the long estuary of mud and sedges;
The line I travel has the English gauge;
    The engine's shadow vaults the little hedges;
    And summer's done. I sign the usual pledges
To be a better poet, better man;
I'll really do it this time if I can.

I'm home again, and goodness knows to what,
    To read the papers and to earn my bread;
I'm home to Europe where I may be shot;
    "I'm home again", as William Morris said,
    "And nobody I really care for's dead."
I've got a round of visits now to pay,
So I must finish this another day.

END OF PART IV

CHAPTER XIV

Letter to Kristian Andreirsson, Esq.

My Dear Kristian Andreirsson,
  In Reykjavik I made you a promise that I would send you my impressions of your country, and now I am back at home I must do my best to fulfil it, a small return indeed for all your unwearied hospitality to us, and for your wife's delicious pancakes. Though I question whether the reac-

tions of the tourist are of much value; without employment in the country he visits, his knowledge of its economic and social relations is confined to the study of official statistics and the gossip of tea-tables; ignorant of the language his judgment of character and culture is limited to the superficial; and the length of his visit, in my case only three months, precludes him from any real intimacy with his material. At the best he only observes what the inhabitants know already; at the worst he is guilty of glib generalisations based on inadequate and often incorrect data. Moreover, whatever his position in his own country, the social status of a tourist in a foreign land is always that of a rentier—as far as his hosts are concerned he is a person of independent means—and he will see them with a rentier's eye: the price of a meal or the civility of a porter will strike him more forcibly than a rise in the number of cancer cases or the corruption of the judicial machine. Finally the remoteness of Iceland, coupled with its literary and political history, make it a country which, if visited at all, is visited by people with strong, and usually romantic, preconceptions. Few English people take an interest in Iceland, but in those few the interest is passionate. My father, for example, is such a one, and some of the most vivid recollections of my childhood are hearing him read to me Icelandic folktales and sagas, and I know more about Northern mythology than Greek. Archbishop van Troil, who visited Iceland in 1772, makes an observation which all tourists would do well to remember—

"You must not", he says, "in this place apply to me the story which Helvetius tells of a clergyman and a fine lady who together observed the spots in the moon, which the former took for church steeples and the latter for a pair of happy lovers. I know that we frequently imagine to have really found what we most think of, or most wish for." He might have further added, that when we fail to find it we often rush to the opposite extreme of disappointment.

I do not intend to expatiate upon the natural beauties of your island: to you they need no advertisement and for the tourist there are many guide books; the Great Geysir will draw its crowds without any help from me. Besides, there is an English poem with the sentiments of which I entirely sympathise.

> Biography
> Is better than Geography,
> Geography's about maps,
> Biography's about chaps.

As I am going to be frank about what I disliked, I must say at once that I enjoyed my visit enormously; that, except on one minor occasion, I met with unvarying kindness and hospitality; and that as far as the people

Farmer

Haymaker

Germanischer Typus

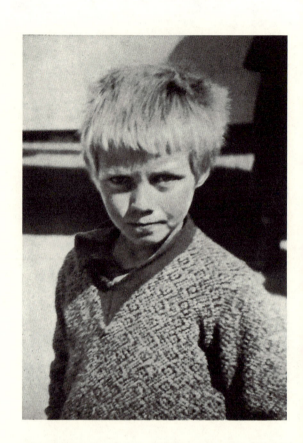

Fisher Girls

themselves are concerned, I can think of none among whom I should prefer to be exiled.

Physique and Clothes

I find the physical standard of the Icelanders, both in health and looks, high compared with most European countries, but not as high perhaps as the Norwegians. On the whole the men seem better looking than the women. It is all the more pity, therefore, that the average taste in clothes should be so poor. I know that Englishwomen are the worst dressed in the world, but that is no excuse for Iceland. I have seldom seen worse clothes, for both sexes, than I saw in the shops in Reykjavik; flashier and more discordant in colour. This is, I know partly a question of money, but not entirely. The Icelandic women could be twice as well dressed for the same expenditure.

Character

This is a silly thing to write about. I can't believe that the character of one nation is much different from that of another, or does not have the same variations. In any case the tourist sees nothing important. Like others before me I admired nearly all the farmers I met enormously; I saw none of that boorishness and yokel stupidity that one sees in the country in England. On the other hand I felt that many of the people in the towns were demoralised by living in them. This is natural. Towns take a lot of getting used to, and one must be much richer, if one is to live decently in them, than one need be in the country. The two obvious faults I noticed were unpunctuality, which is trivial, and drunkenness, which is silly but not to be wondered at when it is almost impossible to get a decent drink in the country. The beer is filthy, wine is prohibitive in price, and there is nothing left but whisky, which is not a good drink.

A Norwegian fish merchant told me that he did not like doing business with Icelanders, but personally I found them more honest than most people I have met. I am told that politics are very corrupt—natural perhaps in a country where everyone knows everyone else personally—but I have no means of verifying or contradicting this.

As regards their emotional life, I found the Icelander, certainly as compared with the Englishman, very direct, normal, and free from complexes, but whether that is a good or a bad thing, I cannot decide.

Manners

The Icelander seems to me to have beautiful natural manners, but rather imperfect artificial ones. By artificial ones, I mean those which do not depend on an instinctive feeling for other people, but have to be learnt for a complicated social life. Mackenzie, writing in 1810, said: "The

unrestrained evacuation of saliva seems to be a fashion all over Iceland."
It seems to be so still.

Wealth and Class Distinctions

It is an observation frequently made by bourgeois visitors that in Ireland there are no rich and no poor. At first sight this seems to be true. There are no mansions like those in Mayfair, and no hovels like those in the East End. Wages and the general standard of living are high in comparison with other countries; and there is less apparent class distinction than in any other capitalist country. But when one remembers that Iceland has an area larger than Ireland, a population smaller than Brighton, and some of the richest fishing grounds in the world, one is not convinced that the wages could not be higher and the differences less. I saw plenty of people whose standard of living I should not like to have to share, and a few whose wealth made them arrogant, ostentatious, and vulgar. In England there are certain traditional ways of living and spending for rich people which at least give them a certain grace. In Iceland there are none.

Education and Culture

The home of some of the finest prose in the world, with a widespread knowledge of verse and its technique, and 100% literacy, Iceland has every reason to be proud of herself, and if I make certain criticisms, it is not because I do not appreciate their achievements, but because from a country which has done so much one expects still more. In education my general impression was that the general standard was high; and I think the custom of students working on farms in the summer should provide the best possible balance of academic and manual education—indeed under these unusual circumstances I should like to see the academic education more classical—Greek and manual labour seem to me the best kind of education. But the higher grades, the sixth form and University teaching do not seem to me so good. I know this is almost entirely a question of money. The only suggestion I can make is that there should be a special school for bright children, picked from all over the island by a scholarship examination.

As regards general culture, it is high, but not as high as some accounts would lead one to believe. While in the country I heard a kitchen-maid give an excellent criticism of a medieval saga, in the towns on the other hand, particularly Reykjavik, there are obviously many people who had lost their specifically Icelandic culture, and had gained no other. In general, while literature seems fairly widely appreciated, there is almost no architecture, no drama, and little knowledge of painting or music.

I know that this is inevitable. I know that the day of a self-contained national culture is over, that Iceland is far from Europe, that the first influences of Europe are always the worst ones, and that the development

Snapped in the Paddock

What the Tourist does not see

Valdimar

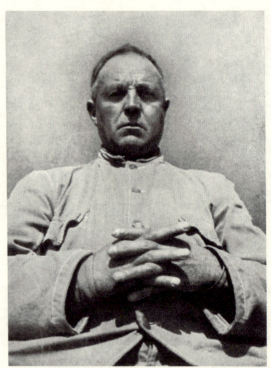

Oddur

of a truly European culture is slow and expensive. But I am convinced that the cultural future of Iceland depends on the extent to which she can absorb the best of the European traditions, and make them her own.

The only suggestions I can make have probably been thought of before, but I give them for what they may be worth.

Owing to currency problems, it is difficult for Icelanders to buy books. Apart from the local town libraries, therefore, there should be one first-class lending library of the best European books, particularly contemporary, serving the whole of the island.

Obviously Iceland cannot afford to buy pictures, but today reproductions are so good that they could with great profit be placed in galleries and schools. Music is more difficult. The Broadcasting Station does much with gramophone records, but could I think do more. I don't like the Scandinavian passion for male choirs, which cuts one off from the vast bulk of choral music.

Lastly, a small country like Iceland should be an ideal place for a really live drama—as in Ireland. This depends solely on writers—of whom there are plenty—and a few enthusiastic amateurs in a small room. To start by building an enormous state theatre which you can't afford to finish, is starting at the wrong end.

General

Most of the books about Iceland which I have read speak as if it were a nation of farmers. In point of fact, the majority live in towns, and pretty grim a town like Siglufjordur is too. To me this is the most important fact about Iceland. The present time is a critical one. I see what was once a society and a culture of independent peasant proprietors, becoming, inevitably, urbanised and in danger of becoming—not so inevitably—proletarianised for the benefit of a few, who on account of their small number and geographical isolation, can never build up a capitalist culture of their own.

A town and a town life which are worth having are expensive, and in a small and not conspicuously wealthy country like Iceland I am inclined to believe that they can only be realised by anyone, let alone the masses, in a socialist community.

Well, then, here are my impressions. I have tried to express them as simply and directly as I could, and can only hope that you will be less conscious of their superficiality than I am.

When next you come to England I shall have my revenge by making you do the same for me.

With kindest regards to your wife and yourself,

Yours sincerely,
W. H. A.

CHAPTER XV

Letter to William Coldstream, Esq.

Now the three ride from Hraensnef to Reykholt where they stayed two nights. Thence they went to Reykjavik and took ship to Isafjördur. Joachim was the vice-consul, a man well spoken of. He found them a motorboat to take them to Melgraseyri in Isafjördardjup. The name of the farmer was Olafur. He had six foster children. Louis fell sick and remained in his bed but Auden and Michael rode to Ormuli where they were very hospitably entertained. After three days they all returned to Isafjördur and dwelt at the Salvation Army Hostel there. They did not go out of doors much but spent the day drinking brandy and playing cards. People said they had not behaved very well. Now it is the end of summer and they sail oversea to England. In the summer Louis and Auden published a book.

This, Bill, is a little donnish experiment in objective narrative.

"But Landscape," cries the Literary Supplement
                    "You must have Landscape":
And the historian of the Human Consciousness;
"You can't put the clock back. Not since Montaigne";
And the reviewer taking the Russians out of a hamper;
                    "It's simply not Tolstoi":
And the professional novelist in a flash;
                    "Too easy. No dialogue."
And the common reader yawning;
                    "I want more love life."

But Landscape's so dull
                    if you haven't Lawrence's wonderful wooziness.
    My private reflections are only what you'd expect from an artist
    and a gentleman.
The poet's eye is not one from which nothing is hid
Nor the straightforward diary of a nice English schoolboy really much use.
And love life—I'm sorry, dear reader—is something
                    I always soft pedal.

But Horrebow came here and wrote a chapter on snakes
                    The chapter has only one sentence.
Hooker came here and made a list of the plants
Henderson came here with Bibles
And looked at the Geysir and thought
                    "The Lord could stop that if he wanted"

Lord Dufferin got tight with the Governor and spoke in dog-latin
And Morris opened his letters from England
                        And wondered at people's calmness.
They can get them all from a public library
This letter's for you.

A reminder of Soho Square and that winter in horrible London
When we sat in the back passage pretending to work
While the camera boys told dirty stories
And George capped them all with his one of the major in India
Who went to a ball with dysentery
                        told it in action
Till we sneaked out for coffee and discussed our colleagues
And were suspected, quite rightly, of being disloyal.
Especially you, whose tongue is the most malicious I know.

But after we'd torn them to pieces, we turned our attention to Art
Upstairs in the Corner House, in the hall with the phallic pillars
And before the band had finished a pot pourri from Wagner
We'd scrapped Significant Form, and voted for Subject,
Hence really this letter.

                        I'm bringing a problem.
Call it as Henry James might have done in a preface
        The Presentation of the Given Subject
The problem of every writer of travels;
        For Life and his publisher hand him his theme on a plate:
"You went to such and such places with so-and-so
And such and such things occurred.
                        Now do what you can."
But I can't.

The substantial facts are as I have stated above
No bandits, no comic passport officials
No hairbreadth escapes, the only test of endurance
A sixteen mile scramble in gumboots to look at dead whales
No monuments and only a little literary history
Gisli the Soursop was killed on the other side of the mountains
No views? O dozens of course. But I sympathise with the sailors
        "Instead of a girl or two in a taxi
        We were compelled to look at the Black Sea, and the Black Sea
        Isn't all it's cracked up to be."

An artist you said, if I remember you rightly,
An artist you said, in the waiting room at Euston
Looking towards that dictator's dream of a staircase

An artist you said, is both perceiver and teller, the spy and the gossip
Something between the slavey in Daumier's caricature
                    The one called *Nadadada*
And the wife of a minor canon.

Very well then, let's start with perceiving
Let me pretend that I'm the impersonal eye of the camera
Sent out by God to shoot on location
And we'll look at the rushes together.

Face of an Icelandic Professor
Like a child's self expression in plasticine
                    A child from the bottom form.
Then a lot out of focus.
Now a pan round a typical sitting-room
Bowl of postcards on table—Harmonium with Brahms' Sapphic Ode
Pi-picture—little girl crosses broken ravine bridge protected by angel.
Cut to saddling ponies—close up of farmer's hands at a girth strap
Dissolve to long shot of Reykholt school
                    Corbusier goes all Northern.
Close up of Gynaecologist Angler offering me brandy
In the next war he said
There'd be one anesthetist to at least four tables.
Mid-shot of fox farm
        Black foxes in coops—white tips to their tails
The rest N. G. I'm afraid.
Now there is a whaling station during the lunch hour
        The saw is for cutting up jaw-bones
The whole place was slippery with filth—with guts and decaying flesh—
                    like an artist's palette—
We were tired as you see and in shocking tempers.
Patreksfjördur by moonlight, shot as the boat left.
Night effects, though I say it, pretty O.K.
Our favourite occupation—the North Pole Café
I've got some shots later of hands of rummy—
        Louis's scandalous luck caused a lot of ill feeling.
Now going up Isafjördardjup—the motorboat cost 40 kronur.
The hills are a curious shape—like vaulting-horses in a gymnasium
                    The light was rotten.
What on earth is all this? O yes, a dog fight at one of the farms
Too confused to show much.
O and this is Louis drawing the Joker as usual.
And here's a shot for the Chief—epic, the *Drifters* tradition
The end of a visit, the motor-boat's out of the screen on the left

The Motorboat cost 40 kronur

Epic, the *Drifters* tradition

Louis

Michael

It was blowing a hurricane.
Harbour at Isafjördur—late summer evening
"Tatty", Basil would call it I think, but I rather like it.

Well. That's the lot.
As you see, no crisis, no continuity.
Only heroic cutting could save it
Perhaps MacNaughten might do it
                    Or Legge.
But I've cut a few stills out, in case they'd amuse you.

So much for perceiving. Now telling. That's easy.

Louis read George Eliot in bed
And Michael and I climbed the cliff behind Hraensnef
And *I was* so frightened, my dear.
And we all rowed on the lake and giggled because the boat leaked
And the farmer was angry when we whipped his horses
And Louis had a dream—unrepeatable but he repeated it—
And the lady at table had diabetes, poor thing
And Louis dreamt of a bedroom with four glass walls
And I was upset because they told me I didn't look innocent
(I liked it really of course)
And the whaling station wouldn't offer us any coffee
And Michael didn't speak for three hours after that
And the first motor-boat we hired turned back because of the weather
"A hot spot" he said but we and the vice consul didn't believe him
And that cost an extra ten kronur.
And it was after ten when we really got there and could discover a
         landing
And we walked up the farm in the dark
Over a new mown meadow, the dogs running in and out of the lamplight
And I woke in the night to hear Louis vomiting
                    Something like a ship siren
And I played "O Isis and Osiris" on the harmonium next day
And we read the short stories of Somerset Maugham aloud to each
         other
And the best one was called *His Excellency*.
And I said to Michael "All power corrupts" and he was very angry about it.
And he ate thirty-two cakes in an afternoon
And the soup they gave us the last day tasted of hair oil
And we had to wrap the salt fish in an envelope not to hurt their feelings
And we stayed at the Salvation Army—notices: no cards allowed,
                    So we played in our bedroom

And we drank Spanish brandy out of our tooth mugs, trying to like it
And feeling like schoolboys, hiding our sins from the maid.
And the film that night was in English, and the lovers were very vehement
But the loud speaker was badly adjusted and they squawked like hens
And Louis stood on the quay muttering Greek in his beard
Like a character out of the Cantos—
ἀλλὰ καὶ ὣς ἐθέλω καὶ ἐέλδομαι ἤματα πάντα
οἴκαδε τ᾽ ἐλθέμεναι καὶ ἰδέσθαι νόστιμον ἦμαρ.

But that wasn't the only thing he said
Back at Hraensnef after a heavy silence
He suddenly spoke. "God made the mice," he said
"And the mice made the Scheiss"
And again he said "The dark lady of the Bonnets"
And Michael said "You like nothing
But smoking, drinking coffee, and writing"
And he wrote on my postcard to Christopher "We have our moods."

That's all except the orchestral background
The news from Europe interwoven with our behaving
The pleasant voice of the wireless announcer, like a consultant surgeon
            "Your case is hopeless. I give you six months."
And the statements of famous economists;
Like cook coming in and saying triumphantly
            "Rover's taken the joint, ma'am."
That's all the externals, and they're not my pigeon
While the purely subjective feelings,
The heart-felt exultations and the short despairs
Require a musician. Bach, say, or Schubert.
But here is my poem, nevertheless, the fruit of that fortnight
And one too of Louis's, for comparative reading.
The novelist has one way of stating experience,
The film director another
These are our versions—each man to his medium.

            "O who can ever gaze his fill",
                  Farmer and fisherman say,
            "On native shore and local hill,
               Grudge aching limb or callus on the hand?
               Fathers, grandfathers stood upon this land,
               And here the pilgrims from our loins shall stand."
                  So farmer and fisherman say
                  In their fortunate heyday:
                  But Death's soft answer drifts across

          Empty catch or harvest loss
              Or an unlucky May.

The earth is an oyster with nothing inside it
    Not to be born is the best for man
The end of toil is a bailiff's order
    Throw down the mattock and dance while you can.

"O life's too short for friends who share",
        Travellers think in their hearts,
"The city's common bed, the air,
    The mountain bivouac and the bathing beach,
    Where incidents draw every day from each
    Memorable gesture and witty speech."
        So travellers think in their hearts,
        Till malice or circumstance parts
        Them from their constant humour:
        And shyly Death's coercive rumour
            In the silence starts.

A friend is the old old tale of Narcissus
    Not to be born is the best for man
An active partner in something disgraceful
    Change your partner, dance while you can.

"O stretch your hands across the sea,"
        The impassioned lover cries,
"Stretch them towards your harm and me.
    Our grass is green, and sensual our brief bed,
    The stream sings at its foot, and at its head
    The mild and vegetarian beasts are fed."
        So the impassioned lover cries
        Till his storm of pleasure dies:
        From the bedpost and the rocks
        Death's enticing echo mocks,
            And his voice replies.

The greater the love, the more false to its object
    Not to be born is the best for man
After the kiss comes the impulse to throttle
    Break the embraces, dance while you can.

"I see the guilty world forgiven,"
        Dreamer and drunkard sing,
"The ladders let down out of heaven;
    The laurel springing from the martyrs' blood;

The children skipping where the weepers stood;
The lovers natural, and the beasts all good."
    So dreamer and drunkard sing
    Till day their sobriety bring:
    Parrotwise with death's reply
    From whelping fear and nesting lie,
        Woods and their echoes ring.

The desires of the heart are as crooked as corkscrews
    Not to be born is the best for man.
The second best is a formal order
    The dance's pattern, dance while you can.
Dance, dance, for the figure is easy
    The tune is catching and will not stop
Dance till the stars come down with the rafters
    Dance, dance, dance till you drop.

W.H.A.

Iceland

No shields now
    Cross the knoll,
The hills are dull
    With leaden shale,
Whose arms could squeeze
    The breath from time
And the climb is long
    From cairn to cairn.

Houses are few
    But decorous
In a ruined land
    Of sphagnum moss;
Corrugated iron
    Farms inherit
The spirit and phrase
    Of ancient sagas

Men have forgotten
    Anger and ambush,
To make ends meet
    Their only business:
The lover riding
    In the lonely dale

Hears the plover's
    Single pipe

And feels perhaps
    But undefined
The drift of death
    In the sombre wind
Deflating the trim
    Balloon of lust
In a grey storm
    Of dust and grit.

So we who have come
    As trippers North
Have minds no match
    For this land's girth;
The glacier's licking
    Tongues deride
Our pride of life,
    Our flashy songs.

But the people themselves
    Who live here
Ignore the brooding
    Fear, the sphinx;
And the radio
    With tags of tune
Defies their pillared
    Basalt crags.

Whose ancestors
    Thought that at last
The end would come
    To a blast of horns
And gods would face
    The worst in fight,
Vanish in the night
    The last, the first

Night which began
    Without device
In ice and rocks,
    No shade or shape;
Grass and blood,
    The strife of life,

Were an interlude
   Which soon must pass

And all go back
   Relapse to rock
Under the shawl
   Of the ice-caps,
The cape which night
   Will spread to cover
The world when the living
   Flags are furled.

L.M.

CHAPTER XVI

Letter to Lord Byron

Part V

Autumn is here. The beech leaves strew the lawn;
   The power stations take up heavier loads;
The massive lorries shake from dusk till dawn
   The houses on the residential roads;
   The shops are full of coming winter modes.
Dances have started at the Baths next door
Stray scraps of MS strew my bedroom floor.

I read that there's a boomlet on in Birmingham,
   But what I hear is not so reassuring;
Rumours of War, the B.B.C. confirming 'em,
   The prospects for the future aren't alluring;
   No one believes Prosperity enduring,
Not even Wykehamists, whose golden mean
Maintains the All Souls' Parish Magazine.

The crack between employees and employers
   Is obvious already as the nose on
John Gielgud's face; the keels of new destroyers
   Get laid down somehow though all credit's frozen;
   The Pope's turned protestant at last and chosen,
Thinking it safer in the temporal circs,
The Italian faith against the Russian works.

England, my England—you have been my tutrix—
    The Mater, on occasions, of the free,
Or, if you'd rather, Dura Virum Nutrix,
    Whatever happens I am born of Thee;
    And Englishmen, all foreigners agree,
Taking them by and large, and as a nation,
All suffer from an Oedipus fixation.

With all thy faults, of course we love thee still;
    We'd better for we have to live with you,
From Rhondda Valley or from Bredon Hill,
    From Rotherhithe, or Regent Street, or Kew
    We look you up and down and whistle "Phew!
Mother looks odd to-day dressed up in peers,
Slums, aspidistras, shooting-sticks, and queers."

Cheer up! There're several singing birds that sing.
    There's six feet six of Spender for a start;
Eliot has really stretched his eagle's wing,
    And Yeats has helped himself to Parnell's heart;
    This book has samples of MacNeice's art;
There's Wyndham Lewis fuming out of sight,
That lonely old volcano of the Right.

I'm marking time because I cannot guess
    The proper place to which to send this letter,
c/o Saint Peter or The Infernal Press?
    I'll try the Press. World-culture is its debtor;
    It has a list that Faber's couldn't better.
For Heaven gets all the lookers for her pains,
But Hell, I think, gets nearly all the brains.

The congregation up there in the former
    Are those whose early upbringing was right,
Who never suffered from a childish trauma;
    As babies they were Truby King's delight;
    They're happy, lovely, but not overbright.
For no one thinks unless a complex makes him,
Or till financial ruin overtakes him.

Complex or Poverty; in short The Trap.
    Some set to work to understand the spring;
Others sham dead, pretend to take a nap;
    "It is a motor-boat," the madmen sing;
    The artist's action is the queerest thing:

He seems to like it, couldn't do without it,
And only wants to tell us all about it.

While Rome is burning or he's out of sorts
    "Causons, causons, mon bon," he's apt to say,
"What does it matter while I have these thoughts?"
    Or so I've heard, but Freud's not quite O.K.
    No artist works a twenty-four hour day.
In bed, asleep or dead, it's hard to tell
The highbrow from l'homme moyen sensuel.

"Es neiget die weisen zu schönem sich."
    Your lordship's brow that never wore a hat
Should thank your lordship's foot that did the trick.
    Your mother in a temper cried, "Lame Brat!"
    Posterity should thank her much for that.
Had she been sweet she surely would have taken
Juan away and saved your moral bacon.

The match of Hell and Heaven was a nice
    Idea of Blake's, but won't take place, alas.
You can choose either, but you can't choose twice;
    You can't, at least in this world, change your class;
    Neither is alpha plus though both will pass:
And don't imagine you can write like Dante,
Dive like your nephew, crochet like your auntie.

The Great Utopia, free of all complexes,
    The Withered State is, at the moment, such
A dream as that of being both the sexes.
    I like Wolf's *Goethe-lieder* very much,
    But doubt if *Ganymede*'s appeal will touch
—That marvellous cry with its ascending phrases—
Capitalism in its later phases.

Are Poets saved? Well, let's suppose they are,
    And take a peep. I don't see any books.
Shakespeare is lounging grandly at the bar,
    Milton is dozing, judging by his looks,
    Shelley is playing poker with two crooks,
Blake's adding pince-nez to an ad. for Players,
Chaucer is buried in the latest Sayers.

Lord Alfred rags with Arthur on the floor,
    Housman, all scholarship forgot at last,
Sips up the stolen waters through a straw,

Browning's complaining that Keats bowls too fast,
And you have been composing as they passed
A clerihew on Wordsworth and his tie,
A rather dirty limerick on Pye.

I hope this reaches you in your abode,
  This letter that's already far too long,
Just like the Prelude or the Great North Road;
  But here I end my conversational song.
  I hope you don't think mail from strangers wrong.
As to its length, I tell myself you'll need it,
You've all eternity in which to read it.

END OF PART V

CHAPTER XVII

Auden and MacNeice: Their Last Will and Testament

We, Wystan Hugh Auden and Louis MacNeice,
Brought up to speak and write the English tongue
Being led in the eighteenth year of the Western Peace

To the duck-shaped mountainous island with the Danish King,
At Melgraseyri in Isafjördardjup
Under the eaves of a glacier, considering

The autumns, personal and public, which already creep
Through city-crowded Europe, and those in want
Who soon must look up at the winter sky and weep,

Do set down this, our will and testament:
Believing man responsible for what he does,
Sole author of his terror and his content.

The duty his to learn, to make his choice;
On each the guilt of failure, and in each the power
To shape, create and move, love and rejoice.

Poor prospects now have any who would insure
Against the blight of crops—blood in the furrows—
And who knows which of our legacies will endure?

First to our ancestors who lie in barrows
Or under nameless cairns on heathery hills
Or where the seal-swim crashes the island-narrows

Or in Jacobean tomb, whose scrolls and skulls
Carry off death with an elegant inscription,
The Latin phrasing which beguiles and dulls

The bitter regrets at the loved body's corruption
Or those who merely share the prayer that is muttered
For many sunk together in war's eruption,

To all, clay-bound or chalk-bound, stiff or scattered,
We leave the values of their periods,
The things which seemed to them the things that mattered,

Pride in family and in substantial goods,
Comfort, ambition, honour and elegance,
The jealous eye upon wives and private woods,

The hand alert for vengeance, the brow which once
Contracted was unforgiving, proud of extremes
Not bearing easily the deserter or the dunce.

L.   And to my own in particular whose rooms
Were whitewashed, small, soothed with the smoke of peat,
Looking out on the Atlantic's gleams and glooms,

Of whom some lie among brambles high remote
Above the yellow falls of Ballysodare
Whose hands were hard with handling cart and boat

I leave the credit for that which may endure
Within myself of peasant vitality and
Of the peasant's sense of humour and I am sure

That those forefathers clamped in the boggy ground
Should have my thanks for any Ariadne's thread
Of instinct following which I too have found

My way through the forking paths of briars and mud,
My thanks I leave them therefore double and next
I leave my father half my pride of blood

And also my admiration who has fixed
His pulpit out of the reach of party slogans
And all the sordid challenges and the mixed

Motives of those who bring their drums and dragons
To silence moderation and free speech
Bawling from armoured cars and carnival wagons;

And to my stepmother I leave her rich
Placid delight in detailed living who adds
Hour to hour as if it were stitch to stitch

Calm in the circle of her household gods;
Item, to my sister Elizabeth what she lacks—
The courage to gamble on the doubtful odds

And in the end a retreat among Irish lakes
And farmyard smells and the prism of the Irish air;
Item, to Dan my son whenever he wakes

To the consciousness of what his limits are
I leave the ingenuity to transmute
His limits into roads and travel far;

Lastly to Mary living in a remote
Country I leave whatever she would remember
Of hers and mine before she took that boat,

Such memories not being necessarily lumber
And may no chance, unless she wills, delete them
And may her hours be gold and without number.

W. I leave my parents first, seeing that without them
There's no fame or affection I could win at all
Whatever fame my poems may collect about them.

The Royal College of Physicians in Pall Mall
And a chair in Preventive Medicine, I leave my father,
And the Bewcastle Cross I bequeath to him as well.

The Church of Saint Aidan at Smallheath to my mother
Where she may pray for this poor world and me,
And a paying farm to Bernard, my eldest brother.

Item, to John, my second, my library
And may my lifetime's luck fall on his head
That he may walk on Everest before he die.

Next Edward Upward and Christopher Isherwood
I here appoint my joint executors
To judge my work if it be bad or good.

My manuscripts and letters, all to be theirs
All copyrights and royalties therefrom
I leave them as their property in equal shares.

W. L. We leave to Stanley Baldwin, our beloved P.M.,
The false front of Lincoln Cathedral, and a school
Of Empire poets. As for his Cabinet, to them

We leave their National character and strength of will.
To Winston Churchill Ballinrobe's dry harbour
And Randolph, un bel pezzo, in a codicil.

To Sir Maurice Hankey for his secretarial labour
The Vicar of Bray's discretion; and to Lord Lloyd
We leave a flag-day and a cavalry sabre.

To Vickers the Gran Chaco (for agents must be paid),
The Balkan Conscience and the sleepless night we think
The inevitable diseases of their dangerous trade.

The stones of Kaldidalur to Hambro's Bank
And the soapworks in the County of Cheshire we gladly grant
To Ramsay MacDonald who's so lucid and frank.

To the Church of England Austen Leigh, The Quant-
um Theory, Stanford in B flat and the Chief Scout's horn
A curate's bicycle, and a portable second hand font.

A Year's subscription to the Gospel Magazine
With which is incorporated the Protestant Deacon,
And a Gentle Shepherd hat but not too clean

We leave the Nonconformists, as a Christmas token,
And all the lives by Franco gently stopped
We leave to Rome, and for the doctrines she has spoken

The cock that crew before St Peter wept.
And to each tribal chief or priestly quack
We leave the treachery of his sect or sept.

Item, to the Bishop of London a hockey-stick
And an Old Marlburian blazer; item to Frank,
The Groupers' Pope, we leave his personal pick

Of a hundred converts from Debrett—we think
Most of them, he will find, have quite a song
Of things to confess from limericks to drink;

Item, we leave to that old diehard Inge
A little Christian joy; item, to Sir
Robert Baden-Powell a piece of string;

Item, to the Primate, pillar of savoir faire,
An exotic entourage; item, to Pat
McCormick a constant audience on the air.

Item, to those who spend their lives in the wet
Lost six counties of the Emerald Isle
We leave our goloshes and a shrimping net;

Item, to Lord Craigavon that old bull
With a horse's face we leave an Orange drum
For after-dinner airs, when he feels full;

Item, to De Valera we leave the dim
Celtic twilight of the higher economics
And a new surname among the seraphim;

Item, to all those Irish whose dynamics
Lead them in circles we leave a cloistered life,
A fellowship say in botany or ceramics.

Item, talking of fellowships, we leave
To that great institution of dreaming spires
With all its lost reputations up its sleeve

A kinder clime for academic careers
Than Thames and Cowley afford, say Medicine Hat
Where petrol fumes will spare the uneasy ears

Of undergraduates growing among the wheat;
And we leave the proctors some powerful opera glasses
And half a dozen bulldogs with Lovelock's feet;

Item, to Convocation a bust of Moses,
A lambskin copy of Excerpta de Statutis
And all the howlers of our Latin proses;

Item, to the Oxford O.T.C. our puttees
And to the Oxford Appointments Board some gay
Jobs in Bulawayo or Calaguttis;

Item, to Sir Farquhar Buzzard a raspberry;
Item, to the College of All Souls the game
Of pleonasmus and tautology;

Item, to the Fellows of King's beside the Cam
A bunch of pansies and white violets;
And to all deans and tutors money for jam;

Item, to Wittgenstein who writes such hits
As the Tractatus Logico-Philosophicus
We leave all readers who can spare the wits;

Item, to I. A. Richards who like a mouse
Nibbles linguistics with the cerebral tooth
We leave a quiet evening in a boarding-house

Where he may study the facts of birth and death
In their inexplicable oddity
And put a shilling in the slot for brains and breath.

And Julian Huxley we leave an ant, a bee,
An axolotl and Aldous; item, to Bert-
rand Russell we leave belief in God (D.V.).

Item, we leave a bottle of invalid port
To Lady Astor; item, the Parthenon
On the Calton Hill to Basil de Selincourt.

Item, we leave the phases of the moon
To Mr Yeats to rock his bardic sleep;
And to Dr Cyril Norwood a new spittoon;

And Tubby Clayton can have some gingerpop;
And General O'Duffy can take the Harp That Once
Started and somehow was never able to stop.

We leave a mens sana qui mal y pense
To the Public Schools of England, plus Ian Hay
That the sons of gents may have La Plus Bonne Chance.

L. To Marlborough College I leave a lavatory
    With chromium gadgets and the Parthenon frieze;
W. And Holt three broken promises from me.

W. L. Item, to the B.B.C. as a surprise
      The Great Geysir; the Surrealists shall have
      J. A. Smith as an Objet Trouvé in disguise.

      To the Royal Academy we leave the 7 and 5
      And to the Geological Museum in Jermyn Street
      All metaphysicians and logicians still alive.

Item, the Imperial War Museum shall get
Professor Lindemann; and South K. a drove—
In the Science Block the Jeans and Eddington set;

And to the Natural History Wing we give
The reviewers on the *Observer,* the whole damn bunch,
And Beachcomber and the beasts that will not live.

The Dock, in all respect, we leave the Bench
And Shell Mex House we leave to H. G. Wells
To accommodate his spawn of Uebermensch.

Item, to those expert with clubs and balls
And double bores and huntin' and fishin' tackles
Some kippered tigers for their study walls;

To the Fogerty School some tropes of the Reverend Tickell's,
And the statue of Peter Pan we leave by halves—
The upper to A. A. Milne, the lower to Beverley Nichols.

Item, to Lady Oxford we leave some curves
And a first edition of Dodo; and to that great man
J. L. Garvin the civilisation he deserves.

Item, we leave our old friend Rupert Doone
Something dynamic and his own theatre
And a setting of his Unconscious on the bassoon:

Item, to Daan Hubrecht a Martello tower,
To Hugh M'Diarmid a gallon of Red Biddy,
And the bones of Shakespeare to Sir Archie Flower.

Item, in winter when the ways are muddy
We leave our gumboots tried on Iceland rocks
To the M'Gillicuddy of M'Gillicuddy,

To keep his feet dry climbing in the Reeks:
Item, we leave a portable camping oven
To Norman Douglas, last of the Ancient Greeks;

And to John Fothergill a Corner House in Heaven.
Item, we leave a tube of Pond's Cold Cream
To the débutantes of 1937.

Item, to Maurice Bowra we leave a dome
Of many-coloured glass; item, to Father
Knox a crossword puzzle or a palindrome.

Item, to Compton Mackenzie a sprig of heather,
To James Douglas a knife that will not cut,
And to Roy Campbell a sleeping-suit of leather.

Item, we leave the mentality of the pit
To James Agate and to Ivor Brown,
And to Edith Sitwell we leave her Obiit.

Item, we leave a little simple fun
To all bellettrists and the staff of *Punch*;
And a faith period to Naomi Mitchison.

And to Sir Oswald (please forgive the stench
Which taints our parchment from that purulent name)
We leave a rather unpleasant word in French.

Item, we leave to that poor soul A. M.
Ludovici the Venus of Willendorf
(A taste we neither condone nor yet condemn.)

Item, to the King's Proctor and his staff
We leave a skeleton key and *Die Untergang*
Des Abendlandes—a book to make them laugh.

Item, a vestry-meeting to Douglas Byng,
The marriage of universals to Geoffrey Mure,
And Sir James Barrie to Sir Truby King.

And to that Society whose premier law
Is the Preservation of Ancient Monuments
We leave Sir Bindon Blood and Bernard Shaw.

Item, to Dr Stopes we leave an ounce
Of cocoa-butter and some transcendental love
And may she mix them in the right amounts.

And to the most mischievous woman now alive
We leave a lorry-load of moral mud
And may her Stone Age voodoo never thrive.

And to Evelyn Underhill a diviner's rod;
The Albert Memorial to Osbert Lancaster;
And Messrs Nervo and Knox to the Eisteddfodd.

And to Ladislas Peri we leave a grand career
As sculptor in concrete, God knows what, or brick;
And Bryan Guinness shall have some Burton beer.

Item, an antidote for camera shock
And a low-brow curiosity in objects to all
Painters and sculptors in metal, wood, or rock.

To modern architects who can design so well
Kitchens and bathrooms, a gentle reminder that
Material pangs are not the only pains of Hell.

To all the technique that composers now have got
We add a feeling for the nature of the human voice
And the love of a tune which sometimes they have not.

To our fellow writers, to the whole literary race
The Interest itself in all its circumstances
That each may see his vision face to face.

To our two distinguished colleagues in confidence,
To Stephen Spender and Cecil Day Lewis, we assign
Our minor talents to assist in the defence

Of the European Tradition and to carry on
The Human heritage. [W.] And the Slade School I choose
For William Coldstream to leave his mark upon.

W. L. To the Group Theatre that has performed our plays
We leave the proceeds of the Entertainment Tax
To pay for sets, and actors on week-days.

W. To the Post Office Film Unit, a film on Sex
And to Grierson, its director, something really big
To sell, I offer with my thanks and my respects.

For my friend Benjamin Britten, composer, I beg
That fortune send him soon a passionate affair.
W. L. To Barbara Hepworth, sculptress, we leave Long Meg

And her nine daughters. A pure form, very pure,
We leave Clive Bell, and to Ben Nicolson a post
At Murphy's where he'll soon make good, we're sure.

May the critic I. M. Parsons feel at last
A creative impulse, and may the Dictatorship
Of the Holy Spirit suppress the classic past

Of Herbert Read. To Peter Fleming a cap
For exploration. We find him very jolly
But think mock modesty does not improve a chap.

We leave the Martyr's Stake at Abergwilly
To Wyndham Lewis with a box of soldiers (blonde)
Regretting one so bright should be so silly.

We hope one honest conviction may at last be found
For Alexander Korda and the Balcon Boys
And the Stavisky Scandal in picture and sound

We leave to Alfred Hitchcock with sincerest praise
Of *Sabotage*. To Berthold Viertel just the script
For which he's waited all his passionate days.

We wish the cottage at Piccadilly Circus kept
For a certain novelist, to write thereon
The spiritual cries at which he's so adept.

To Lord Berners, wit, to keep his memory green
The follies of fifty counties upon one condition
That he write the history of the King and Queen.

L.   And I to all my friends would leave a ration
Of bread and wit against the days which slant
Upon us black with nihilistic passion.

Item I leave my old friend Anthony Blunt
A copy of Marx and £1000 a year
And the picture of Love Locked Out by Holman Hunt.

Item to Archie Burton I leave my car
Which took the count at a crossroads in King's Heath
And bringing me twice in jeopardy at the bar

All but left me a convict or a wraith;
Item I leave a large viridian pot
Of preserved ginger to my dear Ann Faith

Shepard who shall also have my Bokhara mat
And Graham Shepard shall have my two cider mugs,
My thirty rose-trees and, if he likes, my hat.

Item I leave my copies of *Our Dogs*
To Mrs Norton who lives at Selly Hill:
And to Victor Rothschild the spermatozoa of frogs.

Item my golf clubs to Ernest Ludwig Stahl
Which after a little treatment with emery paper
Should serve him well around the veldt and kraal;

And Vera Stahl his sister I leave an upper
Seat at Twickenham for the Irish match
To be followed by a very recherché supper.

And Mrs Dodds I leave a champion bitch
And a champion dog and a litter of champion pups
All to be born and weaned without a hitch:

And Professor Dodds I leave the wind which whips
The Dublin Mountains and the Knockmealdowns
And may he forgive my academic slips.

Item to Betsy my borzoi a dish of bones
And 7/6 for her license for next year
And may her name be scratched on the Abbey stones:

Item to Littleton Powys more and more
I leave my admiration and all the choice
Flowers and birds that grace our English shore.

Item to Wilfred Blunt a pretty piece
Of the best rococo and a crimson shirt
Appliquéd all over with fleurs-de-lys:

Item to J. R. Hilton a Work of Art
And a dream of the infinitesimal calculus
Bolstered on apples in an apple-cart.

Item to Mr and Mrs McCance a mouse
That will keep their cats in one perpetual smile:
Item to Moore Crosthwaite a concrete house

Built by Gropius: item to George Morell
Perpetual luck at the dogs: item to Tom
Robinson a blue check homer that flies like hell

And makes his fortune: item a quiet room
To Denis Binyon to practise his Hellenistic
Greek in readiness for the Day of Doom:

W. L. Item to dear John Waterhouse a gymnastic
Exercise before breakfast every day
(A better cure for the figure than wearing elastic)

And a grand piano under a flowering tree
To sate his versatile and virile taste
From the Hammerklavier to the Isle of Capri.

Item to Gordon Herrickx a titan's wrist
Strong to the evening from commercial stone
And may his glyptic fantasy persist:

Item, to Robert Medley some cellophane
And a pack of jokers; item, a box of talc
To Geoffrey Tandy in case he shaves again.

Item to Humphrey Thackrah a flowered silk
Dressing-gown and a bottle of Numero Cinq:
Item to Isiah Berlin a saucer of milk:

L.   Item to Lella Sargent Florence a drink
After hours and a salad of chicory:
Item to my cousin Oonagh a coat of mink:

Item to the Brothers Melville the artist's eye
And may their beliefs not hamper them for ever:
Item to Guy Morgan and also Guy

Burgess and Ben Bonas and Hector MacIver
And Robert Dunnett and Norman Cameron
I leave a keg of whiskey, the sweet deceiver:

Item I leave to my old friend Adrian
Green Armitage who now is a stockbroker,
A jolly life as an English gentleman:

Item to Helen Cooke I leave an acre
Of Cornish moor to run her spaniels in
On perfect terms with the local butcher and baker:

Item I leave a sun which will always shine
To Elspeth Duxbury and a ginger cat
Which will always be washed and groomed by half-past nine:

Item to Ivan Rowe a gallon pot
Of Stephens' blue-black ink: item to Walter
Allen I leave the tale of a tiny tot

On the Midland Regional and from the welter
Of hand-to-mouth journalism and graft
I hope his brains afford him sufficient shelter;

Item to Edith Marcuse I leave a deft
Hand at designing and an adequate job,
And to Coral Brown camellias on her right and left.

Item to Mrs Hancock a koala cub:
Item to Cicely Russell and R. D. Smith
The joint ownership of a Shropshire pub:

Item to Bernard and Nora Spencer a path
To a life of colour, ample and debonair:
Item to old John Bowle a Turkish bath:

Item to Diana Sanger an open fire
A wire fox terrier and a magnolia tree;
And to Ruthven Todd the works of Burns entire.

Item to Curigwen Lewis the Broadway sky
Blazing her name in lights; item to Jack
Chase my best regards and a case of rye:

Item to C. B. Canning a private joke:
Item a clerihew to Christopher Holme
And may he not be always completely broke:

Item to David Gretton a lovely time
Arranging broadcasts from the Parish Hall:
Item to May Lawrence a gin and lime:

Item to Francis Curtis, once Capel,
I leave my wonder at his Oxford Past
Which to my knowledge was without parallel:

W. L. Item to John Betjeman (the most
Remarkable man of his time in any position)
We leave a Leander tie and Pugin's ghost

And a box of crackers and St Pancras Station
And the *Church of Ireland Gazette* and our confidence
That he will be master of every situation.

A Chinese goose to Harold Acton we advance.
W. Item my passport to Heinz Nedermeyer
And to John Andrews, to rub with after a dance,

As many L.M.S. towels as he may require.
W. L. Item to E. M. Forster a bright new notion
For a novel with a death roll, O dear, even higher.

And to St John Ervine, ornament of the nation,
His Ulster accent and les neiges d'antan
And a little, if possible, accurate information:

And some new games with time to J. W. Dunne,
To Andy Corry a six-foot belemnite,
And to Noel Coward a place in the setting sun;

To Dylan Thomas a leek on a gold plate;
Item we leave to that great mind Charles Madge
Some curious happenings to correlate;

Item to the *New Statesman* a constant grudge
And a constant smile saying "We told you so",
And to John Sparrow a quarter of a pound of fudge.

Item, the falling birthrate we leave to Roy
Harrod and Maynard Keynes for pulling together;
To Brian Howard a watch and the painted buoy

That dances at the harbour mouth (which is rather
The poésie de départs but sooner or later
We all like being trippers); item to Father

D'Arcy, that dialectical disputer,
We leave St Thomas Aquinas and his paeans—
W. To Neville Coghill, fellow of Exeter, my tutor,

I leave Das Lebendigste with which to form alliance
And to Professor Dawkins who knows the Modern Greeks
I leave the string figure called the Fighting Lions.

W. L. To the barrister, Richard Best, to wear on walks
A speckled boater; to Geoffrey Grigson of *New Verse*
A strop for his sharp tongue before he talks.

A terrible double entendre in metre or in prose
To William Empson; and we leave his own
Post mortem to any doctor who thinks he knows

W. The Inmost Truth. And the New Peace he has won
To Gerald Heard—and to the teacher Maurice Feild
A brilliant pupil as reward for all he's done.

To Geoffrey Hoyland, whose virtues are manifold
An equal love for every kind of nature,
W. L. And to John Davenport a permanent job to hold.

W. For Peggy Garland someone real in every feature,
To Tom her husband, someone to help; and a call
To go a dangerous mission for a fellow creature

To Nancy Coldstream. I hope John Layard will
Find quick ones always to put him on his feet
To Olive Mangeot a good lodger and, till

The revolution cure her corns, a set
Of comfortable shoes: to Sylvain, her younger son,
My suits to wear when it is really wet.

My Morris-Cowley to carry chickens in
To Peter Roger, with a very fine large goat.
And a Healer's Prize for Robert Moody to win.

W. L. We leave with our best compliments the Isle of Wight
To Robert Graves and Laura Riding, because
An Italian island is no good place to write.

We leave to the Inland Revenue Commissioners
The Channel Islands: for these charming men
Will find there many an undeserving purse.

W. I leave the wheel at Laxey, Isle of Man,
To Sean Day-Lewis, and the actual island leave
To Mrs Yates of Brooklands, to rest there when she can.

W. L. The County of Surrey as it stands we give
To Sapper; and all the roadhouses in Herts
To Hilaire Belloc that he may drink and live.

To Quinton Hogg the wardenship of the Cinque Ports,
And the holy double well of Saint Clether to all
Who suffer guilty feelings and irrational thoughts.

To Sebastian Sprott we offer Mortimer's Hole
W. To snub-nosed Gabriel Carritt the Beetle and Wedge
And T.F.C. may keep the letter that he stole.

W. L. To Mayfair, Crowland Abbey's river-lacking bridge
As symbol of its life. To Crossman, Councillor,
We leave High Office, and a wind-swept northern ridge.

We leave to Cowper Powys Glastonbury Tor
The White Horses to the Horse Guards, and the vale of Evenlode
To all those shell-shocked in the last Great War.

For pacifists to keep the brutal world outside
We've Offa's Dyke, and the caves at Castleton for parents
Who dream of air-raids and want a place to hide.

Item, we leave to Professor Sargant Florence
Dartington Hall and all that is therein.
And Dartmoor Prison to Sir Herbert Pethick Lawrence.

W.   To Rex Warner, birdman, I leave Wicken Fen
And Hillborough Dovecote. To Sydney Newman give
The Coronation Organ to play now and then.

W. L. The twin towers of the Crystal Palace we would leave
To Leonard and Virginia Woolf, and Boston Stump
To Ernest Jones, round which they each may weave

Their special phantasies. To every tramp
We leave a harvest barn, a private drive
And a fenced deer park where he may make his camp.

Snowdonia to Michael Roberts with our love,
To Constant Lambert the Three Choirs Festival,
And the Vale of Eden with the Pennine scarp above

To the children of the London East End. Sweet Boars Hill
To Poets Laureate, past, present, and to come.
As for the parts of our bodies in this will

We allot them here as follows: to the Home
For Lost Dogs and Cats our livers and lights,
And our behinds to the Birmingham Hippodrome.

And our four eyes which cannot see for nuts
We leave to all big-game hunters and to all
Apprentices to murder at the butts;

Our feet to hikers when their own feet fail;
To all escapists our islands of Langahans;
And to Imperial Chemicals a pail

Of what in us would otherwise join the drains;
The Watch Commitee can have our noses and
The British Association can have our brains;

Item our ears, apt for the slightest sound,
We leave those Statesmen who happen to be debarred
From hearing how the wheels of State run round;

To Major Yogi-Brown our navels we award
And our pudenda we leave or rather fling
Our biographers and The Thames Conservancy Board;

Lastly our hearts, whether they be right or wrong,
We leave neither to scientists nor doctors
But to those to whom they properly belong.

Our grit we beg to leave all sanitary inspectors,
Our faith, our hope, our charity we leave The League
To help it to do something in the future to protect us.

Our cheerfulness to each square-headed peg
That lives in a round hole, and our charm at its best
To those who cannot dig and are ashamed to beg.

Our powers of parrot memory we offer to assist
Examinees. Our humour, all we think is funny,
To Dr Leavis and almost every psycho-analyst.

To the Bishop of Bradford our discretion, if any;
And our carnivorous appetites we give away
To Professor Gilbert Murray. Item, our many

Faults to all parents that their families may see
No one expects them really to be good as gold.
After due thought, we leave our lust in Chancery,

     Our obstinacy to the untamed and wild.
W. I leave to my ex-pupils whether bright or dull
     Especially to every homesick problem child

     All the good times I've had since I left school.
     And hope that Erika, my wife, may have her wish
     To see the just end of Hitler and his unjust rule.

W. L. To all the dictators who look so bold and fresh
     The midnight hours, the soft wind from the sweeping wing
     Of madness, and the intolerable tightening of the mesh

     Of history. We leave their marvellous native tongue
     To Englishmen, and for our intelligent island pray
     That to her virtuous beauties by all poets sung

     She add at last an honest foreign policy.
     For her oppressed, injured, insulted, and weak
     The logic and the passion proper for victory.

     We leave our age the quite considerable spark
     Of private love and goodness which never leaves
     An age, however awful, in the utter dark.

We leave the unconceived and unborn lives
A closer approximation to real happiness
Than has been reached by us, our neighbours or their wives.

To those who by office or from inclination use
Authority, a knowledge of their own misdeed
And all the hate that coercion must produce.

For the lost who from self-hatred cannot hide,
Such temporary refuge or engines of escape
From pain as Chance and Mercy can provide

And to the good who know how wide the gulf, how deep
Between Ideal and Real, who being good have felt
The final temptation to withdraw, sit down and weep,

We pray the power to take upon themselves the guilt
Of human action, though still as ready to confess
The imperfection of what can and must be built,
The wish and power to act, forgive, and bless.

EPILOGUE

For W. H. Auden

Now the winter nights begin
Lonely comfort walls me in;
So before the memory slip
I review our Iceland trip—

Not for me romantic nor
Idyll on a mythic shore
But a fancy turn, you know,
Sandwiched in a graver show.

Down in Europe Seville fell,
Nations germinating hell,
The Olympic games were run—
Spots upon the Aryan sun.

And the don in me set forth
How the landscape of the north
Had educed the saga style
Plodding forward mile by mile.

And the don in you replied
That the North begins inside,
Our ascetic guts require
Breathers from the Latin fire.

So although no ghost was scotched
We were happy while we watched
Ravens from their walls of shale
Cruise around the rotting whale,

Watched the sulphur basins boil,
Loops of steam uncoil and coil,
While the valley fades away
To a sketch of Judgment Day.

So we rode and joked and smoked
With no miracles evoked,
With no levitations won
In the thin unreal sun;

In that island never found
Visions blossom from the ground,
No conversions like St Paul,
No great happenings at all.

Holidays should be like this,
Free from over-emphasis,
Time for soul to stretch and spit
Before the world comes back on it,

Before the chimneys row on row
Sneer in smoke, "We told you so"
And the fog-bound sirens call
Ruin to the long sea-wall.

Rows of books around me stand,
Fence me round on either hand;
Through that forest of dead words
I would hunt the living birds—

Great black birds that fly alone
Slowly through a land of stone,
And the gulls who weave a free
Quilt of rhythm on the sea.

Here in Hampstead I sit late
Nights which no one shares and wait
For the 'phone to ring or for
Unknown angels at the door;

Better were the northern skies
Than this desert in disguise—
Rugs and cushions and the long
Mirror which repeats the song.

For the litany of doubt
From these walls comes breathing out
Till the room becomes a pit
Humming with the fear of it

With the fear of loneliness
And uncommunicableness;
All the wires are cut, my friends
Live beyond the severed ends.

So I write these lines for you
Who have felt the death-wish too,
But your lust for life prevails—
Drinking coffee, telling tales.

Our prerogatives as men
Will be cancelled who knows when;
Still I drink your health before
The gun-butt raps upon the door.

L.M.

APPENDIX

Total Area: *c.* 39,760 square miles
Total Population: *c.* 115,000
National debt: 41,938,000 kronur
National income: 14,312,000 kronur
Principal creditor: Hambro's Bank

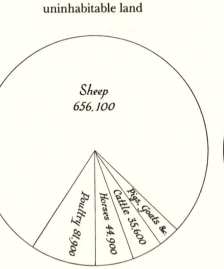

1. Relation of habitable to
   uninhabitable land

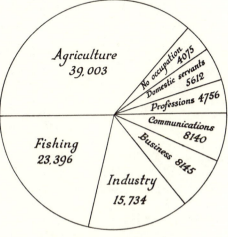

2. Kinds of habitable land

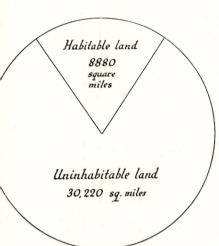

3. Livestock

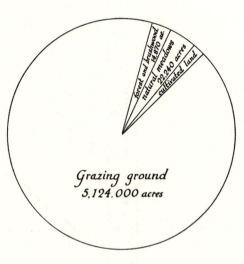

4. Distribution of population
   by occupation

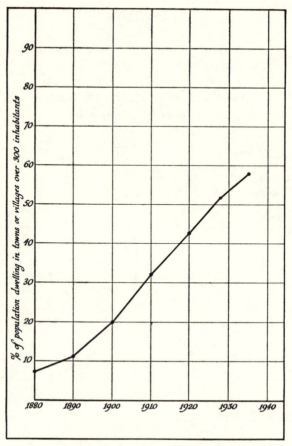

5. Graph showing urbanisation

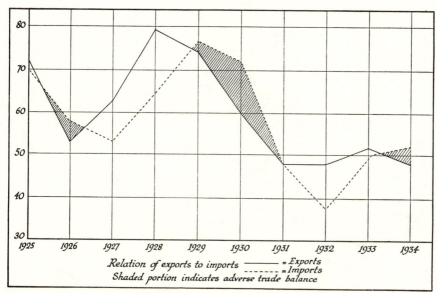

6. Graph of exports and imports

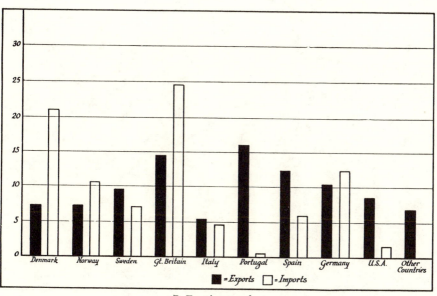

7. Foreign trade

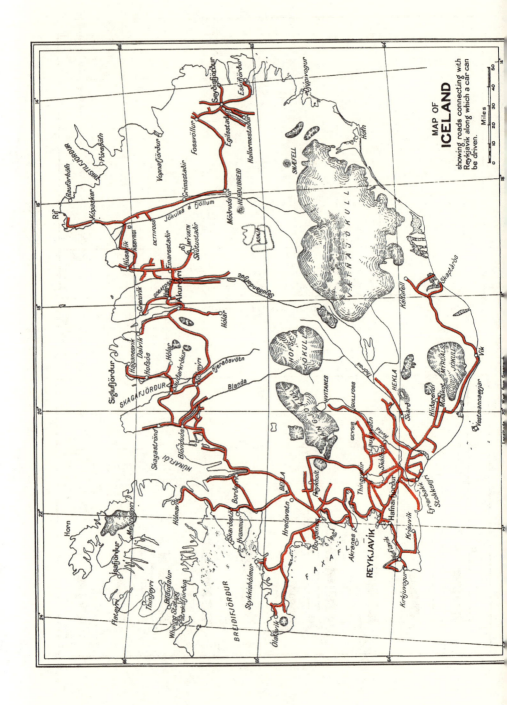

MAP OF
ICELAND

showing roads connecting with
Reykjavik along which a car can
be driven.

Miles
0   10   20   30   40   50

ESSAYS AND REVIEWS

1937–1938

Impressions of Valencia

The pigeons fly about the square in brilliant sunshine, warm as a fine English May. In the centre of the square, surrounded all day long by crowds and surmounted by a rifle and fixed bayonet, 15 ft. high, is an enormous map of the Civil War, rather prettily illustrated after the manner of railway posters urging one to visit Lovely Lakeland or Sunny Devon. Badajoz is depicted by a firing-party; a hanged man represents Huelva; a doll's train and lorry are heading for Madrid; at Seville Queipo de Llano is frozen in an eternal broadcast. The General seems to be the Little Willie of the war; in a neighbouring shop window a strip of comic woodcuts shows his rake's progress from a perverse childhood to a miserable and well-merited end.

Altogether it is a great time for the poster artist and there are some very good ones. Cramped in a little grey boat the Burgos Junta, dapper Franco and his bald German adviser, a cardinal and two ferocious Moors are busy hanging Spain; a green Fascist centipede is caught in the fanged trap of Madrid; in photomontage a bombed baby lies couchant upon a field of aeroplanes.

To-day a paragraph in the daily papers announces that since there have been incidents at the entrances to cabarets, these will in future be closed at nine p.m. Long streamers on the public buildings appeal for unity, determination and discipline. Three children, with large brown eyes like some kind of very rich sweet, are playing trains round the fountain. On one of the Ministries a huge black arrow draws attention to the fact that the front at Teruel is only 150 km. away. This is the Spain for which charming young English aviators have assured us that the best would be a military dictatorship backed by a foreign Power.

Since the Government moved here the hotels are crammed to bursting with officials, soldiers and journalists. There are porters at the station and a few horse-cabs, but no taxis, in order to save petrol. Food is plentiful, indeed an hotel lunch is heavier than one could wish. There is a bull-fight in aid of the hospitals; there is a variety show where an emaciated-looking tap-dancer does an extremely sinister dance of the machine-guns. The foreign correspondents come in for their dinner, conspicuous as actresses.

And everywhere there are the people. They are here in corduroy breeches with pistols on their hip, in uniform, in civilian suits and berets. They are here, sleeping in the hotels, eating in the restaurants, in the cafés drinking and having their shoes cleaned. They are here, driving fast cars on business, running the trains and the trams, keeping the streets clean, doing all those things that the gentry cannot believe will be properly done unless they are there to keep an eye on them. This is the blood-thirsty and unshaven Anarchy of the bourgeois cartoon, the end of civil-isation from which Hitler has sworn to deliver Europe.

For a revolution is really taking place, not an odd shuffle or two in cabinet appointments. In the last six months these people have been learning what it is to inherit their own country, and once a man has tasted freedom he will not lightly give it up; freedom to choose for himself and to organise his life, freedom not to depend for good fortune on a clever and outrageous piece of overcharging or a windfall of drunken charity. That is why, only eight hours away at the gates of Madrid where this wish to live has no possible alternative expression than the power to kill, General Franco has already lost two professional armies and is in the process of losing a third.

The New Statesman and Nation, 30 January 1937

Royal Poets

The Muse of Monarchy. Eric Grant. 5s.

I suppose every humble and loyal subject has often wondered what it would feel like to be King, what one would think about when one woke up alone in the morning or in the middle of the night, and whether one would ever be able to push away the cares of state for a moment to reflect upon what I. A. Richards has summarised as the isolation of the human situation, the facts of birth and death in their inexplicable oddity, the inconceivable immensity of the universe, man's place in the perspective of time, and the enormity of his ignorance. "Of course", we assure ourselves, "I should not change very much; I should never allow myself to lose my private integrity".

The idea of a king writing poetry is therefore peculiarly fascinating to us, because poetry is, for royalty, a private not an official occupation, and we open *The Muse of Monarchy* in the hope that it will tell us something about the private life of our rulers. I'm afraid it doesn't.

On the whole the poems fall into two divisions: light poems, most of which I fancy were written in comparative youth (it is unfortunate that the actual composition dates of the poems are unknown), and poems writ-ten in disaster. Both, unfortunately, read as poetical exercises rather than genuine expressions of feeling, and therefore, the lighter ones are the best.

Henry VIII learned something from his tutor Skelton, and

> Adieu mine own lady
> Adieu my special
> Who hath my heart truly
> Be sure and ever shall.

achieves its object in the way that Anne Boleyn's poem in imprisonment does not:

> Fare well my pleasures past
> Welcome my present payne.

is not adequate to her situation in the way that Henry's poem is to his. The trouble is we know too much about the authors not to be critical of them when they attempt the serious.

Henry VI may declare that "Kingdoms are but cares," but then as we know from the history books, he was a weak king; Edward II that:

> A Father's scourge is for our profit meant
> I see thy rod and, Lord, I am content.

but then he lost Bannockburn; Henry VIII:

> I hurt no man, I do no wrong;
> I love true where I did marry.

but we know better; and Charles I, we feel, was a self-deceiver when he wrote:

> Nature and Law, by thy divine decree
> (The only root of righteous loyalty)
> With this dim diadem invested me.

What is impressive, however, about this collection is the high level of technical accomplishments. If, as poetry, it is not particularly exciting, as verse it is extremely well made. These kings and queens were cultured people; they knew enough about the art of writing to have a real appreciation of poetry, and, more, of contemporary poetry. Their models were the poets of their own time. Henry VIII imitates Wyatt, Elizabeth Campion, Charles I Marvell, Charlotte Sophia Tom Moore.

With the coming of the Hanoverian House, this connection between the court and the poetry of the nation seems to have been lost. If Queen Victoria ever wrote pastiches of "In Memoriam", she must have burnt them. One wonders whether this royal interest will ever be revived and whether the Archbishops and the general public would welcome it if it were. Perhaps it would be unconstitutional.

The Listener, 28 April 1937

A Review of *Illusion and Reality*, by Christopher Caudwell

Illusion and Reality. By Christopher Caudwell. Macmillan. 18s.

We have waited a long time for a Marxist book on the aesthetics of poetry. *Axel's Castle* was a beginning but it was about individual matters, not fundamentals. Now at last Mr Caudwell has given us such a book.

Illusion and Reality is a long essay on the evolution of freedom in Man's struggle with nature, and of the parts that art and science play in that evolution since both are concerned in their different spheres with making man conscious of necessity, of the necessity of his affective instincts and the external forces of Nature, without which knowledge he is a slave:

> A mathematical demonstration cannot be said to persuade. It appears either true or false: if true it simply injects itself into our minds as an additional piece of outer reality. If false, we reject it as mere word-spinning. But if we accept it we are no more *persuaded* of its truth than we are persuaded of the truth of a horse standing in front of us. We do not accept it, we see it. In the same way, in art, we are not persuaded of the existence of Hamlet's confusion, or Prufrock's seedy world-weariness. . . . We feel so-and-so and such and such. We are no more persuaded of their truth than of the truth of a toothache.

After a preliminary discussion of how the mythology of an undifferentiated tribal economy cystallises out with the increase in division of labour and class into science, art, and religion, Mr Caudwell goes on to trace the history of English Poetry from the Elizabethan Period to our own, and to show the relation between its changes in technique and subject matter and the changes in economic production.

The second half of his book is a discussion of the subject-object relation, and of the essentially social nature of words, art and science, an approach which enables Mr Caudwell to make the clearest and most cogent criticism of Freud and Jung, while using their discoveries, which I have ever read.

> Economic production requires association which in turn demands the word. For men to work together, that is, to operate together non-instinctively they must have a common world of *changeable* perceptual reality, and by changeable I mean changeable by their actions; and by changeable by their actions I mean predictable change, such as dawn and eclipse, and locatable change such as "here" and "there". . . . Hence by means of the word, men's association in eco-

nomic production continually generates change in their perceptual private worlds and the common world, enriching both. A vast moving superstructure rises above man's busy hands which is the reflection of all the change he has effected or discovered in ages of life.

Although there is a similar psychological mechanism at work, art is no more neurosis than thought is dream. And the difference is precisely this, that science and art have a social content. The reality around which the extraverted hysteric or cyclothymic distorts the theory is private reality, a reality that contradicts the whole of the social theory of reality in his consciousness. This contradiction instead of leading, as in science, to a synthesis of the private experience with the social theory of reality, demanding a change of both, leads to conduct which denies the social theory of reality. . . . The psychological mechanism of science, because its reality is public and true, produces in the sphere of theory an ego which is the very opposite of that of the cyclothymic extravert—an ego which is drained of affect and quality, which is neutral, passive, and serenely conscious of necessity. Of course this very reality, because it is without the dynamism and appetite of the instincts, requires the emotional reality of art for its completion. It is true, therefore, that a world which tried to live by science alone would deny its theory in practice and show the nerve storms of a cyclothymic, not because science is cyclothymic but because it is only one part of concrete living.

The reality around which the psychasthenic neurotic or schizophrenic distorts the outside world is a private ego, his own private desires and appetites. Around this he arranges a whole mock world (compulsions, phobias, etc.). But the psychological mechanism of art, because its ego is public and noble, produces in the sphere of theory a world which is beautiful and strong. This world, because it is drained of necessity, requires the mechanism of science for its realisation. A world which lived by art alone would deny its theory in practice and live in a beautiful world of dream, while all its actions would produce only ugliness and misery.

I shall not attempt to criticise *Illusion and Reality* firstly because I am not competent to do so, and secondly because I agree with it. Nor shall I summarise it, because a summary always reads like a slick generalisation, and this book requires to be carefully read in its entirety to appreciate the force and depth of Mr Caudwell's argument.

This is the most important book on poetry since the books of Dr Richards, and, in my opinion, provides a more satisfactory answer to the many problems which poetry raises.

New Verse, May 1937

[From *Authors Take Sides on the Spanish War*]

I support the Valencia Government in Spain because its defeat by the forces of International Fascism would be a major disaster for Europe. It would make a European war more probable; and the spread of Fascist Ideology and practice to countries as yet comparatively free from them, which would inevitably follow upon a Fascist victory in Spain, would create an atmosphere in which the creative artist and all who care for justice, liberty and culture would find it impossible to work or even exist.

Authors Take Sides on the Spanish War, 1937

Preface to the Catalogue of Oil Paintings by Past and Present Members of the Downs School, Colwall

This is a collection of paintings by boys who have been through a particular preparatory school. Most of them have been painted at the school, that is to say between the ages of ten and fourteen, but there are also some painted later by old boys at their public schools, and one or two by boys who have become art students.

Most of these paintings were not done during compulsory periods in school but on afternoons set aside every week for chosen hobbies.

The Downs is one of the very few preparatory schools where the boys are taught to paint in oils and the results, in my opinion, fully justify their use as a particularly suitable medium for the young.

I think the most encouraging feature of the exhibition is that little of the work is childishly naive. Painting, as the most physical and manual of the arts, naturally appeals to small children and it is easy enough to have a charming exhibition of their work. But it is gratifying to learn that, with sensible encouragement, boys of not necessarily outstanding artistic ability can continue to paint interesting pictures without having to rely upon an artificially prolonged childishness of vision and technique.

Finally, though no doubt most of these boys will not become professional painters, the result of having painted in oils themselves, is bound to give them a more intimate interest in and intelligent appreciation of the pictorial arts.

I believe the paintings to be enjoyable in themselves but the exhibition should also be of peculiar interest to all leaders of art in this country and especially to those who are concerned about the low standard of art teaching in the great majority of our preparatory schools.

Redfern Gallery, 19–31 July 1937

Education

BY W. H. AUDEN AND T. C. WORSLEY

PART I. FACT

Education is an industry in which something like a hundred million pounds a year are spent.

It is run partly by the State, partly by private enterprise.

It involves four major interests:

(*a*) The State.
(*b*) The Teacher.
(*c*) The Parent.
(*d*) The Child.

A. THE STATE

Public education (except university education) is entrusted to various locally elected councils; these provide for the administration, the staffing, the maintenance and the erection of all public elementary schools (except certain elementary schools, where the buildings and upkeep of the structure, but nothing else, are provided by voluntary, mainly religious, bodies), and they provide some secondary schools and contribute to the maintenance of many others.

Of the total cost, local authorities raise just under half from the rates, while Parliament raises just over half from taxation, and supplies it in the form of grants to the local authorities.

Each Council elected by the ratepayers selects its own education committee, of whom at least a majority must be members of the Council, while the rest may be co-opted for their special knowledge. This committee has its own administrative staff.

The administrative body for Parliament is the Board of Education, with a president who is a member of the Cabinet, and a parliamentary secretary who is a junior member of the Government.

Beyond the statutory requirements, each authority is free to develop its own educational policy, subject to the limitations of (*a*) its own finances and (*b*), if they are insufficient for any project, grants from Parliament which are controlled by the Board.

Control is therefore exercised:

(*a*) By the Finance Committee of the local authority. The Finance Committee is naturally selected from those with financial experience. Consequently the tendency is for them to belong to the employing classes.

(*b*) By the decision of the Board who have to give their approval to any scheme involving a grant. The Board has a further control in that it appoints the inspectors who report on the efficiency of the schools and teachers and act, in general, as liaison officers between the Board and local authorities.

It will be seen that there is no such thing as a State policy for education. The Government of the day can do no more than control the grant from taxation. It cannot dictate policy. The Board can only recommend policy: it cannot dictate it. It can neither appoint nor dismiss teachers.

The real power lies with the local authority.

B. The Teacher

Teaching is an industry which employs over two hundred thousand people.* There are certain *desiderata* for all occupations:

(1) Good pay.
(2) Security.
(3) Reasonable leisure.
(4) Personal freedom.

(1) Pay

This ranges from the £93 a year of the uncertificated woman teacher in an elementary school to the £5,000 a year of the Headmaster of Harrow.†

STATE

The certificated elementary teacher starts at a minimum of £168 and

---

* (1936) In State elementary schools some 160,000 trained and untrained; in grant-aided secondary schools some 24,000. In elementary schools the proportion of women to men is just under 3 to 1. In secondary schools 0.92 to 1.

† Although the number of uncertificated teachers is supposed to be decreasing, there is still one uncertificated for every five certificated teachers in elementary schools.

rises to a maximum of £408. If he is lucky and becomes a head teacher his salary ranges from £348 to £606.*

In a secondary school a graduate will start at £234 and rise to £480 (London has higher rates). As a head, the minimum will be £600.

In short, if you are teaching in a State elementary school your average salary will be about £5 a week.

At the outset you will be above the average income level of about two-thirds of the population; after eight years' service, you will be above over 85 per cent; and towards the end, above 95 per cent.

But in considering these figures one must remember that teachers cannot begin earning before they are twenty, and that many of them then have loans to repay, and that they have appearances to keep up.

PRIVATE ENTERPRISE

Preparatory Boarding schools. Allowing £100 a year for board and lodging, salaries for assistants range from £180 to £400: a head may bankrupt himself or make his fortune.

Public schools. Many of the minor schools keep to the Burnham scale for secondary schools, but the better known start well above it. A teacher at a good public school starts at about £350, and a house-master may be making over £1,000 a year.

(2) Security

UNEMPLOYMENT†

In 1931 in the industrial class 1 in 7 was unemployed;
in the commercial class 1 in 13;
in the professional as a whole 1 in 17;
in teaching 1 in 49.

PENSIONS

All teachers in State schools contribute 5 per cent. of their salaries to a pension scheme. The retiring age is at or after 60, or on completion of forty years approved service, when they receive a pension and a lump sum.

The average in 1936 (for men) was £199 allowance and £519 lump sum.

Public schools make their own arrangements, and preparatory none.

* For men. The scales for women throughout are slightly lower. The starting salary depends on the length of the training and the type of degree gained.

† But this does not take into account those who train as teachers but do not get a post or have to wait, as often happens, two years or more for a post to fall vacant.

DISMISSAL

In State elementary schools and many secondary this lies in the hands of the local education authority, not of the head teacher or the governing committee, as in some secondary and private schools.

Compared with business or industry dismissal is rare and, except for moral offences, difficult. A local education committee with strong political or religious opinions may play a part in their original appointment. The trade union movement is pretty strong.

In private schools the power of the head is almost complete and arbitrary.

(3) Leisure

The official teaching hours are from twenty-three to twenty-eight hours a week. But this is no indication of the real facts. Corrections, preparation and out-of-school activities make a working day of not less than eight and often ten or eleven hours.

Holidays range from about eight weeks a year for the elementary school teacher to sixteen weeks for a private school teacher.

(4) Personal Freedom

The teacher's private life is a matter of public interest and is therefore more circumscribed than in any other occupation. In conduct and expression of opinion the teacher in a private school is less free than a clergyman. In State schools opinions are less controlled, but sex or drink are matters for dismissal more important than inefficiency.*

To the working class the teaching profession offers an escape from the conditions which they have experienced as children, i.e. it offers higher pay, greater security, better working conditions and less chance of unemployment. Moreover, being a black-coated profession it has a higher social status.*

On the other hand, these advantages are won at the cost of a certain loss in personal freedom.

To the bourgeois, teaching, if it does not appeal as a vocation, appeals because it is easy to enter, comfortable and safe.

* A politically conscious workman is fighting his employer and so is more liable to get dismissed for his opinions than the politically conscious teacher who is not fighting the head, who, like him, is a salaried employee.

* Elementary schools (because presumably they are free) are inferior in social status to secondary schools; and elementary teachers (because presumably they are paid less) are inferior to secondary teachers. The latter tend to speak condescendingly to and of the former. Private school teachers rarely speak to either.

Teaching is, also, one of those occupations which make a particular technical and psychological appeal to certain types of people. It offers special opportunities to all who love power, influence over other people, freedom from contradiction, and the company of the immature.

This is not to pass a moral judgement. The profession has both its healers and its wreckers, its liberators and its tyrants. They must be judged by their results.

On the whole the liberal trend in education offers more opportunities to the wreckers and less to the tyrants.

Of necessity the majority of teachers in State schools must choose their profession from economic motives, though they may later discover in it a vocation. The middle class, having a much wider range of choice, are more likely to enter it as a vocation.

This does not mean that the average private school teacher is better than the State school teacher. On the contrary, because the middle class have a wider choice, the more adventurous choose less sheltered careers. The private and public schools are far too full of the timid, the disappointed and the arrested.

The problem in the State school is different. There, prospective teachers have to decide on their career before the age of 18 in order to obtain the necessary grant to pay for their training. (Of the students in the Faculty of Arts at Birmingham nearly 80 per cent. have climbed from elementary schools, and between 80 and 90 per cent. hope to become teachers.) When they discover at the university or training college what teaching will be like, it is too late to change their minds. They are irrevocably committed unless they can afford to return the money from grants or loans. *

Summary

All educationalists agree that Education should not aim primarily at instilling mere fact, but at training "character," "personality," "citizenship," or whatever their phrase may be. They say, and rightly, that the teacher is more important than the method.

But Education is limited by the average ability of those who practise it, both as to method and subjects taught.

Many of the more progressive techniques make demands which only the exceptional teacher can meet. The predominance of the factual over the humanistic in education persists because it is within the powers of the average teacher to learn how to impart fact; but remarkable personalities do not grow on every bush. Training colleges are not staffed by a gaggle of Platos; nor is it likely that all their students would profit by them if they were.

Perhaps it is fair to say that 10 per cent. of teachers are interested in education, 50 per cent. in their craft, and the rest in neither.

C. THE PARENT

Every parent would like his child to become happy and good and healthy and well-off, and they expect Education to make this possible. Which aim they lay most stress on will depend upon which they are most conscious of lacking themselves.

There are average parents, very poor parents, snobbish parents and civilized parents.

The average parent is the poor parent to whom economic security is the primary aim. He knows that the only chance his child has of escaping from the insecurity of his own life is for the child to win a scholarship in the special-place examination with the probability of becoming a teacher.

As long as teaching is the best future financially and socially that any but the most exceptional working-class child can look forward to, State education will have a teacher-training bias, i.e. it will tend to be abstract and academic and to pay an exaggerated respect to examination results. Cramming and overwork will be common because the parents demand them, and necessarily.* The teacher may complain that they are not in the child's best interest; the parent knows better. He knows that a special place is the only chance and that the odds are 10 to 1 against.

To the very poor parent education is mainly a nuisance which prevents his child from beginning to contribute earnings to the household. The child, he knows, is no nearer getting a good job as the result of having been at an elementary school. Outside specially favourable areas like London where there is a wider range of employment, he or she cannot choose the job to which he is fitted by talent or taste; he must take what is offered.

At the most such a parent hopes that school will keep the child out of mischief.

It is a commonplace observation that the lower middle class, the clerks and the small shop-keepers, are more snobbish than the professional classes and the gentry, but its truth is questionable.

The former have more to gain or to lose and are therefore more conscious of what the latter take for granted. Both are equally determined that their children shall go to schools where they mix with "nice" children only. Most of them want a good standard of instruction as well, but the

---

* It is not uncommon for parents to group together to hire a teacher to give additional lessons in secret outside the school.

second-rate private and public schools are proof that when for financial reasons it becomes a choice between niceness and instruction, niceness frequently wins (especially where the woman wears the trousers). In Ealing, for example, 18,000 children attend the State schools, while there are 5,000 attending private schools, many of them unrecognised by the Board.

(It is only fair to add, however, that one factor which influences many parents is the feeling that sending a child to an elementary school is accepting charity. Nineteenth-century liberalism dies very hard. As long as there are (1) a wide variation in income levels, and (2) free and fee-charging schools, it will survive.)

The parent whose first demand from education is what all headmasters say it should be, namely, to produce civilised and cultured people with a reverence for life and an awareness of values, is a rare bird.

To the majority the question of earning a living must overshadow everything else. To the bulk of the remainder civilisation is their way of life: a good accent, pleasant table manners, and popularity at the golf club. To want more a parent must be civilised himself, and well enough off, or well enough connected, to feel reasonably at ease about his child's economic future.

For all these reasons it might seem to be as well that parents have as little say in education as they do. In the elementary school they have none at all; in the secondary schools they can only remove their children.* In the private and public school they can, it is true, choose the school they like best, but they cannot alter very much inside it. To remove a child in the middle of its school career is an upsetting business. Few headmasters listen willingly to suggestions or complaints. The word headmaster has a frightening association for most, and most do not want to be bothered anyway. They have paid their money and expect to be relieved of responsibility.

But parents are also electors and in both capacities their good will is very important on the side of educational reform.

Cost to Parents

(1) *Age 5–14*

Public Elementary school	Nil.
Private preparatory (Boarding)	£100–£200 a year.
(Day)	Perhaps £8–£20 a term.

---

* If a child wins a free place to a secondary school, the parent has not even this remedy: the parent signs a declaration that he will not remove the child before 16. If he does so, he can be (and is) prosecuted unless an adequate reason is adduced.

(2) *Secondary*

State secondary, 11–16 or over	Average £11–£12 a year.
"Public" schools (Boarding)	£100–£300 a year.

To both types of secondary there are scholarships which partially or wholly remit fees.

N.B. The cost to the State for each child at an elementary school is £12–£13; for each child at a secondary school about £32. Most parents of children at secondary schools when they claim to be "paying for" their child's education are, in fact, receiving a higher cash benefit than parents of children at elementary schools.

D. THE CHILD

In the schools of England and Wales there are over 6,000,000 children being educated.

Of these over 5,000,000 are in State elementary schools. And under 12 per cent. are receiving some form of secondary education after 14.

Yet education, we are told, is the one thing which is to save us from War, Bolshevism, Fascism, the influence of the Sunday Press and the Films, and instil the ideals of Service and Co-operation.

From the child's point of view it is the business of education (1) to help him to discover where his aptitudes lie, and (2) to train him to make the best use of them.

A good deal of work is being done in vocational guidance, but

(*a*) Most children must start work at 14.

(*b*) At this age it is rarely possible to make any but the broadest kinds of distinction, e.g. the theoretically and the practically intelligent; or those with an interest in people and those with an interest in things.

(*c*) The range of opportunity is, in most areas, extremely limited.

Equality of Opportunity

Of the 12 per cent. who receive a secondary education, about half can afford to continue irrespective of their ability. The other half are the siftings of competition.

Every middle-class child who goes to a preparatory school will receive a secondary education.

Only one elementary school child in ten will do so.

Unless one is prepared to argue that

(a) Housing conditions and feeding have no influence upon potential ability, i.e. ability is purely hereditary,

(b) The poor are lacking in ability because if they were not they would not be poor,

one cannot believe that those who succeed in the special-place examination are the only working-class children who could profit by secondary education.

On the contrary, according to the researches of Gray and Moshinsky into the abilities of London school children, taking children of equally high I.Q.s, seven fee-paying pupils will receive higher education for every one free pupil.

Provision for Varying Aptitudes

Far from all able children are academically able, but for a variety of reasons, some economic, some historical, the provision for the academic is about ten times as extensive as that made for the technical.

The child who enters industry and wishes to educate himself for his work must do so in his spare time, unless he is under one of the very few employers who allow children time off in their working hours.

Attitude of the Child

The average elementary school child is anxious to leave school; the average private school child is sorry. The former is anxious to be earning and living a life which appears to him more grown up and exciting. The latter has a fuller and a more exciting life at school than he has at home, or, in many cases, than he is likely to have in his work.

Further, for a middle-class child to leave school early is a social disgrace because it puts him on a par with those who have to.

Most teachers assume that children dislike lessons and, being imitators, the children easily catch this attitude. But, as the work of some progressive educators proves, this is not so.

Children like work which shows results; but they can only be interested in the abstract if they can relate it to their own experience. A Peckham child may have its curiosity aroused about Peckham, but hardly about Budapest.

It is not practicable, and perhaps not desirable, to let the child learn only what it likes; but it is a fact that it learns that best.

It is stupid to make it learn what is unsuitable; from doing so follow most disciplinary troubles. In the senior departments of elementary schools it is found that least external discipline is required in the workshops.

LEAVING AGE

Of the total number of school leavers in any one year:

About 70 per cent. leave at 14, the lowest permissible age.
About 12½ per cent. leave before 15.
About 6 per cent. leave before 16.

ORGANISATION

(a) State

By law every child must receive elementary instruction in reading, writing and arithmetic between the ages of 5–14.

A few progressive local authorities with the help of Voluntary Bodies provide Nursery schools for children from the ages of 2–5. In 1936 there were 81 Nursery schools taking 6,375 children.

The present policy* of the Board is to divide education into Primary (ages 5–11) and Post-Primary (11 onwards).

In the primary stage the children are divided into two departments, Infant and Junior. At 11 there is a break and they are drafted off to different types of schools.

The special-place examination takes on about 10 per cent. to secondary schools; a small proportion go to selective Central schools where they may remain up to 16, while the bulk go on to Senior schools which they leave at 14. But these last two are, for administrative purposes, under the Elementary, not the Secondary code. That is, less money is spent on their equipment, staff and buildings, and they have an inferior social status.

Of this mass a very small proportion (1 in 100) may transfer at 13 to technical schools where they stay until they are apprenticed at 16. For the rest there is some provision for part-time voluntary continuation education at night classes or part-time day classes. But it is most unsatisfactory.

About one-third of elementary leavers enrol for these classes. Thirty-

---

* This reorganization is at present in the process of being carried through, and will take several years. It is based on the Hadow scheme, which required for the purpose the raising of the school age to at least 15. Under the new Act this will be done in 1939, but it is generally considered that owing to the clauses allowing exemptions and the refusal to grant maintenance allowances for poor parents, this Act is largely ineffective.

five per cent. of these do not continue beyond one year, while of second-year students 40 per cent. go no farther.

(b) Private Enterprise

There are a number of the so-called Public Schools which are mostly private foundations (many of them originally for the sons of the poor, now all for the sons of the middle class). They give secondary education from the ages of 13–18. Some of these now receive grants from the State in return for which they have to take a percentage of elementary school scholarship winners; others are. not aided but are recognized by the Board; others stand alone.

They are supplied chiefly by preparatory schools (mostly boarding schools for children from 8–13), the fees of which keep them as a preserve for the middle class. These preparatory schools are nearly all owned and managed by their headmasters who run them as a commercial undertaking.

Finally, there are a number (given by the Board as 8,000, maybe more than 9,000) of private schools which are unclassifiable.

CURRICULUM

Nursery Schools

General health, nursery attention and play; no formal education, but lessons in social behaviour.

Primary

General, on the basis of the three R's. Otherwise each school is free within the limitations of its head-teacher and staff to teach what it likes, subject to the approval of the Board's inspectors. In practice this is largely dictated by the demands of the special-place examination. The usual additional subjects are History, Geography and Drawing. In addition there will be some form of physical training, a variety of light crafts, music, nature study, dancing, etc., *ad lib.*

Post Primary

SENIOR AND CENTRAL

A continuation of the Primary course with the addition of science and perhaps one foreign language, often carpentry for boys and domestic subjects for girls. In some there will be a vocational bias depending on the district (commercial, rural, etc.).

JUNIOR TECHNICAL

There are two types: (*a*) pre-apprenticeship for those who have decided on an industry but not a specified occupation within that industry, (*b*) trade schools for defined occupations. These are successful and popular because (1) they are well and generously staffed, (2) they are free from academic restrictions, (3) there are no examinations, (4) leavers find good employment.

SECONDARY SCHOOLS

General academic education with a view to commerce and professions. The curriculum is dictated by the School Certificate Examination, which is devised by boards of joint school and university authorities.

A school certificate is now almost a universal standard. In certain forms it admits to the universities* and most professions and is demanded by most employers.

The nature of this examination will, therefore, make clear the nature of secondary school curricula.

A successful candidate must have passed in not less than five subjects. The essential subjects are arranged in three groups: (1) English subjects including History and Geography; (2) Foreign languages, including the Classics; (3) Mathematics and Science.

Of the five passes there must be at least one from each of these groups.

For the limited number who stay after they have gained their certificate curriculum is dictated by two other examinations:

(1) The Higher Certificate. The same kind as the other but allowing a higher degree of specialization in one branch of academic learning, History, Classics, Mathematics, etc. It is on the results of this examination that State scholarships to the universities are awarded.

(2) The examinations for the scholarships which the universities offer. They demand a growingly greater degree of specialization in one subject.†

In all schools now there is a general widening of curricula. In most State elementary and secondary schools art and hand-work have an almost equal place with other subjects (while in private schools these are still

---

* The regulations are complicated and the practice varies. But it remains true that almost every secondary school takes the examination or the equivalent. The version of the examination given here is the Oxford and Cambridge. Others differ only in detail.

† The "public" schools are the same as secondary schools in this matter. The preparatory schools are dictated to by the Common Entrance, the examination for entrance to the public schools. This requires elementary English, History, Mathematics, French and Latin.

usually regarded as "extras"); acting and music are general, dancing, craft-work, etc., are common.

Two difficulties are involved:

(1) Examinations. Competition grows increasingly fierce; the examination syllabuses remain fixed with their academic bias. Teachers find that the innovations would crowd out the examination essentials.

(2) Any system must be devised for the average ability of those who have to work it. The subjects chosen and the approach to those subjects must depend on what the average teacher can be taught to teach.

DISCIPLINE METHOD AND TECHNIQUE

The growth of knowledge, particularly knowledge about people, has had its effect on education. Enough is known to show that the earlier certainties are no longer absolute, but not enough for new certainties to have appeared. The result is a more tentative and experimental approach to education. There are still plenty of teachers who know the whole truth and are prepared to back their knowledge with the cane; but doubts are widespread.

Within the limitations which their numbers impose teachers now try to take into account the individual differences of the children and their social background; educational authorities call in the help of experts for difficult children; and it is slowly being realised that under-fed children cannot learn. The Provision of Meals Act of 1906 provides that food may be given to a child who "by reason of lack of food is unable to profit by the instruction given".

This improvement has developed from a change in the attitude of individual teachers rather than from a change in organization or technique. Thus corporal punishment is largely decreasing in State schools, but it is still allowed, and is, no doubt, widely practised, both wisely and unwisely.*

Modern theories about such things as self-government and punishment are not generally practised. Where the old arbitrary attitude to discipline has been modified, the change comes from the individual teacher.

The same is true of more strictly technical class-room method. The wide range of experiment and discovery in method has hardly penetrated the mass of schools. The old methods, modified by the change in the relation of teachers and children, persist.

---

* In State schools it is usually only the headmaster who beats, though he sometimes delegates the duty; he must enter such punishment in a book. In private schools housemasters and often assistant masters are also allowed to, and even where this is not so, boys are allowed to beat other boys.

There are four main reasons:

(1) Tradition. This becomes clearer in a later section. Here it may be observed that education has been handed down from the rich to the poor. The prevailing snobberies of English life result in far too much imitation of the public school tradition by State schools.

(2) Examinations. The rigidity of the examination system makes immediate and stringent demands on teachers. Even when they are aware of "progressive" techniques, they have yet to be convinced that such methods produce results; and it is by results that they feel themselves (rightly or wrongly) to be judged.

How important this fact is can be shown by the fact that when the pressure of examinations is not felt, as in Nursery schools, progressive techniques are used.

(3) Size of classes. Mr W. B. Curry, one of the principal practitioners of progressive education, says that he regards a class of 17 as too large for his purpose. 81 per cent. of classes in elementary schools and 73 per cent. in secondary have more than 20 children. (See below.)

(4) Expense. Progressive methods require a larger number of teachers and a good deal of expensive equipment. A really good library for example is an essential.

In spite of this a good deal of experiment does go on in State schools. Exceptional teachers find ways of getting round the difficulties. But, to repeat, the average teacher, like the average man, is not exceptional; reformers do not take sufficient account of the tax which these methods put on the teacher.

The public and preparatory schools are the most backward in their methods. In their case it is not due to economics but to their social purpose.

The greater part of experimental education is carried out in private schools designed, equipped and financed for the purpose. Such schools can choose their kind of teacher, just as they can choose their children. Moreover, they can afford to be isolated.

The State is often accused of hampering educational progress.

It is no doubt true that the administrators often come to think administration more important than education; and they control the funds. It is the danger of any bureaucracy.

But it must in fairness be pointed out that head-teachers enjoy a remarkable degree of freedom within their own schools; and that the Board of Education (as the reports of its consultative committees and its *Handbook of Suggestions to Teachers* show) is well in advance of the mass of educational practice.

Size of Classes

State (1936)

ELEMENTARY SCHOOLS

Only 9 per cent.	have	under	20	pupils	in	one	class.	
About 21 per cent.	"	"	30	"	"	"	"	
About 36 per cent.	"	"	40	"	"	"	"	
About 30 per cent.	"	"	50	"	"	"	"	
2.3 per cent.	have	over	50	"	"	"	"	
While 42 schools	have	over	60	"	"	"	"	

The congestion in classes is much heaveier in urban than in rural districts.

SECONDARY SCHOOLS (On the grant list)

About 26 per cent.	have	under	20	pupils	in	one	class.	
18 per cent.	"	"	25	"	"	"	"	
31 per cent.	"	"	30	"	"	"	"	
23 per cent.	"	"	35	"	"	"	"	
0.4 per cent.	"	over	35	"	"	"	"	

Private Enterprise

Private preparatory: the classes range from about 10 to 15.
Public schools: the highest are about 30 and the lowest about 8.

Thus it will be seen that education for the rich works on the principle that at the primary age small classes are more essential than at the post primary. In State education the opposite.

Universities

Universities have three functions:

(1) To provide further education for advanced students.
(2) By giving the students opportunities for frequent and unrestricted contact with each other and the senior members of the university, to give a wide general education.
(3) To act as centres for research and scholarship.

In England and Wales there are twelve degree-giving universities and a number of satellite colleges.
The total number of students (full time) is about 40,000.

Financially they depend partly on fees (in the provincial universities less than 30 per cent. of the cost is paid for out of fees), partly on treasury grants (1934–5, £2,000,000), and partly on endowments.

As far as the student life is concerned Oxford and Cambridge differ in many important respects from the other universities.

(1) They are residential. They therefore provide a kind of corporate life which the newer universities, poorer and differently designed, can only imitate badly.

(2) The fees are much higher (£225 per annum is a bare sum for a student to get through on. £300 is adequate).

(3) Consequently they have a social *cachet.**

(4) Consequently at these two there is a proportion of students only there for the social life or not having to bother about earning a living, socialites or sons who will inherit positions. At the new universities these types hardly exist.

(5) They are the strongholds of "liberal," i.e. non-utilitarian education.
   The theory is that mental discipline acquired in any one subject is automatically transferable to any other. Thus a first-class honours degree in classics is the best preparation for the Civil Service.

(6) Graduates from these two have about a 75 to 1 chance of certain jobs, the higher-paid grades of Civil Service, and the higher-paid grades of teaching (the Foreign Office, Public School), etc. Altogether they stand the best chances of employment.
   As a result competition for the scholarships offered by the State and the various colleges, and other bodies, is extremely severe.

(7) Teaching is by means of tutorials and lectures; in the former teaching is direct between the teacher and one or at most five students; the value of the latter is widely questioned.
   Thus the corporate life of the students living in colleges, combined with the tutorial system, makes Oxford and Cambridge the nearest approach to the Greek Academy.

The new universities were founded for a much more utilitarian purpose at the height of industrialism. At Oxford and Cambridge the Humane subjects are far more heavily endowed than in the new universities.

In so far as the balance has been redressed it is because the faculties of Arts at the new universities have become almost exclusively departments for training teachers, subsidized by the State and local authorities for that purpose.

---

* N.B. Even at Oxford and Cambridge some 10 per cent. of the students are in receipt of some sort of financial aid, scholarships, Government Grants and L.E.A. Grants.

This aspect of the new universities, as, to use Professor Dodds' phrase, "simply social ladders," is important. It is almost, though not quite true, to say, he suggests, that they exist to enable certain members of the working class to escape from their class by becoming school teachers.

Being far less heavily endowed they cannot afford the number of teachers necessary for a proper tutorial system; and have to rely too much on lectures.

They are non-resident; and though an attempt is made to compensate for this by hostels and other devices, there is far less opportunity for students to meet each other and their elders, and so help each other to grow.

Besides this the economic pressure on the students is sharper and more insistent, and some measure of economic security is essential for proper university conditions.

This is not to deny that the provincial universities do excellent work, but, compared with the older foundations, they labour under heavy disadvantages.

RESEARCH AND SCHOLARSHIP

Here there is less difference between the older and the newer universities. History at Manchester, Engineering at Birmingham, Medicine at Edinburgh and Agriculture at Reading are recognised as the best of their kind.

Endowments tend to come now from the big industrialists, for they are the only people who can afford them. But this does not mean that it is only the scientific and the technical faculties that will get the money; an industrialist who has had no education himself is as likely to found a chair in Greek as a chair in the Bedaux method; for he is often a sentimentalist. But it does mean that the new universities often have to fight against interference from their rich benefactors, and fight tactfully enough not to lose the money. For, sentimentalist or not, the business man tends to despise the academic mind.

OTHER PROVISION FOR ADULTS

(1) Training Colleges

Prospective teachers have one of three possibilities:

(a) They may go to a university and after completing the ordinary three-year course, they will be accepted in some secondary schools.

(But they would count as uncertificated teachers in elementary schools.)

(*b*) At the end of the three-year course they may spend a fourth year taking a teacher's diploma at the education department attached to each university. This gives a course in the history and theory of education, and some elementary psychology. And there are five or six weeks' apprenticeship teaching. These students are expecting to find posts in secondary schools; they by no means always succeed.

(*c*) They may go to a training college of which there are 74 (51 of them being provided by religious bodies). These colleges take students at the age of 18 or over and give a minimum two-year course covering general education and professional training, including some teaching experience. There are additional one-year courses up to four and by taking them students qualify for being placed at a higher starting point in the salary scale. These colleges are concerned only with elementary school teachers.

Ninety-five per cent. of the students are assisted by State grants or loans. The loans will have to be paid back out of salary when they are in employment.

("Students recognised for grants are required to sign a declaration of their intention to follow the profession of teaching." If they do not become teachers they are expected to pay back the grant.)

(2) Adult Education

There is a large variety of different arrangements for part-time study courses arranged by Local Education Authorities, Universities (extension lectures) and bodies such as the Workers' Educational Association. Many of these originated with a social purpose, namely to help the workers to understand and so change the system.

But all except the National Labour Colleges have now come under the Board of Education, and receive financial assistance from the State in return for a promise to be non-political.

About 2,600 courses, ranging from one-term courses to three-year courses, were supplied in 1936.

About 50,000 men and women enrolled for them.

It is specifically stated in the regulations governing these courses that they must offer a *liberal* education.

Sociology and English are, jointly, the subjects most taken.

SUMMARY

The English educational system, of which this is a sketch (necessarily abbreviated, for the system has grown up in such a typically haphazard manner that its ramifications are extremely intricate), accurately reflects the social system which created it. Broadly speaking, there are the three grades of schools for the three social classes. For the lower class, the manual workers, the elementary schools turning them out at 14; for the lower middle class, the black-coated workers, continued education up to 16 at the State secondary schools; for the middle classes their own separate system, the preparatory and "public" schools up to the age of 18 or even later.

The system is thought of as an ascending ladder (in that order) and the "democracy" in it consists in opening the ladder by means of scholarships and grants, so that, theoretically, any child with sufficient intelligence can reach the topmost rung (a place at Oxford or Cambridge). In practice the number who can do so is strictly limited, if by nothing else, by the laws of supply and demand.

The class structure remains, though there is an opportunity for some to pass from one class to another; what happens to them after they have climbed is another matter. But if all the donkeys cannot get the carrot, it remains true that a small percentage of them can.

It is a mistake to blame this, as is sometimes done, on the educational system, or to imagine that educational reform can change it. The fault is with the prevailing social philosophy. And what is true of the organization of education is also true of the content. A society which despises manual work will give its highest rewards to those who escape farthest from it, and so the most exclusive education that the English provide is that which is, strictly, useless. If the way to avoid manual labour, with its poor rewards and despised position, is to become a teacher or a clerk or a civil servant, an academic bias is forced on the system.

This is reflected by the series of examinations which cut across the whole educational life in a series of horizontal bands. All children in elementary schools take the special place examination at 11 or $11\frac{1}{2}$, since this is the gateway to secondary schools and the escape from the bottom class; and the curriculum of elementary education up to that age is dictated by this examination. The next gateway is the school certificate examination at 16, which leads to the professions and, above all, to the university. This examination, and so the secondary school curriculum, is dictated by the scholarship examinations to the universities, which in turn are dictated to by the final honours schools at the universities, success in which is the passport to the liberal professions.

In short, the curriculum of the elementary school must be directed towards the kind of ability which will give every child the chance of becoming a high-grade civil servant.

N.B. The Spens Report on Secondary Education was published after this pamphlet was written and set up.

If its recommendations are adopted they would do much, within the framework of the present system, to remedy these defects. It proposes universal free education under a new Secondary code embracing the present central and senior schools, for all children beyond the age of 11 up to 16; it suggests redressing the lack of provision for any but academic ability by establishing technical high schools parallel with the present secondary schools, with possibility for the transfer of misfits between the several kinds of schools (cf. our suggestions). It also recommends that the school certificate examination should be divorced from its connection with the universities.

The full adoption of the report would go a long way towards minimizing some of the major inequalities in the present system. But it remains true that, while our society gives its respect and its rewards where it does, the competition for academic education, and the bias to it, is bound to continue.

Our criticism of the report's curriculum proposals are implicit in the suggestions we offer.

PART II. THEORY

All education is a preparation for life. It must teach people how to do the things which will keep them alive, agriculture, hunting, fighting and what not; and it must teach them how to live together, the laws, customs and beliefs of the community.

In a primitive community with an undifferentiated economy, there is no quarrel between the vocational and the social aspect, for, apart from the division of labour between the sexes, all have to do the same things and lead the same kind of life. Religious instruction is practical, and practical instruction religious.

Educational theory begins when society has become differentiated, when different classes are living so differently, and doing such different things that the question arises: "What shall we teach and to whom?"

The Middle Ages

Our present education has developed out of the theory and practice of the Middle Ages. Mediaeval social theory divided society into three classes:

(1) Those who pray.
(2) Those who guard.
(3) Those who work.

Those Who Pray

Their social function was to mediate between God and man; their practical occupation a life of contemplation. That is to say, their life was a mental one, a training of the mind rather than the body, the more so because the flesh was held to be evil. Originally they were vowed to poverty, and in many monastic communities, manual labour was an important part of their life, but their intellectual training was an abstract and philosophical one. Believing that the material world was as straw beside the heavenly mysteries, and that the truth had been revealed once and for all, and that their task was one of interpretation only, they did not pursue a scientific method of inquiry.

In addition, their professional language was Latin. As they were the only literate part of society, they became responsible for education, legal and administrative duties. It is from them that the academic tradition with its bias towards abstract knowledge divorced from action, its preference for interpretation rather than creation, its formalism, and its emphasis on Latin, is derived.

Those Who Guard

Their function was to guard property; their occupation the life of the courtier and the soldier; and their training, a training of the body and the social manners of a governing class. To them the military virtues of physical strength, courage, loyalty and social discipline were important, and neither intelligence nor technical skill of much value. It is on them, with modifications made by Puritanism, that the public school social code is based.

Those Who Work

Their function was to provide society with goods, their occupation manual labour, and their training purely vocational. The peasant child began to work in the fields as soon as he could, and as economic life became increasingly complicated, an organised apprentice system grew up in the skilled trades. For them education was empirical and specialised.

This view of society involves three assumptions:

(1) That the structure of society is static.
(2) That it is just.
(3) That the special aptitudes suited to each class are inherited. (Except of course in the Church, where the laying on of hands took the place of birth-right.)

Christianity was committed to the belief that all human souls were of equal value. To square this with the manifest inequality of social reward, the theologians were forced to explain it by the Fall of Man. Society, then, was corrupt, but it was just. Further, if children are born evil, then they will always tend not to want the things they ought to want, such as learning or courage or manual skill, and must be forced to want them. The traditional disciplinary technique was due partly to ignorance, but was aggravated by an *a priori* doctrine of what the child must be like.

THE RENAISSANCE AND THE REFORMATION

Both had important influences upon education. The study of Greece brought knowledge of an intellectually-educated ruling class and a secular culture. It was not incompatible with being a gentleman to be also a scholar. This encouraged speculation at the expense of authority, but it only intensified the gulf between thought and action, by making learning an aristocratic privilege. The pursuit of disinterested knowledge like pure mathematics and the practice of disinterested action like sport was socially respectable. Applied science or manual labour were not.

The Reformation coincides with the rise to political and economic power of the middle classes, and as a new class they had a new conception of society. Puritanism accepted the first two tenets of mediaeval social theory but denied the third, i.e. it held that:

(1) The structure of society is static.
(2) It is just.
(3) Special aptitudes are not inherited.

It accepted the class stratification, but asserted that the class in which the individual found himself depended upon his own efforts. The Middle Ages had believed, in theory at least, that the beggar was as good as the rich man. The Puritans denied this. The beggar was a beggar because he was wicked. All classes must pray and all classes must work. It is from them, both for themselves, and as employers, that the demand for a more vocational and scientific education and the attack on the Humanities has come.

Rousseau and Romantic Anarchism

The increasing complexity of social and economic life, and their growing moral and physical ugliness, stimulated a reaction which began with Rousseau and is ending with Freud. The fundamental beliefs on which it is based are:

(1) The structure of society is static.
(2) It is unjust.
(3) The individual is born good and is made evil by society. "Man is born free and is everywhere in chains."

The effects of these beliefs on the theory and practice of education have been immense. If the individual is born good, then the child is better than the adult, and it is the adult who must learn from the child.

However questionable in some respects their theories may have been, they had the practical effect of making people study children to see what they were really like, and it is to the followers of Rousseau that we owe most of the advance that has been made in teaching and disciplinary technique.

Comments

(1) The single point upon which all these theories agree, and upon which they are all wrong, is that the structure of society is static and unchangeable.
(2) The Middle Ages were right in supposing that the poor are not necessarily poor because they are wicked, nor the rich necessarily rich because they are virtuous. The Puritans were wrong.
(3) The Puritans were right in supposing that ability or the lack of it are not necessarily inherited. The Middle Ages were wrong.
(4) Rousseau was right in supposing that society is not necessarily just. The Middle Ages and the Puritans were wrong.
(5) The Middle Ages and the Puritans were right in supposing that Society is a necessary fact. Rousseau was wrong.

The Victorian Era

With the middle classes established in the saddle after the industrial revolution, came the consolidation of their private educational system, the reform of the old public schools, the creation of a great many new ones, and a systematisation of the principles on which they were to be run. The public schools before Arnold began to reform them had been tough, barbarian places which produced the kind of brave and unscrupulous adventurers who get an Empire. Arnold's job was to turn them into incubators for the type of narrow-minded, active, unquestioning administrators who would develop and keep it, and the same type was needed for the reformed army and the new Civil Services, all the key positions of a new dominant class.

The contribution of Arnold and his followers was the invention of the prefect system, the emphasis on "character" rather than intelligence, and the discovery of organised games as the best means of developing it. By the prefect system boys were given a training in the theory and practice of authoritarian discipline; while their character-training taught them to regard themselves as natural leaders, owing a rigid loyalty to their group; and as they lived in boarding schools where only their own class was admitted from the ages of 8–18, it was hardly surprising that they identified their group completely with the nation. These features remain to-day the foundations of the public school system (vide *Games*).

A national public education begins at the end of the nineteenth century, when industrial processes demand technically educated masses and recruits for the lower grade executive posts. If the evangelicals of the nineteenth century wanted the poor to be taught to read so that they could read the Bible, the more far-sighted of the bourgeoisie wanted it so that they should understand blue-prints and modern book-keeping. That, instead of either, they should come to understand Karl Marx, was no part of anyone's design, though it was a danger which the die-hards foresaw.

TRANSITION TO DEMOCRACY

The establishment of universal compulsory education created a new problem which the liberal conscience attempted to solve by the "ladder" theory. Government should be by the best men irrespective of class, and the problem was to make access to the highest positions as easy and generous as possible. This theory is a barely concealed "leadership theory," the logical end of which is seen in the modern Nazi training colleges. But it has never been brought to anything like its logical conclusions in England.

The exclusiveness of the public schools was largely retained, and justified on the grounds that their products were the leaders who *served* the nation; while at the other end an attempt was made to limit their exclusiveness by opening them to a small creamed selection of working-class boys. This movement has never touched the more important schools, and the less important, whose finances have forced them to enter it, have never had to admit more than 10 per cent. of their total numbers.

This half-heartedness is defended by the assertion that the public schools have something very precious (their tradition) which might be swamped by too great an influx of the lower classes. This gives the game away. The middle classes *are* the best, but, under this liberal theory, they may recruit into their ranks a small selection from the lower classes who are then submitted to a thorough de-classing process. The class structure remains unaltered, but a certain number of the lower classes are taken out of their class and trained as leaders. But it still remains that to be leader you must be middle class.

Liberal education also implies the academic bias; liberal, in this sense, meaning fit for an Athenian free man as opposed to a slave. And the Athenian tradition that a real free man despises trade as well as manual labour still lingers, rather mustily, in our educational approach.

The practical success of Rousseau's methods in education only shows that if you treat children with a modicum of kindliness and common sense, in other words, if you make the society in which they live a reasonably decent one, they will thrive on it. A good society makes people good, a bad society makes them bad. Therefore if you can discover the factors which make a society what it is, you can educate people to virtue. The failure of education to have any appreciable effect upon the behaviour of adults or nations shows that most people adapt themselves very quickly to whatever society or section of society they happen to fall into. The charming young public school athlete becomes the Great Portland Street tyke.

This is not to say that school society ought to be no better than society outside, but to say that it cannot be; different schools imitate different sections. The State school imitates the mass-production factory; the public school, the army and the Colonial Civil Services; while the progressive school community resembles that of the *rentier* who is free to devote himself to higher things, and is under no obligation to develop his courage or his cunning.

Education can never be more effective than the structure of society as a whole will let it, and the teacher who imagines that you can effectively change education without first changing society will end either by throwing the whole contraption overboard in despair like D. H. Lawrence, or by deceiving himself with a lot of gas about Service like Dr Norwood.

D. H. LAWRENCE, ANTI-IDEALISM, AND FASCISM

All English education pays lip-service to the Liberal ideal, though the public schools have pursued it rather half-heartedly. The most serious attack on Liberal education has been made by D. H. Lawrence, and the fact that the Fascist countries appear on the surface to be putting his theories into practice makes their study extremely important to socialists.

Very briefly summarised they amount to this:

(1) Man fell when he became self-conscious.
(2) Mental life and physical life are at odds; each secretly despises the other.
(3) Idealism, the running of the instinctive life by the self-conscious mind, corrupts life.
(4) Europeans have lived so long under the rule of idealism that they have become deranged, and think they want what they ought to want. They are, most of them, self-conscious neurasthenic ninnies, afraid of life.
(5) Every individual is unique, with his unique needs. You cannot live by a set of Sunday School rules.
(6) Very few people either really want or are suited to a life of thought. Most can only learn a few tricks.
(7) The aim of education should be to help people to realise their deepest instinctive needs.

Education should therefore:

(1) Turn its back on the whole academic tradition. The majority of pupils will need no more than the three R's. The basis of training should be the primary manual trades, farming, building, tinkering, cooking, etc., not book-learning nor ornamental arts and crafts.
(2) Train the body and spirit by the tougher sports like boxing and swimming which develop courage and personal pride. Gymnastics begin at the wrong end by setting out to train the body through the mind.
(3) Select its candidates for mind-training very carefully.

Many of Lawrence's observations are true, and perhaps several of his practical suggestions are sound, but his refusal to admit that on the whole people are like what they are because society is like what it is instead of the reverse makes his conclusions dangerous. As a matter of observation it is true that book-learning has a bad effect on many people, and that manual work is viewed with horror. But it is not true to say:

(1) That you know that mental activity *must always* be only suited to a few.
(2) That you know who they are.

It is a very attractive doctrine for an authoritarian state, because once you begin by saying that some people are born to think and therefore to rule, while the mass are born not to think but to carry out the way of life which the thinkers decide is best for them, it is a short step to saying that those who are actually ruling are born to think and those who oppose them must not be allowed to think. It is Plato's old problem of how to secure rule by the Good Men. No one can decide who they are, and no one has ever succeeded in convincing those who are in power that they are bad or that they are incompetent to judge who is.

Headmasters of old schools and new schools alike are always proclaiming that their aim is to produce leaders. This only shows that they are conceited. Every teacher knows in his heart of hearts that he has not the slightest idea of what effect he is having, that he is working largely in the dark, that on most of his pupils he has no effect at all, and probably a bad effect on half the rest.

It also shows that they are reactionary. The leaders of the second generation are the rebels of the first. A leader is the very last person they would recognise or like to see in their schools; what they want is a pleasant-mannered yes-man with executive ability.

We come back again to the old fallacy that there can be a state of society which is final and absolutely just. The moment we forget that

(1) All forms of society are imperfect,
(2) Some are better than others,

that is to say, if we become romantically utopian or other-worldly, if we deny the movement of history, we surrender to the first tyrant who can seize power.

Loyalty and intelligence are mutually hostile. The intelligence is always disloyal. There must always be a conflict between the loyalty necessary for society to be, and the intelligence necessary for society to become. The question of whether there are some people who are followers by nature, and others who are leaders, can only be discussed when education up to the age of maturity is open to all.

Meanwhile the important part of Lawrence's attack is his attack on the school curriculum. Every educationalist agrees that education should be general and not vocational, yet, in fact, everyone receives a vocational education in academic teaching. It is not a question of whether some people do not need an academic training but of whether all people do not need a practical manual one in some real trade, and need to realise that the mind is only a part of the whole man.

PART III. SUGGESTION

Since Education can never be much better than the social system within which it functions, the improvement of the latter must take precedence over everything else. Until every child has the same educational opportunities, until equal social value is put upon all forms of employment, until class distinctions are obliterated, all suggestions for educational reform, except on quite minor points, must seem highbrow and unreal. What follows presupposes radical social changes, and is only offered tentatively as matter for discussion.

I. TRAINING COLLEGES AND TEACHERS

Teachers are unique in receiving a vocational training from the age of 5. No one would expect a fifteen-year course in typewriting and shorthand to produce the perfect secretary, yet that, in effect, is the way in which we train teachers.

It would be hard, for instance, to think of a worse course than segregating teachers by themselves as happens in those training colleges which are not attached to a university. The teacher should know more about life than other people; he knows less. Sometimes he realises this; his pupils always do.

The training colleges offer a little text-book psychology, some instruction in the theory and technique of teaching, and uplift about the citizens of to-morrow. The psychology a teacher needs is that of a sensitive, observant, intelligent man or woman of the world, or else that of a fat, stupid, kindly saint; not potted McDougall. And this cannot be taught. Given the right soil, it grows by friendship with all kinds of people, by love affairs, by an active life. Similarly, all the teaching technique you can teach in a lecture hall cannot amount to more than a few tricks. Technique and personality are inseparable; what one learns, one learns by practice and by personal apprenticeship to those who are good at their profession. We suggest therefore:

(1) That intending teachers should have several interviews with some really experienced person to find out for themselves what sort of a person they are, and if they really want or are suited to become teachers. How one is to find the interviewer is a question. One hesitates to suggest the psychologists, as there are so few that one trusts. But the truly wise men must be found. In the event of intending teachers deciding against continuing, they should be under no obligation to return State grants, and if they are still due to receive them for further training, they should get them.

(2) That the valuable part of the training course is the practical part; this should be much longer than the six months or six weeks that students get at present, and they should be sent to work under the personal guidance of adult and experienced teachers, the choice of teacher to vary with the personality of the pupil and the type of school in which he or she intends to teach.

(3) That in so far as theoretical instruction is needed, the staff of training colleges should be frequently changed, and consist of school

teachers temporarily seconded to the job. The training-college post should never be a dead end.

(4) That under no circumstances should the teacher in training be made to live in conditions where the company is confined to other pupil teachers.

(5) That before a teacher starts on his career, not less than a year should be spent in some totally different kind of life. What this would be would vary of course very much from area to area and teacher to teacher. For some it might be employment in industry, for others a social service job, for others foreign travel, etc.

(6) That provision should be made for entering the teaching profession from other occupations, experience in the latter to count fully in assessing increment allowances. That, in general, as much use as possible should be made of the part-time teacher.

(7) That in not less than every five years, every teacher should have a sabbatical term, and in not less than every ten a sabbatical year, with pay.

(8) That teaching hours should be such as to encourage teachers to do research or any other work of their own, no matter how apparently remote from their job.

II. The Pre-Primary School

(1) That it is probable that most children begin the three R's too early. A small child's wish to read is often a sign that it is unhappy or bored.

(2) That up to the age of seven, and perhaps later, little is wanted but good facilities for play, the company of other children of both sexes, fresh air, and as little interference as possible, except for careful medical attention. It is truer of this age than of any other, that if you look after the body the mind will look after itself.

III. 7–11

(1) That the proper school for this age is certainly a day school, and probably co-educational.

(2) That the basic subjects are English Language (not Literature), Arithmetic, and Nature Study, which in the town means study of people, trains, buses, etc.

(3) That dramatics, singing, and painting are also extremely important subjects for this age-group.

(4) That foreign languages, history, geography, civics, etc., are probably unsuitable as having no relation with the child's experience. There are better outlets for imagination.

(5) That children of this age are capable of doing simple unskilled manual jobs, and where the school needs them, they should be encouraged to carry them out.

IV. 11–15

(1) That it is an interesting comment upon Fascism that many of the theories and practices which it prescribes for adults may be well adapted to the needs of adolescents. The emphasis on physical adventure and physical toughness, the segregation of the sexes, the distrust of intellectualism, the love of ritual, the gang and leader organisation, all apply to many boys and girls from 11 to 16.

(2) That no democracy can survive unless a very large percentage of its citizens take an interest in what are commonly called things of the mind, read widely, think dispassionately and so on. At present it is an unfortunate fact that a large percentage, even of those who receive higher education, do not take this interest, and there is some evidence to show that it is during adolescence that such an interest is developed or lost. There is no justification for assuming that this is inevitable until much deeper research has been undertaken on the most suitable curricula for adolescents.

Accepted tradition assumes that for those who can afford to prolong their education beyond 14 or 15 such an education should be academic. While, on the contrary, it seems very likely, even for many who will afterwards adopt an academic career, that at this particular age the basis of education should be physical, and technical, and intellectual work a private hobby rather than an official lesson. In the present state of our psychological knowledge this can remain no more than a theory.

(3) That all that can be done at present is to build up a really adequate technical-school system parallel to the secondary one, with proper facilities for transfer of misfits in one or the other up to the age of 14.

(4) That in the former the training should be based for boys on learning a manual trade, and for girls on domestic science, except for those with particular gifts.

(5) That even in the secondary schools there should be a certain amount of group constructional work, building, digging, etc., provided that the things constructed have a real social use.

(6) That both sexes should be taught biology from a human angle.

(7) That if there is a case for the boarding school, it is at this age.

(8) That, in general, more damage is done by being compelled to learn things to which the particular individual is hostile or unsuited, at this

age, than at any other, and that therefore the guiding principle should be to allow people to put their *main* energies at this time into what most interests them, while ensuring that they do not neglect entirely either body or mind. The adolescent, in fact, should specialise more, and the 15–18 age group should have a more general education than at present.

V. 15–18

(1) That as far as freedom and general living conditions go, schools should be run on university lines, i.e. pupils would be expected to work much on their own, and to be treated as reasonable human beings.
(2) That there should be different kinds of education for different kinds of ability, but as far as possible within the same school buildings.
(3) That while those preparing for a technical career would continue practical work, they are now fitted for full theoretical instruction.
(4) That a course in social and economic history and geography should be compulsory for all students, technical or academic.
(5) That an examination, corresponding to the present School Certificate, but with a much wider range of subject choice should be taken by all (except Scholarship candidates) at about 18.

VI. Universities

(1) That the tutorial system should be extended as far as possible, and the number of lectures much curtailed.
(2) That while the college system should be encouraged, the life of the university should not be divorced from the life of the town. It should take its full share in municipal administration. There should be university seats on the Town Council.
(3) That the students should be represented on some sort of consultative committee with the governing body.

VII. Discipline

(1) That the problem of discipline is so bound up with material facts such as size of classes, buildings, grounds, etc., and psychological questions such as the proper type of curriculum, that its discussion in the abstract is largely unreal.
(2) That while a democracy is bound to accept the principle that discipline by consent is preferable to discipline by coercion, it must be

remembered that a degree of coercion enters into all human rela-
tionships, and that moral coercion can be more damaging than physi-
cal coercion.

(3) That it is possible that the child passes through various phases, cor-
responding to various types of social organisation, e.g. that in the
pre-primary and primary stage he is a romantic anarchist, in adoles-
cence an authoritarian (and therefore a rebel also), and after sixteen
potentially a rational democrat.

(4) That if this is true, the proper kind of adult authority in the first
stage would be paternal, supplying material needs and protecting
from physical damage, in fact, rather like the "good" employer. That
education should be through voluntary play, but that on the other
hand the child should not be expected to bother about questions of
self-government. That in adolescence discipline should be stricter,
external and from above downwards, and finally after sixteen by ra-
tional argument and democratic self-government.

VIII. GAMES

(1) Children and most adults naturally enjoy using their bodies freely
and progressively more skilfully. When they do not it may be because
of revulsion at or rebellion against the bogus moral values attached,
physical defects, or premature mental development due to loneli-
ness, emotional troubles, compensation, or mistaken parental insis-
tence. Precocious mental activity upsets the psycho-physical balance.

(2) Most boys like tough and dangerous sports and games and ought to
have the opportunity to indulge in them.

(3) Games offer opportunities for the development of valuable quali-
ties, endurance, courage, etc. (It is doubtful if they *teach* them. Thus
Rugby football confirms a timid boy's cowardice more often than it
teaches him courage.)

(4) They provide emotional outlets. A ritualistic game like cricket is
exhibitionistic, and adolescents are always self-regarding. Tough
games like Rugger release hate and love. This is valuable.

(5) In a game the players experience emotions of fear, excitement, and
triumph. These experiences create a deep and lasting bond between
those who have shared them. For this reason such things as village
cricket so praised by the England-lovers mitigate class-feeling. They
do not, of course, remove it. It is only in a classless society that the full
value of games can be realized.

The importance of games and sports is obscured in many "progressive"
educational theories, because the whole subject has been so mishandled
by the public schools.

The Public School Tradition propagates two fallacies:

(1) That "it is the team-spirit which *alone* builds character" (Dr Norwood).
(2) That no game in which the individual stands out has educational value.

The Team Spirit

A little observation of public schoolboys, both at school and afterwards, soon shows that those who excel at games are not conspicuously virtuous. If that theory were true, England would not only be a much better country than it is, but it would be led by a band of blues. On the contrary, public schoolboys form the section of the community who are most prone to demand competition rather than co-operation internationally and nationally, the potential militarists and strike-breakers.

But this is not the fault of games, as the opponents of them sometimes suggest.

The Team-spirit, like the School-spirit, the House-spirit, the Old-boy-spirit, is a form of harnessing loyalty to a group.

A public school is situated in one locality and most of the boys are drawn from other localities. The school has no natural place in the district; it only provides a certain amount of small trade, and it is notorious that there is often a feud between the public school and the inhabitants of the town or countryside where it is placed.

A natural community spirit would graft the school on to the community life of the locality. This is impossible because the school draws its members entirely from one class.

Since a community spirit is desirable, the school proceeds to manufacture an artificial one of its own.

Its apologists claim that the spirit once learnt will be gradually extended. They imagine an ascending staircase of loyalties leading from the smallest group, the team, through the house, the school, the nation, up to the lonely figure of Christ at the top. The fact that this progression seldom occurs in practice never seems to disturb them; it is a beautiful dream.

What really happens is that the various "spirits" manufactured in the first place to compensate for a lack of real community spirit, reinforce the one unifying social factor, the isolated one-class nature of the schools.

All this is more important than the actual number of children in public schools would indicate, because

(1) The public schools product occupies at least 60 per cent. of strategic positions (e.g. officers in the armed forces).
(2) Many State schools are deceived into imitating this aspect of the public school tradition (e.g. the house system).

(3) The policy of giving scholarships from elementary schools to public schools and universities, while these institutions remain as they are, results in a creamed selection of working-class children being submitted to a powerful re-classing process.

A community sense would be invaluable, if the nation were a harmonious community. The public school practice serves only to intensify the class differences.

Individualism

Dr Norwood says: "Lawn tennis, fives, rackets, golf, are also good in their place, good games, but mainly hygienic in their value." That is, a team game is morally better than any "individualistic" one. But one may observe that:

(1) Individualism is a far greater element of team games than is usually admitted. Any game involving more than one player demands co-operation, and conversely in any game the good player will shine. The only difference in this respect between tennis-doubles and Rugby football is that in the latter there are nearly eight times the number of players. Would the team-spirit protagonists prefer games with 200 a side?

(2) What is true of the adolescent is not necessarily true of an adult or a young child. Team games correspond to a real need in the adolescent. He naturally likes games where one gang fights another. But what is true for boys between 11 plus and 16 has been universalised into a truth for people of all ages, and exalted into a morality; with the result that many people come to dislike all games because they were made to play team-games too soon; and those who are good at team-games, by continuing to play them when adult, suffer from arrested development.

A SHORT TERM PROGRAMME

But at present most of this must remain in the air. In the event of a Socialist Government being returned to power without a radical change in the class system and the private ownership of capital, we suggest the following points should be an essential part of its educational programme. In addition, of course, to the obvious demands for better buildings, more playing fields, more teachers and smaller classes:

(1) A serious tackling of the Teacher-Training problem.
(2) Compulsory inspection of all private schools with power to close. It

is sometimes argued that this would endanger certain schools where valuable experiment is being done, which a reactionary or short-sighted government would be more likely to close than the really reactionary and inefficient ones. There is always a risk of this, but it is negligible compared with the urgent problem of the inefficient private school which is far more common than the good one, as the class of parent which can just afford a cheap private school is a larger class than the richer parent who can pay for the best.

(3) The raising of the school-leaving age to 16, with full provision of maintenance allowances.

(4) That, if making State elementary education compulsory for all would, in the present state of England, raise such a dust that no government could survive, this must be an objective which is never lost sight of, as it probably has more to do with class feeling on its psychological side in this country than any other factor. We shall never have a country even remotely resembling a democracy till we do, however excellent some of the preparatory schools may be.

(5) The raising of the leaving age not to mean a secondary education for all of the academic kind now offered by the secondary school. In particular, there should be a full development of the Junior Technical school.

(6) Separation of the School Certificate Examination from University Entrance examinations. The former to have a range which would cover technical as well as secondary curricula. Further, instead of the present practice of a pass or a fail, the certificate should take the form of a document stating how the candidate has done in each subject and including a teacher's testimonial.

(7) All employers in all trades to be compelled to provide facilities for their employees to attend Day Continuation classes up to the age of 18.

(8) State grants for higher education to be awarded on general or special ability and to carry with it no obligation to enter the teaching profession.

(9) Equal financial status for all types of teachers, male or female, elementary or secondary, with provision for family allowances.

(10) Provision for transfer of teachers from one kind of school to another. Every teacher should have some experience of both elementary and secondary teaching.

(11) Full provision of Nursery schools and child guidance clinics.

N.B. It is often suggested that a Socialist Government should compel the public schools to take a percentage of free-place children. This underestimates the power of the public school tradition. It would not result in the democratisation of the public schools, but in the conversion of favoured working-class children into sound public school men. None are so reactionary as those who are afraid of falling.

Written around November 1937; published as
Education: To-Day—and To-morrow, 1939

A Good Scout

Bare Knee Days. By F. Haydn Dimmock. Boriswood. 12s. 6d.

If those who discover early in life what they want to do, are able to do it, and are never disappointed, are the truly fortunate, then Mr Dimmock is a very lucky man. As a schoolboy his imagination was fired by the Boy Scout Movement:

> In imagination I was a pioneer pushing my way through impenetrable jungle with the stars as my compass; then a backwoodsman of the great forests with my shelter of brushwood and my cooking fire and the smell of wood-smoke and the aroma of sizzling bacon in my nostrils. That was the life, real life. That was what Baden-Powell was offering to us—the outdoor life away from the towns, the right to do the things people told us not to do.

And today, after a lifetime of editing *The Scout,* lecturing, camping, Jamborees in Birkenhead, Jamborees in Budapest, Jamborees in Holland, riding on the footplate, or helping to run a cruising Scout train, with only one short break on the Western Front when he was badly wounded, he can still say:

> I ask no more of God or man than health and strength to enjoy many many more glorious Bare-Knee Days.

Mr Dimmock is a fine example of a good Scout: brave, jolly, hardworking, easily moved by spectacular ritual, just, and good with boys. He has travelled widely and has some good stories to tell, particularly one about his host at one lecture engagement whose sons had been killed in the war, and who suffered in consequence from strange fits of absentmindedness.

If one puts the book down with a feeling of disquiet, it is not the fault of the author, but of the great movement which he represents. Scouting has done a great deal for town children—Mr Dimmock gives some excellent instances—it gets them out into the open air, it teaches them to be observant and self-reliant. But does it teach them to think? Uplift about service is insufficient. Mr Dimmock visits Hungary and Poland, for example, neither of them countries conspicuous for their social justice. He is quite rightly impressed by the warmth of their welcome, but never once does he seem to criticise or even to be curious about the real state of these countries; he passes from the peasant's hut to the hunting lodge without a query. Why should camp life be *real* life as opposed to *artificial* town life? Most of us have to live in towns and need to be taught how. All civilised life is artificial; i.e. it is life which is not ruled by the forces of Nature, but by one's own free will, and no one can use that properly who has not acquired self-knowledge and the habit of reason. The Chief Scout in his foreword to this book suggests his panacea:

> Dive into good comradeship with a lot of cheery fellows, join in their activities, and become, like them, normal.

One suspects that the Chief Scout prefers Plato to Socrates. Good comradeship, cheeriness, action, are all good, but are they, in a democracy, enough? As for normality, when one considers the normal state of the world today, one is not reassured.

The Listener, 8 December 1937

In Defence of Gossip

Let's be honest. When you open your newspaper, as soon as you have made sure that England hasn't declared war, or been bombed, what do you look at? Why, the gossip columns! These Names make News, the Londoner's Diary, Behind the Headlines, Personality Parade, or whatever it is. And as for books, if you had to choose between the serious study and the amusing gossip, say, between Clarendon's History of the Rebellion and John Aubrey's Scandals and Credulities, wouldn't you choose the latter? Of course you would! Who would rather learn the facts of Augustus' imperial policy than discover that he had spots on stomach? No one.

Few of the human passions can be guaranteed to last. Sooner or later we all grow too old for love, and even the joys of eating and drinking depend upon the caprices of our digestion. Tobacco? Yes, possibly, but the only pleasure we can absolutely count on to last as long as life itself is the one which distinguishes us from the beasts, the pleasure of curiosity; and, of all the exciting and interesting things which happen round about us, the behaviour of our neighbours is the most fascinating. I know that there are people who would rather find a lesser spotted woodpecker in a wood than their churchwarden with a chorus girl in a teashop, but these are the real eccentrics.

Then again, a lot of us have work we are interested in, but that's shop, and what a bore the fellow is who *will* talk shop in general company, the stockbroker who holds forth about bulls and bears to people who have never got nearer one than the Zoo—so unEnglish, don't you think? Or the lady who insists on giving you the latest bulletins from her nursery: the baby-snob, she's a terror.

No, shop can be the most absorbing of all forms of conversation, but for heaven's sake, let's keep it in its proper place.

Then there are other kinds of bores. There's the lecturer with his over-powering voice and supreme contempt for your intelligence. "It's all as simple as A.B.C. really", he begins, and so it is, and quite as dull. And there's the strong silent man or woman, the most conceited species of all. "I don't see any point in talking," he seems to suggest, "unless one has something worth saying. I'm just a plain simple fellow; I can't keep up with all you clever chaps," meaning of course, "If I were to open my mouth you'd be amazed at the wisdom and scandal which would come out of it. But you are unworthy to receive it." The lecturer is bad enough, but the strong silent man is infinitely worse. Still waters run deep. What a rotten proverb! Silence is the camouflage of the stupid. You can take any-body in with it, but you must have the right sort of face.

The only way to deal with the lecturer or the self-conscious oyster is by the direct personal remark, as the lady did, who, when sitting at table with a very pompous bishop, suddenly remarked in a clear voice: "He's got a face like the inside of an elephant's foot."

But you and I, I hope, are not bores. Whatever our consciences may say, whenever we meet our friends, as soon as the conventional inquiries about health and babies are over, we settle down to a cosy little gossip.

I saw John the other day. You know he's engaged.

I did hear something about it. She's very rich, isn't she?

Yes. Her parents are perfectly furious. He turned up at a party at their house in a hired dress suit!

How's that friend of his? The one who's so worried about his hair?

Oh, David, you mean. I saw him last week at a cocktail party. He was tight, and insisted on talking French all the time. But it wasn't very good French. He'll be as bald as a coot in a few years' time. Talking of David, how's Helen?

Not drinking quite as much as she used to. I think she's lovely, don't you?

Yes, but, Christmas! How stupid!

That's the trouble. She knows she's a bore.

The one I'm sorry for is that child of hers, left alone all day with that ogre of a nurse. My dear, she positively eats him. And so on and so on. We all do it, and no policeman or clergyman will ever stop us. But gossip is still listed officially as a vice, the kind of thing we do ourselves, but punish children for doing.

Well, is it really a vice? Never, we are told, say anything about other people that you wouldn't like to hear said about yourself. This is ridiculous and impossible. If we were really to act on this, we should never say anything about anybody except that he or she was the nicest, most beautiful and intelligent person in the whole world, because nobody is satisfied with less praise. We all really think that we are the nicest person in the world; if we didn't we should commit suicide. Perhaps at the bottom of our hearts we suspect that this isn't true, but we quite rightly expect our friends to behave in our company as if it *were*. We are not so foolish as to expect *them* to believe it, though. We all know that they'll say something very different, and perhaps nearer the truth, the moment our back is turned, just as we shall about them, but who cares? As long as we don't actually *hear* the catty remark, we are happy. It's this that stops most of us from reading other people's letters and listening at keyholes. We are terrified of coming across some unflattering reference to ourselves as in those horrifying advertisement strips. "James asked me how I like his book: I had to pretend I'd read it," or "Poor Jean is under the illusion that she still looks twenty-three." You know the kind of thing.

Gossip has fallen under a cloud because of the people who abuse it. I remember once as a small boy when my elder brother repeated at a tea-party, where a certain lady was present, a remark of my aunt's to the effect that the lady smelt. For the next few days, to all his toys, to his sponge and toothbrush and all his belongings, he found a paper pinned on which were written the words, "Never Repeat". As my aunt was an inveterate gossip, whose stories often were only remotely connected with the truth, we both thought this rather unfair at the time, but now I think the punishment was just. The person who ruins gossip is the person who repeats it back to its victim. That's every bit as bad as writing anonymous letters.

Another objection raised to gossip is that it causes mischief. As the result of a loose tongue, someone loses his job or divorces her husband. This is not the fault of *gossip*, but of the *kind of people* one gossips *with*. There are some kinds of people in whose presence you should shut up like an oyster: people with strong moral views, members of Watch-Committees or Purity Leagues, natural policemen, schoolmasters. If you really mind what people do you have no right to gossip.

But there's no reason whatever why gossip should make mischief. As a game played under the right rules it's an act of friendliness, a release of the feelings, and a creative work of art.

I began by saying that an interest in one's neighbours is common to all the human race. Common, too, at least to all nice people, is a love of conversation and a dislike of being alone. There are people who would rather play bridge or tennis or do something rather than talk, but I think that rather unfriendly, don't you? Still worse is the person who sits in the corner saying nothing, and then goes home and writes it all up in a little black diary. He is a spy, and should be treated as such. No, you can be quite sure that the person who dislikes talking, dislikes the entire human race, himself included, which is worse than the person who talks shop all the time, who at least likes himself.

A friendly person is interested in other people, and tries to talk about the things which interest them. Cut out gossip and there'll be no conversation left except shop, smoke-room stories, and the most vapid kind of tea-table talk. I'd rather be dead.

Secondly, gossip is the greatest safety valve to the emotions that exists. Psychologists tell us that we all nourish secret grudges, hatreds, jealousies, resentments against even our nearest and dearest, and that the cure lies in getting them off our chests. When we gossip, we do for nothing in the street or the parlour what we should have to pay two guineas an hour for doing in the consulting room. How often I have worked off some ill-feeling against a friend by telling some rather malicious stories about them, and as a result met them again with the feeling quite gone. And I expect you've done the same. When one reads in the papers of some unfortunate man who has gone for his wife with a razor, one can be pretty certain that he wasn't a great gossip. Very few gossips end in asylums or the condemned cell. It is cheaper than going to a doctor, and much nicer than actually having a row with our friends.

Lastly, gossip is creative. All art is based on gossip—that is to say, on observing and telling. The artist proper is someone with a special skill in handling his medium, a skill which few possess. But all of us to a greater or less degree can talk; we can all observe, and we all have friends to talk to. Gossip is the art-form of the man and woman in the street, and the proper subject for gossip, as for all art, is the behaviour of mankind.

Like other arts, there are many different kinds of technique. There's the complete fairy tale. This is the commonest way of gossiping about prominent public figures, because we don't really know anything about them. Of course, we begin by saying that we got it from a friend who has a friend in the Foreign Office, but that's only a conventional opening like "Once upon a time." The fault about most of these kinds of stories is that they aren't nearly daring enough. If you are going to tell a story which you know no-one will seriously believe, let it be a good one. To say that you have it on the most reliable authority that a certain Dictator is off his head won't interest anyone, but if you say that he has just made a brown wire-haired terrier, called Bungy, headmistress of a large girls' school; and proceed to describe the school prizegiving with a wealth of circumstantial detail, and in a very penetrating voice, you'll have the whole tea-shop listening to you. The secret of this kind of story is detail and more detail, preferably as extraordinary as possible.

If you are gossiping about someone you know, there is either the realistic or the poetical treatment. For the novice, the realistic is probably the safest, and should generally be used, anyway if the story is a really juicy one. If you have the good fortune actually to catch the Squire's wife kissing the chauffeur, or to see the bailiffs sitting in the Jones' hall, it's unlikely that you can improve on the story by any embellishments. The trouble is that, in most cases, the actual facts one has to go on are too slight to make a good tale by themselves. The true masters of gossip start with some little thing that either has happened or might have happened, and develop it. Let me take an imaginary example. Senator Gogarty tells somewhere of how he sat in a train in Ireland with the late Mr George Moore. Moore was looking out of the window, and waxed lyrical about the scenery. "I would give £5 to be able to go on looking at that view", he said. "Well, you shall," said Gogarty, and pulled the communication cord. According to Gogarty, Moore was very angry indeed. Now this incident happened, but supposing it hadn't. The basis of the story is Moore's remark about the scenery. That must be true, but suppose Gogarty only thought, either at the time, or later: "What fun it would be to take Moore at his word". Would it matter? Not in the least. The story would be spoilt without completing it. In fact, it was his artistic duty to complete it.

No, don't let's confine our gossip to the clumsy and untidy truth. Let us leave that to the timid and the dull. Gossip should soar on wings. The world of gossip should be a Land of Cockaigne, and its inhabitants heroic figures well over life size.

Oh yes, and while we're on the subject of technique, there are two faults which the beginner should avoid. Never be arch, by which I mean, never start like this:

"I had an interesting talk with X the other day."
"What did she say?"
"Oh I promised not to tell you.
"Oh come on."
"No, really, I can't ———!"

Etc., until everyone is bored. It's bad manners, like keeping people waiting for their dinner.

The other fault to avoid is the *apologetic* opening. Phrases like:

"I suppose it's *cruel* to say it, but ———"
"You know I'm *devoted* to her, but ———"
"I don't *usually* gossip, but ———"

It's a sign of bad style and of an unpleasant nature. Let your gossip be Yea, Yea, and Nay, Nay.

The great subjects for gossip are Love, Crime, and Money. Few of us, unfortunately, know many criminals, and reliable information about other people's finances is difficult to get hold of, so we generally have to fall back on love, which is a pity, as it tends to get rather monotonous. The ideal situation for the born gossip would be a village containing a mad vicar, a squire who was the terror of every parent with a daughter, a squire's wife who was being blackmailed by her chauffeur, a cocaine-taking doctor, a beautiful blonde girl in the pay of a foreign power, a sinister professor who never came out of his house, and an ex-convict or two; but, alas such villages only exist in detective stories. And we must put up with our own little village where nothing more happens than that the vicar is too high-church for the vestry, the squire's son has failed in his school certificate, the doctor danced several times with the beautiful blonde girl at the village institute dance, the professor is only an unmarried old entomologist with small independent means, and now and then someone is fined for poaching.

Well, never mind. Skilfully handled, you can make quite a lot of that. Remember, never hesitate to invent, but invent *in detail*, never gossip to people who'll run off straight away to the victim, never gossip to people with moral principles, and don't have any conscience about being a gossip. If it is a fault, which I don't believe, it is a fault that is shared by the entire human race.

BBC National Programme, 13 December 1937;
The Listener, 22 December 1937

Introduction to
The Oxford Book of Light Verse

I

Behind the work of any creative artist there are three principal wishes: the wish to make something; the wish to perceive something, either in the external world of sense or the internal world of feeling; and the wish to communicate these perceptions to others. Those who have no interest in or talent for making something, i.e. no skill in a particular artistic medium, do not become artists; they dine out, they gossip at street corners, they hold forth in cafés. Those who have no interest in communication do not become artists either; they become mystics or madmen.

There is no biological or mathematical law which would lead us to suppose that the quantity of innate artistic talent varies very greatly from generation to generation. The major genius may be a rare phenomenon, but no art is the creation solely of geniuses, rising in sudden isolation like craters from a level plain; least of all literature, whose medium is language—the medium of ordinary social intercourse.

If, then, we are to understand the changes that do in fact take place, why in the history of poetry there should be periods of great fertility, and others comparatively barren, why both the subject-matter and the manner should vary so widely, why poetry should sometimes be easy to understand, and sometimes very obscure, we must look elsewhere than to the idiosyncrasies of the individual poets themselves.

The wish to make something, always perhaps the greatest conscious preoccupation of the artist himself, is a constant, independent of time. The things that do change are his medium, his attitude to the spoken and written word, the kind of things he is interested in or capable of perceiving, and the kind of audience with whom he wants to communicate. He wants to tell the truth, and he wants to amuse his friends, and what kind of truth he tells and what kind of friends he has depend partly on the state of society as a whole and partly on the kind of life which he, as an artist, leads.

When the things in which the poet is interested, the things which he sees about him, are much the same as those of his audience, and that audience is a fairly general one, he will not be conscious of himself as an unusual person, and his language will be straightforward and close to ordinary speech. When, on the other hand, his interests and perceptions are not readily acceptable to society, or his audience is a highly specialised one, perhaps of fellow poets, he will be acutely aware of himself as the poet, and his method of expression may depart very widely from the normal social language.

In the first case his poetry will be "light" in the sense in which it is used in this anthology. Three kinds of poetry have been included:

(1) Poetry written for performance, to be spoken or sung before an audience [e.g. Folk-songs, the poems of Tom Moore].
(2) Poetry intended to be read, but having for its subject-matter the everyday social life of its period or the experiences of the poet as an ordinary human being [e.g. the poems of Chaucer, Pope, Byron].
(3) Such nonsense poetry as, through its properties and technique, has a general appeal [Nursery rhymes, the poems of Edward Lear].*

Light verse can be serious. It has only come to mean *vers de société*, triolets, smoke-room limericks, because, under the social conditions which produced the Romantic Revival, and which have persisted, more or less,

---

* A few pieces, e.g. Blake's *Auguries of Innocence* and Melville's *Billy in the Darbies*, do not really fall into any of these categories, but their technique is derived so directly from the popular style that it seemed proper to include them. When Blake, for instance, deserts the proverbial manner of the *Auguries* for the eccentric manner of the Prophetic Books, he ceases to write "light verse."

ever since, it has been only in trivial matters that poets have felt in suffi-cient intimacy with their audience to be able to forget themselves and their singing-robes.

II

But this has not always been so. Till the Elizabethans, all poetry was light in this sense. It might be very dull at times, but it was light.

As long as society was united in its religious faith and its view of the universe, as long as the way in which people lived changed slowly, audi-ence and artists alike tended to have much the same interests and to see much the same things.

It is not until the great social and ideological upheavals of the sixteenth and seventeenth centuries that difficult poetry appears, some of Shake-speare, Donne, Milton, and others. The example of these poets should warn us against condemning poetry because it is difficult. Lightness is a great virtue, but light verse tends to be conventional, to accept the atti-tudes of the society in which it is written. The more homogeneous a soci-ety, the closer the artist is to the everyday life of his time, the easier it is for him to communicate what he perceives, but the harder for him to see honestly and truthfully, unbiased by the conventional responses of his time. The more unstable a society, and the more detached from it the artist, the clearer he can see, but the harder it is for him to convey it to others. In the greatest periods of English Literature, as in the Elizabethan period, the tension was at its strongest. The artist was still sufficiently rooted in the life of his age to feel in common with his audience, and at the same time society was in a sufficient state of flux for the age-long beliefs and attitudes to be no longer compulsive on the artist's vision.

In the seventeenth century poetry, like religion, had its eccentric sports. Milton, with the possible exception of Spenser, is the first eccentric Eng-lish poet, the first to make a myth out of his personal experience, and to invent a language of his own remote from the spoken word. Poets like Herbert and Crashaw and prose-writers like Sir Thomas Browne are minor examples of the same tendency. Marvell and Herrick are "tradi-tional" in a way that these others are not, even though the former often use the same kind of tricks.

The Restoration marks a return both to a more settled society and to a more secure position for the artist under aristocratic patronage. His so-cial status rose. When Dryden in his "Essay on the Dramatic Poetry of the Last Age" ascribes the superiority in correctness of language of the new dramatists to their greater opportunities of contact with genteel society, he is stating something which had great consequences for English poetry. With a settled and valued place in society, not only minor poets, but the greatest, like Dryden and Pope, were able to express themselves in an easy manner, to use the speaking-voice, and to use as their properties the images of their everyday, i.e. social, life.

Their poetry has its limits, because the society of which they were a part was a limited part of the community, the leisured class, but within these limits, certain that the aim of poetry was to please, and certain of whom they had to please, they moved with freedom and intelligence.

This ease continued until the Romantic Revival which coincided with the beginning of the Industrial Revolution. From a predominantly agricultural country, where the towns were small and more important as places for social intercourse than as wealth-producing centres, England became a country of large manufacturing towns, too big for the individual to know anybody else except those employed in the same occupation. The divisions between classes became sharper and more numerous. At the same time there was a great increase in national wealth, and an increase in the reading public. With the increase in wealth appeared a new class who had independent incomes from dividends, and whose lives felt neither the economic pressure of the wage-earner nor the burden of responsibility of the landlord. The patronage system broke down, and the artist had either to write for the general public, whose condition was well described by Wordsworth in his preface to the *Lyrical Ballads,*

> A multitude of causes, unknown to former times, are now acting with a combined force to blunt the discriminating powers of the mind, and, unfitting it for all voluntary exertion, to reduce it to a state of almost savage torpor. The most effective of these causes are the great national events which are daily taking place, and the increasing accumulation of men in cities, where the uniformity of their occupations produces a craving for extraordinary incident, which the rapid communication of intelligence hourly gratifies;

or if he had an artistic conscience he could starve, unless he was lucky enough to have independent means.

As the old social community broke up, artists were driven to the examination of their own feelings and to the company of other artists. They became introspective, obscure, and highbrow.

The case of Wordsworth, the greatest of the Romantic poets, is instructive. While stating that he intended to write in the language really used by men, in particular by Westmorland farmers, whenever he tries to do so he is not completely successful, while in his best work, the *Odes* and *The Prelude,* his diction is poetic, and far removed from the spoken word. The sub-title of *The Prelude, The Growth of a Poet's Mind,* is illuminating. Wordsworth was a person who early in life had an intense experience or series of experiences about inanimate nature, which he spent the rest of his poetical life trying to describe. He was not really interested in farm-labourers or any one else for themselves, but only in so far as they helped to explain this vision, and his own relation to it. When he objects to eighteenth-century diction as "artificial," what he really means is artificial for his particular purpose. The diction of the Immortality Ode would be as artificial for Pope's purposes as Pope's was for Wordsworth's.

Wordsworth's case is paralleled by the history of most of the Romantic poets, both of his day and of the century following. Isolated in an amorphous society with no real communal ties, bewildered by its complexity, horrified by its ugliness and power, and uncertain of an audience, they turned away from the life of their time to the contemplation of their own emotions and the creation of imaginary worlds—Wordsworth to Nature, Keats and Mallarmé to a world of pure poetry,* Shelley to a future Golden Age, Baudelaire and Hölderlin to a past,

> . . . ces époques nues
> Dont Phoebus se plaisait à dorer les statues,

the Pre-Raphaelites to the Middle Ages. Instead of the poet regarding himself as an entertainer, he becomes the prophet, "the unacknowledged legislator of the world," or the Dandy who sits in the café, "proud that he is less base than the passers-by, saying to himself as he contemplates the smoke of his cigar: 'What does it matter to me what becomes of my perceptions?'"

This is not, of course, to condemn the Romantic poets, but to explain why they wrote the kind of poetry they did, why their best work is personal, intense, often difficult, and generally rather gloomy.

The release from social pressure was, at first, extremely stimulating. The private world was a relatively unexplored field, and the technical discoveries made were as great as those being made in industry. But the feeling of excitement was followed by a feeling of loss. For if it is true that the closer bound the artist is to his community the harder it is for him to see with a detached vision, it is also true that when he is too isolated, though he may see clearly enough what he does see, that dwindles in quantity and importance. He "knows more and more about less and less."

---

* Mr Stephen Spender, in his essay on Keats in *From Anne to Victoria*, has analysed the gulf between the world of the poems and the world of the letters. Keats's abandonment of "Hyperion" with the remark that there were too many Miltonic inversions in it, is a sign that he was becoming aware of this gulf. When the subject-matter of poetry ceases to be the social life of man, it tends to dispense with the social uses of language, grammar, and word-order, a tendency which Mallarmé carried to its logical conclusion.

Browning is an interesting case of a poet who was intensely interested in the world about him and in a less socially specialized period might well have been the "easiest" poet of his generation, instead of the most "difficult."

It is significant that so many of these poets either died young like Keats, or went mad like Hölderlin, or ceased producing good work like Wordsworth, or gave up writing altogether like Rimbaud. "I must ask forgiveness for having fed myself on lies, and let us go. . . . One must be absolutely modern." For the private world is fascinating, but it is exhaustible. Without a secure place in society, without an intimate relation between himself and his audience, without, in fact, those conditions which make for Light Verse, the poet finds it difficult to grow beyond a certain point.

III

But Light Verse has never entirely disappeared. At the beginning of the Romantic age stand two writers of Light Verse who were also major poets, Burns and Byron, one a peasant, the other an aristocrat. The former came from a Scottish parish which, whatever its faults of hypocrisy and petty religious tyranny, was a genuine community where the popular tradition in poetry had never been lost. In consequence Burns was able to write directly and easily about all aspects of life, the most serious as well as the most trivial. He is the last poet of whom this can be said. Byron, on the other hand, is the first writer of Light Verse in the modern sense. His success lasts as long as he takes nothing very seriously; the moment he tries to be profound and "poetic" he fails. However much they tried to reject each other, he was a member of "Society", and his poetry is the result of his membership. If he cannot be poetic, it is because smart society is not poetic. And the same is true, in a minor way, of Praed, whose serious poems are as trivial as his *vers de société* are profound.

IV

The nineteenth century saw the development of a new kind of light poetry, poetry for children and nonsense poetry. The breakdown of the old village or small-town community left the family as the only real social unit, and the parent-child relationship as the only real social bond. The writing of nonsense poetry which appeals to the Unconscious, and of poetry for children who live in a world before self-consciousness, was an attempt to find a world where the divisions of class, sex, occupation did not operate, and the great Victorian masters of this kind of poetry, Lewis Carroll and Edward Lear, were as successful in their day as Mr Walt Disney has been in ours. The conditions under which folk-poetry is made ensure that it shall keep its lightness or disappear, but the changing social conditions are reflected in its history by a degeneration both in technique and in treatment. The Border ballad could be tragic; the music-hall song cannot.* Directness and ease of expression has been kept, but at the cost of excluding both emotional subtlety and beauty of diction. Only in America, under the conditions of frontier expansion and prospecting and railway development, have the last hundred years been able to produce a folk-poetry which can equal similar productions of pre-industrial Europe, and in America, too, this period is ending.

The problem for the modern poet, as for every one else to-day, is how to find or form a genuine community, in which each has his valued place and can feel at home. The old pre-industrial community and culture are gone and cannot be brought back. Nor is it desirable that they should be. They were too unjust, too squalid, and too custom-bound. Virtues which were once nursed unconsciously by the forces of nature must now be recovered and fostered by a deliberate effort of the will and the intelligence. In the future, societies will not grow of themselves. They will either be made consciously or decay. A democracy in which each citizen is as fully conscious and capable of making a rational choice, as in the past has been possible only for the wealthier few, is the only kind of society which in the future is likely to survive for long.

In such a society, and in such alone, will it be possible for the poet, without sacrificing any of his subtleties of sensibility or his integrity, to write poetry which is simple, clear, and gay.

For poetry which is at the same time light and adult can only be written in a society which is both integrated and free.

Editorial Note and Acknowledgements

Certain notes should be added on the editorial methods and arrangement which have been followed. To avoid overlapping, no poem which appears in *The Oxford Book of English Verse* is included (with the exception of a poem by Thomas Jordan which appears here in a fuller version). Many of the poems in that anthology, particularly in the earlier sections, are, of course, "light" in the sense in which the word is used here.

The order of the poems is chronological. Poems of known authorship are arranged by the dates of their authors' births, but more varied criteria have been used to determine the position of the large number of anonymous poems, ballads, and songs which the volume contains. The earliest versions of the ballads and nursery rhymes have been used, except where later versions were more complete, or of greater literary merit. The nursery rhymes have generally been placed at the date of the earliest extant

---

* Kipling, who identified himself with British middle-class imperialism, as Pope identified himself with the 18th-century landed gentry, wrote serious light verse; and it is, perhaps, no accident that the two best light-verse writers of our time, Belloc and Chesterton, are both Catholics.

version, but when there is evidence that a rhyme existed earlier, it has been placed at the earlier date. The vexed question of ballads has been settled, in some cases perhaps rather arbitrarily, by dividing them according to the general evidence of their antiquity between the sixteenth and seventeenth centuries. Folk-songs have been grouped mainly in the late eighteenth and early nineteenth centuries: many of them could undoubtedly claim a much earlier position, but the forms in which we know them, and in which they were first collected, belong as a rule to this later period.

Details of the sources of poems not easily accessible, and some of the evidence of date, are given in an index at the end of the volume; but there are some poems, particularly in the modern period, for which the editor has had to rely on an oral tradition, often still changing, for his text.

The impossibility of adequately modernising poems of the Middle English period has made it necessary to reproduce in their original forms all poems up to the early sixteenth century. From that point onwards poems have been modernised in spelling and punctuation, and the editions from which they are taken have been given in the index only when they are not to be found in the authors' collected works.

The editor's thanks are due to Madame Olive Mangeot, Miss Hedli Anderson, and Mr John Betjeman for many valuable suggestions, to Mr J. A. W. Bennett of Merton College for checking the early texts, and to Mrs A. E. Dodds, to whose industry, scholarship, and taste he owes more than he finds it comfortable to admit.

The Oxford Book of Light Verse,
edited by W. H. Auden, 1938

Jehovah Housman and Satan Housman

A.E.H. A Memoir. By Laurence Housman. Cape. 10s. 6d.

Heaven and Hell. Reason and Instinct. Conscious Mind and Unconscious. Is their hostility a temporary and curable neurosis, due to our particular pattern of culture, or intrinsic in the nature of these faculties? Can man only think when he is frustrated from acting and feeling? Is the intelligent person always the product of some childhood neurosis? Does Life only offer two alternatives: "You shall be happy, healthy, attractive, a good mixer, a good lover and parent, but on condition that you are not over-curious about life. On the other hand you shall be attentive and sensitive, conscious of what is happening round you, but in that case you must not expect to be happy, or successful in love, or at home in any company. There are two worlds and you cannot belong to them both. If you belong to the second of these worlds you will be unhappy because you will always be in love with the first while at the same time you will despise it. The first world on the other hand will not return your love because it is in its nature to love only itself. Socrates will always fall in love with Alcibiades; Alcibiades will only be a little flattered and rather puzzled."

To those who are interested in this problem, A. E. Housman is one of the classic case histories. Few men have kept Heaven and Hell so rigidly apart. Jehovah Housman devoted himself to the emendation of texts of no aesthetic value and collected thunderbolts of poisoned invective in notebooks to use when opportunity arose against the slightest intellectual lapses; Satan Housman believed that the essence of poetry was lack of intellectual content. Jehovah Housman lived the virginal life of a don; Satan Housman thought a good deal about stolen waters and the bed. Jehovah Housman believed that slavery was necessary to support the civilised life; Satan Housman did not accept injustice so lightly.

> But they've pulled the beggar's hat off for the world to see and stare,
> And they're taking him to justice for the colour of his hair.

But they had one common ground upon which they could meet; the grave. Dead texts; dead soldiers; Death the Reconciler, beyond sex and beyond thought. There, and there only, could the two worlds meet.

Mr Laurence Housman's memoir of his brother records a great many interesting facts from which the reader must construct his own theory of what happened to Housman to cause this division, of why, for instance, he did not work for Greats, and why he did not allow his family to come to see him in those critical years from 1882–1892. But however fascinating such speculations may be, they are of minor importance. What happened to Housman happens in one way or another to most intellectuals, though few exhibit the symptoms in so pure a form.

> The stars have not dealt me the worst they could do;
> My pleasures are plenty, my troubles are two.
> But oh, my two troubles they reave me of rest,
> The brains in my head and the heart in my breast.
>
> O grant me the ease that is granted so free,
> The birthright of multitudes, give it to me,
> That relish their victuals and rest on their bed
> With flint in the bosom and guts in the head.

Yes, the two worlds. Perhaps the Socialist State will marry them; perhaps it won't. Perhaps it will always be true that

Wer das Tiefste gedacht, liebt das Lebendigste,
Hohe Tugend versteht, wer in die Welt geblickt
   Und es neigen die Weisen
Oft am Ende zu Schönem sich.

Perhaps again the only thing which can bring them together is the exer-
cise of what Christians call Charity, a quality for which, it will be remem-
bered, neither Jehovah nor Satan Housman had much use, but of which
perhaps they were both not a little frightened.

New Verse, January 1938

Chinese Diary

BY W. H. AUDEN AND
CHRISTOPHER ISHERWOOD

I.—HANKOW

From the point of view of a journalist, or indeed of anybody who likes to
be on the spot while history is being made, Hankow is, at this moment,
undoubtedly one of the half-dozen most interesting places in the world. It
is the Barcelona of China. True, it is not the official seat of the Govern-
ment, for the President has retired to Chungking; and it has not the stra-
tegic importance of Canton, that gateway by which a large proportion of
foreign war supplies must reach the Chinese Army; but it is to Hankow
that you must come if you want to get some idea of how China is fighting
this war, and to meet the men and women who are directing her efforts.

   Cut off from the sea by the Japanese occupation of the Yangtze river-
mouth, Hankow has still two important links of communication with the
outside world, the daily air-service from Hong Kong, and the Canton–
Hankow railway. So far, the Japanese have left the air-service alone, per-
haps for fear of more international incidents. The railway, of course, is
bombed, but with extreme inefficiency.

   It was by railway that we first arrived, one morning early in March, at
the Wuchang station. Wuchang is on the south bank of the river, Hankow
on the north: we stumbled down to the ferry-boat in a tearing bliz-
zard. After the steamy warmth of Canton, it was like finding oneself
suddenly in pre-war Siberia; for the buildings along the Bund are all
Occidental—the warehouses, offices and consulates of the former Eu-
ropean concessions—and most of the restaurants and bars are kept by

Russian emigrants, a fat defeated tribe, who lead a melancholy indoor life of gossip, tea-drinking, Mah-Jongg and cards.

At Wuchang, live General Chiang Kai-Shek and his wife—"The Generalissimo" and "Madame" as Mr Donald, their Australian friend and adviser, invariably calls them. Mr Donald, who started life as a journalist, appears to occupy the position of a kind of oracle—an oracle of commonsense. One half-expects to meet an adventurer, a diplomat or a sycophant, and finds instead a matter-of-fact, downright, middle-aged man, kindly and hospitable, with a weakness for patent medicines, who will eat nothing but European food, who speaks only English. Mr Donald's ignorance of Chinese, people tell you, is his greatest asset, in this land of plots and secrets.

Through Mr Donald's kindness, we were privileged to drink tea with Madame herself—that charming, super-efficient and highly formidable lady, whose American mission-training has equipped her with a perfect command of the English language and an almost terrifying social poise. "Do poets like cake?" she asked. We assured her that we did. "I thought, perhaps, that they preferred spiritual food." The cakes were delicious. (Did Mr Donald choose them, we wondered.) After tea, Madame answered our questions with the ease and affability of a professional lecturer. The Generalissimo himself we saw only for a moment. Quiet, bald, seemingly gentle and shy, he was led by Madame on to the balcony to pose, arm in arm, for yet one more photograph. Under the camera's eye, he stiffened visibly, like a schoolboy who is warned to hold himself upright.

China has certainly collected an oddly-assorted bunch of friends and helpers. At the far end of the Bund, in the former Japanese Concession, General von Falkenhausen, the German military adviser, has his headquarters. Here, you find yourself in old Potsdam, amidst the heel-clickings, the stiff bows and the monocles—though the General himself, a lean elderly man in pince-nez, has more of the Prussian schoolmaster about him than the Reichswehr officer. Much has been written and speculated about the German advisers' role in Chinese affairs and the nature of their relations with the Nazi Government, but there can be no doubt that their advice is given loyally and disinterestedly, even if it is not always taken.

And at the other extremity of the international quarter, at a distance from the Germans which may well be regarded as symbolic, lives Miss Agnes Smedley, that veteran friend and chronicler of the Red (now 8th Route) Army. Miss Smedley is not so optimistic as the General. She fears, and perhaps with reason, for the ultimate future of the Chinese Communists when this war is over.

What a day one might spend in this extraordinary city! Breakfasting with Comrade Po Ku of the 8th Route Army; lunching with a dyspeptic munitions agent who shows you photographs of the Shanghai corpses; having tea and exchanging rumours with the foreign journalists; trying to interview the Russian airmen, who never open their mouths, or the charming and enthusiastic Chinese intellectuals, who seldom shut them; dining with the British Admiral who, parted from his ship by the Yangtze boom, has become an ardent collector of antiques; passing the evening at the Chinese opera, or a Russian cabaret, or the German Club. And, at last, when everybody else has gone to bed, and the evening air-raid was over, you might, if you had the constitution of an ox, return to the journalists again, and sit drinking Chinese wine out of small metal tea-pots, and boasting in three languages, until dawn.

II.—The Front Line

Early on the morning of March 27th we left Hsiuchiou, in rickshaws, for the northern front. To anybody wishing to visit a battle-area whose location and extent are vague, rickshaw-travel is strongly to be recommended. Trains get held up, lorries demand roads, horses cannot carry much baggage; but in a rickshaw you are your own master—you can make detours, take short cuts across open country, and, if enemy planes come over, a single bound will land you safely in the ditch.

Where was the War? We asked at every village, but nobody could tell us for certain. There was still no sign of it when, late that afternoon, we bumped downhill into Li Kwoe Yi. Somewhere, in that marvellously peaceful valley which opened beyond, dotted with labouring coolies in their brilliant blue clothes and big straw hats, were the Japanese. The blossom was just beginning on the slopes, and the landscape reminded us strongly of the Thames near Oxford. Not a gun was to be heard; not a puff of smoke to be seen.

Ahead of us a soldier was riding. We stopped him to ask how and why his pony had turned bright green. He explained that the Army camouflages all its white horses against aircraft, and directed us to General Chang-Tschen's headquarters, in a village at the foot of the hills, a mile or so away.

General Chang-Tschen received us with the grave politeness of an elderly university professor—his first words were an apology for the supper he was about to offer us. While it was cooking he explained the situation. We were nearer to the Front than we had supposed, for the Chinese were actually holding the south bank of the Grand Canal, hardly two miles distant. Han Chwang, on the northern canal bank, was in Japanese hands. "But there are also many Chinese troops north of the canal," the General added. "They are surrounding the Japanese at various points.

When these have been taken, we shall advance." At this moment the bell of the field-telephone rang. "Ah . . ." murmured the General, apologetically. "We have information that the Japanese will soon begin to fire their gun. Please do not be alarmed. It is only a very small gun. . . ."

After supper, mounted on tiny ponies, we trotted across the fields by the light of the setting sun, towards the lines. In the distance the boom of the unalarming "small gun" could be heard, like the slamming of a far-away door. We dismounted in another village, now occupied only by troops and barking dogs, where we were introduced to more officers, with the inevitable exchange of visiting-cards. From this point, we were told, we must advance in single file, on foot—a precaution perhaps deliberately staged by our hosts to provide us with an extra thrill; for here, as we later discovered, we were not merely out of sight of the enemy but also out of range. The great earthworks, in the twilight, looked absolutely deserted; they were sad with all the boredom and tragic idleness of war. Then their inhabitants, some of them boys of fifteen, emerged from straw-lined holes to salute us as we passed. "How do they recognise an officer?" we asked—for, at the Front, there is no distinction of uniforms —and were answered: "An officer is recognised by his face."

Next morning we visited the front-line itself. The sun shone brightly. It was hot and sinister and deadly quiet. Crouching in dug-outs under the shattered railway bridge, and amongst the ruined huts opposite Han Chwang village, the men talked in whispers, for the Japanese were so near that you could have thrown a stone into their lines. Nevertheless, tea was produced from somewhere, and we bowed and smoked and chatted. "England has helped China very much in this war," the officers told us politely; and we had to protest, all too sincerely, that England hadn't helped nearly enough.

It is difficult for a foreigner to assess Chinese morale, for cocksureness and boasting in the Western manner are rare. The average officer speaks of China's chances with an air of gentle deprecation; and yet he is ultimately confident, or, at least, hopeful. "The Japanese fight with their tanks and planes," one of them told us, "but we Chinese fight with our spirit." When we had seen everything we were asked for our opinion of the trench system. The officers seemed actually disappointed when we praised it: they would really have welcomed even a foreign civilian's suggestions and advice.

As we walked back towards Li Kwoe Yi, the newly arrived battery of Chinese guns opened fire over our heads, bombarding Han Chwang village. The Japanese replied, but the Chinese battery was far beyond their range. For the first time the advantage in equipment did not lie with the enemy. The battle, which was to culminate in the Chinese victories of a week later, had just begun.

III.—The Lung-Hai Railway in War-Time

The Lung-Hai Railway was built by the Belgians and runs east and west through the wheat-growing districts immediately south of the Yellow River, from Pa Chi, about one hundred miles west of Sian, to Hsiuchiou. Beyond Hsiuchiou, the track has been torn up, to check a possible Japanese advance. At Chongchow, in Honan, the Lung-Hai links up with the Pin-Han line to Hankow. These two lines form the only artery for moving troops along the Yellow River front, and for carrying eastward such war material as may enter China from Russia, via Chinese Turkestan. The Japanese have repeatedly bombed and shelled it, but, so far, traffic has never been seriously dislocated.

We made several journeys along this line. Here is one of them:

Wednesday. The sky is cloudless and the midday sun very hot, although it is only the end of March, as the westbound "express" steams into Chongchow. Chongchow station has suffered more than most from air-raids. The waiting-room is in ruins. In the street outside, all that is left of the Hotel of Flowery Peace is a mass of bricks and one tottering wall. The streets are quiet, because business is only carried on at night.

Our Belgian locomotive has been camouflaged with daubs of mud; the roofs of the third-class carriages are black with refugee passengers. On every journey, we are told, two or three fall off and are killed. Hardly have we got into our compartment, when the air-raid warning sounds, and we have to hurry to the station dug-out, while the train pulls out to hide somewhere in the country. The station dug-outs are roomy concrete structures: many of them were built as long as two years ago, when the Chinese began to realise that war was sooner or later inevitable. This particular air-raid is a false alarm, so we start—only an hour late. A last-moment rush of refugees for the already over-crowded train-roofs is beaten off by station officials with sticks. The victims merely laugh: their padded coats are so thick that the blows raise only a cloud of dust and lice.

To-day we are in luck. The train stops only a few minutes at each station. (On an earlier journey, we once waited six hours at a place called Democracy: a young officer got so bored that he began firing at the rooks with his revolver, and was severely reprimanded in the waiting-room.)

We are passing through the loess region: precipitous sand-canyons, cave-dwellings, fantastic sand-pinnacles resembling Lot's wife. Often, the canyons are artificially terraced for wheat-growing: from the distance the hills look like some old Babylonish city.

There is no dining-car. Meals are cooked in a box-car: the boys bring us hot face-towels and endless cups of weak tea. They tell us that, barring accidents, we shall be in Sianfu to-morrow morning, if the train can get to

Lo Yang by dusk; for the section between Lo Yang and Tungwan can only be travelled in the dark. Here the line runs close beside the Yellow River; and the Japanese are on the north bank with their guns sighted on the track.

Towards evening the hills flatten down into a broad fertile valley of orchards and green wheat. It is six o'clock and we are already running into Lo Yang. A soldier leans out of a troop-train and lays two fingers side by side: "England and China," he shouts, "together. Italy and Japan, together too."

Thursday. Something has gone wrong. We wake up to find ourselves in a small station, halfway between Sian and Lo Yang. There has been an accident farther down the line. Nobody knows the details, or how long we shall have to wait. The train moves out of the station for safety and stops in a ravine between two tunnels. Within half an hour, a complete market-town has sprung up around us: peasants sell cigarettes, tea and all sorts of food—boiled chickens varnished red with soya bean, sausage-shaped waffles, hard-boiled eggs. Child beggars gather under the windows, intoning a litany of want and staring at the foreign devils through swollen, trachema-infected lids. Most of the passengers clamber down and sit about chatting, or go to sleep on the shady side of the line. The engine-driver produces some straw and makes a bed for himself under his engine, where he lies reading a book.

Friday. We have moved during the night, but only one station. As we have found several bed-bugs we decide to have a real spring-clean of the carriage. While the car-boys are washing the windows, we take out all our bedding, beat it with walking-sticks, and hang it up on the station fence in the sun. The idea catches on, and soon the station is festooned with clothing. Madame Chiang Kai-shek, we feel sure, would have approved.

By now the car-boys are very friendly: they bring along a gramophone and some records of Chinese singing, which sound startlingly like Donald Duck. We have begun Chinese lessons, which are followed by a delighted crowd on the platform. One of the boys produces, but cannot play, a flute.

Saturday. Again, we have scarcely moved at all during the night. We get a lift on the breakdown train to see the accident. On the edge of a steep embankment, two hundred feet above the Yellow River, we find an engine lying on its side amidst torn-up track. Half-way down the slope is a splintered carriage. A wheel came off a truck, derailing the whole train: nine people were killed, fifteen seriously injured. But a new track has now been built, skirting the wreck, and we shall leave this evening.

Fuel has run out, the meat is high and there is no sugar, only some sticks of what tastes like Edinburgh rock; but a bottle of whisky has appeared, unearthed from the box-car like a gift from a better world. All the lights on the train are put out, as we move off for our last rabbit-dash past the Japanese guns. The train gathers speed, roaring through tunnels and deep cuttings, swaying precariously over high bridges. The carriage is filled with sulphur and smuts. Suddenly we come out of a tunnel and see the Yellow River below us and, across the river, brilliant and isolated in the huge dark countryside, like some pretentious roadhouse, the Japanese searchlights. But there is no shot. We plunge into another tunnel, and soon we are passing at high speed through the derelict sidings of Tungwan station, where no train ever stops now. We are clear. Passengers begin to talk and light candles. To-morrow morning, we shall breakfast in Sianfu.

IV.—MISSIONARIES IN THE WAR AREA

Late last autumn, Chengtingfu, in the province of Hopeh, was occupied by Japanese troops. At the Catholic mission station, ten missionaries, French, Belgian, Spanish and Italian, had given shelter to a number of Chinese women refugees. A party of Japanese soldiers, it appears, came to the mission and demanded the women. The missionaries seem to have persuaded them to go away: overnight, the women were smuggled out of the town. But next morning the soldiers returned, and furious at having been tricked, murdered all the foreigners. This crime, later investigated by consular officials, was finally admitted, in essentials, by the Japanese authorities themselves.

It was exceptional, no doubt; and every war must necessarily produce such outrages—nevertheless, the prospects are certainly not pleasant for those foreign missionaries and doctors who find themselves planted in the path of a possible Japanese advance. "What we shall do if they come," was a constant topic of conversation at all the mission stations we visited along the Yellow River line; and everywhere our hosts faced the emergency with a matter-of-fact courage which amazed us. There was no question of running away. A mission compound offers the only hope of refuge to a mass of children and of women who will, if left in their own homes, most likely be raped.

At one town, not more than twenty miles from the firing line, we found two mission doctors, an American lady and gentleman, both nearing seventy, preparing for the decisive moment. "We're bricking up all the compound gates," they told us, "except this one. If the Japs come into the town, we shall take it in turns to stay by the gateway, day and night." It is most important, everyone agrees, that the invaders shall be received by a foreigner. You mustn't show that you're frightened, you must argue with them, you must be firm but very polite, you must offer them tea. The technique is now well established, for missionaries who have already "crossed the line" have managed to send letters of advice to their colleagues on the Chinese side. It is very important, of course, to get hold of an officer as soon as possible; the officers are generally courteous and amenable, though they cannot always control their own troops. A few are Christians, and some have even been persuaded to post notices on the hospital gates, officially forbidding entrance.

Meanwhile, the mission hospitals are busy: most of them are full of air-raid victims or of wounded soldiers. Without the assistance of the mission doctors, the Chinese army would be in a bad way indeed, for, outside their hospitals, there are few surgical instruments and hardly any of the portable X-ray sets so vitally necessary in searching for buried shell-splinters and bullets. There is always the air-raid risk. All hospital roofs are clearly marked with their national colors; yet the American Baptist mission at Chengchow had two bombs dropped recently inside its compound. Very few hospitals have dugouts large enough to accommodate all their patients, even if they could be moved in time.

V.—What Is Going to Happen?

With very few exceptions—such as a Catholic priest who said that only Japan can bring Law and Order, and a banker who said that both sides were natives, so what did it matter—the Europeans we have met, even the Germans, have been pro-Chinese, and increasingly confident that, in the long run, China will win. Foreign military attachés who four months ago thought her finished are now extremely optimistic and everyone agrees that the Japanese invasion has at least done one thing: it has unified the Chinese nation as it has never been unified before. The Central Government generals, the generals from Kwangsi, reactionaries and communists, former bandit leaders and anti-bandit societies like the Red Spears, are now fighting side by side. Generalissimo Chiang Kai-shek is a national hero, as the crowds outside the photographer's window in any obscure little town will testify.

But it would be a mistake to imagine that a Chinese victory is either certain or imminent. Apart from their manifest inferiority in airplanes, tanks, guns, etc., the Chinese appear to have certain psychological characteristics which, from a military point of view, are defects. In the first place, they seem curiously passive; prepared to resist, but hardly to attack. Again and again, we gather, their German advisers have urged them to take the offensive; but, until recently, with little success. In the second place, the Confucian tradition of the gulf between the scholar and the common people is still very strong. There are still far too many people in China—students, professional classes, wealthier business men—who regard the war as a coolies' war; and one gets very sick of hearing: "There are four hundred million Chinese. We have plenty of common soldiers to do the fighting. Our job is to educate ourselves for the task of reconstruction after the war"—particularly when one remembers that it is these very students who have been most ardent in demanding war against Japanese aggression. One staff officer said to us, laughingly: "You think our soldiers very brave, but they don't know they are brave. They set no value on their lives. If you asked *me* to take a rifle and fight, of course I wouldn't do it!"

On the other hand, the war has shown clearly that the Japanese army is not the wonderful fighting machine that some imagined. Its air force is ludicrously ineffective, its discipline poor, and it suffers from a swollen head. Despising the Chinese, it has organized solely for an uninterrupted advance, and has pushed on in small units, regardless of its communications and its rear. Further, in the occupied areas, instead of pacifying the population by decent behavior and small concessions, which would not, in the beginning, have been difficult, it has, by its brutality, done everything to antagonize the common people, who, however much they may have hated the Chinese war-lords, find the Japanese infinitely worse. "Give me four divisions of European troops" said a military expert, "and I could drive every Japanese out of China in six months."

It is rumored that the Japanese would like to stop now; keeping, of course, Manchuria, Peking and Shanghai. The Chinese assert that they will continue fighting until they have won all of these back, but whether they will, it is hard to say. Anything less, however, can only mean another war in the future.

As to what will happen in the event of a decisive Chinese victory, it is again impossible to be certain of anything. At the moment, men are fighting on the same side, and behaving indeed as if they were the closest personal friends, who for the past twelve years have been trying to kill each other. Take the Communists, for instance. At the moment, their military help is valuable, and not only Kuomintang officials but even Hong-Kong business men will assure you that, after all, they are not so bad as they have been painted, and that, in any case, they are not real communists at all. But, when asked what role they think the Communists will play after the war, they become ominously vague. "It is not a question of the government working with the Communists," Madame Chiang told us. "It is a question of the Communists working with the government."

But two things seem fairly clear. It will take at least five years to reorganize the country after the war, a work in which, presumably, all parties should be able to coöperate. And the problems of a vast illiterate population, a language which prolongs the process of education by at least two years in comparison with the West and habits of corrupt administration which are by no means dead, make a democratic government in our sense impossible for many years to come. The greatest probability would seem to be some form of centralized military dictatorship.

The New Republic, 1 June 1938; *The New Statesman and Nation*, 25 June and 16 July 1938

Meeting the Japanese

BY W. H. AUDEN AND
CHRISTOPHER ISHERWOOD

If you have just spent four months in the interior of wartime China, visited two fronts, a dozen military hospitals, and the sites of many air-raids, it becomes difficult to remember that you are supposed to be an impartial neutral, whose country maintains "friendly diplomatic relations" with each of the two belligerent governments. For us, in Canton, in Hankow, along the Yellow River, the Japanese were "the enemy"; the Chinese anti-aircraft were "our" guns, the Chinese planes "our" planes, the Chinese army was "we." Most of the foreigners in China feel that way nowadays, even the officials.

In the course of our travels, we had met only two Japanese. One of them was sitting in the corner of a railway carriage on the Lung-Hai line, tied up with rope like a parcel, surrounded by his guards. He had been captured somewhere near the Grand Canal, and was being taken down to Hankow to be questioned by the authorities. Prisoners in this war are a kind of zoological rarity; we gaped at this one with furtive and somewhat shamefaced curiosity—a sheepish, moon-faced youth, who spoke neither Chinese nor English, as isolated in his captivity as a baby panda. There was nothing we could do for him, except to put a cigarette between his lips, and go away as soon as was decently possible. The other Japanese was also a prisoner. We were taken to see him on our way up to the South-eastern front. He was tall and handsome, with a large mustache and considerable dignity. He had been a schoolmaster before the war, and one felt that he was not sorry to be out of it. The Chinese journalists who accompanied us were impressed chiefly by his size. As one of them ambiguously remarked: "He must be the Longfellow of Japan."

It seemed strange and unnatural, therefore, to be sitting down to lunch with four Japanese civilians in the dining-room of the Shanghai Club. The four Japanese were all distinguished personages, a consular official, a business man, a banker, and a railway director; they gave us the collective impression of being stumpy, dark brown, bespectacled, mustached, grinning, and very neat. We had resolved, of course, to be extremely tact-ful. To make any reference, however indirect, to the war would, we felt, be positively indecent.

But the Japanese, evidently, had no such qualms. "You have been travel-ing in China?" said one of them, right away. "How interesting. . . . I hope you had no inconvenience?" "Only from your airplanes," we replied, forgetting our resolutions. The Japanese laughed heartily; this was a great joke. "But surely," they persisted, "you must have found transport and living conditions very primitive, very inefficient?" "On the contrary," we assured them, "extremely efficient. Kindness and politeness every-where. Everybody was charming." "Oh yes," the consular official agreed, in an indulgent tone. "The Chinese are certainly charming. Such nice people. What a pity . . ." "Yes, what a pity!" the others chimed in. "This war could so easily have been avoided. Our demands were very reason-able. In the past, we were always able to negotiate these problems amica-bly. The statesmen of the old school—you could deal with them, they understood the art of compromise. But these younger men, they're dreadfully hot-headed. Most unfortunate . . ." "You know," continued the consular official, "we really love the Chinese. That is the nice thing about this war. There is no bitterness. We in Japan feel absolutely no bitterness towards the Chinese people." This was really a little too much; the last remnants of our prearranged politeness disappeared. It was hardly surprising, we retorted, with some heat, that the Japanese didn't feel bitter. Why should they? Had they ever had their towns burnt and their crops destroyed? Had they ever been bombed? Our four gentlemen had no answer ready. They merely blinked. They didn't appear in the least offended. Then one of them said, "That is certainly a most interest-ing point of view."

They wanted to know about the morale in Hankow. Was there much enthusiasm? What possibility was there of a negotiated peace? None, we declared, with spiteful relish. Chiang would continue to resist—if neces-sary, to the borders of Thibet. They shook their heads sadly, and drew in their breath with a sharp, disappointed hiss. It was a pity . . . a great pity. . . . And then—we had been expecting it—out came the Bolshevik bogey. Japan was really fighting on China's side, to save her from herself, to protect her from the Soviets. "And from Western trade competition," we might have added, but it wasn't necessary. For, at this moment, through the window which overlooked the river, the gun turrets of *H.M.S. Birmingham* slid quietly into view, moving upstream. In Shanghai, the visual statements of power politics are more brutal than any words.

Like formidable, excluded watchdogs, the real masters of Shanghai in-habit the dark, deserted Japanese Concession or roam the ruined wilder-ness of Chapei, looking hungrily in upon the lighted populous international town. On Garden Bridge, their surly sentries force every Chinese foot passenger to raise his hat in salute. Incidents are of almost weekly occurrence: a foreign lady is insulted, an innocent naturalist is arrested as a spy. Representations are made—"through the proper channels"; apologies are gravely offered and accepted. Out driving one day, in a district occupied by the Japanese, we saw two soldiers with drawn bayonets prodding at a crowd of women and children. We stopped. Here, we thought, is a chance of witnessing an atrocity at first-hand. Then we noticed a third soldier, with a basket. The Japanese were—distributing food.

On the voyage home, we stopped at Nagasaki for a few hours, and later had time for one night in Tokyo before rejoining our boat at Yokohama. There are few signs of the war here, beyond the posters which advertise heroic military films. In the streets of the towns we passed through, there were still plenty of able-bodied young men in civilian clothes. Many of the public lamps of Kobe are not lit at night—a precaution, we were told, against air-raids—but the shops shine brightly enough to illuminate the entire city. As we entered the Tokyo station, a troop-train was leaving for China, amidst cheering and waving banners. As far as we could judge, the enthusiasm wasn't being produced to order.

Some Chinese believe that Japan is tired of this war. We wish we could agree with them. Ten Japanese soldiers have committed suicide. No doubt. But suicide proves nothing. It is the national reaction to all life's troubles: an officer's reprimand, a love affair gone wrong, a quarrel, a snub. Twenty Japs were seen by a peasant, sitting round a fire in a wood: "they looked very sad, and one of them said, 'I am tired of this war.'" No doubt. Were there ever any soldiers, anywhere, who didn't grumble, since the days of Julius Caesar? No, Japan isn't tired of this war. Not yet. She won't be tired until the steadily approaching economic crisis is upon her, until the Chinese make some effective air-raids on her munitions factories, until she has been forced to call another million men to the colors. She won't be tired until the fall of Hankow (if Hankow does fall) proves to her—as we hope and think it will—that you cannot beat China merely by occupying her cities. For we believe that China can be beaten only when her morale and newly found unity have been broken, and that is a task which all the robber nations of the earth, banded together, might well fail to accomplish.

New Masses, 16 August 1938

Escales

BY W. H. AUDEN AND
CHRISTOPHER ISHERWOOD

This ship is like a hospital. Miles from land, home, love, sanity, we lie limp in our deck chairs, gazing out dully across a sea which is as boring and hopeless as an incurable spinal disease. The nurses are very attentive. All the meals are at unnatural, invalid hours.

Beneath our conversation, our eating, our thoughts, the engines throb, deep down, like a fever. This voyage is our illness. As the long days pass, we grow peevish, apathetic, sullen; we no longer expect, or even wish to recover. Only, at moments, when a dolphin leaps or the big real birds from sunken Africa veer round our squat white funnels, we sigh and wince, our bodies gripped by the exquisitely painful pangs of hope. Maybe, after all, we are going to get well; we are going to arrive . . . But the relapse is immediate and violent. We shuffle off to the bar for our evening medicine: brandy and ginger ale.

We wake to the immediate sense of a changed vibration: the ship is beating through shallow, sandy water. Port Said glitters up over the horizon into the oblique sunshine. The water-front houses, from the distance, are like a denture of brilliant teeth, waiting to devour the traveler. But the teeth, on closer inspection, are not so brilliant, after all: their backs are revoltingly dirty, many are decaying, several are false. Long before we have berthed, the deck is swarming with carpet-sellers, fountain-pen merchants, touts for dancing halls and hotels. Conjurers produce chickens from empty cups. A pickpocket steals a pair of spectacles. Everybody gesticulates and screams.

We hire a car and drive to Cairo. The Delta country is as flat as Holland. Strings of Arabs, gaudily robed, with shambling camels, wander along the edges of the waterways, looking as incongruous as extras who have lost their way to the location of a Biblical film. In the middle distance are herons, bulrushes, flat-topped hovels roofed with straw and mud—and, in glimpses beyond, the desert, a slow-heaving, silvery gray ocean, obscurely reflecting the sky.

CAIRO: that immense and sinister Woolworth's, where everything is for sale—love, lottery tickets, clothes hangers, honor, justice, indecent postcards, bootlaces, disease—as much and as cheap as you like, till the buyer goes mad with boredom and guilt. And behind it, at the end of a tram ride, the three Pyramids, looking ugly and quite new, like the tip-heaps of a prosperous quarry. For a long time, we couldn't find the Sphinx at all. Stumbling over the litter of recent excavations, we came upon it suddenly,

smaller than its photographs, in a pit. There it lies, in the utter stillness of
its mortal injuries; the flat cruel face of a scarred and blinded baboon,
face of a circus monstrosity, no longer a statue but a living, changing crea-
ture of stone. A camera, if cameras had been invented, could have shown
how that face has changed through the centuries, growing old and blind
and terrible in the blaze of the sun, under the lash of the wind and the
desert sand. Once, no doubt, it was beautiful. Long ago, it could see. Now
it lies there mutilated and sightless, its paws clumsily bandaged with
bricks, its mane like an old actor's wig, asking no riddle, turning its back
upon America—injured baboon with a lion's cruel mouth, in the middle
of invaded Egypt.

DJIBOUTI: Brown emery-paper mountains heaped with thunder clouds
in the background of the gulf, and a flat foreshore where a few buildings
stand, very distinct and defiant in the glare, as though Life had estab-
lished itself here, step by step, cell by cell, in face of superhuman diffi-
culties, and might not be able to hold the position. A wireless station, a
group of salt stacks like conical white tents, three petroleum tanks, some
Arab dhows stranded in the cracked tidal mud—and always the wheeling
sea hawks, which seem to the traveler to be screaming unintelligible, nos-
talgic news of home.

This is an outpost, a self-contained world where you could spend your
life, and marry and take to drink and drugs and die—*une vie.* "People
really live here," was our first amazed thought; and here were the people,
approaching us in launches steered by tall stork-legged Negroes in scarlet
and orange turbans, with the tricolor trailing exhausted at the stern. All
the characters of Somerset Maugham translated into French—the
shriveled but still elegant woman of thirty-five who is the mistress of an
eighteen-year-old boy in spotless ducks . . . and her husband, a hateful,
red-faced furry-eared brute in canvas shorts, who knows about it all, and
drinks Pernod and doesn't care. Last, terrible in white and gold, comes
General X. Like every French officer of high rank, he has the air of being
invisibly crippled; one arm is tucked woodenly into his breast. He gives a
curt, stiff salute—his face absolutely expressionless, his eyes and little
mustache quite dead—and climbs the staircase to the first-class smoking
room, almost unnoticed, like a plague.

The natives of Djibouti are really black, with a soft, nocturnal black-
ness; their legs and forearms, emerging from snowy white robes, are like
fragments of another element, pieces of midnight—your eyes seem to
penetrate the outer surface, to gaze into their very depths. They walk
superbly—approaching you from a distance across the dusty fields like
the proud but courteous envoys of a great kingdom, attended by an obse-
quious camel or a herd of evil-eyed white goats.

In a hut near the camel market, our guide told us, it was possible to see the Belly Dance. Would we care to go there? We agreed, of course; for this, surely, would be the real thing, rank and hot from the bowels of Africa, and not to be compared with the miserable wriggling and posturing we'd seen already in Brussels, Paris and Berlin. Our guide opened the door in a high wicker fence and led us into what looked like a small chicken run. He clapped his hands, and a dozen girls came running across the street, laughing and stumbling, in their huge flowered skirts. We must choose three, the guide said. They stood giggling in a row: the ones who had not been chosen ran off immediately, very gay, not seeming in the least offended.

Then the bargaining began. *Trois cent? Deux cent cinquante?* No we said, ridiculous! We moved toward the door. The Negresses flung themselves against it, laughing riotously. *Cinquante*, we said. *Non, soixante! Non, non, cinquante! Soixante! Cinquante! Soixante! Non! Oui! Non!* But, already, they were scrambling out of their clothes. Stark naked, with their nozzle breasts which look as if they were made to unscrew, their drum bellies and absurd little legs, they suddenly appeared much younger, mere children. Facing each other, they started to clap hands, like children playing pat-a-cake, stamping the earth with their heels and chanting in high gay wailing voices. But hardly had they executed a dozen steps before one of them shouted: *Soixante!* and they all laughed, as if at a dirty, forbidden joke. The clapping and stamping continued: *Soixante!* More clapping and laughter. *Soixante! Cinquante!* we cried. *Non, soixante!* It was plain that none of them had the faintest notion how to do the Belly Dance, or, indeed, any kind of dance whatsoever. Getting tired of the shouting and stamping, they decided to try the effect of a little romance. They tried to persuade us to sit down on a couple of upturned buckets—with the air of sirens who invite you to relax upon a voluptuous divan littered with rose petals; we were so weak with laughing that we could no longer even speak. *Soixante?* they pleaded once more, but already they were losing interest— for bargaining, like dancing and love, was only another children's game. Quite suddenly, the game was over; they dived into their clothes, took our fifty-franc note, giggled and let us out.

COLOMBO: The shabby white buildings of an abandoned international exhibition. On the breakwater, an immense neon sign: "Ceylon for Good Tea." Groves of weary palm trees, like damp mops. The air is warm and stale.

The center of town is drab and clean and English, with macadams, red pillar boxes, traffic signals, gasoline stations and punctual buses. And the Singhalese officials, wearing their clipped mustaches and correct tropical drill suits, are marvelously disguised as British empire-builders. But the suburbs are gay and crowded—the superb, brittle torsos of slim laughing natives jostle aimlessly down ramshackle lanes of shops crammed with all the gaudy, eye-catching trash of the East. Beyond the town, the countryside—despite the banana groves, the rubber plantations, the turquoise or scarlet flash of outrageous blossoms—reminded us strangely of the Thames Valley. It was as if, in the night of some freak summer, Kew Gardens had broken loose, pouring its grosser vegetation over the southern counties, strangling England's trees and grasses, scaring her shy weak flowers into terrified obscurity. Here and there, exotic shrubs on the lawns of old manor houses or country rectories have joined the insurrection, established local revolutionary committees. Next morning, human beings look out of their foliage-darkened windows to find that their race dominance is over: the dictatorship of the plants is secure from Yarmouth to Torquay. Yes, in this country, blood is inferior to chlorophyll, and all men, white or brown, are slaves, working their lives away in the dank stench of an all-powerful vegetable kingdom.

One of our fellow passengers is a beautiful Parisian girl, traveling out to rejoin her husband, a planter in French Indo-China. This morning, as we reached the mouth of the river, and the pilot came on board with the mail, she had news that he was lying in a hospital, seriously injured in a motor smash, two days ago. We know that this is a lie: he is already dead. The news has spread all over the second class.

We are all watching her, covertly, as the ship enters Saïgon harbor. She must guess the truth already, from our glances and whispers; even her best friends avoid her, like an infectious disease. She paces the deck in an agony of impatience, her eyes brilliant with tears. Now and again she takes the binoculars from a passenger's hand, without a word of thanks or apology, and focuses them on the shore.

It is through her eyes that we take our first impression of the town. The huge brown kites don't care, they circle ceaselessly over the wide muddy river, swooping sometimes as if to snatch the round straw hats from the heads of coolies in the sampans. The crew of a British tramp steamer are chipping paint with brutally indifferent hammers. The crowd on the quay, waving and laughing, in their light clothes, shout gleefully to friends on board: "How's Mother?" "Well." "How's Father?" "Splendid." "How's the family?" "Oh, we're all fine." They are mocking her, with their youth and health and joy. And the stolid façade of the waterfront—the big white hotel, the feathery trees, the warehouses, the French advertisements: how she will loathe them from this day onward! Perhaps the single word "Job" will epitomize the whole sunlit scene—will afflict her with agony and nausea for the rest of her life.

Hong Kong harbor, in a chilly, drizzling fog. This might be Scotland, or the coast of Norway. Junks with patched, dragon-wing sails drift past, ancient and forlorn as wrecks fished from the bottom of the sea. A Japanese liner rests on her side in a rocky creek, beached by last autumn's record typhoon. The island towers up out of the mist, with Hong Kong at its foot—cruisers like watchdogs guarding the monumental banks, Queen Victoria's statue fixes China in a rigid stare; here, surely, is the ugliest city ever built upon the earth.

On the wharf, two bored coolies are holding a banner: "Welcome to the Islington Corinthians." The members of the Hong Kong football team are waiting to receive their opponents. But where will they disembark? First the gangway is placed here, then there, then a hundred yards further down; the banner follows it patiently, sagging in the middle. The football captain runs up and fusses and scolds; it is straightened, just in time. The team utters a dutiful cheer.

On this island, boiled shirts and banks, a cenotaph, soda fountains, American movies and English tea; over there, beyond the streaky ocher mountains, somewhere, a war. Not recovered, not even convalescent, we are routed out of our hospital into the uncomfortable, familiar world. After all, incredibly, we have arrived.

Harper's Bazaar, October 1938

The Sportsmen: A Parable

Long ago, on a certain tract of country, some men were out shooting. The country was pretty open, so that who secured the biggest bag depended mainly upon who was the best shot. Perhaps the standard of marksmanship was not very high:—the sportsmen were only the best shots from the village, who had come out for a bit of shooting in the slack season between harvest and ploughing. They were out to shoot duck, for they knew that no one in their senses would want to eat anything else; and their sporting instincts were not very English: it is hard enough to hit a duck at all, they would have argued, and if one is lucky enough to spot one sitting, so much the better.

A few hundred years passed, and men were still shooting over the same country. This had now become much overgrown, which was more favourable for some kinds of birds than the open country and less so for others: some new species had appeared, and some old ones died out. Another result of the growth of vegetation was that now some of the butts were much more advantageously placed than others, so that even a good shot, if he got a bad butt, might be unlucky. The sportsmen had changed too. Though most of them still shot duck to sell in the open market, the best shots had been hired by the village squire who preferred partridge, a

taste with which they were inclined to agree; in fact, it was they who had
first persuaded him to try one for a change. They still hadn't dared try
and sell him a grouse which, in their opinion, tasted even better, and
which they always took home with them when they were lucky enough to
hit one. The standard of marksmanship was high, as it well might be,
seeing that most of them did nothing else, and wouldn't have known what
to do with a sickle if they saw one.

They were proud of their job, and determined to keep up a high stan-
dard of skill and sportsmanship, so that those who took shots at sitting
birds were fined and regarded as outsiders.

Another few hundred years passed. The country had now become so
densely wooded that from most of the butts it was only possible to see a
tiny circle of sky immediately overhead, and the bags so small that both
the village and the squire had almost forgotten what birds tasted like, had
stopped sending out any more sportsmen, and were living on tinned food
sent down in vans from the city. Such sportsmen as there were, were now,
most of them, boys from rich homes who had run away because they did
not get on with their parents and were attracted by the idea of a wild life
in the woods, with an occasional eccentric who, even when he was in the
nursery, had a passion for playing with toy firearms. It was now so diffi-
cult to hit anything, that those who went on shooting at all, became very
fine shots indeed. And, as no one wanted any birds any more anyway, the
sportsmen had begun to feel that the only excitement in shooting lay in
the skill required. It had become a point of honour not to fire at a com-
mon bird or an easy target, even if they should see one. Each had his own
set of rules: one would only fire at birds a thousand feet up; another
neglected all but woodpeckers with white tails; a third always took aim
standing on his head. And how they quarrelled over the relative merits of
their different methods in the Sporting Quarterly.

Now about the time I am describing, a curious thing happened. Ru-
mours began to reach the village of a far country where the inhabitants
had cleared the land of timber, so that duck had once more become plen-
tiful and shooting parties were again in fashion. Stirred by the news,
some of the villagers formed a party and went out into the woods to fell
the trees, despite the threat of the squire to prosecute them if they did.
There they met the few remaining sportsmen and began to tell them what
they had heard; how, in that far country, he who brought home the big-
gest bag of duck was fêted by the village and handsomely rewarded.
When they heard this, the sportsmen were divided in their opinions.
Some said: "I would rather die than shoot such an ugly bird as a duck."
Others said: "The squire is my first cousin, and I am expecting a legacy
when he dies; I mustn't do anything that would offend him." And all
these retired in dudgeon to their butts. One, an older man and, perhaps,

the finest marksman of them all, stood for a long time in silence and then said: "I think you are right in what you say, and I wish you every success in your efforts to clear the country and encourage the duck to breed as they used to, but I must ask you to forgive me if I do not help you. For many years now I have been spending all my waking hours in the study of ea-gles. I do not know if there are any others who share my passion; I do not suppose that there will ever be many who feel as I do about these rare and beautiful birds; but for me, it is my vocation and my life. So I must ask you to excuse me." And having said this, he went his way.

Those who remained behind, asked the villagers what they should do, as they rarely saw any duck nowadays. The villagers replied that the first thing necessary was to fell the trees and clear away the undergrowth and they suggested that the sportsmen should lend a hand with this. A few thought this a reasonable suggestion, but the greater part were alarmed and offended, saying: "Me turn woodcutter. I am a sportsman." And in-deed, when one looked at them, one was inclined to feel that they were right. Most of them would have been very unskilful woodcutters. So they, too, retired to their butts. There, in the days that followed, they had plenty of time to reflect upon what had been said on all sides, and one or two began to keep an eye open for duck, thinking: "How surprised and impressed the village would be, if I were to stroll in one evening with a couple of fine duck over my shoulder." But watch as they might, they seldom saw a sign of one, and, even when they did, they were so accus-tomed to trick targets that they missed. This was very humiliating to crack shots such as they were. "Bah!", they said, "those villagers are a stupid lot: if they want duck, they shall have them"; and, putting their guns aside, they sat down to model duck out of clay and old newspapers, using to guide them some coloured plates which they had torn out of ornithologi-cal textbooks in their fathers' libraries.

When the models were finished and dry, they returned with them to the village, and said: "Look what we have shot." Some of the younger villagers who had never seen duck except in a museum were impressed, and praised the sportsmen highly for their skill; but the older and wiser among them fingered the models, and smelt them, and said: "These are not duck; they are only clay and old newspapers."

New Verse, Autumn 1938

[Message to the Chinese People]

BY W. H. AUDEN AND
CHRISTOPHER ISHERWOOD

During the recent crisis in Europe, it may well have seemed to you that the West had forgotten China. This is not true. In these tragic and difficult days through which we are living, we would like to tell you, the Chinese nation, that there are people in England, and not a few of them, who know that the struggle in which you are so heroically engaged, is an essential part of the struggle for Freedom and Justice which is going on in every country in the world. We realize that you are fighting, not only for China, but for us, and that the issue of the Sino-Japanese conflict cannot but have the most profound effect upon the peoples of America and Europe. We pledge ourselves to do all that lies in our power, little—we confess it with shame—though it may be, to assist China and to try to persuade those more influential and powerful than us to do the same.

During the earlier part of this year we spent four months travelling about your country and no words express our admiration of your courage and patience in the face of a well-armed and merciless enemy. In such a war victory will lie with those whose powers of endurance are greatest.

We pray, not only for your sake but also for our own, that, confident in the justice of your cause, you will never lose heart, however desperate the situation may appear, but fight on to that victorious conclusion which is the hope of every decent man and woman in this country.

The Far Eastern Magazine, April 1939

Men of Thought and Action

The Coming Victory of Democracy. By Thomas Mann.
Secker and Warburg. 2s. 6d.
Days of Hope. By André Malraux. Secker and Warburg. 7s. 6d.

To-day, when one cannot open a newspaper without reading of some new triumph of the anti-democratic Powers, it is only too easy to despair, and those who despair will always fail.

Here are two writers, one German and one French, who have not lost faith in democracy, and this fact alone would make their work important to us.

The Coming Victory of Democracy is the expanded text of a lecture he gave in America, and with it is printed the magnificent open letter to the Dean of Bonn University, written by Herr Mann when he was deprived of his doctor's degree.

The lecture is the best brief statement of what democracy means which I have read.

It is insufficient to define the democratic principle as the principle of majority rule and to translate democracy literally—all too literally— as government by the people, an expression of double meaning which could also signify mob rule, for that is more nearly the defini- tion of Fascism. . . . We must define democracy as that form of gov- ernment and society which is inspired above every other with the feeling and consciousness of the dignity of man.

In man nature becomes conscious . . . in him nature opens a door to the spiritual, questions, admires and judges itself. . . . To become conscious means to acquire conscience, means the knowledge of what is good and what is evil. . . . In humanity nature becomes responsible.

Humanity will no longer mean a tolerance that ensures every- thing—even the determination to destroy humanity. Face to face with fanaticism incarnate, a freedom which through sheer goodness and humane scepticism no longer believes in itself will be irrevocably lost. . . . Freedom must discover its virility.

Democracy must continue to develop the bourgeois revolution, not only politically but also economically. . . . One must desire as one de- sires a necessity that liberal democracy will develop into social democ- racy, from the economic as well as the spiritual point of view.

Days of Hope is about a country where "Freedom has discovered its viril- ity." Monsieur Malraux is not only one of the most distinguished French novelists, but was also in command of the International Air Force fighting for the Spanish Government, and this rare combination of the sensibility of the writer with the experience of the man of action has produced an epic which, in my opinion, is likely to emerge as one of the greatest books of our generation. To sensibility and experience one should also add faith. It is curious that the Great War produced no really outstanding novel. Perhaps one reason for this is because, in that war, no one had a clear idea of and belief in what they were really fighting for. Malraux and the Spaniards have, as it is this faith that binds all the different scenes and characters into an attractive whole.

Days of Hope is an epic rather than a novel in that it sets out to give a panoramic picture of the war as a whole, rather than a study of the development of a few individuals. Hundreds of characters appear, Anarchists, Communists, peasants, Fascists, and the scene shifts from Madrid to the Alcaza, from the Alcaza to Barcelona, from the execution-ground to the café.

If you want to know what it feels like to be bombed or to take part in a bombing raid, what people talk about during a civil war and how they behave, read this book. Dialogue and description are equally convincing, and from the opening scene in the telephone exchange at Madrid until the end, it is as exciting as a murder trial. Because it was written by an active fighter for the Spanish Government, you must not think that the Government is painted in sham snow white. Inefficiencies, cruelties, intrigues, the conflict between Anarchists and Communists, between those who want to *be* something and those who want to do something, are not glossed over, but through all the mess and muddle, the amazing courage and determination of the Spanish people shines out very clearly, so that if you choose to call it so, *Days of Hope* is propaganda—propaganda for the truth.

As an experiment I asked three leading Birmingham booksellers for this book, and not one had it in stock. This is a disgrace to us all. Do buy it, or insist on your library getting it at once, and persuade everyone you know to read it.

The Town Crier (Birmingham), 14 October 1938

Ironworks and University

Living. By Henry Green. Dent. 2s. 6d.
Goldworthy Lowes Dickinson. By E. M. Forster. Arnold. 10s. 6d.

Neither of these books is new—one is five, the other nine years old—but both deserve to be read much more widely than they are.

There was an iron foundry in Tysely. The son of the owner, after being educated at Eton and Oxford, went into the works as an employee to learn the business. *Living* was the fruit of that experience. In this novel, Mr Green has attempted to give a cross section of life in all the classes connected with the factory, from the big employer down through the works manager and the skilled workers to the unskilled hands; their hopes, their loves, their failures.

This involves him in the difficult problem of how to keep four or five threads of story running simultaneously and how to make them harmonise into a single pattern. This Mr Green has solved with great skill and originality. The book is written in a series of paragraphs like cinema "shots", which are then "cut" so that one sets off and illuminates the next, and the total effect is of a continuous, smooth-running narrative, and not, as this kind of book is apt to be, a rag-bag of rapportage. Further, the style of writing is also unusual.

> Just then in iron foundry shop Craigan looked up from big cylinder he was making and beckoned to boy who was one of the boys making cores. This one came up. Craigan said how he would like piece of cake, he said it was easier for boys in foundries now than when he started. Boy said it may have been but all the same wouldn't have been a misery like Craigan in any iron foundry, not to touch him, not since they started. Mr Craigan said that in his young days you could never have said that to a moulder when you were core boy.

The use of reported speech as in the later George Moore, and the omission of the definite article as in Anglo-Saxon poetry, may seem affected and tiresome at first, but as one reads on, one begins to feel that it is absolutely right for this subject.

I should be very interested to know if *Living* as a picture of factory life in Birmingham is as convincing to a factory worker as it is to an outsider.

In *Goldsworthy Lowes Dickinson*, we move from a Birmingham foundry to a Cambridge college, and a don who "was never shipwrecked or in peril, was seldom in great bodily pain, never starved or penniless, never confronted an angry mob nor went to prison for his opinions, nor sat on the bench as a magistrate, nor held any important administrative post, was never married, never faced with the problems of parenthood, had no trouble with housekeeping or servants."

Mr Forster imagines Mephistopheles asking him why he has written a biography of his friend. Was he a great writer? No. Was he an important thinker? Did he accomplish anything material for humanity? No. He worked for the League of Nations and we all know what has happened to that body. All that he can offer in reply are the words of Dickinson's bedmaker: "He was the best man who ever lived", but when one has finished the book, Mr Forster makes us feel that that reply is sufficient.

It is the portrait of a Liberal who believed in reason and love and personal relationships, but learnt from experience not to be too optimistic about their power; of a highbrow who began with an interest in mysticism and a hatred of crowds, who came to realise the necessity of Socialism and political action, and if the "democracy where everyone is an aristocrat" in which he believed seems to us at the present moment a dream of the very distant future, it is we and not Lowes Dickinson who need to be ashamed.

This memoir is written with all the humanity, wit, affection and skill of presentation which one expects from our greatest living novelist.

But these amenities lay at the edge of his life. Its centre was covered with rubbish and worry. And at its opposite edge lay an imbecile boy whom he sometimes kicked in order to ingratiate himself with his schoolfellows. He made no special confession to his parents about this; it was not a crime like the potatoes, nevertheless it haunted him.

He is said to be the only man who could make a Corona type upside down. He struck the keys rapidly and violently, thinking of what he thought and not of what he did, with the result that he doubled lines, halved them, threw capitals in the air, buried numerals in the earth, broke out into orgies of ? ? ? ? or % % % %, and hammered his ribbon to shreds. George becomes "Geroge", Gerald "Gerlad", perhaps "perhpas", and there are even happier transformations, such as husband into "humsband" and soul into "soup".

Goldsworthy Lowes Dickinson is one of Mr Forster's best books and one of the few really distinguished modern biographies.

The Culture of Cities. By Lewis Mumford. Secker & Warburg. 21s.

The Culture of Cities deals with the second necessity mentioned in *The Coming Victory of Democracy*, by Herr Mann, "The development of liberal democracy into social democracy."

Mr Mumford, with the aid of many excellent illustrations, traces the development of the city from its origin as a fort, through the medieval city centred on the Cathedral and the baroque city centred on the palace of the authoritarian prince, to the Coketown of the industrial revolution, and finally to the crazy "megalopolis" of to-day which is not even mechanically efficient, and where a balanced and social life is impossible and man is helpless inside the prison he has made. Helpless, that is, unless he has the knowledge and the technique which he needs to plan a style of living. Mr Mumford calls it the Biotechnic order, which is the servant and not the master of his physical and spiritual needs. Mr Mumford points out that the greatest obstacles to such necessities as decentralisation and regional planning are not technical—cheap electrical power has largely overcome that—but human failings of pride and greed; the pride, for instance, that demands enormous permanent buildings as symbols of national greatness or frontiers based on fake conceptions of race in defiance of the demands of the physical earth; and greed that supports centralisation because it means high ground rents.

But though Mr Mumford does not spare human folly, *The Culture of Cities* is an optimistic book. It shows us clearly that if we have the will, we already have the knowledge and the power to make towns like Birmingham, by which at present we are disgraced before the cats and dogs, only a memory of a necessary past.

Democracies do not ask less of their citizens than the totalitarian states; they ask a great deal more, but it has to be given of their own free-will. They ask every one of us to become rational and active, in the words of Bergson:

To act as men of thought,
To think as men of action.

The Town Crier (Birmingham), 21 October 1938

Democracy's Reply to the Challenge of Dictators

If we are democrats, we must think about all that democracy involves. If you do not believe in it, then it is no use pretending that you are democrats—you had better join the other side.

We are seeing the end of Liberal Democracy, and there are two alternatives to it. One of them is Fascism; the other is something which I shall call Social Democracy. I am not very optimistic about the future of Social Democracy in this country during the next twenty years at least; yet I consider the end of Liberal Democracy a good thing.

Social Democracy and Liberal Democracy have certain things in common:

(1) All democracy, I believe, rests first and foremost on one simple thing—that you believe environment to be more important than heredity. If you do not believe that—and there are many people who do not—you cannot possibly believe in democracy. Man is the only animal who has been able to continue evolution after biological development is finished. He is the only animal capable of using his intelligence and making choices; the only animal whose society can develop from one form into another.

(2) The second belief of democrats is that children differ from their parents; that, while at any given moment people are not equal in talent and ability, the pattern of talent will be altered in the next generation. People who believe that the poor are poor because they are stupid, and that they will have stupid children, will not adopt a democratic form of government.

(3) Democracy also surely believes that moral good, the possibility of moral choice, is not only for the few favoured people, but for the vast majority of ordinary decent men and women. I should like to make a distinction between natural good and moral good. Animals are naturally good in that in what they do they cannot do wrong. When

people fall into a habit, it means that they can make no choice; and when it is a good habit the result is natural good behaviour. A great many people believe that those who are capable of making a moral choice are few, and that the rest of mankind must be disciplined by propaganda and coercion of one kind or another so that they shall become good. This is not the democratic point of view.

These are the three essential theories of democracy. To them the Liberal Democrats added certain other things:

(a) They said that man is born free, that the child is always by nature good and is made bad by society.
(b) One line of Liberalism asserted that man is completely rational and you only have to explain changes to him and he will consider them without being affected by personal and social influences or interests.
(c) Again, Liberal Democracy states that all social coercion is bad. Man is an individual, and the important factor in making society is the individual. To produce the right kind of individual is the task of education. If only I can make my pupils nice, kind, honest people, then, when they come out into the world, the world will be changed in a generation.

Liberal Democracy has failed, and failed completely. None of us who have anything to do with education, I think, can help feeling that we have had a certain success in giving people educational training and enabling them to do certain kinds of tricks and certain kinds of jobs, but that so far as making citizens or influencing the world in any way is concerned we have utterly failed. The reason is that it is the form of society into which children go when they leave school that dictates very largely the kind of persons they are to become. Take three stockbrokers—one from a Secondary School, one from Eton and one from Dartington: I doubt very much whether in 15 years' time you will be able to tell one from the other.

Moreover, because Liberal Democracy spoke of freedom but ignored justice, its results have been social inequality, class war, lack of social conscience, lack of social cohesion, lack of sociality. Nobody feels that they are needed by society. The strongest feeling of the kind and tender is, "Well, I can't do anything about it. I must just be a decent chap, and the tough can go their own way." Liberal Democracy ignored economic methods and we are now reaping the harvest.

Fascism—make no mistake about it—owes its success to the fact that it appeals to the sense of justice of good people. It induces them to swallow something that purports to be real justice. Fascism is the most important problem of the countries of the world to-day. It does not consist simply of one or two men, so that, if Hitler were bumped off, it would disappear. The danger of Fascism arises because Liberal Democracy, by failing to mete out justice in society, has made people feel that freedom is not worth while. Fascism has attacked one by one every tenet of Democracy. It says that heredity is far more important than environment. It says that men are born naturally bad; that the majority, the masses, are incapable of moral choice. Hitler refers in *Mein Kampf* to the "rabbit hearts" of the masses. There are a few who do know the good, and it is their job to rule society and compel the majority of the masses to be naturally good. Fascists, again, say that there is here and now the perfect form of society which will last for ever. The individual can only serve the will of society; he has no rights of his own. Intelligence is of very little importance in comparison with loyalty. What is important is, not that society should be creative, but that it should be unified.

Unless Social Democracy can answer Fascism, Fascism will succeed, and will deserve to succeed. The first thing that Social Democracy must say is that man is not born free or good. What he becomes depends on the kind of society in which he lives. Children are without any kind of social life at all. Take a baby. It is a bundle of unconditioned reflexes, and it only becomes rational when it learns to talk and think through the social media. If a society is based on certain values of profit-making, nothing you can do will prevent the people who live in that society from adopting these values, because the power of the individual is very small. You will say that there is no perfect form of society, but you will not say, "All societies are pretty bad; let me withdraw myself and lead my own life." You will say that some forms of society are better than others and will fight to establish better forms. You will say that the only possible solution to the problem of freedom and unity is social justice, that so long as society is unequal and unjust, democracy, whatever your political form, is a sham. Your new society will expect and demand the right to control the interests of groups which threaten to upset the justice of society, and it will take steps to check those who are now maintaining that injustice.

The effect of such a view on education and on teachers must first be, I think, to make us extremely humble, sceptical and cynical about what we are doing at the moment, because our education is not so far bringing people towards a democratic state. On the contrary, it is encouraging them to become more assertive and less interested in the mass of the people; there is a scramble to get to the top, because people must escape as far as they can from economic pressure. It is no good having a nice progressive school which is like a good society, when your children are going out into a world where economic pressure will immediately attack them. They will not be strong enough to withstand it, and their reaction can only be either to accept it or to refuse to have anything to do with social action.

In the second place, teachers will realise that their first job now is to take part in political action, for as long as society is unequal as it is, the whole idea of democratic education is a sham. Unless all the members of a community are educated to the point where they can make a rational choice, democracy is a sham. The combination of social inequality with democratic forms of government means either mob rule or dictator rule by those who know best how to handle and inflame the mob. The primary demand of all educationists must be for equality of educational opportunity; otherwise, the first law of democracy—that environment should master heredity—is violated.

I know that this will mean that probably, if you do take part in political activity, half of you will lose your jobs. But until teachers are prepared to fight for the kind of society in which the work they do can have real effect, education is not worth considering.

I think teachers are going to be much more interested in adult education and less in child education, because democracy does not imagine that people are finished when they are 14, 18, 21, or whatever age we turn them out, and that after that they have nothing to do but to carry out their jobs. Naturally the Fascist States are extremely interested in child education, because they do not want people to develop on their own. To them, if the child can receive its ideas by the time it is 12, then the chief work is done, apart from vocational training. In a Fascist State the only general education required of the average citizen is military. But in a Social Democracy education has a double task: to train for a particular vocation, and to equip all citizens for an intelligent political life.

Frankly I am not very optimistic about what the bulk of teachers in this country are likely to do. Enormous pressure will be brought—is, as you know, already being brought—to bear on the majority of teachers who work in our state schools to confine their activities to the classroom. There is a temptation for those who work in the more favoured schools, particularly if they are interested in their actual job, to feel that if they can concentrate on their own children in the school, that is the most that can be expected of them. Well, it is not. Nothing will do short of a determination by everybody who is interested and who believes that democracy is a kind of society worth having, to delay no longer in attacking the central problem. And that problem is not one of educational technique; it is primarily a problem of freedom, a problem of social justice.

The New Era in Home and School, January 1939

Nonsense Poetry

The Collected Verse of Lewis Carroll. Macmillan. 8s. 6d.
The Lear Omnibus. Nelson. 3s. 6d.

Everyone who enjoys life, enjoys nonsense or games of thought, just as they enjoy action games like football. In the earliest kind of drama, the mummer's play, characters play with words in phrases like:

I knocked at the maid and the door fell out,

just as they do in the comic film of to-day:

You've sunk so far you could walk under a duck.

The logic of our conscious everyday life, the values of our society, are never so completely satisfying that we do not feel from time to time the need to laugh at and to escape from them, and the less satisfactory they are, the more strongly we shall feel this need. Thus to-day, nonsense, the nonsense, for instance, of Donald Duck or Pop-eye or the limerick, is the only universal art, appealing alike to adults and children, highbrows and lowbrows, Right and Left, Mr Chamberlain (?) and the readers of the *Town Crier.*

It is not an accident that Lewis Carroll and Edward Lear, the two great English masters of nonsense, were both Victorians, for it was in the Victorian age that the atomisation of society into solitary individuals, which is one of the effects of laissez-faire capitalism, first began to be felt actively.

Both came from the upper middle class—Lear gave drawing lessons to Queen Victoria, Carroll was a University don—for it is in that class that social isolation is first felt, as the living conditions of the workers give them more of a community life, and less leisure for reflection. And both were bachelors who were intensely interested in children and family life. When society gets too big and too unjust, it is to the family that even adults must turn for emotional security, and it is the child who seems to them to inhabit a Golden Age before the divisions of sex and class. (Similarly the physically ill seem beyond them. Hence, perhaps, the interest of uneasy capitalists in Medicine.)

The difference between Carroll and Lear may be roughly summed up by saying that one is classical and the other romantic.

Carroll is happier and drier: he accepts the everyday world emotionally but his intelligence finds its pretensions a little absurd, and enjoys suggesting alternative universes. The same interests in logic and mathematics which occupied him in his university career also dominate *Wonderland.*

> They told me you had been to her
> And mentioned me to him
> She gave me a good character
> But said I could not swim.

It is a real looking-glass world, the reversed image of Oxford.

Lear, on the other hand, is the romantic rebel, who finds the real world unbearable; his poems are homesick of a lost happiness.

> Calico Jam
> The little fish swam
> Over the syllabub sea,
> He took off his hat
> To the sole and the sprat
> And the Willaby-wat—
> But he never came back
> He never came back
> He never came back
> He never came back to me.

Compare, for example, their methods of inventing words. Carroll's portmanteau words like "fruminous" (fuming-furious) are intellectual abstractions. Lear's inventions, mostly proper names (Chankley Bore) are governed, like Milton's, by the emotional value of the sound.

Psychologists, of course, have explained their work in terms of sexual frustration; but such private troubles, even if true, are only part of a much wider and more public search for a democratic life, a life of love and affection among ordinary happy people, a life which capitalism, specialisation, and over-academic education made and are still making extremely difficult. Further, if we are Socialists, we must not be prigs and talk contemptuously of escape art. For they succeeded; their work *can* be enjoyed by everybody, it *is* democratic; and it is only Fascists who imagine that they can create a society so perfect that no one will ever want to criticise or escape from it.

The Town Crier (Birmingham), 28 October 1938

Introduction to *Poems of Freedom,*
edited by John Mulgan

Great claims have been made for poets as a social force: they have been called the critics of life, the trumpets that sing men to battle, the unacknowledged legislators of the world. On the other hand they have been accused of being introverted neurotics who find in infantile word-play an escape from the serious duties of adult life, the irresponsible fiddlers deserting a Rome in flames. Both opinions are bosh, but the second is the inevitable reaction from the first. Those who go to poetry expecting to find a complete guide to religion, or morals, or political action, will very soon be disillusioned and condemn poets, though what they are really condemning is their own attitude towards poetry.

Because the medium of poetry is language, the medium in which all social activities are conducted, demands are made on it which it would never occur to people to make on the other arts like painting or music (although, in fact, music is probably a far more effective stimulus to action).

Poets are rarely and only incidentally priests or philosophers or party agitators. They are people with a particular interest and skill in handling words in a particular kind of way which is extremely difficult to describe and extremely easy to recognise. Apart from that, they are fairly ordinary men and women, neither better nor worse, with the same limitations of nationality and class, with the same feelings and thoughts and prejudices. Some have been rich, some have been poor, some intelligent, others stupid.*

Because language is communicable, what they do for society is much the same as what they do for themselves. They do not invent new thoughts or feelings, but out of their skill with words, they crystallise and define with greater precision thoughts and feelings which are generally present in their class and their age. To adapt the saying of the old lady: "We know what we think when we see what they say."

Take for example Timon's speech:

> Why this
> Will lug your priests and servants from your sides,
> Pluck stout men's pillows from below their head:
> This yellow slave

---

* It is true, however, that during the last hundred years, artists have tended to become a social class of their own, in parallel with the general trend to specialisation, or class division, and social organisation, a tendency which has had serious consequences for both the artist and the public, but that is not a question which I wish to raise over this anthology.

> Will knit and break religions; bless the accurs'd;
> Make the hoar leprosy ador'd; place thieves,
> And give them title, knee and approbation
> With senators on the bench;—this is it
> That makes the wappen'd widow wed again.

Nothing is said here that either we or Shakespeare's contemporaries did not already know, but our awareness of the power of money is extended and intensified.

Reading this anthology will teach no one how to run a state or raise a revolution; it will not even, I think, tell them what freedom is. But it is a record of what people in many different social positions, from a peer like Lord Byron to a poor priest like Langland, and in many different Englands, from Wat Tyler's to Stephen Spender's, have noticed and felt about oppression, and so also it is a record of what we still feel. The details of our circumstances of injustice change, so does our knowledge of what is unjust and how best to remedy it, but our feelings change little which is why it is possible still to read poems written by those who are now dead.

> Avenge, O Lord, thy slaughtered saints, whose bones
> Lie scattered on the Alpine mountains cold

was what Milton felt about the Albigensians, but it is equally well what we feel about the Basques, and

> I can't take up my musket and fight them now, no mo!
> But I'm not going to love 'em and that is certain sho!
> And I don't want no pardon for what I was or am,
> I won't be reconstructed and I don't give a damn

will remain a perfect expression of dislike of pompous authority, long after the American Civil War has been forgotten.

The primary function of poetry, as of all the arts, is to make us more aware of ourselves and the world around us. I do not know if such increased awareness makes us more moral or more efficient; I hope not.

I think it makes us more human, and I am quite certain it makes us more difficult to deceive, which is why, perhaps, all totalitarian theories of the State, from Plato's downwards, have deeply mistrusted the arts. They notice and say too much, and the neighbours start talking:

> There's many a beast, then, in a populous city
> And many a civil monster.

Poems of Freedom, edited by John Mulgan, 1938

Foreword to *Poet Venturers:*
A Collection of Poems Written by Bristol School Boys and Girls

I was most interested to hear of this effort on the part of the School boys and girls in Bristol to use their own original work in order to raise money to alleviate the distress which Japanese aggression has caused in China.

Democracy cannot be genuine unless each of us, in his or her sphere, is prepared to serve it with heart and head; at the same time Democracy cannot demand such service; it has to be given of our own free will. But unless we do so give it Democracy is a sham and soon supplanted by forms of Government which demand social responsibility at the expense of freedom. A book of this kind is a hopeful sign that the youth of this country is beginning to realise that it must earn the right to be free.

I, therefore, recommend it to the public for the sake of the poems themselves and for the practical expression of sympathy for their fellow human beings shown by these young people in Bristol.

I hope the booklet will interest many and that, as a result of the sales, a considerable sum will be sent to the Fund for Chinese Medical Aid.

Saturday,　　　　　　　　　　　　　　*13, Court Oak Road,*
October 29th, 1938.　　　　　　　　　*Harborne, Birmingham.*

Poet Venturers, 1938

"The Noble Savage"

Patterns of Culture. By Dr Ruth Benedict. Routledge. 10s. 6d.

I want this week to recommend a book which is not only fascinating to read for itself, but which also has, I think, important implications for any of us who are concerned about the form and future of our own society.

One of the main differences between the Victorians and ourselves is that we have one more science, the science of anthropology, which has modified profoundly our conception of progress.

Before our time, social theorists could assume that there was one culture, one civilisation, the civilisation of Europe, the only one they knew; all other people were savages. For the same reason, there was only one kind of civilised mind, the European, towards which the uneducated and backward portions of the race must inevitably evolve.

The individual inside a culture is always inclined to believe that the latter is the product of individual free will, that he and his neighbours make their society rather than that they are made by it. It is only when he is able to compare it with completely different kinds of social organisation, and to see how different in another culture are its bearers, in their religious beliefs, their ideas of right and wrong, their personal conduct, etc., that he begins to realise the immense power of a cultural pattern to mould the personal characters of individuals.

That is one of the three great contributions to social theory; the other two are the exploding of two fallacies, the fallacy of the Noble Savage, and the fallacy of the Base Savage. Rousseau and other eighteenth century writers who realised some of the shortcomings of their own culture, were able to posit a primitive being unwarped by social pressure, the pristine and good individual. But we now know that all so-called primitive people have extremely complicated and conservative social organisations. Man is not born good or free.

On the other hand, features like cannibalism, polygamy, or tribal war which at one time seemed to be proofs that primitive man was a cruel, ruthless beast, who was slowly tamed by civilisation, are now known to be themselves the products of highly complex civilisations, ritual behaviour patterns which must have appeared quite late in human history.

> Work upward, working out the beast
> And let the ape and tiger die

however admirable in sentiment, has nothing to do with historical fact.

Dr Benedict's book is an account of three different cultures, that of the North-West American Indian, that of the Pueblo Mexican, and that of the Dolu Islander.

The first is a culture organised round war and the military virtues of courage and virility, and might well appeal to our more progressive Nazis. The second is the ideal world of the Peace Pledge Union, a gentle agricultural and artistic society, where people dislike suffering, that it is not done to weep when anyone dies. And Dolu Island is like an asylum for paranoiacs. The one thing there that is a sure sign of not coming out of the top drawer is a willingness to help one's neighbour.

Now the physical differences between these three peoples as between any human beings are very slight. Man finished his biological development long ago. Yet the vast majority of individuals, in each society, accept its ways and values as normal and right and adapt themselves to them, though all cultures make some attempt to find a social niche for those who do not quite fit in; i.e. if you are a North-Western American Indian, and do not like fighting, you can cultivate hysteria and become a respected Shaman.

These three cultures arc instinctive growths; our own is rapidly becoming a conscious one, but we can learn from studying them that if we desire certain values and behaviour, we must create the social patterns which encourage these values and discourage their opposites. The Pueblo Mexicans, who by our standards seem the most desirable, fail because they are so custom-bound that they vegetate, they are no longer a growing, creative society, and though we can learn from them, we have to discover for ourselves how to combine creativeness with gentleness. And from the scientific study of other cultures we must proceed to our own. The Lynds in their study of Middletown America, and Mr Tom Harrisson and the Mass Observers in their study of Worktown England, are beginning to show us what are the real values which our culture promotes, and it cannot be said that so far the truths are particularly cheering.

The Town Crier (Birmingham), 4 November 1938

A New Short Story Writer

Something Wrong. By James Stern. Secker & Warburg. 7s. 6d.

Publishers always tell you that volumes of short stories do not pay; those who read them prefer to find them in magazines and to forget them.

The vast majority of short stories are anecdotes, the every-day incident with the surprising twist at the end, the carefully prepared after-dinner tale. If they are well enough done you catch the inflections and gestures of the expert raconteur who is always being asked out to dinner. They bring quick profits in money and success, for they are easy and amusing to read—once. Maugham is the best living practitioner of this genre. But they do not linger in the memory. They all seem to be told by the same kind of person, the old, old, old man of the world.

On the other hand, if the anecdote is not memorable, neither is the potted novel. One must not feel that if the author had taken more time and trouble, the story could be five times as long. There must be no unsolved or undeveloped situations. For this reason, the kind of plot or idea which suits a novel rarely makes a good short story. The genuine short story writer inhabits another world, a world which wobbles uncertainly between the world of the poem and the world of the novel proper.

As Elizabeth Bowen says:

Peaks of common experience soar past an altitude line into poetry. There is also a level immediately below this in which life is being more and more constantly lived, at which custom crystallises, from which a fairly wide view is at command. This level the short story is likely to make its own.

More particularised then than the poem, more generalised than the novel.

D. H. Lawrence was a master of such a field of experience (and more successful, in my opinion, as a short story writer than as a novelist), but there have been others—Katherine Mansfield, Elizabeth Bowen, Stephen Spender (in *The Burning Cactus*), and now there is Mr Stern.

Something Wrong is a cycle of stories about the experiences of children and adolescents (childhood is usually a better field for the short story than it is for the novel), about the terror and ecstasies, the jealousies and unconscious cruelty of the immature, and about the shadow, now tragic, now horrible, now comic of the adult parental world.

Parents are inclined to regard their children as dream extensions of their personality; the strong-willed child reacts to this by doing the opposite of what is expected of him, often at great damage to himself; while the sensitive child is tortured only too often by the feeling that he is unworthy of his father or mother. "The Broken Leg" is a terrifying study of this common situation.

"Travellers' Tears", perhaps the finest story in the book, is a description of the sudden awakening of a twelve-year-old American boy to a consciousness of beauty and love, an experience which happens to us all but which few can remember clearly. As in a poem, the properties of the story like the South Sea island night and the boy's American accent are determined by the dominating emotion, instead of being determined by the action, as they would have to be in a novel.

But to illustrate Mr Stern's method of approach, let us take "The Holiday". The subject is really "giggling". The chief characters are a colonel, his wife, and their three children, the oldest already grown up. Colonel Moon is a stupid, kindly bore; his wife has a cruel streak which she rationalises as discipline. The family are staying by the seaside, and the children are coming to realise that their parents are imperfect and funny, instead of perfect and alarming.

> Then, as though until that moment she had completely forgotten her husband's existence, Molly Moon said suddenly: "Heavens! Where's Dermott?"
>
> Paul, who was lying quite near his father, started to giggle. "Under the table," he said, and burst out laughing.
>
> On hearing this, Walter was the first to explode. Cake-crumbs shot from his mouth and spattered the cloth. One crumb caught little Billy between the eyes and there was a renewed outbreak of screams and laughter when that child started to yell. . . .

. . . Molly rushed at her son and grabbed him by the collar.

"Go straight back to the car and stay there till we come," she shouted, smacking him on the head. "And you'll go straight to bed when we get home," she added as a parting thrust.

"And as for you, Paul, you jolly well ought to be ashamed of yourself."

"I?" said Paul, turning in surprise. "What have I done now?"

"You know quite well," said his mother, "making that ridiculous remark about daddy being under the table. You knew it would make Walter laugh."

"Yes," said Paul, smiling to himself, "that was precisely why I did make it. We don't laugh enough."

I recommend Mr Stern as one of the most moving and original short story writers who has appeared for a long time.

The Town Crier (Birmingham), 18 November 1938

The Teaching of English

There is a fundamental difference between education in a democracy and education in a totalitarian state. General education in the latter means military service plus political belief rather than political understanding, and the real work of the teacher is limited to vocational training. In a democracy, on the other hand, where every citizen is expected to be able to take part in political life (using "political" in its widest sense), general rather than vocational education is the basis of school life, and the basis of general education is training in the use of one's own language.

The "talk" of a democracy is often contrasted unfavourably with the "action" of a dictatorship. If the democracies are to rebut this charge, they must be able to show that this talk can be a real and indispensable aid to wise and just action, instead of being, as in practice it only too often is, a device to prevent anything practical being done.

Talk can never be anything but futile unless both speaker and listener really understand what is being said, and one has only to open a newspaper or popular magazine, or listen to a sermon or a political speech, to realise that such understanding is extremely rare. Language and understanding are alike vague, and as long as this is the case, talk will remain a hindrance to right action rather than a help.

A great part of the blame for this must be laid on the teachers of English in our schools, and, in the case of the upper class schools, on the teachers of classics. The latter, for example, have encouraged, in the translation into English from Latin and Greek, the use of a literary abstract refined language utterly remote from the every-day spoken tongue of the translator. But it is of the teaching of English that I wish to speak, for that is of importance in every class of school.

Up to the age of nine or ten, until, that is, he has learnt to talk or read and write, the child's training in language is determined, more or less, by its practical necessity of making its every-day wants known to others. In a modern industrial community, reading and writing are almost as necessary as talking, and are learnt relatively easily and efficiently. But only a small percentage of the population advance beyond this stage of elementary understanding.

They may learn a lot more words and some more tricks from their child, but their real understanding of their own language grows very little.

I am inclined to think that this is largely due to the domination of English teaching by the teaching of English literature, the learning about and imposed appreciation of great books which, after all, have mostly have been written by adults about adults for adults.

This kind of teaching is really vocational training for English teachers; it fits the pupil for nothing else, except, perhaps, for becoming a literary critic. Its result is to make the livelier children feel that literature is "bunk", and most of the rest to fake their feelings and conceal their bewilderment—the evidence given by Dr I. A. Richards in *Principles of Literary Criticism* and by Mr Stephen Potter in *The Muse in Chains* is damning and unanswerable. It does not teach them to become creative writers; still less does it train them in their every-day business and personal life to express their thoughts and feelings accurately and honestly. And it is precisely such honesty and accuracy in the ordinary man and woman that democracy requires. We must learn to know and to speak the truth ourselves, and recognise when we are being deceived by others, and it is the duty of the English teacher to begin to train us when we are young. I recommend the following books to teachers as being the most useful that I know for this purpose:—

The London Book of English Prose. By Herbert Read and
Bonamy Dobrée. Eyre & Spottiswoode. 10s. 6d.

An anthology, not of purple passages, but of all the various kinds of prose needed by man, narrative, scientific, and emotive. It ranges from Lincoln's speech at Gettysburg to Army operations orders from Palestine, from a speech by Captain Ahab out of *Moby Dick* to Mr Justice Macnaughten summing up a sharepushing case, from Sir Thomas Malory to Arthur Eddington.

Dictionary of Modern English Usage. By H. W. Fowler.
Oxford University Press. 8s. 6d.

A well-known and excellent corrective both to journalistic sloppiness and to academic snobbery.

Common Sense Tests in English (age group 10–14). By R. O. Swann.
Junior Tests in English (age group 14–18). By R. O. Swann.
Methuen. 1s. 6d. each.

Books of exercises in grammar, description, narrative and common sense, based on the pupil's own experience. Invaluable to every teacher.

Clear Thinking. Jepson. Longmans. 3s. 6d.

Justifies its title.

The Teaching of English. Elton. Cambridge University Press. 2s. 6d.

Contains very useful exercises in vocabulary work.

Matter, Form and Style. O'Grady. Bell. 3s. 6d.

Provides excellent material for précis work and training in logical thinking.

The Town Crier (Birmingham), 25 November 1938

Morality in an Age of Change

Everything that lives is Holy.—Blake

I

(1) Goodness is easier to recognise than to define; only the greatest novelists can portray good people. For me, the least unsatisfactory description is to say that any thing or creature is good which is discharging its proper function, using its powers to the fullest extent permitted by its environment and its own nature—though we must remember that "nature" and "environment" are intellectual abstractions from a single, constantly changing reality. Thus, people are happy and good who have found their vocation: what vocations there are will depend upon the society within which they are practised.

There are two kinds of goodness, "natural" and "moral". An organism is naturally good when it has reached a state of equilibrium with its environment. All healthy animals and plants are naturally good in this sense. But any change toward a greater freedom of action is a morally good change. I think it permissible, for example, to speak of a favorable mutation as a morally good act. But moral good passes into natural good. A change is made and a new equilibrium stabilised. Below man, this happens once for each species; the change toward freedom is not repeated. In man, the evolution can be continued, each stage of moral freedom being superseded by a new one. For example, we frequently admire the "goodness" of illiterate peasants as compared with the "badness" of many townees. But this is a romantic confusion. The goodness we admire in the former is a natural, not a moral, goodness. Once, the life of the peasant represented the highest use of the powers of man, the farthest limit of his freedom of action. This is no longer true. The townee has a wider range of choice and fuller opportunities of using his power. He frequently chooses wrongly, and so becomes morally bad. We are right to condemn him for this, but to suggest that we should all return to the life of the peasant is to deny the possibility of moral progress. Worship of youth is another romantic pessimism of this kind.

(2) Similarly, there is natural and moral evil. Determined and unavoidable limits to freedom of choice and action, such as the necessity for destroying life in order to eat and live, climate, accidents, are natural evils. If, on the other hand, I, say, as the keeper of a boarding-house, knowing that vitamins are necessary to health, continue, for reasons of gain or laziness, to feed my guests on an insufficient diet, I commit moral evil. Just as moral good tends to pass into natural good, so, conversely, what was natural evil tends, with every advance in knowledge, to become moral evil.

(3) The history of life on this planet is the history of the ways in which life has gained control over and freedom within its environment. Organisms may either adapt themselves to a particular environment—e.g. the fleshy leaves of the cactus permit it to live in a desert—or develop the means to change their environment—e.g. organs of locomotion.

Below the human level, this progress has taken place through structural biological changes, depending on the luck of mutations or the chances of natural selection. Only man, with his conscious intelligence, has been able to continue his evolution after his biological development has finished. By studying the laws of physical nature, he has gained a large measure of control over them and in so far as he is able to understand the laws of his own nature and of the societies in which he lives, he approaches that state where what he wills may be done. "Freedom", as a famous definition has it, "is consciousness of necessity."

(4) The distinguishing mark of man as an animal is his plastic, unspecialised "foetalised" nature. All other animals develop more quickly

and petrify sooner. In other words, the dictatorship of heredity is weakest in man. He has the widest choice of environment, and, in return, changes in environment, either changes in nature or his social life, have the greatest effect on him.

(5) In contrast to his greatest rivals for biological supremacy, the insects, man has a specialised and concentrated central nervous system, and unspecialised peripheral organs, i.e. the stimuli he receives are collected and pooled in one organ. Intelligence and choice can only arise when more than one stimulus is presented at the same time in the same place.

(6) Man has always been a social animal living in communities. This falsifies any theories of Social Contract. The individual *in vacuo* is an intellectual abstraction. The individual is the product of social life; without it, he could be no more than a bundle of unconditioned reflexes. Men are born neither free nor good.

(7) Societies and cultures vary enormously. On the whole, Marx seems to me correct in his view that physical conditions and the forms of economic production have dictated the forms of communities: e.g. the geographical peculiarities of the Aegean peninsula produced small democratic city-states, while the civilisations based on river irrigation like Egypt and Mesopotamia were centralised autocratic empires.

(8) *But* we are each conscious of ourselves as a thinking, feeling, and willing whole, and this is the only whole of which we have direct knowledge. This experience conditions our thinking. I cannot see how other wholes, family, class, nation, etc., can be wholes to us except in a purely descriptive sense. We do not see a state, we see a number of individuals. Anthropological studies of different communities, such as Dr Benedict's work on primitive American cultures, or that of the Lynds on contemporary Middletown, have shown the enormous power of a given cultural form to determine the nature of the individuals who live under it. A given cultural pattern develops those traits of character and modes of behavior which it values, and suppresses those which it does not. But this does not warrant ascribing to a culture a superpersonality, conscious of its parts as I can be conscious of my hand or liver. A society consists of a certain number of individuals living in a particular way, in a particular place, at a particular time; nothing else.

(9) The distinction drawn by Locke between society and government is very important. Again, Marx seems to me correct in saying that sovereignty or government is not the result of a contract made by society as a whole, but has always been assumed by those people in society who owned the instruments of production.

Theories of Rights arise as a means to attack or justify a given social form, and are a sign of social strain. Burke, and later thinkers, who developed the idealist theory of the state, were correct in criticising the *a priori*

assumptions of Social Contract and in pointing out that society is a grow-
ing organism. But, by identifying society and government, they ignored
the power of the latter to interfere with the natural growth of the former,
and so were led to denying the right of societies to revolt against their
governments, and to the hypostatisation of the *status quo*.

(10) A favorite analogy for the state among idealist political thinkers is
with the human body. This analogy is false. The constitution of the cells
in the body is determined and fixed; nerve cells can only give rise to more
nerve cells, muscle cells to muscle cells, etc. But, in the transition from
parent to child, the whole pack of inherited genetic characters is shuffled.
The king's son may be a moron, the coal heaver's a mathematical genius.
The entire pattern of talents and abilities is altered at every generation.

(11) Another false analogy is with the animal kingdom. Observed from
the outside (how it appears to them no one knows), the individual animal
seems to be sacrificed to the continuance of the species. This observation
is used to deny the individual any rights against the state. But there is a
fundamental difference between man and all other animals in that an
animal which has reached maturity does not continue to evolve, but a man
does. As far as we can judge, the only standard in the animal world is
physical fitness, but in man a great many other factors are involved. What
has survival value can never be determined; man has survived as a species
through the efforts of individuals who at the time must often have
seemed to possess very little biological survival value.

(12) Man's advance in control over his environment is making it more
and more difficult for him, at least in the industrialised countries with a
high standard of living, like America or England, to lead a naturally good
life, and easier and easier to lead a morally bad one.

Let us suppose, for example, that it is sometimes good for mind and
body to take a walk. Before there were means of mechanical transport,
men walked because they could not do anything else; i.e. they committed
naturally good acts. Today, a man has to choose whether to use his car or
walk. It is possible for him, by using the car on an occasion when he ought
to walk, to commit a morally wrong act, and it is quite probable that he
will. It is despair at finding a solution to this problem which is responsible
for much of the success of Fascist blood-and-soil ideology.

II

(1) A society, then, is good insofar as

(*a*) it allows the widest possible range of choices to its members to
follow those vocations to which they are suited;

(*b*) it is constantly developing, and providing new vocations which
make a fuller demand upon their increasing powers.

The Greeks assumed that the life of intellectual contemplation was the only really "good" vocation. It has become very much clearer now that this is only true for certain people, and that there are a great many other vocations of equal value: human nature is richer and more varied than the Greeks thought.

(2) No society can be absolutely good. Utopias, whether like Aldous Huxley's Brave New World or Dante's Paradiso, because they are static, only portray states of natural evil or good. (Someone, I think it was Landor, said of the characters in the *Inferno*: "But they don't want to get out.") People committing acts in obedience to law or habit are not being moral. As voluntary action always turns, with repetition, into habit, morality is only possible in a world which is constantly changing and presenting a fresh series of choices. No society is absolutely good; but some are better than others.

(3) If we look at a community at any given moment, we see that it consists of good men and bad men, clever men and stupid men, sensitive and insensitive, law-abiding and lawless, rich and poor. Our politics, our view of what form our society and our government should take here and now, will depend on

(a) how far we think the bad is due to preventable causes;

(b) what, if we think the causes preventable, we find them to be.

If we take the extremely pessimistic view that evil is in no way preventable, our only course is the hermit's, to retire altogether from this wicked world. If we take a fairly pessimistic view, that badness is inherited (i.e. that goodness and badness are not determined by social relations), we shall try to establish an authoritarian regime of the good. If, on the other hand, we are fairly optimistic, believing that bad environment is the chief cause of badness in individuals, and that the environment can be changed, we shall tend toward a belief in some sort of democracy. Personally I am fairly optimistic, partly for reasons which I have tried to outline above, and partly because the practical results of those who have taken the more pessimistic view do not encourage me to believe that they are right.

(4) *Fairly* optimistic. In the history of man, there have been a few civilised individuals but no civilised community, not one, ever. Those who talk glibly of Our Great Civilisation, whether European, American, Chinese, or Russian, are doing their countries the greatest disservice. We are still barbarians. All advances in knowledge, from Galileo down to Freud or Marx, are, in the first impact, humiliating; they begin by showing us that we are not as free or as grand or as good as we thought; and it is only when we realise this that we can begin to study how to overcome our own weakness.

(5) What then are the factors which limit and hinder men from developing their powers and pursuing suitable vocations?

(*a*) Lack of material goods. Man is an animal and until his immediate material and economic needs are satisfied, he cannot develop further. In the past this has been a natural evil: methods of production and distribution were too primitive to guarantee a proper standard of life for everybody. It is doubtful whether this is any longer true; in which case, it is a moral and remediable evil. Under this head I include all questions of wages, food, housing, health, insurance, etc.

(*b*) Lack of education. Unless an individual is free to obtain the fullest education with which his society can provide him, he is being injured by society. This does not mean that everybody should have the *same* kind of education, though it does mean, I think, education of some kind or other, up to university age. Education in a democracy must have two aims. It must give vocational guidance and training; assist each individual to find out where his talents lie, and then help him to develop these to the full—this for some people might be completed by sixteen—and it must also provide a general education; develop the reason and the consciousness of every individual, whatever his job, to a point where he can for himself distinguish good from bad, and truth from falsehood— this requires a much longer educational period.

At present education is in a very primitive stage; we probably teach the wrong things to the wrong people at the wrong time. It is dominated, at least in England, by an academic tradition which, except for the specially gifted, only fits its pupils to be schoolteachers. It is possible that the time for specialisation (i.e. vocational training) should be in early adolescence, the twelve-to-sixteen group, and again in the latter half of the university period; but that the sixteen-to-twenty age group should have a general education.

(*c*) Lack of occupations which really demand the full exercise of the individual's powers. This seems to me a very difficult problem indeed. The vast majority of jobs in a modern community do people harm. Children admire gangsters more than they admire factory operatives because they sense that being a gangster makes more demands on the personality than being a factory operative and is therefore, for the individual, morally better. It isn't that the morally better jobs are necessarily better rewarded economically: for instance, my acquaintance with carpenters leads me to think carpentry a very good profession, and my acquaintance with stockbrokers to think stockbroking a very bad one. The only jobs known to me which seem worthy of respect, both from the point of view of the individual and society, are being a creative artist, some kind of highly skilled craftsman, a research scientist, a doctor, a teacher, or a farmer. This difficulty runs far deeper than our present knowledge or any immediate political change we can imagine, and is therefore still, to a certain extent, a natural rather than a moral evil, though it is obviously much aggravated by gross inequalities in economic reward, which could be remedied. I don't myself much like priggish phrases such as "the right use of leisure." I agree with Eric Gill that work is what one does to please oneself, leisure the time one has to serve the community. The most one can say is that we must never forget that most people are being degraded by the work they do, and that the possibilities of sharing the duller jobs through the whole community will have to be explored much more fully. Incidentally, there is reason for thinking that the routine manual and machine-minding jobs are better tolerated by those whose talents are for book learning than by those whose talents run in the direction of manual skill.

(*d*) Lack of suitable psychological conditions. People cannot grow unless they are happy and, even when their material needs have been satisfied, they still need many other things. They want to be liked and to like other people; to feel valuable, both in their own eyes and in the eyes of others; to feel free and to feel responsible; above all, not to feel lonely and isolated. The first great obstacle is the size of modern communities. By nature, man seems adapted to live in communities of a very moderate size; his economic life has compelled him to live in ever-enlarging ones. Many of the damaging effects of family life described by modern psychologists may be the result of our attempt to make the family group satisfy psychological needs which can only be satisfied by the community group. The family is based on inequality, the parent-child relationship; the community is, or should be, based on equality, the relationship of free citizens. We need both. Fortunately, recent technical advances, such as cheap electrical power, are making smaller social units more of a practical possibility than they seemed fifty years ago, and people with as divergent political views as the anarchists and Mr Ford are now agreed about the benefits of industrial decentralisation.

The second obstacle is social injustice and inequality. A man cannot be a happy member of a community if he feels that the community is treating him unjustly; the more complicated and impersonal economic life becomes, the truer this is. In a small factory where employer and employees know each other personally, i.e. where the conditions approximate to those of family life, the employees will accept without resentment a great deal more inequality than their fellows in a modern large-scale production plant.

III

(1) Society consists of a number of individual wills living in association. There is no such thing as a general will of society, except in so far as all these individual wills agree in desiring certain material things, e.g. food and clothes. It is also true, perhaps, that all desire happiness and good-

ness, but their conceptions of these may and do conflict with each other. Ideally, government is the means by which all the individual wills are assured complete freedom of moral choice and at the same time prevented from ever clashing. Such an ideal government, of course, does not and could not ever exist. It presupposes that every individual in society possesses equal power, and also that every individual takes part in the government.

(2) In practice, the majority is always ruled by a minority, a certain number of individuals who decide what a law shall be, and who command enough force to see that the majority obeys them. To do this, they must also command a varying degree of consent by the majority, though this consent need not be and never is complete. They must, for example, have the consent of the armed forces and the police, and they must either control the financial resources of society, or have the support of those who do.

(3) Democracy assumes, I think correctly, the right of every individual to revolt against his government by voting against it. It has not been as successful as its advocates hoped, firstly, because it failed to realise the pressure that the more powerful and better educated classes could bring to bear upon the less powerful and less educated in their decisions—it ignored the fact that in an economically unequal society votes may be equal but voters are not—and secondly, because it assumed, I think quite wrongly, that voters living in the same geographical area would have the same interests, again ignoring economic differences and the change from an agricultural to an industrial economy. I believe that representation should be by trade or profession. No one person has exactly the same interests as another, but I, say, as a writer in Birmingham, have more interests in common with other writers in Leeds or London than I have with my next-door neighbour who manufactures cheap jewelry. This failure of the geographical unit to correspond to a genuine political unit is one of the factors responsible for the rise of the party machine. We rarely elect a local man whom we know personally; we have to choose one out of two or three persons offered from above. This seems to me thoroughly unsatisfactory. I think one of our mistakes is that we do not have enough stages in election; a hundred thousand voters are reduced by a single act to one man who goes to Parliament. This must inevitably mean a large degree of dictatorship from above. A sane democracy would, I feel, choose its representatives by a series of electoral stages, each lower stage electing the one above it.

(4) Legislation is a form of coercion, of limiting freedom. Coercion is necessary because societies are not free communities; we do not choose the society into which we are born; we can attempt to change it, but we cannot leave it. Ideally, people should be free to know evil and to choose

the good, but the consequences of choosing evil are often to compel others to evil. The guiding principle of legislation in a democracy should be, not to make people good, but to prevent them making each other bad against their will. Thus we all agree that there should be laws against theft or murder, because no one chooses to be stolen from or murdered. But it is not always so simple. It is argued by laissez-faire economists that legislation concerning hours of work, wages, etc., violates the right of individual wills to bargain freely. But this presupposes that the bargaining powers of different wills are equal, and that each bargain is an individual act. Neither of these assumptions is true, and economic legislation is justified because they are not.

But there are other forms of legislation which are less justified. It is true that the individual will operating in a series of isolated acts is an abstraction—our present acts are the product of past acts and in their turn determine future ones—but I think the law has to behave as if this abstraction were a fact, otherwise there is no end to legislative interference. Take the case, for instance, of drink. If I become a drunkard, I may not only impair my own health, but also that of my children; and it can be argued, and often is, that the law should see that I do not become one by preventing me from purchasing alcohol. I think, however, that this is an unjustifiable extension of the law's function. Everything I do, the hour I go to bed, the literature I read, the temperature at which I take my bath, affects my character for good or bad and so, ultimately, the characters of those with whom I come in contact. If the legislator is once allowed to consider the distant effects of my acts, there is no reason why he should not decide everything for me. The law has to limit itself to considering the act in isolation: if the act directly violates the will of another, the law is justified in interfering; if only indirectly, it is not. Nearly all legislation on "moral" matters, such as drink, gambling, sexual behavior between adults, etc., seems to me bad.

(5) In theory, every individual has a right to his own conception of what form society ought to take and what form of government there should be and to exercise his will to realise it; on the other hand, everyone else has a right to reject his conception. In practice, this boils down to the right of different political parties to exist, parties representing the main divisions of interest in society. As the different sectional interests cannot form societies on their own—e.g. the employees cannot set up one state by themselves and the employers another—there is always coercion of the weaker by the stronger by propaganda, legislation, and sometimes physical violence; and the more evenly balanced the opposing forces are, the more violent that coercion is likely to become.

I do not see how in politics one can decide *a priori* what conduct is moral, or what degree of tolerance there should be. One can only decide which party in one's private judgement has the best view of what society ought to be, and to support it; and remember that, since all coercion is a moral evil, we should view with extreme suspicion those who welcome it. Thus I cannot see how a Socialist country could tolerate the existence of a Fascist party any more than a Fascist country could tolerate the existence of a Socialist party. I judge them differently because I think that the Socialists are right and the Fascists are wrong in their view of society. (It is always wrong in an absolute sense to kill, but all killing is not equally bad; it does matter who is killed.)

Intolerance is an evil and has evil consequences we can never accurately foresee and for which we shall always have to suffer; but there are occasions on which we must be prepared to accept the responsibility of our convictions. We must be as tolerant as we dare—only the future can judge whether we were tyrants or foolishly weak—and if we cannot dare very far, it is a serious criticism of ourselves and our age.

(6) But we do have to choose, every one of us. We have the misfortune or the good luck to be living in one of the great critical historical periods, when the whole structure of our society and its cultural and metaphysical values are undergoing a radical change. It has happened before, when the Roman Empire collapsed, and at the Reformation, and it may happen again in the future.

In periods of steady evolution, it is possible for the common man to pursue his private life without bothering his head very much over the principles and assumptions by which he lives, and to leave politics in the hands of professionals. But ours is not such an age. It is idle to lament that the world is becoming divided into hostile ideological camps; the division is a fact. No policy of isolation is possible. Democracy, liberty, justice, and reason are being seriously threatened and, in many parts of the world, destroyed. It is the duty of every one of us, not only to ourselves but to future generations of men, to have a clear understanding of what we mean when we use these words, to remember that while an idea can be absolutely bad, a person can never be, and to defend what we believe to be right, perhaps even at the cost of our lives and those of others.

The Nation, 24 December 1938; *I Believe:*
The Personal Philosophies of Certain Eminent
Men and Women of Our Time, 1939

George Gordon Byron

George Gordon Byron, one of the three English writers with a European reputation, the other two being Shakespeare and Oscar Wilde, was born in respectable lodgings in London on January 22nd, 1788, and died in Greece thirty-six years later, a major poet, a brilliant letter-writer, and a rich man, after a lifetime of unhappiness, travel, and love-affairs.

On neither side was the stock particularly stable. The Byrons were sensual, irresponsible, and charming. His uncle spent days fighting toy naval battles with his man-servant, and used to stage races of cockroaches up and down his own body. His father eloped with a married woman, and on her death, married the poet's mother for her money, which he soon spent.

The Gordons were passionate, unhappy, and cruel; many of them had ended on the scaffold. Catherine Gordon fell wildly in love with Captain Byron, a love that he did not return, and when their son was born, they had already separated, meeting only to have violent rows. Owing, probably, to the carelessness of the midwife, George Gordon Byron was born with a deformed foot.

At the age of ten he succeeded to the title and left Aberdeen Grammar School for the more select Harrow. Cambridge followed Harrow; and, soon after, came a Grand Tour of Portugal, Albania, and Greece, during which he wrote the first two cantos of *Childe Harold*, the publication of which in 1812 made him the literary lion of fashionable London.

At the beginning of 1815 he married an heiress, Miss Milbanke; but, as had been the case with Byron's own parents, the lady was more in love with him than he with her, and within little more than a year they had parted, and there was a scandal. Socially ruined, he left England for good to settle in Italy, where he wrote his greatest poem, *Don Juan*. In 1823 he was drawn into politics, into the struggle of the Greeks to win independence from Turkey. He left Italy to join the Greek Army at Missolonghi; three months later he caught a chill and died on April 19th, 1824. There is little doubt that the popular feeling aroused by his death was an important factor in determining the decision of the British Government to support the Greek cause.

The source of the poetic gift is a mystery: it is possible that, had Byron's foot been cured by modern surgery, or had his parents got on with each other, he would never have written a line. On the other hand, there are plenty of cripples and children of unhappy parents who write bad poetry or none. The study of a poet's biography or psychology or social status cannot explain why he writes well, but it can help us to understand why his poetry is of a particular kind, why he succeeds at one thing and fails at another: no study of Byron the man, for example, will ever explain the excellence of *A Vision of Judgment,* but it will partially explain why *A Vision of Judgment* is unlike the *Ode on the Intimations of Immortality in Early Childhood.*

Byron spent his early years in comparative poverty with a mother who alternately hit him and covered him with kisses, and a Calvinist nurse who spoke to him of Hell-fire and predestined damnation. Periodically there were visits from his father and parental rows. Unhappiness sharpens a child's wits, and he soon realised that his parents were violent and odd people, that his ancestors were violent and odd too, and that his deformity made him different from other children. Further, as usually happens when the parents are separated, he idealised the absent one, the father. Out of this background came the Byronic Hero: father made him handsome and dashing, mother made him passionate, nanny made him doomed, ancestors and the little lame foot made him aristocratic yet the bitter enemy of society.

He is a dream-figure and, like all dream-figures, even Dante's Beatrice, theatrical and a bit of a bore, which is why *Childe Harold* and *Manfred,* in spite of great incidental beauties, have not worn well. *Don Juan,* on the other hand, is a success because in that poem the hero is not really the hero at all, but a passive figure to whom certain experiences happen, a device enabling Byron to get down to the business for which his talents were really suited, a satirical panorama of the ruling classes of his time.

Byron was an egoist and, like all egoists, capable of falling in love with a succession of dream-figures, but incapable of genuine love or fidelity which accepts a personality completely. This did not prevent his writing good love poetry like *Hebrew Melodies.* In fact, nearly all love poetry is dream-figure poetry. Love may stimulate an artist indirectly and intensify his general vision of life; it does not often make him write love poems: their source is more commonly egoism or frustrated lust.

But Byron was not only an egoist; he was also acutely conscious of guilt and sin. Sometimes these two traits ran in harness, and their conjunction brought out the worst in him, both in his personal life and in his art; the self-conscious Satanism of his affairs, and the worst parts of *The Corsair.* At other times they were in opposition, and the conflict brought out the best; *Don Juan* and the Greek expedition.

Byron had one great virtue which everyone recognised in him from his earliest years; he had immense physical and moral courage. Even his worst errors were those of a brave man; he was never cautious or afraid of making a fool of himself either in his art or his life, nor was he a disingenuous careerist, qualities which distinguish him from a greater poet whom in many ways he resembles, Alexander Pope, who could have written the attack on Southey, but never the great lines against the Duke of Wellington.

No egoist can become a mature writer until he has learnt to recognise and to accept, a little ruefully perhaps, his egoism. When Byron had ceased to identify his moral sense with himself and had discovered how to extract the Byronic Satanism from his lonely hero and to turn it into the Byronic Irony which illuminated the whole setting, when he realised that he was a little ridiculous, but also not as odd as he had imagined, he became a great poet. For Byron was not really odd like Wordsworth; his experiences were those of the ordinary man. He had no unusual emotional or intellectual vision, and his distinctive contribution to English poetry was to be, not the defiant thunder of the rebel angel, but the speaking voice of the tolerant man-about-town.

His literary influences were Pope, Gay, Tom Moore, Hookham Frere, and perhaps Chateaubriand: from these he fashioned a style of poetry which for speed, wit, and moral seriousness combined with lack of pulpit pomposity is unique, and a lesson to all young would-be writers who are conscious of similar temptations and defects.

Written October 1938; *Fifteen Poets*, 1941

China

You want to know why I went to China—well, I'll tell you. I wanted to know what China was like during the war and what the Chinese people were like.

I stopped at Hankow. Then I went up the Yellow River. There were two war fronts at that time—one along the Yellow River and one near Shanghai; I visited them both, by train, car, walking and once by rickshaw. The authorities gave me every facility to travel and wherever I went both soldiers and civilians seemed genuinely glad to see English people—and grateful.

A soldier leaned out of a troop train, laid two fingers side by side and shouted "England and China together". I arrived late one night in the pouring rain at a ruined village which the inhabitants were expecting to have to evacuate at any moment, as the Japs were advancing. I found a number of them standing out in the rain holding up a banner with the English word "Welcome" written on it.

Train-travelling in China in wartime is more comfortable than you would think. There is always a teapot in the compartment which is never allowed to be empty, and if the train does sometimes stop for days at a time, a market springs up round it at once, where you can buy chickens, eggs, peanuts, etc.

Talking of food, a Chinese dinner table looks as if it were set, not for eating but for a lesson in water-colour painting, with little dishes of coloured sauces, and chopsticks like brushes and paint rags to wipe the chopsticks on. Many of the dishes, such as bird's-nest soup and ancient eggs, I found delicious but I drew the line at black beetles. My final impression was that in China nothing was specifically eatable or uneatable. You could begin munching a hat or bite a mouthful out of the wall. Equally you could build a hut with food provided at supper.

I had a good many air raids, particularly in Hankow. At night I would go up on to the roof to watch the searchlight beams plotting the sky like dividers, till suddenly they intersected and there the Jap planes would be, isolated in light like the bacilli of some fatal disease. There was one big air battle in April just after lunch. I put on sun glasses and lay on my back on the lawn of the British Consulate. A shell burst near a Japanese bomber. It flared against the blue like a struck match. Down in the road the rickshaw coolies were delightedly clapping their hands. Then came the whining roar of another machine, hopelessly out of control, and suddenly a white parachute mushroomed out over the river. Probably a Chinese plane this time, for the Japs, it is said, are not allowed parachutes. A leaflet fluttered down onto the roof of the Consulate. It assured the Chinese that Japan was their truest friend.

There is little trench fighting in this war, and the actual front is often impossible to find. No one seems to know if the next village is in the hands of the Chinese or the Japanese. The Chinese soldiers wear a blue padded uniform like an eiderdown quilt; they generally have a couple of hand grenades stuck into their belts like chianti flasks, and on their backs a paper umbrella or a sword like a gigantic fish knife. Some of them can have been no more than fifteen years old. The Army medical service is pretty primitive and most of the serious surgical work at the time of my visit was being done by the mission hospitals.

What is the Chinese War like? Well, at least it *isn't* like wars in history books. You know, those lucid tidy maps of battles one used to study, the flanks like neat little cubes, the pincer movements working with mathematical precision, the reinforcements never failing to arrive. War isn't like that. War is bombing an already disused arsenal, missing it and killing a few old women. War is lying in a stable with a gangrenous leg. War is drinking hot water in a barn and worrying about one's wife. War is a handful of lost and terrified men in the mountains, shooting at something moving in the undergrowth. War is waiting for days with nothing to do, shouting down a dead telephone, going without sleep and sex and a wash. War is untidy, inefficient, obscene, and largely a matter of chance.

Midland Magazine, BBC Midland Home Service,
16 January 1939; *The Listener*, 2 February 1939

JOURNEY TO A WAR

Terror Bequeathed: Cartoon by Yet Chian-yu from the magazine
"War-time Cartoons"

Journey to a War

BY W. H. AUDEN AND
CHRISTOPHER ISHERWOOD

[*1938*]

To E. M. Forster

Here, though the bombs are real and dangerous,
And Italy and King's are far away,
And we're afraid that you will speak to us,
You promise still the inner life shall pay.

As we run down the slope of Hate with gladness
You trip us up like an unnoticed stone,
And just as we are closeted with Madness
You interrupt us like the telephone.

For we are Lucy, Turton, Philip, we
Wish international evil, are excited
To join the jolly ranks of the benighted

Where Reason is denied and Love ignored:
But, as we swear our lie, Miss Avery
Comes out into the garden with the sword.

FOREWORD

Early in the summer of 1937, we were commissioned by Messrs Faber and Faber of London and by Random House of New York to write a travel book about the East. The choice of itinerary was left to our own discretion. The outbreak of the Sino-Japanese War in August decided us to go to China. We left England in January 1938, returning at the end of July.

This was our first journey to any place east of Suez. We spoke no Chinese, and possessed no special knowledge of Far Eastern affairs. It is hardly necessary, therefore, to point out that we cannot vouch for the accuracy of many statements made in this book. Some of our informants may have been unreliable, some merely polite, some deliberately pulling our leg. We can only record, for the benefit of the reader who has never been to China, some impression of what he would be likely to see, and of what kind of stories he would be likely to hear.

It would take too long to mention all those to whom we are indebted, but we should like particularly to thank:

Mr Sloss (Vice-Chancellor of Hongkong University), the Rev and Mrs Geoffrey Allen, Mr Basil Boothby, Mr William Spring, the Military Governor of Che-kiang, the Provincial Government of Kinhwa, Dr Ayres, Dr Brown, Dr Gilbert, Dr MacFadyen, Sir Archibald and Lady Clark Kerr—for their hospitality;

Mr Blunt (H. M. Consul-General at Canton), Mr Moss (H. M. Consul-General at Hankow), the Governor of Kwan-tung, Mr Wu Ti-chen, Mr Hollington Tong, Dr Han Li-wu, Miss Agnes Smedley, Mr France, Mr Edgar Snow, Mr Freddy Kaufmann, and Mr Rewi Alley—for information and introductions;

The Hankow Film Studios, for two stills from *Fight to the Last;*

Mr C. C. Yeh, for the cartoon used as our frontispiece;

Major Yang and Mr Zinmay Zau, for Chinese poems;

Mr Hughes of Oxford, for assistance in translation; and, last but not least, our Boy, Chiang, for his faithful and efficient service.

W.H.A.
C.I.

December 1938.

London to Hongkong

The Voyage

Where does the journey look which the watcher upon the quay,
Standing under his evil star, so bitterly envies?
When the mountains swim away with slow calm strokes, and the gulls
Abandon their vow? Does it still promise the Juster Life?

And, alone with his heart at last, does the traveller find
In the vaguer touch of the wind and the fickle flash of the sea
Proofs that somewhere there exists, really, the Good Place,
As certain as those the children find in stones and holes?

No, he discovers nothing: he does not want to arrive.
The journey is false; the false journey really an illness
On the false island where the heart cannot act and will not suffer:
He condones the fever; he is weaker than he thought; his weakness is real.

But at moments, as when the real dolphins with leap and abandon
Cajole for recognition, or, far away, a real island
Gets up to catch his eye, the trance is broken: he remembers
The hours, the places where he was well; he believes in joy.

And maybe the fever shall have a cure, the true journey an end
Where hearts meet and are really true: and away this sea that parts
The hearts that alter, but is the same, always; and goes
Everywhere, joining the false and the true, but cannot suffer.

The Sphinx

Did it once issue from the carver's hand
Healthy? Even the earliest conquerors saw
The face of a sick ape, a bandaged paw,
A Presence in the hot invaded land.

The lion of a tortured stubborn star,
It does not like the young, nor love, nor learning:
Time hurt it like a person; it lies, turning
A vast behind on shrill America,

And witnesses. The huge hurt face accuses,
And pardons nothing, least of all success.
The answers that it utters have no uses

To those who face akimbo its distress:
"Do people like me?" No. The slave amuses
The lion: "Am I to suffer always?" Yes.

The Ship

The streets are brightly lit; our city is kept clean:
The third class have the greasiest cards, the first play high;
The beggars sleeping in the bows have never seen
What can be done in staterooms; no one asks why.

Lovers are writing letters, sportsmen playing ball;
One doubts the honour, one the beauty, of his wife;
A boy's ambitious; perhaps the captain hates us all;
Someone perhaps is leading the civilized life.

It is our culture that with such calm progresses
Over the barren plains of a sea; somewhere ahead
The septic East, a war, new flowers and new dresses.

Somewhere a strange and shrewd To-morrow goes to bed
Planning the test for men from Europe; no one guesses
Who will be most ashamed, who richer, and who dead.

The Traveller

Holding the distance up before his face
And standing under the peculiar tree,
He seeks the hostile unfamiliar place,
It is the strangeness that he tries to see

Of lands where he will not be asked to stay;
And fights with all his powers to be the same,
The One who loves Another far away,
And has a home, and wears his father's name.

Yet he and his are always the Expected:
The harbours touch him as he leaves the steamer,
The Soft, the Sweet, the Easily-Accepted;

The cities hold his feeling like a fan;
And crowds make room for him without a murmur,
As the earth has patience with the life of man.

Macao

A weed from Catholic Europe, it took root
Between the yellow mountains and the sea,
And bore these gay stone houses like a fruit,
And grew on China imperceptibly.

Rococo images of Saint and Saviour
Promise her gamblers fortunes when they die;
Churches beside the brothels testify
That faith can pardon natural behaviour.

This city of indulgence need not fear
The major sins by which the heart is killed,
And governments and men are torn to pieces:

Religious clocks will strike; the childish vices
Will safeguard the low virtues of the child;
And nothing serious can happen here.

Hongkong

The leading characters are wise and witty;
Substantial men of birth and education
With wide experience of administration,
They know the manners of a modern city.

Only the servants enter unexpected;
Their silence has a fresh dramatic use:
Here in the East the bankers have erected
A worthy temple to the Comic Muse.

Ten thousand miles from home and What's-her-name,
The bugle on the Late Victorian hill
Puts out the soldier's light; off-stage, a war

Thuds like the slamming of a distant door:
We cannot postulate a General Will;
For what we are, we have ourselves to blame.

Travel-Diary

1

On February 28th, 1938, we left Hongkong in the *Tai-Shan*, a river-boat, bound for Canton.

At this time, Canton could be reached by two alternative routes: the river-line or the Kowloon–Canton railway. The railway was being bombed, almost daily, by Japanese planes operating from an aircraft-carrier anchored somewhere off Macao; but these attacks did very little to disturb traffic. Most of the bombs fell wide of their mark. If the track was hit, gangs of coolies, working at amazing speed, could repair it within a few hours. The river-boats, which were British-owned, had never been bombed at all.

It was a fine, hot, steamy morning. We breakfasted on board, and hurried out on to the deck, eager to miss none of the sensational sights which had been promised us. Friends in Hongkong, who had made the trip, had described how Japanese planes, returning from a raid, might swoop low over the *Tai-Shan*, playfully aiming their machine-guns at our heads. Or perhaps we should actually see the Japanese warships engaged in an artillery duel with the Bocca Tigris forts. If only we could get some photographs! We were secretly determined to try, despite the printed warning against cameras which we had read in the dining-saloon: "During the critical time of the country, anything might be considered as a wrong deed or subjected to a guilty movement. . . ."

One's first entry into a war-stricken country as a neutral observer is bound to be dream-like, unreal. And, indeed, this whole enormous voyage, from January London to tropical February Hongkong had had the quality—now boring, now extraordinary and beautiful—of a dream. At Hongkong, we had said to each other, we shall wake up, everything will come true. But we hadn't woken; only the dream had changed. The new dream was more confused than the old, less soothing, even slightly apprehensive. It was all about dinner-parties at very long tables, and meetings with grotesquely famous newspaper-characters—the British Ambassador, the Governor, Sir Victor Sassoon. We seemed to be in a perpetual hurry, struggling into our dinner-jackets, racing off in taxis to keep appointments for which we were already hopelessly late. And always, like dreamers, we were worried—listening in a daze to instructions or advice which we knew, only too well, we should never be able to remember in the morning. There were warnings, too; some of them as fantastic as any nightmare: "Never mix with a Chinese crowd, or you'll get typhus." "Never go for a walk alone, or they may shoot you as a spy."

Now, as the *Tai-Shan* steered out of the harbour, towards the big whitewashed rock which marks the passage into the mouth of the West River, we made another effort to shake ourselves free from the dream. "Well," Auden said, "here we are. Now it's going to start."

Here we were, steaming smoothly into the estuary of the broad, softly-swimming river, steaming away from the dinner-tables, the American movies, the statue of Queen Victoria on the guarded British island, steaming west into dangerous, unpredictable war-time China. Now *it*—whatever it was—was going to start. This wasn't a dream, or a boys' game of Indians. We were adult, if amateur, war-correspondents entering upon the scene of our duties. But, for the moment, I could experience only an irresponsible schoolboyish feeling of excitement. We scanned the river-banks eagerly, half-expecting to see them bristle with enemy bayonets.

"Look! A Japanese gunboat!"

There she lay, murderously quiet, anchored right across our path. We passed very close. You could see the faces of her crew, as they moved about the deck, or polished the sights of a gun. Their utter isolation, on their deadly little steel island, was almost pathetic. Self-quarantined in hatred, like sufferers from a fatally infectious disease, they lay outcast and apart, disowned by the calm healthy river and the pure sanity of the sky. They were like something outside nature, perverse, a freak. Absorbed in their duties, they scarcely gave us a glance—and this seemed strangest, most unnatural of all. That is what War is, I thought: two ships pass each other, and nobody waves his hand.

The river narrowed in. Here were the Bocca Tigris forts. Ranged along the fertile shore, and rising out of the shallow golden water on their leafy islands, they looked utterly deserted, harmless and picturesque as the ruins of a hundred-year-old campaign. It was hard to believe that they were equipped with modern weapons which had actually inflicted considerable damage upon the Japanese ships. Behind them, in the middle of the river, stood a small grey mountain shaped like a swimming turtle. The sailors began to take soundings. A young American journalist told us that river-boats sometimes ran aground here. In the course of our conversation, he mentioned casually that he had been on the *Panay* at the time of the incident. Thrilled and goggling, we were prepared to hang upon his words; but he was bored and tired—homesick, weary of China and the war. He was giving Canton its last chance. If a real story didn't break within a fortnight, he'd do his best, he said, to get sent back to the States. We retired, not wishing to bother him further, and viewed him from a respectful distance, with awe. A disillusioned journalist is the Byron, the romantic Hamlet of our modern world.

It was very hot. As we approached Canton, the scenery reminded us of the Severn Valley—there were willows and fruit-trees; an old country house standing within a walled garden had the sadness and charm of a mortgaged English estate. Great junks passed us. They resembled Elizabethan galleons, towering up sheer out of the water, architectural, richly carved, top-heavy. They were dangerously crowded with passengers, and, apparently, sailing backwards. Even a little green gunboat seemed uniquely Chinese, with its slender, quaintly tall funnels—less like a warship than some exotic sort of water-beetle. On the deck of a British steamer, a man in white ducks was practising drives with a golf-club. Warehouses began to crowd along the banks; many of them had Union Jacks, swastikas, or Stars and Stripes painted upon their roofs. We imagined a comic drawing of a conscientious Japanese observer looking down in perplexity from a bombing-plane upon a wilderness of neutral flags, and finally espying a tiny, unprotected Chinese patch: "Don't you think", he says, "we might be able to fit a little one in, just there?"

Canton has two semi-skyscrapers which first appear, at some distance, rising above the fields. The river near the landing-stages was infested with launches, sampans, and skiffs, creaking and bumping together in an apparently hopeless traffic-jam. Our steamer barged its way patiently through them towards the shore. The sampans were often navigated by a whole family of men, women, and children, each punting or rowing furiously in a different direction, and screaming all the time. Somehow or other, we elbowed our way down the gang-plank, and out through a quayside mob of police, customs officials, travellers, porters, and onlookers, to the waiting car which the British Consul-General had most kindly sent to meet us.

The British Consulate is in the foreign concession, on the river-island of Shameen. For once, we had to admit—remembering the horrors of Colombo, Singapore, Hongkong—the British had shown some good taste. Shameen is delightful: its houses are well-proportioned and unpretentious, with large airy verandahs and balconies, and there is a wide central avenue of lawns and trees. You cross to the island over a narrow sandbagged bridge; strongly guarded, for the foreigners fear a stampede of Chinese into the concession, in the event of a large-scale air-raid or a Japanese attack. British and American gunboats were moored alongside the outer shore. Their crews were playing football—hairy, meat-pink men with powerful buttocks, they must have seemed ferocious, uncouth giants to the slender, wasp-waisted Cantonese spectators, with their drooping, flowerlike stance and shy brilliant smiles.

We were to stay at Paak Hok Tung, a village half a mile down the river. American and English missionaries have made a settlement there. Walking up the tidy path between playing-fields, college buildings, and villa gardens, you might fancy yourself at home in one of the pleasanter London suburbs. And it was in a pleasant, cultured suburban drawing-room that our missionary host and hostess gave us tea. Had we had a nice journey? Yes, thank you, very nice. Any trouble at the customs? Well, unfortunately, yes: Auden had had to pay thirty dollars duty on his camera. Oh, how tiresome; but you'll get it back. Was it usually so hot in Canton at this time of year? No, it wasn't. Five days ago, it had been quite chilly.

Somewhere, from far away across the river, came a succession of dull, heavy thuds; felt rather than heard. And then, thin and distinct, the whine which a mosquito makes, when it dives for your face in the dark. Only this wasn't a mosquito. More thuds. I looked round at the others. Was it possible that they hadn't noticed? Clearing my throat, I said as conversationally as I could manage: "Isn't that an air-raid?"

Our hostess glanced up, smiling, from the tea-tray: "Yes, I expect it is. They come over about this time, most afternoons. . . . Do you take sugar and milk?"

Yes, I took both; and a piece of home-made sultana cake as well, to cover my ill-bred emotion. It was all very well for Auden to sit there so calmly, arguing about the Group Movement. He had been in Spain. My eyes moved over this charming room, taking in the tea-cups, the dish of scones, the book-case with Chesterton's essays and Kipling's poems, the framed photograph of an Oxford college. My brain tried to relate these images to the sounds outside; the whine of the power-diving bomber, the distant thump of the explosions. Understand, I told myself, that those noises, these objects are part of a single, integrated scene. Wake up. It's all quite real. And, at that moment, I really did wake up. At that moment, suddenly, I arrived in China.

"They're moving off now," our hostess told me. She had the kindly air of one who wishes to reassure a slightly nervous child about a thunderstorm. "They never stay very long."

After tea, she and I went for a walk. It was already beginning to get dark. We climbed a small hill behind the village, overlooking the Canton valley. Beneath us lay the great sprawling city, and, all around it, in the dusk, the mysterious, wooded Kwantung plains. Along the horizon, miniature mountains poked up their little hat-like peaks. It was the landscape of *Alice through the Looking-Glass.* Here you might make a Lewis Carroll walking-tour, coming unexpectedly upon the strangest of people engaged in the queerest of tasks—two old men trying to put a rat into a bottle, a woman pouring water through a sieve. And yet all these topsy-turvy occupations, when one came to inquire into their purpose, would prove, no doubt, to be eminently practical and sane. The Chinese, we had been told, do nothing without an excellent reason.

As we walked home, our hostess discussed the students at the Paak Hok Tung theological college. The teaching of Christian theology, she said (and we were to hear this repeated by many other mission-workers), is a difficult problem in China. The motives which bring the Chinese student into the western mission-school are likely to be mixed. On the material side, he has much to gain: knowledge of a European language, initiation into Occidental ways, the possibility of a good job. Christianity, since the conversion of Chiang Kai-shek, is politically fashionable, and is likely to become even more so in the future, if the present régime survives this war.

And, even supposing that the student is earnest in his intentions, he will find Christian theology hard to digest. The Chinese mind is not naturally attracted to the Myth. It is preoccupied with practical ethics. It asks to be given the seven rules for the Good Life. It is far more interested in this world than in the possibilities of the next. And so these young men—however quickly they may acquire the theological technique, however cleverly they answer their teacher's questions—are apt, in later life, to backslide into philosophical paganism.

Our hosts had been disappointed in the attitude of the young Cantonese intellectuals towards the war. Before the fighting began, they had taken the lead in anti-Japanese propaganda, and demanded the use of force. But now few of them seemed inclined to go into the trenches. "This", they said, "is a coolies' war. Our job is to educate ourselves for the task of reconstruction which will come later." Nevertheless, there is a good deal to be said on the students' side. China can ill afford to sacrifice her comparatively small educated class. And it must be remembered that, for the Cantonese, the land warfare was taking place in an area hundreds of miles distant, inhabited by a people whose language they could not even understand.

Next day, we were woken by mixed noises—the far-off explosions of the morning air-raid and the strains of our host's harmonium from the neighbouring chapel. Directly after breakfast we left by launch for the city. The Consul-General had lent us his car to pay an official visit to the Mayor, Mr Tsang Yan-fu. This was our first attempt at a professional interview, and we were anxious not to disgrace ourselves. Seated proud but nervous behind the consular chauffeur, and the fluttering Union Jack on the bonnet, we wondered what questions we should ask him. The streets swept past, some westernized, some purely Chinese, all hung with the long inscribed shop-banners, golden, scarlet, and white, which make every town in this country seem permanently *en fête*. The crowds were enormous; every road was blocked with foot-passengers, rickshaws, carts. We saw few signs of air-raid damage. For several months now, the Japanese had dropped no bombs on the centre of the city—attacking only the railway-stations, the flying-field, and the suburbs. There were piles of sand-bags at the entrances of the larger hotels.

The Mayor's office was a huge building, guarded by boys with automatic pistols. The sentries returned our tentative smiles with the blank glare of armed idiocy peculiar to very young troops. Like most of the soldiers we had seen in the streets, they looked about fifteen years old.

Mr Tsang Yan-fu received us in his private bureau, alone. He was dressed in the simple, becoming blue uniform of a government official, without medals or gold braid, which resembles the costume of an English chauffeur. The Mayor's smooth round face was split permanently, it seemed, by an immense grin; like a melon from which a slice has been cut. It was hardly necessary for us to interview him: he interviewed himself, laughing all the time:

"We not wan' to fight Japan. Japan wan' to fight *us*! Ha, ha, ha! Japan velly foolish. First she wan' to be number *tree* power. Then number *two*. Then number *one*. Japan industrial country, you see. Suppose we go Japan, dlop bomb—woo-er, boom! Velly bad for Japanese, I tink? Japanese come to China. China aglicultural country. Japanese dlop bomb—woo-er, boom! Only break up earth, make easier for Chinese plough land! Much people is killed of course. Velly cruel. But we have lots more, yes? Ha, ha, ha, ha!"

At this moment, we were deafeningly interrupted by the air-raid sirens. They were just outside the window. Mr Tsang became almost unintelligible with amusement; he shook violently in his chair: "You see? The Japanese come to dlop bombs on our heads! We sit here. We smoke our cigarettes. We are not afraid! Let us have some tea!"

But the raiders didn't, on this occasion, reach Canton after all. We were disappointed, for we had been hoping to see the Mayor's luxury dugout, said to be one of the wonders of the city. Auden took some photographs, for which Mr Tsang obligingly posed; and we bowed ourselves out of the room.

We both liked Mr Tsang. If this was typical of China's attitude towards the Japanese, it was certainly an example to the West—with its dreary hymns of hate, and screams of "Baby-killer", "Hun", "sub-human fiends". This scornful, good-natured amusement was, we agreed, exactly the note which a cultured, pacific country should strike in its propaganda against a brutal, upstart enemy. Mr Tsang's kind of humour, if properly exploited, should win China many friends abroad.

That evening there were guests at dinner—among them a Chinese colonel and his wife. The Colonel was a somewhat enigmatic figure; his communicative manner and fluent American English may have hidden as many secrets as the traditional reticence of the Orient: "You have a nice place here, Reverend. It's simple but it's good. . . . How much you pay for that cabinet, excuse?" He was perfectly willing to discuss anything—Chinese music, the war, his wife. They had been affianced to each other at the age of two; for their respective fathers were friends, and wished to perpetuate the memory of their affection. Since childhood, the Colonel hadn't seen his fiancée until the age of twenty-six. Then he returned from Russia, and they were married immediately. "So you don't have any marriages for love?" a lady in the party asked, with less than English tact.

And: "But you have been very lucky, Colonel," our hostess put in hastily. The Colonel bowed: "Thank you, Madam."

He then informed us that Canton now had a considerable force of chaser planes. During the past fortnight, eleven Japanese had been brought down. The Government had offered a reward to anybody who could bring down a plane; as a result, anti-aircraft defence had become a local sport, like duck-shooting. When the planes came over, everybody blazed away—even the farmers with their blunderbusses in the fields. One Japanese pilot, flying incautiously low, had been wrecked by a hundred-year-old mortar in a junk. On another occasion, when two Japs had made a forced landing, the peasants ambushed them, and would even have succeeded in capturing one of the planes in perfect working-order, if a third Jap hadn't swooped down and destroyed it with a bomb.

At dinner, the Colonel entertained us single-handed. He told us how, during a visit to London, he had walked through Limehouse, and seen a Chinese notice: "Best opium fresh from Yun-nan", prominently displayed in a doorway, under the nose of a patrolling bobby. He knew all about cooking, and showed our hostess how to prepare a fish. Certainly, he assured us, you could get roast dog. Snake wine was good for rheumatism. He invited us all to his house to eat ancient eggs.

The Colonel, it appeared, was a noted singer. After dinner, he was persuaded, without much difficulty, to oblige. In Chinese opera, he explained, there are various styles of singing, adapted to the different stock characters; and he undertook to give us samples of each. The romantic hero emits sounds like a midnight cat, the heroine a thin nasal falsetto; the bandit is quite terrifying—the volume is small, but the effort involved would have put Caruso to shame. Before our fascinated eyes the Colonel's face turned from yellow to purple, from purple to black; his veins bulged like ropes. But just when it seemed that he would injure himself seriously and permanently, he burst out laughing—with a gesture of comic indignation towards his placid, bespectacled wife: "How shall I sing", he exclaimed, "when she looks at me like that?"

We had been invited to lunch, next day, with General Wu Teh-chen, the ex-mayor of Shanghai, now Governor of Kwantung Province.

General Wu lived on the outskirts of the city, in a comfortable but unpretentious concrete villa. Mr Tong, the Governor's secretary, welcomed us in the hall—a smiling, moon-faced man, so soft and gentle that one could barely resist the impulse to stroke his cheek and offer him a lump of sugar. He told us that the Governor would soon be down, and introduced us to the half-dozen other guests; both English and Chinese. A swarthy, efficient-looking young man in blue uniform proved to be Mr Percy Chen, whose book on the first phases of the present war we had read during our stay in Hongkong. (One sentence in it had particularly pleased us: the author is speaking of the incident at the Marco Polo bridge—"Shortly before midnight, the manœuvres developed towards realism, and live ammunition was used on both sides." Surely, the outbreak of a war has never been more tactfully described?)

Mr Chen spoke English perfectly. He had been a barrister of the Middle Temple, and had spent eight years in Russia. Indeed, as he himself confessed, his life had been lived so much abroad that he felt himself to be almost a foreigner in China. He was very critical of the Japanese strategy. There was no co-ordination, he said, between the various commands: whole divisions would often advance without orders. All the Chinese present were anxious to know what we thought of Mr Eden's resignation and its possible effect on British foreign policy in the Far East.

General Wu now came into the room, and we were introduced. The Governor was a strongly-built man, in a loosely-fitting brown uniform, with talkative, informal manners. His eyes, behind thick horn-rimmed glasses, were earnest and sometimes puzzled. He spoke with hesitation, feeling for his words, and looking round the whole company, as if for support: "The war is the biggest disconception China has ever suffered. The peoples lose their homes and walk. But it makes them a nation. This is the one thing China gets from the war. . . . After the war, the bankers spend the money on the countries."

We began to move into the dining-room, still talking; there seemed to be no special order of precedence. All this informality, admirable as it was, disappointed us a little. Both Auden and myself were still steeped in the traditions of *The Chinese Bungalow*. We had even rehearsed the scene beforehand, and prepared suitable compliments and speeches. The Governor should have said: "My poor house is honored." And we should have replied: "Our feet are quite unworthy to rest upon your honourable doorstep." On which, the Governor, had he known his stuff, would have cracked back: "If my doorstep were gold, it would hardly be fit for your distinguished shoes." And so on. Perhaps, after all, it was a good thing that General Wu was unacquainted with the subtleties of European stage-Chinese, or we might never have reached the lunch-table.

One's first sight of a table prepared for a Chinese meal hardly suggests the idea of eating, at all. It looks rather as if you were sitting down to a competition in water-colour painting. The chopsticks, lying side by side, resemble paint-brushes. The paints are represented by little dishes of sauces, red, green, and brown. The tea-bowls, with their lids, might well contain paint-water. There is even a kind of tiny paint-rag, on which the chopsticks can be wiped.

You begin the meal by wiping hands and face with hot moistened towels. (These towels are, perhaps, China's most brilliant contribution to the technique of material comfort; they should certainly be introduced into the West.) Then comes the food. It is served in no recognizable order of progression—fish does not necessarily follow soup, nor meat fish. Nor can the length of the meal be foreseen by the guest. His favourite dish may well appear at the very end, when he is too bloated even to taste it. *Hors-d'œuvre* delicacies remain in presence throughout—and this, too, is like painting; for the diners are perpetually mixing them in with their food, to obtain varying combinations of taste.

To-day we had shark's fin soup (one of the great soups of the world; quite equal to minestrone or borsch), lobster, chicken, rice, and fish. The drink, which was served in small metal teapots, resembled Korn or Bols. It was made from rose-petals and maize. The Governor had considerately provided us with knives and forks, but these we declined to use. We had eaten already with chopsticks in Hongkong, and were anxious for more practice. In China, it is no social crime to drop your food on the table. When a new dish comes in, the host makes a gesture towards it with his chopsticks, like a cavalry-commander pointing with his sabre to an enemy position, and the attack begins. This scramble, so informal yet so scrupulously polite, is the greatest charm of a Chinese meal; and even the most expert eater can hardly avoid making a certain amount of mess. One of the English guests was showing me how to pick up a shrimp patty, when he let it fall on to the carpet. His face was promptly saved by Mr Tong, who exclaimed: "Ah, that shrimp must be alive!"

Hot brown rice-wine followed the rose-petal gin. The Governor raised his glass to us: "Welcome to China!" The Minister of Agriculture, who was sitting next to Auden, began to discuss the rice-problem. Before the war, much of the rice consumed in Kwantung Province was imported from the north. Now there was a shortage, because these areas had been occupied by the Japanese. The Government was therefore encouraging the Cantonese to use sweet potatoes as a substitute. It had issued a wartime cookery-book, explaining what could be done with the available foodstuffs. Remembrance-days had been instituted, on which no rice might be eaten. Originally, these days were to commemorate certain important dates in the Sino-Japanese dispute—beginning with the invasion of Manchuria; but the Governor had decided that these would be too difficult to remember. Now the no-rice rule came into force simply on every fifth day. To check the spread of beri-beri, the sale of polished rice had been prohibited altogether.

Both the Governor and the Minister were interested in rural education. The country schools, said General Wu, were not designed to make their pupils eager to migrate into the towns; they aimed at producing good and contented farmers. Auden, who had read in a local paper that morning that the farmers had rioted against a new agricultural station, asked if the peasants, in general, resented the introduction of scientific farming methods. The Governor denied this: "But we must not expect them to come to us," he said. "We must go to them."

Somebody mentioned Hitler's Reichstag speech. "I think Germany is very silly," said General Wu. "She says that Japan defends against Bolshevism; unless Japan would fight, China goes Communist. But Germany is wrong. China will not go Communist; but if war continues a long time, Japan she goes Bolshevist. China has four hundred million peoples, Japan one hundred million; but there are more Communist agitators in Japan than in whole of China."

"So you think Communism's impossible in China?" Auden asked.

"China agricultural country. I have thousand acres. I have ten sons. They have only hundred acres. In China there are no big landlords. Every Chinese man must have a house, he must marry; then he has credit with society."

Here General Wu was interrupted by a servant, who brought a message to say that the Japanese were raiding the railway, near the frontier between Kwantung and the New Territories. "The Japanese mind", he observed, "is funny. It can get everything without war, but it must make war. Japan doesn't think like other nations. . . . But Great Britain," he appealed suddenly to us, "she can stop this war?"

Yes, we agreed, she could stop it. But would she? Ah. . . . There was a moment's embarrassed silence. Then the Governor tactfully indicated that lunch was over.

We spent the next two days chiefly in shopping and wandering about the city. Neither of us could ever tire of walking the streets: there was so much to see. The commonest shops seemed to be barbers and apothecaries, whose windows exhibited deer-horn (to cure impotence) and strange, twisted roots, like mandrakes, in glass cases. There were bizarre placards, in English: "New Life Cars." "Street-Sleepers' Association." "Blood Protection Co. Ltd." The food-shops were fascinating, too. Auden gazed in horror at the edible black-beetles, I at the tubs of live swimming snakes. If I had to eat snake, I said, I thought I should really go mad. Auden determined to trick me into doing so at the first possible opportunity.

All around us crowded and jostled the Cantonese, in their light pyjama-clothes—a small, gay, elegant people, of great physical beauty. The more fashionable girls had had their hair curled and permanently waved, which didn't suit them, however. Some of the very young children wore brilliant scarlet jackets and parti-coloured jockey-caps; their naked buttocks, pushing out through the divided breeches, were smeared with dirt from the road. We noticed a few whose faces were powdered and rouged; this is sometimes done, we were told, on the child's birthday.

On the advice of our hosts, we bought two camp-beds, complete with mosquito-nets, which folded neatly into canvas sacks. Another big sack would hold the bedding, and could be used, later on, for our necessary clothes as well. These beds proved, later, to be invaluable. (At the present moment, they are ornamenting a doss-house, somewhere in New York.)

We had also to provide ourselves with visiting-cards, in English and Chinese. Without cards, travel in China would be difficult in the extreme. A friend in Hongkong had supplied us already with phonetic Chinese names—Au Dung and Y Hsiao Wu: in Canton, we got them printed.

On our last evening we were invited to dine with the captain of a British gunboat, anchored off Shameen. The captain was fond of flowers; there were plenty of them in his tiny cabin, and orange-trees in tubs stood on the few square feet of deck around the gun. You had to be careful, he told us, when buying flowers in the Canton markets; the blossoms are often wired on, so are the roots. On the whole, his opinion of Chinese honesty was low.

The chief function of the gunboats, in peace time, is the protection from pirates of British-owned ships. The gunboats are flat-bottomed, drawing only five feet of water, and they can steam far up the river. They are capable of doing fourteen knots; but this speed is inadvisable, for it washes away the banks, and they are likely to be fired on, in retaliation, by angry farmers. They are built in England, and their voyage to the East is something of an adventure; if the sea is rough, they are towed, with all hatches battened down; if smooth, they proceed under their own steam.

The dinner was excellent, with caviare and French wines. We caught a glimpse of a lonely, formal, self-contained existence; and wondered what an American or a French naval officer would make of the captain—he was so much more subtle, more intelligent than his cultivated Bertie Wooster drawl. ("The shooting-season opened with a fine bag. We got five pirates; two of 'em in the water.") When it was time for us to go, the ship's private sampan rowed us ashore. The old lady, its owner, had decorated the basket-work roof with photographs of football teams and British crews.

We were to leave Canton next day, March 4th, by rail for Hankow. The train was scheduled to start at 6 p.m. Earlier in the afternoon we went round to the British Consulate to say goodbye. The Consul wasn't particularly cheerful. Yesterday, he told us, the line had been heavily bombed and cut by the Japanese. Trains took anything from five to seven days to make the journey; you might even be turned out of them altogether and compelled to spend the night in an obscure provincial village. A lady who had just arrived from Hankow had assured him that she wouldn't make the trip again for ten thousand pounds. "Not, of course," the Consul added, smiling, "that I want to discourage you."

We protested that we weren't discouraged—that the air-raids would help to pass the time, and a night in the paddy-fields would provide excellent copy. Nevertheless, as we approached the Canton railway station, I began to cast nervous glances at the sky. It was a warm, windless evening—perfect weather for the Japs.

Along the road near the line hundreds of coolies squatted humbly in the dust: these, it appeared, never aspired to get on to the platform at all. Only, at the very last moment, when everybody of any consequence was already on board, they might be allowed to scramble over the fence and mingle in one desperate fighting rush for the few remaining places in a cattle-truck. Many of them, obviously, would be left behind. Several would very likely break an arm or a leg.

The station building was small, shabby, and crammed with soldiers. It smelt very bad indeed. A group of police officers in smart black-and-silver uniforms challenged us smilingly. But they didn't want to see our tickets, or even our passports; they merely demanded from each of us a visiting-card. These cards, somebody told us later, are the perquisites of the officials who collect them; they like to show them to their wives, and boast about the interesting people they have met.

Thanks to the influence of Governor Wu, our reservations were the best obtainable on the train: a two-berth coupé in the first-class coach. This coach was almost the only one in the immensely long train whose roof was painted with camouflage: we speculated on the advantages and disadvantages of our presumed invisibility from the air. The station officials were nervous too, perhaps; for our departure was punctual to the minute. As we drew slowly down the platform, soldiers and police stood to attention and saluted. One of the passengers—a pale, calm young man, with a long whippet-nose and protruding under-lip—bowed in silent acknowledgment; he was evidently an important Government official. The whole effect was slightly sinister—like watching your own military funeral from the gun-carriage itself.

Our train puffed leisurely out through the suburbs, into the open country. At this stage of the journey I blessed the driver's caution; for the Consul had added to my nervousness by tales of bombed bridges imperfectly repaired with bamboo stakes. Besides, if the Japanese came over, you could jump out of the window without the slightest risk. Standing in the corridor we made friends with a Chinese bank-director who assured us that, all being well, we should reach Hankow in two days and three nights only. Our spirits rose considerably.

Actually we saw the traces of only one air-raid, at a small station where we stopped soon after dark. A bomb had landed right beside the track; the ruins of the waiting-room were scattered around its crater. If there were other such ruins we must have passed them after we had gone to bed. There were many hold-ups and long waits. By night we travelled much more slowly than by day.

There was no restaurant on this train, but the stewards provided plenty of food. There was even a special European menu. This we rejected, after one trial, as too nasty—until the boredom of the Chinese dishes drove us back to it, later on. In any case, we weren't particularly hungry.

About breakfast-time we stopped at a mountain station near the Kwantung–Hu-nan provincial border. A big crag, wrapped in mist, towered above the track. Peasants brought baskets of fruit for sale—they looked like miniature oranges. In defiance of Hongkong's warnings against dysentery we ate them skin and all.

All that day, we rumbled through the fertile, blood-coloured valleys of southern Hu-nan, bathed in hot sunshine. Charming, compact villages of grey and white houses clustered round their square watch-towers, which resembled the towers of English country churches. There were rookeries in the copses, and haystacks built round the tree-trunks. The paddy-fields mounted the gentle hill-slopes, terrace by terrace, like tarnished mirrors reflecting the sky. Here and there big gangs of coolies were working on the track. As we passed, one of them forcibly pulled down his friend's trousers, exhibiting him, grinning, to the entire train.

The stewards hurried up and down the corridor with hot face-towels, bowls of rice, cups of tea. As the journey progressed the tea grew nastier, tasting increasingly of fish. The two armed guards in the corridor—one of them surely not more than twelve years old—peered into our compartment to watch the foreign devils screaming with laughter at mysterious jokes, singing in high falsetto or mock operatic voices, swaying rhythmically backwards and forwards on their seats, reading aloud to each other from small crimson-bound books. The swaying was an exercise which we had invented, in a vain effort to ward off constipation; the books were *Framley Parsonage* and *Guy Mannering*. Neither was a great success. We admired Scott's skill in spinning out the story; Trollope we found merely dull. He seemed interested exclusively in money, and the appalling consequences of signing your name on a bill. By the middle of the second day we had finished them both. We had nothing else to read, and our voices were too hoarse for any more singing. The journey ceased to amuse.

After Changsha the weather turned cloudy and much cooler. The peasants on the stations wore huge turbans, like figures in a Rembrandt biblical painting. Soldiers toiled past, in their heavy equipment, patiently clutching paper umbrellas. We had rain-swept glimpses of the vast Tung-ting Lake. (How strange to remember that in London, only three months ago, I had placed my finger on it in the atlas, and said, "I wonder if we shall ever get as far as *here?*")

Early next morning we arrived at Wuchang. The thermometer had dropped during the night, and we staggered out of the station into a driving blizzard. The causeway and the stone stairs down to the ferry were slippery with ice. Coolies jostled blindly against us, with the averted, snot-smeared, animal faces of the very humble, the dwellers in Society's smallest crevices, the Insulted and Injured. Auden's paper umbrella had broken in the storm; it wrapped itself round his head like a grotesque kind of hat. Slithering and cursing, we crowded into the hold of the listing steamer and stood, jammed too tight to move, amidst straw baskets, rifles, soldiers, peasants, and sacks. This was not the moment to fuss about infection or lice. On the distant shore, the buildings of Hankow stood grim and black against the low clouds; before us swept the Yangtze, a terrible race of yellow waves and tearing snow. We had arrived, it seemed, at the very end of the world.

2

March 8.

Today Auden and I agreed that we would rather be in Hankow at this moment than anywhere else on earth.

Stark and blank along the northern shore, the buildings of the old treaty port present their European façades to the winter river. (Only the French Concession still officially exists; and the authorities are preparing to barricade it with barbed wire and big wooden gates in the event of a Japanese attack.) There are consulates, warehouses, offices, and banks; British and American drug-stores, cinemas, churches, clubs; there is a good lending library, a Y.M.C.A., a red-light street of cafés—Mary's, the Navy Bar, The Last Chance. Around all this the Chinese city stretches for miles, a warren of ramshackle, congested streets, out to the race-track, the air-field, and the snow-covered Hu-Peh plains.

The clothing-shops, the cafés, and the restaurants are kept by White Russian emigrants. You see two or three of them behind nearly every bar—a fat, defeated tribe who lead a melancholy indoor life of gossip, mah-jongg, drink, and bridge. They have all drifted here somehow—by way of Mongolia, Hongkong, or the United States—and here they must stop; nobody else will receive them. They have established an insecure right to exist—on Nansen passports, Chinese nationality-papers of doubtful validity, obsolete Tsarist identity-certificates as big as table-cloths, or simply their mere impoverished presence. Their great pallid faces look out into the future, above innumerable cigarettes and tea-glasses, without pity or hope. "Their clocks", says Auden, "stopped in 1917. It has been tea-time ever since."

In the slushy streets the raw Siberian wind stings the cheeks of the hurrying crowd—Europeans in fur-lined coats, Chinese in skin caps with ear-guards like airmen's helmets. The rickshaws are fitted with hoods and carriage-lamps—as though, by some process of age and desiccation, hansom-cabs had shrunk to the size of prams. Coolies stagger in and out of doorways, balancing cases slung on springy bamboo poles. They encourage each other with sharp rhythmical cries: "Hoo, ha, ah, hoo, hi, ha!" Soldiers in uniforms of blue quilt pad silently by, splashed with mud from passing cars, their thin sandals sodden in the melting snow.

This is the real capital of war-time China. All kinds of people live in this town—Chiang Kai-shek, Agnes Smedley, Chou En-lai; generals, ambassadors, journalists, foreign naval officers, soldiers of fortune, airmen, missionaries, spies. Hidden here are all the clues which would enable an expert, if he could only find them, to predict the events of the next fifty years. History, grown weary of Shanghai, bored with Barcelona, has fixed her capricious interest upon Hankow. But where is she staying? (Everybody boasts that he has met her, but nobody can exactly say.) Shall we find her at the big hotel, drinking whisky with the journalists in the bar? Is she the guest of the Generalissimo, or the Soviet Ambassador? Does she prefer the headquarters of the Eighth Route Army, or the German military advisers? Is she content with a rickshaw-coolie's hut?

Perhaps she is nearer than we think—at the neighbouring house in the compound of the British Consulate-General, where T. V. Soong sometimes confers far into the night on the problematical future of the Chinese Dollar. The Consul has offered us the hospitality of a big empty room, in which we can pitch our camp-beds. Downstairs, in an atmosphere of Winchester, Racine, service gossip, and Chinese vases—all of them museum-pieces; a few disconcertingly ugly—we discuss our future plans. We have decided to go north: first to Cheng-chow, and thence to some point on the Yellow River front. To do this, we shall need a servant-interpreter. The Consul has found us one already, a friend of his own Number One Boy. His name is Chiang.

Chiang is one of the few Chinese we have seen whose appearance could be described as middle-aged. He has the manners of a perfect butler. His English leaves much to be desired, and he does not even pretend to be able to cook. Nevertheless, we have engaged him, for expenses and forty dollars a month. Before the deal was concluded, the Consul warned him, at our request, that we were going into the war area. Would he be frightened? "A servant", Chiang replied, "cannot afford to be frightened."

This afternoon we paid a visit to Bishop Roots, the American bishop of Hankow. Bishop Roots has spent a lifetime in China. Within a few weeks he is going to retire. Lately the bishop's ideas have moved sharply towards the Left; he describes himself as a "Christian revolutionary". A short time ago his daughter caused a local sensation by journeying to the north-west to visit the red Eighth Route Army, now officially incorporated into the Chinese forces. Since Miss Agnes Smedley came to stay with the bishop his house has been nicknamed "The Moscow–Heaven Axis".

Bishop Roots is bald, sententious, and oracular in the grand American manner. He reproved us gently for our interest in the immediate outcome of the war. "You've got to think in terms of five hundred years. . . . This country has an historic part to play in the future of the world. Here the great stream of western culture which sprang from Greece and Rome, was modified by Judah and absorbed technics, will meet that other great humanist stream which sprang from Confucius, was modified by India and did not absorb technics. This will be the birthplace of the new world-civilization, and the Chinese realize it. . . . Only a revolution in men's hearts, a new idealism—such as the Oxford Group Movement is attempting—can save the world from destruction. I believe it must come. . . . Thank you for visiting me. I like to have a talk with newcomers, before any one else gets hold of them. . . . Miss Smedley, I'm afraid, is out."

March 9.

This afternoon we attended the press conference. It is held daily, at five o'clock, in the offices of Mr Hollington Tong, Hankow's publicity chief.

The narrow stuffy room was crowded with camp-stools, and half-filled by a long table, on which stood tea-cups, chocolates, and cigarettes. The correspondents of the various foreign newspapers lounged or chatted in groups, frowning as they puffed disgustedly at their pipes. Nearly all of them were American or Australian; we were the only English present. And there was a pale, worried-looking boy from Berlin, in a black shirt, breeches, and dispatch-rider's boots.

The first two or three minutes were embarrassing. The old hands viewed us with inquisitively hostile eyes. We hastened to explain that we were not real journalists, but mere trippers, who had come to China to write a book. The hearty, square-shouldered, military-looking man to whom we had addressed ourselves slapped us both on the back: "These young fellows", he shouted to the others, "are desperate to go to the front at once." The great news-men smiled, weary but indulgent. "Why, isn't that just fine?" some one drily observed. "I don't mind telling you," the military-looking man continued, "I haven't been to the front myself. But I've been darn near death several times." We flattered him with timid grins.

Presently, to our delight, two friends walked in—Capa and Fernhout (we had got to know them both during the voyage from Marseilles to Hongkong. Indeed, with their horse-play, bottom-pinching, exclamations of "Eh, quoi! Salop!" and endless jokes about *les poules*, they had been the life and soul of the second class.) Capa is Hungarian, but more French than the French; stocky and swarthy, with drooping black comedian's eyes. He is only twenty-three, but already a famous press-photographer. He has been through most of the civil war in Spain. Fernhout is a tall, blonde young Dutchman—as wild as Capa, but slightly less noisy. He worked with Ivens and Hemingway as a camera-man on the film *Spanish Earth*. Ivens was with them now. We hadn't met him before. He is a good deal older than the others, small, dark, with sparkling little eyes. The three of them have just arrived in Hankow direct from Hongkong, by air.

They are waiting here for their equipment, which is being sent by rail, before starting for the north-west. They are going to make a film about the life of a child soldier, a "little red devil", in one of the mobile units of the Eighth Route Army. They hope to leave Hankow sometime next week.

The daily news-bulletin was read by Mr T. T. Li, the official mouthpiece of the Government. He resembles the most optimistic of Walt Disney's Three Little Pigs. The word "defeat" has no place in his mouth. Every Japanese advance is a Chinese strategic withdrawal. Towns pass into Japanese hands in the most tactful manner possible—they simply cease to be mentioned. He reads very fast, and keeps losing the place in his papers: "Of seven planes brought down by Chinese ground forces, fifteen were destroyed by infantry." Nobody bothered to question the arithmetic, or, indeed, to pretend any interest whatsoever. Any scraps of genuine news would be circulated later, when the journalists had dispersed to the bars for a pre-dinner drink.

The lecture over, we approached Mr Tong himself, with a request for the Government passes which are necessary for any journey to the north. Mr Tong listened gravely; his eyes tired and calm behind his tinted, rimless spectacles. Yes, everything should be arranged; though he doubted whether we should get permission to visit Sian. It would be several days, in any case, before the passes were ready.

An immediate consequence of our visit to the press conference has been the arrival at the Consulate, during dinner, of an enormous packet. It contains all the press bulletins of the China Information Committee for the past three months. We are supposed, apparently, to study them before tomorrow afternoon. Auden calls them "our lessons".

March 10.

This morning we went to interview Mr Donald, friend and adviser to the Generalissimo and Madame Chiang Kai-shek. Mr Donald is living, at present, in a flat on the Bund—a large, ramshackle place, guarded by quantities of slightly conspiratorial secretaries, menservants, and messenger-boys. He received us in his bedroom. He was just recovering from a bad cold, and a whole chemist's shop of bottles was laid out on the table by the bed. Donald is a red-faced, serious man, with an Australian accent and a large, sensible nose—a pleasant surprise; for most of our informants had led us to expect an oily, iron-grey, evangelical figure, with a highly developed manner. He neither boomed nor snapped; but lectured us, as we desired, on the war-situation, clearly and concisely, with the aid of a big map. We talked chiefly about the possibilities of Russia giving military assistance to the Chinese. Donald said that the extent of this assistance has been much exaggerated. Nevertheless, he thinks that the Japanese are likely to make a drive on Sian, in order to prevent possible Russian supplies coming into China. If the Sian–Lanchow road were cut, these supplies would be obliged to take an interior route of extreme difficulty, over the mountains.

We asked him what part the Communists are likely to play after the war. He counter-questioned: "What do the Communists stand for? Can they, in fact, be called Communists at all?" In his view, Communism ceased to exist in China after the withdrawal of Borodin.

Donald's own career has been extraordinary. He was a *Times* correspondent in Harbin. Then he became adviser to Chang Hsueh-liang, the "Young Marshal"; and later the "foreign friend" of Chiang Kai-shek himself. He says habitually: "We think this," "we decided that," and "I said to the Generalissimo," "the Generalissimo said to me," although neither can speak the other's language. Donald's well-known ignorance of Chinese has, no doubt, been a great protection to him in this country of plots and secrets. He hears no more than is good for him to hear. He is the man whom everybody can trust.

As we were going he asked us about our plans. We told him of our proposed journey to the north. Donald looked dubious and shook his head: "Well, I wish you luck. But it's a hard road. A hard road." He paused, then added, in a lower, dramatic tone: "You may have to eat Chinese food."

We laughed. He might have been about to warn us against nameless horrors. "But surely", asked Auden, "you eat it yourself?"

"*Chinese* food!" Donald's face contracted with disgust. "Never touch the stuff! It ruins my stomach."

March 11.

Mr Donald has given us an introduction to General von Falkenhausen, the chief of Chiang Kai-shek's German military advisers. This afternoon I took a rickshaw and started out to look for his headquarters.

They were somewhere out in the old Japanese Concession, at the far end of the Bund. But the address had been mis-spelt, and we wandered backwards and forwards for a long time. Many of the houses in this part of the city have been commandeered by the Chinese Army since their owners fled to Japan. Soon after the outbreak of war, the police made a raid and discovered that the Concession had been the centre of a big illicit drug-traffic.

All along the streets raw recruits were being drilled. They were mere boys, awkward-looking and unnaturally stout in their quilted uniforms, their poor yellow hands turned rubber-grey by the cold. They seemed to be performing all kinds of outlandish physical exercises. A single recruit knelt on one knee opposite his N.C.O., and the two regarded each other in silence for minutes on end, as though the private were being hypnotized. A little further on another N.C.O. barked out an order, and his whole squad slightly and elegantly advanced one foot, in an attitude which suggested ballet-dancing, combined with a sort of stolid ferocity. My coolie rambled this way and that, stopping frequently to ask the way, which everybody told him and no one knew. We kept passing and repassing the same platoon. In my newly-made riding-boots I tried, unsuccessfully, to look very stern and official. Presently I had to laugh; the recruits grinned back. I gave them a mock salute, which they returned. Their officers shouted at them, but they were smiling, too. Just when discipline threatened to become seriously disorganized I noticed that we were passing the General's house for the third time.

The General was out, but his A.D.C. received me—a mountainous figure, with clipped silver hair, a gold bracelet as thick as a bicycle-chain, and a monocle screwed several inches into his face. Even in his tweed jacket and flannel trousers he was unmistakably the Reichswehr officer. And his office, despite its thick Japanese matting, was a bit of old Potsdam, with secretaries coming in and out, heel-clicking, jerking forward their bodies in stiff, formal bows.

Most of the Germans have been in China for several years. They belong to the pre-Hitler emigration period, when an ambitious officer could foresee no adventurous military career in his own country, and often preferred to go abroad. Between them they have built up all the more modern units of the Chinese Army, and it is only natural that they should want to remain to see it in action. Nobody we have so far met has ever seriously suggested that they could be suspected of disloyalty to China, despite the Anti-Comintern Pact. Nevertheless, their position at the present moment, amidst this weird collection of helpers and allies, is certainly ambiguous. What does Berlin think of their activities? What does Moscow? Does Chiang himself entirely trust them? Perhaps not. At any rate their advice is not always taken; but this may be due to the jealousy which native generals invariably display towards their foreign colleagues—as in Franco's army in Spain.

The A.D.C. thought that China could certainly win this war—if only her troops would "stand up straight and do as they're told." But he sometimes sighed, one suspected, for three or four crack German divisions to put some stiffening into the Chinese resistance. From military matters our talk wandered back to the Harz Mountains. Wernigerode, which we both knew, was the A.D.C.'s native town.

Auden and I are to come back and see General von Falkenhausen tomorrow morning.

March 12.

When we arrived at headquarters the A.D.C. greeted us: "Well, gentlemen; you've heard the news?"

No, we said, we hadn't.

"Last night the German Army marched into Austria."

The bottom seemed to drop out of the world. But the A.D.C. was taking it very calmly. "Of course," he said, "it had to happen. And now I hope that England and Germany will be friends. That's what we Germans have always wanted. Austria was only causing trouble between us. A good thing the whole business is settled, once and for all."

He led us, still rather dazed, into another room, where General von Falkenhausen was sitting. "Here they are, Excellency." He bowed and left us alone.

The General looks more like a university professor than a Prussian officer. He wears pince-nez; a gaunt, grizzled man of about fifty-five. We asked him the routine question: could China win?

"Well," said the General, "I am an optimist. I am an optimist for three reasons. First, because I am a soldier. A soldier is a professional optimist. Secondly, because, if I were not optimistic, I could not give confidence to those around me. Thirdly, because the present situation really affords grounds for optimism." He thinks that the Yellow River line is strong; and that Hankow can be easily defended—there are plenty of troops. When I asked him (more for the sake of saying something than because I really wanted to know) where he had been during the battle for Shanghai, he smilingly refused to answer. Why, neither of us can imagine.

As we walked home the whole weight of the news from Austria descended upon us, crushing out everything else. By this evening a European war may have broken out. And here we are, eight thousand miles away. Shall we change our plans? Shall we go back? What does China matter to us in comparison with this? Bad news of this sort has a curious psychological effect: all the guns and bombs of the Japanese seem suddenly as harmless as gnats. If we are killed on the Yellow River front our deaths will be as provincial and meaningless as a motor-bus accident in Burton-on-Trent.

Meanwhile our daily round had to continue. We had got an appointment with Miss Agnes Smedley.

We found her in an upstairs bed-sitting-room at Bishop Roots's house, staring dejectedly into the fire. She is really not unlike Bismarck, with her close-cropped grey hair, masculine jaw, deeply-lined cheeks and bulging, luminous eyes. "Hullo," she greeted us, listlessly: "What do you two want?"

We introduced ourselves, and she began to cross-examine us, mockingly rather than aggressively: "What's your background?" "Are you a leftist?" "Do you poetize?" Our answers seemed to amuse her. She shook a little, unsmiling, with the faintest kind of laughter; but all the time she held us, suspiciously, with her fearless, bitter grey eyes. We got a bad mark, I could see, when we admitted that we were staying at the British Consulate; and another when we told her we had just been visiting the German military advisers. "What are they plotting now?" she asked. We protested that General von Falkenhausen was certainly quite above suspicion. "I don't trust any German!" exclaimed Miss Smedley, passionately.

It is impossible not to like and respect her, so grim and sour and passionate; so mercilessly critical of every one, herself included—as she sits before the fire, huddled together, as if all the suffering, all the injustice of the world were torturing her bones like rheumatism. She has just suffered a great personal disaster. Her notes and photographs, taken during her latest visit to the Eighth Route Army, have all disappeared in the Chinese post. "There's plenty of people here", she commented, darkly, "who didn't want them to arrive."

Towards the end of our interview she appeared to soften a little. Auden's untidiness pleased her, I think. "After all," one could see her reflecting, "they're probably quite harmless." "Do you always", she asked ironically, "throw your coats on the floor?" Before we left she wrote us an introduction to the Hankow office of the Eighth Route Army.

The press conference this afternoon was particularly dreary. Austria cast its shadow over us all, and the glib evasions of the official war-bulletin made our hearts sink with boredom and apprehensive despair. We sneaked out early in the middle of an immense tactical lecture by a Chinese correspondent lately returned from the front.

This evening we called at the offices of the Eighth Route Army. They, too, are in the former Japanese Concession, not far from the German headquarters. Everything seemed very friendly and informal. We spent a quarter of an hour with Comrade Po Ku, the Army's Hankow representative, sitting on stools in a bare little room, and drinking glasses of hot water into which a few tea-leaves had been dropped. Po Ku himself took part in the Long March across the Grasslands to the North-West. He is frail-looking, gentle-voiced, and gay, with a slight squint. His movements appear somewhat numbed, as though he had stayed far too long out in the snow.

Po Ku asked if we were thinking of visiting the Eighth Route Army. We said, "No—so many journalists have been up there already, and written about it so well. Besides, the journey requires more time than we could possibly allow." Po Ku agreed, but suggested that after we return to Hankow we might travel down to the south-eastern front. Another Communist army (the new Fourth Army) is being formed at Nanchang. If we cared to, he would give us the necessary letters. We agreed that this might be a very good idea.

March 13.

This evening we have seen our first Chinese opera. We were the guests of Mr Hsiao Tung-tze, managing director of the Central News Agency. Mr Hsiao has been more than kind to us already: he has promised to present each of us with an album of Chinese operatic records to take home to England.

Tonight they were performing the original Chinese version of the westernized play called *Lady Precious Stream*. We arrived late, during the big scene in which Lady Precious Stream recognizes her husband on his return from fighting the barbarians of the west.

The theatre was packed. Every one in the audience was laughing, talking, shouting across the auditorium to greet his friends. People kept coming in and going out. Attendants ran round with hot face-towels and glasses of tea. It seemed nearly impossible to hear a single word from the stage: but no doubt this didn't matter, because the public knew the whole play by heart. As Auden remarked, it was like hearing Mass in an Italian church.

The performance was highly artificial and ritualistic—a mixture of song, ballet, fairy-story, and knock-about. The dresses were gorgeous: scarlet, orange, or green silk, embroidered with fantastic flowers and dragons. The head-dress is symbolically important: Generals in command of armies wear four flags planted on their heads, like the regimental colours in a military chapel; the hero has a kind of pin-cushion crown, stuck with flowers; the barbarian princess trails two enormously long peacock feathers from her hair, like an insect's antennae. The female roles are played by men—their faces transformed by make-up into pink and white masks. The sleeves of their robes are cut so that they fall almost to the floor. The gestures made by the actors in flapping these sleeves, to express anger or contempt, are an important technical feature of the drama, and are closely watched by connoisseurs in the audience. Emperors wear long beards, villains comic masks. There is hardly any attempt at scenery; only a single back-drop, some cushions, and a few chairs. The stage-hands lounge at the back of the stage, in full view of the spectators, occasionally coming forward to place a cushion, adjust the folds in an actor's robe, or offer a bowl of tea to refresh one of the singers after a difficult passage. This tea-drinking has become, in the course of centuries, an integral part of the performance. It is said of an actor: "He drinks his tea beautifully." The actors also show great dexterity in handling the cushions on which they kneel in moments of supplication or despair; when they have finished with them they skim them nonchalantly back to the stage-hands, with a flick of the wrist, like quoits.

There is a certain amount of spoken dialogue, but the opera consists chiefly of sung recitative, within a five-note compass. The orchestra is seated upon the stage itself: there are several percussion instruments, a violin, and a sort of bagpipe. The singing is thin, reedy, nasalized; to western ears it startlingly resembles Donald Duck. We were quite unable to distinguish the gay from the tragic, or the bridge-passage from the climax. But the audience, despite its chatter, was evidently following the music with critical attention; for, at certain points, it broke into the kind of applause which, in Europe, greets a very pretty high C.

Our Chinese hosts did their best to explain the story. Some women flap their sleeves. "The wives are despising her for not having a husband." Lady Precious Stream utters some piercing, Disneyesque sounds. "Now she is reconciling filial piety with her wifely duty." A general is sent to kill the hero; they engage in a ballet-fight. The hero, to our surprise, is beaten. But he has won a moral victory, for the general repents and begs his forgiveness. The old Emperor, father of Lady Precious Stream, is deposed, and the hero takes the throne. His frumpish old mother is honoured; the villain is led out to execution. The old Emperor sulks a bit, but gives in at last with a good grace. Lady Precious Stream receives a little flag to show that she is now Wife Number One.

March 14.

This afternoon Mr Donald took us to have tea with Madame Chiang Kai-shek.

We crossed the river to Wuchang in the lace-curtained cabin of a private Government launch. The guards all sprang to attention and saluted as we stepped on board; Donald leading the way, looking very grand and ministerial in his fur coat with its black astrakhan collar. His cold was still bothering him, he told us.

The Generalissimo and Madame are living, at present, in the old provincial army headquarters. Our car passed under a stone gateway, flanked by painted lions, circled a lawn beneath which a solid-looking dug-out had been built, and stopped before the guarded doors of the villa. Donald took us straight upstairs to wait in a small sitting-room, furnished in sham walnut, like the interior of an English road-house. From the bare wall the photograph of Dr Sun Yat-sen looked down, decorated with the crossed flags of the Republic and the Kuomintang. In the corner stood a cabinet full of cutlery and dusty champagne-glasses; on a table a cellophane box enclosed a huge birthday-cake, at least two feet high. Yesterday, Donald told us, was Madame's birthday. The cake was a present from the ladies of Hankow. Madame was going to send it to a home for refugee children.

A servant brought in the tea-things and, a few moments later, Madame herself appeared. She is a small, round-faced lady, exquisitely dressed, vivacious rather than pretty, and possessed of an almost terrifying charm and poise. Obviously she knows just how to deal with any conceivable type of visitor. She can become at will the cultivated, westernized woman with a knowledge of literature and art; the technical expert, discussing aeroplane-engines and machine-guns; the inspector of hospitals; the president of a mothers' union; or the simple, affectionate, clinging Chinese wife. She could be terrible, she could be gracious, she could be businesslike, she could be ruthless; it is said that she sometimes signs death-warrants with her own hand. She speaks excellent English, with an intonation which faintly recalls her American college-training. Strangely enough, I have never heard anybody comment on her perfume. It is the most delicious either of us have ever smelt.

We began by congratulating her upon her birthday.

"Ah . . ." she smiled and shook her head, with a simplicity which was none the less attractive for being artificial: "I hoped no one would know. . . . A man likes to have birthdays. A lady not. It reminds her that she is getting old."

We sat down at the tea-table. "Please tell me," said Madam, "do poets like cake?"

"Yes," replied Auden. "Very much indeed."

"Oh. I am glad to hear it. I thought perhaps they preferred only spiritual food."

The cakes were extremely good. (Had Donald chosen them, we wondered?) Madame herself ate nothing. Behind her mask of vivacity she looked tired and far from well. We chatted about England, about our journey, about our impressions of China. When we had finished she said: "And now perhaps you would like to ask me some questions?"

We answered that we should like her to tell us something about the New Life Movement.

In Hongkong we had heard our first reports of this curious moral crusade, launched by the Generalissimo and his wife, four years ago—and they had been most unfavourable. Priggery and hypocrisy, it seemed, were flavoured unpleasantly with police bullying. A specimen frock, showing the correct length of sleeve for a chaste woman, had been exhibited in Peking. A young English traveller had been reprimanded in the streets of Sian for smoking a pipe out of doors. Some people even had had their teeth compulsorily scrubbed. Mixed walking, it was rumoured, was forbidden in the cities of the interior.

(This public segregation of the sexes is, of course, nothing new in China. As the essay of a modern Hongkong student so charmingly put it: "In the days of Confucius everything was well managed in the Land of Loo. The coffin-cloths were fine and thick. Men and women walked on opposite sides of the street.")

Mr Tsang, the Mayor of Canton, had been more reassuring: "New life is not *under* and not *over* human nature." But, so far, every one we had met, Chinese and European alike, had seemed slightly vague about the exact character of the Movement itself.

Folding her hands and lowering her eyes to the table Madame now began to deliver what was evidently, to her, a familiar lecture. For centuries, she told us, the Chinese people had been ruled by a despotic governing class. Therefore, when China became a republic, they had very little idea of how to govern themselves. The officials of the old imperial order had possessed a definite moral code which, in theory at least, they acknowledged as binding—however often they may have failed to put it into practice. But this moral code died with them, and a period of chaos ensued, which was a fertile breeding-ground for Communist propaganda. And so the New Life Movement was inaugurated in a speech by the Generalissimo himself at Nanchang, in 1934. According to Madame, it was the sight of the desolation wrought by the Communists in Kiangsi Province and the feeling that something must be done for the peasants which roused the Generalissimo to action.

(Elsewhere we have heard a different and more convincing explanation. When the Nanking Government suppressed the Communists it still had to reckon with the effects of their propaganda amongst the common people, who had come to respect them and to learn from them a different way of life. The New Life Movement was therefore, according to this view, a direct attempt to compete with the Communist platform of economic and social reform, substituting a retreat to Confucius for an advance to Marx. In a sense Madame herself admitted this when she said: "We are giving the people what the Communists promised but couldn't perform.")

The New Life Movement is based on the practice of four moral virtues: *Li* or Reason, *I* or Propriety of the Outward Man, *Lien* or Moral Judgment, and *Chih* or Conscience. It aims at instilling into the people ideals of civic responsibility and social service. Volunteers have been sent out to check administrative corruption, clean city streets, and generally raise the standard of public health. Hospitals and relief-works have been established. Mah-jongg and opium-smoking have been forbidden. Government officials are not allowed to visit brothels.

Madame, we were bound to admit, made all this sound eminently practical and sensible: "To Europeans, our virtue of Outward Propriety may seem rather silly. But China has forgotten these things, and so they are important." We repeated some of the stories we had heard of reformist extravagance, and she agreed that they were probably quite true. Some of the followers of the Movement had been stupid, over-zealous, dizzy with success; but the Government certainly did not encourage them.

We asked her whether, after the war was over, the Government would be prepared to co-operate with the Communists. "It is not a question", Madame replied, "of our co-operating with the Communists. The question is: Will the Communists co-operate with *us*?" "I had two Communist women to tiffin today," she added. "I told them: 'As long as the Communists want to fight for China we are all friends.'"

Just as we had said good-bye and were leaving the room, an officer came up the stairs. It was the Generalissimo himself. We should hardly have recognized in this bald, mild-looking, brown-eyed man, the cloaked, poker-stiff figure of the news-reels. In public and on official occasions, Chiang is an almost sinister presence; he has the fragile impassivity of a spectre. Here in private he seemed gentle and shy. Madame led him out on to the balcony to pose, arm-in-arm, for yet another photograph. Under the camera's eye he stiffened visibly, like a schoolboy who is warned to hold himself upright.

On the way back to Hankow we discussed the Movement and the Chiang régime. Could China ever be cleaned up? Auden, himself a veteran enemy of compulsory hygiene, was sceptical. We laughed as we pictured Chiang, Madame, and Donald flying frantically about the country by aeroplane, clearing out the drains in one city, buttoning up the coats in another, starting a trachoma-clinic in a third. By the time they had finished the first city would be filthy again and the coat-collars in the second already beginning to come apart.

"As long as you fight for China", Madame had told the Communists, "we are all friends." No doubt. But what does she mean by "China"? Is this struggle to be a mere "coolies' war", fought to make the country safe for a continuance of the rule of the "Soong Dynasty", the small and all-powerful clan of bankers to which Madame herself belongs? Can Chiang, with his long record of Communist-suppression, ever form a permanent alliance with men like Mao Tse-tung and Chou En-lai, whose whole lives have been devoted to the workers' struggle? It is certainly hard to believe.

Nevertheless, it is impossible not to feel that the leadership of the Chiangs is vital for China, as long as this war continues. And Madame herself, for all her artificiality, is certainly a great heroic figure. There is one story about her which particularly pleases us. A few months ago the Japanese proposed some extremely impudent peace terms; their offer was made through the medium of a neutral foreign ambassador. The ambassador came to tea and delivered his prepared speech. There was an awkward silence. Somewhat embarrassed, the ambassador added: "Of course, I give you this message without any comment." Madame looked at him: "I should hope so," she said quietly. Then, switching on all her charm: "Tell me, how are your children?" This was the only answer the Japanese ever received.

March 15.

This evening, as we were walking home to dinner, the air-raid sirens began to scream. One of them, the loudest, bellowed from far away across the river, like a sick cow. The bare trees in the snowy consulate garden had seemed heavy with black leaves; but the leaves were rooks, and now, startled up into the orange evening sky, they circled hither and thither, weaving gigantic intricate patterns. The police began to clear the streets, hustling rickshaw-boys into the cover of archways and doors. The abandoned rickshaws were lined, like kneeling camels, along the gutters of the already deserted road. It was a solemn, apprehensive moment, as if before an eclipse of the sun.

With the Consul and several others we climbed to the roof of one of Hankow's highest buildings, the American bank which stands on the Bund, near to the British Consulate. The electric current had already been switched off, so the lift wasn't working, and we had to grope our way up flight after flight of stairs in the pitch darkness. On the roof there was plenty of light, for the brief dusk was over and the moon was full.

The brilliant moon lit up the Yangtze and the whole of the darkened city. The streets lay empty and dead, except when a lorry, carrying soldiers or ambulance-workers, tore down them, shrieking its brakes at the corners. Already the sirens had sounded for the second time—announcing that the raiders had crossed the inner danger-zone and were within twenty minutes' flying-distance of Hankow. Now at any moment they would be here.

A pause. Then, far off, the hollow, approaching roar of the bombers, boring their way invisibly through the dark. The dull, punching thud of bombs falling, near the air-field, out in the suburbs. The searchlights criss-crossed, plotting points, like dividers; and suddenly there they were, six of them, flying close together and high up. It was as if a microscope had brought dramatically into focus the bacilli of a fatal disease. They passed, bright, tiny, and deadly, infecting the night. The searchlights followed them right across the sky; guns smashed out; tracer-bullets bounced up towards them, falling hopelessly short, like slow-motion rockets. The concussions made you catch your breath; the watchers around us on the roof exclaimed softly, breathlessly: "Look! look! there!" It was as tremendous as Beethoven, but *wrong*—a cosmic offence, an insult to the whole of Nature and the entire earth. I don't know if I was frightened. Something inside me was flapping about like a fish. If you looked closely you could see dull red shrapnel-bursts and vicious swarms of red sparks, as the Japanese planes spat back. Over by the aerodrome a great crimson blossom of fire burst from the burning hangars. In ten minutes it was all over, and they had gone.

"Afraid we didn't put up a very good show tonight," said a British naval officer, as we stumbled downstairs. "Looks as if they caught the home team on the ground."

He was right. We heard later that six Chinese planes had been destroyed before they had had time to take the air.

3

Two days later, at seven o'clock in the morning, we left Hankow by train for Cheng-chow.

Our servant Chiang accompanied us to the station. Already before dawn he had arrived at the Consulate to report for his first day of duty—a demure and dignified figure, in his patent leather shoes, black silk robe, spotless linen and European felt hat. His grandeur tacitly reproved our shabbiness—Auden's out-at-elbow sports-coat, my dirty, baggy flannels. We were unworthy of our employee. He was altogether a gentleman's gentleman.

At the ticket-barrier, Chiang began to exhibit his powers. Herding the coolies with our baggage ahead of him he flourished our government passes (stamped with the Generalissimo's own chop) beneath the awed nose of the sentry. We should have lost face, no doubt, had we deigned to present them ourselves. Then, when everything was arranged, Chiang stepped aside, with a smiling bow, to let us pass. This, his unctuous gesture seemed to say, is how Big Shots board a brain.

No sooner had we settled into our compartment, than Chiang bustled off, to carry on the process of face-making among the car-boys. "My masters", he undoubtedly told them, "are very important personages. They are the friends of the Generalissimo and the King of England. We are travelling to the front on a special mission. You had better look after us well, or there might be trouble." The car-boys, no doubt, knew just how much of this to believe; but their curiosity was aroused, nevertheless, and they all came to peep and smile at us through the corridor window. We may have undone Chiang's work a little by winking and waving back. But perhaps we were not unimposing figures, with our superbly developed chests—padded out several inches by thick wads of Hankow dollar-bills stuffed into every available inner pocket. This seemed a dangerous way to carry money, but traveller's cheques would have been useless in many of the places to which we were going.

This train was in every way superior to those running on the Canton–Hankow line. In peace-time it would have taken you through to Peking. Nowadays it went no further than Cheng-chow: the railway bridge over the Yellow River had been blown up to check the Japanese advance. There was a handsome dining-car, with potted plants on the tables, in which we spent most of the day. This dining-car had only one serious disadvantage: there were not enough spittoons. Two of the available five were placed just behind our respective chairs, and the passengers made use of them unceasingly, clearing their throats before doing so with most unappetizing relish. In China, it seems, children learn to spit when they are two years old, and the habit is never lost. True, the New Life Movement discourages it, but without any visible effect. Even high government officials of our acquaintance hawked and spat without the least restraint.

Our journey was quite uneventful, despite the usual prophecies of air-attack. The train ran steadily on through the golden-yellow landscape. The snow had all disappeared, and the sun was hot; but it was still winter here, the trees were leafless and the earth bare and dry. All around us spread the undulating, densely inhabited plain. At a single glance from the carriage-window, one could seldom see less than two hundred people dotted over the paddy-fields, fishing with nets in village ponds, or squatting, on bare haunches, to manure the earth. Their gestures and attitudes had a timeless anonymity; each single figure would have made an admirable "condition humaine" shot for a Russian peasant-film. What an anonymous country this is! Everywhere the labouring men and women, in their clothes of deep, brilliant blue; everywhere the little grave-mounds, usurping valuable square feet of the arable soil—a class-struggle between the living and the dead. The naked, lemon-coloured torsos, bent over their unending tasks, have no individuality; they seem folded and reticent as plants. The children are all alike—gaping, bleary-nosed, in their padded jackets, like stuffed, mass-produced dolls. Today, for the first time, we saw women rolling along, balanced insecurely as stiltwalkers on their tiny bound feet.

We arrived in Cheng-chow after midnight, two hours behind time. The moon shone brilliantly down on the ruined station, smashed in a big air-raid several weeks before. Outside, in the station-square, moonlight heightened the drama of the shattered buildings; this might have been Ypres in 1915. An aerial torpedo had hit the Hotel of Flowery Peace; nothing remained standing but some broken splinters of the outer walls, within which people were searching the débris by the light of lanterns. All along the roadway street-vendors were selling food, under the flicker of acetylene flares. Chiang told us that Cheng-chow now did most of its business by night. In the daytime the population withdrew into the suburbs, for fear of the planes.

A few yards down the main street from the square we found an hotel with an intact roof and an available bedroom. The proprietor warned us that we should be expected to leave it at 8 a.m.; during the daytime all the hotels were closed. Chiang bustled about, giving orders to everybody, admirably officious to secure our comfort. The beds were unpacked and erected, tea was brought; with his own hands he steadied the table by placing a piece of folded toilet-paper under one of the legs. Where would he sleep himself, we asked. "Oh, it doesn't matter," Chiang replied, modestly smiling. "I shall find a place." He seemed positively to be enjoying this adventure. We both agreed that we had got a treasure.

I slept very badly that night, dozing only in five-minute snatches until dawn. From the station-sidings came the mournful wail of locomotives, mingling with cries of the nocturnal street-hawkers and the constant shuffling and chatter of people moving about downstairs. Through a window beside my bed I could see the ragged bomb-hole in the roof of the next-door house, and the snapped beam-ends poking up forlornly into the clear moonlight. Why should the people of this town assume that the Japs would only attack during the daytime? Tonight, for example, would be ideal. . . . And I remembered how Stephen Spender had told me of a very similar experience he had had during a visit to wartime Spain. Meanwhile, in the opposite bed, Auden slept deeply, with the long, calm snores of the truly strong.

Immediately after breakfast we set out for the American Mission Hospital. The Consul-General in Hankow had given us an introduction to Dr Ayres, its chief. Cheng-chow, viewed by daylight, seemed less dramatic, but infinitely more depressing. It stands at the junction of China's two main railway lines: the Pin-Han, running north and south; the Lung-Hai, running east and west. In peace time, Cheng-chow exploited its key-position to the full. It was a city of gangsters, gamblers, prostitutes, and thieves. All trains, we had been told, stopped there for twenty-two hours—simply in order to give the passengers time to visit the drug-dens and the brothels. When, at intervals, an agitation arose to speed up the train service, the principal hotel-keepers and opium-joint-proprietors would send a delegation to Nanking with a suitable bribe, to plead for the maintenance of the original schedule.

The houses of the main streets were pretentious, sinister, and shabby, coated all over with a peculiarly evil-smelling, sticky dust which blew in clouds about the town. We pushed our way down the long, straggling market-lane which led to the hospital gates. At intervals, amidst the booths and shops, were shallow dug-outs, barely a yard deep and no larger than a dog-kennel, roofed over roughly with planks, earth, and straw. In my jaundiced, sleepy mood, everything I noticed seemed miserable and corrupt. Every third person in the crowd appeared to be suffering from trachoma, or goitre, or hereditary syphilis. And the foodstuffs they were buying and selling looked hateful beyond belief—the filthiest parts of the oldest and most diseased animals; stodgy excrement-puddings; vile, stagnant soups and poisonous roots.

It was a relief to find ourselves in Dr Ayres's sitting-room, with all its wild, grass-widower's untidiness—odd shoes, old coats, sweaters, and surgical instruments scattered everywhere; used razor-blades and tea-cups on the mantelpiece; medical books sandwiched between last year's copies of the *Saturday Evening Post*. The place certainly needed a feminine hand. It was dirty, but with the kind of dirt to which we were accustomed. We felt at home at once.

Dr Ayres himself, a charming, drawling southerner from the State of Georgia, welcomed us like old friends expected for months. He was just having breakfast, and presently in burst his colleagues—Dr Hankey and Dr McClure.

"Boy," cried McClure, rubbing his hands, "I've got a kidney today! Gee, what luck!"

"Oh, Bob," said Hankey protestingly. "You might let me do it!"

"No, *Sir!* I want to have a stab at it myself."

Hankey, we discovered during the course of the meal, was a newcomer to China. He was an Englishman, and had volunteered for war-work direct from Guy's. Tall, lanky, and young, beaming behind his thick spectacles, he amused and delighted the others by his enthusiasm for every novelty. Everything thrilled him—bomb-craters, pagodas, stomach-wounds, the faces of old beggars: he was perpetually whipping out his camera for a photograph.

McClure was a stalwart, sandy, bullet-headed Canadian Scot, with the energy of a whirlwind and the high spirits of a sixteen-year-old boy. He wore a leather blouse, riding breeches and knee-boots with straps. Born in China, educated in Canada, he had earned his college fees by working as a stevedore and a barber. Before the war he had had his own hospital at Wei-hwei, north of the Yellow River. It was now in Japanese hands. At present he was acting as a co-ordinator of Red Cross services; and visiting, in this capacity, all the hospitals and mission-stations up and down the Lung-Hai line.

After our second breakfast we were taken round the premises. In the compound Dr Ayres had built a big thatched emergency-hut to accommodate the overflow of wounded. Most of the in-patients were suffering from bomb-injuries: fractured legs and arms. Trunk-wounds, the doctors told us, were mostly fatal; the victims were usually brought in too late, and died of sepsis. The Japanese had been very active in the Cheng-chow region lately, attacking not only the town itself, but many of the surrounding villages. McClure himself had had an extremely narrow escape, only a week or two before: the ferry-boat in which he was crossing a river had been destroyed a few moments after he had jumped into the water. Two bombs had been dropped here in the mission compound, just beside the enormous outspread American flag.

The operating-theatre was a scene of lively, rough-and-ready activity. The work of six surgeons had to be done by three—and quickly; there was no time for professional niceties. People strolled in with telegrams or parcels, and remained to help, to the best of their ability; there was something for everybody to hold: a leg, a towel, or a bucket. In the general confusion, while Ayres's back was turned for an instant, one of the operating-tables upset. The patient's head hit the floor with a resounding crack. He looked slightly dazed, but didn't complain.

At lunch McClure told us that he was leaving that evening to visit some hospitals in the direction of Kai-feng. Kwei-teh would be his first destination. Why shouldn't we go with him? We agreed that we should like to, and went upstairs to Dr Ayres's bedroom to lay in some reserves of sleep.

After a late supper we started out. Chiang was silent this evening, and inclined to be unhelpful; perhaps he was intimidated by McClure's dynamic presence. We were semi-apologetic about the extent of our baggage, uneasily suspecting that McClure considered our possession of beds and a private servant as slightly sissy. He himself carried only a small suitcase. When we reached the station half a dozen coolies sprang out of the darkness, each struggling for a bag. McClure punched one of them hard on the jaw. The man wasn't a bona-fide porter, he explained later, but a railroad thief.

The train, we were told, would leave at ten minutes to two. We had several hours to wait. The platform, unlighted, crowded with troops, was bitterly cold. But McClure's energy warmed us like a brazier.

Himself a Presbyterian, he had no use for dogma in mission-work; it was silly to bother the Chinese with theological language which they couldn't understand. Phrases like "washed in the Blood" merely disgust them; "the King of Heaven" suggests to their minds only a sort of super-tax-collector. "If you stand up on a soap-box you only get hold of the loafer who's on the look-out for an easy job. The people we want are the farmers. And they're too busy to come and listen to a lot of talk. This crusader-stuff is the bunk."

"In this century mankind's got to choose between alcohol and the combustion-engine. You can't run both. The hospitals are full of saps who try to. If you want to go fast you've got to live clean. . . . Reminds me of a funny thing. I used to work in Formosa, you know. One day an old man came into my clinic. Said he couldn't remember his age; thought he must be close on eighty. 'Why, boy,' I said, 'you've got a physique like man of twenty-five!' And he had, too. Magnificent! Well, I thought to myself, here's a chance to teach the students something. So I had them all come in. 'See here,' I said to them, 'this is what you get from living clean. Look at him—and now take a look at yourselves!' Then I asked the old man: 'You don't smoke, I suppose?' 'No, never.' 'And I guess you don't drink, either?' 'I do not.' 'Don't play around with women?' No, he didn't care to do that, any more. 'Well,' I said, 'to what do you attribute your wonderful health? Tell these gentlemen, please.' So he thought for a minute, and then he said: 'Twice every day I take a little opium. There's nothing like it.' That certainly was one on me, eh—with my Y.M.C.A. stuff?"

Two o'clock came, and half-past, and there was still no train. But Mc-Clure didn't despair. The station-master had assured him that a troop-train would be passing through Cheng-chow at three. "That suits me all right. They're apt to be a bit overcrowded. We'll have to sit on the roof, I guess. . . . Only thing—if the Japs come over you've got to jump. Quick. Those trains are loaded full of ammunition. You wouldn't have a chance. Not a chance."

The troop-train, not altogether to my disappointment, never arrived. Propped against each other, like sacks, on a hard wooden bench, we dozed and froze patiently until seven o'clock. Then we returned to the mission-hospital for breakfast. At nine McClure was back in the operating-theatre, tinkering away at the casualties with unimpaired vigour.

At tea-time we came in to find McClure and two bearded Italian mission-aries listening with grave faces to the wireless. The Italians had brought news that Kwei-teh had already fallen; even the Chinese newspaper admitted that the Japanese had captured a town only twenty-five miles further north. But the wireless-bulletin told us nothing new; and we agreed that we had better attempt the journey, at any rate as far as Kai-feng. "Whatever happens," said McClure joyfully, "we'll be in the thick of it!"

Tonight a train was promised for eleven o'clock. At twelve-thirty we were told that it had actually reached the North Station, only a mile away. McClure decided that he and I should walk there, along the track, leaving Auden and Chiang to look after the luggage. In this way we should be more likely to get seats. As we set out it began to rain. Several hundred yards down the line there was a most unpleasant bridge, open to the water beneath. You had to cross it by stepping delicately from girder to girder, hoping that the gaps, invisible in the darkness, would be roughly equidis-tant. "What shall we do", I asked timidly, "if the train comes now?" "Jump it," replied McClure promptly, and proceeded to explain the proper technique of jumping trains, if you didn't want a broken neck.

But, to my surprise and relief, the train actually was waiting. McClure efficiently identified it from among a dozen others. We even found a sleeping-compartment with four vacant berths. At first he was inclined to turn up his nose at so much unnecessary comfort; but I cunningly pleaded with him to accept it for the sake of Auden, who, I hinted, was far from well.

Auden, meanwhile, had had an alarming experience. After a visit to the station lavatory at the far end of the sidings, he had returned to find that Chiang and our luggage had utterly disappeared—swallowed up in a vast, amorphous mass of sleeping soldiers and refugees which grew perpetually larger, like a nightmare fungus, and threatened gradually to cover the entire platform. It had taken him an hour's search to find them again. "I really began to be afraid", he told us, "that I'd lost you all for ever."

At nine o'clock next morning we reached Min-Chuan—a name which, translated, means "Democracy". It was no more than a loop-line, a signal, and a hut, set down, without apparent object, beside a bedraggled grove of willows, in the midst of an immense mud plain. Auden called it "The Bad Earth".

We had plenty of time to dislike the view, for we stayed at Democracy six and a half hours. Why, nobody could tell. McClure predicted that the Japanese must be advancing up the line, and that presently we should all have to retreat to Cheng-chow on foot. His morale, we couldn't help noticing, was slightly impaired. Indeed, he admitted this himself. "It's because", he explained, "my system's running short of sugar. If I can only get something sweet, I'll be all right. What I need, right now, is a box of candy."

Out of the rainy mist, as if in answer to his request, a crowd began to gather. They were neighbouring peasants who had come to sell their wares, scenting from afar the presence of our train. Standing in the drizzle, in their fur hats and straw capes, they offered boiled chicken varnished red with soya beans, sausage-shaped waffles made from bean-flour, grey vermicelli, sugar-cane and hard-boiled eggs. We bought eggs, waffles, and a stick of cane, which McClure sucked contentedly. Its tonic effect upon him was almost immediately apparent. Soon the Bad Earth was forgotten, and we were listening to a further instalment of his lavishly-illustrated autobiography. Our only hope was that it would continue until this journey was over.

In Cheng-chow he had bought a lorry and run it into a quicksand, while disembarking from the Yellow River ferry. Within half an hour the sand had been up to the instrument-board, but they had got it out, nevertheless. "I had to take it apart and clean it, nut by nut. And, boy, when I'd got it apart, I couldn't put the darned thing together again! So I went to Peking, and worked in a Chevrolet garage for a month—learning how."

"One time I was medical adviser to a General. A real old bandit. Boy, was he tough? Wouldn't pay his fees. After a while, when he owed me five hundred dollars, they told me he was going to give me a testimonial tablet. Of course, I knew what that meant. In this country, if you give a man a tablet, it cancels all your debts. So I went around to the tablet-carver, and I said: 'That tablet's not going to be ready till I say the word.' Sure enough, every day that old bandit would send word to ask how the tablet was getting along. And every day the carver would tell him: 'One of the characters isn't just how I want it. I guess I'll do it again.' Was he mad? But I got my money all right, in the end."

At half-past three, without the least warning, the train moved forward. We had almost forgotten that it possessed an engine and wheels. McClure told us that eastern Ho-Nan is the great wheat-growing district of China. The Chinese is essentially a market-gardener. He cultivates wheat as the English grow roses. He makes a hole for each single plant, and fills it with night soil. In consequence the yield per acre is very high. The Anglo-American Tobacco Company, said McClure, once sent out a party of experts to show the Chinese how to grow tobacco. But, at the end of two years, their experimental farm, equipped with all the latest scientific methods, couldn't produce as big a crop as the Chinese did, on their own.

Where the Chinese failed, he thought, was in their utter lack of co-operative spirit. When the crops are ripe each peasant has to guard his little plot with a gun. If he falls asleep for a moment his neighbours will steal some of it—and the whole village will think this right and proper. When McClure himself had started a co-operative irrigation scheme with electric pumps, the project had had to be dropped, because it would have necessitated closing some wells and deepening others; and no one was prepared to have his own well closed. Similarly, a superior kind of peach has recently been brought to China, but it cannot be grown unless an entire community is ready to agree to its introduction. Otherwise, local jealousy would be such that the fruit would all be stolen before it was ripe.

Fights over property are not uncommon. For example, a woman has a hen. When she is feeding it a neighbour's hen runs up to share the grain. The two women have words and exchange blows. The owner of the hen then tells her son, who immediately attacks the son of the neighbour. Finally, every member of both families joins in, and there follows what McClure calls "a knock-down and drag-out", in the course of which several people will probably be wounded or killed.

Cheating in business, he added, was nearly universal. Clay beans were manufactured, at considerable trouble and expense, to adulterate bean flour. Wheat was made heavier by the addition of tacks and scrap-metal.

The magnetic separator of a flour-mill in this district removes at least one hundred and fifty pounds of metal a day.

Towards five o'clock we arrived at Shang-kui, Kwei-teh's nearest railway station. The distance between Kwei-teh and Shang-kui is about five miles; we covered it in rickshaws, along a flat, rough road, lined with trees. The buildings of the Church of Canada Mission Hospital stand in their own large compound-garden, beyond the air-field, just outside the city. It seems strangely touching, in the midst of the alien plain, to come upon these prim, manse-like walls of grey brick, so isolated, so stubbornly Anglo-Saxon, despite the pointed, upcurving eaves of their corrugated iron roofs. After the drill-ground bareness of Cheng-chow, the garden itself seemed wonderfully fruitful and pleasant. The trees were full of birds—crows and beautiful blue-jays, with white throat-collars and long sky-blue tails.

McClure entered like Father Christmas, with a double postman's knock, and soon, amidst back-slappings and kidney-punchings, we were being introduced to his two Canadian colleagues, Dr Gilbert and Dr Brown.

Our first questions were, naturally, about the Japanese. Where were they? But nobody in Kwei-teh exactly knew. They might arrive at any moment to attack the city—or they might be still a long way off. The railway line to Sü-chow appeared to be unbroken, as yet. Trains were going daily east. Here they had had very few air-raids. Shang-kui station was occasionally bombed, but without much damage, so far.

Next afternoon, after a much-needed night of unbroken sleep, we all walked into the city, to call on the Roman Catholic bishop and on the local American Baptist missionary, Mr White. Seen from outside, Kwei-teh is a town of great beauty; its four massive walls, flanked by corner watch-towers, are surrounded by a wide, reedy moat. The gateways are plastered with advertisements. But these huge, boldly-daubed characters decorate rather than disfigure Chinese architecture—at any rate, to our western eyes. Within the walls is a maze of muddy, stinking streets. This place would be a death-trap in an air-raid. Life seemed unbearably cramped and confined; we were both conscious of a mild claustrophobia. "It gives you an idea", said Auden, "of what Europe must have been like in the Middle Ages."

The bishop, a rotund and cheerful pro-Franco Spaniard, welcomed us with a bottle of cherry-brandy. "This is the one good thing", he told us, "that comes out of Russia." He was not displeased at the prospect of a Japanese conquest. The Japanese, he said, would bring law and order to China.

Mr White was an altogether more sympathetic figure—pleasant-looking, quite young, with tooth-paste-advert teeth. Unlike the other

Protestant missionaries, he had kept his family with him—a wife and two small children. They invited us to lunch next day. The American flag in his garden had stuck half-way up the pole. McClure volunteered, of course, to shin up and get it down. McClure was in his element here. When the centrifugal pump at the hospital went wrong, he knew why; when the gas-plant failed, he could put it right; when the engine was making the wrong kind of noise, McClure detected it at once. Dr Brown, his friend since college days, provided a mock-admiring audience for all these feats of energy and skill.

On the way home Dr Gilbert told us that this countryside was once overrun with bandits. Since the war, however, there had been fewer. In China the bandit is usually a soldier out of work. But the road to the station was still unsafe after nightfall. Local men of property, coming up to Kwei-teh in rickshaws, had been attacked and robbed; the rickshaw-coolies simply ran away. And Dr Brown himself, driving the ambulance-truck down to Shang-kui late one evening, had been shouted at to stop, and fired on when he refused. McClure, needless to say, pooh-poohed the danger. Bandits were easy enough to deal with, he told us. You merely had to strike first. He had been cycling near Cheng-chow one evening when he spotted some suspicious characters lurking on the road ahead. "I didn't hesitate. I drew my gun right away, and fired a couple of shots into the air. Those bandits did the vanishing trick, all right! Man, I'll bet they're running yet!" The moral of this story was that both Auden and myself should carry automatic pistols. It wasn't the first time we'd heard this piece of advice, but we had no intention of following it.

Dr Gilbert then went on to tell us of a local missionary and his wife who happened, a few years ago, to be on a train which was just drawing into Shang-kui station. By the merest chance they decided to leave the coach in which they were travelling and move forward to another, where they could find more comfortable seats. As the train arrived, the two back coaches, which they had just quitted, were uncoupled, and promptly raked with machine-gun fire. The station authorities had got word that they contained some notorious bandits. The bandits were killed, all right; but so were many innocent passengers. The Mayor of Kwei-teh later expressed his regret that this should have been so. "It was", he agreed, "very unfortunate for the Pooblic."

Auden offered his cigarettes, which Dr Gilbert accepted, somewhat coyly. The standards of Kwei-teh hospital were liberal enough, in comparison with many others; but, even here, nicotine had the daring attraction of a minor vice. Elsewhere in the mission-field, so we had heard, the sternest taboos prevailed. Mission-doctors were obliged to smoke in secret, like schoolboys. If they were discovered there would be a public prayer-meeting for the salvation of their souls. In some places a doctor caught drinking a glass of wine by his minister would be liable to lose his job altogether. (It must be added that, in the course of our Yellow River journey, we witnessed few serious signs of this stupid and contemptible tyranny—no doubt because the tyrants themselves had been the first to abandon their posts and run away from the danger-zone. In general, only the best type of missionary had remained.)

We were just finishing breakfast next morning when Dr Brown invited us to attend service in the hospital chapel. The hymn they were singing had, as its refrain, the words, "Arise! Arise!" In Chinese it sounded like: "*Chee-ee-ee-ee lai!*" This tune, set to different words, is a favourite song of the Eighth Route Army. The Chinese minister, seeing that there were foreign visitors in the congregation, made the service last as long as he possibly could.

Afterwards, in the operating-theatre, we watched McClure and Brown at work. The patient had a vaginal-urethral fistula, sustained in child-birth. We took the opportunity of examining her feet. A girl's feet are generally bound at the age of four or five. All toes except the big toe are turned under the foot, and fastened in this position. Subsequent growth will then only have the effect of raising the arch, forming a deep groove across the centre of the sole, which is very liable to sores. The custom of foot-binding is gradually dying out in China. Most of the bound feet we saw in Kwei-teh were those of middle-aged or elderly women.

While he operated McClure kept up a running commentary for the benefit of the amused and slightly scandalized Canadian Sister. "Let's have something to kneel on. . . . You see, Sister, I'm more devotional than you think. . . . Now the torch. . . . Let your light so shine. . . . Oh boy, that's good! Sponge, Brother. . . . More light in the north-east. . . . Phew, I'm sweating. This is worse than two sets of tennis. . . . Now then, Bunty pulls the strings. Which string shall you pull, Brother? If you were in a sailing-ship, you'd be sunk. . . . Well, that's fixed the exhaust. We'll do the differential tomorrow. . . ."

Opposite the hospital buildings, there was a small enclosed plot of land, half kitchen-garden, half municipal park, which contained an obelisk commemorating the foundation of the Chinese Republic. Brown had heard that some bandits had been executed there the day before, so we went over to look. In the park were an old lady and some soldiers, eating their midday meal under a fruit-tree. "Their heads are over in that ditch," they told us. We hunted about for some time but could find nothing. "Oh well," remarked the old lady, casually, "then the dogs must have got them."

Brown thought it more likely that the bandits' relatives had carried off the heads, during the night. The Chinese, like the Japanese, have a horror of leaving a headless corpse behind them, for, without a head, they cannot hope to enter the next world. Even after a surgical amputation, the doctors have to offer the severed limb to the patient. He will probably wish to keep it until his death, when it will be buried with him. This is why, after a penal decapitation, the heads are usually stuck on poles above the city gates, out of reach of the victims' families.

In Kwei-teh, as elsewhere, the authorities' scale of punishments is fatally simple. In order to scare his cook, who had stolen and re-sold a large quantity of the hospital's sugar, Brown once reported him to the Mayor. Happening to glance out of the window next morning, he was just in time to prevent the cook being led out to be shot. When, later, he expostulated, the Mayor seemed surprised: "But I thought you wanted me to punish him?"

We lunched, as arranged, with the Whites. There was another guest, a Baptist minister from further down the line. We had fruit-juice, meat-loaf, salad, and cake. It was a resolutely cheerful little American household; Mrs White was educating her daughter with the aid of correspondence-school books. One couldn't help wondering what would have happened to them six months from now. If the Japanese came, the Whites had arranged to take refuge in the hospital-compound. Neither of them seemed in the least nervous at the prospect.

The meal opened with a slight misunderstanding. "I have a lot of bandits in my field," the Baptist minister told us.

"How very unpleasant for you," said Auden sympathetically. "Do they steal your vegetables?"

The minister looked somewhat puzzled until Mr White explained: "It's the mission-field he means."

The conversation then became professional: "In Loyang he heard the Gospel, and it took root." "He was quite a skilled silversmith, but when he became a Christian he refused to make dragons and other works of the Devil. So he lost his job." "The Japanese remind me of that text in Ezekiel xxix: 'But I will put hooks in thy jaws, and I will cause the fish of thy rivers to stick unto thy scales.'"

The Whites had a young fox-terrier. Mr White put a small piece of cake on the table, and asked: "Do you want it?" The dog cocked its ears but didn't move. "Are you a Catholic?" Mr White asked it. There was no response. "Are you an Anglican?" "Are you a Presbyterian?" "Are you a Seventh Day Adventist?" "Are you a Mormon?" Mr White turned to us proudly: "Now watch. . . . Are you an American Baptist?" The terrier jumped for the cake at once.

"But did you notice", said Mr White, "how he nearly made a move when I mentioned the Adventists? I'm kind of worried about him."

Next day was a brilliant warm spring morning. This is the time of year when the coolies begin to discard some of their heavy winter clothes and the lice, emerging from the padding, seek other hosts. "In the spring", the Chinese say, "the louse can fly."

From the road outside came the continual pig-squeal of wheelbarrows going past. To quote McClure, all Chinese wheelbarrows squeak, because the squeak is cheaper than the grease. Also, the boss can tell at once if one of his coolies quits work.

At crack of dawn McClure had set off to visit a mission-station somewhere to the south, riding Dr Brown's push-bike. McClure is one of the great apostles of the bicycle. He trusts it over any kind of country, as other men trust the horse. Dr Brown maintains, however, that, owing to the state of the roads, most of McClure's cycling is done on foot. We were more than sorry to see him go.

Really, the proceedings of the Chinese are so mysterious as to fill one, ultimately, with a kind of despair. During the morning Auden heard an explosion and ran out into the road to see what had happened. All he could see was an officer haranguing his men, and a group of peasants who were burning an old book. Then a woman rushed up and prostrated herself before the officer, wailing and sobbing. The officer raised her to her feet and, immediately, the two of them began talking quite naturally, as though nothing whatever had occurred.

Numbers of wounded soldiers arrived in rickshaws from the northern front. They had been several days *en route,* and a few of the rickshaws contained corpses. The wounded were all bandaged in the roughest possible way. Often a bit of dirty wadding from somebody's coat had been simply stuffed into the wound. Dr Brown told us that the warm intestines of a freshly-killed chicken are a favourite Chinese antiseptic.

Today we had decided to start trying to leave for Sü-chow. The being-about-to-start appeared to be an important phase of any journey through this part of China. Brown drove us that afternoon to Shang-kui, to interview his friend Mr Lin, the Sectional Engineer. Mr Lin was a charming, shock-headed gentleman, fervently patriotic: he had taken a vow, he told us, not to cut his hair until the Japanese had been driven right out of China. "When Shan-Tung is retaken, I cut a little. When Hopeh is retaken, I cut more. When Manchukuo is retaken, I cut all." He spoke vehemently of the Japanese atrocities against women: "Everywhere they are going, the Japanese committing adultery." "Manchukuo was the beginning," he said. "Then came Abyssinia. Then Spain. And now, you see, the Germans have take Australia without firing a single shop."

We inquired about our journey. Mr Lin assured us that there would be a train—there were always two trains to Sü-chow every day. True, it might be late, very late—it might even arrive tomorrow morning; nevertheless, it would be today's afternoon train. Meanwhile, if we wished, we could sleep at his house, so as to be nearer the railway station.

Dr Brown then took us for a walk round Shang-kui. It was a wretched little place, muddy, overcrowded, and infested with hens. We inspected the bath-house, where you were scrubbed in a big communal pool of steaming water, by little boys; and then conducted to a curtained-off apartment, where you could have your toes massaged, drink tea, and get a woman. One of the customers was covered with a syphilitic rash. Nobody minded being looked at; we merely felt embarrassed by our own clothed presence. The whole building was filthy and smelt heartily of urine. A third-class bath, we were informed, cost six cents, including tip.

We then went into a Chinese military hospital—actually a square of miserable, windowless huts, grouped round the sides of a compound. The wounded lay in their uniforms, on straw—three men often beneath a single blanket. The orderly told us that they had hardly any dressings or antiseptics, and no proper surgical instruments at all. We found eleven men lying in a room barely fifteen feet long and eight broad. In one hut the sweet stench of gas-gangrene from a rotting leg was so violent that I had to step outside to avoid vomiting. There was no X-ray apparatus here, of course, so very few of the bullets could be extracted. Those who were badly wounded could only be left to die. Indeed, it argued a strong constitution if they could get to the hospital at all. Some were stranded near the battlefield because they hadn't a dollar to pay for carriage.

Almost all the patients were apparently cheerful—despite the darkness, the stink of urine-sodden straw, the agonizing jolts which their wounds must continually have received from their bedfellows. Indeed, they thanked us for our kindness in coming to see them. Our visit upset all of us—and particularly Brown, who was much worried over his half-formed decision to leave Kwei-teh and join the Eighth Route Army, where he would have to work under similar conditions. I think the sight of these men finally made up his mind for him. He told us that when we returned from Sü-chow he would probably be ready to start.

We returned to the mission hospital for supper, and set off again at ten o'clock, loaded with presents of food from Dr Gilbert and the Sisters. Brown drove very fast, skidding wildly all over the muddy road; but nobody tried to stop us.

Mr Lin made us very comfortable. We erected our beds in his outer office. A boy brewed unending cups of tea, and we sat talking far into the night—chiefly about Confucius, of whom Mr Lin was an ardent disciple. "Confucius say: 'One must live without hurting others.' Very bright." On the wall of the office was a framed Chinese character, executed in sweep-

ing brush-strokes, with a thick, bushy tail—somewhat resembling an im-
pressionist drawing of a cat. Mr Lin told us that it signified "Going for-
ward smoothly, step by step." Certainly, we agreed, this was an admirable
motto for a railway engineer.

4

March 24.

We slept soundly, woke, breakfasted. Still no train. It arrived at last,
about 10.30 a.m. Just as we had got all our luggage on board, a large bell
on the roof of a neighbouring building began to toll—the local warning
of an air-raid. So, with several dozen others, we retired to the station dug-
out, a fine structure of concrete and wooden piles, with three rooms and
two exits, built by Mr Lin himself, in 1936, when the Chinese, seeing that
war was sooner or later inevitable, had begun to make their preparations.
The dugout was fitted with telephones; and a long, dramatically candle-lit
conversation followed with various stations further down the line. At the
end of half an hour we were told that the Japanese weren't coming af-
ter all.

So we started. Mr Lin's influence had procured us a free pass to Sü-
chow, and the station master came in person to see us off. We left Shang-
kui with faces much enlarged.

The carriage roofs, as usual, were black with passengers. On every jour-
ney, we are told, two or three of them fall off and are killed. At the last
moment, dozens of people tried to clamber on to the train, and were
beaten off with sticks. The train-guards even chased particularly agile
boys right along the platform, thrashing them unmercifully. But this, it
seemed, was only a kind of game, for the victims' padded coats were so
thick that the blows only raised a cloud of dust and lice; and pursuer and
pursued roared with laughter.

Our journey took up the whole of the day. There were the usual cups of
tea, the usual damp towels (we no longer wipe our faces with them, how-
ever, for McClure has warned us of the danger of trachoma-infection),
the usual hour-long halts. The stations were mostly small, and much alike,
with their rookeries, their basket-ball pitches, their food-vendors, their
lurid or cryptic anti-Japanese cartoons. At one place a young officer got
so bored that he began firing at the rooks with his revolver, and was se-
verely reprimanded by a hastily improvised court-martial in the waiting-
room. Chiang enjoyed himself hugely as face-maker and gossip-bearer.
This time, he told the car-boys, quite pointlessly, that we were doctors—
much to our alarm; for we expected at every station to be summoned to
perform major operations upon the wounded. "But at least", said Auden,
"we'd be better than nothing." So we agreed, if called upon, to have a try.

Not far from Sü-chow we passed an armoured train, its metal sides plastered with a camouflage of mud. Behind it was the Generalissimo's special coach. He and Madame, we learnt later, had been in Sü-chow, attending a military conference.

Presently Chiang came running excitedly to tell us that a Japanese prisoner had been taken on board our train. He had been captured somewhere near the Grand Canal. The Generalissimo had personally ordered that he should be kindly treated, and sent down to Hankow for cross-examination. He would go there on the return journey. Prisoners in this war are a kind of zoological rarity; we gaped at this one with furtive and somewhat shame-faced curiosity. A stout, round-faced youth, tied up with rope like a parcel, he seemed as isolated in his captivity as a baby panda. His half-dozen guards grinned at him cheerfully, but he looked sheepish and scared, as well he might—for one of them was negligently twirling a pistol on his index finger. It threatened at any moment to go off and shoot somebody in the foot. The Japanese, said Chiang, had been a tailor in civil life, but this was probably invented, for the prisoner spoke only his native language, and no one present could understand it. There was nothing we could do for him except to put a cigarette between his lips and go away as soon as was decently possible.

We arrived at Sü-chow at about half-past nine in the evening. Here, too, the station buildings have been damaged by air-raids, but not very seriously. No sooner had we emerged into the darkened street outside than we were set upon by a mob of rickshaw-coolies, yelling and snatching for our baggage. Chiang dealt with them most efficiently, though his methods are the very opposite of McClure's. In three or four minutes the bargaining and scuffling were over, and we were bumping over the cobbles, into the city.

We had arranged to stay the night at the Garden Hotel, chiefly because Chiang had been told, on the train, that it was the headquarters of General Li Tsung-jen. Li Tsung-jen and Pai Ch'ung-hsi are jointly in command of the Chinese armies in this zone: the soldiers refer to them as "The Two". Before the war these generals were the virtual dictators of Kwang-si Province, and the avowed enemies of the Generalissimo. That they and their troops are fighting up here in the north, hundreds of miles from their home, is one of the most striking instances of China's solidarity against the Japanese. We are anxious to meet Li Tsung-jen, because we want him to give us passes to visit the front. We have a letter of introduction to him from the all-providing Mr Hollington Tong.

General Li wasn't at the Garden Hotel, after all; but we decided to stop there, nevertheless. The hotel itself was full; we were given a room in a sort of garden pavilion. The place was draughty and cold; we unwisely tried to light the stove, which nearly smoked us out into the street. But, as

Auden remarked, it was better to die like Zola than like Captain Scott. And soon, despite the intimate noises which reached us, through the matchboard walls, from the rooms of our fellow-guests, we had both sunk into the heavy dreamless sleep of semi-asphyxia.

March 25.

This morning there was an air-raid, of which we saw and heard very little. The bombs seemed to be dropping at a considerable distance. When it was over we started off to call on Dr MacFadyen, of the Presbyterian Mission Hospital. We had a letter to him from Dr Brown.

Sü-chow is an attractive city of one-story houses with narrow, cobbled streets. It stands along the old bed of the Yellow River, which is several feet higher than the town itself. The police here are armed with flat swords; they carry them slung on their backs in short red sheaths.

When we arrived at the hospital Dr MacFadyen was out, so we went on to the house of his colleague, Dr Greer. This hospital has a very large compound. Besides the main building, the annexe, and the doctors' houses, there is a clinic for women, which is Dr Greer's special charge.

Dr Greer herself, a white-haired, apple-cheeked lady of seventy from the Southern States is, even on casual acquaintance, plainly one of the great figures of the China Mission. She wears a Chinese robe, with flat-heeled leather shoes and several pairs of thick woolen stockings. She welcomed us like long-lost grandsons, clapping her hands as she chatted, to hurry on the servants in their preparation of an emergency lunch.

Married to a missionary, but now a widow, she has spent the whole of her adult life here in Sü-chow, and today her sons and daughters are also missionaries, working in different parts of the country.

"You saw my clinic as you came by? My husband and I wanted that bit of ground for twenty years. And here's how we got it. . . ."

There had been trouble in the city at that time. Sü-chow was in the hands of a bandit army. The plot of land in question had been occupied by bandit-soldiers. Dr Greer's husband was in bed, very sick. One night, dozing beside him, Dr Greer awoke to see one of the bandits standing in the corner of the bedroom, holding her husband's revolver. Her first thought was, "He's going to kill my husband!" So she rushed at him. They struggled. The bandit threw her off and dashed out of the room. Dr Greer's husband woke up, exclaiming that they'd all be murdered. Dr Greer hastily gave him his medicine and an injection; then seized the poker and charged downstairs to continue the battle. But now she heard screams coming from her children's room. The bandit had run through it, dropping the revolver on the bed. "So back I ran—like an old hen after her chickens." Meanwhile, the bandit had jumped from a window into the garden and escaped. When Dr Greer's husband got well he complained to the bandit's general, who not only apologized, but immediately withdrew his soldiers from the neighbouring plot, and so the Greers were able to buy it, cheap. Dr Greer's only comment on this story is: "I guess the Lord must have given me strength."

On Dr Greer's advice we installed ourselves, uninvited, in Dr Mac-Fadyen's house. He would, she assured us, be only too glad of a bit of company, for his wife was away. Any qualms we may have felt were dispelled when, presently, the Doctor himself returned. He also is American, and also elderly—a burly, bullet-headed man, in shabby, greenish-black clothes, with twinkling eyes and a rich southern accent. He seemed to take our presence as a matter of course. "Well, well," he greeted us, "I kind of thought it wouldn't be long before some more of you newspaper-boys got around here." (The last "newspaper-boy" to visit Sü-chow was an American journalist. He stayed here a week, as the guest of Dr MacFadyen, trying to get permission to go up to the front. The authorities made so many difficulties and excuses that he finally returned to Hankow in despair.)

Sü-chow, it appears, is in no immediate danger of falling. But the enemy are not more than thirty miles to the north, and they are advancing from the south-east as well. If and when the Japanese occupy the city Dr Greer and Dr MacFadyen will remain. They plan to give shelter, in their compound, to a large body of female refugees.

The technique of receiving the Japanese is now well established in missionary circles. Letters of advice on this subject have even found their way from one side of the line to the other. It is very important, everybody agrees, that a foreigner shall be present when the invaders enter a town. When the attack is expected you must brick up all your compound-gates but one. (They are doing this at Sü-chow already.) This gate must always be left open or it may be broken down. During the critical period one or other of the white missionaries must remain in the gate-house all day and sleep there at night. When the first soldiers arrive they must be given tea. You must argue with them patiently, you must be firm but very polite, and on no account must you show that you are frightened. It is important to get hold of an officer at the earliest possible opportunity. With luck he may even post a notice forbidding soldiers to enter your compound. Mission reports agree that the officers—especially if they are Christians—will be courteous and amenable, but they cannot always control their own troops. The common soldiers are all right if they aren't drunk. The Japanese, in general, are very easily intoxicated, however, and then the trouble begins. The lives of the male inhabitants will probably be spared, but most of the women will almost certainly be raped, so it is the women who must be got into the mission-buildings. What drunken and really undisciplined troops will do when they find themselves deprived of girls is uncertain.

In one well-authenticated instance the missionaries themselves were murdered.

Dr Greer and Dr MacFadyen know all this and accept it as a matter of course. Their unsensational heroism would seem even more extraordinary if it weren't paralleled by many similar cases. At this very moment, for example, a missionary named Hoskyns, who is well over seventy, remains at his post in Y-Hsien, with two elderly ladies. The town is being besieged, and a big artillery battle is said to be in progress.

This afternoon we went to headquarters to see Li Tsung-jen. Li's secretary, Major Pan, received us, a handsome, gentle young man with a puzzled scowl, who spoke adequate English. On the basis of demanding twice as much as one expects to get, we asked for a private car to take us to the front, and an interpreter to accompany us. Major Pan scowled and looked worried. It was he, we learnt, who had had to deal with the American journalist. Perhaps he foresees that we shall be an even greater nuisance. Finally he took us in to meet General Li himself.

Li speaks no English. He is a very polite, nut-brown man, with an enormous mouth and deeply intelligent eyes. Through our translator we asked for passes to the front. Li replied that the front was extremely dangerous. We answered that we didn't mind. Li bowed. We bowed back. Tea was drunk. The interview closed on a note of polite obstructionism.

A few hours later, to our surprise, a soldier came round to the hospital with a couple of signed permits.

March 26.

We have changed our plans. It is no good badgering the unfortunate Major Pan, whose final suggestion was that we should go up to the front by train and return the same day—this would mean spending only a few hours in the trenches. Also, the movements of the troop-trains are worse than uncertain. So we have arranged, through Chiang, to hire rickshaws and travel quite independently, by road. Major Pan, whom we have seen again today, to get road permits, is more discouraging than ever. The road, he says, is liable to attack by Japanese mobile units operating behind the Chinese lines. However, after much bowing and tea, the permits were signed.

This morning there was a big air-raid on the station and the centre of the town. The planes were overhead for nearly half an hour. But we could hardly tear ourselves away to look at them, so deeply were we engrossed in the treasures of Dr MacFadyen's library. Auden is reading *Bleak House.* I have a novel by Oppenheim, called *Michael's Misdeeds.*

Dr Greer came in later. A bomb, she told us, had dropped just beside the mission church during the service. The glass in the windows had all been shattered, but the congregation was on its knees, and no one was hurt. She had been at the station distributing tracts to a regiment of soldiers who were leaving on a troop-train. They had all clamoured: "We want a little book!" And she'd said: "If you snatch you won't get one!" So they hadn't snatched.

Dr Greer thinks that the Japanese came over this morning because they are trying to destroy the new guns which are passing through Sü-chow on their way up to the line. So far, apparently, they haven't succeeded.

Dr MacFadyen tells us that there is an earlier city of Sü-chow, buried about twenty-five feet underground by a flood six hundred years ago. At the bottom of the well in his garden there are ruins of a house from which he has excavated all kinds of utensils and implements. Floods have always been a great danger in this region. The dyke along the former Yellow River bank is very old. It is strengthened with a mixture of lime, sand, glutinous rice, and pig's blood—the ancient Chinese form of cement. At the north gate of the city there is a curious bronze ox—placed there as a charm against floods. When the water begins to rise the ox is supposed to bellow.

China, says Dr MacFadyen, is a terrible place for growths and tumours. In the hospital he has a whole museum of bladder-stones. One of his patients had a polypus growing out of his nose, so long that you could wind the pedicle round his neck. He once removed a three-pointed stone which was sticking simultaneously into the navel, the rectum, and the urethra. Another patient had a tumour on his back weighing sixty pounds. It resembled a meal-sack. Whenever the man sat down the weight of it pulled his feet up into the air. All these phenomena are due, largely, to neglect; few people will come into the hospital until things have progressed so far that they are already freaks. In some cases the relatives are opposed to medical treatment, because they imagine that the sick man brings them luck. In others, the patient himself grows positively to like his own affliction.

March 27.

At half-past seven this morning we left Sü-chow in our four hired rickshaws—two for ourselves, one for Chiang, and one for the baggage. The rickshaw-coolies had agreed that they could make the journey to the front easily in one day.

At the north gate we stopped for several minutes, while Auden photographed the bronze ox from every conceivable angle. A big crowd gathered to watch us, laughing and chatting, as well they might: we certainly make an extraordinary trio. Auden, in his immense, shapeless overcoat and woollen Jaeger cap, seems dressed for the Arctic regions. Chiang, neat as ever, might be about to wait at a Hankow consular dinner-party. My own beret, sweater, and martial boots would not be out of place in

Valencia or Madrid. Collectively, perhaps, we most resemble a group of characters in one of Jules Verne's stories about lunatic English explorers. Even our oddly-shaped canvas sack, riding ahead of us in its rickshaw like a fat, sullen emperor, might be supposed to contain one of Verne's fantastic contraptions for investigating the bottom of the sea or flying from the earth to the moon.

The weather was grey and cloudy. As we left the city behind us the sirens began to wail, and we congratulated ourselves on having avoided the delay of the morning air-raid.

Alternately walking and riding, we reached Mao Tsun, the first village marked on the sketch-map which MacFadyen had prepared for our journey. The road was flat and easy, winding across the cultivated plain, with low hills on our left and, on our right, the high embankment of the railway. A few miles out of Sü-chow we had crossed an elaborate trench-system, as yet empty and unguarded, evidently designed to defend the city from the north. We passed a boy leading a donkey with a small red cloth on its back. Chiang, even more officious than usual, stopped to warn the boy that he must remove the cloth at once, or its bright colour would be likely to attract the attention of Japanese airmen!

Beyond Mao Tsun the road got very rough and the country wilder and less inhabited. We had to walk most of the way to Liu Chuan. The sun came out, bright and hot; I shed my sweater, Auden his overcoat and cap. All the while I was keeping a faintly uneasy eye alert for the Japs, but there was no sign of them, either in the air or among the barren folds of the hills.

At Liu Chuan we ate our midday meal at a table in the middle of the street, for the hovel which was the village's only restaurant swarmed with flies. The crowd round our stools was so dense that you couldn't move an elbow without touching a human body. The children were the most inquisitive; the chins of the smallest were ranged along the table-edge, a row of decapitated heads, smeared with mucus and dirt. They scuffled silently for the scraps we threw them, nearly overbalanced by the huge drum-bellies which are due to enlarged spleen. The grown men looked on, smiling and commenting, from behind. Our occasional accidents with the chop-sticks—we are now getting comparatively skilful—amused them greatly.

Chiang questioned everybody but could get very little definite news. The fighting, most people seemed to think, was going on just north of Han Chwang, where the railway line crosses the Grand Canal. We could certainly push on as far as Li Kwo Yi, and spend the night there. Then we should be able to visit the trenches next day, on foot. Here, in Liu Chuan, they had heard the guns very plainly during the night. But now there wasn't a sound.

Liu Chuan was full of soldiers but we met no troops on the road beyond—only an occasional army lorry and groups of refugee peasants going south, laden with sacks. The low empty hills crowded in; we climbed slowly to the top of a shallow, stony pass. Here and there, in the middle distance, we saw a sentry posted at some vantage-point which commanded the windings of the track. The railway was no longer visible; it had curved away to the east. Once, very faintly, I fancied I heard the boom of a gun.

From the top of the pass the view opened. We were looking down the slopes to Li Kwo Yi, with the Grand Canal beyond, and the valley where Han Chwang must lie: not a shot to be heard, not a puff of smoke to be seen—the meadows still and peaceful in the afternoon sun, the blossom beginning on the hill-sides and, in the distance, a blue range of mountains. Auden made me laugh by saying thoughtfully: "I suppose if we were over there we'd be dead."

From here we looked down on War as a bird might—seeing only a kind of sinister agriculture or anti-agriculture. Immediately below us peasants were digging in the fertile, productive plain. Further on there would be more peasants, in uniform, also digging—the unproductive, sterile trench. Beyond them, to the north, still more peasants; and, once again, the fertile fields. This is how war must seem to the neutral, unjudging bird—merely the Bad Earth, the tiny, dead patch in the immense flowering field of luxuriant China.

"Surely", I exclaimed, "that horse is *green*?" And so it was. We overtook the soldier who was riding it. He explained that all army horses, if they are white, are camouflaged in this way against aircraft. He told us, also, that we shouldn't be able to get to Han Chwang: the northern part of the village is actually in the hands of the Japanese. The southern half, on this side of the canal, is in the Chinese front lines.

On the bridge, just outside Li Kwo Yi, sentries stopped us and examined our passes and cards. We were told that we must first see General Chang Tschen, whose headquarters are at Ma Yuan, a village about two miles to the east. So we set off along a field path running roughly parallel to the canal, towards the village, or group of villages, lying on the edge of the plain under the hills. The sun was just beginning to sink, and Ma Yuan, in the distance, with its walls and rookeries and square, church-like towers, looked so lovely that we could almost cheat ourselves into believing that this wouldn't, on closer inspection, prove to be just another huddle of mud and bamboo huts. From a mile away it couldn't have appeared more beautiful and august if it had housed the combined culture of Oxford, Cambridge, and the Sorbonne.

And indeed, despite the soldiers, the horses, the hens, and their symphony of smells, there was something very academic, dignified, and gentle about the bespectacled officers who received us. General Chang

Tschen himself is mild and stout, in carpet slippers. His first words were an apology for the quality of the supper we were about to eat. It was taken as a matter of course that we should spend the night in Ma Yuan as his guests.

"So you wish to visit the front? Ah. . . ." The officers looked puzzled and mildly discouraged. "The front is very dangerous." "Yes, we have heard that." "Ah. . . ." There was a pause of polite deadlock. We felt very apologetic for our own obstinacy. Then the telephone rang and the General answered it, in accents which, to our western ears, have always the ring of resigned, dignified despair: "Wa? Wa? Ah. . . . Ah. . . . Ah. . . ." Then a sigh, as though of extreme pain: "Aah. . . ." "We are told", he informed us, "that the Japanese will soon begin to shoot with their gun. Please do not be alarmed. It is only a very small gun. . . ."

By the time we had finished supper it was already after six o'clock. The General's A.D.C. came to tell us that we might pay a visit to the front immediately before dark. Auden, Chiang, three or four officers, and myself made up the party. Mounted on small Chinese ponies we trotted away over the fields. Auden, during his visit to Iceland, had become a daring, if somewhat unorthodox, horseman. Chiang and I were beginners; indeed, Chiang had never ridden before in his life. But there was no difficulty in keeping your seat on these docile little animals; no sooner had we started than they fell into line, nose to tail, like a circus-troupe.

We dismounted at a ruinous and practically deserted village much nearer the canal. Dusk was gathering, and I narrowly escaped decapitation by a slack field-telephone wire which hung across the street. Here were more officers: there was a five-minute pause for introductions, the exchange of visiting-cards, handshakes, and salutes. "You are now", the A.D.C. told us impressively, "in the third Chinese line."

We admired it duly, and asked if we might be taken on to the second. The A.D.C. hesitated, and sighed. We were certainly difficult to please. In the second line, he warned us, we should be within range of the Japanese gun. We persisted, however, emboldened by the sight of a soldier on the top of the distant earthworks, standing casually, black against the sky. If the Japs couldn't hit him they must be very bad shots indeed.

So, in single file, we advanced across the fields on foot towards another village. Here and there, in a small shallow pit, a soldier would be crouching, with his rifle beside him: why he was posted there neither of us could imagine. Our guides insisted that we should keep well apart; but this precaution seemed unnecessary because, as we later discovered, we were entirely invisible to the enemy. Perhaps the A.D.C., in his kindly way, wished to give us the maximum thrill for our money.

The second line is well constructed—amazingly so, considering that it has all been dug within the last week. It runs right across the plain at an average distance of about half a mile from the canal itself. The front line is the actual canal bank, which ends, to the west, on the shores of the big, shallow Y-Shan lake. The Japanese have, in fact, occupied nearly the whole of Han Chwang—for the southern suburb is extremely small; their main stronghold is the railway station. But this Grand Canal front is only in the nature of a barrage or dam, for beyond it, to the north, Chinese mobile units are besieging the enemy (and Mr Hoskyns) in Y-Hsien, and attacking them at several other points. Provided, in fact, that the canal-line holds, the Japs are cut off, and will be destroyed piecemeal. General Chang Tschen's idea is, it seems, to clear up these centres of their resistance before ordering a general advance northwards. The Japanese are estimated to have between three and four hundred men in Han Chwang itself: the Chinese rather more. And reinforcements are expected tomorrow.

We inspected the whole of the second line, and asked to be taken on to the first; but it was already getting very dark, so we didn't press the point. From the canal an occasional shot rang out, and once or twice, like the slamming of a great door, came the boom of the unalarming "small gun". In the twilight the earthworks looked mournful and deserted. They might have been the remains of some vast engineering scheme, abandoned long ago. As we picked our way along them a soldier would now and then emerge from his straw-lined hole, to salute. Most of these boys looked pitifully young. We asked what they were doing so near the front line. Did they ever have to take part in an attack? Our guides assured us that they were only orderlies, and seldom exposed to any real danger.

We plodded back across the fields, dog-tired by this time, to the village where we had left our ponies. The ride back to Ma Yuan was much more exhilarating, for the horses, smelling supper, broke their circus-formation, and cantered through the darkness over the uneven plough-land. We passed a shuttered and apparently deserted farmhouse, inside which a dog was furiously barking. I wondered if its refugee owners had left it locked in there by mistake. As we approached Ma Yuan a party of horsemen rode out to challenge us. It was lucky that the A.D.C. was well in front, and could give the password before any misunderstandings arose.

General Chang Tschen has assigned us a room in one of the commandeered houses of the village. It is still furnished with tables and stools; in the corner stands an immense lacquered Chinese bed. It feels very hard, and we prefer our own. Chiang has just put them up. He himself is going to sleep on the table. This evening he seems depressed. He got terribly bumped during his ride and is now feeling very stiff. Also he was scared, we think, at the prospect of visiting the front line tomorrow: we have reassured him by saying that he needn't come with us. This may also ease our way in negotiating with the officers, for Chiang does all our interpreting here, and he isn't above editing our requests and the Chinese replies.

A soldier has just been in to warn us not to go outside our own yard during the night. A sentry, as he put it, might make a stupid mistake.

I am beginning to feel an extraordinary affection for my bed. It gives a kind of continuity to this whole journey which is very reassuring. No matter whether we are sleeping at the Consulate or at Dr MacFadyen's, or in this hut, it is always the same bed—and so I am always at home.

March 28.

Woke soon after dawn to the crowing of a rooster, the braying of a donkey, and the chirping of a tame cricket which hangs in a little cage outside the door. During breakfast we continued our argument with two of the officers about the proposed front-line visit. "If you go", said one of them, as though this were a startling and final ultimatum, "we are afraid we cannot guarantee to protect you." "But we do not ask for protection." Another difficult pause. "Please tell them", said Auden to Chiang, "that a journalist has his duty, like a soldier. It is sometimes necessary for him to go into danger." This heroic sentiment, or Chiang's rendering of it, had a surprising effect. Quite suddenly they gave us up: we were altogether too tiresome for any further comment. Very well, we might start in an hour.

Meanwhile there was time for a stroll round the village. It was a glorious, cool spring morning. On a waste plot of land beyond the houses a dog was gnawing what was, only too obviously, a human arm. A spy, they told us, had been buried there after execution a day or two ago; the dog had dug the corpse half out of the earth. It was rather a pretty dog with a fine, bushy tail. I remembered how we had patted it when it came begging for scraps of our supper the evening before.

We asked whether there were many spies about. Yes, quite a number. The peasants round here are very poor and the Japanese offer them handsome rewards for treason. How had this particular man been caught? He was a peasant who had crossed the Grand Canal by night and come to Ma Yuan to get news. He had been so indiscreet as to ask the General's cook where the General lived. The cook, who suspected him already, had exclaimed: "Oh, you spy!" And the peasant had hung his head and blushed. He was arrested immediately. This is Chiang's version of the story—obviously garbled. But no doubt, from time to time, there really is a miscarriage of justice. The Chinese take no chances.

We started at half-past eight. When the horses were brought round Chiang insisted on mounting one of them—the largest—and posing for his photograph. He was anxious to have a souvenir of his equestrian exploits. We then arranged that he and the rickshaw-coolies should proceed direct to Li Kwo Yi and wait there until we rejoined them later.

Our own route was the same as yesterday evening. There were the same semi-farcical precautions: the advance in single file across the fields and some dramatic dodging along communication trenches, only to emerge from them right on the crest of the sky-line as brilliantly illuminated targets. Finally we reached the canal bank itself. But this part of the front— as one of the officers, who spoke a little English, had to admit—was only occupied by the Japanese at night, when almost all the real fighting and raiding takes place. During the daytime the Japs retire into Han Chwang village.

Gradually we made our way westwards towards the shattered railway bridge, the village, and the lake. All the soldiers rose at our approach and saluted. We asked how they recognized an officer, for there is no apparent difference in uniform. "An officer", said our guide, "is recognized by his face."

By this time the sunshine was very hot. Our walk was long and rough; I envied Auden his rubber shoes and bitterly repented of the vanity which had prompted me to wear my own uncomfortable, slightly oversize boots. Reaching the bridge we scrambled down into the dug-out which the Chinese have constructed right under the railway embankment. The men here talked in whispers, for the Japanese have machine-guns posted in the row of ruined cottages beyond. You could easily throw a stone across the canal into their positions.

Among the huts of the southern suburb we stopped to drink hot water and take group-photographs of the commander and his staff. The commander insisted that we should pose with them: "Your families", he said, "will be very pleased to know that you have been so brave." Visiting-cards were liberally exchanged. Our pockets bulged with them. As the hot-water party progressed our hosts began an excited conversation in Chinese. Auden and I, left to our own devices, found ourselves discussing the poetry of Robert Bridges. *The Testament of Beauty* can seldom have been quoted in less appropriate surroundings.

At length it was time to go on. Our guides led us to the extreme end of the village, a spit of land projecting into the lake. Twice, crouching and running, we crossed streets which were protected only by curtains of matting from the enemy's eyes. There was a little shrine with two holes made by shell-fire in its roof. The last house on the opposite bank of the canal was said to be full of troops, but Auden popped his head above the parapet and took two pictures without getting shot at. "I don't believe", he whispered to me, "that there are any Japs here at all."

His words were interrupted by three tremendous detonations. The newly-arrived Chinese guns, somewhere near Li Kwo Yi, had opened fire. The officers said that we must start back immediately; at any moment now the Japanese would reply. We were bustled out of the village in company

with a soldier who was ordered to escort us back into safety. We said good-
bye to our hosts, thanking them hastily but sincerely for all their hospi-
tality and patience.

As we trudged over the fields, lying bare and empty in the sunshine, the
bombardment continued. More Chinese guns opened fire from the east.
The Japanese fired back, shelling the trenches we had left. The Chinese
guns were far out of their reach—they seemed to have a range of at least
seven miles. We could hear the great slam of the explosion, then the
express-train scream of the shell right over our heads, then the dull crash
of the burst, and a black, escaped genie of smoke would tower, for a mo-
ment, above the roofs of Han Chwang, or the open countryside beyond.
Whenever this happened the soldier grinned at us delightedly.

Presently the firing slackened and stopped. From the north came the
drone of approaching planes. The Japanese were out looking for the Chi-
nese guns. They circled the sky several times, passing quite low above us.
Whenever they came over, the soldier signalled to us to lie down. It was an
unpleasant feeling lying there exposed in the naked field: one couldn't
help remembering the many anecdotes of aviators' caprice—how a pilot
will take a sudden dislike to some solitary figure moving beneath him, and
waste round after round of ammunition until he has annihilated it, like
an irritating fly. Auden seized the opportunity of catching the two of us
unawares with his camera. "You looked wonderful", he told me, "with
your great nose cleaving the summer air."

In Li Kwo Yi we found Chiang and the coolies waiting. The village
authorities gave us lunch on a lavish scale—twenty-seven boiled eggs were
provided for three people. Just as we had finished eating the bombard-
ment recommenced; its concussions shook the window frames. The pros-
pect of another visit from the Japanese planes speeded up the rickshaw-
boys considerably; they pulled us to the top of the pass in record time.
They were pleased to have got out of the danger zone, but also, it seemed,
proud to have been in it. All the way down to Liu Chuan they chattered
gaily to each other and sang. Through Chiang we questioned them about
their wages. The general exodus from Sü-chow during the first threat of
Japanese invasion had created a rickshaw boom. Coolies had charged
eight dollars to take passengers to the railway station. Some of them made
as much as twenty-four dollars a day.

We reached Mao Tsun without incident about six o'clock. A troop-train
was just leaving and we were lucky enough to get a lift in it, through
Chiang's diplomacy with the station-master, back to Sü-chow in time for
supper. We paid off the coolies, who would return to the city on foot
next day.

We both agree that it is nearly impossible for casual foreigners like our-
selves to assess Chinese military morale. Judged by western standards the

impressions brought back from a visit like this are bound to be superficially depressing. In Europe one is so accustomed to cocksureness and boasting that the reticence of a Chinese officer seems positively defeatist. While we were at the front this morning our guide said: "Over there are the lines to which we shall retreat." "But you *mustn't* retreat," Auden interjected, in spite of himself, rather severely. The Chinese merely smiled. And later, when we had seen everything, we were asked for our opinion of the trench system. The officers seemed genuinely disappointed when we praised it, and I don't think this was only politeness. They would really have welcomed even an ignorant English civilian's suggestions and advice.

The average Chinese soldier speaks of China's chances with an air of gentle depreciation, yet he is ultimately confident or, at least, hopeful. "The Japanese", said one of them, "fight with their tanks and planes. We Chinese fight with our spirit." The "spirit" is certainly important when one considers the Chinese inferiority in armaments (today's new guns were a remarkable exception) and their hopeless deficiency in medical services. European troops may appear more self-confident, more combative, more efficient and energetic, but if they had to wage this war under similar conditions they would probably all mutiny within a fortnight.

5

Next afternoon as I was writing up our travel notes Auden (who had been out to call on Major Pan) rushed in to say that a train for the west was leaving in half an hour. We packed in a scramble, said good-bye to Dr MacFadyen, and got to the station with only a couple of minutes to spare.

This train, we discovered, was the very same in which we had come from Kwei-teh to Sü-chow five days before. Chiang and the car-boys greeted each other delightedly like old friends, and he set to work at once intriguing that we should all be given free passes for the journey. The ticket-collector proved very amenable. After a glance at the Generalissimo's chop he bowed himself out of our compartment. Our one ungrateful regret was that we had ever been so silly as to buy tickets on this railway at all.

We now intended to travel straight through to Sian, covering almost the entire stretch of the Lung-Hai Railway. The minimum length of this trip, under present conditions, would be one whole day and two nights. But at Tung-kwan, where the line runs close beside the Yellow River, the Japanese had mounted guns on the northern shore, so this part of the journey had always to be made during the darkness and might cause twenty-four hours' delay. McClure, with all the relish of a Job's comforter, had told us about Tung-kwan already: "Why, boy, it's nothing but a shooting-gallery. The

Japs have their guns sighted on the track. And they've got searchlights, too. If once they spot you you haven't a chance—not a chance."

In the middle of the night we stopped at Shang-kui. Dr Brown was rather on our consciences; we had half-promised to pay him and Dr Gilbert a visit when we returned from Sü-chow. But we couldn't face the prospect of abandoning our train and at length compromised by telling Chiang to get on the telephone to Kwei-teh Hospital and ask Dr Brown if he was ready to join us at once. After a long time Chiang returned to say that only the night-watchman seemed to be awake, and that he could get no satisfactory reply.

All next morning we ran steadily westwards. The train had become a model of punctuality; nowhere did we stop longer than a quarter of an hour. Even the ill-omened "Democracy" was left behind without undue delay. The car-boys, Chiang told us, were optimistic. If we could reach Loyang by six o'clock, they said, we should pass Tung-kwan during the night and be in Sian next day before noon.

Beyond "Democracy" the sandy plain is desert to the horizon, patched here and there with scanty green, where peasants scratch miserably for their living, like fowls. One-wheel carts, drawn by donkeys, toil over the waste, creaking as if their frames were loaded with the whole immense weight of the sky. We passed Kai-feng. By mid-day we were in Cheng-chow. We noticed that the sidings behind the station were full of derelict railway trucks, splintered and smashed by bombs.

Now the loess region begins. We skirted the gaping sand-canyons, guarded by fantastic sandy spires and pinnacles—an entire landscape of Lot's wives. The cliff-faces are dotted up and down with the dark entrances of cave-dwellings. Here and there the slope has been architectured into terraces, upon which wheat is growing. The walls of the terraces are strengthened with a kind of mud-stucco, so that, from a distance, the hillside resembles an old Babylonish city.

Presently the canyon-country flattens down into a broad rich river valley of orchards and green parks. Sails move slowly above the waters of the hidden stream. There are wells everywhere; donkeys plod round them in circles, working the wooden irrigation-wheels. The poorer farmers, who cannot afford them, are raising the water by windlass. Here and there, breaking the monotony of the countless blue-clad figures, you catch sight of a pair of scarlet trousers or a coat. "Surely you must admit", the bland evening seems to say, "that these people are happy and good?"

We reached Loyang punctual almost to the minute. The platform was crowded with troops. A soldier leant out of the opposite train-window laying his forefingers together and shouting something which made the others laugh and applaud. "England and China", Chiang translated, "together! Italy and Japan together, too!"

I slept uneasily that night—in my trousers and shirt: not wishing to have to leave the train and bolt for cover in my pyjamas. Auden, with his monumental calm, had completely undressed. There were frequent shuntings and stops, excited conversations in the corridor, darkened stations where men gesticulated mysteriously with lanterns and electric pocket-lamps. At last I tired of waiting for Tung-kwan—if, indeed, we hadn't passed it already—and relapsed into a long, boring, travel-nightmare which did not leave me until dawn.

We both woke with a start in full sunny daylight. Where were we? Certainly not in Sian. Certainly not past Tung-kwan, even; for, away to our right, spread the broad beach of the Yellow River. On our left was a little station: we read its name-board, Ling Pao. The station buildings were pitted with shrapnel-holes and all the windows were smashed. A piece of loose iron on top of the water-tank, camouflaged with branches, clattered in the hot violent wind. Behind the station in a sandy hollow lay the mean, dusty village. Chiang came in with bad news. There had been a railway accident farther down the line. We shouldn't be able to move on till eight o'clock that night.

We did move, nevertheless, into a deep cutting between two tunnels, where the train could take shelter from a possible attack by enemy planes. The other passengers seemed to take the delay much more philosophically than we did. They scrambled up the steep slopes of the cutting or went to sleep on the shady side of the line. The engine driver got out a bundle of straw—perhaps kept specially for this very purpose—and lay down comfortably under his locomotive to read a book. The sun blazed down, the bottom of our ravine was heated like a brick-oven. Presently a string of peasants came trooping through the tunnel from Ling Pao, and, within half an hour, the cutting was a market resounding with the screams of women and boys crying their wares.

Peevishly anxious for news, we asked Chiang to fetch the conductor. He arrived, apologetically smiling. Yes, it was quite true, there had been an accident. An engine had run off the rails. They were laying a loop of new track around the wreck. We should probably be able to start tomorrow at noon. "*Tomorrow, at noon!*" we echoed in dismay. "What's the good of that? You can't pass Tung-kwan by daylight." The conductor smiled vaguely, bowed, and left us.

Meanwhile the car-boys had ceased hovering at the door of our compartment; they now came boldly inside and sat down. They seemed to have nothing whatever to do. The liveliest of them was called Chin-dung; his long floppy hair framed a charming, flat-nosed, impudent face. Chin-dung was exceedingly vain: he was eternally combing his hair or admiring his figure in the glass. He wore a thick rubber belt, like a bandage, which squeezed his pliant body into an absurdly exaggerated Victorian wasp-waist. None of the car-boys spoke English, but they made themselves perfectly at home, prying into our luggage, examining and trying on our clothes, eating nuts, spitting seeds with their teeth, and helping themselves liberally to our cigarettes.

After lunch—without the least warning, and leaving a good quarter of its passengers behind on the cutting slope—the train moved off. But it was only backing through the tunnel into Ling Pao to water the engine. It stayed there several hours. Chin-dung presented us with a signed photograph of himself looking loutish and rather touchingly ridiculous in his best holiday suit of clothes. The other car-boys soon joined him, bringing with them a portable gramophone which played wailing opera-airs. We both began to feel that we had lived in this compartment for the whole of our lives.

Towards evening the train raised our wildest hopes by starting again—this time in the right direction. It carried us as far as the next station, a bleak upland village, standing back from the river, whose name-board, in the gathering darkness, we couldn't read. We christened it "Wuthering Heights", and fell asleep early, to the whining of the wind between the motionless carriage-wheels.

"Wuthering Heights" was certainly preferable to Ling Pao. The morning air when we woke was cool and fresh. But poor Auden was in a terrible state: his legs and arms were covered with bug-bites. The bugs must be nesting in the upholstery of the shabby old Belgian sleeping-berths. We decided to have a radical spring-cleaning. First we called for basin after basin of hot water and washed ourselves all over. Then we set Chin-dung and the other car-boys to scrubbing the windows, while we ourselves took all our bedding out on to the platform, beat it with our walking-sticks, and hung it on the station fence to air in the sun. At first the Chinese passengers looked on, giggling with amazement. Then they began to follow our example. In a short time windows were being washed and bedding hung out down the whole length of the train. We felt sure that Madame Chiang Kai-shek would have approved.

After lunch we moved on a few more miles to the next station, Wen Chung Shan. It lay in the cup of a vast sand-plateau, high above the river. There was nothing here but the station buildings, and a few bamboo huts. Walking along the platform to stretch my legs I was accosted by one of the passengers, a sly, spotty boy with hair like a Japanese doll. He glanced quickly to left and right, nipped me suddenly and painfully in a sensitive place and murmured: "Nice girl?" I smiled and followed him to the station exit, curious to see how the nice girl would be produced. From one of the huts beside the line an old woman emerged on minute bird-like feet, leading by the hand a child of ten. She beckoned invitingly. I laughed, shook my head, and turned back towards the train.

Meanwhile Auden was teaching Chin-dung English. They were learning the parts of the body, naming them alternately in English and Chinese. A big crowd of passengers and beggars looked on, roaring with laughter whenever the anatomical lesson reached an intimate area. Chindung was rather stupid, but some of the younger spectators were very quick. They capered about the platform, slapping themselves all over and shouting the new, rude, foreign words.

But the lesson soon ceased to be a joke and became a hearty nuisance. Thrown back upon each other's well-worn company, we got through the long hours as we could best contrive—emptying out our heads like wastepaper baskets for the least scrap of amusement or interest. We told the old anecdotes, each secretly hoping that the other would remember or invent some new detail, however palpably untrue. We improvised parodies and limericks. We lost ourselves in interminable arguments and speculations: "What would happen if the world ran out of oil?" "What would you describe as the unhappiest day of your life?" "Does a man become a different person in a different place?" "If I know that I have no soul does that prove that nobody else has one, either?"

Meals were our greatest solace. Constipated though we were we could still eat, and the food provided by the kitchen-truck was, considering the circumstances, excellent. Our chief luxury was the American coffee which we had brought with us from Hankow in tins; Chiang always prepared this himself. Tonight there was no electric current on the train: we had to eat by candle-light. Chin-dung came in with a Chinese flute which neither he nor any one else present could play. His efforts to do so were so painful that at length we had to turn him out of the compartment altogether.

"Is there anything else you would like?" Chiang asked. And Auden answered jokingly: "Yes. Bring us some whisky." To our astonishment Chiang returned with a bottle of Red Label three-quarters full. He had found it in a corner of the kitchen-truck, where it must have been lying unnoticed for months.

During the night we reached Pan Tao, about fifteen miles distant from Tung-kwan itself. Another day of boredom and inaction seemed inevitable. But after breakfast we discovered that a breakdown train was leaving Pan Tao immediately for the scene of the accident. Mr Wong, the Inspector of Railways from Sian, was on board. He kindly agreed to take us with him. Mr Wong spoke fluent French; he had worked with the Belgian engineers when this part of the line was built, between 1931 and 1936.

We asked Mr Wong about the Japanese at Tung-kwan. He was very reassuring. Oh yes, they shelled the line but they didn't do much damage. As for searchlights, they had them certainly, but didn't use them often. Mr Wong pointed out some shrapnel-holes in the iron wall of the truck in which we were travelling. This train had been fired on early yesterday morning, but nobody was hurt. "Had the Chinese any guns?" we asked. "Certainly. Now we have some big guns." "I suppose", said Auden, "you shell the Japanese?" "No, we don't do that. You see, we don't want the Japanese to know that we've got them."

Three miles beyond Pan Tao the line emerged from its deep cutting on to an exposed, curving ledge, built out from the sandy slope of the hills. Far beneath, at the foot of the precipice, lay a big village surrounded by trees and cultivated fields, spreading down to the beaches of the Yellow River, whose golden-red bluffs showed through a faint haze behind the northern shore. Right ahead, towering into the western sky, was a jagged chain of gigantic blue mountains. This might have been the valley of Ruskin's fairy story. No one could possibly have chosen a more beautiful spot for a disaster.

The derailed locomotive lay on its side right on the very edge of the embankment amidst wreckage and twisted track. One coach had slithered half-way down the steep sand-slope beneath. We asked Mr Wong exactly how the accident had happened. Two trains, he said, had been travelling west, one very close behind the other. As they rounded this curve a wheel had come off a truck on the rear train. Its driver, hearing the noise, had imagined that the Japanese were firing at him from across the river and had accelerated so violently that he collided with the train in front and crashed off the rails. Nine people had been killed and fifteen seriously injured. We asked if there were many accidents on the Lung-Hai line. "Oh no," said Mr Wong, "we've only had two in the last three weeks."

The new loop-track was laid already. Throughout the long, hot morning, we watched the travelling crane as it laboriously shifted the position of the damaged engine. Mr Wong took us down to lunch in the village: the hut in which we ate was papered entirely with old copies of American "tabloids" and magazines, shipped out here by the ton and sold for such architectural purposes. Wherever you looked, the crimes of gangsters and the love-secrets of divorcées were proclaimed from the bamboo walls.

During the afternoon, without any warning, a Japanese aeroplane appeared, flying straight towards us out of the north-western sky. The breakdown gang stopped work and watched it without attempting to take cover. But many of the onlookers scattered, and three or four of the most panic-stricken actually glissaded right down the embankment slope to the village in a cloud of sand. The Japanese pilot was only scouting, it seemed. He changed his course and headed along the railway, flying east.

We returned to Pan Tao on foot, walking down the track. By the time we arrived it was already getting dark. Supper was a somewhat cheerless meal that evening; the car-boys had run out of firewood, so all the food was cold. There was no more sugar, either. Chiang brought us some sticks of candy to dip in our coffee. They looked like blackboard-chalk and tasted of Edinburgh rock.

About half-past nine everything was ready to start. The guards hurried from compartment to compartment, extinguishing all the candles. We took up our positions in the corridor at a window which I had insisted on opening, for fear of shattered glass. Auden, of course, was certain that nothing would happen. "I *know* they won't shoot," he kept repeating, until I began to be superstitiously afraid that the demons of the air would hear him and take offence.

We stopped twice at blacked-out stations where officials shouted excitedly to the engine driver, as though giving him last-minute warnings and instructions. "They won't shoot," Auden repeated. The train gathered speed, lurching so violently from side to side that I began to agree with him—we should probably be derailed long before we reached Tung-kwan at all. Putting out our lights had been an altogether superfluous precaution, for the glare from our stokehole lit up the entire cutting, and swept the huge, flickering shadow of the engine along its flying banks. The scream of the whistle, announcing our approach, must have been audible for miles. The corridor was a fog of sulphur and smuts.

There was a curious sense of relief, even of pleasure, in those final moments. There was nothing we could do either to hinder or to assist. Everyday life, so complex and anxious, was soothingly simplified to the narrowness of a single railway track. Our little egotisms, our ambitions, our vanities, were absorbed, identified utterly with the rush of the speeding train. The cutting deepened, and a tunnel swallowed us in roaring darkness. Now. . . .

We burst out of it into clear starlight; the high embankment rose sheer from the river's edge. And there, right opposite, blazing from the blackness of the opposite shore like the illuminations of a pretentious roadhouse, were the Japanese searchlights. We yelled at them and waved our arms, suddenly hysterical as a drunken charabanc party: "Come on! Shoot! Shoot!" Then another tunnel choked our shouting with its fumes. A couple of minutes later we were clattering crazily over the points past the deserted sidings of Tung-kwan station. And soon after the guard came to tell us that we might relight our candles. We were safe. The train slackened speed a little. The passengers began to get ready for bed. "You see," said Auden. "I told you so. . . . I knew they wouldn't. . . . Nothing of that sort ever happens to *me*." "But it does to *me*," I objected; "and if it had this time you'd have been there, too." "Ah, but it didn't, you see." "No. But it might." "But it didn't."

There is no arguing with the complacency of a mystic. I turned over and went to sleep.

We arrived in Sian without further incident at half-past seven next morning.

Our first impressions of the city were formidable. As we left the railway station its gigantic town-wall towered ahead, extending to left and right as far as the eye could see till it was lost in the thick, clammy, morning mist. We might have been about to enter a gaol. And here, at the gate, were the gaolers, surly and unsmiling—typical soldiers of the sullen north-west. Despite Chiang's well-proven technique, they were not to be appeased with a mere flourish of visiting-cards. They demanded our military passes and examined them suspiciously for a long time before they let us through.

The Guest-House at Sian must be one of the strangest hotels in the world. A caprice of Chang Hsueh-liang created it—a Germanic, severely modern building, complete with private bathrooms, running water, central heating, and barber's shop; the white dining-room has a dance-floor in the middle, and an indirectly rose-lit dome. Sitting in the entrance-lounge, on comfortable settees, you watch the guests going in and out, with the self-assured briskness of people accustomed to luxury and prompt service, inhabitants of a great metropolis. Those swing-doors might open on to Fifth Avenue, Piccadilly, Unter den Linden. The illusion is nearly complete.

Nearly, but not quite. For, now and then a tattered rickshaw-coolie, popping his head in to joke with the page-boys, reminds you of what is really outside.

Sian has shrunk too small for its own immense penitentiary-walls. Most of the houses are mere shacks, dwarfed by the crazy old medieval gate-towers. Like shabby, dispirited spectators of a procession, they line the edges of the wide, rough, cart-track streets. Everywhere there are plots of waste ground littered with ruins. When the sun shines the city is swept by great clouds of dust blowing down from the Gobi desert; when it rains the whole place is a miserable bog. Beyond the walls, all along the southern horizon, you can see the broken line of the big, savage, bandit-infested mountains.

If Cheng-chow smells of disease, Sian smells of murder. Too many people have died there throughout history, in agony and terror. In 1911 the Chinese population fell upon the Manchus and massacred twenty-five thousand of them in the course of a single night. In 1926 the city endured a terrible seven-months' siege. The Guest-House itself has been the scene of more than one execution.

At the time of our arrival the guests of the hotel were, almost exclusively, military or official—little band-box officers, slim and smart and chattering; older, more responsible men, whose hair was cropped close to the skull, who wore felt slippers and whose uniform hung loosely on them like crumpled pyjamas. There were only four Europeans—Mr Smith, the British postmaster, and Dr Mooser, with his two Swiss colleagues of the League of Nations commission, which was to advise the Chinese Government on the prevention of infectious diseases.

Mr Smith was something of a local character. Without his tragic grimaces and dramatic, story-telling gestures, no foreign party was quite complete. He had worked for several years in Harbin and his description of the postal services there and in Shen-si Province was fascinating. The posts in Shen-si are conveyed by runners who cover amazing distances in record times. The runners make their own non-aggression pacts with the local bandits and are very seldom molested. Transport other than by foot presents enormous difficulties. Even Mr Smith was often quite unable to get trucks when he wanted them from the Provincial Government, owing to the petrol shortage.

Trucks interested us, too. We hoped, somehow, to get a lift in one when we left Sian, as far as Cheng-tu. From Cheng-tu we planned to reach Chung-king and so return, by river-boat down the Yangtze, to Hankow. The only alternative was to go by bus from the rail-head at Pao-ki. But Dr Stockley and Dr Clow, the two Scotch surgeons at the Mission Hospital, told us that this would be nearly impossible. Pao-ki was crammed with refugees already, all waiting to get away. There were only two buses, each holding fifty people, and the company had issued three thousand tickets up to date.

We went for advice to Mr Russell, the missionary, one of the oldest and most experienced foreign residents in Sian. Tall, thin, grave, blue-eyed, looking much younger than his years, Mr Russell was guilty of one mild eccentricity: there were three clocks in his house, each set to a different time. Time, anyhow, is a tiresome factor in Sian life. There is post-office time, which regulates the activities of the town, and Shanghai time (three-quarters of an hour later) which the railway authorities observe. To these Mr Russell had added London time. When last he returned to China from leave he found himself unable for sentimental reasons to alter his own watch.

Mr Russell promised to take us to see the secretary of the Military Governor, who would, perhaps, be ready to help us. But we should have to wait a little; for next day, April 5th, was Ching Ming, the festival of The Sweeping of the Graves. All the officials would be leaving town to hold a service at the tombs of the Jo emperors, and the Government offices would be closed.

Instead he showed us the Pe-lin museum, known as the Forest of Tablets. Among them is the famous Nestorian Tablet, which proves the existence of Christianity in classical China. Some of the engraved stones are wonderfully beautiful—the lines could hardly be more flowing and delicate if they were painted with a hair-brush on silk. Outside the museum was a little shop where rubbings of the tablets were for sale. While we were admiring them and drinking tea with the shopkeeper, a raid began on the air-field outside the city. The Japanese dropped about twenty-five bombs. There was no anti-aircraft fire or any attempt at resistance by the Chinese planes.

Mr Russell was a very interesting companion. He had worked in the China Mission for the last thirty years, partly here, partly at Yen-an-fu, which, since 1936, has been the capital of the Chinese Soviet Republic in the north-west. During this period he had acquired an intimate knowledge of bandits, their code of morals, their peculiarities and their tactics.

On one occasion the bandits raided Yen-an itself and were only persuaded, through Mr Russell's intervention, to withdraw on condition that they should be sent a certain number of rifles and a certain quantity of ammunition from the arsenal of the city militia. After a great deal of argument the militia were talked into agreement, against the vote of a minority, who exclaimed: "Rather than give up our arms we'll become bandits ourselves!" and immediately deserted into the hills. The city authorities then deputed Mr Russell and a Catholic missionary to ride out to the bandits' mountain stronghold, taking the arms with them, loaded on a donkey. They arrived towards nightfall, after the donkey had collapsed, and they had been obliged to pile the rifles across their own saddles. In the twilight they narrowly escaped being shot at by the bandits' outposts. But they were recognized in time and escorted to a cave, where they were hospitably received. During the night three fully armed men entered the cave. Mr Russell and the priest woke up expecting to be murdered immediately. But the three bandits had not come to kill them. They were tired of their life with the gang and wanted to escape to another province. Would the missionaries give them letters of safe conduct to show to the Government authorities? They also had another request: they wished to become Christians. But here a delicate problem arose: how many were to be Baptists, how many Roman Catholics? This the priest solved very simply by baptizing all three of them into the Roman Church. Mr Russell politely made no objection.

Next day both missionaries rode back to Yen-an. They found the city authorities in high spirits. The mayor explained gleefully that they had played an excellent trick on the bandits. The cartridges which they had sent them had all been emptied of powder and the rifles damaged so that they couldn't be used. Wasn't it clever? "No," said Mr Russell. "Not clever at all. It was very stupid, and I'm afraid you'll regret it." The mayor laughed at his fears. Even if the bandits did attempt reprisals, he said, they would never be able to enter the town. A strong force of Government troops were already on their way to protect it.

But the Government troops never arrived and soon the bandits returned. Coming home late one evening, Mr Russell found several of their leaders sitting waiting for him in his own study. This time he really expected instant death. But the bandit chiefs were quite friendly. "We know you are our friend," they told him. "You played fair with us. It wasn't your fault about the rifles—you didn't know. . . . But now you must not interfere. Stay here indoors and you will be safe." Mr Russell pleaded with them but it was of no use. The bandits were determined on revenge. So he stayed indoors and survived the big massacre of the population which followed.

From this day onwards his friendship with the bandits was secure. When he wanted to visit his mission-stations in the south of the province it wasn't even necessary for him to warn the bandits in advance: they knew of all his comings and goings through their spies. He would ride into a village and find it apparently quite deserted: not a shop open, nothing for sale. But a man would sign to him from a doorway, and there, inside the house, a meal would be waiting. "We have been ordered to get it ready for you," he was told. Indeed, such was Mr Russell's prestige that a Chinese general who had a journey to make through dangerous country came and appealed for his protection. The general wanted to bring an armed bodyguard, but this Mr Russell refused. "Either you take your soldiers," he told the general, "or you take me alone." The general chose Mr Russell. When they had gone some distance they met a party of men on the road and stopped to talk to them. The general never knew until after they had arrived at their destination that these were the bandits themselves.

Mr Russell supplemented the account Dr Stockley had already given us of the siege of Sian in 1926. A Chinese war-lord attacked the city in April and held it blockaded until November, when the defenders were relieved by the "Christian General", Feng Yü-hsiang. The length of the siege surprised and dismayed the missionaries, who had expected it to be an affair of days. Many peasants from the outlying villages were trapped inside the town, but these Mr Russell managed to evacuate, in parties of two hundred, through the lines of an enemy commander who was less intransigent than his allies. Here again Mr Russell's good intentions were the cause of trouble, for his Chinese secretary took advantage of the truce to smuggle into Sian a message from the besiegers hidden in a melon. The message was addressed to some disloyal officers among the garrison. It invited immediate surrender on favourable terms. But the melon was opened by the city guards and its secret discovered. Mr Russell himself was viewed with suspicion, and he had the greatest difficulty in saving his secretary from execution.

In October the foreign women and children were allowed to leave Sian. The men could have left too, but they decided to remain in order to protect and feed the refugees who were living in their compounds. Food was now very scarce. The missionaries had bought supplies of wheat earlier in the siege. They had to keep them buried in their gardens in stone jars, for every day the soldiers came to search. "If you can find it", Mr Russell told them, "you can have it!" But the soldiers couldn't find anything. The missionaries dared only eat at night, grinding the flour with their own millstones. During September and October thousands of people died of hunger, collapsing suddenly as they went about their business. Corpses lay where they had fallen in the streets.

When the city was at last relieved there was a great rush to the south gate. Mr Russell said that never, as long as he lived, would he forget the sight of the first village carts, stacked high with fruit and vegetables, being mobbed by the starving townspeople.

Throughout the siege the missionaries in Sian got no word or sign of help from the British authorities, and this, Mr Russell felt, was a good thing in the long run, for it did much to convince the Chinese that the missionaries had no connection with the British Government, and were not, in any sense, its agents or spies.

Sian is remarkable for its rickshaws. They have blue or white hood-covers, embroidered with big flowers, of an oddly Victorian design. We used the rickshaws a good deal, out of laziness, despite Dr Mooser's warning that their upholstery often contained typhus-lice. Typhus is one of the great scourges of Shen-si Province. One of Mooser's two colleagues, an engineer, went down with it soon after his arrival, but, thanks to an inoculation, the attack was comparatively slight.

Dr Mooser himself was a stocky figure, eagle-eyed, with a bitter mouth and a smashed, rugged face. He wore a leather jerkin, riding-breeches, and big strapped boots. He rushed at life, at China, at this job, with his head down, stamping and roaring like a bull. The dishonesty and laziness of the average Chinese official was driving him nearly frantic. "While I'm here", he bellowed at his assistants, "you are all Swiss. When I go away you can be Chinese again, if you like—or anything else you Goddam well please."

Not that Mooser had much use for his countrymen either, or, indeed, for any Europeans at all. "The Swiss are crooks, the Germans are crooks, the English are the damn lousiest crooks of the lot. . . . It was you lousy bastards who wouldn't let ambulances be sent to China. I have all the facts. I shall not rest until they are published in the newspaper." With his colleagues he spoke Swiss dialect, or English—boycotting High German, the language of the Nazis.

Dr Mooser had established several refugee camps in Sian, as well as a delousing station. The refugees were housed in empty buildings. As soon as could be arranged they were sent off into the country and distributed amongst the neighbouring villages. There were about eight thousand of them in the city, including one thousand Mohammedans, who had a special camp to themselves. These people belonged mostly to the middle class of China—nearly all of them had a little money. The really poor had no choice but to stay where they were, and await the coming of the Japanese. The really rich were already safe in Hongkong.

There was no doubt of Mooser's efficiency. The camps were well run, the floors and bedding clean, the children's faces washed, and there was hardly any spitting. Mooser was a great favourite with the children. Whenever he visited them his pockets were full of sweets. "I had to sack three camp commandants in the first week", he told us. "They call me The Chaser."

Mooser didn't quite know what to make of us—especially after he had heard from me that Auden was a poet. He had no use for poetry because "it changes the order of the words". While he was working in Mexico he was summoned to the bedside of an Englishman named David H. Lawrence, "a queer-looking fellow with a red beard. I told him: 'I thought you were Jesus Christ.' And he laughed. There was a big German woman sitting beside him. She was his wife. I asked him what his profession was. He said he was a writer. 'Are you a famous writer?' I asked him. 'Oh no,' he said. 'Not so famous.' His wife didn't like that. 'Didn't you really know my husband was a writer?' she said to me. 'No,' I said. 'Never heard of him.' And Lawrence said: 'Don't be silly, Frieda. How should he know I was a writer? I didn't know he was a doctor, either, till he told me.'"

Dr Mooser then examined Lawrence and told him that he was suffering from tuberculosis—not from malaria, as the Mexican doctor had assured him. Lawrence took it very quietly. He only asked how long Mooser thought he would live. "Two years," said Mooser. "If you're careful." This was in 1928.

6

April 6.

Today there are some interesting new arrivals at the hotel. They are the four members of the German medical mission, which has come to inspect the war areas. The mission is headed by Dr Trautmann, the son of the German Ambassador to China. They all came clumping in, dressed, with truly national tactlessness, in a kind of German Army Medical uniform. They keep very much to themselves, sitting at a table in the corner and calling loudly for beer.

The uniforms have already created the worst possible impression. People here are convinced—no doubt most unjustly—that the Mission has political motives. But Dr Trautmann and his colleagues seem quite unaware of the difficulties they are about to encounter. They have announced their intention of going north to visit the Eighth Route Army. It seems most unlikely that they will get permission to do so. And Dr Mooser certainly won't help them. Whenever they appear he glares across the room at them like a tiger about to jump.

This morning, with Mr Russell, we went to call on Mr Liu Yin-shih, of the Ministry of Pacification. Mr Liu presented us to General Chiang Ting-wen, the military governor. General Chiang speaks no English: Mr Liu translated. We asked the usual questions: what did he think of the situation? when would the Chinese attack? what would be the outcome of the war? And received the usual answers—polite, optimistic, vague. The General told us one interesting detail, however. It seems that the Japanese forces opposite Tung-kwan are very small and therefore obliged to do a good deal of bluffing. They move trucks up and down the shore, creating an appearance of great activity—but the trucks are full of stones. There are also wooden figures set up to represent soldiers. The General laughed as this was translated to us, with the chuckling, indulgent air of placid superiority which the Chinese so often assume when the Japanese are spoken of.

We asked Mr Liu to transmit to the General our request for seats in a lorry to Cheng-tu. The General merely smiled and passed this off with a compliment: Mr Liu was to tell us how greatly he admired our spirit in undertaking this adventurous journey. But Mr Liu himself, when we talked to him alone later, seemed more helpful. He promised to let us have definite news in a day or two.

Our dealings with the military on the Sü-chow front have accustomed us to being saluted: it is a form of vanity which grows on you very quickly. Indeed, I am now quite piqued when soldiers don't salute. Today, for instance, I found myself glaring at a young sentry who was lolling against the barrack-gates, so ferociously that, after two or three seconds, he sprang guiltily to attention and presented arms.

We both hope that the transport problem will soon be settled. Life in this hotel is alarmingly expensive, and its comforts are making us daily less inclined to return to the tiresome little hardships of our journey. The food here is pretentious, dull, and bad. Every day there is chicken, and every day there is pork. There are also eggs and ham. Sometimes the ham gets into the soup, which is made of chicken, and always thick white. The fish is high. There is one bottle of whisky in the bar, which we are steadily drinking: it should last our time. *Après nous*, the unspeakable Shanghai sherry—for the duration, presumably, of the war.

The menu is full of weird items: "Ham egg." "Hat cake." "Lemen Pie." "FF Potatoes." After the meal cocoa is served, in small coffee-cups.

April 7.

This morning Mr Liu kindly sent a staff officer to escort us round the various sights of Sian. The staff officer's presence was necessary in case we should wish to take photographs—for here, in Shen-si, the regulations are very strict.

We had intended to begin with the Drum Tower, which stands in the middle of the town, but just as we were climbing its steps the air-raid alarm sounded. The Drum Tower is used as an observation post, so the officer said that it would be better to return there later. We would drive out first to see the Big Goose Pagoda, about a mile outside the city walls. The people of Sian take air-raids very seriously. The police drive them helter-skelter off the streets with sticks, and the general atmosphere of alarm is consequently much greater in Sü-chow or Hankow.

Ahead of us, bumping along the road which led from the city gate, was a motor-bus. Just outside the city Auden stopped our car to photograph some Mohammedan tombs. To our surprise the bus stopped too, and out of it jumped twenty figures in blue overalls, nearly all of them Europeans, blonde-haired, snub-nosed, chattering in Russian. They scattered over the fields, shouting to each other, laughing, turning somersaults, like schoolboys arriving at the scene of a Sunday-school picnic. Our guide told us that they were Russian mechanics from the air-field, and that they are always evacuated like this when a raid is threatened.

Here was a partial answer to one of the questions we have been asking everybody about the extent of Russian aid to China. Many Chinese deny categorically that there are any Russians in Sian at all. Others have told us that it is the Russian mechanics who won't allow civil planes of the Eurasia Company to land on the aerodrome, because the Eurasia pilots are mostly Germans. We have also heard that trains are going through the station every night loaded with Russian munitions and trucks which have come into China across northern Sinkiang. It seems nearly impossible to get any definite information.

The Big Goose Pagoda, like nearly everything else we saw this morning, is a thousand years old—so our guide told us. It is less ornate, more massive, simpler in outline, than the kind of pagoda you see in travel magazines. From the top, looking out over the fields, you can see the traces of a much larger city, the Sian of the T'angs. The Pagoda used to stand on its outskirts. On the highest story there is a little shrine, and on the wall behind it—as in so many other appropriate and inappropriate places— somebody has scribbled one of the conventional anti-Japanese drawings: China as a giant martyr, stuck full of swords and pestered by a tiny Jap aeroplane which buzzes round his head like a wasp. On reaching the bottom of the Pagoda stairs I had a violent attack of cramp, and for the rest of the morning could only hobble. Auden suggests that it is probably the prelude to some rare Oriental disease.

After this we saw the Little Goose Pagoda, which is a semi-ruin, split down the middle by an earthquake, and the Mohammedan mosque in the city, and the Drum Tower. This afternoon we drove out to Lintung, a famous hot springs resort lying right under the mountain, in the direction of Tung-kwan. We bathed at the bath-house in its willow-pattern garden of pools and bridges. The water has no very remarkable properties: it neither stinks nor fizzes, nor is it in the least discoloured. But it is nice and warm.

It was here that the Generalissimo was arrested by the commander of the Young Marshal's bodyguard on the 12th of December, 1936. You can still see the dent of a bullet in one of the scarlet wooden pillars outside his sleeping-pavilion, and high above, on the mountain path, the rocks bear an inscription in red characters telling how, at this spot, Chiang Kai-shek, who had escaped from the bath-house in his nightshirt, was caught by the pursuing soldiers.

Beyond Lintung is the largest tomb in China, that of the Emperor Ch'in Shih Huang Ti (200 B.C.), who burnt the scholar's books at a spot where grass has never grown since. According to legend, he had a marvellous palace, illuminated by candles which would burn for a thousand years, and protected by mechanical archers who shot unwelcome guests. On the mountain-top, we were told, is a beacon with a "Wolf! Wolf!" story attached to it. The beacon summoned the Emperor's generals in time of danger, and the Empress lit it for a joke. The generals, arriving and finding that they had been tricked, were cross, naturally. So that, later, when the Empress was really in the hands of bandits, they saw the fire and didn't come. So she died.

When we got back to the hotel I decided to have a massage. We arranged with the manager that one of the coolies from the neighbouring bath-house should be sent up to our room. A speciality of this country is toe-massage, which is simply toe-pinching—and how they can pinch! The coolie also played a syncopated drum-rhythm on my legs, producing a series of quite loud hollow pops, interspersed with arpeggios of astonishingly painful thumb-stabs. Then with finger and thumb he carefully felt for, grasped, and tweaked my ulnar nerves. I yelled. It was like a violent electric shock. But the coolie didn't even smile. His terrifying, impersonal ferocity reminded me of the demons you see in temple-paintings, devouring the bodies of the damned. Perhaps he did my cramp good. At any rate, I feel very stiff.

April 8.

Today it is raining heavily. The city is a wilderness of mud through which the rickshaws toil with their hoods up—long hoods which protect the coolie as well as his passenger, who sits, invisible and blind, behind a high waterproof bib.

This afternoon we have been to see Mr Liu again, and our last hopes of getting down to Cheng-tu are destroyed. We should be obliged to charter an entire truck, and it would cost at least three hundred dollars. So we have decided to go back to Hankow the day after tomorrow by rail.

Mr Liu was very friendly. He begged us to stay and talk. He used to be a professor of modern history at Nanking University. He speaks good English, and is extremely intelligent and widely read.

Without our even asking—for the subject is so taboo as to seem almost indecent—he talked quite openly about the Russian military supplies. The Russian trucks, says Mr Liu, bring them as far as Tiwha, where the Chinese trucks meet them. The journey from Tiwha to Sian sometimes takes three weeks. Aeroplanes are often flown across from Russian territory direct to Lanchow. But Russia only supplies thirty per cent of China's petrol: the rest comes from the Americans and the English via Hongkong.

We asked Mr Liu's opinion of the possible duration of the war. He predicted another fifteen months. Then, if China still held out, Japan's finances would collapse. "But what about China's finances?" we asked. Mr Liu smiled: "China has no finances. That is our strength. . . . China doesn't pay silver. She imports arms entirely on credit." After the war China would need the Western Powers for many years to come. They would get their money back on reconstruction and economic development. Extra-territorial rights would have to be abolished, of course. He assured us that China would never make peace until Manchuria had been restored to her.

Asked what kind of government he would like after the war, he became a little vague. Oh yes, there would be a Parliament with three parties: Kuomintang, Social Democrat, Communist. But it was plain that he expected friction between the Communists and Chiang Kai-shek before long. And, of course, the country would, in practice, be governed by a military dictatorship. Outer Mongolia and Thibet would remain outside the direct influence of the Government. They were valuable as buffer-states. No, there could be no real democracy, at present. The electorate wasn't sufficiently educated. Elementary primary education has begun in certain provinces, but it is concerned for the moment chiefly with inculcating patriotic principles. Reading and writing will come later.

We asked whether there is any form of conscription in China. Oh, no, Mr Liu replied, it wasn't necessary. China has far more able-bodied soldiers than she can possibly use. The coolies volunteer everywhere, and they are brave as a matter of course—they set no value on their lives. "If you asked *me*", Mr Liu added jokingly, "to take a rifle and fight, I wouldn't do it, of course!" He believed that education tended to make the Chinese unsuitable for military purposes. The officers who have been trained at

West Point or in England expect their men to wash themselves and brush their teeth—and the men don't like it. Returning to the subject of conscription, Mr Liu also told us that the carrying-on of the family is such an important article of Chinese religious feeling that the eldest son never becomes a soldier.

(Mr Liu's remarks may be true of Shen-si Province, but we have heard elsewhere that compulsory military service is very strictly enforced. You can only avoid it by paying for somebody else to go in your place. Thus the richer members of a village will club together and subscribe enough to buy its necessary quota of recruits from the poorer families which badly need the money.)

This evening we went up to Mooser's room to drink with a party of Chinese doctors and the Swiss. Somebody told the story of how another foreign medical expert arrived in Sian, alone: he spoke no Chinese, so on leaving the station he got into a rickshaw and waited to see what would happen. The rickshaw-coolie took him straight to General Staff Headquarters, where he was immediately arrested and locked in a room for several hours, until an English-speaking officer arrived, and the matter was explained.

While we were talking, fire-crackers began to explode all over the city. And presently we got the news of the big Chinese victory on the Grand Canal front, at Tai-erh-chwang. We were all excited, except for one of the Chinese doctors, who became sad and thoughtful. He had a Japanese wife.

April 9.

Today, as we were sitting in the hotel entrance-lounge, in walked Dr Brown. He is on his way north to join the Eighth Route Army and will leave for Yen-an tomorrow, with one of the Swiss doctors.

Dr Brown was in the highest of spirits. He seemed to have grown ten years younger. He told us how, shortly after we left Kwei-teh, Dr Gilbert, who was cycling home one evening, was stopped by bandits within a few hundred yards of the hospital gates. They took away his money and his watch but didn't hurt him. The bandits hadn't been caught.

April 10.

This afternoon at five o'clock we left Sian by train for Hankow. Dr Mooser and the Swiss engineer are travelling in the next compartment. They are going down to a medical conference at Changsha. Trautmann and his Germans are also on board. Having failed to reach Yen-an they are making for Sü-chow. This is the same old train, and Chin-dung and his friends have lost no time in re-establishing their claims on our cigarettes. They are, luckily, a little awed, however, by our fellow-passenger—

an important military official who reclines in the opposite bunk, reading poetry with an air of extreme fastidiousness. When the car-boys look in, he eyes them distastefully and touches his temples with a handkerchief moistened in eau-de-Cologne. From Chiang we learn that he has been up in the north-west, supervising the transport of Russian munitions. Unfortunately he speaks hardly any English, and is obviously much too grand to be cross-examined through an interpreter.

We are rather annoyed with Chiang just now. The long, lazy stay at Sian has corrupted him. He has become bossy, impudent, and careless. When he packed this morning he left a number of our things behind in the hotel. Now, as the losses are discovered, he takes refuge in his bad English until we could gladly box his ears.

"So you didn't pack the soap, Chiang?"

Chiang looks at us and smiles: "Yes."

"Well, where is it, then?"

"I don't know."

"But you *must* know. Look for it."

Chiang looks, not very carefully. His manner suggests that the search is quite hopeless.

"Did you pack it, or didn't you?"

"Yes."

"You mean you *did* pack it?"

"No."

April 11.

During the night we arrived at Hwayin Hsien, one of the last stations before Tung-kwan. We shall stay here until this evening. A train has just come through from the east with one of its windows smashed by shell-fire—otherwise no damage. In the distance you can hear the booming of artillery. The Chinese batteries have revealed themselves at last. They are said to have put one of the Japanese guns out of action already.

Hwayin Hsien is a pretty little town with clean cobbled streets and several ancient shrines. Behind it towers a sacred mountain, a magnificent blue crag like a shattered molar tooth thrust up from the pine-forests beneath. Cavalry units are quartered here and the plain is dotted with cantering riders. From every pool and ditch frogs sound their tiny klaxons in the brilliant sunshine. All this morning we have been lying in the grass smoking and talking a few hundred yards from the train, under the shadow of the town wall. There was an air-raid warning, but no Japanese appeared. Now and then a group of passing soldiers and peasants would stop and speak to us. When we showed that we didn't understand they would make the signs of Chinese characters with their forefingers on the palms of their hands. Though there are so many dialects in China, the written language is almost universally understood—and so the country people believe that English is merely yet another dialect. This sign-language has been tried on us over and over again.

April 12.

Here we are back at "Wuthering Heights". We passed Tung-kwan safely during the night. More sitting about, more English lessons with the car-boys, more short strolls with one eye on the train. Quite literally, we don't trust it any further than we can see it. It is liable to start without the least warning at any moment. At a station where we stopped earlier this morning it very nearly succeeded in leaving Dr Mooser and his colleagues behind.

Auden did a lot of photography among the platform crowd. Shortly after his return from one of these camera-expeditions we looked out of the window to see a beggar rolling on the ground and roaring as though in fearful pain. The Englishman, he yelled, had stolen his spirit and put it into his little box. He wanted five dollars compensation. We were both rather alarmed by this new form of blackmail, but the onlookers seemed to be on our side. They merely laughed.

April 13.

We reached Loyang at noon. Chiang came to tell us that we should stay here six hours in order to reach Cheng-chow at the correct time. The train would leave at exactly twenty-five minutes past six. "Rubbish!" said Auden. "I bet you a dollar it doesn't!" Chiang smiled blandly.

Chiang and I went into the town during the afternoon. I wanted to buy a tea-pot as a present to an English friend. We examined hundreds. The heat was stifling. Later we drank tea, and Chiang told me about his wife and children. They are still in Nanking, and apparently quite safe, though he hasn't had news of them for some time. Chiang himself fled from Nanking before the Japanese occupation; he was afraid of being conscripted for forced labour. It must be said for him that he really is eager to improve his English. Nearly every day he brings us a list of words which he has heard us use and wishes to have explained. This afternoon he was particularly anxious to know how to describe his job. After we had exhaustively discussed the meanings of "interpreter", "valet", "servant", "butler", "major-domo", "steward", "guide", and "travelling-companion", Chiang decided that "valet" was the most suitable and the nicest of all.

The train started at 6.25, to the minute. Auden handed over his dollar. We wondered if the engine-driver was going to get a commission.

We were in Cheng-chow by half-past ten. The Hankow express was already waiting, but the doors of the first-class coach were locked. However, the attendant recognized us and, perhaps remembering our enormous tipping-powers, let us into a sleeping-compartment in defiance of the regulations. Chiang, stingy as ever, had underpaid the luggage-coolies. While they were arguing two station-guards ran up, smacked the coolies' faces and drove them away with their rifle-butts before we had had time to interfere.

April 14.

At breakfast in the dining-car we met Mr Jao, a live-wire, hard-drinking Chinese war-correspondent who had been with us in Hankow when we visited the opera. Mr Jao has just returned from the front. He was one of the first to enter Tai-erh-chwang after its recapture by the Chinese troops. When they got into the town they found everything dead—men and women, ducks, dogs and cats. One house only was left intact. Its owner, instead of being thankful, had come round to headquarters crying and scolding because one of her chairs had been smashed.

Some troops, passing a shell-hole near the road to Tai-erh-chwang, thought they saw something move. It was a wounded Japanese soldier, who had covered himself in blankets and was attempting to hide. They shouted to him to give himself up, but he refused and opened fire on them. After a battle lasting nearly an hour the Japanese was killed.

Despite the reward of 160 dollars offered for every prisoner taken alive, very few Japanese are ever captured. They are told by their officers that the Chinese behead their prisoners, so they prefer to commit suicide before the enemy arrives. Some Japanese corpses are even found with notes attached to their clothing, begging the Chinese not to cut their heads off after death.

April 20.

We have been back in Hankow now for nearly a week.

Spring has transformed the entire city. It is Siberian no longer; it is sub-tropical. The weather is as warm as an English July. In six weeks the period of real clammy heat, which makes a Hankow summer nearly intolerable for Europeans, will have begun.

The trees are all in leaf, the gardens are full of blossom. The rickshaws have folded back their hoods and the rickshaw-coolies run sweating, stripped to the waist. The troops have removed the padding from their uniforms or exchanged them for light cotton clothes. The civilians begin to appear in white drill jackets and shorts.

In the early evening there is usually a little knot of spectators round the gates of the British Consulate, peering into the garden, where the neat, athletic figure of the Consul-General is to be seen, practising with his golf-clubs. The exquisite accuracy of the Consul's putting seems somehow very reassuring, amidst all the chaos and inefficiency of wartime China. Perhaps the Chinese onlookers feel this, too.

The fine weather favours the air-raids by day and by night. The Japs are now not only a danger but a positive nuisance. If Auden and I go out shopping in different parts of the town we have always to arrange an emergency rendezvous—for there is usually no time to return to the Consulate, and the alternative may be an hour of solitary boredom standing in a doorway or sitting in a café, waiting for the "all clear" to sound. The night-raids are worse, with their false alarms and endless delays. Twice we have hardly slept at all. I have moved my bed out on to the balcony so as to be able, at any rate, to watch the planes without getting up. When the raid is over, a Chinese plane, with a red and a green light on its wing-tips, circles over the city, to guide the defenders back to the air-field. Looking for this plane we stare so hard into the sky that soon the stars themselves appear to move. I see them dancing in front of me long after I have shut my eyes in an angry and hopeless attempt to fall asleep again.

April 21.

Today, having written up our Yellow River material and finished a series of newspaper articles, we reopened our social life by attending a tea-party at the Terminus Hotel. Mr Han Li-wu had arranged it in order that we should meet the leading Chinese intellectuals at present in Hankow. The intellectuals were grouped at small tables, in parties of five or six, and our hosts moved us gently but firmly one to another, whenever an interesting conversation was beginning to develop. The gathering was certainly most distinguished. We were honoured by the monumental presence of Feng Yü-hsiang, the "Christian General" (who is said once to have baptized a whole regiment of his troops with a fire-hose). Feng speaks no English—nor does he need to. He is one of those huge, benevolent human whales whose mere silence is all-sufficient. Our compliments were translated to him and he beamed. Then everybody else talked English, disregarding him completely, and he continued to beam. Strangely enough he had a perfect right to be there, for he is also a poet. He writes verses in peasant dialect about country life, and war. Once the declared enemy of Chiang Kai-shek, he now forms part of the military united front—but so far, it seems, the Government has given him very little to do.

Other notable guests were Messrs Tien Shou-chang, the dramatist, Hoong, the translator, and Mou Mou-tien, the best modern poet, we are told, in China. A lady named Miss Chen Ye-yun, M.A., talked super-enthusiastically about women's war-work. She was lively, dry, and neat—very little different from her counterpart type in Europe. Towards the end of the meal we were interviewed by a young journalist on the *Ta Kung Pao,* one of China's leading newspapers. He had the exotic name of Macdonald (anglicized from Ma Tong-na). This westernization of names is quite usual, it appears, among the intellectuals. What did we think of Chinese morale, customs, morality? What of the military situation? What of the new type of Chinese woman? We answered most inadequately, but it didn't matter—Mr Macdonald was already writing before we had opened our mouths.

Meanwhile, at another table, Mr Tien was having the poem he had written in our honour translated by Mr Hoong.

> Really, the ends of the world are neighbours:
> Blood-tide, flower-petals, Hankow spring,
> Shoulder to shoulder for civilization fight.
> Across the sea, long journey, how many Byrons?

Not to be outdone, Auden replied with a sonnet which he finished writing yesterday, on a dead Chinese soldier.

We both find functions of this sort extremely tiring. There is no lack of goodwill on either side—indeed, the air positively vibrates with Anglo-Chinese *rapprochement*—but are we really communicating with each other at all? Beaming at our hosts we exchange words: "England", "China", "Poetry", "Culture", "Shakespeare", "International Understanding", "Bernard Shaw"—but the words merely mean, "We are pleased to see you." They are just symbols of mutual confidence, like swapping blank cheques. Never mind. It is all in a good cause. So we move from table to table, trying to say something to everybody, and our faces ache with smiling. One smiles so little, it seems, in the West. For a newcomer to China the muscular effort is enormous.

We had just time to change our clothes for the party which was being given by the Admiral and the Consul-General in a luxury flat over the Bank. The Admiral is in command of all the gunboats on this part of the Yangtze River. His hobbies are photography and collecting Chinese vases. ("I don't know if it's Ming, Sing, Ting, or Wing—but I like its shape.") Hankow is full of British naval officers, most of whom are parted from their ships by the Wuhu boom: they lead an unnatural, widowed life of office-work, polo-playing, gossip, and drinks, ruled by a meaningless but unexacting discipline which demands only that they shall wear the correct uniform at certain hours of the day. We like nearly all of them very much indeed. "You're idealists," they tell us, "but you can't alter human nature." A few of them come into the Consulate regularly for their meals. Auden plays to them on the piano. They teach us new songs and the ritual of "Cardinal Puff".

The Admiral, with his great thrusting, naked chin (he detests beards) and the Consul-General, looking like a white-haired schoolboy, received their guests. There was Sir Archibald Clark Kerr, the British Ambassador, Scottish but funny, with the deprecatory, amateur air which marks the born diplomatist. There was Lady Kerr, his wife, a tiny Chilean blonde, whose absurd beauty lent a brilliant, theatrical lustre to the whole proceedings. There was Mr Jarvis, the American Consul—owner of an anthology of seventeenth-century lyrics, which Auden has borrowed, and which a puppy at the Consulate began to eat during the night, getting as far as Milton (Mr Jarvis was very nice about this). There was Peter Fleming and his wife the actress, Celia Johnson, charming in her thick horn-rimmed spectacles. Fleming with his drawl, his tan, his sleek, perfectly brushed hair, and lean good looks, is a subtly comic figure—the conscious, living parody of the pukka sahib. He is altogether too good to be true—and he knows it. This time Fleming is in China as a correspondent of *The Times;* he has just returned from Chung-king, where the Ambassador was paying his first official visit to the President of the Chinese Republic.

The party was a great success. Towards the end of the evening somebody took a goldfish out of its bowl, and sprinkled it with pepper.

April 22.

An extract from today's News Bulletin:

With the tide of war surging on many fronts the "permanent wave" is now at its very ebb in China. This is one of the numerous harbingers of China's final victory in her war of self-defence, for from the ebbing of the "permanent wave" have already arisen hundreds of thousands of Chinese girls bravely and conscientiously taking their share of their country's all-front resistance. . . .

War has introduced a new concept of beauty in China. Girls with pencilled brows like moths, powdered face, manicured finger-nails and toe-nails and above all with the "permanent wave" in their hair, no longer command admiration. They are often considered unpatriotic. In present-day China the true wartime beauty in a woman must carry a martial air. She uses no cosmetics on her face and her hair is pressed backward under a smart cap that matches her army uniform. . . .

Chinese girls, crazy for modernity, borrowed the curliness in their hair from the barber shops. With the change of affairs prevailing in wartime, many of the barber shops in China have shelved their paraphernalia for hair waving.

In Hankow, for instance, such paraphernalia is in operation only in a small number of barber shops located in the French Concession, where are concentrated most of Hankow's singsong girls. These fair ones have to continue to keep their hair waved for the simple reason that they have to live.

But even the singsong girls have changed their style. They want the "permanent wave" that would turn their hair into the likeness of an airplane—the airplane that is fighting in the air against the Japanese.

True to the patriotism into which their hair is shaped, the singsong girls in Hankow have done laudably for their country's cause by helping in raising funds in the interest of China's wounded soldiers and refugees.

You can see the singsong girls any evening, dancing with their friends and customers at the "Wee Golf Restaurant". (The "Wee Golf" is so-called because it has, or had, a midget golf-course on the premises. There is also a "Majestic Golf Restaurant" further down the street.) The singsong girls are not, as we had at first imagined, professional prostitutes. Indeed, it is very difficult to start an affair with one of them. Introductions, and a period of courtship, are necessary; and, if the girl doesn't like you, she won't have you. In general, the Chinese aren't very highly sexed—so people tell us. The average young man will be quite content to spend the evening dancing, flirting, and drinking tea with his girl friend. Sex is an affair of jokes and compliments and gaiety; a graceful minor art, harmless, pretty and gentle as flower-painting on a fan. Most of the girls are attractive, but few are really beautiful: as a rule their faces are too broad and flat. Nearly all of them have superb figures. They wear sleeveless Chinese gowns of patterned silk, tight under the armpits, with a high collar clasped close round the throat. The gown falls to the ankles, but its sides are slashed, so that the wearer's legs when she moves are visible right up to the knee.

This morning we were visited by Mr C. C. Yeh, a shy young man whom we met yesterday at the literary tea. He is the author of a book of short stories in Esperanto, *Forgesitaj Homoj*, written under the pseudonym of "Cicio Mar". Yeh was once a pupil of Julian Bell, when Bell was a professor at the Wuhan University. Like Macdonald he belongs to a propaganda group in the political department of the Military Council. This group includes a number of writers who, until recently, have been in prison for their liberal or left-wing opinions. Yeh himself was in Japan when the war started. The Japanese police arrested him on the suspicion that he was an anarchist. "You must not mind", he told us, "if I seem a little stupid sometimes. You see, they struck me very often upon the head." Like all these amazingly tough Chinese revolutionaries he gives one the impression of being gentle, nervous, and soft.

While we were talking, in burst a spring vision—Agnes Smedley, in a light, girlish dress. She was triumphant and gay. Her manuscript has turned up after all, most mysteriously, in New York; and the new Red

Army book will soon be published in England, Russia, and the States. She seemed delighted to see us back and invited us to come and see her at her new room. (She has moved from the "Moscow-Heaven Axis", for Bishop Roots has already left Hankow.) She is now living in the Chang Gai—the same street as the Eighth Route Army Headquarters. "But the coolies around there call it Pa Lu Gai—'Eighth Route Street.' When you take a rickshaw don't ask for Chang Gai. Just say 'Pa Lu Gai', and see if they understand. I want to find out if it's known all over the town." We promised that we would.

In the afternoon we drive out with the Ambassador, Lady Kerr, and a professor named Kuo, to visit the Wuhan University. It is on the south side of the river, near Wuchang. The university buildings are quite new: they were started in 1931. Their neo-Chinese style of architecture brilliantly combines the old horned roofs with the massive brutality of blank concrete. From the distance the huge central block, with its rows of little windows, standing magnificently in a wild hilly park beside a big lake, reminds you of pictures of Lhasa. Actually this effect of size is achieved by a clever architectural fake—what appear to be the tops of great square towers are, in reality, comparatively small buildings set upon the crest of the hill, so that they rise above the lower façade. The interior is disappointing, chiefly, no doubt, because the war has cut short the work of decoration.

There are only a few students, most of them post-graduates, at Wuhan nowadays. A part of the buildings is even being used as a barracks. Education is cheap. A student needs no more than two hundred Chinese dollars a year for his fees, board and lodging included. Even very poor boys, we are told, are often able to get into the university. For family sentiment in this country is so strong that the most distant relatives feel themselves bound in honour to subscribe something towards the education of a really promising scholar.

About a dozen professors and their wives received us: they seemed particularly delighted that Lady Kerr had come. After we had seen everything we were given tea at a small guest-house in the grounds. Beneath their politely assumed gaiety the professors all seemed apprehensive and sad. They are wondering, no doubt, what will become of the university if Hankow falls. Wuhan has been their life-work, and the ambition has only so recently been realized. Must all they have struggled for be lost again, so soon? Nevertheless, today is not tomorrow; and they have no wish to sadden their honoured guests. So they giggled and chattered, pressing us to immense helpings of the rich cream-cakes. (We had an uneasy feeling that this extravagant banquet must have cost them a good part of their month's wages.)

Before we said good-bye each member of our party was presented with an inscribed silk scroll, on which was painted a panorama of the Wuhan buildings. And Ling Su-hua, wife of Professor Chen, gave Auden and myself two fans, which she had painted that afternoon. They represent landscapes near the lake. On my fan Madame Chen has written two lines from an old poet:

> The mountain and the river in the mist not broken in pieces.
> We should only drink and forget this immense sorrow.

Beneath which she herself has added:

> During this country struggle
> I paint in wonder to forget my sorrow.

Madame Chen is a great admirer of the works of Virginia Woolf. She has given us a little box to take back to Mrs Woolf as a present. Inside it is a beautifully carved ivory skull.

April 23.

Macdonald came in to see us this morning. His interview with us at the tea-party was printed in the *Ta Kung Pao* yesterday, together with a manuscript facsimile and Chinese rendering of Auden's sonnet. Macdonald had been specially praised by his editor for getting this interview, and was feeling very pleased with himself. He translated it all to us, word by word: "Mr Tien then read his poem to Mr Au and Mr Y, who were very much influenced. Then Mr Au read his poem, and everybody was very much influenced."

We got Macdonald to retranslate the Chinese version of the sonnet. The translators had evidently felt that one line:

> Abandoned by his general and his lice,

was too brutal, and maybe, even, a dangerous thought (for generals never abandon their troops under any circumstances). So, instead, they had written:

> The rich and the poor are combining to fight.

Today is St George's Day, and we devoted the rest of it to the Navy. There was a lunch-party at the Consulate, a cocktail-party at the Race Club, and a supper in one of the Russian dance-restaurants (known collectively to the British officers as "The Dumps").

Lunch was argumentative and political. Somebody present believed that Franco was a gentleman and a sportsman, because he played a good game of golf, and had attended a British Consul's funeral in the Canary

Islands on his way to start the rebellion in Morocco. Somebody else gave an interesting analysis of Chiang Kai-shek's Easter Speech. He believed that the Government's removal of the ban on religious teaching in mission schools suggests that the New Life Movement will now become more specifically Christian. Perhaps, also, the Chiangs' Christianity will prove an increasingly effective political weapon to counter the propaganda of the Anti-Comintern Pact. The old accusations against the Communists and their allies of "godlessness" are getting more and more difficult to sustain. Mao Tse-tung himself is said to have attended Mass as a gesture of goodwill towards the missionaries. Perhaps the historian of the future will have to thank Bishop Roots.

Not only the Race Club buildings but even the grounds surrounding them might well be in the heart of Surrey. Here, as Auden remarked, all trace of China has been lovingly obliterated. We drank to "St George's Day—England's Day", and looked forward to "the match tomorrow with our brother Scots, and an excellent tiffin with the St Andrew's Society". We were chiefly impressed by the surprising number of English civilian residents still remaining in Hankow.

Today is also the eve of the Russian Orthodox Easter. Just before midnight we joined the group of onlookers at the doors of the Russian church, which stands a little way down the road from the British Consulate. The church itself was crammed. From the interior came whiffs of incense and hot leather—the nostalgic perfume of exile. Nearly the whole of the White Russian colony must have been assembled, including the taxi-girls from "The Dumps". Their high-boned faces, illuminated by the candles which each member of the congregation held in his or her hand, looked beautiful and cold and pure. Many of the taxi-girls were accompanied by their men friends, heavy, blue-chinned figures in dinner-jackets, waiting, somewhat impatiently, for midnight, when custom would permit them to exchange the ambiguous Easter kiss.

7

We now began to make plans for our visit to the south-eastern front—if, indeed, it could be described as a "front" at all. The Japanese forces were working their way inland from Shanghai, thrusting forward like the spokes of an irregularly-shaped fan. To the north-west the fan covered Nanking; to the west it approached Wuhu, where the Chinese had barred the Yangtze with their boom; to the south-west it touched Hang-chow. About the country which lay in between these points information was contradictory and vague. The Japs would advance along a valley and retreat again. They would occupy a village or a railway station, and hold it like a fort in the midst of an area overrun with hostile guerilla units. It was even said that with a knowledge of the lie of the land you could easily penetrate their lines, unchallenged, to the very outskirts of Shanghai itself.

We, too, hoped eventually to reach Shanghai without having to return to Hankow and make the usual journey via Hongkong. The river-ports of Ningpo and Wenchow were still open. From either of them we ought to be able to get a boat direct to the Bund of the International Settlement.

Next morning we went to see Agnes Smedley in her new home. She was living in an otherwise deserted building, a former military headquarters. After wandering down empty and semi-ruinous passages it was strange to come upon her gay, prettily-furnished room, with its vases and screens. When we arrived, Capa and Po Ku were both with her. Miss Smedley's first question was: Had we remembered to ask the rickshaw-coolies for the Pa Lu Gai? Yes, we had; and they had brought us here without hesitation. Miss Smedley was delighted. She seemed to regard this as a definite victory for the workers' cause.

Capa had just returned with the others from Tai-erh-chwang. He had got a lot of pictures, and Ivens had shot a whole section of his film. But Capa was dissatisfied. He had found the Chinese face unsatisfactory for the camera, in comparison with the Spanish. He was plainly longing to return to Spain. "I'd like to get back to Paris for the Fourteenth of July", he said wistfully, "and dance in the streets. Then off to Madrid. . . ." But, meanwhile, he was accompanying Ivens and Fernhout to Yen-an and the north-west. He wanted us to help him send off his photographs uncensored to America, where they would be published as a book.

"You make much money!" said Po Ku with an explosive, giggling laugh. Po Ku laughs at everything—the Japanese, the war, victory, defeat. We asked for the latest news of the Eighth Route Army. What were conditions like nowadays? "Terrible!" Po Ku giggled. "They have no shoes!" "*No shoes!*" echoed Miss Smedley, with a moan of the wildest despair. She began to pace the room with her hand to her mouth. "Tell me, Po Ku, what shall we do? *No shoes!* I must cable to America at once!"

They began to discuss the shoe problem. In Hankow there is a type of rubber-soled sandal which can be bought wholesale, very cheap. They argued expertly about its merits and defects. It was fascinating to watch them—both, in their different ways, so practical, so deadly earnest: the smiling East, the melodramatic West. The Red Army, one sees, is Agnes Smedley's whole life—her husband and her child. "When I was with them", she told us, "for the first time I felt at one with the universe." Here in Hankow she was miserably homesick for the north-west. But here she could do more to help by keeping in touch with sympathetic organizations abroad. And so she stayed.

We talked of the south-eastern front, and Po Ku repeated his promise of a letter to the Communist Fourth Army headquarters at Nanchang. He said also that he would try to arrange an interview for us with Chou En-lai.

In the afternoon of the next day we drove out to the suburbs to visit Hankow's film-studio—the largest of its kind in wartime China. There were two buildings: a big shabby villa, once the property of a Chinese general, now used for dark-rooms and the accommodation of the actors; and the more recently built studio itself. In the garden half a dozen young actors and technicians were playing netball beside a dismantled set representing a shell-wrecked village. Dresses were hung out to dry on a clothes-line. The whole place looked very domestic and untidy and cheerful. Our hosts explained that no work was done during the daytime, because of air-raids. After dark the shooting in the studio would begin.

Mr Lo, the sound-engineer, showed us round. Neither he nor any of his colleagues had studied abroad, nor had they ever imported foreign advisers. He had learnt everything out of books, constructing his own sound-recording apparatus and enlarging-camera. This home-made equipment was excellent. Technical problems had been solved with astonishing economy and ingenuity. We particularly admired the interior set itself. It was the living-room of a farm-house, prepared for a wedding, with an eye for detail which would put most western art-directors to shame. The properties had none of that unnatural newness which is such a besetting vice of the English studios. Mr Lo showed us a whole arsenal of machine-guns, rifles, and uniforms, most of which had been actually captured by the Eighth Route Army from the Japanese.

At present the studio was producing only war-films. Just now they were at work on the story of Shanghai's "Doomed Battalion". It would be called *Fight to the Last*. We were shown some of the rushes. The war-scenes were brilliant. The producer had an astonishingly subtle feeling for grouping; his weakness lay in the direction of the actors themselves—he had indulged too often the Chinese talent for making faces. All these grimaces of passion, anger, or sorrow, seemed a mere mimicry of the West. One day a director of genius will evolve a style of acting which is more truly national—a style based upon the beauty and dignity of the Chinese face in repose.

Besides these fragments we were shown several news-reels. There were the ruins of Tai-erh-chwang; the entry of the Chinese troops into the town; a woman's naked body, horribly mutilated; a speech to the soldiers by Feng Yü-hsiang (who must surely, to judge by his tones and gestures, be one of the best orators in China); and an amusing and touching shot of some Manchurian prisoners dancing for joy on finding that they were not to be executed. One of the prisoners was a White Russian. A considerable number of them, we were told, are fighting in the Japanese Army.

In the evening Miss Smedley came round to see us at the Consulate, deeply depressed. The Police have just raided the bookshops in Hankow and Chung-king, and confiscated large quantities of Left-wing and Communist literature. Even General Feng Yü-hsiang's poems have been banned, because he writes about the poor. It is difficult to tell just who gave the order for this police action; probably one of Chiang's more reactionary advisers. It may not mean very much, but it is disheartening. It shows that there are still people in the Government who can't forget the old feuds.

Agnes Smedley took a very serious view of the matter. She feared that these raids might indicate a change of policy towards the Communists on the part of the Kuomintang. She suspected even that the Eighth Route Army was being deliberately kept short of money and equipment, lest it should become too important as a military and political factor when the war was over. She told us also that three prominent Chinese business men in Shanghai had just been caught organizing a kidnapping racket to supply the Japanese brothels with Chinese women.

We paid another visit to General von Falkenhausen's headquarters. Our friend the A.D.C. was in an indignant mood. He had just read the news of an interview given by a prominent American journalist to the Press in Shanghai. The journalist had praised China's solidarity, adding that Germans and Russians were "fighting side by side". "Never in my life", the A.D.C. assured us, "have I spoken to a Soviet Russian!"

That same morning we had been shown a report issued by the German Chamber of Commerce in Shanghai. It was a tactfully worded but extremely thorough criticism of Berlin's Far Eastern policy. The German Government's support of Japan, it claimed, was responsible for the ruin of German business interests in China. Many firms were failing already. By the end of the year they would have closed down altogether.

We had tea with Mr Han Li-wu. He was anxious to invite a delegation of British artists and writers to visit China in the near future and wanted us to suggest some suitable names.

From another informant we had heard, unofficially, that Japan was already angling for peace terms on the basis of the pre-war *status quo*. We asked Mr Han if he thought that China would agree to let Japan keep Manchukuo. Mr Han replied that this depended largely on the attitude of the British Government. If Britain insisted China might have to agree.

In one of "The Dumps" that evening we talked to the proprietor, an ex-Cossack officer in the Tsarist army. "Well, thank goodness," he said, "I shall be finished with this place next Friday for ever! I've got a job as instructor to a cavalry unit at Loyang. There'll be six of us working together—three of them are Soviet officers from the Red Army." "Won't that be rather awkward for you?" we asked. "Of course not," said the proprietor, "why should it be? All those politics are a thing of the past. If Japan attacks Russia I shall join the Red Army myself." He told us how, a few days before, he had talked to one of the Soviet airmen at present in Hankow. "Are you a Communist?" he had asked the airman. "Naturally." "Then I suppose you're an internationalist?" The airman had laughed: "Me an internationalist? No! I'm a Russian."

For some time we had been anxious to have an interview with Du Yueh-seng. At length next morning, through Macdonald, this was arranged.

Before the war Du Yueh-seng was one of the most influential Chinese politicians in Shanghai. A Big Business chief after the classic American pattern, Du not only employed labour, he controlled it. His political organization, the Green Jade Band, held the Chinese city in a state of undeclared martial law. In the International Settlement also, Du was a great power behind the scenes. After the Communist *coup d'état* in 1927 which put Chiang Kai-shek into power, it was Du and his men who helped Chiang to turn upon his former allies, and kill or drive into exile all the most dangerous radicals among them. When the Japanese entered Shanghai they destroyed much of Du's property, and thereby made for themselves an implacable enemy. Du was now a high Government official, holding an important position on the Red Cross Central Committee. He was said to be completely illiterate.

To visit Du's flat was to enter a strongly-guarded fortress. At least a dozen attendants were posted in the hall, and, when we sat down to talk, there were others who stood in the background behind our chairs. Du himself was tall and thin, with a face that seemed hewn out of stone, a Chinese version of the Sphinx. Peculiarly and inexplicably terrifying were his feet, in their silk socks and smart pointed European boots, emerging from beneath the long silken gown. Perhaps the Sphinx, too, would be even more frightening if it wore a modern top-hat.

Du speaks only Chinese, but several of the doctors present were able to translate our conversation. We talked entirely about the Red Cross. We were told that there were eight thousand qualified doctors in China: eighteen hundred of them were engaged in Red Cross work. Though arrangements were still very imperfect a number of mobile operating units had already been sent out, and were working in or near the front lines. Du asked us for our own experiences and impressions, and nodded his head slowly and heavily as they were translated to him. As we stood up to go he said something to one of the doctors, who told us: "Mr Auden and

Mr Isherwood, Dr Du Yueh-seng wishes to say how much he appreciates your interest in China's Red Cross. He wishes to thank you—in the name of humanity."

One of the top names on Du Yueh-seng's 1927 black list had been that of Chou En-lai, organizer of the armed insurrection and the general strike. Auden was lucky enough to meet him next morning, quite by chance, when he went round to the Pa Lu Gai to photograph Agnes Smedley. That Miss Smedley had agreed to be photographed at all was a great concession. "If you weren't a leftist writer", she told Auden, "I shouldn't let you do this. I hate my face."

Today she was in a cheerful mood because Chou En-lai had written an article exposing the lies of the Whampoa clique—the extreme Right wing of the Government. Kao Tzse, head of the Second Bureau of the Political Department, had published a pamphlet purporting to be the verbatim account of a speech by Po Ku. According to this pamphlet Po Ku had frankly admitted that the Communists had been guilty in the past of murdering many innocent people. It also pretended that he had told his audience that the United Front was only a tactical formation, to be dissolved when it had served the Community Party's purpose.

Chou En-lai believed that the longer the war continued the more complete would be China's victory, and the closer would be the understanding between the Communist Party and the Kuomintang. What he most feared was a compromise peace between the Kuomintang and Japan at the Communists' expense. He was not at all satisfied with the munitions situation. Many private firms had offered their services and asked for government support—but nothing had been done.

When Auden left, Miss Smedley gave him an apple and a card to the New Fourth Army headquarters in Nanchang. To our lasting regret the photographs he had taken of her were all blurred or spoilt.

This, April 29th, was our last day in Hankow. It was also the birthday of the Emperor of Japan. The Japanese celebrated it in their usual manner with a big air-raid. When they arrived, the "home team" was already up to meet them—twenty of the newly-delivered Gloucester Gladiators and thirty Russian machines.

Soon after lunch the sirens began to blare. We put on our smoked glasses and lay down flat on our backs on the Consulate lawn—it is the best way of watching an air-battle if you don't want a stiff neck. Machine-guns and anti-aircraft guns were hammering all around us, but the sky was so brilliant that we seldom caught a glimpse of the planes unless the sun happened to flash on their turning wings. Presently a shell burst close to one of the Japanese bombers; it flared against the blue like a struck match. Down in the road the rickshaw coolies were delightedly clapping their hands. Then came the whining roar of another machine, hopelessly out of control; and, suddenly, a white parachute mushroomed out over the river while the plane plunged on, down into the lake behind Wuchang. This must have been a Chinese, for the Jap pilots, it is said, are not allowed parachutes. They are even rumoured to be padlocked into their cockpits.

Guided by the gesticulations of the rickshaw-boys we ran to another part of the garden in time to watch two planes manœuvring for position. They emitted long streamers of smoke as if writing advertisements. Then another plane, a Japanese, came tumbling out of the eye of the sun, shot to pieces, and turning over and over like a scrap of glittering silver paper. A spent explosive bullet hit the road in front of the house with a tremendous crack. (For a moment we really thought that the Consul-General must have gone mad and opened fire on the enemy with his shot-gun.) Today the Japs annotated their bombs with propaganda leaflets; one of them fluttered down to rest on the roof of the Consulate. It assured the Chinese that Japan was their truest friend.

As soon as the "All Clear" had sounded we telephoned for a car and drove at top speed down twisting, crowded lanes to the banks of the Han River. On the opposite shore smoke was still rising in clouds from the buildings of the Hanyang Arsenal, and from the slum-suburbs which surrounded it. The Japanese had dropped many of their bombs here—a striking proof of the inefficiency of the Japanese Intelligence Service, for the Arsenal had been evacuated several months before and was now practically disused.

The current of the muddy little river as it swirls round the bend into the Yangtze is terribly swift. People are frequently drowned here. We wondered how we should get across, and regarded with deep misgivings the crazy old sampan in which a boy of twelve and a one-eyed crone were offering to ferry us over. But there was no time to waste. The old lady worked us upstream like a rock-climber, grappling her way from one moored sampan to the next with her boat-hook; then out we shot, obliquely, into the middle of the river. As we approached the further bank, with the speed of a motor-car, a serious crash seemed almost inevitable, but the little boy broke the shock with a glancing stab of his bamboo pole, and, a moment later, we were scrambling up the steep mud bank below the Arsenal wall. One of the bombs had blown a derelict boiler clean over this wall and dropped it into the water, all but sinking a small cargo-steamer. Naked coolies, up to their waists in the current, were already working to shift it.

There was a crowd outside the Arsenal gates amidst the havoc of plaster, tiles, and splintered bamboo which, an hour before, had been a row of cottages. A flourish of passes and cards got us past the police guards into the grounds of the Arsenal itself. The authorities were certainly doing their job efficiently: the wounded had long since been removed, and the fire brigade had things well under control; only one small building was still actually in flames. Judging from the size of the bomb-craters the Japanese had wasted a big sum of money.

Over by the other gate lay five civilian victims on stretchers, waiting for their coffins to arrive. They were terribly mutilated and very dirty, for the force of the explosion had tattooed their flesh with gravel and sand. Beside one corpse was a brand-new, undamaged straw hat. All the bodies looked very small, very poor, and very dead, but, as we stood beside one old woman, whose brains were soaking obscenely through a little towel, I saw the blood-caked mouth open and shut, and the hand beneath the sack-covering clench and unclench. Such were the Emperor's birthday presents.

We heard later that five hundred civilians had been killed in the raid and thirty planes destroyed—nine Chinese and twenty-one Japs. Several other Japanese planes had been seriously damaged and were not expected to be able to reach their base. That night Hankow celebrated its greatest aerial victory.

The Navy and our friends from the Consulate gave us a tremendous send-off. We staggered on board the river-steamer for Kiukiang just as the gangways were going up. Later I found myself involved in a semi-maudlin, semi-aggressive conversation with two German passengers who assured me solemnly that never, under any circumstances could England and Germany be friends. Germany would never forget how she had been treated, in the Far East, at the outbreak of the 1914 war. I retired to bed, having lost the argument. I am never much good at defending the British Empire, even when drunk.

There was time to shave, dress, have breakfast, and be heartily sick before Kiukiang swam smoothly round the curve of the river—a pretty Europeanized waterfront of balconied houses and trees, with H.M.S. *Gnat* lying in the foreground at anchor, flat as a nursery tea-tray laden with clean white crockery.

On the river-stairs we were accosted by a big, bald man with the face of a good-humoured don or judge; he wore horn-rimmed glasses, sports jacket, Chinese stockings and shorts. This was Mr Charleton, proprietor of Journey's End, an hotel (or, as he preferred to call it, an inn) situated several miles from Kiukiang, in the Kuling hills.

We had heard of Journey's End, of course, already. It was advertised regularly in the Hankow English newspaper:

JOURNEY'S END

850 feet above sea level. Up here, all is fresh, clean, and beautiful. The Mount Lavinia of the Yangtze Valley. Grilled rainbow trout. Crab home-grown salads. Fresh prawn curries.

Sunrise

Fresh as a maid, all grace and beauty,
Cool as the trout in our Lien Hwa Tong,
Green as the grass of our lakeside pasture,
Gold as the comb in our wild bees' home.

Eventide

Red as the rays of an Iceland sunset,
Tired as a child at bedtime's hour:
Dark, dark as the mane of a blue-black Arab:
Quiet, all quiet as a leopard's paw.

Such days and nights in China's Switzerland are both fine things, little brother: Come and see for yourself.

"Good morning, sir," (this was to Auden). "Are you by any chance a relation of the author? Your wife is German, I believe? You wonder how I know? Heard it over the bamboo wireless. News travels fast in this country." (This, as we discovered later, was a typical example of Mr Charleton's love of mystification. He had, as a matter of fact, been told all about us by one of our fellow-passengers a few moments before.) "You're an author too, sir?" (Charleton turned to me.) "You really must forgive me for not knowing. I live in Sleepy Hollow. I say, I do hope you're not angry with me? I ought to have said: Are you both, by any chance, relations of the authors? Never mind—you two youngsters must bear with an old man who's got one foot in the grave. I hope when you come to my age you'll be able to say: I enjoyed every minute of it! Oh, I've been very lucky. I've had a wonderful life. I'm the wickedest man in the world. My father was the most upright man I ever knew: he was a manager of the Bank of England. I knew Brooke, you know. We were at Cambridge together. I admit I'm a gambler. I could have had anything I wanted from life. Anything. But I played too hard and I lived too hard. They offered to make me a don. Not because I was a great scholar; it was for my rowing. I made a fortune in Shanghai. Lost every penny of it. Who cares? What is success if you're miserable? I'm the happiest man alive!"

I suppose we had already agreed to stay at Journey's End. Or perhaps we hadn't. Anyhow, here we were, bundled into an ancient car with steering-gear like a roulette wheel, bumping through the green countryside, towards the lucid blue of the Kuling mountains. From the village where we stopped Charleton led us uphill, along a path which crossed and recrossed the mountain stream by stepping-stones and tumbledown rustic bridges. The house, with its deep porches, stood on a terrace, looking down the glen. Beneath it the torrent had been dammed to make a swimming-pool ("like swimmers into cleanness leaping", Mr Charleton had quoted in his latest advertisement). On a board in the garden he had painted Dorothy Frances Blomfield Gurney's notorious lines:

> The kiss of the sun for pardon,
> The song of the birds for mirth.
> One is nearer God's heart in a garden
> Than anywhere else on earth.

Running out to meet us came a drilled troop of house-boys in khaki shorts and white shirts, prettily embroidered with the scarlet characters of their names. Mr Charleton's boys were famous, it appeared, in this part of China. He trained them for three years—as servants, gardeners, carpenters, or painters—and then placed them, often in excellent jobs, with consular officials, or foreign business men. The boys had all learnt a little English. They could say: "Good morning, sir," when you met them, and commanded a whole repertoire of sentences about tea, breakfast, the time you wanted to be called, the laundry, and the price of drinks. When a new boy arrived one of the third-year boys was appointed as his guardian. The first year, the boy was paid nothing; the second year, four dollars a month, the third year, ten. If a boy was stupid but willing he was taken on to the kitchen staff, and given a different uniform—black shirt and shorts. All tips were divided and the profits of the business shared out at the end of the year.

The boys also learnt boxing, and were allowed to use the swimming-pool daily, unless one of them had been responsible for a dirty spoon or fork. They also were taught to be quiet. Any boy who shouted lost a good conduct mark. As Mr Charleton said: "God has given you a pair of beautiful legs, and He meant you to use them. If you've anything to say come up close and say it." Boys were summoned by striking with a small hammer one of the numerous shell-cases which were disposed about the house and grounds. On the subject of dress Charleton exercised a more than military strictness. On certain days all the boys were obliged to wear their stockings up to the knee; on others the stockings were rolled down to the ankles. "It depends", he explained, "on my mood."

Our rooms were large and the beds very comfortable. Each bedroom was provided with a Bible and a volume of pornographic French literature. If you stayed at Journey's End long enough you could work through twenty of them at least. "You'll have tiffin under the camphor-tree; it keeps off the insects," said the headmaster (for surely this was a preparatory school?) or the abbot (for perhaps, after all, it was a monastery). "This is Hu Sur-chen. He'll look after you. Each guest has a boy attached to him." Hu Sur-chen smiled faintly. He was a delicate-looking youth of nineteen, unusually shy for a Chinese.

So we had tiffin under the camphor-tree, aware, in a trance of pleasure, of the smell of its leaves; of the splash of the stream over the stones; of the great gorge folding back, like a painting by Salvator Rosa, into the wooded hills behind the house. There were snipe to eat, and rainbow trout. It was all far, far too beautiful to be real. "If I make the sign of the Hammer and Sickle", I said, "everything will disappear." And Auden agreed: "It's the Third Temptation of the Demon." One could arrive for the week-end and stay fifteen years—eating, sleeping, swimming; standing for hours in a daze of stupified reverence before the little Ming tomb in the garden; writing, in the porch, the book that was altogether too wonderful to finish and too sacred ever to publish; pleasantly flagellating the flesh by a scramble up the mountain to the Lily Cave and the Dragon Pool; and, in the evening, inventing imaginary sins to repent of, under the expert guidance of the schoolmaster-abbot.

Chiang, it seemed, had also succumbed to the Third Temptation. Never had he been so lazy—though, indeed, there was nothing whatever for him to do. He spent the day lounging in a deck-chair, or gossiping with the servants of Mr Kung (brother of the great banker), who, excepting Herr Meyer, one of the German military advisers, was Charleton's only other guest. Mr Kung is said to resemble Confucius, whose lineal descendant he is. He reminded us strongly of Balzac.

Charleton admirably refrained from bothering his visitors. Although the place was so small he respected their privacy. If he saw you didn't want to talk he passed your chair with a simple fascist salute. Sometimes he made suggestions: would you like to walk to Kuling, or take a bath? If you agreed he raised his thumb with the gesture of an emperor at the Roman games. But if you were in the mood for conversation you could have that, too. Too inconsequent to be for a moment boring, he sideslipped from Cambridge into Shanghai, from big business to small pleasures, from the blood-sports to the fine arts, from Love to Death. He was sure that he would die soon, he told us. He had lived, played, gambled, worked too hard. Never mind. He was ready for the call.

Herr Meyer was not ready for the call, however. He wanted most emphatically to get well, to finish his job, to return to his wife and children in

Hanover. He was a dumpy, sensible, good-natured, middle-aged man; the most senior of all the German advisers. He had been through every recent campaign and survived their risks until, recently, an attack of typhus had affected his heart. He was optimistic about the outcome of the present war. His own troops were stationed at Loyang, and he would go there at the end of his convalescence in a few days' time. He had been training the same corps ever since he came to China. Meyer repeated what we had heard already in Hankow—that the German advice had been frequently disregarded, that promises of supplies had sometimes been broken, that there had been far too much red tape, that the Japanese could have been defeated long ago. He did not believe that Manchukuo could be recaptured. He was certain that a Japanese victory would mean the end of foreign influence in the Far East.

The relationship between Meyer and Charleton was the only noisy thing at Journey's End. They made up for their respective lack of English and German by shouts and laughter. The chief cause of their serio-comic friction was one of Charleton's house-boys. Meyer had offered the boy a job but stipulated that he must come away at once. Charleton insisted that the boy should stay at Journey's End till September to help with the summer visitors. Meyer retaliated with typically German banter about the hardness of his bed, the badness of the food, the heat of his room, and the number of insects. Charleton, who didn't understand a word, roared: "That's a nasty one!" or "Sorry! I don't speak Welsh!"

Next morning the Demon began to exercise his power. We were to have left for Nanchang, and we didn't. It was chiefly my fault: I had wanted to go up to Kuling, the mountain village which is the missionaries' holiday resort. But today the clouds were down on the hills; the gorge was choked with mist; and the swimming-pool, after a night of heavy rain, was pouring itself out over the rocks like a miniature Niagara.

Were we, perhaps, going to stay on here for ever? The rain was so soothing. . . . After all, why go to Nanchang? Why go anywhere? Why bother about the Fourth Army? It could take care of itself. What was this journey? An illusion. What were America, England, London, the spring publishing season, our families, our friends, ambition, money, love? Only modes of the First Temptation of the Demon—and why should one temptation be better than another? True, our cash would run out, but Charleton wouldn't let us starve. He'd put us into shorts, and we should wash the dishes and clean the thunder-boxes and take out guests for walks. Later we'd learn to fish and hunt mountain leopards and shoot snipe. We should become real hill-men, and perhaps even beat Charleton's record time up to Kuling—one hour and thirty-five minutes. "No, no!" cried Auden, almost in despair. "We must leave tomorrow morning!"

In the afternoon Hu Sur-chen took us to see the Iron Pagoda—which wasn't, as we had expected, a building, but a three-foot monument in a temple a few miles away. The priests at the temple gave us tea. On the way back there was a thunderstorm, and the rain fell in torrents. We arrived home happily drenched, feeling like old Journey's End boys already.

In the sitting-room was a stuffed dog—once Mr Charleton's prize-winning spaniel, "Lady Lovable". Being in a surrealistic mood we made it sit with us at supper. There was something very sinister about "Lady Lovable": one of her glass eyes had fallen out, the other glared at us with the ferocity of a Chinese dragon. Auden said that she would probably visit us during the night, dragging her paralysed hindquarters after her, with a dry slithering sound, along the passage to the bedroom door.

After supper Mr Charleton drank Chinese wine and was nearly overcome by the extraordinary happiness of his life. "We've all had that picture, 'Love Locked Out', in our rooms!" he shouted at Herr Meyer, who replied that the lemonade had been adulterated with petroleum. The rain poured down on the roof, and the insects descended upon us in myriads—there were beetles in the tea, midges in the air, and great whiskered creatures trying to crawl out of the beer-glasses. "Haven't I given you three tins of *pâté de foie gras* at three dollars fifty each?" cried Charleton; and Meyer retorted: "At Christmas I shall come back with a couple of friends and smash this lousy hole to bits." "I'll never have another Fritz inside my door," said Charleton. "The last one couldn't pay his bill—and do you know what he left me instead? A German flag!" At this point the house-boys created a diversion by bursting the bathroom boiler. "The whole place is flooding," observed Charleton, philosophically, "I don't care. I hope you two kids will have a grand life. Drink to the poor old man next Christmas Eve. I shall be dead by then. God bless."

During the night the Demon left us abruptly in a tremendous gust of wind which flung wide the bedroom doors and extinguished the lamps. It was no longer difficult to tear ourselves away from Journey's End. Next morning even the novices of this all-too-charming monastery appeared in a more prosaic aspect—they were merely Chinese servants awaiting their cumshaws. Having received them they giggled shamefacedly—as Europeans giggle over Sex—and asked for a little, a very little, just a trifle more.

So Charleton gave us his last Roman salute and away we drove down to the station at Kiukiang, only to find that the train had left an hour before its advertised time, and that there was no other that day. If we had been true poets—the kind of poets Charleton respected—we should, no doubt, have laughed gaily and wandered off, hand in hand, into the fields to make each other crowns of wild flowers. But, alas, in our fussy, materialistic way, we were cross. Kiukiang had nothing to offer us beyond two beds in the China Travel Hotel. It was drizzling. The *Gnat* had sailed away. And Auden felt ill. The after-effects of an attack of dysentery were undermining his iron nerves. He remarked that our room would be a peculiarly suitable place to die in. We spent a sombre afternoon chain-smoking, talking about diseases, and reading a three-volume edition of Motley's *Rise of the Dutch Republic*. Motley depressed us both intensely with his catalogue of tortures, massacres, and battles. "And it's exactly the same nowadays," Auden exclaimed. "Really, civilization hasn't advanced an inch!"

In the evening we went to the cinema. The big picture was about a Chinese weakling who turned traitor to his country and agreed to make signals to Japanese aircraft in exchange for cocaine injections given him by a fiendish Jap doctor. He was shot, of course, and the audience clapped. And then the avenging Chinese troops captured the town—and everybody clapped still louder. We both wondered how long it would be before we were applauding similar trash, only a shade more sophisticated, at all the London cinemas.

8

May 3.

The sun was shining this morning. The junks in the creek outside our hotel hosted their great tattered dragon-wing sails. Kiukiang seemed charming again, and curiously Dutch. We caught the train with plenty of time to spare: it left shortly after eight.

The Kiukiang–Nanchang railway has none of the drama of the Lung-Hai. There were no air-raid alarms, no long halts. The carriage roofs are painted with large spots, like a nursery rocking-horse. The countryside is as green as Devonshire, with flowering hedges, and little hills and lanes. We noticed that the faces on the station platforms were less typically Chinese (according to western ideas) than in the other provinces we have visited. The eyes are larger and rounder. The noses are straight, even, sometimes, hooked or beaky.

The Burlington Hotel at Nanchang is more up to date even than the Sian Guest-House, and considerably cheaper. The food is good, too. As befits the birthplace of the New Life Movement, the hotel prohibits gambling, prostitutes, shouting, musical instruments, and opium on its premises. There is a beautifully bound copy of the Bible in Chinese on the writing-table in my bedroom.

May 4.

After breakfast we started off to find the headquarters of the New Fourth Army. The outward appearance of Nanchang is most deceptive.

From across the river it looks almost as imposing as Hankow. The Burlington Hotel stands on a fine broad ring-boulevard, laid out with grass and planted with trees soon after the proclamation of the New Life Movement. But the inner town remains filthy, tortuous, and picturesque; stinking lanes, full of pot-holes, wind their way round evil-smelling, stagnant lakes. After nearly an hour of inquiries we discovered the house we were looking for—a half-empty mansion with big, weed-grown courtyards, near to the Three-Eyed Well. Anything less military could hardly be imagined. We were received very politely by two men and about a dozen little boys, who told us that all the responsible officers were away somewhere near the front, but that they would be returning to Nanchang soon.

Next we went to the offices of the Salt Gabelle to call on M. Berubé, who is a friend of the Consul-General in Hankow. The Chinese manager most kindly lent us a car to drive out to a little camp of ply-wood huts, standing in a fir-plantation about a mile outside the city. M. Berubé and his staff have moved there to escape the air-raids, which have been very frequent and have caused a great deal of damage. This camp used to belong to an Italian firm of aircraft manufacturers. The Italians were found to be in league with the Japanese, so they had to leave in a hurry. Berubé has nicknamed the place "Frascati's".

A confirmed Anglophile, small and dapper and facetious, he speaks excellent idiomatic English. During the war he served with the French Air Force: his father was a spy in Copenhagen. He has an English wife. He prefers P. & O. boats to the Messageries Maritimes because there is more discipline, and the passengers are obliged to dress for dinner. He quoted with relish a dictum of Anatole France: "A British boat is a floating democracy. A French boat is a drifting demogogy." His most thrilling adventure in China was his capture by bandits on the Shanghai–Peking express in 1923.

In the afternoon we went round to the American Mission Hospital so that Auden could be examined. This is the largest hospital we have so far seen in China. Among the patients who were waiting to be treated was a round-faced young Chinese, about twenty years old, whose eyes had an expression of the most painful anxiety and bewilderment. He came up with his brother to speak to us: "Please can you tell me the fact?" "What fact?" we asked. "The fact about thinking. Is it done by radio-waves? I am very nervous." The brother explained to us that their whole family had been killed in an air-raid, and that the young man was suffering from shock. He hoped to get treatment here in the hospital. He had been a clerk in the post office, and spoke good English. "I'm going to find out", he told Auden, "whether you are a radio man. Can you, please, introduce me to the President? I want to know if I'm still in the experiment. Then I shall be comforted."

May 5.

We returned to the hospital again this morning. The doctors, here as elsewhere, are admirable and efficient; but there is a most unpleasant lady missionary, smug and fat, who displays a blasphemous professional familiarity with the Almighty, whom she evidently regards as the private property of the American Nonconformists. She is not, we are glad to hear, a regular member of the hospital staff, but only in Nanchang on a visit.

After tea we visited the Governor of Kiang-Si Province, Mr Hsiung Shih-hueh. Slim and erect, in his plain blue uniform and elastic-sided shoes, the Governor looks a mere boy, nearly twenty years younger than his age. His pale oval face and sloe-black eyes have the repose of a great actor or a Buddhist saint. As Auden said, his mere presence would make him a fortune on any stage.

The results of the interview were not very encouraging. The Governor thanked us for our visit, and hoped that we shouldn't be detained very long in Nanchang. He plainly didn't approve of our plan to leave China via Ningpo. The bridges along the Kin-hwa–Ningpo road were broken. If we attempted the journey, he regretted that he could not guarantee us against "something very unfortunate". We had much better return to Hongkong. However, he promised to make further inquiries, and to let us know in a few days' time. We asked if we might be allowed to visit the propaganda-school for cadets which, we have heard, exists in Nanchang. After some consultation, the Governor replied that this was unfortunately impossible, "owing to the political situation". We bowed ourselves out.

May 6.

At the Out-patients' Department of the hospital today we again saw the young man who is worried by "the fact about thinking". The fat lady missionary came up to talk to him, and his brother told her of the family tragedy. She simply didn't listen. "Don't worry," she told the young man. "Leave it to Jesus. You go home to your father and mother and eat some of mother's good food. Jesus will look after you all right."

Never forgetting our admiration for the missionaries of the Yellow River, it is only fair to tell the story we heard recently from an American airman in Hankow. Some years ago the airman and a friend were flying near Loyang. The weather shut down, so they made for the nearest emergency landing-field, on the outskirts of a small, dirty town. The airman suggested that they should try to get a bed at the mission-station, and, sure enough, the missionary received them hospitably, and showed them up to a bedroom, where they shaved, washed, and changed their clothes. They didn't see their host again until the evening. Downstairs, supper was ready: the food looked good, and they were both very hungry. Then

the missionary, having said Grace, suddenly asked: "Do either of you gen-
tlemen smoke?" The airman didn't, but his friend did. "Do you drink?"
Yes, they both took a drink occasionally. "Then I'm sorry," said the mis-
sionary, "there's no place for you under this roof." They could hardly
believe their ears; but the missionary wasn't joking. Out they had to go,
leaving the supper uneaten, to sleep on chairs in the local Chinese inn.
"And now tell me", our informant concluded, "what would *you* have said
to that missionary?"

May 7.

Yesterday afternoon we went shopping with Berubé. Auden bought his
favourite kind of panama hat. This particular example is made, appar-
ently, of cardboard. It certainly won't survive the first shower. Berubé was
so much amused that he has written an indecent poem about it, which he
brought us today.

This morning Auden went again to the hospital and returned in a state
of delighted fury against the lady missionary. Hearing that we were off to
the front she had said: "Are you insured with Jesus? Jesus has positively
guaranteed eternal life. . . . This life" (holding up her thumb) "is just a
teeny span." Auden wishes he had bitten it.

We have now decided to leave at once for Kin-hwa. It is no good waiting
for the result of the Governor's inquiries, or the return of the Fourth Army
officers to Nanchang. If we can't get through to Ningpo or Wenchow later,
well, we can't. There will be plenty of time to bother about that after we
have visited the south-eastern front.

Today we at last met Wingeter, the American engineer and civil pilot
who is working at the air-field here. Wingeter lives at the Burlington, and
it is a great pity we didn't get to know him sooner, for we both like him
very much. Wingeter is leading a lonely, worried life—uncertain whether
to return to New York and rejoin his wife, or renew his contract here. He
and Berubé are the only English-speaking westerners, apart from the
missionaries, in Nanchang. On the air-field there are a number of Russian
pilots, but they keep very much to themselves, and are constantly being
changed. After a few months' service a pilot returns to Russia and a new
man comes out to take his place. When the Japanese attack Hankow the
Nanchang planes often fly out to cut off the raiders' retreat. If the
Nanchang air-field itself is bombed the Russians take up their heavy
bombers and fly them away out of danger until the raid is over. But the
Chinese guards remain on the field, ready to run out and plant flags in
the bomb-craters, so that the Russians, on their return, may be able to
make a safe landing. Wingeter says that the Chinese behave on these occa-
sions with incredible bravery. Many of them get killed. If there is a night-
raid Wingeter jumps into his car and drives out to the hills, for the Bur-

lington is too near the air-field to be safe. A bomb has actually destroyed one of the houses on the boulevard just opposite the hotel.

Chiang suggested that we should try to get free passes on to the train to Kin-hwa. So we went along to interview the Director of the railway. By this time it was already a quarter past seven, and the train was due to leave at eight o'clock, so the interview was somewhat unnerving: we had only a quarter of an hour in which to get through the handshaking, the bowing, the card-exchanges, the tea-drinking, and all the other slow-motion phases of Chinese politeness. At last the passes were signed, and we dashed in Wingeter's car to the station. Luckily the train started ten minutes late.

May 8.

When we woke early next morning the train was crossing a wide valley of paddy-fields. The rising sun struck its beams across the surfaces of innumerable miniature lakes; in the middle distance farmhouses seemed actually to be floating on the water. Here and there a low mound rose a few feet above the level of the plain, with a weed-grown, ruinous pagoda standing upon it, visible for miles around. Peasants with water-buffaloes were industriously ploughing their arable liquid into a thick brown soup.

We arrived in Kin-hwa at about four o'clock in the afternoon. Hardly had we stepped out of the train when we found ourselves surrounded by a group of soldiers and police. An officer, running up and saluting, requested us to come into the station guardroom. "We have been expecting you," he explained. "We have been down to meet two trains already." Somewhat bewildered we followed him. More officers were introduced. "And now", said one of them, who appeared to be the local chief of police, "I shall escort you to your hotel. A room has been reserved."

We glanced at each other nervously. "Do you think", Auden whispered, "that we're really under arrest? They'd probably be far too tactful to tell us so." "Perhaps they think we're spies," I said. "Anyhow, we shall never know—until we're actually taken out to be shot." "Oh, they'd never shoot us. Far too crude. We shall simply disappear."

The truth, of course, proved to be far less dramatic. A letter from somebody in Hankow, a wire from Hollington Tong, a mention of our names in the Nanchang paper have combined to convince the Kin-hwa authorities that we are people of importance—and we are going to be treated as such. From now on we must resign ourselves to fulfilling all the obligations of public characters.

It has started already. Hardly had we dumped our bags in the bedroom of the bungalow China Travel Service hotel, when the first official caller was announced—the Kin-hwa Director of the railway. He was followed by the chief of police, who looked into tell us that a special constable had been put permanently at our disposal. He would sit in the entrance-lounge all day, awaiting our orders. What, exactly, does one do with a special constable, we wondered, as we thanked the chief of police profusely.

Next came Mr T. Y. Liu, the secretary of the civil government, and correspondent to the *South-Eastern Daily News*. He is a gnome-like little man, with the delicate bones of a very young child, and the weird, upcurving eyes of an immemorially ancient Chinese dragon. In some moods he has the face of a sixteen-year-old boy; in others he sits blinking and yellow as a man of eighty. Mr Liu, we feel already, is to be our great friend in Kin-hwa. And he will come with us to the front. As he himself says: "When I am in danger I have no fear."

After much tea—this evening all records for tea-drinking were easily broken—we drove out with Mr T. Y. Liu to visit General Huang Shao-yung, Governor of Che-kiang Province. The Governor's headquarters are in a small village at the foot of the mountains. By the time we had arrived there it was already quite dark. Guided by soldiers with flashlights, we crossed an unevenly paved bridge over the mountain-stream, and stumbled through a garden to the door of a cottage. Just inside the cottage hung a linen curtain upon which was projected, as in a post-war German horror-film, the huge, distorted, crouching shadow of the Governor himself.

The Governor wasn't at all horrific, however. He was a ponderous, crop-haired man with a jolly laugh, somewhat resembling a Prussian officer of the least formidable type. He offered at once not only to give us passes to visit the front but to send us there in his own car. We could see everything, we gathered, quite easily and quickly, and be back at Kin-hwa within two or three days. The Governor also explained the military situation. He seems to think that we shall have no difficulty in getting down to Ningpo when this journey is over.

This evening we dined at the hotel with Mr Liu, his wife, and a charming, boyish major who has been wounded three times in the fighting round Shanghai. "Major Yang", we were told, by way of introduction, "does not fear death." Major Yang speaks no English; he could only smile and repeatedly raise his glass to our health. He and Mr Liu drink cognac as though it were a light table-wine. We did our best to follow suit. Meanwhile, T. Y. Liu described the very serious operation he had undergone two years ago in Shanghai. By the end of the meal Auden and I were so drunk that we even ventured to criticize the Chinese habit of spitting. Mr Liu agreed that it was disgusting, unpatriotic, and must be stopped. He and Major Yang continued to spit, with the utmost relish, throughout the rest of the evening.

May 9.

This morning we made a ceremonial tour of the town, accompanied by Liu, Yang, Chiang, and suite—including our private constable. Kin-hwa is, perhaps, the most attractive small city we have so far visited in China.

The narrow, flagged streets are wonderfully clean, and the shops are so well stocked that they might well be transported bodily into a museum, to exemplify the various crafts and trades. There was nothing you couldn't get, from a fan to a jade sealing-stone. Auden bought two tiny embroidered scarlet jackets for a godchild, but there our purchases ended, because it became quite clear that the municipal government will insist on paying for everything we ask for in this town. The Governor has already sent word that we are his guests as long as we care to stay at the China Travel hotel.

At the municipal government office we were received by the city governor and the chief of police, and shown the dug-out in which many of the employees had sheltered when a big Japanese bomb landed in the garden. At present it was full of water, a fact which the chief of police discovered too late, when he had stepped into it, up to his knees. The Japanese, we are told, never bomb the city nowadays; but they sometimes attack the railway station.

We lunched at a restaurant which has just been opened by refugees from Hang-chow. (Before the war started Hang-chow used to be the provincial capital of Che-kiang. Since the Japanese occupation the Government has moved to Kin-hwa.) The building itself is very pretty. Its pillars are scarlet and turquoise blue, festooned with tiny electric bulbs and coloured paper streamers—like the entrance to a fun-fair. Here the politeness-game, which we had been playing all morning, reached its height. We were a party of twelve, and, for some time, it looked as if we should never get upstairs at all—there was so much playful scuffling to yield the places of honour, so much bowing, so many "after you"s. As a pro-British gesture, our hosts insisted on eating the European menu—a suffocating cavalcade of soup, chicken, Mandarin fish (on a Chinese list of dishes, every fish seems to be described as "Mandarin"), pork, more chicken, more fish, and sweets. Toasts were drunk and re-drunk in every conceivable combination, till our heads swam. We kept swapping specially dainty morsels with our neighbours. Auden and I developed a private game: it was a point of honour to praise most warmly the dishes you liked least. "Delicious," Auden murmured, as he munched what was, apparently, a small sponge soaked in glue. I replied by devouring, with smiles of exquisite pleasure, an orange which tasted of bitter aloes and contained, in its centre, a large weevil. On the whole the food was very nice, but our hosts disparaged it out of courtesy—and of course we had to protest: "Horrible stuff, this. We must apologize. . . ." "No, no! Not horrible. Wonderful!" "Very poor after your English cookery." "English cookery disgusting! Chinese cookery marvellous!" "We are so sorry." "The best lunch we ever had in our lives." "Miserable." "Excellent." "Bad." "Good." "Bad." "No!" "Yes!" And so on. We kept it up throughout the meal.

After lunch, stuffed and intoxicated, we staggered home to rest, but

not for long. We had promised to address the three hundred students
who are being trained in Kin-hwa as teachers and propagandists. The
students will go out into the villages of the surrounding countryside and
explain to the peasants the causes and aims of the war. It is strange to
have to talk to an audience which does not understand a single word you
are saying. One's natural instinct is to shout at them as though they were
deaf, or simply to make horrible faces and wave the arms like a windmill.
"After this war", Auden bellowed, "you will have to fight a more terrible
enemy than the Japanese. You will have to fight disease, bad housing,
illiteracy, dirt. . . ." "You must win this war", I boomed, "to save China, to
save Japan, to save Europe." At the end of every five or six sentences, we
had to pause, to let Mr Liu or the chief of police translate. Goodness
knows what they said to the audience. It seemed to us that they were
making quite a different speech, much longer, all on their own. When we
had finished the Governor thanked us. He wanted, he said, to give us
three letters stating China's case—one to show to England, one to Japan,
and one to the world. I took this literally, at first, and had an alarming
vision of ourselves toiling up and down embassy staircases all over Lon-
don. But the letters, it later appeared, were only figures of speech.

What did the students make of us? Most of them listened attentively. A
few were giggling or drawing pictures. One or two were asleep. While we
were having tea after the ceremony a good many of them came in with
autograph albums for our signatures.

We went on to inspect the military hospital, which is in a magnificent
old temple on the outskirts of the city. Each ward is a shrine, with a gigan-
tic plaster Immortal towering benevolently above the beds. These figures
have real horsehair beards. The hospital is fairly well equipped. The
operating-theatre is very clean but there is no X-ray apparatus, and all the
water must be brought from a neighbouring well.

May 10.

Before nine o'clock this morning the Governor's car, a splendid Nash
saloon which was once the property of the mayor of Hang-chow, came
round to call for us at the hotel. There were six of us in the party—T. Y.
Liu, Major Yang, the chauffeur, a freckled boy with projecting teeth, and
ourselves. The boy is a rather mysterious figure. We tried to prevent his
coming with us, for the car, when all our luggage had been put into it, was
already overcrowded; but we were assured that his presence was abso-
lutely necessary. He had to carry a brandy bottle, he knew the road (this
was untrue) and he "could find gasoline". Auden suggested that he must
be a new type of dowser.

Chiang we were leaving behind. He would be of no use to us, for Liu
talks fluent English—and we haven't forgotten his obstructionism at Han

Chwang. This arrangement certainly suited Chiang. He will have a wonderful time at Kin-hwa while we are away, running up bills at the Governor's expense and enjoying our reflected glory.

The chauffeur reminds us of a character in a novel by D. H. Lawrence—the groom in *St Mawr*, or one of those "dark", sinister Mexicans in *The Plumed Serpent*. Indeed, with his square, heavy figure and brilliant, dangerous smile, he looks more like a Mexican Indian than a Chinese. When the car started his eyes glazed over in a mindless, sub-human stare. His foot sank heavily on the accelerator, and remained there, despite the twistings of the road, until he had deposited us at the brink of a river, about three miles beyond the city.

During this first stage of the journey we had two rivers to cross. The car was ferried over them on a raft propelled by bamboo punt-poles. It is advisable to get out of your car while making such a passage, for the current is strong and the raft very small. Mr Liu told us that a motor-bus had recently been upset in the middle of the stream, drowning all its passengers.

There was plenty of water traffic: small junks with a single sail, and caravans of long, narrow long-rafts shaped like Canadian toboggans—drawn by gangs of coolies who plodded slowly along the bank, at the end of an immensely long rope.

At Lanchi—a town with several very beautiful pagodas, eighteen miles from Kin-hwa—we came to our third river, and had to wait, because the troops of the Nineteenth Division were crossing in the opposite direction. They were on their way from the south-eastern to the Tsin-pu front. The Nineteenth is a crack division from Fu-kien and Sze-chwan which fought at Shanghai.

We sat on the bank and watched them scrambling ashore from sampans, with their ponies, and machine-guns, and cooking-pots. They had the air of real, hardened soldiers, inveterate and practical as tramps. Experience had taught them exactly what equipment to carry—a thermos flask, a straw sun-hat, chopsticks, an umbrella, a spare pair of rubber shoes. A face-towel hung from each man's belt, like a dish-clout, together with two or three hand-grenades which resembled miniature Chianti bottles. Gaining the shore they formed immediately into a straggling line and marched off, shuffling shabbily and quickly along, with their feet muffled in old rags, laughing and joking—perfectly adapted, it seemed, to their life of hardship, dirt, and pain.

Beyond Lanchi the road leaves the river-valley and turns off into the hills. Soon we were hurtling round the curves of a mountain pass. The scenery was superb, but we were too frightened even to look out of the window. Instead, Auden tried to distract our thoughts from the alarming Present by starting a conversation about eighteenth-century poetry. It was no good: we could remember nothing but verses on sudden death. Meanwhile, the road twisted and struggled, and the car clung to it like a mongoose attacking a cobra. Pedestrians screamed, cyclists overbalanced into paddy-fields, wrecked hens lay twitching spasmodically in the dust-storm behind us. At every corner we shut our eyes, but the chauffeur only laughed darkly as befitted one of the Lords of Death, and swung us round the curve with squealing brakes. Neither Major Yang nor Mr Liu showed the least symptoms of nervousness. "The road is very difficult," Mr Liu observed peacefully, as we shot across a crazy makeshift bridge over a gorge, rattling its loose planks like the bars of a xylophone. "It wouldn't be difficult", I retorted, "if we weren't driving at seventy miles an hour."

We stopped at a small town for gasoline and a late lunch. In the square was an ambulance-truck full of wounded—the first we had seen that morning. Mr Liu bought some tablets of Tiger Balm, the cure-all tonic which is advertised all over China. He was feeling in need of them because, as he explained, he had slept badly the night before. "If I sleep well I am very strong. If I do not sleep I can do nothing." Today he seemed actually to have shrunk into a little ivory-faced manikin, with a big wet baby's underlip. Nevertheless, he remained the perfect host. "You are the guests of China," he kept repeating. "We must try to satisfy you. You are our friends."

After this short respite the D. H. Lawrence *Todesfahrt* continued. But we were braver now. With food inside us we ventured to admire the view. There were water-mills in the river far below. The hills were cultivated to their summits; the striped, wheat-covered folds of the mountains looked like yellow corduroy. "Oh, my Gard!" exclaimed Mr Liu, and was abruptly and violently carsick. A few miles further on Major Yang, who had been looking very thoughtful, followed his example.

Towards the end of the afternoon we descended into the plain. There were more villages here, and a good many buses and lorries. Twice our chauffeur escaped a head-on collision by inches. "The Chinese", somebody once told us, "are very lucky drivers." But not always. Along this part of the roadside we counted five hopelessly shattered wrecks.

A little further on we passed an embankment where a line of track was under construction. "That", Mr Liu told us, "is the secret railway." We were much intrigued: "Why is it secret? Who is it secret from? How can you keep a railway secret?" we asked. "It is secret," Mr Liu replied.

Just after six o'clock we reached Tunki—the end of today's journey. We are staying at the Yellow Mountain Hotel, whose trellised verandah overhangs the shallow, straggling river, with a background of dark, bumpy mountains stained by the setting sun. All along the bank, women are washing clothes in the pebbled stream; there are willow-groves along the shore; in a distant field some soldiers are playing blind-man's buff. This might be a small town in the north of Italy. Tomorrow, says Mr Liu, we shall go up to the front by car, returning to Kin-hwa the day after.

About half an hour after I had finished writing the above, there was a clatter in the passage and the sound of some one talking English. This was Dr Lim, head of the China Red Cross. He was in Dr Mooser's party when we travelled back to Hankow from Sian. Dr Lim was educated abroad and speaks English in preference to Chinese. He was dressed like a rover scout, in smart grey shorts and a jaunty forage-cap. "I heard you were here," he told us. "I saw Peter Fleming in Nanchang. Has he arrived yet?"

"Fleming?" The name was echoed by a young Chinese who, at this moment, strode into the room. "Which of you gentlemen is Mr Fleming?"

"Neither." We introduced ourselves. The young man, who was Mr T. C. Liu, of the *Central News*, seemed displeased.

"What are you doing here?" he asked.

"We want to go to the front."

"Oh. . . ." Mr T. C. Liu frowned. "But they didn't say that any other journalists were coming. I'm very surprised."

He had no reason to be surprised, we retorted; we had nothing to do with him. Our guide was Mr T. Y. Liu (whom we now introduced). We were travelling to the front quite independently.

But our tone failed to impress Mr T. C. Liu. He was in charge here and nobody, not even an unwelcome guest, should escape his jurisdiction. He has a smooth, adolescent face, whose natural charm is spoilt by a perpetual pout and by his fussy school-prefect's air of authority. His eyes behind their horn-rimmed glasses are as nearly priggish as it is possible for Chinese eyes to be.

Negligently tossing his hat and mackintosh to the servant who followed him, he unfolded a large sheet of blank paper on our bedroom table. "Tomorrow", he announced, "a representative of General Ku will come here to answer any questions. But now I will try to explain the general strategic situation to you with a simple map." Producing a pencil, postulating our interest as a matter of course, he drew highroads, shaded in towns, arrowed troop movements; lecturing us like the brilliant sixth-form boy who takes the juniors in history while the headmaster is away. Everything was lucid and tidy and false—the flanks like neat little cubes, the pincer-movements working with mathematical precision, the reinforcements never failing to arrive punctual to the minute. But war, as Auden said later, is not like that. War is bombing an already disused arsenal, missing it, and killing a few old women. War is lying in a stable with a gangrenous leg. War is drinking hot water in a barn and worrying about one's wife. War is a handful of lost and terrified men in the mountains, shooting at something moving in the undergrowth. War is waiting for days with nothing to do; shouting down a dead telephone; going without sleep, or sex, or a wash. War is untidy, inefficient, obscure, and largely a matter of chance.

We asked about the New Fourth Army and were told that, two days ago, they had been moved to the Wuhu front. The officers we had tried to see in Nanchang left Tunki yesterday, to return there. "But why do you wish specially to see the Fourth Army?" said T. C. Liu reprovingly. "It does not differ from the other units, except that it has a more highly developed propaganda machine. Wuhu is very quiet just now. The most active sector is near the Tai Lake. That would be more interesting for you, I think."

We got rid of him at last, on the understanding that he would come back in the morning with some one from headquarters. Then we could decide what we wanted to do.

We are now wondering if it will be possible to leave for the front before he returns.

May 11.

Charming as this hotel is, it isn't ideal to sleep in. It is being used as an unofficial military headquarters, and the coming and going of messengers was continuous throughout the night. Mah-jongg players kept up a perpetual clatter, banging down their pieces on a table somewhere upstairs. In the early hours of the morning old men and women come wandering into the rooms, selling bread and fruit. The electric light in my bedroom won't turn out at all. If you don't want it you must simply unscrew the bulb.

During breakfast we asked Major Yang if he knew any comic soldiers' songs. He said that he did, but added that, in this war, all the army songs were patriotic and serious. After some persuasion he sang the following verses, which Mr T. Y. Liu translated:

The River Is Full of Red

My angry hair, standing up, pushes my hat.
I stand near the rail of the balcony
And watch the continual rain.
I lift my head to look at the sky, and give a long laugh.
Now I am thirty, my great ambition is anxious and hot.
All the great deeds I did are just like the dust and the soil to me.

Eight thousand *li* of distance;
Nothing but the moon and the clouds.
Don't waste your time.

Don't let your hair grow white.
It makes you sorry.

Then Mr Liu told us the words of a coolies' song:

We get up at sunrise
We go to bed at sunset
We work hard
We plough the field to grow food
We dig the well to get drink—
There is nothing for the King to do.

(I may as well insert here another song which we heard later in Shanghai. It is a song of the Chinese guerilla units which operate behind the Japanese lines. This is Mr Zinmay Zau's translation.)

When the season changed, so changed the strategy,
We took off our uniforms and put on the old cotton cloth.
Let the enemies fire their guns in vain and be happy for nothing;
They will capture an empty city like a new coffin.

Our heroes will put out their wits and tricks
To entertain enemies like fathers:
When they ask for wine we'll give them "Great Carving Flowers";
When they ask for dishes we'll give them "Shrimps and Eggs".

When they get greedy for happiness they become afraid of death,
They won't listen to the orders of their superior officials;
They'll insist that the others should go in front when they go to the
    front:
A handful of tears and a handful of snot.

The enemies will be bewitched to their end:
Aeroplanes won't dare to go into the sky;
Tell them to attack, and they'll retreat;
Tell them to fire and they will let out their wind.

A shout of "KILL!" and we'll fight back,
Rakes and spades will be mobilized:
This time our army will come out from the fields,
They will be like storms and hurricanes.

Tens of years of insults, we now have our revenge;
Tens of years of shame, we now have washed clean:
Those who scolded us, we now will flay their skins;
Those who hit us, we now will pull out their veins.

Those who boasted now will be like dumbs
Eating aloes and galls;
Those who killed and never minded fishy smell.
They will today become mincemeat themselves.

Those who burned our houses
Will now have nowhere to bury their bodies;
Those who raped our girls
Will now have their wives as widows.

Widely opened are the eyes of our God,
What you did to others will now be done to you.
Let's wait for the certain day of the certain month,
When we will have both the principal and interest back without discount.

After breakfast we walked out into the town. In front of a clothing shop a man and a boy were singing a highly syncopated sales-duet about a pair of trousers. All the passers-by grinned at us, and we wondered if there was anybody in the whole street who didn't already know our names and our business in Tunki. When we returned Mr T. Y. Liu informed us: "I have spent the morning with the dictionary and learnt two new words—Jingoism and Rumour."

Here, in Tunki, T. Y. appears to have lost some of his self-confidence—perhaps because he is outside his own province. He seems intimidated by T. C. Liu, and shows no willingness to sneak off without him to the front. Possibly he doesn't exactly know where it is.

T. C. arrived after lunch, accompanied by Major-General Shiu, who is General Ku's chief of staff and head of the military Red Cross in this area. We all crowded somehow into Auden's little bedroom and the map-making began again. Once more we asked about the Fourth Army, and were politely snubbed. T. C. had the whip-hand, and he knew it. We couldn't go anywhere without him.

"How long would it take us to get to the nearest fighting?" Auden asked.

"About ten days, there and back. You would have to walk or ride."

"We were told we could see everything in two or three days."

T. C. looked scornful. He was deciding, one could see, that we weren't really keen. He said firmly:

"If you want to see anything interesting it will take you ten days as a minimum."

"But we're with Mr T. Y. Liu. We don't know if he can keep the car so long. Can you, Mr T. Y.?"

"Can do."

"Oh, very well. . . ."

"Good." T. C. nodded his head triumphantly. "We shall leave tomorrow morning."

9

A few minutes later Peter Fleming himself walked into the room. "Hullo, you two," he greeted us, with the amused, self-conscious smile of a guest who arrives at a party in fancy dress. Though indeed his dress was anything but fancy—for this occasion it was almost absurdly correct. In his khaki shirt and shorts, complete with golf-stockings, strong suède shoes, waterproof wrist-watch, first-aid outfit and Leica camera, he might have stepped straight from a London tailor's window, advertising Gent's Tropical Exploration Kit. "I saw all I wanted to see at Sü-chow," he explained, "so I thought I'd get down here before the rush starts."

Fleming then introduced his companion, Mr Ching, of the Hankow publicity office. Mr Ching was short and sleek and plump. He wore a pretty canary yellow shirt. He looked worried, as if he viewed this journey with considerable misgivings. T. C. Liu greeted him rather haughtily, as he had greeted our own T. Y. Fleming alone he recognized as an equal. It was settled between them that Wuhu and the Fourth Army should not be visited; we were to start tomorrow in the direction of the Tai Lake.

In the afternoon we all went to call on General Ku. The car took us several miles out into the country and stopped in the middle of an almost deserted plain. On foot we made our way along the little dikes which divided the paddy-fields, towards a distant copse. Dusk was gathering, and the over-arching trees formed a proscenium beyond which the General and his staff stood grouped with beautifully theatrical effect. At the edge of the glade we stopped and bowed. The General returned our bow. We advanced a few paces. Our hosts did likewise. More bows. Another advance. We met. We shook hands. It was like a scene from a Shakespearian comedy—or, as Fleming said, like the prelude to a duel.

The interview took place in a wooden hut, round a table loaded with delicacies—fruit, brandy, and expensive imported chocolates. Fleming, as our representative, handled the exchange of courtesies with consummate skill; it was unnecessary for either of us to open our mouths. "Will you please", he asked T. C. Liu, "thank General Ku for seeing us at such a difficult time—and will you apologize for our clothes?" He knew just what questions to ask: "Would the General give us his views on the relative merits and defects of the Japanese soldier?" He knew just how to bring the meeting to a close: "Will you tell the General that, although war correspondents are supposed to be absolutely impartial, we do not think we should be going too far in asking him to drink with us to a Chinese victory?"

Before we left we examined a pile of war material recently captured from the Japanese. It was now quite dark. Holding electric torches we poked about among diaries, photographs, and private letters of dead men. There was a picture of a young cadet, posed in his new uniform; and a letter from a brother which said that they were all praying for his safety, but that it was a noble thing to die for one's country. There were flags, machine-guns, helmets, rifles. Mr T. C. Liu read out translations of the diaries and letters, construing every sentence into a proof of the decay of Japanese morale. On the whole he wasn't very convincing.

We arrived back late for supper, and all drank a good deal of brandy. The brandy had a depressing effect on Major Yang. Presently he said something to T. Y. Liu, who told us:

"Major Yang wishes to apologize."

"Oh, really? Why?"

"Major Yang says he wishes to apologize for being alive."

"But why shouldn't he be alive?"

"He says it is a disgrace for any Chinese officer to have left Shanghai. They should have held it, or died where they stood."

We protested that Major Yang had no reason to apologize. He was a hero. We were proud to be sitting with him at the same table. Major Yang bowed and clasped his hands in the customary gesture of thanks. But he remained gloomy and morose for the rest of the evening. Auden tried to distract his thoughts by asking him about the future of the Communists, but without much success. "If they will follow the three principles of Dr Sun Yat-sen", he told us, "we shall allow them. Otherwise they will have to be suppressed." Fleming sat silently smoking and grinning. From time to time he punctuated the conversation in truly Chinese fashion with a resounding belch.

Next morning the noise outside our doors made all further attempts at sleep impossible. The hotel servants were emptying buckets of refuse on to the heads of the washerwomen squatting along the river bank. Yells and curses mingled with the clatter of the servants' feet, which resembled the clumpings of a country dance. I went out on to the balcony, to find, to my amazement, Fleming still fast asleep. His pillow was a hard leather satchel, in which he carried his writing materials. He didn't wake up until we had nearly finished breakfast.

On the river a man was fishing from a boat with tame cormorants. The cormorants perched all round the gunwale of the boat, squawking and flapping their wings. They had short strings tied to their legs, but were quite free. We watched one of them fighting a free-lance kite for possession of a fish. Somebody told us that a well-trained cormorant costs as much as twenty-five dollars.

At half-past nine we started. There were two car-loads of us: T. C. Liu, Ching, Yang, and a young radio expert named Shien; T. Y. Liu, Fleming, and ourselves. There was a good deal of argument as to who should ride with whom—but we clung firmly to our pet and mascot, T. Y., pointing out that the others would then be able to talk Chinese amongst themselves.

Our first destination was the divisional headquarters near Hwei-chow, a charming house in a large garden which had once belonged to a famous historical scholar. Here we were offered biscuits and bowls of sweet warm milk, before beginning our morning strategy-lesson. Fleming was very conscientious about "lessons". He took exhaustive notes and made us feel ashamed of our laziness. Also, he knew enough Chinese to understand roughly what was being said. He protested, most impressively, when the translation failed to tally with the original. This, needless to say, put T. C. Liu on his mettle. His phraseology became increasingly schoolmasterish and pedantic.

In a building near by there was a Japanese prisoner, a cavalry colonel, who had been captured by Chinese irregulars. Driving behind the Japanese lines, he had had a motor accident, and the irregulars had caught him before he could escape. Presently he came in, shuffling between two guards—a tall crop-haired man, dressed in Chinese uniform and clumsy football boots. He looked ill, and deeply depressed, but he answered our questions with great natural dignity. In civil life he had been a schoolmaster. He had been called up, at the outbreak of the war, to serve in a supply department. Asked who he thought would win, he replied tactfully that it depended on whose morale would last the longest.

T. Y. Liu was chiefly impressed by the prisoner's unusual height. (Even the smallest Chinese sneer at the Japanese as dwarfs.) "I think", he said, "that this man must be the Longfellow of Japan." Today, T. Y. was in the highest possible spirits. When we had lost the way and stopped to wait for the others beside a stream, he lay down under a tree, curled up his legs and kicked—exactly, as Auden said, like the wizened little changeling baby in a fairy story. We roared with exaggerated laughter at his jokes, tickled him, pinched him, and deliberately misunderstood everything he said.

Near Yü-tsien we stopped to have dinner at another divisional headquarters. Swallows flitted round the carved beams of the temple courtyard. We drank Hsaio Shen wine, and a special brand of Tien-mu-shan tea—pale green shoots which barely flavoured the glasses of almost boiling water. T. C. Liu drew one of his sketch-maps and translated the commanding officer's statistics: "In this village sixty per cent of the women have been adulted." "Along this line the Chinese forces will offend the

Japanese." In one engagement, he told us, there had been five hundred Japanese casualties and only eighty Chinese. "Will you congratulate the Major-General", drawled Fleming, "on such an excellent proportion?" We repeated our Chinese victory toast, and were brought water to rinse out our mouths with, after the wine. Along the edge of the courtyard ran a stone gutter into which you could spit or empty slops.

It was then decided to drive on a further ten miles to Tien-mu-shan, the road-head at the foot of the mountains. We could sleep at the hotel there—the proprietor was an old friend of Mr T. Y. Liu—and cross the pass next day to army headquarters at Pao Fu Chun. From Pao Fu Chun it would be another day's journey to Meiki, which was said to be about forty Chinese *li* from the front lines.

At the road-head we were met by a party of soldiers, who led us up a path to the hotel through woods of pine and cedar, silent and strongly scented in the deep blue moonlight. Before the war Tien-mu-shan was a favourite summer resort. It was half-past ten when we arrived, but there was no question of going to bed. Mr Wang, the proprietor, awaited us, fairly bursting with information. We sat down at once to our evening lessons.

Mr Wang was the civil governor of six counties, and he had prepared an exhaustive report on the atrocities of the Japanese against the civilian population. In Mr Wang's area eighty per cent of the houses had been burnt. Out of 1,100 houses in Siaofeng only 200 remained. Out of 2,800 in Tsinan only 3. Three thousand civilians had been killed during the past four months. Children were being kidnapped by the Japanese and sent to Shanghai—for forced labour or the brothels. Out of 110,000 refugees only ten per cent had been able to leave the district. The rest were returning, where possible, to their ruined homes, with money from the Government to buy seeds for the spring sowing. If they belonged to areas occupied by the Japanese they would be given work—either in repairing the roads or in their own handicrafts.

The guerilla units—known as the Red Spears—were very active in this province. The Japanese had tried to counteract their influence and confuse the political sympathies of the peasants by organizing a rival force, called the Fish Spears. The Fish Spears were not being a success, however. So far, they had enrolled only a hundred members.

On this front the Japanese advance-guard was living, literally, in a state of siege. The troops could only venture out from their strongholds in large bodies, or they ran the risk of ambush. A seventeen-year-old Red Spear had caught ten enemy soldiers drinking in a cottage and killed them all with a sword. A peasant named Da Man had been ordered by a Japanese officer to guide him back to his unit. To reach the unit it was necessary to ford a river; the officer told Da Man to carry him across on his back. In mid stream Da Man threw the officer into the water and bashed his head in with a stone. "Oh, jolly good!" exclaimed Fleming, in the tone of one who applauds a record high jump or a pretty drive to leg.

We got up at five o'clock next morning and went down to an ample but unappetising breakfast of chicken and warm lager beer. As a rule the Chinese do not carve a chicken, they chop it transversely into slices, so that even the tiniest morsel contains a fragment of bone.

After breakfast the coolies came round with carrying-chairs mounted on long bamboo poles. T. C. Liu announced, in advance, that he would never make use of the chairs: "My psychology does not allow me to do so." For the moment, in any case, everybody was prepared to walk. Fleming supervised our departure with his customary efficiency. One saw his life, at that moment, as a succession of such startings-out in the dawn. He stood pulling at his pipe, giving orders to the coolies, tying up loose ends, adjusting the weight of bags, encouraging each member of the party with a joke or a word. At the bottom of the path the horses were waiting. We said good-bye to Major Yang, who had decided not to accompany us. He was afraid of straining his newly-healed wounds.

The way up the pass was no more than a winding mule-track, very steep in places, and slippery with mud from mountain streams. Far below us the torrent rushed over the boulders. Lizards with blue tails flickered across the path and there were dragon-flies and tiger-beetles, turquoise and viridian. Fleming eyed the copses for signs of game and delighted us by exclaiming: "How I wish I had my rook-rifle!" Our preliminary defensive attitude towards him—a blend of anti-Etonianism and professional jealousy—had now been altogether abandoned. He, on his side, confessed to a relief that we weren't hundred per cent bolsheviks: "I'd expected you two to be much more passionate." Laughing and perspiring we scrambled uphill; the Fleming Legend accompanying us like a distorted shadow. Auden and I recited passages from an imaginary travel-book called "With Fleming to the Front".

Near the top of the pass we stopped to rest at a farmhouse. Auden went inside and came bounding out again with loud cries of dismay, nearly knocking over an old woman. "My God!" he exclaimed. "It's full of bees!" The old woman was astonished and angry at his behaviour—neither she nor the rest of the family seemed to mind the bees at all. She hobbled off, muttering to herself. "If we'd been Japanese", I told Auden, "this could be turned into a first-class atrocity story."

Because of the bees we had to sit outside in the hot sun drinking bowls of icy spring-water, and eating bean-cakes. The water tasted delicious. It was the first we had drunk, unboiled, since we entered China.

At the summit of the pass, which is 4,000 feet high, we stopped again and waited for the others to catch up with us. The long climb, like Life, had strung them out. Already it was possible to predict how they would behave during the rest of the journey. T. C. Liu and Shien, the radio-expert, were wiry and tough; T. Y. Liu and Ching were going to be the lame ducks. T. Y., who had told us yesterday that he could walk a hundred *li* a day, was now complaining that he hadn't slept well, and that a horse had trodden on his foot. He sat sulkily huddled in one of the chairs, his yellow goblin face shrunken to a pair of cheek-bones and a pout of misery. T. C. Liu was unsympathetic. "A horse trod on *my* foot, too," he said scornfully, "but *I* don't mind!" Poor Ching was too exhausted to be able to utter a word. He had plodded all the way on foot and looked as if he had lost pounds of weight already. Fleming, seeing his distress, suggested that he should give up the march and return to Tien-mu-shan on one of the horses. This he indignantly refused.

On our way down the other side of the pass Auden and I tried riding in the chairs. But this was nearly as tiring as walking, for our bearers were obliged to tilt us at such acute angles, as they stepped expertly down from rock to rock, that we had to strain every muscle to prevent ourselves from falling out. So we took to our feet again. At about half-past three that afternoon we limped into Pao Fu Chun, the beautiful little village at the foot of the gorge, standing among trees beside the stream.

Army headquarters were in the old temple with its cool white court-yards and elaborately-carved wooden pillars. Fleming, who had out-walked us all, sat chatting and drinking tea with the General and his Chief of Staff. He was the only one of us who had covered every yard of the distance on foot, and he looked as fresh and sleek as ever.

Auden, as was hardly surprising, felt tired and ill. The tea and warm rice-wine, which we now drank on empty stomachs, were altogether too much for him. When the orderlies brought supper he rushed out of doors to be sick. Throughout the meal he sat pale and shuddering, with eyes averted from a dish of small, blanched, slippery creatures which stood in the middle of the table. "It's those dreadful *efts,*" he muttered. "I daren't look at them, or I shall do it again." The General, unaware of what was wrong, repeatedly pressed Auden to taste the "efts". Auden, with a smile of polite agony, refused to do so. He spent the rest of supper with a handkerchief stuffed into his mouth.

After the meal we were all eager for bed. But, as we were undressing, T. C. Liu came to announce that the "Anti-Japanese Corpse" of Siaofeng had arrived to give us details of the Japanese atrocities in their town. So we struggled wearily into our clothes and went out to greet them—six men and a woman, all wearing their best clothes, and lined up, as Auden said, like a village choir.

Siaofeng had been occupied by the Japanese three times: in December, in February, and in March. When the regular Chinese troops had been forced to retire the local anti-Japanese corps had remained. Apparently harmless farmers and peasants, they were, in reality, dangerous enemies of the invader. They had a highly-organized intelligence service, which co-operated with the Chinese General Staff. At night the Japanese were sniped at (for the irregulars had hidden stores of arms), bridges were blown up, cars were damaged. The Japanese, of course, had made terrible reprisals. Whole villages had been burnt. There had been mass-executions of men, women, and children.

When the Siaofeng delegates went on to speak of the decay of Japanese morale they were less convincing. Here, as elsewhere, we had the impression that the Chinese were merely saying what they themselves wished to believe. Ten Japanese soldiers had committed suicide in a temple. No doubt. But suicide proves nothing. It is the national reaction to all life's troubles—an officer's reprimand, a love-affair gone wrong, a quarrel, a snub. Twenty Japs had been seen by a peasant sitting round a fire in a wood. "They looked very sad, and one of them said: 'I am tired of this war.'" But were there ever any soldiers anywhere who didn't grumble, since the days of Julius Caesar?

While we were listening, Fleming passed me a piece of paper. It was a memorandum, drawn up in the best Foreign Office style, tactfully suggesting that our expedition should be split up into two parties—those who wished to push on to Meiki and reach the front as quickly as possible, and those who were more interested in investigating the civilian problems in the rear. By this means Fleming hoped to save the faces of T. Y. Liu and Ching, and to speed up our march. We all signed the memorandum and agreed that it should be shown to the others as soon as the meeting was over.

But the memorandum wasn't altogether a success. T. Y. Liu was offended. Nothing, he protested, would induce him to forget his "Chinese Duty" of accompanying Auden and myself, if necessary, into the jaws of death. T. C. Liu was catty. (He still continued, despite our protests, to address Fleming as "Mr Framing" and myself as "Mr Isherman"—which, for some obscure psychological reason, annoyed me enormously.) Ching was in frank despair. He admitted that he had a weak heart, and ought never to have come, but he wouldn't agree to travel more slowly than the rest of us. Perhaps he feared that the news of his failure would somehow reach Hankow. Only Shien, as ever, remained placid and cheerful. He was the youngest member of the party, and had a gay, charming disposition. He spoke very little but giggled quietly to himself.

Our camp-beds were left behind in the car at Tien-mu-shan. Tonight we had to sleep on planks. Auden and I soon settled down uncomfortably enough, but, for Fleming, the day wasn't over. Opening his typewriter, he started work on a long dispatch. We fell asleep to the tireless rattle of the keys.

The first light woke us, striking down into the courtyard round which we were sleeping. Somewhere in the woods behind the temple a bird mockingly repeated four distinct notes. Auden said that they meant "All men are fools." He was still feeling tired and unwell.

Fleming (whom we now addressed, with the brand of humour only permissible on walking-tours, as "Frame-Up") had taken Ching aside for a short but firm talk. He now announced to us all: "Mr Ching has been very heroically concealing a weak heart. I have persuaded him, much against his will, to return to Tien-mu-shan. We all sympathize with him in his disappointment, knowing how keen he was to get to the front." So honour was satisfied. Mr Ching started off up the pass, accompanied by one of the chairs. The rest of us walked into the village, where extra horses and chairs were waiting. In Ching's place, an officer from head-quarters was to accompany us to the front. An elderly, cheerful man, he was referred to, somewhat cryptically, as "the Business Master". As we set off, Fleming told us: "I have a bullet for the woman in the shape of a bottle of whisky."

Walking and riding along the valley we reached Siaofeng. Outside the town the Mayor was waiting to receive us. The local ambulance corps lined the road and stood to attention as we passed. The Mayor led us through street after street of ruins; a wilderness of brick-heaps and rub-bish, as hopeless as an unsolved jig-saw puzzle. The streets were crowded, now, to welcome our party, and everybody seemed lively and gay. Business was being carried on as usual. All around the little town the fields were being cultivated; the fertile countryside was in strange contrast to the desolation within. The Mayor told us that the Japanese had special burning-squads, who carried out their work carefully and systematically. Perhaps for this reason there were few actual signs of fire. The buildings simply looked smashed.

After a second breakfast we pushed on again along what looked like an unfinished motor-road, now overgrown with grass. At a booth near the city an old woman was selling food, tea, and cigarettes. T. Y. Liu warned us against a certain brand of cigarettes called *Pirates*. Some consignments of them were said to have been poisoned by the Japanese. Auden, the ever-inquisitive, immediately bought a packet. We both smoked them but neither suffered any bad results. (The poisoning story was probably non-sense, anyway. But we had already heard, on much better authority, that the Japanese had poisoned several junk-loads of salt, destined for a dis-trict near the south-eastern front.)

Ti-pu, our next stopping-place, was more badly damaged, even, than Siaofeng. Nevertheless, I was able to buy a pair of socks. My feet, by this time, were covered with blisters, and I was glad when my turn came to ride one of the fat, obstinate little horses. The horses knew what was before them, it seemed. Nothing would induce them to hurry. They were saving their strength.

Beyond Ti-pu the road shrank to a narrow flagged path winding through rice-fields and dense bamboo groves. Thin rain began to fall. Strings of peasants passed us in single file, heavily burdened with their household goods, making their slow way back towards safety. Now and then we met wounded, carried on rough bamboo litters, who regarded us with bloodshot incurious eyes. We began to have that ominous, oppressive feeling experienced by travellers who are going alone in the wrong, un-popular direction—towards a glacier or a desert. I strained my ears for the first sound of the guns.

But we were still a long way from the lines. At four o'clock we reached Anchi. Here hardly more than a dozen houses remained standing. In one of them the Mayor received us. We sat in his bedroom drinking Chinese gin. The gin was of terrific strength. It was exactly what we needed to get us over the last lap of our day's journey, for the rain was now falling in torrents.

At five o'clock we set out again. I rode ahead, with T. C. Liu, Shien, and the "Business Master". Drunk and drenched to the skin we shouted to each other, sang, and joked. Later, turning maudlin, I sentimentally em-braced my horse and told it, in German, the story of my life. In no time, it seemed, we were crossing the slippery, high-arched pack-bridge which spans the river just outside Meiki.

On the outskirts of the town a little group of people stood waiting un-der umbrellas in the downpour. They were supporting a banner on which was printed the English word "Welcome". Like deliverers we rode slowly down the waterlogged street. Meiki seemed comparatively undamaged. The population crowded in the doorways, grinned and stared. Many saluted.

We were shown upstairs to a candle-lit room, with a charcoal brazier, round which we could strip and get dry. Later, we were told, uniforms would be brought into which we could change. Meanwhile, the steam from our clothes and naked bodies made the atmosphere as thick as a Turkish bath. Presently Auden and Fleming arrived. They had walked the whole way, deep in an argument about Soviet Russia. They were in the highest of spirits and muddy from head to foot. In fact, everybody was cheerful except T. Y. Liu, who had ridden in a covered chair and hadn't got wet at all. We made a mock fuss of him but failed to brighten him up. He sat curled on a stool, pouting and groaning.

The news was vague and bad. The divisional commander was too busy to see us. He would try to come round later. He had telephoned through to Anchi that afternoon, only to find that we had started an hour before. He had wished to prevent our leaving Anchi, for Meiki was already in danger. The Japanese had suddenly attacked from the direction of Hu-chow, and heavy fighting was going on only twenty-five *li* away.

We waited. At last the commander himself appeared. Although very polite he couldn't conceal his dismay at our presence. We were tiresomely notorious foreigners, who might add to his responsibilities by getting killed. Our proper place was on a platform in London—not here, amongst exhausted and overworked officers and officials. We might have to leave, he warned us, in the middle of the night. The evacuation of the civilian population had started already. Touched, and rather ashamed of myself, I thought of those men and women who had wasted their last precious hours of safety, waiting to welcome us with their banner in the rain. The promised uniforms never arrived, and our luggage was too wet to un-pack. A soldier brought blankets. We threw ourselves on to the plank beds and tried to sleep.

Soon after midnight I was started out of an uneasy, drunken doze to see three soldiers disappearing into the room where Fleming was lying. When they came out again a moment later I was too fuddled to be certain whether or not Peter was with them. The bastard, I thought soggily, he's sneaking off to visit the front without telling us. Or maybe the Japs are here. Anyhow, I was too lazy to care. So I dozed off again to the sound of falling rain, the creaking of the old wooden house, the endless gossiping murmur of soldiers round the fire in the neighbouring room.

When I woke again about 4 a.m., it was still pitch dark. The Chinese were getting up. The brazier had gone out. Paddling across the wet floor we searched wretchedly by candle- and match-light for our clothes. My trousers were still soaked, my shirt had a large burn on the front—it had lain too near the coals—my shoes were shrunken and stiff with mud. The others were no better off, though the Chinese had plenty of dry clothes to change into, and their hairless faces looked fresh and clean beside our own dirty stubble beards. Auden stole T. C. Liu's stockings. Peter dog-gedly prised open his drenched suède shoes. Slightly hysterical after this, our third night of insufficient sleep, we laughed and joked at the doleful T. Y.'s expense. "T. Y., art tha sleeping there below?" T. C. Liu, mean-while, was telephoning to divisional headquarters. After grinding at the instrument for some minutes like a coffee-machine, he extracted a few grains of the blackest possible news. The general couldn't see us. He was too busy to make any statement. We were to leave immediately.

"Not without our breakfasts," said Fleming firmly. To Auden and my-self he whispered that such delaying tactics gave us our only possible chance of seeing anything at all. T. Y. Liu announced that he would leave Meiki at once by chair. He hadn't slept for a fortnight. He was very ill indeed.

But was there any breakfast to be had? The whole house seemed to have gone suddenly dead. Only a couple of orderlies, fidgeting at the door, remained unwillingly at our disposal. Following Peter's cue, we continued to demand food, and an interview with some responsible staff officer, until even T. C. Liu, who was certainly no coward, began to look a trifle green. Divisional headquarters, he told us, would soon be retiring to Anchi: we could speak to the general there. The Japanese were now only ten *li* away from the town. They would probably attack as soon as it got light.

It did get light. Still we dawdled. I began to feel exceedingly uncomfortable. T. Y. Liu had already left, and there was a rumour that all the horses and chairs had followed him. At half-past seven a little food was reluctantly brought: we ate it with obstinate deliberation. Meanwhile Peter held forth, for the benefit of T. C. Liu, on the waste of his valuable time, *The Times*'s time, in visiting this front, where one saw nothing and where all information was withheld. T. C. was only too easily drawn by this kind of teasing; he controlled his temper and his impatience with difficulty. I wondered what would have happened, by this evening, to the handsome furniture of the upper rooms, and discussed, with Auden, the ethics of pocketing a pair of jade animals to save them from the fate worse than death.

By eight o'clock we had finished eating. There was nothing to do but leave. It was a grey, lowering morning. My feet were so painful that I could barely hobble along the streets: despite the evacuation order there were plenty of people still about. They regarded our bedraggled departure quietly. I felt like the last, lame, ship-deserting rat. A few civilians tried to propitiate Fleming with a promise of some "unofficial information"— but this consisted only in showing him a couple of soaked newspapers on a ruined wall.

The chairs and horses had waited for us after all. I got on to my little brown pony, which seemed nearly as tired as I was, and away we plodded, along the muddy, straggling field-paths. The whole countryside was sodden like a sponge. The clouds were low over the hills, with occasional streaks of sunshine. It was stuffy and warm. Away behind Meiki, we heard sudden bursts of gunfire. The atmosphere of retreat, coupled with our hangovers, depressed us all—all except Peter, who marched indefatigably ahead, with his tireless, springy stride, puffing at his pipe. He was smoking a cheap brand of Chinese tobacco which smelt, as he himself said, like the burning hair of an old actor's wig.

T. C. Liu had insisted, with some show of reason, that the fall of Meiki—if Meiki did fall—would be unimportant and even strategically advisable: the Japs were to be lured down into the valley and destroyed there by the time-honoured pincer-movement. But nowhere along the whole route did we see any evidences of serious military preparation. We met hardly any troops, except city guards and the wounded.

We got to Anchi about ten o'clock. T. Y. Liu had already arrived. T. C. Liu had proposed staying there to await developments, but it now appeared that the authorities, although most hospitable, were anxious to pass us still further back. The divisional commander had telephoned from Meiki, requesting our immediate evacuation. Our whole party was against this. T. C. Liu pointed out that we couldn't ask the coolies to go on. They had stayed up the whole night, having been warned that we might wish to start at any moment. T. Y. Liu was even more emphatic. If he didn't get some rest, he said, he would be seriously ill, and he curled up to sleep on somebody else's bed.

T. C. had now become very portentous and secretive. He had long conferences with the Mayor. It was evident that he was getting information which he wouldn't transmit. Peter retaliated with semi-humorous bullying: "All this reticence is creating a most deplorable impression, Mr Liu. It's quite obvious that the Chinese have been defeated." "No, not defeated," T. C. pedantically insisted. "This is a strategic withdrawal."

The authorities now played a new card. The weather, they pointed out, was clearing; the Japanese aeroplanes were therefore to be expected, and the municipal offices—clearly visible as one of the few buildings left standing among the ruins—would almost certainly be bombed. Immediately a party was formed—headed by T. Y. Liu—demanding instant evacuation. Peter teased them, reminding T. Y. of his exhaustion and T. C. of his solicitude for the coolies' comfort. The coolies, needless to say, were roused at once. So off we started, after saying good-bye to the heroically placid Mayor, who was quietly awaiting yet another occupation of his town, and the probable destruction of its few remaining houses.

Auden and I now relapsed into the chairs. Fleming, with the flattering brutality of a born leader, had extracted T. Y. from one of them and had even persuaded him to march at his side. We advanced by a shorter route through the lonely countryside. The coolies strode along, relieving each other with trained adroitness. We gazed at their bulging calves and straining thighs, and rehearsed every dishonest excuse for allowing ourselves to be carried by human beings: they are used to it, it's giving them employment, they don't feel. Oh no, they don't feel—but the lump on the back of that man's neck wasn't raised by drinking champagne, and his sweat remarkably resembles my own. Never mind, my feet hurt. I'm paying him, aren't I? Three times as much, in fact, as he'd get from a Chinese. Sentimentality helps no one. Why don't you walk? I can't, I tell you. You bloody well would if you'd got no cash. But I *have* got cash. Oh, dear. I'm so heavy. . . . Our coolies, unaware of these qualms, seemed to bear us no ill-will, however, At the road-side halts they even brought us cups of tea.

We arrived in Siaofeng well before dark, and were welcomed as warmly as on the previous morning. T. Y. Liu was very cocky: "You see," he told us, "I am stronger than you!" T. C. Liu was full of excitement about an anecdote he had heard on the road: a woman had brewed tea and had sent out her little son to offer it, free, to passing soldiers. As Peter commented, it was significant of the former Chinese attitude to soldiers that this action should still be considered so remarkable.

After supper we were asked to address the Government employees and civilian volunteers on our impressions of the war zone. The audience stood to attention while we spoke. T. C. Liu translated.

The day ended with an argument about our future route. T. Y. wanted to get back to the road-head by the way we had come; T. C. wanted to make a detour which would involve a further three days' march. This time Peter and I supported T. Y. We got our own way—much to the relief of my own swollen feet.

Next morning we were told that Meiki had fallen. The Japanese had occupied it almost exactly twelve hours after our departure.

We started at six in far higher spirits. Everybody had slept reasonably well, the weather was fine, and our horses could be urged into a smart trot. As they approached Pao Fu Chun (which they perhaps misguidedly believed to be the end of their day's journey) they even had bursts of cantering. There was the necessary spice of ill-feeling, *en route*, because T. Y. Liu had taken one of the chairs after we had offered them to a party of wounded soldiers.

At the temple we stopped for lessons. Or rather, we sat sulkily while T. C. Liu, the prize scholar, received private tuition—most of which, he told us loftily, he wasn't allowed to pass on. He had met a colleague from the *Central News*, and the clique-atmosphere thickened. When our hosts offered us breakfast T. C. refused it without consulting us, and was rebuked by Peter. "Surely", T. C. retorted, "it is a matter of common sense that one does not require two breakfasts?" We protested that we did. T. C. said nothing, but went away for a specially private conference with a staff officer. Presently he returned. "Is there any news?" Fleming asked. "There is one piece of news", replied T. C., with a spiteful smile, "which will interest you greatly: milk is being prepared, and some eggs."

We started at ten o'clock for the long toil up the pass. I had bought some Chinese shoes in Pao Fu Chun which carried me like magic, and I set off on foot to overtake Peter, whom I found, at last, bathing his feet in the stream. Auden, he told me, was far ahead. Obeying some Nordic *Excelsior*-urge, he was racing, stripped to the waist, for the summit. He awaited us there, amidst a crowd of coolies, who were carrying boxes of ammunition over the mountain, down to Pao Fu Chun. The size and weight of the ammunition-boxes appalled us, but the coolies, with the worst half of their journey behind them, still seemed comparatively fresh. They greeted us gaily with friendly gestures and smiles. It was only later, when we had reached the first farmhouse on the other side of the pass, and were drinking tea, that T. C. Liu told us that the coolies had asked him whether we were Italians or White Russians. If so, they said, they would follow and arrest us. T. C. added, with some satisfaction, that T. Y. Liu had taken another route, a much more difficult one, on the advice of his chair-bearers, and had disappeared. Quite probably he had been robbed and murdered. We expressed more than mere polite concern at this news, for our coats and rucksacks were in the bottom of T. Y.'s chair.

My feet now collapsed utterly. The Chinese shoes had been too small, and I must have bruised my big toe on the rocks, for the toe-nail had turned quite black. I should have to take a chair down to the road-head. This was explained to the bearers (there were only two of them today) and they agreed, although passengers are not usually carried down the upper part of the path, which is narrow and very steep. What followed was quite absurdly alarming. The chair hung poised, for enormous moments, on the strength of the front man's ankles. A cough or a sneeze, it seemed, would send all three of us headlong over the precipice. But my bearers had the balance of trained acrobats, and we got down to Tien-mu-shan without accident. On arrival I made them a speech of thanks, through T. C. Liu, and gave them a bonus. They seemed pleased and genuinely surprised.

The cars took us to Yü-tsien, a grubby, noisy little town, with a rat's nest of an hotel, where Mr Ching, in a kimono, had been nursing his heart, and Major Yang his war-wounds and his complicated sense of honour. There was an air-raid alarm, to which nobody paid the least attention, and a crowded supper-party in our bedroom, where hatchets were buried in bowls of rice. T. Y. Liu, neither robbed nor murdered, cleared his reputation at enormous length: he hadn't taken the wounded soldiers' chairs, they had refused them; and he had walked *all* the way over the mountain. "So you see," he concluded, "I am not cruel at all." T. Y. addressed T. C. as "My dear brother". Toasts were drunk. T. C. was thanked for his efficiency, Shien for his endurance, Peter for his leadership: the examination results were published, and everybody came out equal top.

After supper Fleming, Auden, and I explained to T. C. Liu our views on Chinese propaganda. Atrocity stories, we told him, would make little impression on the West—people had heard too many of them already. And the decay of Japanese morale was a subject which was better left alone. T. C. listened carefully and thanked us. He seemed really anxious to get advice. We felt warmly towards him this evening. Whatever might be said against his manners he was certainly a person whom one could admire and respect. We said good night in a friendly spirit.

Good night, but not to sleep. A hand-drum operated by a night-watchman was followed by a mating cat, Mah-jongg clatter, a rain-storm, door-slamming, a baby, a dog, and power-diving mosquitoes. In the morning I found that my underlip had swollen into a great flap of hard, hanging flesh. I amused myself by twisting it grotesquely to scare children who peeped through the door, but they only laughed at me. Auden had been bitten, too. We both reproached our Chief, who had promised, on the word of an explorer, that there would be no insects.

We left for Tunki at a fairly civilized hour. The hotel-boy who packed our things had solemnly poured the last drops from a cognac bottle over the bed, as though performing some magical rite. The journey was uneventful. T. Y. Liu, in wonderful spirits, told us: "I am never sorry." He spoke too soon, for presently he was sick. We stopped to get petrol near a restaurant where they were cooking bamboo in all its forms—including the strips used for making chairs. That, I thought, is so typical of this country. Nothing is specifically either eatable or uneatable. You could begin munching a hat, or bite a mouthful out of a wall; equally, you could build a hut with the food provided at lunch. Everything is everything.

We arrived at Tunki about midday. Our chief object in returning there had been to interview General Ku, but we couldn't. He had gone away, and no other member of the staff was available. The newspapers, we found, made no reference to the fall of Meiki.

At supper we drank cognac and began an argument on the meaning of the word Civilization. Had China anything to learn from the West? Peter thought not. "The Chinese", he kept repeating, "have got everything taped." "Surely," I protested, "you can't pretend that the coolie is well off, in his present condition? Isn't he ever to hear Beethoven? Or see your wife act?" "Oh," said Peter airily, "he's got them both pretty well taped." Auden was more for providing the coolies with meals from a really good French restaurant. He had decided, finally, against Chinese food.

T. Y. Liu, Yang, Fleming, Auden, and I left Tunki early next morning for Kin-hwa. It had stopped raining, but the road was very soft and treacherous; the rivers we had to cross were all swollen. When we reached the last of them the ferrymen refused altogether to take the car over, so we had to make a detour which brought us into Kin-hwa on foot. It wasn't very far. Just outside the town there was a little amateur ferry over some flood-water, operated by small boys, who punted us in circles until some of the passengers snatched the poles from their hands and helped themselves.

Meanwhile T. Y. had run the whole gamut of his moods. Pre-vomitory sadness (Fleming and Auden had had undecided bets on whether he or Yang would be sick first) was followed by promises and apologies: "I have tried to satisfy you. I will do everything possible to help you. It is my

Chinese duty." After we had passed the provincial border into Che-kiang he became rather haughty and showed us his seal with the official chop. But the walk from the ferry was too much for him: he relapsed into the blackest of sulks.

Peter, to our great regret, left Kin-hwa by train that same evening, for Nanchang. We had all three enjoyed our expedition together. As Auden said, summing it up: "Well, we've been on a journey with Fleming in China, and now we're real travellers for ever and ever. We need never go farther than Brighton again."

Two days later—this was May 20th—we were able to leave Kin-hwa by bus for Wenchow. The alternative route was closed because it seemed likely that the Japanese were about to attempt a landing near Ningpo. The municipal government, hospitable to the last, had arranged that the chief of police should accompany us. A soldier was sent to buy our tickets and reserve our seats on the bus.

At the bus station we said good-bye to Chiang and to T. Y. Liu. Chiang was returned to Hankow with a handsomely-worded testimonial in his pocket: it recommended him to all who wished to make a tour of the Chinese war-areas. T. Y. we presented with our three volumes of Motley, suitably inscribed. "God bless you, my dear friends!" were his parting words.

The journey was unexciting. Ten miles out from Kin-hwa a Japanese aeroplane appeared, but showed no interest in our bus. At Lishui we were told that we should have to stop the night; a bridge farther down the road had been broken by floods and wouldn't be repaired till morning. We called on the Chief of Police, the city Governor, and the Canadian Catholic Mission. The Canadian Bishop, Monseigneur McGrath, gave us a copy of his book on mission-work in Che-kiang Province, *The Dragon at Close Range*.

The Catholic Fathers at Lishui had no hospital, only a dispensary and a school. There had been no serious air-raids here, they told us, so far; though the Japanese sometimes bombed the air-field. Once they had machine-gunned and killed a dog. On the whole life at the mission-station seemed very happy and pleasant. The countryside was beautiful: the younger and more athletic Fathers toured it on their bicycles. All of them were fond of a day's fishing. In the evenings they listened to the gramophone or played darts. They gave us whisky from Shanghai and American cigarettes.

It was interesting to notice, here as elsewhere, how the missionaries had modified their attitude since the war towards Communism and Communists in China. Two years ago, the Fathers themselves admitted, they had regarded the Communists simply as bandits—or, at best, as Robin Hoods, who robbed the rich to feed the poor. Now they were beginning to take the movement seriously, and to recognize the part it might play in determining the future development of the country.

One of the Fathers told us an extraordinary insect-story. A Chinese boy employed at the Mission had been stung by a centipede and was very ill. The Fathers could do nothing for him until their Chinese catechist produced a certain kind of spider which he had found crawling about the roof. This spider, he told them, would suck the poison from the boy's wound. And it did. When the spider had finished sucking, the catechist put it into a bowl of water so that it could eject the poison from its own body. The boy recovered immediately.

We stayed in Wenchow two days, on board the steamer which was to take us to Shanghai. Although Wenchow itself was still in Chinese hands the mouth of its river was guarded by the Japanese, and only vessels of friendly nationality were allowed to pass in and out unmolested. So the Chinese steamers had taken on foreign officers and got themselves de-naturalized: some German, some Italian, some Portuguese. Our ship had been built in Hongkong and had certainly never been outside the China Seas: nevertheless, she was registered at Trieste, had acquired a new Italian name, and had exchanged her Norwegian captain for an Italian. The old captain remained on board, however, and continued to navigate in the tricky channels of the river mouths. He wore civilian clothes and was, officially, a passenger.

A cabin port-hole is a picture-frame. No sooner had we arrived on board than the brass-encircled view became romantic and false. The brown river in the rain, the boatmen in their dark bat-wing capes, the tree-crowned pagodas on the foreshore, the mountains scarved in mist—these were no longer features of the beautiful, prosaic country we had just left behind us; they were the scenery of the traveller's dream; they were the mysterious, *l'Extrême Orient*. Memory in the years to come would prefer this simple theatrical picture to all the subtle and chaotic impressions of the past months. This, I thought—despite all we have seen, heard, experienced—is how I shall finally remember China.

The time passed slowly and agreeably. Released from the tyranny of our journey, we indulged the minor vices, over-eating and over-sleeping. It was a luxury to allow oneself to feel mildly ill. Lounging against the rail we watched children playing on the wharf below. We amused ourselves by dropping coins and ten-cent notes on to the quayside, and waiting to see how long it would be before they were noticed and picked up. It was remarkable that hardly any of the children and dock-labourers who found the money looked up to see where it had come from—either be-

cause they feared it might be reclaimed, or from a natural piety which
accepted all Heaven's gifts without question. One coin landed near a very
dirty little boy of four or five years old—so near that it seemed certain he
must have seen it. But, for a long time, he made absolutely no move,
except to glance furtively to left and right. Then, very slowly, without ever
looking downward, he worked the coin over the ground with his toe into a
position from which he could pick it up. Having pocketed it he rose to his
feet and toddled off with an air of extreme unconcern. The perfection of
his technique—so matter-of-fact that it wasn't even sly—was one of the
most shocking things I have ever seen in my life. It told the whole story of
the coolie's animal struggle for existence.

The Norwegian ex-captain told us yarns of Spitsbergen, where he had
once navigated the ice-breaker *Krassin,* and of his fights with Chinese pi-
rates, as a customs officer, in Bias Bay. He and the Italian officers got on
very well together. He played operatic airs on the piano in the saloon, and
the Italian captain sang in a fine fruity tenor. He could also give a really
marvellous imitation of a hen laying an egg. The Italian captain was one
of those handsome, hook-nosed men who talk about women as if they
were a kind of wine, or a choice brand of cigar.

On May 23rd we sailed down the river soon after lunch, but it was
already dusk when we passed out of the estuary, skirting between the
bald, lonely islands, behind which an armed Japanese transport-steamer
was lurking, like a highway robber. The Japs signalled to us to ask where
we were going. "If they tell us to stop", said the Captain, "I shall refuse."
"But won't they fire on you?" Auden asked. The Italian laughed: "I'd like
to see the bastards try it! I should wireless to one of our warships. She
could be here in two hours—and she'd send planes ahead of her."

Somewhat to our regret, however, the Japanese allowed us to pass with-
out further inquiry.

Two days later, when we had finished breakfast and come up on to the
bridge, the ship was already steaming up the Whangpoo River. The Nor-
wegian pointed out to us the ruins at Woosung, where the first fighting
took place after the Japanese had made their landing. It was strange and
shocking to see lorry-loads of Japanese soldiers moving along the river-
bank, and to pass Japanese freighters and ferry-boats plying with the
peaceful self-assurance of an enemy who had come to stay. The blood-
spot flag, which we had last seen lying disgraced on the ground amidst the
war-trophies at Tunki, now hit the eye brazenly from every angle, as it
fluttered from the poles of buildings and ships. A Japanese aeroplane
passed overhead, and it seemed unnatural and wrong that we didn't have
to scamper for cover. In half an hour we should have reached Shanghai.

10

Shanghai. May 15–June 12.

Seen from the river, towering above their couchant guardian warships, the semi-skyscrapers of the Bund present, impressively, the façade of a great city. But it is only a façade. The spirit which dumped them upon this unhealthy mud-bank, thousands of miles from their kind, has been too purely and brutally competitive. The biggest animals have pushed their way down to the brink of the water; behind them is a sordid and shabby mob of smaller buildings. Nowhere a fine avenue, a spacious park, an imposing central square. Nowhere anything civic at all.

Nevertheless the tired or lustful business man will find here everything to gratify his desires. You can buy an electric razor, or a French dinner, or a well-cut suit. You can dance at the Tower Restaurant on the roof of the Cathay Hotel, and gossip with Freddy Kaufmann, its charming manager, about the European aristocracy or pre-Hitler Berlin. You can attend race-meetings, baseball games, football matches. You can see the latest American films. If you want girls, or boys, you can have them, at all prices, in the bath-houses and the brothels. If you want opium you can smoke it in the best company, served on a tray, like afternoon tea. Good wine is difficult to obtain in this climate, but there is enough whisky and gin to float a fleet of battleships. The jeweller and the antique-dealer await your orders, and their charges will make you imagine yourself back on Fifth Avenue or in Bond Street. Finally, if you ever repent, there are churches and chapels of all denominations.

We ourselves have alighted on one of the topmost branches of the social tree: we are staying at the British Ambassador's private villa in the French Concession. This villa is the property of an important shipping firm. It is known as their Number One House. Cream-coloured and eminently pro-consular, with cool solid Corinthian porticoes, it stands calmly in a big garden of shaven lawns and Empire Exhibition flower-beds. Everything is in perfect working-order and modelled to scale. There is a limousine full of petrol in the garage, complete with a real live chauffeur, wearing white cotton gloves. There are Settlement police to guard the front gate, correctly equipped down to the last detail. There are Chinese servants who can say "Your Excellency", and bow from the waist. On special occasions they wear coats of lemon-coloured silk. All the doors open and shut, the telephone rings, and the bath-taps turn on and off.

The Ambassador and Lady Kerr are, like ourselves, perfect strangers in this life-size doll's house. It will continue to function years after we are all dead. Nevertheless, they play up splendidly—returning the salutes of the guards at the gate, changing their clothes at the right hours, accepting the food and the service with fine nonchalance. It is only occasionally that one takes them unawares, resting for a moment in the lemon and cream drawing-room amidst the vases and lacquered screens, between tea with the Dutch Ambassador and dinner with the Naval Attaché, and realizes that they are an ordinary married couple, tired and not always in the best of health, who rely profoundly upon each other's intuitions and moods. Lady Kerr reads detective stories. Sir Archibald owns thirty-two pipes. They are the only objects in this vast museum which seem really and intimately to belong to him.

It is the Ambassador's turn to give an official garden-party. The preparations are elaborate. They require the co-operation of the ladies of the British colony, the Seaforth Highlanders, the Embassy staff. Invitations are sent out. The drinks and the cold buffet are organized. The portico is decorated with flags. Bowing deeply, the doll-butlers usher in their national enemies, the bandy-legged, hissing Japanese generals. Everybody is present, including the journalists. Next morning, the local newspapers will carry photographs of the most distinguished guests. Out on the lawn the Scottish pipers play their airs.

Everything goes off like clockwork. It is a beautifully-contrived charade, the perfect image of another kind of life—projected, at considerable expense, from its source on the opposite side of the earth. Such functions, no doubt, are well worth the money they cost, for here and there, amidst the regulation small-talk, a serious word is exchanged, a delicate but pointed hint is dropped. This afternoon certain minute but important readjustments have been made in the exquisite balance of international relationships. At any rate, thank goodness, it hasn't rained.

But gaily as the charade-players laugh, and loudly as they chatter, they cannot altogether ignore those other, most undiplomatic sounds which reach us, at intervals, from beyond the garden trees. Somewhere out in the suburbs, machine-guns are rattling. You can hear them all day long. Everybody in the Settlement knows what they mean—the Chinese guerilla units are still active here in the enemy's stronghold. But if you are so tactless as to call the attention of the Japanese officers to these noises they will reply that you are mistaken—it is only their own troops at firing-practice.

The International Settlement and the French Concession form an island, an oasis in the midst of the stark, frightful wilderness which was once the Chinese city. Your car crosses the Soochow Creek: on one side are streets and houses, swarming with life; on the other is a cratered and barren moon-landscape, intersected by empty, clean-swept roads. Here and there a Japanese sentry stands on guard, or a party of soldiers hunts among the ruins for scrap-iron. Further out, the buildings are not so badly damaged, but every Chinese or foreign property has been looted—

and no kind of wild animal could have made half the mess. At Medhurst College, once a mission-school in the Ling-Ping Road, books and pictures have been torn up, electric-light bulbs smashed, wash-basins wrecked. On the fringes of the city civilians are still living; one hears many stories of their ill-treatment at the hands of the Japanese. Out driving one day we noticed two soldiers with drawn bayonets prodding at a crowd of women and children. We stopped. Here, we thought, was a chance of witnessing an atrocity at first hand. Then we saw a third soldier, holding a basket. The Japanese, in their own inimitably ungracious way, were distributing food.

Like formidable, excluded watchdogs, the real masters of Shanghai inhabit the dark, deserted Japanese Concession, or roam the lunar wilderness of Chapei, looking hungrily in upon the lighted populous international town. On Garden Bridge their surly sentries force every Chinese foot-passenger to raise his hat in salute. Incidents are of weekly occurrence: a foreign lady is insulted, an innocent naturalist is arrested as a spy. Representations are made "through the proper channels"; apologies are gravely offered and accepted.

Inside the Settlement, too, an underground, deadly political struggle is going on. The Japanese never cease their intrigues to form a puppet-government which is, one day, to rule China under their orders. Blackmail and bribes coerce or tempt a few prominent Chinese to negotiate with the enemy, but the would-be traitors seldom live long enough to be of much use to their new masters, for patriotic terrorists are always on the alert. Going into the Cathay Hotel one morning for a cup of coffee, we found a little crowd round the entrance gazing at a pool of blood. A Chinese business man, notorious for his pro-Japanese sympathies, had been leaving the building when he was fired at by gunmen: his White Russian bodyguard had shot back, and a battle followed, in which several people were killed. The business man himself had been badly wounded in the throat. Next time, most probably, he won't escape alive.

The perimeter of the international town is guarded by a mixed force of foreign troops. The defence sector allotted to the Seaforth Highlanders runs north from Soochow Creek to the railway station; going round their pill-boxes and sentry-posts one gets some idea of the extraordinary position in which the British troops found themselves last winter during the attack on Shanghai. The direct line of advance lay through the international zone, and neither the Japanese nor the Chinese would believe that the British weren't going to let the enemy cross it to turn their flank. So they opened fire on each other across the corners of the defence sector, and the British soldiers, right in the line of the shooting, were often unable to leave their pill-boxes for twenty-four hours at a stretch. The walls of all the posts are dented with bullet-marks.

The Shanghai fighting culminated in the rearguard action fought by the "Doomed Battalion", which was occupying the Chinese Mint Godown, to the west of the Thibet Road bridge. The British General, Telfer-Smollett, saw that if the Chinese persisted in holding the Godown some of the Japanese shells were certain to explode across the creek, in Soochow Road and beyond, so he urged their evacuation. The Chinese commander replied that he could evacuate only under direct orders from the Generalissimo himself. Madame Chiang was first approached. "No," she said, "they must die that China may live." But General Telfer-Smollett persisted, and the Generalissimo at length agreed that the battalion should be withdrawn. The Japanese were also willing, for the Mint Godown commanded their flank, and its resistance was holding up their advance.

A night was fixed for the withdrawal of the Chinese troops into the International Concession. The telephone lines to the Godown and to the Japanese headquarters had not been broken, so Telfer-Smollett was able to keep in constant communication with both sides. At the last moment the Japanese rang up to say that they refused to guarantee the safe passage of the battalion: they were angry because the Chinese had continued to fire all through the afternoon and had inflicted serious losses. So they trained their machine-guns and searchlights down the Thibet Road, which the evacuating troops would have to cross to reach the international zone. At the end of the road, beside the bridge, stood a British pill-box, directly in the line of fire.

General Telfer-Smollett came, with his staff, to superintend the withdrawal personally. He was taking cover behind the Bank of China Godown on the opposite side of the road, and here he received the Chinese, as they dashed across into safety. The Japanese fired all their machine-guns at once: the Chinese got their chance of escape while the guns were being reloaded. Eventually the entire battalion was able to withdraw, bringing its weapons and ammunition, with the loss of only seven men. Some people will tell you that the British troops in their pill-box, tired of being shot at, returned the Japanese fire, and even put a machine-gun out of action. This is officially denied. Anyhow, the Japanese, in the darkness and confusion, could hardly be certain where the bullets were coming from. The battalion, in accordance with a previous agreement, was interned in the International Settlement and will remain there until the end of the war.

Here we were, sitting down to lunch with four Japanese civilians in the dining-room of the Shanghai Club. This lunch had been arranged for us by a prominent British business man—and, of course, we agreed in advance, we should do nothing to embarrass or compromise our host. We would both be very tactful indeed. To make any reference, however indirect, to the war would, we felt, be positively indecent.

Fortified by a drink at the Long Bar (needless to say, it proved to be far shorter than we had expected) we advanced to meet our fellow-guests. The four Japanese were all distinguished personages—a consular official, a business man, a banker, and a railway director. The consular official was smooth-faced, and looked rather Chinese; the others gave us the collective impression of being stumpy, dark brown, bespectacled, moustached, grinning and very neat.

The Japanese, evidently, did not share our scruples: "You have been travelling in China?" asked one of them, straight away. "How interesting. . . . I hope you had no inconvenience?" "Only from your aeroplanes," I replied, forgetting our resolutions. The Japanese laughed heartily: this was a great joke. "But surely", they persisted, "you must have found the transport and living conditions very primitive, very inefficient?" "On the contrary," we assured them, "extremely efficient. Kindness and politeness everywhere. Everybody was charming." "Oh yes," the consular official agreed in an indulgent tone, "the Chinese are certainly charming. Such nice people. What a pity. . . ." "Yes, what a pity!" the others chimed in: "This war could so easily have been avoided. Our demands were very reasonable. In the past we were always able to negotiate these problems amicably. The statesmen of the old school—you could deal with *them*, they understood the art of compromise. But these younger men, they're dreadfully hot-headed. Most unfortunate—" "You know," continued the consular official, "we really love the Chinese. That is the nice thing about this war. There is no bitterness. We in Japan feel absolutely no bitterness towards the Chinese People." This was really a little too much. The last remnants of our prearranged politeness disappeared. It was hardly surprising, we retorted, with some heat, that the Japanese didn't feel bitter. Why should they? Had they ever had their towns burnt and their women raped? Had they ever been bombed? Our four gentlemen had no answer ready. They merely blinked. They didn't appear in the least offended, however. Then one of them said: "That is certainly a most interesting point of view."

They wanted to know about the morale in Hankow. Was there much enthusiasm? Enormous enthusiasm, we replied. What chances were there of a negotiated peace? None, we declared, with spiteful relish—Chiang would continue to resist, if necessary, to the borders of Thibet. The Japanese shook their heads sadly, and drew in their breath with a sharp disappointed hiss. It was a pity . . . a great pity. . . . And then—as we had been expecting—out came the Bolshevik Bogey. Japan was really fighting on China's side—to save her from herself, to protect her from the red menace. "And from Western trade competition," we might have added, but it wasn't necessary. For, at this moment, through the dining-room window which overlooked the river, the gun-turrets of H.M.S. *Birmingham* slid quietly into view, moving upstream. In this city the visual statements of power-politics are more brutal than any words. The Japanese had followed the direction of our eyes. Lunch ended in a moment of thoughtful and slightly embarrassed silence.

Mr Rewi Alley is a factory inspector and official of the Public Works Department—a stocky New Zealander with light cropped ginger hair and a short rugged nose. For seven years he has been working to improve conditions in the hundreds of Chinese factories around Hongkew—and now everything is wrecked. The Japanese have destroyed seventy per cent of China's industry. Some of the luckier concerns have been able to crowd into the International Settlement, and reopen there. Most of these factories are very small—two or three rooms crammed with machinery and operatives. The majority of the operatives are young boys who have been bought from their parents outright for twenty dollars: they work from twelve to fourteen hours a day. Their only wages are their food, and a sleeping-space in a loft above the work-room. There are no precautions whatever against accident or injury to health. In the accumulator factories, half the children have already the blue line in their gums which is a symptom of lead-poisoning. Few of them will survive longer than a year or eighteen months. In scissors factories you can see arms and legs developing chromium-holes. There are silk-winding mills so full of steam that the fingers of the mill-girls are white with fungus growths. If the children slacken in their work the overseers often plunge their elbows into the boiling water as a punishment. There is a cotton mill where the dust in their air makes T.B. almost a certainty. Alley has had its owner into court three times but he has always managed to square the judge. Accidents are invariably found to be due to the carelessness of the workers involved. There is no compensation and no insurance.

Before the war industrial conditions, though still very bad, were slowly improving. Now the destruction of so much plant has created enormous supplies of surplus labour. (In the silk factory, for example, women's wages have fallen from thirty to twenty cents a day.) The Japanese, in Alley's opinion, will exploit the Shanghai workers even more brutally than the Chinese owners have exploited them in the past. They will flood the markets with cheap goods and so gradually lower working-class standards of living all over the world.

If you tire of inspecting one kind of misery there are plenty of others. Refugee camps, for instance—triple tiers of shelves under a straw roof. These hovels would disgrace the dirtiest Chinese village. On each shelf lives, cooks, eats, and sleeps an entire family. A single hut will hold about five hundred people. There is often only one source of water-supply for a whole camp, a fire-hose main in the street: the queue to it reaches into dozens all day long.

Since the Japanese occupation of the outer city, the International Settlement has been dangerously overcrowded. There is no restriction on sub-letting: the minimum sleeping-space on a floor may cost one dollar sixty cents a month. When the British wished to clear a single street a hundred yards long for defensive purposes they were told that this would mean evicting fourteen thousand people. Under present conditions Alley estimates that forty thousand refugee children must die during the next twelve months from under-nourishment and epidemics. Cholera has started in Shanghai already.

Then there is the problem of the rickshaw-coolies. Their standard of life is hardly better than that of the refugees themselves. The profession is recruited chiefly from the country boys who leave their homes and come to Shanghai because they have been told that it is a "gold- and silver-making place". The number of rickshaws in the International Settlement is limited to ten thousand. You can buy a rickshaw for fifty to seventy dollars. Then you must register it. The registration-plate costs, officially, five dollars. But these plates, being limited in number and absolutely essential, change hands many times, always at a profit. They have been known to fetch five hundred dollars apiece. The rickshaw-owner hires out his machines to the coolies at the rate of seventy cents a day. (Often a rickshaw is operated by two coolies working on alternate days.) The war has hit the rickshaw trade severely. The midnight curfew has reduced the number of business hours, and the Japanese occupation has restricted the area of traffic—for no rickshaw can now pass the limits of the international zone. The coolie may expect a profit of from thirty to sixty cents: this, if he is sharing his rickshaw, must keep him alive for two days. Often he is unlucky; his registration-plate or his pawn-tickets are stolen or he gets into trouble with the police over some traffic regulation and is fined. Having no reserves it is nearly impossible for him to make good these losses. So he sinks further and further into debt. As one coolie told a Chinese worker who was taking us round the slums: "Our life seems to be fastened down with live hooks."

During the past few years, however, something has been done to help the coolies. Four rickshaw-pullers' mutual aid centres have been started in Shanghai. At these centres they can rest, drink tea, have a bath and get medical attention. They are run by the Municipal Council. Each coolie pays five cents a day for his membership. He gives the money to his rickshaw-owner, from whom the Council collects it.

Tucked away in unobtrusive corners, unnoticed and almost forgotten, are the crippled remains of the soldiers who fought to defend Shanghai. We have visited one such hospital with Alley: all its patients have lost an arm or a leg. They are being taught simple trades—soap-making, stocking-knitting, or the manufacture of crude artificial limbs; but the chief doctor, a missionary, doesn't approve of education and tries to get them sent away before they can learn much. Most of them, if they recover, have no future but begging. All day long the unfortunate patients are pestered by Chinese evangelists, who lecture them, lay hands upon them, and try to persuade them to sing hymns. Without much success, however. The other day, we are told, the patients went on strike and tore up all their Bibles.

The soldiers were astonishingly cheerful, and all anxious to be photographed. One boy was a remarkable artist. He drew portraits and caricatures. He had fought in the "Doomed Battalion". His younger brother, he told us, had been eaten alive in Shan-si Province by a wolf.

The hospital authorities have circulated a questionnaire among the patients to discover their reasons for joining the army. The results are as follows:

Economic reasons	36
Economic reasons + admiration of military career	26
Patriotism	23
Family difficulties	23
Conscription	16
Homeless	9
Wish to suppress local bandits	7
Deceived by promises of reward	1
Vanity	1

Allen is convinced that China cannot hope to win this war unless she develops an industrial co-operative movement in the interior of the country. During the past thirty years Chinese industry has been concentrated in the coastal area, but the coast towns and the big river ports are now all occupied or threatened by the Japanese. Sooner or later, all China's industrial plant will fall into the enemy's hands unless it is removed in time to the inner provinces.

Japan is planning the economic colonization of China, nothing less. Already she has published schemes for the building of new canals, railways, cotton and silk mills. In Hongkew and the other occupied districts of Shanghai she is reopening her factories. Of the 130,000 operatives now employed in Shanghai ninety per cent are working for the Japanese.

The flight into the international zone is no solution of China's economic problems. Even if the Chinese in the Settlement retain some measure of political freedom their operations can only strengthen the Shanghai area as an economic base for the Japanese war-machine. Their communications with the interior are becoming increasingly difficult and may soon be cut off altogether. And yet, during the first four months of 1938, over 400 new

Chinese factories were established in the western district of the Settlement, while less than fifty industrialists moved their plants elsewhere.

The Chinese Government, as Alley points out, has had great success in developing the agricultural co-operative movement—consumers, marketing, and credit co-operatives. It has thereby strengthened the rural purchasing power. In addition to this the local market has been automatically protected as a result of the blockade enforced by war conditions on the import of foreign goods.

The peasants of the interior are therefore able to buy manufactured articles as never before. But there is little or nothing to buy. The enormously reduced Chinese industrial production is quite unable to meet this increased demand. What is now urgently needed is the reorganization of industry on the same basis as the successfully reorganized agriculture. China requires 30,000 industrial co-operatives.

The planners of the industrial co-operative movement propose the establishment of three "zones of economic defence". First, the big static units—the heavy industries, equipped with elaborate machinery and employing many workers. These will be engaged chiefly in making munitions. Because of their size they cannot easily be moved, so they should be located far out of reach of the enemy, in the extreme western provinces. Secondly, the medium-sized units, situated between the front and the rear. These should be semi-mobile, and equipped with machine-tools. Thirdly, the "guerilla" units. These co-operatives should use only light, easily portable tools. Their function would be to provide articles of immediate necessity to the military forces.

Since the Japanese army strikes only along easy lines of communication—a highroad, a railway, or a river—it should be possible for the "guerilla" units to operate around and even behind the enemy's positions. If the Japanese have occupied a large town, Chinese industrial co-operatives could still function in the neighbouring villages, providing manufactured articles necessary for the farming population. They would thus prevent areas adjacent to the Japanese garrisons from becoming economically colonized by Japanese goods. Their value, as centres of patriotic propaganda, would therefore be enormous.

Industrial co-operatives would also solve the refugee problem. They could absorb thousands of homeless and workless peasants, and divert the millions of dollars now being spent on refugee camps in the occupied areas, where destitute Chinese are merely kept alive until such time as the Japanese wish to exploit their labour power.

The difficulties in carrying out this scheme are, of course, immense. Chinese industry can only be transplanted and decentralized with the fullest co-operation of the industrialists and the workers themselves. The

Chinese are no fonder of moving than anybody else. Many will have to leave their homes and even their families behind them, and set off on a roundabout journey to distant parts of the country, where their native dialect is unintelligible, and where they feel themselves as isolated as an Italian farmer in Wales. In many cases the Government will have to carry out its projects by force: plant, tools, and the means of transport will have to be commandeered. The propaganda-drive for industrial migration will have to be redoubled. Above all, money will be needed—money for transport, money for compensation, money to buy portable machinery, Delco-plants, and charcoal-burning engines. The organizers of the movement plan to appeal to the League of Nations, and to the labour parties of friendly foreign States, for technical and financial aid. We only hope that they won't be disappointed by the results.

In this city—conquered, yet unoccupied by its conquerors—the mechanism of the old life is still ticking, but seems doomed to stop, like a watch dropped in the desert. In this city the gulf between society's two halves is too grossly wide for any bridge. There can be no compromise here. And we ourselves, though we wear out our shoes walking the slums, though we take notes, though we are genuinely shocked and indignant, belong, unescapably, to the other world. We return, always, to Number One House for lunch.

In our world, there are the garden-parties and the night-clubs, the hot baths and the cocktails, the singsong girls and the Ambassador's cook. In our world, European business men write to the local newspapers, complaining that the Chinese are cruel to pigs, and saying that the refugees should be turned out of the Settlement because they are beginning to smell. In our world "the only decent Japanese" (as all the British agree in describing him) defends the wholesale bombing of Canton on the ground that it is more humane than a military occupation of the city. In our world, an Englishman quite seriously suggests that the Japanese should be asked to drive the Chinese farmers from a plot of land enclosing a grave-mound which spoils the appearance of the garden.

And the well-meaning tourist, the liberal and humanitarian intellectual, can only wring his hands over all this and exclaim: "Oh dear, things are so awful here—so complicated. One doesn't know where to start."

"I know where *I* should start," says Mr Alley, with a ferocious snort. "They were starting quite nicely in 1927."

Picture Commentary

UNITED FRONT

The Chiangs   Madame

Li Tsung-jen (from the south)

Feng Yü-hsiang (from the north)

Du Yueh-seng (capitalist)

Chou En-lai (communist)

SOLDIERS AND CIVILIANS

Sian   Kiang-si

PROVINCIAL GOVERNORS

Staff Officer

Divisional Commander (Chang Tschen)

Officer (Major Yang)

Men

With legs

Without

CHILDREN IN UNIFORM

Railway Engineer (Shang-kui)

City Mayor (Canton)

Chauffeur

Press Bureau

T. Y. Liu

T. C. Liu

REPORTERS

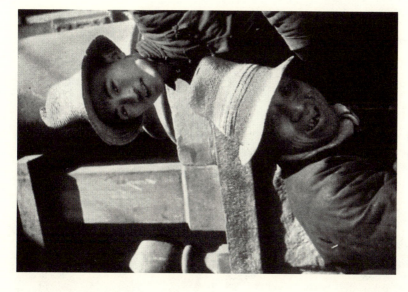

Coolies

Intellectual (C. C. Yeh)

FOREIGNERS

Ambassador (Sir Archibald Clark Kerr)

Adviser (W. H. Donald)

Press Photographer (Capa)

Special Correspondent (Peter Fleming)

Shanghai Business Man

White Russian Restaurant Proprietor

Catholic

Protestant

MISSIONARIES

Swiss (Dr Mooser)

Canadian (Dr Brown)

DOCTORS

Italian Captain

British Sailor

Japanese sentry

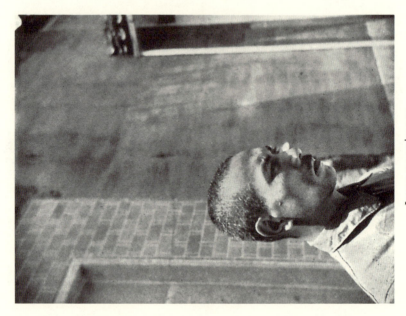

Japanese prisoner

WAR ZONE

In the Trenches

Temple in front line

Japanese front line

Enemy planes overhead

Chiang

The Innocent

The Guilty

Dynamited Railway Bridge

Houses (Chapei in Shanghai)

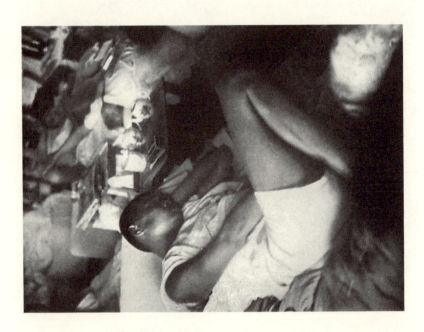

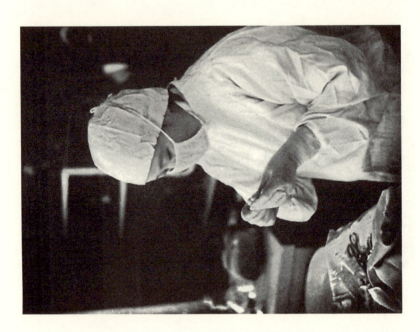

In Hospital

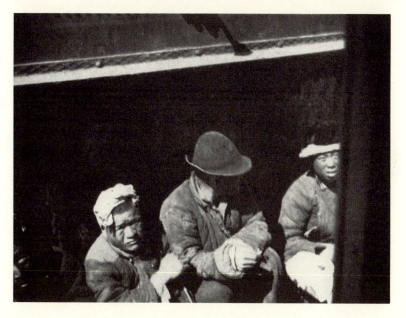

Refugees en route

Refugees in camp

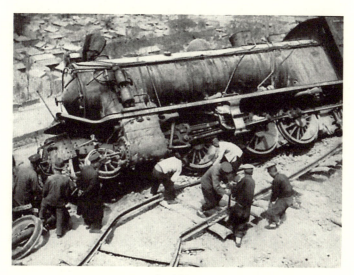

Accident

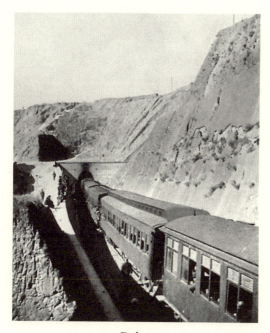

Delay

Passengers

Car-boy

Train Parasites

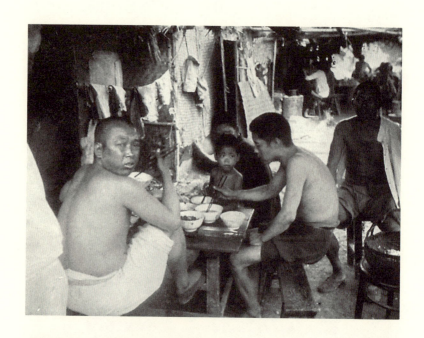

La Condition Humaine

Stills from *Fight to the Last*

Unknown Soldier

In Time of War

A Sonnet Sequence
with a verse commentary

I

So from the years the gifts were showered; each
Ran off with his at once into his life:
Bee took the politics that make a hive,
Fish swam as fish, peach settled into peach.

And were successful at the first endeavour;
The hour of birth their only time at college,
They were content with their precocious knowledge,
And knew their station and were good for ever.

Till finally there came a childish creature
On whom the years could model any feature,
And fake with ease a leopard or a dove;

Who by the lightest wind was changed and shaken,
And looked for truth and was continually mistaken,
And envied his few friends and chose his love.

II

They wondered why the fruit had been forbidden;
It taught them nothing new. They hid their pride,
But did not listen much when they were chidden;
They knew exactly what to do outside.

They left: immediately the memory faded
Of all they'd learnt; they could not understand
The dogs now who, before, had always aided;
The stream was dumb with whom they'd always planned.

They wept and quarrelled: freedom was so wild.
In front, maturity, as he ascended,
Retired like a horizon from the child;

The dangers and the punishments grew greater;
And the way back by angels was defended
Against the poet and the legislator.

III

Only a smell had feelings to make known,
Only an eye could point in a direction;
The fountain's utterance was itself alone;
The bird meant nothing: that was his projection

Who named it as he hunted it for food.
He felt the interest in his throat, and found
That he could send his servant to the wood,
Or kiss his bride to rapture with a sound.

They bred like locusts till they hid the green
And edges of the world: and he was abject,
And to his own creation became subject;

And shook with hate for things he'd never seen,
And knew of love without love's proper object,
And was oppressed as he had never been.

IV

He stayed: and was imprisoned in possession.
The seasons stood like guards about his ways,
The mountains chose the mother of his children,
And like a conscience the sun ruled his days.

Beyond him his young cousins in the city
Pursued their rapid and unnatural course,
Believed in nothing but were easy-going,
And treated strangers like a favourite horse.

And he changed little,
But took his colour from the earth,
And grew in likeness to his sheep and cattle.

The townsman thought him miserly and simple,
The poet wept and saw in him the truth,
And the oppressor held him up as an example.

V

His generous bearing was a new invention:
For life was slow; earth needed to be careless:
With horse and sword he drew the girls' attention;
He was the Rich, the Bountiful, the Fearless.

And to the young he came as a salvation;
They needed him to free them from their mothers,
And grew sharp-witted in the long migration,
And round his camp fires learnt all men are brothers.

But suddenly the earth was full: he was not wanted.
And he became the shabby and demented,
And took to drink to screw his nerves to murder;

Or sat in offices and stole,
And spoke approvingly of Law and Order,
And hated life with all his soul.

VI

He watched the stars and noted birds in flight;
The rivers flooded or the Empire fell:
He made predictions and was sometimes right;
His lucky guesses were rewarded well.

And fell in love with Truth before he knew her,
And rode into imaginary lands,
With solitude and fasting hoped to woo her,
And mocked at those who served her with their hands.

But her he never wanted to despise,
But listened always for her voice; and when
She beckoned to him, he obeyed in meekness,

And followed her and looked into her eyes;
Saw there reflected every human weakness,
And saw himself as one of many men.

VII

He was their servant—some say he was blind—
And moved among their faces and their things;
Their feeling gathered in him like a wind
And sang: they cried—"It is a God that sings"—

And worshipped him and set him up apart,
And made him vain, till he mistook for song
The little tremors of his mind and heart
At each domestic wrong.

Songs came no more: he had to make them.
With what precision was each strophe planned.
He hugged his sorrow like a plot of land,

And walked like an assassin through the town,
And looked at men and did not like them,
But trembled if one passed him with a frown.

VIII

He turned his field into a meeting-place,
And grew the tolerant ironic eye,
And formed the mobile money-changer's face,
And found the notion of equality.

And strangers were as brothers to his clocks,
And with his spires he made a human sky;
Museums stored his learning like a box,
And paper watched his money like a spy.

It grew so fast his life was overgrown,
And he forgot what once it had been made for,
And gathered into crowds and was alone,

And lived expensively and did without,
And could not find the earth which he had paid for,
Nor feel the love that he knew all about.

IX

They died and entered the closed life like nuns:
Even the very poor lost something; oppression
Was no more a fact; and the self-centred ones
Took up an even more extreme position.

And the kingly and the saintly also were
Distributed among the woods and oceans,
And touch our open sorrow everywhere,
Airs, waters, places, round our sex and reasons;

Are what we feed on as we make our choice.
We bring them back with promises to free them,
But as ourselves continually betray them:

They hear their deaths lamented in our voice,
But in our knowledge know we could restore them;
They could return to freedom; they would rejoice.

X

As a young child the wisest could adore him;
He felt familiar to them like their wives:
The very poor saved up their pennies for him,
And martyrs brought him presents of their lives.

But who could sit and play with him all day?
Their other needs were pressing, work, and bed:
The beautiful stone courts were built where they
Could leave him to be worshipped and well fed.

But he escaped. They were too blind to tell
That it was he who came with them to labour,
And talked and grew up with them like a neighbour:

To fear and greed those courts became a centre;
The poor saw there the tyrant's citadel,
And martyrs the lost face of the tormenter.

XI

He looked in all His wisdom from the throne
Down on the humble boy who kept the sheep,
And sent a dove; the dove returned alone:
Youth liked the music, but soon fell asleep.

But He had planned such future for the youth:
Surely His duty now was to compel;
For later he would come to love the truth,
And own his gratitude. The eagle fell.

It did not work: his conversation bored
The boy who yawned and whistled and made faces,
And wriggled free from fatherly embraces;

But with the eagle he was always willing
To go where it suggested, and adored
And learnt from it the many ways of killing.

XII

And the age ended, and the last deliverer died
In bed, grown idle and unhappy; they were safe:
The sudden shadow of the giant's enormous calf
Would fall no more at dusk across the lawn outside.

They slept in peace: in marshes here and there no doubt
A sterile dragon lingered to a natural death,
But in a year the spoor had vanished from the heath;
The kobold's knocking in the mountain petered out.

Only the sculptors and the poets were half sad,
And the pert retinue from the magician's house
Grumbled and went elsewhere. The vanquished powers were glad

To be invisible and free: without remorse
Struck down the sons who strayed into their course,
And ravished the daughters, and drove the fathers mad.

XIII

Certainly praise: let the song mount again and again
For life as it blossoms out in a jar or a face,
For the vegetable patience, the animal grace;
Some people have been happy; there have been great men.

But hear the morning's injured weeping, and know why:
Cities and men have fallen; the will of the Unjust
Has never lost its power; still, all princes must
Employ the Fairly-Noble unifying Lie.

History opposes its grief to our buoyant song:
The Good Place has not been; our star has warmed to birth
A race of promise that has never proved its worth;

The quick new West is false; and prodigious, but wrong
This passive flower-like people who for so long
In the Eighteen Provinces have constructed the earth.

XIV

Yes, we are going to suffer, now; the sky
Throbs like a feverish forehead; pain is real;
The groping searchlights suddenly reveal
The little natures that will make us cry,

Who never quite believed they could exist,
Not where we were. They take us by surprise
Like ugly long-forgotten memories,
And like a conscience all the guns resist.

Behind each sociable home-loving eye
The private massacres are taking place;
All Women, Jews, the Rich, the Human Race.

The mountains cannot judge us when we lie:
We dwell upon the earth; the earth obeys
The intelligent and evil till they die.

XV

Engines bear them through the sky: they're free
And isolated like the very rich;
Remote like savants, they can only see
The breathing city as a target which

Requires their skill; will never see how flying
Is the creation of ideas they hate,
Nor how their own machines are always trying
To push through into life. They chose a fate

The islands where they live did not compel.
Though earth may teach our proper discipline,
At any time it will be possible

To turn away from freedom and become
Bound like the heiress in her mother's womb,
And helpless as the poor have always been.

XVI

Here war is simple like a monument:
A telephone is speaking to a man;
Flags on a map assert that troops were sent;
A boy brings milk in bowls. There is a plan

For living men in terror of their lives,
Who thirst at nine who were to thirst at noon,
And can be lost and are, and miss their wives,
And, unlike an idea, can die too soon.

But ideas can be true although men die,
And we can watch a thousand faces
Made active by one lie:

And maps can really point to places
Where life is evil now:
Nanking; Dachau.

XVII

They are and suffer; that is all they do:
A bandage hides the place where each is living,
His knowledge of the world restricted to
The treatment that the instruments are giving.

And lie apart like epochs from each other
—Truth in their sense is how much they can bear;
It is not talk like ours, but groans they smother—
And are remote as plants; we stand elsewhere.

For who when healthy can become a foot?
Even a scratch we can't recall when cured,
But are boistrous in a moment and believe

In the common world of the uninjured, and cannot
Imagine isolation. Only happiness is shared,
And anger, and the idea of love.

XVIII

Far from the heart of culture he was used:
Abandoned by his general and his lice,
Under a padded quilt he closed his eyes
And vanished. He will not be introduced

When this campaign is tidied into books:
No vital knowledge perished in his skull;
His jokes were stale; like wartime, he was dull;
His name is lost for ever like his looks.

He neither knew nor chose the Good, but taught us,
And added meaning like a comma, when
He turned to dust in China that our daughters

Be fit to love the earth, and not again
Disgraced before the dogs; that, where are waters,
Mountains and houses, may be also men.

XIX

But in the evening the oppression lifted;
The peaks came into focus; it had rained:
Across the lawns and cultured flowers drifted
The conversation of the highly trained.

The gardeners watched them pass and priced their shoes;
A chauffeur waited, reading in the drive,
For them to finish their exchange of views;
It seemed a picture of the private life.

Far off, no matter what good they intended,
The armies waited for a verbal error
With all the instruments for causing pain:

And on the issue of their charm depended
A land laid waste, with all its young men slain,
The women weeping, and the towns in terror.

XX

They carry terror with them like a purse,
And flinch from the horizon like a gun;
And all the rivers and the railways run
Away from Neighbourhood as from a curse.

They cling and huddle in the new disaster
Like children sent to school, and cry in turn;
For Space has rules they cannot hope to learn,
Time speaks a language they will never master.

We live here. We lie in the Present's unopened
Sorrow; its limits are what we are.
The prisoner ought never to pardon his cell.

Can future ages ever escape so far,
Yet feel derived from everything that happened,
Even from us, that even this was well?

XXI

The life of man is never quite completed;
The daring and the chatter will go on:
But, as an artist feels his power gone,
These walk the earth and know themselves defeated.

Some could not bear nor break the young and mourn for
The wounded myths that once made nations good,
Some lost a world they never understood,
Some saw too clearly all that man was born for.

Loss is their shadow-wife, Anxiety
Receives them like a grand hotel; but where
They may regret they must; their life, to hear

The call of the forbidden cities, see
The stranger watch them with a happy stare,
And Freedom hostile in each home and tree.

XXII

Simple like all dream wishes, they employ
The elementary language of the heart,
And speak to muscles of the need for joy:
The dying and the lovers soon to part

Hear them and have to whistle. Always new,
They mirror every change in our position;
They are our evidence of what we do;
They speak directly to our lost condition.

Think in this year what pleased the dancers best:
When Austria died and China was forsaken,
Shanghai in flames and Teruel retaken,

France put her case before the world; "Partout
Il y a de la joie." America addressed
The earth: "Do you love me as I love you?"

XXIII

When all the apparatus of report
Confirms the triumph of our enemies;
Our bastion pierced, our army in retreat,
Violence successful like a new disease,

And Wrong a charmer everywhere invited;
When we regret that we were ever born:
Let us remember all who seemed deserted.
To-night in China let me think of one,

Who through ten years of silence worked and waited,
Until in Muzot all his powers spoke,
And everything was given once for all:

And with the gratitude of the Completed
He went out in the winter night to stroke
That little tower like a great animal.

XXIV

No, not their names. It was the others who built
Each great coercive avenue and square,
Where men can only recollect and stare,
The really lonely with the sense of guilt

Who wanted to persist like that for ever;
The unloved had to leave material traces:
But these need nothing but our better faces,
And dwell in them, and know that we shall never

Remember who we are nor why we're needed.
Earth grew them as a bay grows fishermen
Or hills a shepherd; they grew ripe and seeded;

And the seeds clung to us; even our blood
Was able to revive them; and they grew again;
Happy their wish and mild to flower and flood.

XXV

Nothing is given: we must find our law.
Great buildings jostle in the sun for domination;
Behind them stretch like sorry vegetation
The low recessive houses of the poor.

We have no destiny assigned us:
Nothing is certain but the body; we plan
To better ourselves; the hospitals alone remind us
Of the equality of man.

Children are really loved here, even by police:
They speak of years before the big were lonely,
And will be lost.

        And only
The brass bands throbbing in the parks foretell
Some future reign of happiness and peace.

We learn to pity and rebel.

XXVI

Always far from the centre of our names,
The little workshop of love: yes, but how wrong
We were about the old manors and the long
Abandoned Folly and the children's games.

Only the acquisitive expects a quaint
Unsaleable product, something to please
An artistic girl; it's the selfish who sees
In every impractical beggar a saint.

We can't believe that we ourselves designed it,
A minor item of our daring plan
That caused no trouble; we took no notice of it.

Disaster comes, and we're amazed to find it
The single project that since work began
Through all the cycle showed a steady profit.

XXVII

Wandering lost upon the mountains of our choice,
Again and again we sign for an ancient South,
For the warm nude ages of instinctive poise,
For the taste of joy in the innocent mouth.

Asleep in our huts, how we dream of a part
In the glorious balls of the future; each intricate maze
Has a plan, and the disciplined movements of the heart
Can follow for ever and ever its harmless ways.

We envy streams and houses that are sure:
But we are articled to error; we
Were never nude and calm like a great door,

And never will be perfect like the fountains;
We live in freedom by necessity,
A mountain people dwelling among mountains.

Commentary

Season inherits legally from dying season;
Protected by the wide peace of the sun, the planets
Continue their circulations; and the galaxy

Is free for ever to revolve like an enormous biscuit:
With all his engines round him and the summer flowers,
Little upon his little earth, man contemplates

The universe of which he is both judge and victim;
A rarity in an uncommon corner, gazes
On the great trackways where his tribe and truth are nothing.

Certainly the growth of the fore-brain has been a success:
He has not got lost in a backwater like the lampshell
Or the limpet; he has not died out like the super-lizards.

His boneless worm-like ancestors would be amazed
At the upright position, the breasts, the four-chambered heart,
The clandestine evolution in the mother's shadow.

"Sweet is it," say the doomed, "to be alive though wretched,"
And the young emerging from the closed parental circle,
To whose uncertainty the certain years present

Their syllabus of limitless anxiety and labour,
At first feel nothing but the gladness of their freedom,
Are happy in the new embraces and the open talk.

But liberty to be and weep has never been sufficient;
The winds surround our griefs, the unfenced sky
To all our failures is a taciturn unsmiling witness.

And not least here, among this humorous and hairless people
Who like a cereal have inherited these valleys:
Tarim nursed them; Thibet was the tall rock of their protection,

And where the Yellow River shifts its course, they learnt
How to live well, though ruin threatened often.
For centuries they looked in fear towards the northern defiles,

But now must turn and gather like a fist to strike
Wrong coming from the sea, from those whose paper houses
Tell of their origin among the coral islands;

Who even to themselves deny a human freedom,
And dwell in the estranging tyrant's vision of the earth
In a calm stupor under their blood-spotted flag.

Here danger works a civil reconciliation,
Interior hatreds are resolved upon this foreign foe,
And will-power to resist is growing like a prosperous city.

For the invader now is deadly and impartial as a judge:
Down country footpaths, from each civic sky,
His anger blows alike upon the rich, and all

Who dwell within the crevices of destitution,
On those with a laborious lifetime to recall, and those,
The innocent and short whose dreams contain no children.

While in an international and undamaged quarter,
Casting our European shadows on Shanghai,
Walking unhurt among the banks, apparently immune

Below the monuments of an acquisitive society,
With friends and books and money and the traveller's freedom,
We are compelled to realize that our refuge is a sham.

For this material contest that has made Hongkew
A terror and a silence, and Chapei a howling desert,
Is but the local variant of a struggle in which all,

The elderly, the amorous, the young, the handy and the thoughtful,
Those to whom feeling is a science, those to whom study
Of all that can be added and compared is a consuming love,

With those whose brains are empty as a school in August,
And those in whom the urge to action is so strong
They cannot read a letter without whispering, all

In cities, deserts, ships, in lodging near the port,
Discovering the past of strangers in a library,
Creating their own future on a bed, each with his treasure,

Self-confident among the laughter and the *petits verres,*
Or motionless and lonely like a moping cormorant,
In all their living are profoundly implicated.

This is one sector and one movement of the general war
Between the dead and the unborn, the Real and the Pretended,
Which for the creature who creates, communicates, and chooses,

The only animal aware of lack of finish,
In essence is eternal. When we emerged from holes
And blinked in the warm sunshine of the Laufen Ice Retreat,

Thinking of Nature as a close and loyal kinsman,
On every acre the opponents faced each other,
And we were far within the zone where casualties begin.

Now in a world that has no localized events,
Where not a tribe exists without its dossier,
And the machine has taught us how, to the Non-Human,

That unprogressive blind society that knows
No argument except the absolute and violent veto,
Our colours, creeds and sexes are identical,

The issue is the same. Some uniforms are new,
Some have changed sides; but the campaign continues:
Still unachieved is *Jen,* the Truly Human.

This is the epoch of the Third Great Disappointment:
The First was the collapse of that slave-owning empire
Whose yawning magistrate asked, "What is truth?"

Upon its ruins rose the Universal Churches:
Men camped like tourists under their tremendous shadows,
United by a common sense of human failure,

Their certain knowledge only of the timeless fields
Where the Unchanging Happiness received the faithful,
And the Eternal Nightmare waited to devour the wicked.

In which a host of workers, famous and obscure,
Meaning to do no more than use their eyes,
Not knowing what they did, then sapped belief;

Put in its place a neutral dying star,
Where Justice could not visit. Self was the one city,
The cell where each must find his comfort and his pain,

The body nothing but a useful favourite machine
To go upon errands of love and to run the house,
While the mind in its study spoke with its private God.

But now that wave which already was washing the heart,
When the cruel Turk stormed the gates of Constantine's city,
When Galileo muttered to himself, "*sed movet*",

And Descartes thought, "I am because I think",
Today, all spent, is silently withdrawing itself:
Unhappy he or she who after it is sucked.

Never before was the Intelligence so fertile,
The Heart more stunted. The human field became
Hostile to brotherhood and feeling like a forest.

Machines devised by harmless clergymen and boys
Attracted men like magnets from the marl and clay
Into towns on the coal-measures, to a kind of freedom,

Where the abstinent with the landless drove a bitter bargain,
But sowed in that act the seeds of an experienced hatred,
Which, germinating long in tenement and gas-lit cellar,

Is choking now the aqueducts of our affection.
Knowledge of their colonial suffering has cut off
The Hundred Families like an attack of shyness;

The apprehensive rich pace up and down
Their narrow compound of success; in every body
The ways of living are disturbed; intrusive as a sill,

Fear builds enormous ranges casting shadows,
Heavy, bird-silencing, upon the outer world,
Hills that our grief sighs over like a Shelley, parting

All that we feel from all that we perceive,
Desire from Data; and the Thirteen gay Companions
Grow sullen now and quarrelsome as mountain tribes.

We wander on the earth, or err from bed to bed
In search of home, and fail, and weep for the lost ages
Before Because became As If, or rigid Certainty

The Chances Are. The base hear us, and the violent
Who long to calm our guilt with murder, and already
Have not been slow to turn our wish to their advantage.

On every side they make their brazen offer:
Now in that Catholic country with the shape of Cornwall,
Where Europe first became a term of pride,

North of the Alps where dark hair turns to blonde,
In Germany now loudest, land without a centre
Where the sad plains are like a sounding rostrum,

And on these tidy and volcanic summits near us now,
From which the Black Stream hides the Tuscarora Deep,
The voice is quieter but the more inhuman and triumphant.

By wire and wireless, in a score of bad translations,
They give their simple message to the world of man:
"Man can have Unity if Man will give up Freedom.

The State is real, the Individual is wicked;
Violence shall synchronize your movements like a tune,
And Terror like a frost shall halt the flood of thinking.

Barrack and bivouac shall be your friendly refuge,
And racial pride shall tower like a public column
And confiscate for safety every private sorrow.

Leave Truth to the police and us; we know the Good;
We build the Perfect City time shall never alter;
Our Law shall guard you always like a cirque of mountains,

Your Ignorance keep off evil like a dangerous sea;
You shall be consummated in the General Will,
Your children innocent and charming as the beasts."

All the great conquerors sit upon their platform,
Lending their sombre weight of practical experience:
Ch'in Shih Huang Ti who burnt the scholars' books,

Chaka the mad who segregated the two sexes,
And *Genghis Khan* who thought mankind should be destroyed,
And *Diocletian* the administrator make impassioned speeches.

Napoleon claps who found religion useful,
And all who passed deception of the People, or who said
Like Little *Frederick*, "I shall see that it is done".

While many famous clerks support their programme:
Plato the good, despairing of the average man,
With sad misgiving signs their manifesto;

Shang-tzu approves their principle of Nothing Private;
The author of *The Prince* will heckle; *Hobbes* will canvass,
With generalizing *Hegel* and quiet *Bosanquet*.

And every family and every heart is tempted:
The earth debates; the Fertile Crescent argues;
Even the little towns upon the way to somewhere,

Those desert flowers the aeroplane now fertilizes,
Quarrel on this; in England far away,
Behind the high tides and the navigable estuaries;

In the Far West, in absolutely free America,
In melancholy Hungary, and clever France
Where ridicule has acted a historic role,

And here where the rice-grain nourishes these patient households
The ethic of the feudal citadel has impregnated,
Thousands believe, and millions are half-way to a conviction.

While others have accepted *Pascal*'s wager and resolve
To take whatever happens as the will of God,
Or with *Spinoza* vote that evil be unreal.

Nor do our leaders help; we know them now
For humbugs full of vain dexterity, invoking
A gallery of ancestors, pursuing still the mirage

Of long dead grandeurs whence the interest has absconded,
As Fahrenheit in an odd corner of great Celsius' kingdom
Might mumble of the summers measured once by him.

Yet all the same we have our faithful sworn supporters
Who never lost their faith in knowledge or in man,
But worked so eagerly that they forgot their food

And never noticed death or old age coming on,
Prepared for freedom as *Kuo Hsi* for inspiration,
Waiting it calmly like the coming of an honoured guest.

Some looked at falsehood with the candid eye of children,
Some had a woman's ear to catch injustice,
Some took Necessity, and knew her, and she brought forth Freedom.

Some of our dead are famous, but they would not care:
Evil is always personal and spectacular,
But goodness needs the evidence of all our lives,

And, even to exist, it must be shared as truth,
As freedom or as happiness. (For what is happiness
If not to witness joy upon the features of another?)

They did not live to be remembered specially as noble,
Like those who cultivated only cucumbers and melons
To prove that they were rich; and when we praise their names,

They shake their heads in warning, chiding us to give
Our gratitude to the Invisible College of the Humble,
Who through the ages have accomplished everything essential.

And stretch around our struggle as the normal landscape,
And mingle, fluent with our living, like the winds and waters,
The dust of all the dead that reddens every sunset;

Giving us courage to confront our enemies,
Not only on the Grand Canal, or in Madrid,
Across the campus of a university city,

But aid us everywhere, that in the lovers' bedroom,
The white laboratory, the school, the public meeting,
The enemies of life may be more passionately attacked.

And, if we care to listen, we can always hear them:
"Men are not innocent as beasts and never can be,
Man can improve himself but never will be perfect,

Only the free have disposition to be truthful,
Only the truthful have the interest to be just,
Only the just possess the will-power to be free.

For common justice can determine private freedom,
As a clear sky can tempt men to astronomy,
Or a peninsula persuade them to be sailors.

You talked of Liberty, but were not just; and now
Your enemies have called your bluff; for in your city,
Only the man behind the rifle had free-will.

One wish is common to you both, the wish to build
A world united as that Europe was in which
The flint-faced exile wrote his three-act comedy.

Lament not its decay; that shell was too constricting:
The years of private isolation had their lesson,
And in the interest of intelligence were necessary.

Now in the clutch of crisis and the bloody hour
You must defeat your enemies or perish, but remember,
Only by those who reverence it can life be mastered;

Only a whole and happy conscience can stand up
And answer their bleak lie; among the just,
And only there, is Unity compatible with Freedom."

Night falls on China; the great arc of travelling shadow
Moves over land and ocean, altering life:
Thibet already silent, the packed Indias cooling,

Inert in the paralysis of caste. And though in Africa
The vegetation still grows fiercely like the young,
And in the cities that receive the slanting radiations

The lucky are at work, and most still know they suffer,
The dark will touch them soon: night's tiny noises
Will echo vivid in the owl's developed ear,

Vague in the anxious sentry's; and the moon look down
On battlefields and dead men lying, heaped like treasure,
On lovers ruined in a brief embrace, on ships

Where exiles watch the sea: and in the silence
The cry that streams out into the indifferent spaces,
And never stops or slackens, may be heard more clearly,

Above the everlasting murmur of the woods and rivers,
And more insistent than the lulling answer of the waltzes,
Or hum of printing-presses turning forests into lies;

As now I hear it, rising round me from Shanghai,
And mingling with the distant mutter of guerilla fighting,
The voice of Man: *"O teach me to outgrow my madness.*

It's better to be sane than mad, or liked than dreaded;
It's better to sit down to nice meals than to nasty;
It's better to sleep two than single; it's better to be happy.

Ruffle the perfect manners of the frozen heart,
And once again compel it to be awkward and alive,
To all it suffered once a weeping witness.

Clear from the head the masses of impressive rubbish;
Rally the lost and trembling forces of the will,
Gather them up and let them loose upon the earth,

Till they construct at last a human justice,
The contribution of our star, within the shadow
Of which uplifting, loving, and constraining power
All other reasons may rejoice and operate."

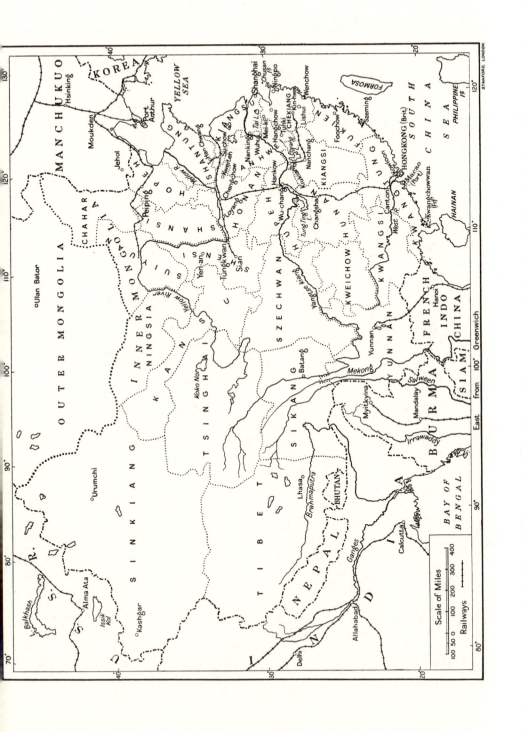

STANFORD, LONDON

APPENDICES

Auden as Anthologist and Editor

THIS appendix lists books, magazines, and broadcasts for which Auden gathered and introduced work by other writers. In addition to the published and broadcast items noted below, Auden had a hand in the preparation of *Prose Pieces and Poems,* by Anthony Abbott, published by Victor Gollancz in 1929. This was a collection of poems by an Oxford undergraduate who died at nineteen in March 1928. A note on the verso of the title page states, "Grateful thanks are due to Mr D. A. Sington and Mr W. H. Auden, for their kind help in the arrangement of these Verses and Essays."

Auden also began work on a few editorial projects that he never completed. The first of these was a three-volume study of preparatory-school, public-school, and university life that he and Isherwood conceived probably early in 1928 (see Appendix V). The study was to consist entirely of personal letters, excerpts from school and university magazines, and other documents that would display the unexamined attitudes fostered by English schools and universities. All that survives of this project, and probably all that was ever completed, was a notebook now in the Berg Collection of the New York Public Library, titled "Letters[:] Public School", in which Auden transcribed letters from Old Marlburnians to the Marlborough School magazine, and letters written from South America to Auden's Oxford friend Gabriel Carritt by one of Carritt's Sedbergh schoolmates. Auden also included cuttings from the magazine of his own preparatory school, the *St Edmund's School Chronicle.* One of these cuttings is a report in the June 1917 number titled "The Field-Day in the Devil's Punch Bowl", which describes Auden's participation in the drill of the school's Rifle Club.

In late 1936 or early 1937, in another notebook now in the Berg Collection, Auden transcribed dozens of quotations from representatives of youth groups, churches and other religious organizations, Nazi and fascist parties, and other statements of conservative and right-wing positions. No record exists of Auden's purpose in copying these passages, but it may have been for a collection comparable to his earlier project.

Late in 1937 or early in 1938 Auden apparently made plans to compile for Faber & Faber an anthology of poetry for children. On 8 February 1938 his agents prepared a memorandum of agreement for the book, but Auden had left a few weeks earlier on his journey to China, and nothing came of the project after he returned in July. T. S. Eliot reminded him in a letter of 6 January 1939 that he had planned to undertake this work after his return from China, but Auden, who was about to leave for America, seems never to have mentioned the book again in his letters to Eliot.

Oxford Poetry 1926

This annual anthology, begun in 1910, was edited by undergraduates. The volume for 1926 was edited by Charles Plumb and Auden, who wrote their preface probably early in the summer of 1926 (see p. 739). The book was published in November 1926 by Basil Blackwell; an American edition was published by D. Appleton, New York, in 1927. Auden included three of his poems in the volume.

Charles Plumb recalled: "I met him [Auden] in the rooms of a mutual friend in . . . Exeter [College] and was so taken with his conversation and evident brilliance that I realised that he would be an ideal editor of the next volume of Oxford Poetry . . . for which Basil Blackwell had asked me to recommend a colleague. I don't think I had ever seen any of his own writing" (letter to Mendelson, 27 August 1975).

Auden may have helped set the tone of a note headed "Oxford Poetry" that appeared in the *Cherwell*, 15 May 1926, p. 92:

> The Editors of *Oxford Poetry* are now ready to receive contributions c/o Basil Blackwell. We understand that this market shows a firmer tone and that profusion of words without some mental control will meet a steely refusal. As someone said, amongst poems at Oxford just now there are too many of "these 'ere finicky contraptions."

Oxford Poetry 1927

The volume, edited by Auden and C. Day-Lewis, was published in November 1927 by Basil Blackwell; an American edition was published by D. Appleton early in 1928.

Auden chose Day-Lewis as coeditor, with Basil Blackwell's approval. A request for contributions, under the heading "Oxford Poetry, 1927", appeared in two undergraduate weeklies, the *Isis*, 15 June 1927, and the *Cherwell*, 18 June 1927:

> The Editors are now ready to receive contributions. They would be grateful to intending contributors if these would forward their MSS. before the end of term, or earlier if possible.—W. H. AUDEN, C. DAY-LEWIS, *Editors*.

(In the *Isis*, "editors" was not capitalized.)

Auden and Day-Lewis began their preface in late June or early July, and Auden may have revised or completed it later in July (see p. 739).

Each of the editors solicited from his closest friend a poem meant to appear anonymously at the end of the alphabetical sequence of named authors. Auden wrote to Isherwood in June 1927:

> I am editing Oxford Poetry this year. I shall not contribute other than a lengthy very highbrow and possibly offensive preface. Do write us a poem for it, to go in under anon.

Isherwood sent a short poem, "Souvenirs des Vacances", for which Auden thanked him in a letter written early in July: "Thanks awfully for the Souvenirs, which will do admirably." The other anonymous poem in the volume, "An Ornithological View of Existence", was almost certainly commissioned by Day-Lewis from Rex Warner, who was a passionate bird-watcher. Five more serious poems by Warner appeared in the volume under his name. After telling Isherwood that he would not contribute to the volume, Auden included one of his own poems, and Day-Lewis contributed one of his.

The Larchfieldian

Auden was a master at the Larchfield Academy in Helensburgh from April 1930 through June 1932. He probably took some part in editing the school magazine, the *Larchfieldian*, which had been begun or revived by the school's headmaster in 1927 and continued publication through 1931. No copy of the magazine is known to survive. Auden may have worked only on an issue that appeared in December 1931. He told Michael Roberts on 11 December 1931: "I have been very busy setting examinations and correcting proofs of a school magazine." The *Helensburgh and Gareloch Times*, 30 December 1931, reported in its column "Notes on the Way" that a new issue of the *Larchfieldian* recorded the progress of the boys in scholastic work, playing field, and gymnasium—"a record of considerable value". The same column noted that C. Day Lewis (who had by this time dropped the hyphen), Auden's predecessor at the school, had just published *From Feathers to Iron*, and that Day Lewis's closest affinity was with Auden "who is apparently the direct inspiration of one of the best poems in the book". It seems likely that Auden arranged for this publicity, in the same way that he had probably arranged to plant in an earlier column a report of Naomi Mitchison's favorable review of his 1930 *Poems*. (I am indebted to Stan Smith for much of this information.)

The Badger

Auden began working as a master at the Downs School, Colwall, in September 1932, and soon after he arrived started organizing a school magazine. Until he left the school in July 1935, Auden anonymously shepherded five biennial numbers of the *Badger* through the press, and apparently selected most of the contents. The first five numbers contained unsigned prefatory notes probably written by Auden and the headmaster, Geoffrey Hoyland, who encouraged the magazine's creation. Hoyland's half-brother and successor, W. F. Hoyland, wrote in the Autumn 1959 number that Auden "was largely responsible for launching *The Badger*".

The first number, dated Spring 1933, opened with the following note. (Here, and in the remaining notes, the hanging indents of the original are reduced to block paragraphs and the first few words of each paragraph are reduced from capitals to ordinary text.)

APOLOGY

THE BADGER makes his bow. He is late in appearing, choosing to remain in his burrow until his new coat and other embellishments were ready rather than to appear earlier without them.

A School magazine is apt to be a deadly affair, dull as ditch water. THE BADGER would rather die than be dull, and he *will* die, for all his new coat, if Downians past and present do not keep him alive and lively by their contributions.

THE BADGER will not be content to print, year by year, dull records of forgotten matches and painstaking essays that had better have been left to the waste-paper basket. His aim is to bring together within his covers the *live* work of past and present Downians, together with just enough of chronicle and comment to keep us all in touch with one another and with the School.

What rot! you may say when you read some of the contributions to this first number. Well, why not? If you are an Old Downian you wrote a deal of rot yourself when you were here—and are probably doing so still, if the truth were known. If you are a *present* Downian there is no doubt on the matter at all and no more to be said.

Let us agree that live nonsense is better than dead wisdom and that it is fitter that THE BADGER's pages should contain the natural outpourings of Smith Minor, even if they be nonsense, than his painful attempts to write like his elders and betters (who often, if they did but know it, write worse nonsense themselves). Besides, among the chaff you may well, if you search carefully, find grains of wheat and of that which is better than wheat, for Smith Minor sometimes sees and thinks and even says things that are hidden to the Important Smith Major—things that are very worth while indeed.

So THE BADGER would like to publish work by eight-year-olds and nine-year-olds and ten-year-olds and any-year-olds. He wants First Form boys and Sixth Form boys and Old Boys and Staff, past and present, to send him their work, poetry or prose or pictures, for his future numbers. So long as the work is alive it will be printed—if there is room.

The cover and various headpieces, tailpieces and ornaments appearing in this number have been designed for us by Mr Claughton Pellew. Those past or present Downians who are skilled at woodcuts or pen and ink designs will perhaps, from time to time, send us contributions of the same kind from which blocks can be made. Nothing will be more welcome, for they will be of permanent value to THE BADGER.

Finally, if you climb a new mountain or discover a new fungus or in any other way achieve adventure in body, mind or spirit, will you tell us about it?

THE EDITORS.

The second number, dated Autumn 1933, included verses by Auden (signed "Anon.") about a junior matron at the school. The magazine opened with this prefatory note, which, as in all later numbers edited by Auden, lacked the laconic signature, "The Editors", that had appeared in the first number:

APOLOGIA

THE BADGER bows again. He thanks his many friends for their kind and generous greeting to his first number, and makes bold to present his second. Comments and criticisms will be very welcome, for he is anxious to improve himself and please his readers.

The first number has produced a crop of letters and messages from old Downians, some of whom have been out of touch with the School and its doings for many years.

One has been unearthed in the middle of New York, and has the distinction of being the very first Downian of all, for (as Mrs Jones reminds us) when the School was first opened he made a point of turning up the day before so as to make certain of being the first boy.

Another writes from New South Wales, and after sending us his congratulations adds a request for "a couple of panoramic views of the School— the whole of it—with all the new buildings, gadgets, and attachments thrown in. You see, I'm sure that half of the three hundred old Downians have forgotten what their old school looks like, and some of them don't possess television sets to see over *14,000* miles."

We will do our best with the panoramic view, but Einstein will have to produce a new theory and practice of relativity if we are to get all the school buildings into one picture.

The illustrations in this number include, as we promised, the work of both past and present Downians. Michael Mounsey is, so far as we know, the first O.D. to exhibit in the Royal Academy, and we are glad to reproduce one of his wood engravings as our frontispiece. In this and future numbers we shall add the age instead of the Form of boy contributors in brackets after their names, and in the case of Old Downians, the year of leaving.

We are glad to print two articles by Old Downians, and we hope that more of them, especially those who live or travel over seas, will send us contributions.

We owe a number of new head and tail pieces to Mr Pellew, and others to Mr Telfer, while one has been supplied by a boy still at the School. Such adornments are always welcome contributions.

The third number, with this prefatory note, appeared in Spring 1934:

PROLOGUE

It was Apologia last time, and Apology the time before; will someone invent a suitable word that is less pompous than "Editorial"?

A prologue is the preface to a play. This number of THE BADGER is largely composed of play, so perhaps the word is not so ill-fitting. Boys have been playing with words, fitting them together into shapes that are pleasing, or with ideas that chime together even if they seem inconsequent.

It may seem strange that Bishops should be coupled with railway engines, moons with glass-cases, and a worm with a penny; but is it any stranger than that we should eat cucumber with salmon and red currant jelly with mutton, or than the familiar partnerships between cats and fiddles, cows and moons, and the walrus and the carpenter?

THE BADGER, be that as it may, contains in this issue an unusual amount of young boys' work. You may think there is too much of it, or you may like it; in either case the Editors will be glad of your criticism.

The flow of contributions is increasing, and several articles have been squeezed out in consequence. The hobby report, promised in our last number, will appear more appropriately next Autumn with an account of the work shown in the Exhibition. The library section, with reviews of new books, has also been held over till October.

Finally, THE BADGER is not at present a paying proposition, and is running at a loss. We do not intend to close down; on the contrary we mean to expand our pages and our scope as time and experience advance, but we appeal to all our readers, especially Old Downians, to help to make our circulation as wide as possible.

The fourth number, dated Autumn 1934, included the first part of Auden's "In Search of Dracula" (p. 72), and opened with the following note. ("Adam", a sculpture of a child sitting on a plinth, is on the grounds of the school.)

APOLOGIA

Christmas numbers of prominent periodicals frequently appear in the early Autumn, so it is but redressing the balance when the Autumn number of THE BADGER appears at Christmas. Moreover, it gives THE BADGER the opportunity of wishing his readers a Happy Christmas, which obviously could not be done in October.

THE BADGER appears in a new coat, designed for him by Mr Feild. The various legs, arms, and heads which appear on the cover are, we are assured, authentic portions of present Downians and do fit together somehow.

The balance of Old Downians' and present Downians' contributions is still too much in favour of the latter. We hope that more and more O.Ds., as time goes on, will send us accounts of their adventures.

Two members of the staff, together with an O.D., disappeared into the mists of Central Europe in a Morris (more vocal than dependable) during the Summer holidays. Something of what they did may be gathered from "In Search of Dracula"—to be continued in our next.

The frontispiece in this issue is a photograph of the oil painting by Dr T. H. Somervell which now hangs in the Library as a memorial to J. D. Hoyland.

Our spring number which, true to type, will probably appear early in the Summer term, will contain more literary items and one or two that have been crowded out of this issue, including the overdue Library section, and a photograph of "Adam".

If your subscription is due, will you send it in to the Secretary at the School? That will help us to balance the budget.

The Spring 1935 number, with the photograph promised in the preceding issue, and the second part of "In Search of Dracula", opened with this note:

PROLOGUE

This may be described as a modest attempt at an "Art Number" of THE BADGER. We are illustrating a number of oil paintings done by boys during the past twelve months.

The art work in the School is showing an interesting development, as will be seen from the pictures we reproduce. Besides putting down on canvas what they see, some boys are making the attempt to put down what they feel.

It is a pity that colour reproduction is beyond the resources of THE BADGER, for such a painting as "Toothache" depends more on its colour values than on its form.

Some may feel that pictures composed of abstract forms and colours that do not represent real objects are not suitable for adorning their drawing-room walls. This may be true, but it does not follow that the painting of them is not very worth while.

By way of contrast and complement to the boys' work we reproduce a painting by an Old Downian and one by Mr Feild. A boy's photograph also finds a place for the first time; we hope there will be many such in the future.

So much for art. With this number we reach the half-way point in Mr Jones's memories of "The Downs in Times Past". We hope if possible to include in future numbers one or two photographs of the school in early days.

Auden continued to write topical verse for the *Badger* after he left the school in 1935. One poem appeared in the Autumn 1935 number, and two more, together with his preface to the exhibition of paintings by Downs School pupils at the Redfern Gallery (p. 388), in the Autumn 1937 number, after he had filled in as English master during the summer term, from May through July.

THE POET'S TONGUE

Auden compiled this anthology in collaboration with John Garrett, who had been an undergraduate at Exeter College, Oxford, and probably met Auden through Auden's tutor Nevill Coghill. The anthology was perhaps the issue of a brief affair between Garrett and Auden in the autumn of 1934, when Garrett was head of English at Whitgift School in Croydon, and they jotted down in a Wimbledon pub a list of the poems they would like to see in an ideal anthology for use in schools, a book that would be arranged in an arbitrary sequence of alphabetical order of first lines. (In 1935 Garrett founded the Raynes Park County Grammar School nearby; Auden wrote a school song for him in 1936.) Auden and Garrett conceived an anthology in two volumes, one for younger children, the other for older ones, and on 17 October 1934 Garrett presented the preliminary plans to G. H. Bickers of George Bell & Sons. Bell published the two volumes on 20 June 1935, with the volumes described on the title page as "First Part" and "Second Part". A one-volume trade edition, with four paragraphs omitted from the introduction, appeared on 8 August 1935, but the trade edition was an afterthought to a book primarily designed for school use. A few months before publication, T. S. Eliot heard a rumor that Auden was compiling an anthology of verse, and asked if it might be offered to Faber & Faber, who were themselves contemplating such an anthology; Auden replied on 23 March 1935: "Yes I am doing an anthology for Bells but it's purely a beaks' affair so I don't imagine it would conflict with yours."

Auden apparently sent an early version of the preface and selection to Bell in February 1935. In an internal memorandum, Bickers listed various problems with these. Of the preface he wrote: "This won't do at all. The Preface is not the place to lecture compilers of anthologies, or teachers of English in schools, on the error of their ways. Nor to tilt at class consciousness and the snobbish origins of traditional culture." (All memos and correspondence about the anthology are in the Bell archives at the Reading University Library.) At Garrett's suggestion, Bickers visited Auden at the Downs School on 15 March 1935, and Auden agreed to write a new preface after school broke up at the end of the month, and to prepare a final list of contents. In the following week Auden sent Garrett a list of contents (apparently with only a few texts copied out), and on 28 March Garrett apparently delivered this to Bell, with further texts copied out by Garrett's pupils.

Preparation was delayed while the publishers had some poems typed, attempted to track down others, and sought copyright permissions. Ezra Pound refused to take less than five pounds for any piece, no matter how short, and was dropped without regrets; but Garrett lamented in a letter to Bickers the necessity of dropping Noël Coward's "Mad Dogs and Englishmen" for similar cause.

During the next few weeks Auden revised the selection and sent the texts of some elusive poems (including, copied in his own hand, the hymn from a Scottish Psalter printed as item 39 in Part I). At Garrett's suggestion he wrote to A. E. Housman for permission to reprint some poems, which Housman had at first refused, and got Housman's assent. Auden sent the finished introduction probably on 7 April, and also sent an index of subjects, which, at his suggestion, was combined with the author index for the first volume. He sent a similar index of subjects for the second part around 7 May; this was, at his suggestion, printed separately from the second part's author index. Auden also sent a combined subject index for both parts, but Bickers dropped this as an annoyance to schools that assigned only Part II.

A letter from Bickers to Auden on 29 April notes that Auden "had at one time contemplated having (in Book II, at any rate): (a) a chronological chart; (b) a map of England showing distribution of Poets; (c) giving professions as well as the dates of the authors." Bickers discouraged Auden from proceeding with these. The list of "Book Suggestions" at the end of Part II was evidently Auden's work. Bickers, with Garrett's approval, wrote Auden on 21 May 1935 suggesting that it was "tactfully desirable" to add P. H. B. Lyon's *The Discovery of Poetry*. Auden wired back: "You please yourself think book vile myself", and it was not added.

After the two volumes were ready Bickers and the editors began discussing a combined edition for adults. Bickers proposed simply binding the two parts in one volume with a new preface. Auden, in a letter of 7 June, preferred to combine the two parts in a single alphabetical sequence, with some omissions and additions. Garrett visited Auden around 10 June, and reported to Bickers that Auden wanted to prepare an adult edition with many selections replaced. Bickers eventually decided that a rearranged and revised edition would be prohibitively expensive to prepare, and proceeded with plans for the simple combined edition. Bickers suggested that Auden write a new conclusion to the introduction, but Auden wired him on 10 July: "Believe introduction should simply end [at the word] dictate"—that is, at the final word of the paragraph beginning "In compiling an anthology" (p. 108). Bickers agreed, but added the final paragraph from the original introduction.

In a letter sent from Iceland in July 1936 Auden told Bickers: "I want to see you when I come back about a new edition of the Poet Stung". He seems not to have followed up on the idea.

During preparations for the book, Auden and Garrett began making preliminary plans for a schoolbook on English composition that Bickers hoped to publish. Bickers wrote Auden on 2 May 1935: "I am very pleased to hear that you are willing to tackle the *English Composition*." On 7 June, when Auden told Bickers that he would send further suggestions for the proposed one-volume edition of *The Poet's Tongue*, he added: "Similarly as regards the Composition book, where I have ideas about an illustrated book which I should like to discuss with you." Bickers invited himself to visit Auden to talk about the book, and Auden replied in late June: "Yes, do come in July about the composition book as I should like to get started on it in August if possible." Bickers visited Auden at the Downs School on 24 July, and arranged the next day to send a variety of existing composition books. Early in August Auden asked to be sent a copy of *Folk Tales of Many Nations* (probably F. H. Lee's *Folk Tales of All Nations* or Lillian Gask's *Folk Tales from Many Lands*), but nothing more seems to have been heard of the project.

The March of Time Series

In October 1936, when the publishing house of Longmans, Green introduced this series of illustrated books, Auden and Arthur Elton were listed as editors. Auden's name appeared only on the first title, *Why Aeroplanes Fly*, by Arthur Elton and Robert Fairthorne, and he never had any further contact with the publishers. The unsigned introduction to the first title noted that "it is the aim of the editors to lay before the reading public a detached, simple and untechnical explanation of the world we live in—its mechanics, its social organisations, its methods of government. It is their aim to bring alive the ordinary things of the world, and to reveal the complex workings of society which too many people take for granted." When further volumes were published late in 1939 Auden's name was dropped because the publishers received no replies from him in response to their letters about the series.

Arthur Elton was a film director who worked with Auden at the G.P.O. Film Unit in 1935 and 1936. He and Auden perhaps conceived the series before Auden left the Film Unit in February 1936. Auden mentions Elton briefly in *Letters from Iceland* (p. 280).

Poetry: English Number

The January 1937 number of *Poetry: A Magazine of Verse*, the American monthly published in Chicago, was a special "English Number, edited by W. H. Auden and

Michael Roberts". Michael Roberts was the schoolmaster and poet who had compiled the most prominent anthologies of Auden's generation of writers, *New Signatures,* 1932, and *New Country,* 1933, and had recently edited *The Faber Book of Modern Verse,* 1936; in 1932 he had coedited with Basil Bunting an earlier English number of *Poetry.* Roberts had become friendly with Auden while working on these anthologies, and Roberts's wife, Janet Adam Smith, had befriended Auden when, as deputy editor of the *Listener,* she published his poems and reviews.

Around the spring of 1936, Roberts invited Auden to coedit another English number of *Poetry.* Auden replied in an undated letter: "If we're paid, I should be delighted to help edit the Monroe booklet". (Harriet Monroe was the editor of *Poetry* until her death in September 1936.) Roberts then solicited work from poets who were in their forties or younger, and in June 1936 sent a sheaf of poems to Auden, who replied in an undated letter:

> Thank you for the enclosures. As far as I am concerned, this is my list of likes in order.
>
> | | |
> |---|---|
> | [Rex] Warner | The 4 Bird poems |
> | [James] Reeves | Christmas |
> | | A Matter of Discipline |
> | Dylan Thomas | Seed at Zero |
> | | Now Say Nay |
> | [Ronald] Bottrall | Transmutability |
> | [Graham] Hough | Heliograph |
> | [Roger] Roughton | Poem |
>
> I feel I must be getting very old and stuck in liking what I liked when we were boys together [*Auden and Roberts first met as adults*], because [David] Gascoyne means nothing to me. Thomas is exciting up to a point but I wish I didn't feel the excitement was simply the exhilaration of being very tight. I know Reeves is like Graves but genuine not bogus Graves. [John] Lehmann's poems seem to be bogus Stephen [Spender], and I've never been able to see anything in Herbert Read. How old is Mr/Miss [Ll(ewellyn).] Wyn Griffith? He might do something but not yet.

Auden then left for Iceland, and did nothing about the special number until 16 September, the day after he returned, when he wrote Roberts: "Will send you some stuff in a few days. Do you really want an article? and, if so, on what? I leave you to choose."

In an undated letter written perhaps a week or two later, he commented on other poems that Roberts had sent him:

> By [Clifford] Dyment I suppose you mean [George] Barker. I like the last half of the Spender, but find the spectacle of Stephen trying to be heterosexual acutely embarrassing. You couldn't screw another one out of him could you? Barker I leave to you as I don't understand a

word. Bits but only bits seem to me incantational. Really surrealism at
this time of day is a cough drop I can't swallow. I like [Edwin] Muir
and [T. W.] Eason. Agree with you about Bowel Sion [Lilian Bowes
Lyon]. [Richard] Church might I think scrape a pass if you're hard
up. I enclose a poem of my own ["Journey to Iceland"] for your vig-
ilant eye. Sorry for the misprints in F 6.

Not long after this, perhaps in late September or early October, Auden replied
to another group of poems sent by Roberts:

I like all these except the Herbert Read. He never seems to me to feel
and think in words; everything has a translated effect about it. As a
great admirer of and believer in [Charles] Madge, I wish he could get
a little easier. I've always thought the sonnets about Austria, and the
sun, in the Faber book ["Loss" and "Solar Creation", printed in Rob-
erts's *The Faber Book of Modern Verse*] the two best sonnets of our time.
I like this [William] Empson poem; all the same I could shake him.
    The Iceland poem is appearing in the Listener. Does this matter?
    Christopher and I are busy completely altering Ransom's character
in F 6.
    O yes, you must have some MacNeice.
    On thinking it over, I'm too fed up with prose generalisations to do
an article. I hope you don't mind, but the thought of churning one
out makes me feel ill.

Perhaps sometime later in October, Roberts sent the essay, "Aspects of English
Poetry: 1932–1937", which he had written for the special number. Auden re-
sponded in an undated letter:

Good. But just one point about poetry and propaganda. The real
reason why artists are not good party men, is that the artist qua artist
is a voyeur. He doesn't wish to change his subject matter. He has a
propagandist effect only because he shocks. He is the little boy who
runs into the drawing room and says "I saw Aunt Emma in her bath
without her wig". Dante enjoyed hell. He didn't want to reform it. Of
course no artist is a "pure" artist in this sense. He does as a person
have reactions and it is good that they enter, because pure art is like a
pure chemical element. It doesn't react, i.e. it's unreadable. (This is
my objection to the [Laura] Riding argument.)

Roberts did not incorporate this point into his essay, but, in evident agreement
with Auden's previous letter, he referred in the essay to "Charles Madge's poem
about Vienna (which is one of the best sonnets of our time)".
    Probably in late October or in November Auden sent Roberts another list of

preferences, apparently with a manuscript of his poem "O who can ever praise enough":

Michael Roberts	All except *In the Strange Isle*
Roughton	Sliding Scale
Dyment	Straight or Curly
Bottrall	Lost Heaven

But really you know, except for yourself, I find all this terribly depressing. Roughton is a would-be-clever little ass but he does at least think of poetry as something to be spoken which the others don't. And most of it is so *dull*. But perhaps I'm becoming Blimpish.

As for myself, I've very little stuff, as the Iceland book is swallowing most of my immediate activities. Still here is a [?small] little piece for what it's worth.

(This last letter is in the University of Chicago Library; the others are in a private collection.)

Except for David Gascoyne, John Lehmann, and Herbert Read, all the poets whose poems Auden mentioned in his letters were represented in the special number, although some poems were substituted for those in the early list of poems. Roberts evidently was unable to obtain a contribution from MacNeice. The special number included a "London Letter" by William Empson, Auden's review of William Plomer's poems (see pp. 166–67), and reviews by C. Day Lewis and Empson. Roberts also supplied checklists of recent books of poems, anthologies, and critical studies.

Geoffrey Grigson wrote anonymously in *New Verse*, February–March 1937, that the special number had been "edited by W. H. Auden and (principally, we suspect) Michael Roberts".

Up the Garden Path

This collection of bad verse and bad music, compiled by Auden and Benjamin Britten, was broadcast in the BBC's Regional Programme on Sunday morning, 13 June 1937. A BBC internal memo, dated 14 May 1937, describes the planned broadcast as "an anthology of trash in poetry and music. Mr [John] Cheatle has discovered that Mr W. H. Auden, for poetry, and Mr Benjamin Britten, for music, have made a hobby of collecting such material, and has got their agreement to help him. They will provide material and help him to put the script together, and have expressed their willingness to do the work for (for them) a small fee. I suggest 12 guineas each."

The program, subtitled "A Recital of Verse and Music", lasted 35 minutes. It was presented by John Cheatle, and sung and spoken by Charlotte Leigh, Denis Arundell, Felix Aylmer, and V. C. Clinton-Baddeley; at the piano were Henry Bronkhurst and Denis Arundell. The summary of the broadcast in the BBC Written Archives Centre give this list of the contents (lightly emended):

MUSIC

Funeral March	Chopin
Bump	Heinrich Frobel [Friedrich Fröbel]
April Morn	Music by Robert Batten, words by John Dowers Boosey
Study	[Henri] Bertini; album copyright 1911, Augener
Les Cloches du Monastère	[L. J. A.] Lefébure-Wély
Night Hymn at Sea	Music by A. Goring Thomas, words by J. Williams [?and] Mrs Hemans
Il Corricolo	Durand de Grau

POEMS

"Flo's Letter"	Anon.
"The Toys"	Coventry Patmore
"King Robert"	Longfellow
"The Uninvited"	Anon.
"Blackbird"	T. E. Brown
"The Bells"	E. A. Poe
"The Female Friend"	The Rev. Cornelius Whur
"Temple of Nature"	Erasmus Darwin
"Napoleon and the British Soldier"	Thomas Campbell
Selections from	Shakespeare

The "Night Hymn at Sea" apparently attributed to both J. (or Isaac?) Williams and Felicia Hemans was in fact by Mrs Hemans alone. The two anonymous poems have not been identified.

POEMS I ENJOY

Auden's contribution to this series was broadcast in the BBC Regional Programme on 11 November 1937. He was invited to select and introduce some poems early in October 1937. In reply to his lost letter of acceptance, Ian Cox of the BBC wrote on 9 October 1937: "We are delighted to hear that you are willing to take part in the series 'Poems I Enjoy'. . . . In my letter of 29th September I suggested provisionally the week beginning 6th December as a possible one for this transmission. I find now that Thursday, 11th November, from 6.40–7.0 p.m. on the Regional wavelength is vacant and I am wondering if you could possibly accept this time instead of the other."

Auden replied, probably in mid-October 1937:

I have been away, so have only just [*word missing where a hole is punched in the page*] your letter. I shall be in London on Tuesday [?19 October]. Can we meet then. I ring you up [*sic*] as soon as I arrive.

I enclose my proposed programme. I want to make the comments very short. I hope indeed that you will have another speaker than myself. The order is

(1) Crooked man.   Nursery rhyme.
(2) Fairest Isle.   Dryden.
(3) A Terre   Wilfred Owen
(4) Kangaroo   D. H. Lawrence
(5) Wellington   Byron.
(6) The Rebel.   Anon.

P.S. Please don't lose the copies.

After writing out this list, Auden wrote new numbers to the left of the originals so that the sequence of (4) and (5) were reversed. "The Rebel" was probably the poem that Auden included in both *The Poet's Tongue* and *The Oxford Book of Light Verse* under the title "The Rebel Soldier".

After the broadcast, probably on 13 November 1937, Auden told A. E. Dodds: "The B.B.C. banned three poems I chose for a programme last week." Evidently because the broadcast occurred on Armistice Day, the BBC had rejected the poems by Owen and Lawrence and "The Rebel". Auden introduced and commented on the poems, which were read by Giles Playfair and V. C. Clinton-Baddeley. The summary of the twenty-minute broadcast in the BBC Written Archives Centre gives this list of the contents.

There was a crooked man   Nursery Rhyme
Song of Venus ["Fairest Isle"]   Dryden
Easter 1916   Yeats
"At Timon's Villa let us pass a day"
    (60 lines from Satires)   Pope
Kangaroo   D. H. Lawrence
A Poison Tree   Blake
"How pleasant to know Mr Lear" Edward Lear

THE OXFORD BOOK OF LIGHT VERSE

This anthology was published in October 1938. Auden first proposed it to Charles Williams at Oxford University Press on 28 July 1937. Williams reported to Sir Humphrey Milford, the press's publisher, on 30 July ("O.B.M.V." is *The Oxford Book of Modern Verse*, edited by W. B. Yeats):

I met W. H. Auden for the first time at Oxford on Wednesday. He is an extraordinarily pleasant creature, and we found ourselves in passionate agreement against the more conservative poets, such as Binyon, Richard Church, and even a doubtful Wilfred Gibson. We talked of the O.B.M.V., against which he raised the usual objection that it was not of the same authority as the other Oxford Books of verse. In some surprise I asked him whether he and his friends had any respect for any of them, but he did seem to feel, anyhow for the 15th, 16th and 17th Century books, that they were an adequate and important collection. He then went on to say that he very much wanted to do an Oxford Book of Light Verse. I murmured something to the effect that books of light verse were always very depressing when they were actually before one.

His scope would include such poems as Chaucer's *Wife of Bath*, some of Burns, and the right pieces from *Don Juan*. I suggested that there was a lot of interesting pre-Chaucerian lyrics which would be worth examining, and he agreed. His main point, as it developed, was that light verse of this kind (the doubtful borderline would be *L'Allegro*) showed the difference between the sensibilities of the various periods even better than more solemn stuff. I agree with this, because great tragedy always has a kind of similarity about it, whereas lighter stuff enjoys its own distinctions. His view therefore is that such a book may be a contribution to criticism as well as a collection of poems.

(All letters to and from employees of Oxford University Press quoted in this section are in the archives of the press.)

On 20 September 1937 Williams reported that Auden had looked in again (with Isherwood) to ask about progress toward acceptance of his idea. "His main reason for inquiring was that he is free from any other work for the autumn and could make a beginning if we wished." Auden visited again on 28 September, and was told by John Mulgan that the press had agreed to publish the book. Auden replied to Mulgan's confirmation letter, probably on 2 October 1937:

> Dear Whelgan,
>
> I hope I've got your name right. It looks rather like ULULGAU, but then all signatures do.
>
> Terms you suggest quite OK by me. I must still offer a solemn warning about length. Remember I have to cover the same period of time as the Quiller Couch [*Oxford Book of English Verse*], and represent more than lyrics only. I know I've got to have extracts from long works but I hate them to be only snippets.
>
> If possible I should like £100 advance (irrespective of copyright) before the Mss is finished but must leave that to your clemency.
>
> Perhaps you would prepare me some forms of application for copyright as you did for Yeats. Do I just send them to the publishers in the case of the dead as well as the living, who will then forward them to the literary executors?

Mulgan, in a letter in which he typed out his signature, agreed to the advance, and warned Auden to write to publishers, not authors, for permission. When Mulgan later sent a contract, Auden replied, on 3 December 1937:

> Many thanks for the contract. This seems fine in every way, except the stipulation as to length. I will do my best to keep that down, but if the book is to be worth anything, it must be a parallel book to the

Quiller-Couch. What I should prefer is for you to see the selection as I make it, and then see if I can convince you as [to] its length. If I can't then I can shorten it. The selection is almost finished.

I do want advice on one point. What is the copyright position as regards such things as Folk-songs. Does the collector, e.g. Cecil Sharp hold this or are they free from copyright?

Auden wrote Mulgan again, probably in the last days of December 1937:

I hope you have quite recovered from your flu. I'm going to Spain next week, for a fortnight, but on my return I am very anxious to see you. Could I come down to Oxford.

As I told you I did not think it certain that the Light verse book would be completely ready for the press, nor will it. The selection is made, copyrights applied for (but not paid) and a rough preface written. There is a great deal of anonymous stuff, and the question of dating that is very difficult. I have to leave for China as per contract by the end of Jan., so I want to discuss all these problems with you.

(Auden dropped his plans to visit Spain with Isherwood when the Spanish Government's delay in issuing travel permits made it impossible to fit in the visit before their scheduled departure for China.) During this time, A. E. Dodds had volunteered to do much of the work of preparing the manuscript. An undated note to her reads: "Here are two more poems and the order list. Please emend anything where necessary. It is extremely good of you take all the trouble" (all letters to A. E. Dodds are in the Bodleian Library). Another undated note to her reads:

Many thanks. Here is Dunbar shortened. Sent you proper version of I have a young sister ["I have a yong suster"] yesterday.

Oh yes, and will you add to the collection Samuel Butler's "O God, O Montreal". And if

(a) Anything else good occurs to you put it in.

(b) Anything doesn't seem good enough, cut it out.

After Auden left for China in January 1938, A. E. Dodds took over the work of preparing the typescript for the press. On 2 February 1938, after looking through Auden's Middle English section, she wrote Mulgan: "*Versions*. All Mr Auden's typescript needs checking. He gave me the references from memory and a good many are wrong." She sent the press the typescript of the section of the book up to Edmund Spenser on 17 February, and may have sent the rest of the book around March. After Auden returned from China in July, A. E. Dodds continued to work on the book. In an undated note Auden asked: "Don't send me proofs unless there is any difficulty. I couldn't bear it."

Work continued on the book while Auden spent August and September in Brussels. He wrote to Mulgan on 15 August 1938, probably with a proof of his "Editorial Note" and replies to questions:

Many thanks for your letter. I return herewith the editorial note with an extra paragraph of acknowledgements.

I should like if it is considered possible and in taste to dedicate the book to Professor E. R. Dodds.

I hear you decided to say where *everything* comes from. O dear. . . .

P.S. Did you get in the second Chesterton? Quite understand about Après la Guerre. The English are like that (*Not* New Zealand [Mulgan's home country] I hope). Fukkit passes because it's medieval and scholars are past hope.

The dedication "To Professor E. R. Dodds" did appear in the book. The second Chesterton was one of his two poems included in the book, either "Ballade d'une Grande Dame" or "Citizenship". "Après la Guerre" (a widely known song, printed in *Songs and Slang of the British Soldier: 1914–1918*, ed. John Brophy and Eric Partridge [1931]) was evidently judged too crude a masculine jest to be included; and, despite Auden's assurances, "fukkit", a word in Dunbar's "In secreit Place this hyndir Nycht", caused problems later (see below). The press's insistence on softening the language of ballads and other anonymous poems in the book led Auden to protest to A. E. Dodds on 29 August 1938: "For God's sake please stop the Press making the broadsheets etc suitable for the B.B.C."

Meanwhile, the decision to identify all sources added to A. E. Dodds's burdens. Auden's letter to her on 29 August listed a few sources. On 31 August he told her: "I don't know who Austin was, and it didn't say in that grubby little booklet the name of which I have forgotten which I found in the Margaret Street Library [in Birmingham]. Anyway I'm sure it wasn't Alfred. Let's call him Samuel." She and the press decided to drop Austin's poem instead.

After the book appeared, buyers noticed the language of Dunbar's "In secreit Place this hyndir Nycht". The scholar who annotated the early poems, J. A. W. Bennett, had not translated "fukkit", but he did translate two terms as "penis". As Auden later told Dr Edward Kallman in a letter of 1 June 1939 (letter at the Harry Ransom Humanities Research Center at the University of Texas at Austin):

I've had to cut a beautiful love poem of Dunbar's out of the second English edition because the travellers said it dished the book with the girls' schools. It's all the fault of the learned Oxford ninny who did the glossary, and was so conscientious he translated all the dirty words.

When he was told that the poem had to be cut, Auden wrote Mulgan from Brussels on 12 December 1938 (letter in the possession of R. G. Mulgan):

Re Light Verse, I am reluctant to cut the exquisite poem of Dunbar's which is better than the English deserve, but quite realise its commercial necessity. I have no Dunbar here, so suggest either asking Mrs Dodds to choose one or getting yourself or anyone else whose taste you trust in the O.U.P. to do so. May I leave it in your hands?

If it is possible to make alterations in a reprint I should like to cut *Three something rats in three something hats,* and to add William Plomer's *Murder on the Downs* from *Visiting the Caves* published by Jonathan Cape.

In the second impression of the book, published in December 1938, Dunbar's poem was replaced by his "The Ballad of Kynd Kittok", and two stanzas were added to the beginning and one removed from the end of the book's excerpt from his "Quod Dunbar to Kennedy". The other substitution that Auden requested was not made.

In 1973 Jon Stallworthy wrote to Auden on behalf of the press to invite him to prepare a new edition of the book. Auden replied on 31 July: "Thank you for your letter. I would like to do a new *Oxford Book of Light Verse,* but it will take me at least a year, since I want to radically revise the whole thing. After all, it came out many years ago and I have read a great deal more since." On 5 September 1973 Auden wrote to Edward Mendelson:

As you know, in the thirties I edited *The Oxford Book of Light Verse.* The Clarendon Press are now suggesting a new edition. This will mean, of course, radical revision. In the nearly forty years since I compiled it, much excellent light verse has been written, more in America, I believe, than in England. Then, even in the original anthology, many excellent poems were omitted for the simple reason that I had not read them.

In such an undertaking, I think two heads better than one. Would you be willing to collaborate with me on the new book?

No work was done on a new edition, and Auden died later the same month.

Reported Lectures

THIS appendix includes detailed reports of Auden's otherwise unpublished talks and lectures. Brief, unspecific reports are not included here but are listed in "Interviews, Dialogues, and Conversations with W. H. Auden: A Bibliography", by Edward Mendelson, *Auden Studies 2* (1994).

POETRY AND FILM

Auden delivered this lecture on 7 February 1936 under the auspices of the North London Film Society, at the Y.M.C.A. on Tottenham Court Road. The announced title was "Poetry and the Film". The version printed under the title "Poetry and Film" in *Janus*, May 1936, is described there as an "authorized report of a lecture to the North London Film Society", and may have been made partly from Auden's manuscript. It displays some of his characteristic punctuation. The North London Film Society, whose president was Andrew Buchanan, screened documentary and art films for its members, and during the winter and spring of 1935–36 organized a series of lectures on the art and technique of film. *Janus* was a little magazine published in London under the editorship of John Mair and John Royston Morley. Auden's lecture appeared in its second and final issue, together with work by Dylan Thomas, Gertrude Stein, and others. Emendations and corrections are printed within square brackets.

The Industrial Revolution was responsible for the formation of two classes; a class of people composed of employers and employed, those actively employed in industry, and a class of people living apart from industry but supported by its profits—the rentier class. A distinct type of art arose more or less representative of the outlook of this section of the public, developing through Cézanne, Proust and Joyce. But co-existent with this rentier art was the art of the masses expressing itself in the music-hall. This popular art of the music-hall has been taken over and supplanted by the film.

The film's essential factor is its power to concentrate on detail. The stage has to confine itself to stylised make-up, broad gestures and generalised presentation, on account of the distance separating audience from the scene; but the film, by means of the moving camera, close-ups, etc., can characterise its material more thoroughly and minutely without fear of the effect being lost on the audience. If a peasant is photographed at work in a meadow the scene is definite because it is localised naturally by the visual detail presented in the shots. To show a similar scene on stage requires a much more broad effect. The film gives the concrete visual fact, while the stage gives an idea, a suggestion, of the fact.

Certain disadvantages and advantages result from the second essential characteristic of the film—its continuous forward movement in time. Owing to this particular movement, the success of an attempt to convey factual information by means of film is doubtful. If a suitable test [were] carried out as to the relative educational value of film or book, it would prove films to be valuable as stimulants of interest, but not as substitutes for the kind of factual instruction that a book or a teacher can give. Another danger for the film to guard against is preoccupation with types; for types are generalisations of people and such generalisation does not give a film a chance to use its special power of selecting and emphasising detail to build up a complete character. It is the essence of the camera that it deals with the immediate present. For this reason, a third mistake for films to make is to try to deal with historical material.

The proper concern of film is the building up of a general impression by means of particular detail; the analysis of character; and the material that contemporary life offers.

The use of sound raises the question of the relation of visual images to word images. The visual image is a definite one, whereas verbal images are not sharp; they have auras of meaning. A visual image cannot be made to mean a number of things, nor can a word image be confined to one thing. For this reason, highly developed metaphors cannot be included in the film medium. Where there is a combined image, e.g.— "Beauty's ensign yet Is crimson in thy lips and in thy cheeks, And death's pale flag is not advanced there", the different images would have to be split up for film presentation, and the resulting effect would be more in the nature of a simile. By putting two shots side by side, a furnace can be likened to a chess-man. But to get over an abstract idea, as distinct from a visual similarity, the sound track would have to hold the abstraction as complement of the concrete visual image. In the film, *The Scottish Mail-bag* [*Night Mail*] (on which Mr Auden has recently been working) a shot of mail-bags is accompanied by the words, "listen to the postman's knock, for who can bear to feel himself forgotten".

Because the sound sense and the visual sense of a film have a direct relation to each other, an audience finds it easy to follow an intricate visual continuity providing the sound does not make too many demands on its attention. But a strong sound image added to a strong visual image tends to cancel out both.

The G.P.O. Film Unit has been experimenting with the chorus, using it for detached comments on the action. And it was found that if such a chorus was to be used and be audible it was dangerous to use more than one voice. A need for more volume meant, not an increase in the number of the chorus, but either the one voice to be amplified, or the same voice re-recorded and super-imposed on itself. For the different timbres of a number of different voices coming together left the words inaudible.

There are a number of ways poetry can be used in film. The most obvious way is as a general emotional commentary. Mr Auden had just contributed to a publicity film, *By the Sea-side*, in which poetry had been applied in this way; one of the shots seemed to him to be particularly good in its impact. The scene was the departure of people from the hot and dusty city to a coast. Someone is carrying a tennis racket, and as the net of the racket fills the scene covering all the bustle and heat, the words "like a cool fish in a grotto" are heard from the sound track.

Poetry can also be used to express the thoughts of characters, in rather the same way as Eugene O'Neill introduces the "interior" voice in *Strange Interlude*.

Actual poetic dialogue is impracticable chiefly on account of the big technical difficulties in making the visual and verbal continuity correspond.

Another interesting development would be an adaptation of the thought-stream technique to films, a method similar to that in the novels of Henry James. For example, while people were moving within a scene, the sound could all [?be] generalised descriptions, or abstract references, through a third voice quickly recognisable as coming from outside of the actors.

But whichever method is adopted one necessity must be observed—the spoken poetry must bear some relation, whether of similarity, indirect reference or contrast, to what is seen. For without a quickly grasped connection, the poetry and its place in the film is meaningless.

The generally accepted metrical forms cannot be used in films, owing to the difficulty of cutting the film exactly according to the beat without distorting the visual content. Mr Auden even found it necessary to time his spoken verse with a stop-watch in order to fit it exactly to the shot on which it commented—although the pan shot does offer a means of getting the visual rhythm to follow the rhythm of the poetic line. Trucking in or out, varying the sound volume, provides another means of gaining the same effect.

Mr Auden's last point was the difficulty of finding the right kind of support to enable such experiments to be carried out. It is financial support that is required for these experiments, without restriction on the director's independence of outlook either by commercial or departmental policy.

The Craft of Poetry

On 5 November 1937 Kathleen Isherwood (Christopher's mother) recorded some extracts from a lecture titled "The Craft of Poetry" that Auden gave that day at

Queen Mary's Hall in Great Russell Street. Her diary (now at the Harry Ransom Humanities Research Center) gives this account:

> He gave a very good and interesting lecture with *many* quotations by heart, but somehow, partly perhaps from being shortsighted he did not get into touch quite in the same way as C[hristopher] though the audience found more perhaps to enter into their notebooks. He began with "the handicap of a poet for being one", maintained that poetry could never be taken quite seriously though it reflects on human behaviour or it can tell a story—the actual technique comparatively easy—the difficulty, to find the right words in which to express it. But the patience, character and will-power necessary to the novelist is not to the poet. It is according to *what* is being said, some must be blank verse, others in couplets, or ballads—to find the right form is one of the difficulties and to express what you would say, you must have had parallel emotions, if not the same—to write of murder you need not necessarily have murdered anyone, but can go through the sensation in killing a fly that you might feel in killing your Mother-in-law! A poet must be an engineer and spy, and have memories, "but first and foremost it is 'play', do not let us take poetry too seriously."

SPAIN

At Shrewsbury School, on 30 October 1938, Auden gave a lecture under this title, which was reported by A[lexander] N[eil] S[kinner] in the school magazine, the *Salopian*, 19 November 1938:

> On October 30th the 1918 Society was addressed by W. H. Auden, who spoke on "Spain." He began by issuing a warning against his own bias in favour of the Government and against our laziness over the Spanish problem, whose importance was recognised in Germany and Italy. He went on to describe the Spanish character, melancholy but courteous: this he illustrated by a reading from the poet Lorca.
>
> He pointed out that Spain was trying to solve in four years problems that had taken us four hundred—Land Distribution, Education and Social Services, the right of a part to secede (as Ireland) and the quarrel of Church and State. The churches were not burnt, he said, by Communists nor Fascists, but as a mark of spontaneous hatred by the people against a wealthy landlord, the Church. Mr Auden then gave a brief history of Spain, emphasizing her backwardness and the resulting aristocratic rule, ending with the recent revolutions, the elections of 1936 and the war. This he summed up in two readings from the novelist Bernanos, one illustrating the necessity for organisation of the "Spirit of Spain," the other a most dramatic description of a night air-raid on Talavera, from a bombing-plane.
>
> Mr Auden concluded with another warning; that we should not support General Franco because he plays golf, and that those who support the right cause may be blackguards, their opponents may be "awfully nice people," but that does not prevent them from being "just plain wrong."
>
> We were very grateful to Mr Auden for a lecture that was extraordinarily

interesting throughout, and our only sorrow was that he could not go on for ever, to tell us more of the war and of intervention, which he had only mentioned. Surely the Society could let lectures as enthralling as this begin earlier, and afford its members an extra half-hour?

THE FUTURE OF ENGLISH POETIC DRAMA

This lecture was delivered in Paris, at the Sorbonne, on 8 December 1938, to l'Association France–Grande Bretagne, at the invitation of its Comité des Relations Intellectuelles. The lecture was reported in the association's journal *France–Grande Bretagne,* July–August 1939, under the title "The Outlook for 'Poetic Drama'".

The French reporter of Auden's talk on poetic drama seems to have been baffled by his speaking style and Oxonian accent; the published text contains some garbled and nonsensical passages that I have emended as best I could. Some of the emendations are, by necessity, drastic. For example, the reported text makes Auden allude to modern studies of culture such as "Middleton's 'The Links'". No such study exists, and Auden almost certainly meant to refer to "the Lynds' *Middletown*" or "*Middletown* by the Lynds". (In other lectures and essays late in 1938 he mentioned this study by Robert S. Lynd and Helen Merrell Lynd of a typical American city; see pp. 473 and 479.) Some of the apparently garbled passages I have let stand, although a bracketed "?" marks the points where the confusion seems greatest. I am unable to make anything satisfactory out of one especially defective sentence in a generally confused passage about dramatic characters—a sentence that in the printed text begins: "It is no use calling them, striving in a ravel for something you cannot arouse people's interest, unless those people are real characters. . . ." Possibly Auden meant to convey something rather like this: "It is no use calling them [by allegorical or collective names like] 'striving' or 'Rabble' or something; you cannot arouse people's interest unless those people are real characters. . . ." Many of the obscure and awkward sections of the text may in fact be accurate transcriptions of Auden's partly improvised lecture, so I have not tried to clean up the informalities of his syntax. But I have silently corrected evident errors in transcription, altered and added punctuation for the sake of clarity, and, where the emendation seems doubtful, added or substituted words or parts of words within square brackets. All footnotes are editorial additions.

It is for a double reason that I am extremely sensible, firstly, of the honour that has been done to me in being requested to address you this evening, and, secondly, I am doubly sensible of my incapacity, for two reasons. First of all I am an Englishman, and I cannot but be aware when I come to your city of Paris that I am in some degree a provincial, belonging to a fringe of that European culture of which Paris is the centre. As I walk your streets, I am constantly reminded of the presence of the great dead to whom Paris was a spiritual home, and by great dead I do not only mean Frenchmen, but all Europeans. I think particularly, for example, of Baudelaire, Rimbaud, Heine, etc., names but for whom the history of the poetry of my country would be very different. And if I have reason to feel humble before France, which is the landmark, the continued centre, and the guardian of European culture, I have another reason, which is my age. In looking through the list of lecturers in this series, I realize that I am the youngest of them. Now, after the war there was a feeling that the world belonged to the young. Well, if there is anything that the last eight years have taught us, I think it is that the world does not belong to the young, that never has there been a time when, on the one hand, it has been more difficult to attain maturity, and, on the other hand, when maturity was more necessary. It is, alas, too common a case for the vices of age to overcome the inexperience of youth, because, while science has not succeeded in prolonging, I mean in retarding, physical decay very much, yet the process of attaining an intellectual and emotional maturity in our civilization becomes longer every year. So that, too often, before an individual has attained maturity, before he has outgrown the folly of youth, he is overtaken by those characteristic vices of age which are love of comfort and a conscience stained by disingenuous complacencies.

Now, the title of this lecture has been called "The Future of English Poetic Drama". It is obviously impossible to state the future of any spiritual movement because one is almost certain to be proved wrong; one is always tied up with the conception of one's own thought. I think, for example, of Mr Wells's work on *Things to Come*, and, amidst many remarkable prophecies, if one looks at the clothes in which the people are dressed, I cannot seriously believe that the world will ever come to wearing that kind of toga.

So, really, when one says: "I have come to speak of the future of this or that," after all one really means: "I am going to consider problems which are perhaps bothering you and which are bothering myself." Students are familiar with the examiner who disposes of certain questions which he himself cannot solve and which he expects the students to solve for him. So, this evening I would like to consider certain problems which bother me. To you they may seem very simple and childish and already solved, and something may come of it.

I cannot speak as a literary historian, I am no scholar. I cannot speak with the experience of Mr Bernard.* I speak as a beginner in the dramatical art and as an amateur who has made many mistakes and will make a great many more before he has done. You see it is so difficult, because it always seems to me that perhaps the striking personal discovery, may, after all, be one of the commonplaces of trivial knowledge, and again, what seems to me of immense public importance may really be a purely private dream. So that, before I start, really I must explain one or two things about myself as regards dramatic writing.

For various reasons, some accidental, some personal, the plays that I

* [Jean-Jacques Bernard, the dramatist, who introduced Auden's lecture.]

have written are in collaboration with Mr Christopher Isherwood, who is a prose writer, a novelist, while I write verse. So that if this evening I suggest to you that a possible form of drama for the future is one that combines prose and verse, that is partly dictated by the fact that my collaboration has been one between verse and prose. Secondly, we have certain interests in common which one may call partly political and partly psychological. Here I mean those factors in social life which are not directly personal, like sex or parenthood, which affect and limit character and even the ordinary passions themselves. So, I again suggest to you this evening that the drama of the future will probably deal with some such themes. There again, I am really talking about something which I myself feel I must do. But, after all, thought does not occur in a vacuum. What happens [to] occur to people as their own private belief [h]as a curious habit of turning up when history requires it, just as is the same case with inventions. They do not appear until there is an economic necessity for them, though the amount of inventive talent at any time in the world's history is not likely to vary very much. Yet, at this certain point, when it becomes necessary, invention does occur, so that when one has an idea it is extremely unlikely that it is purely original, and I think therefore there is to-day a certain amount of objective and poetic kind of drama that I wish to discuss, as it is of some value to us at this time.

In the first place, there is, on the side of writers themselves, a growing interest in the drama and in a poetic drama. In Germany, while Germany was free, there was Brecht and Toller, in England there has been Mr Eliot and Mr Spender, in America there has been Mr Odets and others, who on their side, interested in poetry, have also become interested in drama and who also have become interested in subjects either religious or political, which differed from the conventional drawing-room comedy of their time. And from the side of the public, there is the pleasant and direct evidence of box office receipts.

I refer to the success, for example, of Mr Eliot's *Murder in the Cathedral*, which, if one compares it with *Becket* of Tennyson, on the same subject, does show a change in the attitude of the public. There are a number of people now who welcome a different kind of drama.

I would like to divide my enquiry this evening into three parts:

Firstly, what is the nature of the stage as a medium, what can it do, what can't it do, what can it do best?

Secondly, what is the nature of the theatrical subject, what kind of things make good subjects for plays?

Thirdly, certain details and problems of theatrical technique.

Let me then begin with the stage as a medium. Now, such discussions, I know, remind one awfully of discussions in cafés—these long drunken arguments, very late at night, which begin, "I suppose . . .", on the notion of pure poetry, or whether it is good or necessary for morale or propaganda. But there is a certain amount of justification for discussing the laws of limitation of a medium, particularly such a highly artificial medium as that of the drama, because, of course, as in life, there are no rules that you can write down, except the purely unpoetical rule of success or failure. Yet, as also in life, in order to be free it is necessary to study those factors and forces which limit one's freedom. For example, it is impossible to learn to fly until one understands the law of gravitation.

I don't want to talk now about the drama of the past, but the drama of to-day has two great media with which it has to compete. I refer to the novel and the cinema. Let us, for a moment, compare the dramatic medium with the medium of the novel.

To start with, drama, of course, is a public medium; that is to say it demands the cooperation of a large number of people, not necessarily very intelligent, it requires many pieces of apparatus, and it requires a building of considerable size. Secondly, as compared to the novel, it is continuous and irreversible. You cannot stop and say: "I would like to have that bit over again." [As] well, as it costs money, the subject and the treatment of that subject must be of sufficient general interest to get enough people together to pay. I know that sounds very simple, but it is a problem which often is neglected. And furthermore, the subject and the treatment must be of such a kind that they are understandable to people at half-past-eight or nine o'clock at night, after a comparatively good dinner. Now, the more characters and the more apparatus you require, the more popular, of course, must be the subject. If you have a musical comedy, you can employ a great many people and pieces of machinery, but if you wish to write a play about miners in Alaska, then you have better write something requiring only two or three actors and, as scenery, some curtains. I think this is very childish, but it is a reason, for example, why Hardy's *Dynasts* is not very likely to be performed often.

Again, as compared with the novel the time is very limited. A play must not last less than an hour and a half or people will not think they are getting their money's worth, and it must not last more than three hours or they will miss their last train.

Most important in plays are the actions done by people in a limited space. The actions that you can really do in a stage space are limited. You cannot eat a whole meal, ride a bicycle, or drive a motor-car; you cannot do anything except the preliminaries of love-making; you cannot expect actors to do anything that involves physical injuries to themselves. I once, for example, read a play by a young man which was about a man on a golf course. While he was out playing golf, his friends were sitting at the bar and thought what a good joke it would be when he came back to tell him that his wife had died. So, when he came back they said to him: "Your wife has had an accident", upon which the hero took his golf club and beat his brains out with it. That is more than you can expect any actor to do. Compared with a novel, roughly speaking, you can say that it is very much more expensive and must be more popular and less subtle. Secondly, your action is very much more limited—that is, the possible kind of things that can happen on the stage.

Now, let us compare it with the cinema. The cinema, as regards expense and time is like the theatre and a great deal more so, which has a very important social effect because the cinema as a medium is the most realistic and most truthful of all media. On the other side, it is so expensive that it can only be paid for by people who have very good reasons not to wish the truth to be known. It is impossible to imagine a cinema at present that is not either run by the State or by very rich people of some kind of another. I happen to feel this very strongly for having worked a little for the General Post Office in the production of a film. To show the kind of difficulties which arises, I will tell you this one story, because it explains why films sometimes are not as good as they might be. We had to take some pictures of people in a trunk telephone exchange.* It was supposed to be New Year's Eve. I found out that these people were very tired and worked in their shirt sleeves. So I got them into shirt sleeves, got the cameraman, and when the supervisor came he said: "We can't show government officials in their shirt sleeves."

Then, on the other hand, in many ways the film is very much more like the novel. First of all, you get the flexibility, by moving the camera, you can alter the way in which you move. And what is still more important than that, both the novel and the film—and the film even more so—show man in direct relation to nature. There he is on the screen, with fields, hills, streets, etc., about him, so that you can use them as a sort of a comment of the film or, at least, leave it as a question mark. It is like the novel also in its treatment of time. The cinema and its capacity to face physical action is also something which the stage cannot do.

So the chief difference, to start with, between the drama and other media, like the novel and the film, is that in the novel and in the film you can show a man directly in relation to nature, while on the stage you cannot. The novel and the film, if you like, are like a river and the drama is a series of avalanches. The novel is a park, the film is a window looking out on the world, but the stage is a box, it is a prison. We are in this prison with the audience, and the actors are in it too, and the important thing is that the actors can't get out and we share their imprisonment. We demand the release of the captives from the tragedy, in fact, out of a feeling of

---

* [Evidently a reference to the film *Calendar of the Year;* see *Plays,* p. 672.]

extreme claustrophobia. Here, on this narrow stage, surrounded by sham scenery, sham lighting, sham objects, we have a few imprisoned people; and what I think also is, that the stage is supremely conservative in the relation between man's free will and the forces which limit and frustrate that will. That is one reason why I am talking about drama at all to-night, because drama is impossible if you believe that man's life is completely determined and he has no free will at all. If you have no free will and no possibility of making a choice, the dramatic suspense disappears at once. On the other hand, if you are completely liberal and believe that man's will is absolutely uncontrolled, the stage falls to bits and does not mean anything.

The drama is a form [for] the culture which holds temperately to the belief in the free will of man; it also is humble and is aware of all those forces which limit it. It is therefore why drama is not a form for a completely *laisser-faire* community, nor is it a form for totalitarian states, which much prefer the cinema. It is a form for social democracy.

There are so few things—that is unfortunate—that people on the stage can do: they can sing, they can dance, they can gesticulate, they can talk. Gesticulation is so much more suited to and much more subtle on the screen, and the most important thing they can do is to talk. The spoken word is the basis of drama, and within these limits—four walls and sham lighting, these little actions that are possible—the dramatist must hold the mirror up to nature, make a criticism of life, reveal beauty, terror, pity, what you will. So one of the first problems for the dramatist is how to release the captives, that is to say, how are you to relate these characters to a larger life to which they belong. Here they come on the stage as if they came out of trunks, and you have got to show that they did not come out of trunks. Now, in comedy this is done in various ways. Firstly there is the epigram, the witticism: "Did I meet you in Trouville?"—"I have never been in Trouville."—"Neither have I."—"Then it must have been two other people!" Then there is the forgiveness, which is a very important thing in comedy, the unmasking of vice followed by forgiveness, and lastly there is marriage which takes place off the stage. The difference, it seems to me, between comedy and tragedy is that [in comedy] the characters are aware of their lack of freedom. It is always the situation of the rich uncle arriving at the wrong moment and so on, and it is at the end of the play that they discover that they were freer than they thought, while in tragedy they continually believe that they are free until they discover that they were not as free as they thought.

The releases in tragedy are, first of all, death; then there is poetry which lifts the private suffering of the private individuals on the stage into the suffering of all men in such a situation. In poetry you can say, for instance: "Boys and girls Are level [now with men] . . . [And] there is nothing left [remarkable] Beneath the visiting moon."* Such a language breaks down the sides of the stage and releases our feeling of imprisonment.

In later drama, which is not poetic, the great contribution, in the way of release, was made by Ibsen. It is the symbolical object or symbolical phrase. It has been employed, of course, by others. You have *The Seagull* by Tchekov, *The Wild Duck* by Ibsen. The most successful of Ibsen's symbols, the key which leads one out into a form of beauty and terror, are phrases like, "The joy of life is God's", or that terrifying remark in *The Wild Duck*, "The woods avenge themselves", or a remark which comes in John Gabriel Borkman's soliloquy.†

Then, let us think of the question of subject or theme. What subjects now are likely to be most profitable, dramatically, most fruitful? Many people, of course, when they think of a play, think of something about adultery, involving a number of rather well-to-do people, but that, after all, is a relatively recent idea. We are now living at the end of a period which began with the Renaissance, an age of liberty and freedom without unity or justice. It was a period which saw certain important things. It saw first of all that every individual is unique, it believed in the freedom of the will; it was interested in the rational contrast[?] of the intellectual part of man which is and was unique individually; and it did not really believe in society, in unity, in loyalty. And parallel with the growth of belief in the importance of the individual, and [*i.e.,* ?there was] economic change and the gradual atomization of society, until the only social group that remained—the only social, emotional unit—was that, again, of the family. It was a development which, in the end, was to prove a very difficult one, I think, for the dramatist; firstly because along with the interest in character—which did produce at once a great efflorescence of drama—in the end, those who were really interested [in character] turned to a more subtle medium, the novel.‡ Other poets turned—horrified by the complexity and ugliness of their society and bewildered by its past—they turned away to contemplation of their own feelings and to writing of lyric, often beautiful, often obscure poetry.

When the drama began to rise during the nineteenth century, the problems were essentially family problems, that is to say, [the] fight for truth and justice and so on, which is always going on in different ways. At that

---

* [I have rearranged and emended this sentence, which in the printed text reads: "in such a situation, boys and girls, on level. In poetry you can say for instance: 'There is nothing left beneath the shining moon . . .'"]

† [Conceivably Borkman's phrase "the treasure sank back into the deep again", from his long speech—not quite a soliloquy—near the end of Act IV.]

‡ [The printed text reads "a more subtle medium than the novel."]

time it was directly a personal matter that beliefs and customs which belonged to a previous society had survived into the family. Such things, for example, as the subjection of women, and contempt [?for them], were really something which could take place in the family. It was possible for a character to confront her father and say: "I will leave the house!" and for one to feel that an immense moral victory had been gained. It was a personal matter between those two people. Now, when we hear, as we heard in September, Mr Hitler say in this crisis: "There is nothing but two men, myself and Dr Beneš, and what happens is a matter between us two", we know that he is talking nonsense. Recent advances of knowledge in various fields, politics, psychology and economics, have revised our conception of human character and of the different fields of interest over which we look; and, for example, if you take a modern book on culture dealing with ancient culture, [or] a modern study such as *Middletown* [by] the Lynds, they have shown how enormously the social structure and the cultural power of an age contribute to dictate individual characters and the kind of liberty which is permitted, not only [the] liberty of the actual kind of characters which survive in a society. Psychologists generally have shown that not only are we conscious and unique, but that we all bear with us an unconscious in which we are very much like each other, much more than we thought, and there the dramatist has another field of interest that is putting him back. Not only are people unique, but they are also alike and also less free than they thought. The economists have also drawn our attention to the fact, which is quite a common-sense fact but easy to forget, that the kind of characters we have and the kind of way we behave with our wives and our children may have a very close connection with the way in which we earn our living. A stockbroker, maybe, will have more to say than a tradesman.

And lastly, politically, the struggle to avoid limitation, about which—as I ventured to suggest—the dramatist is much concerned, that is, the struggle between destiny and free will, now taking place very obviously and materially in the outer world. It is an age of physical revolution, so that a campaign which at one time was confined to the boudoir is now taking place before the barricades; and that is bound, whether we like it or not, to affect our field as artists.

When we were in China and heard the news about Austria, it was extraordinary the way one felt this China war turned out to be a provincial scuffle. The dramatist to-day must show man in relation to nature; he must show that he is not wholly rational, not wholly irrational, [nor that]* he is wholly determined. He must show the reaction in private and public life, the influence of public life upon the character, upon the individual

* [A conjectural emendation for the printed text's "if".]

and upon society. This he must show, or want to show; and this struggle is taking place in the political field. Now, I do not mean that for that reason one must throw characterization overboard. The stage stands or falls by a few characters standing on the stage. It is no use calling them "Striving" or "Rabble" or something; you cannot* arouse people's interest, unless those people are real characters, because you can never go back, and one thing you have gained is the recognition of individual uniqueness. But we have to combine that now with the realization of collectivity as well.

One of the ways in which, I think, it can be brought about is by the use of poetry, because poetry is a medium which expresses the collective and universal feeling. Now, this can be used in various ways. It can be used as chorus, which is sung or spoken, as for example in *Murder in the Cathedral*. Music has the effect of even more generalizing the emotion, so that if you want to get a general effect, I think music is useful and is going to take a large part. There are some technical difficulties: if you have a number of people singing it is difficult to hear a word they say, and that is a technical problem which has not been completely solved yet. Then you can use characters speaking and try to adapt the kind of speech to the kind of character. That can, of course, only be done very broadly. It was done in medieval drama. There is a lot to learn in that kind of thing.

The trouble about blank verse is that characters when they get excited talk exactly like each other. That is the difficulty with verse—to find a method by which you can differentiate speech and characters.

One can also use soliloquy in which characters reveal themselves or comment on the action of the play. I think there is the danger in a play with a soliloquy in verse because it is extremely difficult to get any characterization.† Many attempts have been made to get a ritual kind of drama—people with masks and moving in graceful gestures—but I personally feel that they are doomed to failure. I think one has to accept the fact that plain art is to be performed by nice-looking and rather vain people.

Again, poetry unalloyed tends, if one is not very careful, to introduce a rather holy note. You cannot have poetry unless you have a certain amount of faith in something; but faith is never unalloyed with doubts and requires prose to act as an ironic antidote.

The problem of writing a play in which verse and prose are combined is difficult and I think not yet solved. There is a certain conception of having different parts of the play on different levels. It is a question whether you are to move from a prose or poetry level. You can either do it in

---

* [The printed text reads "calling them, striving in a ravel for something you cannot"; see headnote.]

† [This is emended from the printed text, which reads: "danger in a play that a soliloquy infers because it is extremely difficult to get any equalization."]

different scenes, one scene on a level, one scene on a different level; or [have] one character who has a greater degree of consciousness and is therefore capable of breaking into verse; or you must find a situation in which the characters are not their normal, everyday selves, such as dreams, or madness. I think that probably to choose as a subject a political subject is a mistake, because history is always now more terrible and more moving than anything you an possibly invent and more extravagant than anything you can imagine. It is impossible now to write about contemporary time unless you took a part in it yourself, because the trouble about trying to write is that one simply does not know enough, or there are very few people who do. Perhaps if you want to do that (I only say this as [*i.e.,* ?of] a subject) it is better to take a parallel of historical interest.

On the whole, I think one must have selected a general kind of subject—a few people, belonging to strata which the dramatist knows well, possibly a family, but treated in a different way [from] which they were treated in a drawing room comedy.

As to scenery, I think this element is important, and I think, from certain experiments which we have made, that if you are to have different levels and different scenes, that [the] visual element must be consistent. If you alter the scenery with the change in the behaviour or language the play falls into little bits. I do not think realistic setting is necessary now, especially as we have to compete with the cinema, but a few objects to establish a sense of reality [are].

Now, what will happen to the stage, I do not know, but I do know this: that the search for a dramatic form is very closely bound up with something much wider and much more important, which is the search for a society which is both free and unified. I spoke at the beginning of this lecture about Paris as the centre of culture, but for more than a century Paris has stood for a great deal more than that for the people to whom liberty and social justice seemed something very precious, who have turned their eyes constantly towards your city; and we, in England, realize very clearly that what happens here affects us enormously. If we sometimes, at this moment, look towards France in apprehension mingled with hope, it is because we realize that while these values have disappeared in one country after another, we know that unless they are safeguarded here, in our country liberty, culture, drama are made impossible.

Auden on the Air

THIS appendix lists Auden's broadcast talks and readings. Auden's two compilations for broadcast, "Up the Garden Path" and his contribution to the series "Poems I Enjoy", are described in Appendix I, and his radio script *Hadrian's Wall*, which was broadcast in the BBC Regional Programme, 15 November 1937, is printed in this edition in the volume of Auden's plays.

During his visit to Spain in 1937 Auden broadcast propaganda for the Government radio in Valencia, probably in the second half of January or the second half of February; no further information about these broadcasts survives. There seems to be no basis for a report (in the *Daily Telegraph*, 19 August 1982) that Auden appeared in "Cover to Cover", a film made by the National Book League for a television broadcast on 27 August 1936.

Auden apparently first spoke before the microphone in a discussion, "Do we read too much and think too little?", listed in the BBC's summary of the day's broadcasts as "by Wystan Auden and E. G. Hilton", BBC Midland Regional Programme, from Birmingham, 20 January 1934. No further details survive of this thirty-minute broadcast.

Auden read four of his poems during the interval of a concert by the City of Birmingham Orchestra in the BBC Midland Regional Programme, from Birmingham, 22 March 1934. Typescripts, tearsheets, and a manuscript are in the BBC Written Archives Centre. The poems were "Coming out of me living is always thinking" [Part II of "1929"], "'O where are you going' said reader to rider", "Out on the lawn I lie in bed", and "Enter with him . . .". (The BBC's internal "programme as broadcast" summary also lists, between the first and second poems, "There are some birds in these valleys" and "Watching in three planes from a room", but they are not among the manuscripts in the Written Archives Centre and are not checked off in the summary, as are the other four.) The manuscripts in the Written Archives Centre include the first four poems listed above and "Sweet is it, say the doomed, to be alive though wretched", which Auden probably did not have time to read. His handwritten introductory comments are: "The five poems I am going to read are in their chronological order of composition. The earliest was written in the summer of 1929 and the latest this year."

Auden read six of his poems in a program of "Music and Poetry", in the BBC Midland Regional Programme, from Birmingham, on 17 January 1936. The poems, which he read in the intervals of a concert by the Birmingham Philharmonic String Orchestra, were "Seaside", "May with its light behaving", "Our Hunting Fathers", "A Bride in the 30's", "In the Square", and "The Malverns".

Auden read his introductory comments on the poems he selected for "Poems I Enjoy", in the BBC Regional Programme, from London, on 11 November 1937 (see p. 706). The text of his comments has not survived.

Auden's talk "In Defence of Gossip" was broadcast in the BBC National Programme, from London, on 13 December 1937 (see p. 425).

Auden and Isherwood spoke for ten minutes about *The Ascent of F 6* in "Speaking Personally", on BBC Television, from London, on 12 October 1938. No text survives.

Auden read his poem "In the Square" in "The Modern Muse", a broadcast by modern poets (with MacNeice, Spender, Dylan Thomas, and others), in the BBC National Programme, from Manchester, on 18 October 1938.

Auden gave a talk on his visit to China in *Midland Magazine,* in the BBC Midland Regional Programme, from Birmingham, on 16 January 1939 (see p. 489).

Public Letters Signed by Auden and Others

THIS section lists letters to the press and other documents signed by Auden but probably not written by him. It also includes the text of a draft letter of protest that Auden prepared for use by himself and others, but which apparently was never printed.

DER THOMAS MANN-FONDS

Under this title an appeal for support of a fund for exiled German writers was printed in the Prague weekly *Die neue Weltbühne*, 11 February 1937. The Czech-German typography, with "ss" instead of "ß", is that of the original.

Der Thomas Mann-Fonds,

eine unter dem Patronat des Dichters stehende Organisation zur Unterstützung emigrierter deutscher Schriftsteller, wendet sich an die Öffentlichkeit mit der Bitte um finanzielle Förderung.

Der Name drückt aus, dass die verödende Unduldsamkeit einer die Gewissensfreiheit des Geistes leugnenden Staatstolalität auch vor verehrungswürdiger Lebensleistung, vor Trägern festgegründeten Weltansehens nicht haltmacht. Indem er Erinnerungen wachruft an beste deutsche Tradition, bedeutet er einen Appell an alle Sympathie und Dankbarkeit, welche die Welt dem schöpferischen deutschen Geiste in Zeiten seiner sittlichen Autonomie und Selbstverantwortlichkeit je und je entgegengebracht hat,—eine Mahnung, diesen Geist, sofern er auch heute noch in Freiheit wirkt, dafür aber freilich des staatlichen Rückhaltes entbehrt und in der Heimat unterdrückt und verpönt ist, zu schützen, zu stützen und am Leben zu erhalten.

Des Interesse der Welt an solcher Erhaltung ist evident. Es hat nichts, mit politischer Polemik zu tun, sondern ist eine einfache Feststellung, auch von denen nicht zu bestreiten, die zu ihr Anlass geben, dass ein nationales Schrifttum einzig im Stande der Freiheit von Bedeutung oder auch nur von irgendwelchem Interesse für die Mitwelt ist. Eine in den Dienst einer politischen Machtkonzentration gezwungene, eine diktatorisch gegängelte und befuchtelte Literatur ist moralische wertlos und uninteressant, weil ihr kein Vertrauen zukommt, weil ihr die natürliche Voraussetzung jeder echten Produktion, das unmittelbare Verhältnis zum Weltgeiste, fehlt und sie in jeder ihrer Äusserungen in dem nicht abzuwehrenden Verdachte steht. Erzeugnis des Ausweichens, des Zugeständnisses und des bedrückten Notbehelfs zu sein. Wer in aller Welt sich dem deutschen Geist um der freien Beiträge willen, welche die allgemeine Kultur von ihm empfing, zu Dank verbunden fühlt, muss wünschen, dass ausserhalb des Machtbereiches einer mit den Vorbedingungen des Schöpferischen unbekannten Partei- und Staatsbevormundung ein deutsches Schrifttum am Leben bleibe.

In diesem Sinn ergeht unser Anruf. Das Brot des Exils ist bitter zu essen, und es ist karg. Da die Bücher der meisten im Auslande wirkenden deutschen Schriftsteller im ihrem Lande verboten sind und so ihr nächstes natürliches Publikum nicht mehr erreichen, ist der Lebenskampf verzweifelt geworden. Viele der Besten werden zu einer übersteigerten Produktion getrieben, die früher oder später die Qualität ihrer Arbeit schädigen muss. Unter der Peitsche der Not reift kein Werk. Die Verlage, die sich der exilierten Literatur annehmen, führen eine bedrohte Existenz. Bald wird es ihnen völlig unmöglich sein, anderes zu publizieren als das kommerziell unmittelbar Einträgliche. Dem Autor, der neue, unerprobte Wege geht, wird der Mund verschlossen, am meisten den Jungen, noch Unberühmten.

Hier vor allem muss der Thomas Mann-Fonds helfen. Ein kompetentes Lektorat, dessen Zusammensetzung alljährlich wechselt, wird den Verlegern Werke dieser Art empfehlen und aus den Mitteln der Stiftung die nötigen Vorschüsse leisten. Wer im Versinken ist, dem soll unmittelbar gegeben werden. Aber nicht genug kann betont werden, dass es sich um mehr handelt als um Hilfe für den einzelnen leidenden Autor: nämlich darum, einem der Humanität verbundenen und aller Humanität werten Deutschtum, das heute im Reich nur in Ausnahmefällen, unbemerkt und ungeehrt, sich äussern kann, behilflich zu sein, der Zeiten schwere Ungunst zu überdauern.

Die Unterzeichneten befürworten bei der internationalen Öffentlichkeit die Zahlung von Spenden an den Thomas Mann-Fonds auf das Konto: *Thomas Mann-Fonds, Schweizerischer Bankverein, Zürich,* für die ČSR.: *Thomas Mann-Fonds, Bank für Handel und Industrie, Prag I.*

Martin Andersen-Nexö, W. H. Auden, Menno ter Braak, Lion Feuchtwanger, Otokar Fischer, Bruno Frank, Leonhard Frank, Sigm. Freud, André Gide, Julien Green, E. J. Humm, Aldous Huxley, Oskar Kokoschka, Josef Kopta, J. B. Kózak, Universitätsprofessor und Abgeordneter, Jaroslav Kvapil, Heinrich Mann, Thomas Mann, André Maurois, Hans Mühlestein, Alfred Neumann, Jules Romains, Ignazio Silone, Upton Sinclair, Anna Maria Tilschová, Karel Weigner, H. G. Wells, Fr. Werfel, Stefan Zweig

SPAIN: THE QUESTION

Nancy Cunard probably composed the text that appeared under this title on a broadside that she sent out as a request for contributions to the pamphlet *Authors Take Sides on the Spanish War*. She posted perhaps two hundred copies from Paris in June 1937, and reprinted the text in the pamphlet at the end of the year, together with 148 replies (see p. 388). The text also appeared in an advertisement for the pamphlet in the *Left Review*, December 1937. Although Auden's printed signature appears below the text, he may have seen it for he first time when he received the broadside (see the notes on his reply, p. 805). The text below is the broadside version: the word "SPAIN" appears vertically to the left of the question itself. The version in the pamphlet has trivial differences in the text, and omits the note to the recipients at the lower left of the broadside.

SPAIN

THE QUESTION

WRITERS and POETS of ENGLAND, SCOTLAND, IRELAND and WALES

It is clear to many of us throughout the whole world that now, as certainly never before, we are determined, or compelled, to take sides. The equivocal attitude, the Ivory Tower, the paradoxical, the ironic detachment,
will no longer do.

We have seen murder and destruction by Fascism in Italy, in Germany—the organisation there of social injustice and cultural death—and how revived, imperial Rome, abetted by international treachery, has conquered her place in the Abyssinian sun. The dark millions in the colonies are unavenged.

Today, the struggle is Spain. To-morrow it may be in other countries—our own.

But there are some who, despite the martyrdom of Durango and Guernica, the enduring agony of Madrid, of Bilbao, and Germany's shelling of Almeria, are still in doubt, or who aver that it is possible that Fascism may be what it proclaims it is:
"the saviour of civilisation".

This is the question we are asking you: Are you for, or against, the legal Government and the People of Republican Spain? Are you for, or against, Franco and Fascism? For it is impossible any longer to take no side.

Writers and Poets, we wish to print your answers. We wish the world to know what you, writers and poets, who are amongst the most sensitive instruments of a nation, feel.

To be able to print you all we want a message from you, a statement in not more than 6 lines. We ask you to phrase your answer on Spain, on Fascism, in this concise form, to send it us as soon as you receive this—in no case later than July 1,—addressed to:

Nancy Cunard, Co Lloyds,
43, Boulevard des Capucines, Paris

The collection of answers will be published forthwith. A copy will also be sent to all those who reply.

PARIS—JUNE 1937

SIGNED
Aragon
W. H. Auden
José Bergamïn
Jean Richard Bloch
Nancy Cunard
Brian Howard
Heinrich Mann
Ivor Montagu
Pablo Neruda
Ramón Sender
Stephen Spender
Tristan Tzara

CHRISTOPHER SPRIGG MEMORIAL

Under this heading the following appeal was printed in the *New Statesman and Nation*, 26 June 1937. It also appeared in the July 1937 number of *Left News*, the monthly bulletin of the Left Book Club, and perhaps elsewhere:

Sir,—May we ask for the hospitality of your columns to bring to your readers' notice an Ambulance Fund which is being raised in memory of Christopher St John Sprigg, a young poet and novelist who has been killed fighting in Spain with the International Brigade?

Though only 29 years of age, Christopher Sprigg had a remarkable record of literary achievement. He was the author of seven novels of distinction and had also written a number of aviation text-books. His last published work, *Illusion and Reality*, issued posthumously under his pen-name of "Christopher Caudwell," has everywhere been recognised as the most brilliant Marxist analysis of the nature of creative literature ever written in English. Of its young author, *Punch*'s reviewer has written:

This country has lost with "Christopher Caudwell" an original and constructive thinker, and just possibly the human race in an hour of change a potential leader.

A quiet, friendly and cheerful young man, and an active worker on the Peace Council, no one could have dreaded or detested war more than did Christopher Sprigg. But greater still was his devotion to the ideals of democratic freedom, and early last December he left England quietly for Spain, there to enlist as a machine-gunner in the newly formed British Battalion of the International Brigade. He was killed in the defence of Madrid on February 12th, heroically covering the withdrawal of his company from an untenable position on the Valencia Road at the sacrifice of his own life.

The purpose of the Fund now being raised in his memory is to provide an ambulance urgently needed for attachment to the English-speaking battalions of the Spanish People's Army, and it was thought that some of your readers might, perhaps, wish to associate their gifts to the Spanish People's cause with the name of this gallant young English writer who gave up a most promising literary career, and has now given life itself, for that same cause.

Donations—and none can be too small to serve—should be sent to the Fund's Hon. Treasurer, The Viscount Churchill, Christopher Sprigg Memorial Fund, at 24 New Oxford Street, London, W.C.1.

Signed: J. B. Priestley   W. T. Layton
            (Chairman)   Ethel Mannin
            W. H. Auden   D. N. Pritt
            Julian Huxley   Hugh Walpole
            Storm Jameson   Leah Manning
                                (Hon. Sec.)

Christopher Sprigg Memorial Fund,
   London, W.C.1.

Mr Wyndham Lewis's Works

Under this heading the following letter to the editor was printed in *The Times*, 22 December 1937:

Sir,—Many years have passed since the strange mind of Wyndham Lewis began to invigorate English painting and letters.

Mr Lewis is now holding his first exhibition since 1921 and it seems to us an appropriate time to suggest that Lewis's deep and original art should be publicly recognized. Social change has made it inevitable that in these days the place and duties of the private patron should be handed over, in a large degree, to the public galleries; and those rarer artists whose vision and energy are too great to be confined in small and decorative pieces must depend on the wise discernment of the galleries more and more.

We believe Wyndham Lewis to be such an artist, and we are convinced that ever serious painter and serious writer in England is much in debt to his integrity, and to the originality and strength of his vision; and we hope that the opportunity of acquiring a representative work by him for the national collection will not be overlooked.

Yours, &c.,

Henry Moore, Eric Gill, Paul Nash, Mark Gertler, Edmund Dulac, Edward Wadsworth, P. H. Jowett, Randolph Schwabe, John Piper, Serge Chermayeff, Raymond McGrath, Arthur Bliss, Michael E. Sadler, T. S. Eliot, W. H. Auden, Herbert Read, Rhondda, Rebecca West, Naomi Mitchison, Stephen Spender, Geoffrey Grigson.

An Unpublished Letter about John Hampson

Around March 1936 Auden drafted a letter of protest against the withdrawal of John Hampson's recently published novel *Family Curse* from a Birmingham subscription library, perhaps the Birmingham Library, but possibly the W. H. Smith lending library. Auden was on friendly terms with Hampson (whose real name was John Simpson), and later, in May 1936, arranged for Hampson to marry the German actress Therese Giehse so that she could obtain a British passport. Auden may have been asked to write the letter on behalf of Hampson's supporters and friends, but it seems more probable that he initiated the letter. Two versions of a possible list of signers appear in his handwriting on the notebook page that faces the draft; the legible names include Professor and Mrs E. R. Dodds, Louis MacNeice, [Austin] Duncan-Jones (professor of philosophy at the university), Mrs [Elsie] Duncan-Jones (of the English School at Birmingham University), [A.M.D.] Hughes (emeritus professor of English), "self", [Walter] Allen, [Gordon] Herickx, [John] Waterhouse (see p. 792 for both), [Martin] Gilkes (an extramural lecturer in the English School), Mr and Mrs [Roy] Knight (of the French School), and Helen Gardner.

The letter survives in the form of a rough pencil draft in a notebook now in the Berg Collection. Although the letter reads as if it had been intended for publication, it has not been traced in Birmingham newspapers of the period, and inquiries have produced no record that Hampson's book was ever withdrawn by any Birmingham library. It is conceivable that Auden was misinformed and that the book had not in fact been withdrawn. The text of the draft, lightly emended, follows:

Sir,

Our attention has been drawn to the withdrawal from the Subscription Library of Mr John Hampson's last novel "Family [Curse]".

We should have imagined that the question of indecency was one which was best left to the judgement of the publishers in the case of firms which have an honourable reputation, as in the present issue, or of the police in the case of firms which have not; and that the first duty of a Subscription Library was to provide the public with a representative selection of the best current fiction, and not to pose as the petty guardian of local morals.

The committee presumably have found it indecent; many people whose standards of criticism command wide respect have not. "—" [*quotations from reviews presumably to be added*].

Opinions on what is and what is not indecent may vary so widely that argument is vain but that a library should set itself up to decide whether or no its adult readers will be corrupted by a book that the law permits to be sold openly, and to deny them the exercise of their own choice, is an unjustifiable presumption.

As a Midland author who has done much for the literary reputation of his neighbourhood, Mr John Hampson has a special claim on the Birmingham libraries, and we are unwilling to see a library which has [?for so long] taken an honourable place in Birmingham life add its name to that list of public and local [*illegible word*] who through ignorance or bigotry have made themselves a laughing stock to the world and a byword to posterity.

Lost and Unwritten Work

THIS appendix describes prose works written by Auden that never appeared, and works that he planned to write but never completed.

In the latter part of 1927 or early in 1928 Auden and Isherwood conceived a three-volume study of preparatory-school, public-school, and university life, which would consist entirely of letters, diaries, and personal confessions by schoolboys and undergraduates. In the notebook titled "Letters[:] Public School" (see Appendix I), Auden copied out letters from old boys printed in the Marlborough school magazine, and personal letters sent by brothers and friends to William McElwee, Gabriel Carritt, and others among Auden's circle at Oxford. He also clipped pages from the *St Edmund's School Chronicle*. Isherwood seems to have done no work on this project, and, to the relief of Auden's friends, it was abandoned.

This three-volume study may have been planned at some early point as a composite portrait of a single individual. An untitled, unsigned prefatory note in Auden's hand, preserved among Christopher Isherwood's collection of Auden's letters and manuscripts, may have been written for it. The note has no indication of its date or origins, but it may have been written shortly before Auden used its concluding phrase as the concluding phrase of the preface to *Oxford Poetry 1927* (p. 5):

The history of Evolution is the history of Life's attempt to organise itself so as to meet the demands of an ever-changing environment, and only in so far as this harmony between the unconditioned and the conditioned is attained can progress be said to be made. Yet this progress, of necessity, involves a loss of resiliency; forms which have achieved a high degree of specialisation and harmony in a peculiar set of conditions, find themselves cut off when these are altered, more humble and even degenerate forms becoming their successors. For man, owing to the greatly increased complexity of his environment, the problem is more difficult, and for him, more pressing.

This book is an attempt to follow as accurately and dispassionately as possible the development from childhood to maturity of an individual with whom circumstances brought the writer into close contact.

In that period all the main emotional problems, the reconciliation of the sex and self-assertive instincts with the dictates of a personal or a conventional morality, and the acquisition of a world-picture in true correspondence to the Reality, have to be faced, and further in the same period we may discover a summary of the attitudes towards these problems held by man in his historical development. I have contented myself with description, leaving the psychologist, if he will, to prescribe. Much data is obscure, still more lacking, but by focussing upon a limited field, I have hoped that the main points may stand out the sharper, and some estimation be made of the difficulties militating against the attainment of spiritual autonomy by Man, whose efforts in that direction, whether by way of negation or license, have been so conspicuous in their paucity.

On 6 October 1930 Auden asked Eliot for books to review for the *Criterion,* and Eliot replied on 29 October by asking Auden to suggest from time to time a book that he might write about. Auden set to work on a review of Christopher Isherwood's translation of Baudelaire's *Intimate Journals,* which had been published with an introduction by T. S. Eliot. He sent the review to Eliot on 4 November 1930 with this cover note: "I don't know if you already have a reviewer for Baudelaire's *Journals Intimes* [*sic*]. If you haven't and you think the enclosed would be of any interest, please use it." Eliot thanked him for his "note on Baudelaire", but said he did not want to publish a review of the book in the *Criterion,* and thought the review form was unsuitable for what Auden had to say; he suggested that Auden might study the subject at greater length, while bringing in Baudelaire incidentally.

Auden took up Eliot's suggestion, but abandoned it a few days later. He told his brother John B. Auden on 15 November 1930: "I have been trying to write an article for the Criterion on Puritanism but I shall chuck it. I can't say things that way. Context and contact are everything. Or else joking verse." No trace of the manuscript survives.

In 1932, during his last months as a schoolmaster at the Larchfield Academy, Helensburgh, Auden wrote an essay on public schools in collaboration with Arnold Snodgrass, a friend who had lived across from the school and later became a schoolmaster. Nothing is known about the content of the article, but Auden apparently first planned to publish it as a pamphlet. He told John Auden on 11 April 1932: "I'm hoping at last to make a little money by a pamphlet on the Public Schools. It's really directed against Cambridge. The young intellectuals from your university are so very ponderous just now." By July the article had apparently been accepted for *Life and Letters,* the monthly edited by Desmond MacCarthy, but it never appeared there. On 28 July 1932, Auden invited Snodgrass to visit him in the Lake District: "If it's a question of money, I can advance you some, on what you will get from our Public Schools article which is appearing in Life and Letters in September" (letter in the Berg Collection). In an undated letter to Snodgrass around October 1932, Auden made his last known reference to the work: "Re our P.S. article. Desmond MacCarthy is sitting thereon and won't say anything." Snodgrass had no recollection of the article when asked about it in 1975.

In July 1935 Eliot asked Auden to review *Literature* by Philip Henderson for the *Criterion.* Auden agreed, but never wrote the review.

In the spring of 1937, Brian Howard wrote his mother from Paris: "Did I tell you that Wystan Auden asked me collaborate on a book with him?" (Marie-Jaqueline Lancaster, *Brian Howard: Portrait of a Failure* [1968], p. 373). This may have been the matter that Auden referred to in a postscript to a letter to Nancy Cunard, probably in May 1937: "Will you ask Brian to communicate with me at once on the matter I wrote about" (letter at the Harry Ransom Humanities Research Center). Howard gave no further details in his letter to his mother, but when he tried working on the book again early in 1939, he told his mother that it would be a book of essays by himself, tentatively titled *The Divorce of Heaven and Hell*, that Auden would "go over it before it is published", and that the publisher, Robert Hale, would probably want Auden to write a preface (Lancaster, *Brian Howard*, pp. 396–97). Nothing came of this.

In the spring of 1937 Auden and Stephen Spender made plans to give an American lecture tour during the winter of 1937–38 and write a book on America, presumably to be modelled loosely on *Letters from Iceland*. Through Auden's literary agent Curtis Brown, Ltd, on 31 March 1937 they signed an agreement for the tour with the New York lecture agent W. Colston Leigh, Inc; and a memorandum of agreement with Curtis Brown, dated 19 May 1937, refers to "a book on *America* to be written by the authors following their lecture tour in America". In July 1937, after Auden and Isherwood were commissioned to visit China early in 1938, the lecture tour was postponed until the winter of 1938–39, and then (as Auden told Spender) abandoned by the American agent. (When Auden was in Iceland in the summer of 1936 he mentioned to his guides that he planned to visit New York in the autumn, but his plans for this trip—which did not occur—seem not to have been connected with a lecture tour.)

Probably on 29 September 1938, the last day of the Munich crisis, Auden and Isherwood signed an agreement with John Lehmann at the Hogarth Press to write a book about their travels in America the following year. Lehmann recalled:

> I had arranged with them, in order to help them with the money for their journey, that they should write a kind of travel book, successor to their *Journey to a War*, to be called *Address Not Known*. . . . But the idea of *Address Not Known* was soon abandoned, when both Christopher and Wystan realized they were making a mistake in committing themselves to a book that would be little more than a repetition of something of which they had already exhausted the possibilities, a collaboration that was only keeping them both from the work that was more essentially their own. Before Christmas the plan was dropped and in its stead I made an agreement with Wystan that he should let me publish his next book of poems. (*I Am My Brother* [1960], pp. 14–15)

This second agreement, dated 3 December 1938, was in fact for an unspecified book or books, and late in 1939 Auden gave his next book of poems, *Another Time*, to Faber & Faber, his usual publisher. He apparently intended to give Lehmann the prose book *The Prolific and the Devourer*, which he began and abandoned in the summer of 1939, and in 1940 arranged to give Lehmann *The Double Man*, the book of verse and prose that evolved from *The Prolific and the Devourer*. Auden was however under contract to give his next book of verse to Faber & Faber, who published the book in 1941 under the title *New Year Letter*.

TEXTUAL NOTES

Essays and Reviews

1926–1936

Preface to *Oxford Poetry 1926*

Page 3.

For the history of this anthology see Appendix I above. Auden and Charles Plumb wrote their preface probably early in the summer of 1926, and the volume was published in November 1926 by Basil Blackwell. The controversy mentioned in the opening paragraph began when the preface to *Oxford Poetry 1925* (edited by Patrick Monkhouse and Plumb) argued that earlier volumes had not been representative of Oxford; the controversy then sputtered briefly in the pages of the *Isis* and other undergraduate magazines. The tone of the preface may reflect the difference in taste between the two editors; Plumb's poetry was more traditional than Auden's was.

Preface to *Oxford Poetry 1927*

Page 3.

For the history of this anthology see Appendix I above. Auden and Cecil Day-Lewis wrote the preface in late June or early July 1927 during a one-week visit to Appletreewick, Yorkshire, where they also selected the verse for the collection. The dates of the visit cannot be determined exactly, but they included 29 June. Possibly Auden revised or completed the preface after the trip; he did not mention it in a letter he wrote to Isherwood after he returned home from the trip early in July (in which he thanked Isherwood for a poem written for the volume), but he told Isherwood in another letter, written later in July during a trip to Yugoslavia: "The preface to Oxford Poetry is written and should be as important as the preface to the Lyrical Ballads" (letter in a private collection). The volume was published in November 1927 by Basil Blackwell.

Auden wrote the second paragraph, with the quotation from Christian Morgenstern (which also appears in a verse manuscript written around the same time), and the final paragraph of the preface. Day-Lewis, who wrote the rest, recalled in *The Buried Day* (1960):

> [Auden's] youthful blend of levity and seriousness . . . emerged also in the introduction to *Oxford Poetry 1927*, which we were compiling just now [June or July 1927]. In Chapter II of his autobiography, Stephen Spender gives a most perceptive account of Auden and their relationship at Oxford. But he says, "I possess in my library a copy of *Oxford Poetry 1927*, with an introduction written by Auden which recalls the matter and manner of his conversation at this time." A little further research would have shown Spender that

this volume was jointly edited by Auden and myself: we wrote, in fact, alternate paragraphs of the introduction, and the first of the extracts which Spender quotes from it, as showing "the abstract nature of Auden's thinking", was written by myself and embodies an idea I had thought up all by myself. Spender's second extract, in which "the abstract solemn language suddenly acquires a buffoonish, half-absurd, half-serious quality", was one of Auden's contributions, couched in a series of grandiose, Augustan antitheses (he could reel off paragraphs of Dr Johnson by heart). What Spender has missed, apart from the other editor's name on the title page, is that a note of mockery runs *throughout* the introduction: the editors were in deadly earnest, but they took out an insurance policy, in the form of deliberately portentous prose styles carrying pastiche to the edge of burlesque, against any risk of solemnity or self-importance. (Pp. 178–79)

The two paragraphs quoted by Spender in *World within World* (1951) are the one beginning "A tripartite problem" (including the first of the three lettered sections) and the final paragraph.

In the quotation from Morgenstern the quotation marks follow German convention; the printer of *Oxford Poetry* placed the opening inverted quotation mark at the top rather than the foot of the line, and either the printer or the author omitted the closing quotation mark.

The footnotes to the preface are by the authors.

A Review of *Instinct and Intuition*

Page 5.

This was Auden's first prose work for the *Criterion;* T. S. Eliot had printed *Paid on Both Sides* in the preceding number. Auden probably wrote the review in January 1930; he posted it to Eliot from 21 Cambridge Square, London, where, during that month, he worked briefly as a tutor. In his cover letter (in the Faber & Faber archives) he told Eliot: "Here is the review of Dibblee's book. I'm afraid it's either too long or too short. I hope it's the kind of thing you want."

The text in this edition retains Auden's capitalization; in the final sentence "Lucifer" has no capital in the printed text but probably had one in Auden's manuscript. In the second paragraph "Parsons'" is emended to "Parsons". In the third paragraph both questions have been placed within quotation marks; the original has quotation marks around only the last phase of the first question (these are retained here as single quotation marks) and around the full second question. In the set-off quotation this edition retains Auden's errors in transcribing Dibblee's "in which alone the species can flourish and in which therefore it is fixed" and "some neural path", as well as Auden's minor changes in punctuation. Errors apparently added to the quotation by the *Criterion*'s compositor ("neuval", "afferent, central, and afferent") are corrected. In the paragraph beginning "Mr Dibblee is hard to follow" (p. 6), the sentence "But that they are different" begins a new paragraph in the printed text, presumably through a misreading of the manuscript.

A Review of *The Grasshoppers Come*

Page 7.

Five numbers of *Échanges*, a little magazine published in Paris in French and English, appeared from 1929 through 1931. It was edited by the American writer and patroness Allanah Harper, who wrote a recollection of it, "A Magazine and Some People in Paris", in *Partisan Review*, July–August 1942. Auden's review appeared in the final number, the only one that included a "Chronique des livres". Harper may have got in touch with Auden through his Oxford friend Tom Driberg, who published a long poem in the third number in March 1930, or, less probably, through her close friend Brian Howard. Auden wrote her on 26 September 1931 (letter at the Harry Ransom Humanities Research Center at the University of Texas at Austin):

Thank you very much for your letter. I shall be very pleased to review any of the books you mention. There has been little published lately that seems of particular interest. What about David Garnett's *The Grasshoppers Come*? Also I should particularly like, if it is possible, D. H. Lawrence's posthumous essay on the Apocalypse.

Harper offered Auden only the book by Garnett.

The French compositor, who evidently worked from Auden's manuscript, made minor transcription errors such as "Beaulands" for "Beanlands" in the third paragraph; such errors are silently corrected here. In the first paragraph a period is added after "Forster". In the fourth paragraph a comma replaces the printed text's semicolon after "what they don't mean", and the nonsense word in the printed text's "lached up by private associations" is emended to "linked" (although "backed" is also plausible).

A Review of *The Complete Poems of John Skelton*

Page 8.

Eliot invited Auden to review this book on 15 September 1931. Auden wrote to Christopher Isherwood on 9 October 1931: "I'm so penniless that I've taken to doing a little reviewing. The new edition of Skelton which I have to do is rather good. I'm trying to get Lawrence's Apocalypse." (See the note to his review of *The Grasshoppers Come*, above.) Auden sent the review to Eliot, together with his review of *Edda and Saga* (see below), on 28 October 1931. "I hope they're the sort of thing you want", he told him (letter in the Faber & Faber archives).

The full title of the book was *The Complete Poems of John Skelton Laureate*. In the second paragraph, I have emended "prefer them relegated" to "prefers them relegated"; in the fifth paragraph, "where to stop" to "when to stop"; and in the third paragraph from the end, "eighteenth concept" to "eighteenth-century concept". I have let Auden's minor transcription errors stand and have not altered "Bowery" to "the Bowery", but Lyndsay is corrected to Lindsay and a hyphen has been removed from Wyndham-Lewis.

A Review of *Edda and Saga*

Page 11.

Auden sent this review to Eliot, together with his review of Skelton's poems (see above), on 28 October 1931. It was one of the *Criterion's* shorter notices, which were signed with initials only. In the heading of the review Auden gave Dame Phillpotts her title, not the name printed in the book itself; in *Letters from Iceland* he rendered her name "Dame Philpot" (p. 207).

A Review of *The Prisoner's Soul—and Our Own*

Page 12.

Auden sent the corrected proof of this review to Eliot on 15 May 1932. It was one of the *Criterion's* shorter notices, which were signed with initials only. The full title of the book was *The Prisoner's Soul—and Our Own: Experiences and Observations from a Prison in Oslo*, by Eivind Berggrav, Bishop of Oslo; Auden omitted the dash in his heading. In the text of the review I have let Auden's capitalization stand.

Writing

Page 12.

Auden's friend Naomi Mitchison invited him to contribute the essay on writing to *An Outline for Boys and Girls and Their Parents*, which she was preparing for Victor Gollancz. Auden wrote to Christopher Isherwood on 10 December 1931: "All operations on Bishop [i.e., revisions to their play *The Enemies of a Bishop*] are suspended as I have just undertaken to do the article on Writing for Gollancz's new children's encyclopedia. It is impossible to be more wicked than this." To his brother John he wrote on 14 January 1932: "In order to have riding lessons I've sold myself to the devil by undertaking to do the article on Writing for Gollancz's 'Child's Outline of Modern Knowledge'". He told Stephen Spender on the same day: "I'm busy with this dreadful article for Gollancz now" (letter in the Berg Collection of the New York Public Library). Probably on 15 January 1932 he sent Mitchison a photograph to use for the drawing of him that would precede his essay, and added: "I have actually started your article". (Auden's letters to Mitchison are in the Berg Collection.) He probably sent the manuscript to Mitchison in the latter part of January.

Auden's manuscript exceeded the stipulated word count, so Mitchison made many small cuts and a few larger ones when she typed the text. In her copy of the book, she noted "slight re-write" at the head of Auden's essay. As she said later, "I couldn't leave a lot of the really depressing parts" (quoted by Katherine Bucknell in her introduction to the essay in *Auden Studies 1* [1990]). She probably sent Auden the typescript with requests for further changes and for a brief biographical note around the beginning of March 1932. Auden made the changes and returned the text on 4 March 1932, and probably added the list of suggested reading that appeared, like similar lists in the book, at the end of the essay. Some items on the list may have been supplied by Mitchison; for Auden's opinion of the title by P. H. B. Lyon, see p. 701. He wrote in his cover letter:

Here is the article. I hope over and done with for good. . . .

If you must say anything about me, which I deplore, say this and this only[:]

Wystan Auden (b 1907) writes poetry and teaches at a school in Scotland.

This biography is all that appears in the book; other essayists received longer and chattier descriptions. I have omitted the subtitle Mitchison added for the book: "or, The Pattern between People".

The book was published on 26 September 1932, and quickly became the target of an attack by Arnold Lunn in *Church Times*, which was followed by a protest in the *Morning Post* signed by the archbishop of York, the bishop of Durham, the headmasters of Eton and Harrow, and other clergymen, schoolmasters, politicians, and others. The *Morning Post* protest, published on 6 October 1932, complained of the recommendations Gollancz had gathered from "Christian men and women of a volume which professes to give an outline of history, and mentions Mohammed, Buddha, and Lenin, but does not mention Christ". (The book in fact discussed Christianity but not Christ.) Auden wrote to Mitchison on 10 October 1932: "The Outline raised the wind. I agree with the Bishops that Xrist should not have been omitted. Why not attacked."

Late in his life, Auden told Robert Wilson that this essay was the first piece of writing for which he had received payment (Wilson, "Collecting W. H. Auden," in *Auden Studies 1* [1990]). He apparently forgot that he had been paid for his earlier reviews in the *Criterion*, and that, as Naomi Mitchison recalled, because of the limited sales of *An Outline for Boys and Girls and Their Parents* after the attacks in the press, Gollancz never paid any of the contributors to the book.

Auden's manuscript is now in the Edinburgh University Library. The typescript version from which the text in the book was set is lost. The text in this edition is based on the manuscript, with minimal emendations of Auden's idiosyncratic spelling and light punctuation, and with the passages cut by Mitchison silently restored. The present text also includes a paragraph on metre that appears only in the published text (the paragraph beginning "Accents", on p. 19; the word "Lastly" was also added to the opening of the next paragraph) and incorporates the heavily revised conclusion of the published version in place of the version in the manuscript, which is reprinted below.

I have followed Mitchison in some minor emendations. In the paragraph beginning "Life is one whole thing" (p. 13) Auden wrote "positive electrons . . . central negative electron", which Mitchison corrected. In the paragraph beginning "The more this feeling grew" (p. 13), Mitchison added the words printed here in brackets: "Before he had lost it, when he [was] doing things together in a group, such [as] hunting". At the end of the paragraph beginning "To go back to our sketch" (p. 15), Mitchison added the bracketed words in "Thus sounds would begin to have sense meaning, to stand for things, as well as having meaning as [an expression of] feeling." At the end of the paragraph beginning "How early speech joined up with writing" (p. 17) Mitchison (or Auden in his revisions) added the sentence "Chinese is still a language of this kind." In the sixth sentence of the paragraph beginning "The effect of this has been a mixed one" (p. 18), I have added "as" before "the past history of the language". Later in the same paragraph, the sentence "At present nobody gets such an education" is either Mitchison's or Auden's replacement for the manuscript version, "Such an education is at present almost entirely lacking".

Auden made three attempts to conclude the essay. The manuscript, in place of the concluding section titled "Books and Life" in the printed version (pp. 23–24), has the following two sections, "History of Literature" and "Summary":

HISTORY OF LITERATURE

A book is the child of a marriage between an individual and the group or society in which he lives. Books provide a kind of a history of society.

Unfortunately we have almost no examples from the literatures of any but comparatively modern civilisations, none for example from the great megalithic matriarchal civilisation which starting in Egypt and Mesopotomia overran the entire world previous to our era (except, that is, for what has filtered down to us distorted and overlain with later additions in folk tales and fairy stories). The earliest literatures we have belong to the Heroic age, a stage in the development of societies already patriarchal when increase in size forces them to migrate in small bachelor groups under a leader to find a wife and home elsewhere on conquered soil. Heroic literature consists of epics, long stories in verse of the exploits of these small groups of fighters, which were chanted in the halls of chiefs in the evenings. The size and bachelor nature of these groups, with their common devotion to a leader, and their common interests in fighting, sailing, and farming produces a characteristic literature. In the epic there is no division between "prosaic" and "poetic" (because there is no second-hand experience). Though often complicated in verse form (appreciation of technique is only possible in a leisured community. These people were conquerors forcing the people they conquered to work for them) yet the actions and emotional situations described are simple, fighting, eating, loving, farming, sleeping. It is essentially masculine; women are not of much importance in it except as causers of trouble, setting up a conflict between loyalty to the family and loyalty to the bachelor group. This theme of divided loyalties and the fight against hopeless odds in a narrow place are the commonest tragic situations in the epic. But the appearance, at least the writing down, of these poems is in itself a sign that the day of that kind of society is passing: the migrant group has already begun to settle down: the bond between leader and his men to relax. Listening to these poems they recover for a moment the old feeling of unity; are one with their forefathers; but the moment passes. The group is growing into the feudal state.

The feudal state is too large to exist as a single group; it becomes stratified in layers, King, baron, knight, freeman, serf, each layer having little in common with another. Literature too becomes class-conscious. Instead of a common literature we have one for the "gentle" and one for the "simple". The latter, lacking the necessary degree of leisure and economic security, becomes crude in feeling and rude in form: the former becomes increasingly complicated in form and refined in feeling, but the feelings have no guts, no contact with the earth, full of feeling about feeling.

But the feudal system was international, common to all Europe, professing one religious faith, and Latin as a universal language for scholarship; poems were freely translated from one language into another, and the Catholic Church did its best to unite all classes. If you read Chaucer's *Canterbury Tales* you can't help being struck by the freedom with which pilgrims of every class talk to each other and laugh at each other's jokes. True, a pilgrimage, like a sea voyage, is a special occasion; but to-day cabin would not be so free with steerage.

We must go back for a moment to look at a special kind of society which has arisen at various times in history, and has seldom failed to show great literary activity, the city state (e.g. Athens—Aeschylus, Florence—Dante). It is easy to see why this should be so. The group is a small one, they are all neighbors sharing each other's interests, and near enough to the country not to lose contact with reality. Leisure gives opportunities for the development of an intricate and difficult art. But the city state has never lasted very long. A few years of feverish activity and then—phut. Why, because its leisure is extorted from colonies or a slave class. It is economically parasitic. Sooner or later war or revolution kill it.

To return to the main current of history. The Feudal system broke down and the Reformation broke up religion. Europe became disunited. Not only were there classes, there were nations. And the Renaissance in Italy with its sense of the importance of learning, produced the highbrow, the man who thinks books are everything, and despises those who do not read them.

When nations are forming themselves, they always show great artistic activity (e.g. during the reign of Elizabeth in England). There is something to be done, a state to be re-made, an Armada to defeat, a religion to reform. But in time these aims are reached. The nation as a group is too large to be united except by exceptional circumstances like a war. In peace time its sense of unity evaporates very quickly, and then the isolation is worse than before. Not only are there upper and lower classes;

there are English upper and lower classes and French upper and lower classes; all out of sympathy with each other: a French literature and an English literature. Drama, always a sign that a community is united, disappears. Literature gets more and more shut up in little circles of clever people. Dryden and Pope are very fine poets but they wrote for a highly cultured few, for a rentier class.

But there is worse to come. The Industrial Revolution, taking the people from the country and herding them into the towns, destroys what folk culture and literature there was. The workers, uprooted and oppressed, cease to be creative.

People cease to be people to one another. They are algebraical symbols expressing money values. "How much wages can I get out of x?" "How many hours a day can I make y do?" You are either an employer or an employee; or a shopkeeper doing your dingy little best to cheat both.

What is literature doing? Either losing its nerve, it turns its back on life and begins to eat itself, becomes bookish, writing about writing, impossible to understand unless you have first read all the other books, or else soured and hysterical, prophesies disaster, or turns just nasty.

SUMMARY

Man writes and reads because he is lonely and wants to be re-united with a group. Writing must do two things. It must affect the whole group and the way in which it affects it must be valuable, assisting the group towards a completer and more discriminating life. The larger the group the harder to unite it and the cruder the feelings which do. But it is impossible for people now to exist in small groups *only*. Like the city state, such groups cannot earn the money to live; they become competitive and unequal like the family. I cannot see that such groups are possible except as short-lived oddities, except in a one-class state where the distribution of money and leisure is more or less equal, and where industries have become decentralised so that we are not compelled to herd together in unmanageable masses. Towns must be smaller. I am also inclined to think we read far too much; that if literature is to revive, most of us will have to stop learning to read and write, stop moving from place to place, and let literature start again by oral tradition. One thing is quite certain. We shall do absolutely nothing without some sort of faith either religious like Catholicism or political like Communism. It's not only literature but our lives that are going to pot. We can't sit on the fence much longer. Well?

The "Summary" printed above is the text that in the manuscript replaces a cancelled earlier version, printed below:

SUMMARY

Man wants to write because he is lonely, and wants to be reunited in a group, and he reads for the same reason. Writing must do two things: it must move the whole group; and the way in which it moves them must be valuable, assist the fuller and more discriminating life of the group.

The larger the group the harder it is to affect it, and the cruder the feelings which do. What is to be done?

The best conditions for writing are the same as those for living. Small groups linked up into larger groups. To bind the former to the latter you must have faith, either a religious one like Catholicism or a political one like Communism. The family which is essentially a group based on unequality will have to diminish in power and importance. (It is probable that living in communal dwellings will be no better.) We must have equality of leisure. We shall have to choose. It's not only a question of literature but our future happiness. We can't sit on the fence much longer. Well?

A slightly emended version of the published text appears in *The English Auden* (1977). A transcript of the manuscript, with extensive introductory and explanatory material by Katherine Bucknell and Naomi Mitchison, appears in *Auden Studies 1* (1990).

PRIVATE PLEASURE

Page 25.

This is the first of the reviews Auden wrote for *Scrutiny* from 1932 to 1935, a period when the journal was edited by various groupings of L. C. Knights, Donald Culver, F. R. Leavis, Denys Thompson, and D. W. Harding. This review appeared in the second number. Auden toned down his Lawrentian manner in later contributions. Knights wrote in a memoir:

> I called on, or wrote to, a number of people, some of them established "names", who we thought might be willing to contribute—Joseph Needham, Michael Oakeshott, W. H. Auden, Herbert Butterfield, G. Lowes Dickinson, and I. A. Richards. Auden, unfortunately, was the only one I didn't meet personally. All received me kindly, with real interest in the project, and promised to write something for an early number, as indeed they did. (*The Leavises: Recollections and Impressions,* ed. Denys Thompson [1984], p. 72)

A reissue of the full run was published by Cambridge University Press in 1963. Michael Black, who administered the publication, wrote to the contributors for formal permission to reprint:

> All of them agreed except W. H. Auden, who thought that *Scrutiny* had been a bad influence, did not think his own contributions "were any good", and withheld permission. This might have threatened the whole venture,

but [the Secretary to the Syndics R. J. L.] Kingford suggested that when we had permission from everyone else we should tell Auden and ask him to reconsider. He did so, not wishing to be the dog in the manger; but he made it a condition that a note should be printed saying that republication was "with his consent but against his will". I failed to remember to do this, and Auden presumably forgot that he had asked for it, which was discreet of both of us. (Thompson, *The Leavises*, p. 88)

Auden's letter to Black, written on 11 October 1961, said: "I regret having to inform you that I cannot give permission to reprint any of the six articles of mine which you list, because I do not think that any of them are any good." After receiving Black's second letter, Auden wrote on 21 January 1962: "Since I have no right singlehandedly to spoil your project, I will consent to the inclusion of my piece or pieces in your re-issue of *Scrutiny*, but you must insert a note to the effect that re-publication is with my consent but against my will. I should, no doubt, feel less reluctant, were I more confident that the cultural influence of *Scrutiny* had been a beneficial one" (letters at Cambridge University Press).

PROBLEMS OF EDUCATION

Page 27.

This was Auden's first review for the *New Statesman and Nation*. In the first paragraph I have emended "bland to his own" to "blind to his own" and "vulnerable things" to "valuable things". In the first set-off quotation I have corrected an obvious misreading by the compositor ("as Imperialists" for "and Imperialists") and replaced parentheses with square brackets, but have let Auden's slight abridgement of the original stand. An editor at the *Criterion* asked Auden to review this book together with *Intellectual Crime*, by Janet Chance, but Auden returned them on 24 April 1933 with a note saying: "I reviewed the former for *The New Statesman* and therefore feel it would not be fair to review it again, and I presume you want the two books reviewed together".

A REVIEW OF *The Evolution of Sex* AND
The Biological Tragedy of Women

Page 29.

In the paragraph beginning "These are minor points" the *Criterion* italicizes "Aphrodite of the Foam", evidently because an editor mistook the phrase (from chapter 26 of Lawrence's *The Plumed Serpent*) as the title of a separate work. Auden trivially misquotes the two books under review; his errors are not corrected here, although in the opening quotation his omission of the phrase indicated below by brackets slightly obscures the sense: "springs the development [of each one] of the two sexes". I have added the page reference for the extracted quotation from Nemilov, and have replaced parentheses with square brackets. Auden's omission of the tilde and accent in Marañón was clearly his error and not that of the *Criterion*, which usually respected European spellings. A manuscript of the final paragraph of the review is preserved among Auden's letters to

Stephen Spender in the Berg Collection. In this edition the capitalization in this paragraph follows that of the manuscript instead of the lighter capitalization in the *Criterion*.

GENTLEMAN VERSUS PLAYER

Page 31.

In the first sentence "believing" is an emendation for "behaving". Auden (or *Scrutiny*'s compositor) omitted a few words in the extracts from Churchill. In the penultimate sentence of the second numbered extract, after "crag", this phrase originally appeared between commas: "their venerated 'El Capitan' or 'Il Duce'". In the third sentence from the end of the third numbered extract, "pictorial" is omitted before "battlefield".

A REVIEW OF *The Dark Places of Education*

Page 34.

This was one of the *Criterion*'s shorter notices, which were signed with initials only. On 21 February 1933 Auden wrote to Eliot's assistant at the magazine: "Here is the proof of my review of *Dark Places in Education*. Would you be so kind as to verify the author's name, as I have sold the book and am not dead certain" (letter in the Faber & Faber archives). Auden correctly remembered the author's surname (he omitted the first name), but in his letter and in the heading of the review he misremembered the title, *The Dark Places of Education,* as *Dark Places in Education.* In the final paragraph he restored the definite article, but evidently failed to underline it, because the printed text of the paragraph, in an obvious error, begins: "The *Dark Places in Education* should". I have let stand Auden's misquotations: "To those who" for "For those who" and "the problem of discipline" for "the problem of authority".

A POET TELLS US HOW TO BE MASTERS OF THE MACHINE

Page 35.

This was Auden's one contribution to the *Daily Herald,* the only national Labour newspaper. The byline reads: "by W. H. Auden, one of our younger poets who is also a schoolmaster."

A REVIEW OF *Culture and Environment* AND OTHER BOOKS

Page 37.

In the list of contributions on the front cover of the magazine this review was referred to by the title "What Is a Highbrow?"—the first sentence of the text.

This was Auden's first review for the *Twentieth Century,* the organ of the Promethean Society, a group that formed in London in 1930 for weekly meetings to discuss progressive causes. Auden told Eliot on 28 October 1931 that he had sent a poem "to the *Twentieth Century,* one of those dreadful little papers with a priggish title and no money." The magazine was edited by Jon Randell Evans, who worked as a reader for the left-wing publisher Victor Gollancz but did not share Gollancz's doctrinaire politics. It appeared monthly from March 1931 through August 1933, then irregularly for six further numbers until September 1934. The first number reprinted Auden's "Get there if you can and see the land you once were proud to own" from his 1930 *Poems,* evidently because the editor found in the poem a statement of the society's views. In the same number A. E. Blake wrote:

> Admittedly we owe a great deal to Wells and the ideas he has outlined in "A Modern Utopia," "The Open Conspiracy," and other books. But we have not swallowed his ideas whole. Chiefly we lack confidence in his Big Business Men and his enlightened men of science and all whom he hopes will share with him a journey to Utopia by the Blue Train.

As the depression worsened the magazine occasionally sounded a Marxist but generally anti-Soviet note; in 1932 it reprinted an essay by Trotsky. As the society grew it subdivided into groups that concentrated on the main concerns of the membership; during much of the period from 1931 to 1934 these were the Political and Economic Group, the Sexology Group, the Active Peace Group, the Philosophy and Religion Group, and the Arts Group. The society also helped organize the Federation of Progressive Societies, whose member organizations announced meetings in the pages of the magazine. Among the better-known frequent contributors to the *Twentieth Century* were Havelock Ellis, A. Desmond Hawkins, John Middleton Murray, A. S. Neill, Max Plowman, and Paul Rotha. Many of its literary reviews were written by Hugh Gordon Porteus and Geoffrey West. Auden seems to have had no direct contact with the society, but he contributed poems (including "A Communist to Others") to four numbers in 1932 and 1933, and, in May 1933, the book review reprinted here. (The magazine did not print the poem he told Eliot he had submitted in October 1931, "Walk on air do we? And how!") Among Auden's friends, Naomi Mitchison contributed essays from 1932 to 1934; Stephen Spender contributed a poem and reviews (including an essay-review on Auden's *Poems* and *The Orators*) in 1932; and Cecil Day Lewis contributed a poem and a review in 1934. A brief account of the magazine appears in Julian Symon's essay on Porteus, "Forgotten Man of the Thirties", *Times Literary Supplement,* 26 March 1973.

A REVIEW OF *The Poems of William Dunbar*

Page 39.

On 31 August 1932 Auden asked Eliot if he could review the edition of Dunbar that he believed was about to appear ("Lawrence's letters I suppose are already begged"). The book was sent to him in January 1933; he sent the review on 24 April 1933, and returned corrected proof on 11 May 1933. In transcribing the manuscript the magazine's compositor made minor slips, which are corrected here.

What Is Wrong with Architecture?

Page 41.

Auden's friend John Betjeman worked for the *Architectural Review* from 1931 to 1933 and presumably commissioned this piece. Auden reduced the name Frederic Towndrow to F. Towndrow. I have emended, in the fourth paragraph from the end, "the rush of an age" to "the rush of our age", and, in the second paragraph from the end, "when the problem" to "where the problem". In both cases the printed texts evidently result from common misreadings of Auden's hand.

A Review of *The Book of Talbot*

Page 42.

At Auden's request, T. S. Eliot's secretary sent him on 10 July 1933 a copy of *The Book of Talbot*, "which Mr [Herbert] Read tells me that you wanted to review" for the *Criterion*. Auden's review slightly misquotes the book. I have corrected in the first set-off quotation "are all alive" to "are all akin", and in the second set-off quotation "For seeing" to "Foreseeing"; both probably resulted from the compositor's misreading of Auden's hand. I have left "leapt up from the brake" (for "bracken"), "a being in ebb" (for "at ebb"), and some minor changes in punctuation, all of which were probably Auden's miscopyings. Violet Clifton's elevation to the rank of "Lady Clifton" occurred only in Auden's imagination.

The First Lord Melchett

Page 44.

Auden evidently made a few trivial mistranscriptions of the book under review, which I have let stand.

The Group Movement and the Middle Classes

Page 47.

Richard Crossman, Auden's friend from his undergraduate days, was a philosophy don when he edited the collection *Oxford and the Groups,* published by Basil Blackwell on 23 January 1934. The book was a survey of the Group Movement by twelve authors, two of them active in leading the movement, most of them antagonistic to it, and all members or former members of Oxford University; the movement had its headquarters in the city of Oxford, from which it took its informal name, but had no formal association with the university. Auden's contribution was probably written late in 1933. The text in this edition preserves Auden's footnotes but silently omits footnotes by Crossman that refer the reader to other essays in the collection. The two paragraphs that begin "Lastly, there is" and "Further, that we do not think" (pp. 49–50) may have been a single paragraph in the manuscript; the phrase "that we do not think" in the second of the two paragraphs depends on the phrase "It seems to be generally true" in the first. Auden's quotation from Gerald Heard's *Social Substance of Religion* (p. 53) is silently stitched together from a number of separate passages, although Auden uses only one ellipsis. Auden's "a cause of love" is miscopied from Heard's "a common love", and "after death" is miscopied from "from death". In the final paragraph of the essay I have emended "size when" to "size where".

The Liberal Fascist [Honour]

Page 55.

Graham Greene opened his preface to *The Old School:* "I regard this book rather as a premature memorial, like a family photograph album. . . . Like the family album, this book will, I hope, be superficially more funny than tragic, for so odd a system of education does not demand a pompous memorial." Eighteen writers described the schools they attended, most of them during the Great War and the years immediately following it. The book, subtitled "Essays by Divers Hands", was published by Jonathan Cape on 23 July 1934. Auden probably wrote his essay early in the year and sent it to Greene, who returned it with a request for changes. On 7 April 1934 Auden apparently sent a corrected copy of the manuscript back to Greene with this cover note: "Hope corrections and additions are clear. I haven't added much so fear essay is rather short but I have said all I want" (letter in the Boston College Library).

The manuscript is now in the possession of Gresham's School, Holt. It is headed, in Greene's hand, "The Liberal Fascist. / Gresham's School, Holt. / By W. H. Auden." For the printed text Greene retitled the essay "Honour" and placed the name of the school in square brackets as a subtitle; he followed a similar convention in titling the other essays in the book. In making his corrections before returning the manuscript to Greene, Auden evidently deleted and discarded the original opening page, crossed through the first half of the second page, and wrote in a new opening sentence to replace the original long opening. He also added a slip of paper containing the passage from "Indeed it is impossible" to "true of the staff as well" (p. 56).

The surviving section of the discarded opening passage—approximately one-third of the original passage—begins in the middle of a sentence about the ways in which middle-class pupils at public schools tried to imitate aristocrats. A conjectural opening for the sentence is supplied in square brackets:

[?The personal manner] they imitated was of course not the aristocrat's behaviour in his own circle which was often extremely emotional, but his behaviour to them, in his opinion his inferiors. Anyway, whatever the virtues of the public school type, as an aristocrat he was a fake. And to-day, what with the war, the economic crisis, Freud, and everything else, faith in the type is waning. The average parent to-day is by no means certain that he wants his son to be a gentleman.

The gentleman has been governing the country for years and he has failed. Whether any other type would have succeeded doesn't matter. Some scapegoat must be found, and there he is. Parents are beginning to ask questions, and not only the cranky ones either. The most respectable fathers and mothers, people who twenty years ago would have regarded anything less than Winchester or Rugby as unthinkable, often indeed themselves old boys of such schools, are hesitating. "If", they are saying, "I send my boy to an ordinary public school, will it really fit him for the world he will have to live in?"

That kind of question is the sole excuse for this kind of book, and if, in my account of Gresham's School, Holt, [*continues as in the second sentence of the published text*].

The printed text included various minor misreadings and misplacements of words that Auden inserted above the line; they are silently corrected here. In the fourth paragraph (p. 55) Greene apparently added "almost" before the words "invariably slatternly"; in the paragraph that begins "It is perhaps as well" (p. 57) he added "too" before "terrified to move" and omitted "and even" from the last sentence; and in the paragraph that begins "To the latter" (p. 57), he added "only" before "partiality". Greene omitted the paragraph that begins "It does not of course follow" (p. 57). Greene cut the last phrases of Auden's final sentence, from "but if one of these" to the end, and moved the remaining part of the sentence to the beginning of the final paragraph, so that the paragraph ended "for what they are worth."

"T. E. LAWRENCE"

Page 61.

Now and Then was a quarterly of extracts from, and reviews of, books published by Jonathan Cape. The full title of B. H. Liddell Hart's book under review was "*T. E. Lawrence*" *in Arabia and After* (including the quotation marks). Auden's review was titled in the manuscript "'T. E. Lawrence' by W. H. Auden", and in the magazine "'*T. E. Lawrence*' reviewed by W. H. Auden". A note on the book, added by Rupert Hart-Davis, who prepared the magazine for the press, referred to the book by the same brief title.

The manuscript was formerly in the collection of A. R. A. Hobson, whose collation of the variants between the manuscript and printed versions is the basis of the text in this edition. I have restored Auden's capitalization (except where he reduces capitals in book titles), and have let stand his inconsistent capitalization of "the truly strong man" and its variants. I have also restored most of his chaotic punctuation. This edition refers to [William] McDougall where the manuscript has MacDougal and the printed text has Macdougal. In the third paragraph the printed text has an extraneous "to" in "will bring to us to the freedom"; the word seems to be deleted in the manuscript and is deleted here. In the fourth paragraph, the manuscript has no comma after "the ditch of despair", and the omission may conceivably have been intended. In the fifth paragraph the manuscript perhaps has "or" immediately preceding "better demonstrated", and this reading makes enough sense to include it here. The final paragraph was for obvious reasons omitted from the magazine but is restored here.

LIFE'S OLD BOY

Page 62.

On page 64, line 7, I have let stand the probably authorial punctuation in "born pure in the adult sense, than they are born observant". A page number with transposed digits has been corrected. Auden or the editors of *Scrutiny* omitted the hyphen in Baden-Powell. In the first paragraph, Clarence Hatry was a financier imprisoned in 1930.

A REVIEW OF *The Poetry of Gerard Manley Hopkins*

Page 66.

Auden's heading reduced the title of the book to *Gerard Manley Hopkins* and the author's first two names to initials. (E. E. Phare's married name was Elsie Duncan-Jones; see p. 732.) I have let stand Auden's minor errors of transcription, although I have corrected two probable compositor's misreadings: "No sight which" for "The sight which" and "really the type" for "merely the type" (p. 68). The text includes these emendations: page 67, line 29, "Saurat" for "Seurat"; page 67, line 37, semicolon after "reactions"; page 68, line 32, "about him" for "of his"; page 68, line 37, "take 'The Bugler's" for "take the 'Bugler's"; page 68, line 41, "Reading the poem" for "Reading of the poem"; and page 69, line 2, question mark after "the subjects of the poem". A page reference is corrected and a set of parentheses replaced with square brackets.

A REVIEW OF *Modern Poetic Drama*

Page 69.

Auden's first unsigned review for the BBC's weekly magazine, the *Listener*, was commissioned by its deputy editor, Janet Adam Smith. Auden is identified as the reviewer in the magazine's records of payment in the BBC Written Archives Centre. In the first paragraph "Obéy" is emended to "Obey".

The next number of the magazine (30 May 1934) printed a letter from Laurence Kitchin:

> I should like to draw attention to some of the rash generalisations in your review of *Modern Poetic Drama*. It is obviously unsafe to say, for instance, that the comedy of manners is "definitely antipathetic to poetry", when the example of Ben Jonson is there to prove the opposite. The assertion that characters who speak verse are flat is more absurd still. The characters in *Hamlet* are thoroughly vitalised and differentiated; they are preserved by the verse as if in ice, but they remain three-dimensional. Finally, there is the suggestion that "poetic drama should start with the stock musical comedy

characters". This was the method of the French Romantic drama—notably in the plays of Victor Hugo, which are generally admitted to be failures dramatically. The dramatic poet of the future had better not be "humble and sympathetic" until he is given more reliable advice.

The following number (7 June 1934) printed a further letter from E. Cannell, which began, "Mr Laurence Kitchin fires a big gun at the rather trivial review in your columns"; offered further objections to the review; and concluded: "It is not beyond the powers of poetic genius to 'distance' even your reviewer's rich uncle and mother-in-law, to set what they hope they are and what they are against the human tide of endeavor and frustration . . . and make them live dramatically."

Auden responded in a paragraph that appeared below this letter, under the heading "Our Reviewer replies":

It is difficult in a short review adequately to define one's terms. What Mr Kitchen [*sic*], citing Ben Jonson, calls character, I should call "humour", the hypertrophied moral quality. As to the flatness or roundness of Hamlet, that again is a matter of opinion. Of course, he is "vitalised and differentiated", but that has nothing to do with his roundness. So are the "characters" in Dickens. That the French Romantics failed with the stock music-hall figures was not due to the latter, but to the fact that the writers had no sense of the theatre. I offered them as a suggestion of material, with which to work, for the dramatist to "distance", to use Mr Cannell's word. There is no reason why the dramatist should adopt it unless he wants to. The only reason for making the suggestion is that their popularity and familiarity gives the public a handle to hold on to, and would seem to imply that they have some psychological and perhaps poetic symbolic value.

A Review of *English Poetry for Children*

Page 70.

Auden sent this review to Eliot on 1 May 1934. It was one of the *Criterion*'s shorter notices, signed with initials only. In the first paragraph I have added commas after "those who" and "admirable", and in the last paragraph emended "minature" to "immature" and "periodical" to "prosodical".

In Search of Dracula

Page 72.

This travel diary from August and September 1934 appeared in two numbers of the *Badger*, the magazine of the Downs School; the second installment began with the entry for 22 August. Each was signed "By W.H.A." Auden's companions on the trip were two Old Boys from the school, Peter Roger, who was working for the school as a gardener, and Michael Yates. Auden mentioned the trip in a letter to Naomi Mitchison, probably in the spring of 1934: "I'm off to the Carpathians this summer stimulated I believe by childish memories of Dracula. I hope we get interned" (letter in the Berg Collection). See also the notes to "Psychology and Art To-day", below.

Most of the private references in the diary are to masters at the school: Mr Pup (p. 72) was a nickname for Francis Day, a churchgoing Latin master, later referred to as Mr Day (p. 74); Mr Booge (for Booj, from Boojum, p. 72) was the Second Master, E. C. Coxwell; Stainless (p. 72) was the nickname of Stephen Marriage, a pupil who received his nickname on the model of "Stainless Stephen", a popular catchphrase; Mr Telfer (p. 75) was a part-time science master; the half-wit brother of a friend (p. 77) was Richard Bradshaw-Isherwood, who delivered the loan after Auden telephoned a request to Kathleen Isherwood (Christopher and Richard's mother). Persons mentioned only by their first names include Hedwig Petzold (p. 76), with whom Auden stayed on a visit to Kitzbühel in 1926, and Gerald Heard (p. 77). Full annotations by Richard Davenport-Hines and Nicholas Jenkins appear in *Auden Studies 2* (1994).

This text emends "lodge" to "Lodge" in the first paragraph; in the entry for 16 August, "Beaudelaire" to "Baudelaire"; in the entry for 22 August, "Jhilava" to "Jihlava"; and in the entry for 24 August, "peeks" to "peaks" (although a lost slang term may perhaps have been intended). Auden's quotation marks around titles of books and dramatic works have been replaced by italics, but his omission of articles from some titles has been left uncorrected. It was probably Auden, not the compositor, who omitted the haček in Lučenec and Trenčin.

To Unravel Unhappiness

Page 77.
    Auden's first extract from the book under review contains minor transcription errors. I have corrected the transposition of "potentially so" as "so potentially", but have left his omission of "generally" and two commas in "could, generally at least, control". In the first sentence of the third paragraph "sets" is emended to "set".

Lowes Dickinson

Page 80.
    The first of three of Auden's pieces on Forster's *Goldsworthy Lowes Dickinson;* the second was a 1938 review for *Town Crier* (p. 460); the third was the introduction he wrote for the 1973 Abinger Edition of the book. In the third paragraph, I have removed the comma after "novelist's".

John Skelton

Page 82.
    Katherine Garvin's anthology of forty essays, *The Great Tudors*, was published by Ivor Nicholson & Watson in March 1935. In 1949, when Auden gave Robert Phelps permission to reprint the essay in a collection that never appeared, he

made two slight corrections, both incorporated here: *pompositas* italicized in the third paragraph, and "winning an essay prize or" for "writing an essay prize on" in the fourth. In the quotation from the Proverbs of Alfred (p. 85) the typist or compositor misread the Old English thorn as "p" and, in the third line, "and" as "as". The lines by Abelard immediately after are misremembered from F. J. E. Raby, *A History of Christian-Latin Poetry* (1927). On page 89, line 7, I have emended "fewer poets have used" to "more poets have not used".

Psychology and Art To-day

Page 93.

Geoffrey Grigson's collection of essays *The Arts To-day* was published by Jonathan Cape on 6 September 1935. Auden's essay, the first of eight in the book, was written around October 1934; on 13 October Auden sent a postcard to Grigson, which reads: "Have patience. Essay nearly finished" (postcard in a private collection). Patience was required because Auden had written Grigson on 11 August: "I'm afraid essay won't be ready by Sept 1st. I've had a creative burst and have shoved everything to one side to finish a play [*The Chase*]. Now I'm going off somewhat exhausted to the Carpathians. Better say Oct 1st." (Postcard in the Harry Ransom Humanities Research Center.)

Of the books listed in the manuscript version of the bibliography at the end of the essay, the latest is the Earl of Lytton's *New Treasure*, published in October 1934. Among the five books apparently added to the bibliography at a later stage, perhaps in proof, Maud Bodkin's *Archetypal Patterns in Poetry* was published in November 1934 and Georg Groddeck's *The World of Man* in December 1934. Auden seems not to have given a title to this essay. In the manuscript, now in the Poetry Collection at the State University of New York at Buffalo, an unknown hand has written the title "The Nature of the Artist". In the book, the essay itself is titled "Psychology and Art To-day", but it is listed in the table of contents as "Psychology and Art".

The printed text (reprinted with light editing in *The English Auden*) adheres closely to Auden's manuscript, although with a few errors and confusions. For this edition the text has been newly edited from the manuscript. Where minor emendations are required I have generally followed the printed text, although I have not added its heavier punctuation. Auden's long quotation from Freud (p. 94) is uncharacteristically accurate, but only because, instead of copying it by hand, he simply tore part of a page from an unidentified book that quoted the same passage.

Most variations between the manuscript and the printed text are minor misreadings by the typist or compositor, which are silently corrected here. Notes on the more significant and more doubtful variants and other textual matters follow.

In the footnote on page 93, the manuscript has "but an opportunity for a particular kind of free associational" where the printed text misreads "but as opportunity for a particular kind of associational". On page 94, line 10, the manuscript reads "their phantasies of the group", with the last three words inserted above the line; the printed text has "the phantasies of their group"; this edition emends to "the phantasies of the group". On page 95, line 26, I have followed the printed text in inserting "as he develops"; the addition may be authorial. On page 95, line 34, I have restored the manuscript's "Most people however fit into society sufficiently too neatly" for the printed text's "Most people, however, fit into society too neatly". In the footnote on page 96, the manuscript apparently reads "brute force" instead of printed text's "with force". On page 97 the dream borrowed from Nicoll's *Dream Psychology* is quoted from the book, but the sentence "The patient could give no associations" and the analysis that follows is Auden's paraphrase. On page 98, line 31, the manuscript reads "ignores words, or treatment of symbols and fails", which I have emended by adding a comma after "symbols"; the typist or compositor was confused by a deleted mark of punctuation and, in trying to make sense of the sentence, typed four words, "and facts he fails", for the manuscript's two words, "and fails". On page 99, in item (3), I have followed the printed text in adding parentheses in the first sentence. Also on page 99, I have restored the manuscript version of the final sentence of the paragraph headed "What Would Be a Freudian Literature" in place of the printed version, which reads: "It is only meant to be suggestive, dividing the Christian era into three periods, the first ending with the fifteenth century, the second with the nineteenth, and the third just beginning; including what would seem the typical characteristics of such periods."

The chart on page 100 follows the page layout of the printed text, with the content restored from the manuscript, where the chart follows the section "What Would Be a Freudian Literature". The manuscript version places the numbers 1, 2, and 3 beneath the second through forth columns; the headings "1st Period.", etc., are taken from the book. Auden used the words "Official" and "Opposition" only in the first row of the third column, followed by a large "<" with the upper leg pointing to the phrase that described the official position, and the lower leg pointing to the opposition one. He drew the same sign in the next four rows of the table. The printed text, followed here, replaces the sign with the words "Official" and "Opposition".

On page 101, in item (6), I follow the printed text in adding "consisting", but have emended "all its power", the reading of both the manuscript and the printed text, to "all the power". On page 102, in item (7), I follow the printed text in adding parentheses in the final sentence. On page 103, in item (14), Auden deleted "their" before "impersonal unconscious", but the printed text's addition of "the" in its place is consistent with Auden's usage elsewhere in the essay. On page 103, in item (15), the manuscript reads "force the generalisation [*horizontal mark that may be an illegible word*] the situation, repression, where [*or when*] it will haunt them". My emended version, with parentheses around "repression", attempts to make the best of the confusion; the printed text has "force the generalisation, the situation, the repression, when it will haunt them". On page 104, immediately before the final quotation, Auden inserted the phrase "shall teach man to unlearn hatred and learn love" above the line, between "that art" and "which can enable Freud"; this edition follows the printed text in adding "which" before the inserted phrase.

The bibliography at the end of the essay was retitled in the printed text "Books to Read". The version printed here follows the manuscript in its incomplete listing of publishers' names and its inconsistent use of last names and full names, but follows the printed text in citing Herbert Read's *Art Now* instead of the manuscript's misremembered title *Modern Art*. The printed text also adds Groddeck's *The World of Man* and the four final titles to the manuscript bibliography. Because the manuscript list ends at the foot of the last surviving page, it is conceivable that the last four titles were on a page now lost, but three of the four were published in Britain from November 1934 through March 1935, and Groddeck's *The World of Man*, added earlier in the list, was published in December 1934. Robert Graves's *Poetic Unreason*, also among the last four titles, was published in 1925, and Auden presumably added it to the list as an afterthought.

Introduction to *The Poet's Tongue*

Page 105.

For the history of this anthology, which Auden edited in collaboration with John Garrett, see Appendix I above. The book was published by George Bell & Sons in a two-volume edition for schools on 20 June 1935, with the volumes described on the title page as "First Part" and "Second Part". A one-volume trade edition appeared on 8 August 1935.

In the second paragraph of the introduction the printed text's "between the rhythm" is plausible, but perhaps should read "between the rhythms" . The one-volume edition omits four paragraphs found in the two-volume edition: those beginning "In an anthology", "At the same time", "Again, now that" (p. 108), and the concluding paragraph. In this edition, the final sentence of the concluding paragraph follows the text of the first volume of the two-volume edition; the second volume replaces "the *Second Part*" with "this last Part".

In the second paragraph Auden apparently added in proof the phrase "all muscular effort" after "necessary to all living things", but G. H. Bickers, at Bell, asked if this could be omitted to avoid an overrun; the proposed addition fits awkwardly into the sentence and is not added in this edition. In the second paragraph from the end, Auden originally wrote "adopted an ahistorical, anonymous order"; Bickers suggested in a letter of 2 May 1935 that "ahistorical" be replaced by "alphabetical", and Auden apparently accepted the suggestion.

The Good Life

Page 109.

Auden's essay is the first of eighteen in *Christianity and the Social Revolution*, a book described on the title page as edited by John Lewis, Karl Polanyi, and Donald K. Kitchin; their names are followed on the same page with the names of an "editorial board" consisting of Joseph Needham, Charles E. Raven, and John Macmurray. The book was published by Victor Gollancz on 28 October 1935; some copies were issued in the United States in 1936 by Charles Scribner's Sons. John Lewis's preface begins: "This volume of essays has a definite purpose, and its plan follows from the purpose. It challenges the traditional attitude of Christianity towards the question of radical social change. It also challenges the orthodox attitude of Communism to Religion." Lewis adds later in the preface: "It is the contention of most of the authors of this book that Christianity cannot be ignored by Socialists. It is, in this country, too virile, in spite of all its defects, and too deeply penetrated with social idealism to be scorned either as a foe or an ally." Most of the essays in the book interpret Christianity in Marxist terms and Marxism in Christian terms. Auden's essay is the first in the opening section, "Socialism in Historical Christianity"; the other two sections are headed "Communism and Religion" and "Dies Iræ".

Lewis's preface concludes: "Many unexpected difficulties have delayed the publication of this work, which was conceived in the summer of 1933. To Mr Donald Kitchin's enthusiasm and energy the launching of the project and the gathering of the early contributors was due. Dr Karl Polanyi took up the task when illness prevented Mr Kitchin from carrying on with the work, but his long visit to America rendered it necessary for the present editor to assume final responsibility." Auden probably wrote his essay late in 1934 or early in 1935, certainly not earlier than October 1934, the publication date of *Aspects of Dialectical Materialism*, by H. Levy, John Macmurray, Ralph Fox, R. Page Arnot, J. D. Bernal, and E. F. Carritt, the book from which Auden took the quotation from H. Levy on page 113.

This edition makes the following emendations. On page 110, line 6, a comma is added after "Oppressed classes". On page 111, line 13, I have replaced a comma with a period after "makes such reflections irrelevant", and capitalized "E.g." to make it begin a new sentence; Auden's manuscripts frequently begin a sentence with a lowercase "eg." On page 111, last line, a comma replaces a colon after "who is good".

The quotation on page 113 from Levy slightly reorders the words in the original and replaces Levy's "intelligible" with "intelligent"; the quotation marks within the quotation have been corrected. (For further details of Auden's treatment of this quotation, see page xxxix.) The quotation on pages 116–17 from F. W. Powicke's essay in *Legacy of the Middle Ages*, ed. C. G. Crump and E. F. Jacob (1926), is cobbled together from three separate passages, with trivial misquotations, and a change from Powicke's "Apostolic poverty" to Auden's "evangelical poverty"; a possible miscopying of Auden's hand by the typist or compositor is "a merely professional activity" for Powicke's "or merely professional activity". The quotation on page 117 from Shaw's *Saint Joan* and the quotation on pages 119–20 from Hans Prinzhorn's *Psychotherapy* also have trivial misquotations; in the latter Auden replaced Prinzhorn's "slender bridge of trust" with "slender ladder of trust", although this change is conceivably an error by the typist or compositor.

The essay is signed "by Wystan Auden".

EVERYMAN'S FREEDOM

Page 123.

Auden's heading omitted the initials in the name of Colonel E. A. Loftus, and his extract has some trivial inaccuracies and omissions, not corrected here. Auden also miscopied the chapter title "The Cog in [*not* and] the Wheel".

THE BOND AND THE FREE

Page 125.

Auden's heading reduced Walter Brierley to W. Brierley. I have treated the fourth and fifth sentences of the review as part of the second paragraph; in the printed text they appear in a separate paragraph. The blank lines between some paragraphs in the present text are reproduced from the original.

[FROM THE SERIES "I WANT THE THEATRE TO BE . . ."]

Page 128.

The first of a series of a dramatic manifestos printed under the same title in the programs of the Group Theatre's Westminster Theatre season, 1935–36. The text in this edition is that of Auden's untitled manuscript, now in the Berg Collection. The text in the program has two errors: in the second paragraph from the end, "confessed" for "compressed", and in the final paragraph, "at any rate directly" for "directly at any rate".

A REVIEW OF *Documentary Film*

Page 129.

Auden's authorship of this unsigned review, presumably commissioned by the *Listener*'s literary editor J. R. Ackerley, is confirmed by the paper's records of payment in the BBC Written Archives Centre, and was no secret to Auden's colleagues at the General Post Office Film Unit who made documentaries of the kind described in the book. In the first issue of *World Film News*, April 1936, the column headed "Meetings and Acquaintances, by All Hands" included this unsigned note:

> W. H. Auden, one of the brightest poets of the younger generation, author of *Dance of Death* and *The Dog Beneath the Skin,* and incidentally film assistant at the G.P.O. Film Unit, wades into his documentary masters in a *Listener* review.
>
> Auden says documentary directors are upper middle-class and never likely to understand workers. He says sponsorship by industrial companies, government department[s], etc., will never permit truthful account of their people.
>
> Their description as "upper middle" will surprise and flatter not a few documentary directors. What is more important than paternities is that documentary forces its serfs to live and learn with workmen under working conditions. Few operators in other arts come as close.
>
> Auden also complains that the documentary product lacks human appeal. It is to be noted that human element increases as the apprentices learn their job. As Auden's own apprenticeship matures he may feel less despondent.

This was probably the work of John Grierson, head of the Film Unit, who in the same issue of *World Film News* is listed as the first of six "controllers" of the magazine; the others were Alberto Cavalcanti, Forsyth Hardy, G. D. Robinson,

Norman Wilson, and Basil Wright. The same issue lists Auden and Isherwood among twenty-nine "Correspondents", many of whom seem never to have written for the magazine. Around the time his review appeared, in the middle of February 1936, Auden took an extended leave from the Film Unit to work in Portugal with Christopher Isherwood on *The Ascent of F 6*. While there, late in March, he posted to Grierson his letter of resignation from the Film Unit. The note in *World Film News* was evidently written before Auden's letter arrived.

In the muddled sixth sentence of the review, "entertainment" is perhaps a compositor's misreading of a word like "antagonism".

Psychology and Criticism

Page 130.

This was the first of Auden's book reviews for *New Verse*, the little magazine edited by Geoffrey Grigson, which had already published many of Auden's poems. The review was probably written around March 1936. A pencil draft is in one of Auden's notebooks now in the Berg Collection; the finished manuscript, used as setting copy, is in the Poetry Collection at the State University of New York at Buffalo. The title of the review was added by Grigson. The text in this edition restores a few quotation marks dropped by the compositor, but does not correct Auden's frequent minor errors in transcription. In the extract beginning "There are always", Auden added the italics and miscopied "individual feeling" for "independent feeling". In the paragraph following that extract, "should go to the making" is perhaps a slip for "should go into the making", and it is unclear whether Auden or Grigson altered the manuscript from "but these few" to "but the few". In a probable misreading, the compositor set the last sentence of the paragraph ("I cannot believe") as a separate paragraph. In the sentence in the fifth paragraph that begins "If he means" the compositor misread "enormous" as "human". In the first sentence of the final paragraph the compositor misread "flowering" as "flowers".

A Review of *Questions of Our Day*

Page 133.

Auden is identified as the author of this review in the *Listener*'s records of payment in the BBC Written Archives Centre. In his first quotation from Ellis he omitted "even" after "There may be". A pencil draft of the review is in one of Auden's notebooks in the Berg Collection.

Selling the Group Theatre

Page 134.

This was printed in the first of seven issues of the *Group Theatre Paper*, the Group's monthly newspaper, edited by John Johnson. A brief history of the paper appears in Michael Sidnell's *Dances of Death: The Group Theatre of London in the Thirties* (1984), pp. 171–72. The text in this edition is edited from Auden's manuscript, formerly in Johnson's possession. In the printed text the opening paragraph omits the word "proper"; the sixth paragraph lists four experimental plays, including *Sweeney Agonistes;* and the third paragraph from the end concludes "this kind in England; activities so many and various." The printed text also shows various obvious misreadings of Auden's hand.

HONEST DOUBT

Page 135.

The International Surrealist Exhibition opened in London on 11 June 1936, perhaps a few days after the publication of the number of *New Verse* that contained Auden's pseudonymous questions. Geoffrey Grigson had earlier begun to use the pages of *New Verse* for a campaign against surrealism, and the campaign persisted into later numbers. Auden's manuscript in the Harry Ransom Humanities Research Center is accompanied by an undated note to Grigson: "Thanks for your wire. I can't do you a real article on surrealism, but here are some questions which you can print instead if you like, under the initials given." The pseudonymous initials "J. B." perhaps stand for John Bull.

Grigson added an anonymous parenthetical subhead to the essay: "(We hope to print authoritative answers to these questions about Surrealism in the next *New Verse.*)" In the next number (August–September 1936), under the heading "Honest Doubt", Grigson wrote anonymously: "Owing to illness, the authoritative answers which were promised to the questions about Surrealism, published in the last number of *New Verse* under the heading of 'Honest Doubt', must be postponed to a later issue." They never appeared.

The text in this edition has been edited from the manuscript. The opening allusion to "the pages of The Minotaur" is to the surrealist magazine *Minotaure.* The printed text expands "translation of Rilke" to "translation of Rilke's *Requiem and other Poems*" and corrects Auden's trivial miscopying of the passage quoted. In section B(2)(a), I have inserted "the" in the phrase "task of the revolutionary bourgeois".

[ROBERT FROST]

Page 137.

This is the first of four untitled introductory essays in Frost's *Selected Poems;* the others are by C. Day Lewis, Paul Engle, and Edwin Muir. Rupert Hart-Davis commissioned the essays in the hope of making Frost's poems more saleable in Britain. Auden probably wrote his essay in the first part of 1936; the selection was published by Jonathan Cape on 13 November 1936. The manuscript of Auden's essay was formerly in the collection of A. R. A. Hobson, but was not accessible for use in this edition.

POPE

Page 141.

From Anne to Victoria: Essays by Various Hands, edited by Bonamy Dobrée, was published by Cassell on 18 February 1937. Auden probably wrote his essay sometime in 1936, perhaps just before he left for Iceland in June. On 25 May 1936, a few weeks before his departure for Iceland, he wrote to his former Downs School pupil Dermott Grubb: "I must stop and go on reading about life in the time of the late Queen Anne, as I have to write an article on Pope, about whom I know very little, but—Aedificandum est [the Downs School motto]." On 6 October 1936 he wrote Dobrée, apparently in reference to the proofs of the essay: "Yes, Pope arrived and has been returned to Cassell" (postcard in the Brotherton Collection at the Leeds University Library).

Dobrée's book contains forty-three biographical essays, each with the subject's dates as a parenthetical subtitle, in this instance "(1688–1744)".

Emendations made for this edition include: in the opening sentences, "Wycherley" for "Wycherly" (twice, probably Auden's error); page 142, line 9, in the otherwise trivially inaccurate quotation from Johnson's *Lives of the Poets*, "shirt" for "short"; page 144, line 17, the comma has been removed (perhaps unnecessarily) from "pacific, within their circle"; page 144, line 32, "foibles" for "fables"; page 147, line 33, "conversation" for "conversations" (which is perhaps what Auden wrote); page 151, line 17, "Romantics'" for "Romantic's"; page 153, line 4, "lethargy for me" for "lethargy for use". In Auden's quotations I have corrected slight errors that appear to be the compositor's misreadings of Auden's hand. After the quotation from *Othello* (p. 149) the printed text has two two-sentence paragraphs which I have combined in a single paragraph. Auden wrote Dobrée on 19 March 1937: "Many thanks for letter. Only 3 misprints in my article" (postcard in the Brotherton Collection). The three were perhaps "short", "fables", and "lethargy for use" in the list above.

A Review of the The Book of Margery Kempe

Page 155.

Auden's authorship of this review is confirmed by the *Listener*'s records of payment.

A Modern Use of Masks: An Apologia

Page 157.

A defense of the Group Theatre's production of *The Agamemnon*, translated by Louis MacNeice, with masks, costumes, and designs by Robert Medley. Auden's note was unsigned in the *Group Theatre Paper* but attributed to him in an abridged and slightly normalized version published in *The Times*, 27 October 1936 (early editions only). It is unclear whether *The Times* reprinted the text from the number of the *Group Theatre Paper* dated November 1936 or whether the newspaper had an advance copy. In the version in *The Times* the first sentence of the last paragraph opens "The chorus masks in *Agamemnon* will show. . . ." If the *Group Theatre Paper* appeared later, its omission of "will" perhaps reflected the fact that the play had opened on 1 November. Despite Auden's apologia, the cellophane masks proved unsatisfactory enough to be abandoned after the first night. Auden alludes to them in the "Last Will and

Testament" that he and Louis MacNeice wrote a few weeks later for *Letters from Iceland* (p. 368).

Are You Dissatisfied with This Performance?

Page 158.

This appeared in the program for the production whose design was defended in "A Modern Use of Masks". The phrase "on membership of a club principle" in the fourth paragraph should perhaps be understood as "on the membership-of-a-club principle".

The Average Man

Page 159.

Auden omits the name of the "unknown Victorian", who was James Mottram.

Four Stories of Crime

Page 161.

This is the first of Auden's two reviews of mystery novels for the *Daily Telegraph*, where C. Day-Lewis wrote a weekly review of current novels. The title was evidently supplied by an editor. In the second paragraph "someone" is an emendation for "some one". Auden's statement that Mrs Pym was probably the most unpleasant detective in modern fiction apparently prompted a letter from the literary editor of the paper, Cyril Lakin, to which Auden replied in an undated letter (now in the Edinburgh University Library):

Thank you for your letter. I'm sorry about the rash remark. It happened to be true but I don't expect I read enough adventure stories.

This kind of work is quite new to me, and I shall always be grateful for any tips or warnings.

Poetry, Poets, and Taste

Page 162.

The Highway was the monthly journal of the Workers Educational Association. I have emended some minor slips by the compositor, and have revised the layout so that the first quotation (from *The Duchess of Malfi*) appears set off rather than run in. I have omitted three arbitrarily placed subheads evidently added by an editor.

Adventures in the Air

Page 165.

On 21 October 1936 Auden replied by postcard to a request from J. R. Ackerley that he review this book for the *Listener:* "Send *High Failure* along" (postcard at the Harry Ransom Humanities Research Center). Auden's minor errors in copying from the book are left uncorrected. The review is signed "Wystan Auden".

A NOVELIST'S POEMS

Page 166.

This is a review written for the English number of *Poetry* (Chicago) that Auden prepared with Michael Roberts during 1936 (see Appendix I above). The review was written in October or November 1936. The text is taken from a typescript, now in the *Poetry* collection at the University of Chicago, which was evidently transcribed from Auden's lost manuscript. In the second paragraph an editor added the comma after "In the first place", and the printed text mistakenly reads "subjectives" for "subjective".

CRIME TALES AND PUZZLES

Page 167.

The second and last of Auden's reviews of mystery novels for the *Daily Telegraph*, probably written in the last days of 1936. The title was evidently added by an editor.

Letters from Iceland

§1 History, Authorship, Text, and Editions

Auden and MacNeice wrote most of this book in the autumn of 1936, and it was published by Faber & Faber on 6 August 1937. Auden prepared a slightly revised second edition in the autumn of 1965, but Faber did not publish it until 7 December 1967.

Auden conceived the idea of a travel book about Iceland in April or May 1936. On a visit to Bryanston, Auden had lunch with his former Downs School pupil Michael Yates, who told him that he, three other boys, and a master planned to visit Iceland that summer. Auden almost immediately afterward asked his agents, Curtis Brown, Ltd, to propose a book on Iceland to the publishing firm of Jonathan Cape, and to ask for an advance that would pay for the journey. On 15 May, T. S. Eliot learned about the proposal, and protested to Auden that the book should have been offered to his regular publisher, Faber & Faber. Auden replied in an undated letter:

> The affair Iceland was this way. Capes have for some time tried to persuade me to do a novel, and I refused, but told them that I would like to do something in the travel line. I did no more about this until I had the Iceland idea and told Curtis Brown to do something about it.
>
> Meeting [Frank] Morley [of Faber] by chance the street, I mentioned the idea to him, and that I had told Curtis Brown to negotiate. As the original suggestion for this type of book came from Capes, I told Curtis Brown to let them know.

Eliot, describing himself as still unhappy, replied on 26 May that Faber could do much better with Auden's work if they published the whole of it, and that Cape had proposed that Auden write a novel, not the travel book that he had offered. Auden's response was a brief undated note, evidently accompanying a letter (now lost) that he had obtained from Cape and that released him from his agreement: "Well, that's that," he told Eliot. "I'm very glad to be back again, scolded but happy."

Auden wrote to Michael Yates with the news that Faber had agreed to finance his journey, and that he would arrive in Iceland some weeks before Yates did. He wanted to include in his book an account of the Bryanston party's journey, and asked Yates to ask the master in charge of the party (W. F. Hoyland, whose half brother was Geoffrey Hoyland, headmaster of the Downs School) if he could join them when they arrived in Iceland. He also invited Louis MacNeice to join him in Iceland. MacNeice reported to his friend Anthony Blunt on 24 May that he hoped to start for Iceland with Auden before the end of June; Auden had invited him on

20 May, when, with MacNeice's help, he arranged a marriage between the German cabaret actress Therese Giehse and the Birmingham novelist John Hampson, for the purpose of giving her a British passport. Giehse was part of the cabaret company organized by Erika Mann, whom Auden had married for the same purpose in 1935. In one of his letters printed in the book Auden reported to Mann on 29 July 1937 that he had completed a cabaret sketch for Giehse, which he published under the title "Alfred".

Auden left for Iceland around 16 May 1936. MacNeice joined him around 8 or 9 August, apparently having been delayed by domestic complications. The Bryanston group arrived on 17 August and stayed for ten days. Yates remained with Auden and MacNeice, and the three apparently left for England around 10 September. Auden was back in his parents' Birmingham home on 15 September.

While he was in Iceland Auden wrote "Journey to Iceland" (the poem, not the prose letter to Isherwood that follows it), "Detective Story", "O who can ever praise enough", and probably the verse letter to R. H. S. Crossman, the prose letters to E. M. A. (Erika Mann Auden), and "'O who can ever gaze his fill'"; he also began drafting "Letter to Lord Byron" during his journey. He and MacNeice wrote the rest of the book after their return.

Letters from Iceland arrived at Faber in installments. On 29 September 1936, Auden wrote Frank Morley at Faber, proposing to visit two days later "to show the photos I want in the Iceland book. Though I say it, I think they're rather good." On 9 October 1936 he delivered two postcards, which he had permission to reprint, and a map (which Faber commissioned the map publisher Stanford to redraw). Probably on 4 November he sent prints of his photographs, together with "some diagrams which I want in an appendix at the end. I also enclose a list showing order and arrangement of illustrations." He also proposed to include in one section of the book "marginal pen and ink sketches, about a dozen in all", but these never materialized. In thanking Auden for the prints, Richard de la Mare, at Faber, wrote on 5 November 1936: "It is rather a pity that you have used such a hard pencil for writing your descriptions on the back, as I am afraid the printers may have some difficulty in preventing this from showing".

Auden told his friend Naomi Mitchison on 5 November 1936: "Am up to my ears in a sort of travel book about Iceland. I've never enjoyed writing anything so much before, but I expect that's a bad sign" (postcard in the Berg Collection). On 28 November, he told Eliot: "Byron, a typescript of which should reach you from Curtis Brown soon[,] is for Iceland". Probably early in December he told E. R. Dodds: "Louis has done a lovely eclogue for the Iceland book and the whole thing is finished except the testament we are going to do together. I think the Byron letter (1300 lines) is rather a success. I'll send it you as soon as it comes back from the typist" (letter in the Bodleian Library). Probably early in January he wrote to his friend Arnold Snodgrass: "Just finished a book of letters (verse and prose) from Iceland where I was all summer. Hope you will like the long one to Lord Byron" (letter in the Berg Collection).

MacNeice recalled that Auden left him with a "great chaotic sheaf of illegible manuscript" when he left for an eight-week journey to the Spanish Civil War in January 1937 (unpublished interview with *Time*, February 1963). Many of the errors in the printed book result from failed efforts by MacNeice or an unidentified typist to read the manuscript.

Auden left Birmingham for Spain on 11 January 1937; on the following day, a proof of the Iceland map arrived at his family's Birmingham home from Faber. Auden's father noted some errors in it, which he reported to Richard de la Mare, who replied that Auden had already passed the block of the map, and that a new one would now have to be made.

After Auden returned from Spain early in March 1937 he visited the Lake District with Isherwood, who on 13 March finished writing the questions that Auden answers in Chapter II of the book; these questions and answers, together with the revisions to the stanzas in Chapter XVII about John Andrews (who accompanied Auden and Isherwood to the Lake District) and perhaps to some other stanzas, were probably the only parts of the book written after December 1936. The final typescript may have been submitted in the latter part of March 1937. Perhaps later the same month, an editor at Faber wrote a memorandum stating various objections to the book, to which Auden and MacNeice replied in a note written by an unknown hand and signed in the same hand with the authors' initials. The objections may be inferred from the reply:

We purposely inserted Chapter IV for Tourists among the letters to break the run of letters. We want the book to be as varied as possible as one glances through it. . . .

We are afraid that we entirely disagree with the suggestion that Chapter IX [*the number repeats a mistake in the Faber memorandum*], the Will, is too long. We should have liked it to be longer. The point about the Will is that it should appear very circumstantial and should have long lists of private names intermixed with the public. The bequests are not all supposed to be funny or satirical. We put in our friends because it is *our* will. People who have read it without knowing the people concerned found it quite readable. In any case this is the sort of book where readers are prepared to do a bit of skipping.

This also applies to Chapter XII, Hetty to Nancy, which is not meant merely as a joke but is to serve as an accurate description of an Icelandic trip on ponies. If we cut the jokes, such as they are, the whole thing will become a little heavy, but if we cut the factual detail it will become useless as information.

If any passages in the Will are decided to be libellous would this be corrected if we substituted for the proper names in those passages initials, asterisks or something of the sort?

The typescript of the book contained musical examples, perhaps settings of the Icelandic songs in Chapter XI, which were drawn for Faber by a calligrapher early in April 1937 and sent to MacNeice for comment. Nothing was heard from MacNeice or Auden, and the music did not appear in the printed book.

Faber sent the typescript to the printer in April 1937 and began to send separate sets of galleys to both Auden and MacNeice later in the month. In Auden's corrections to the galleys of Chapter VI ("Sheaves from Sagaland") he had marked the proofs to indicate that the names of each quoted author should be lowered to a separate line. De la Mare replied that he had considered this carefully while preparing the manuscript and wanted to avoid a broken appearance on the page, and he hoped Auden would accept this decision. Auden had also marked the galleys to indicate that the passages about the 1809 Revolution and an Icelandic Supper should go on separate pages, but de la Mare pointed out that only individual chapters usually open with new pages. Auden replied on a postcard a few days later: "O.K. about your lay out."

Around the second week of May, after corrections to the first galleys were received from Auden and MacNeice, the printer began to send page proofs. On 16 May, after Auden had received some page proofs and a corrected proof of the map, he wrote to de la Mare:

> There are three additions to the map I should like, but shall quite understand if this is impossible. (marked in proof).
>
> On looking at the page proofs, I feel strongly that the title of each letter should be on a page to itself. Can this be managed?

This was too much for de la Mare, who replied on 18 May that it was too costly to change the map, unless Auden were willing to pay for a new block. He noted that he had already had a new block made to incorporate the corrections made by Auden's father, and added: "It does seem rather a pity that the original map that you gave me couldn't have been checked more carefully before we had it." About Auden's request for separate title pages for each chapter, he wrote: "I wish too, that you had suggested the half-titles to the chapters in the book when you gave the MS to me, as it is, of course, impossible to put those half-titles in now without wasting a lot of money, and I do not see how we can agree to it unless you say that you are prepared to pay for it." Auden wrote back on 19 May: "I quite understand about the map, but am not at all satisfied about the $\frac{1}{2}$ titles. The typescript certainly had titles on separate sheets and it never occurred to me that you would do anything else. How much would it cost to put them in."

De la Mare replied on 20 May: "What a nuisance this is about the half-titles. My own recollection certainly is that there were none in the manuscript, but I am not sure that if I had found them there I should have supposed that you wanted them, since half-titles to chapters are hardly ever used—and in fact (and please forgive me for saying it) the manuscript came to us in such a muddle that it was not at all easy to get it in proper order for the printers. I know this because I had to do it myself!" The next day, de la Mare told Auden that the half-titles would cost twelve pounds. Auden did not reply, and the chapters did not receive separate title pages.

Meanwhile, the book's rich potential for libel had raised the alarm at Faber. The most obvious problem was a description of Auden's Gresham's School master Reginald Gartside-Bagnall in Part IV of "Letter to Lord Byron". As early as 15 December 1936, soon after Eliot received the typescript of "Letter to Lord Byron", his secretary wrote Auden at Eliot's request "to enquire who 'Bagnall' is, and whether he is alive or dead. If the former he would be glad to know whether you do not think it rather libellous to describe him as half a knave." Auden seems to have made no change in the text at this time, and de la Mare's secretary, D. R. Cowling, asked Auden on 7 May 1937 whether he were libelling his prep school master. Auden replied on a postcard to de la Mare: "As to libel, I'll guarantee private characters if you'll guarantee public ones."

This was not enough for de la Mare, who had also found problems in the "Last Will and Testament". (Probably Auden had first included the surname of T. F. Coade on page 371, instead of merely his initials.) On 24 May 1937 Faber asked the printer not to prepare bound proof copies until Auden's revisions of libellous passages had been received. The printer had already pulled page proofs of a large portion of the book, from Chapter I through most of Chapter XII, but now suspended work on the rest. On 30 May Auden sent to de la Mare proofs of the last part of Chapter XII through the end of the book, with a note saying: "I do hope all the danger libel spots are out now". He evidently removed one danger spot by rewriting the stanza about Gartside-Bagnall so that it began: "Surnames I must not write—O Reginald" (p. 330).

The printer now completed the suspended proof copies and had them bound in wrappers, although one libel remained in the pages that had been printed earlier: in "Letter to Lord Byron", Part I, stanza 16 included the line "The Book Society had not been bought". This was both libellous and impolitic, because the Book Society had selected *Letters from Iceland* as its monthly choice for its subscribers. In the published text, the line reads: "The help of Boots had not been sought" (page 181). It is conceivable that Eliot made this metrically defective change without consulting Auden.

When Auden sent corrected proofs to de la Mare on 30 May 1937 he also enclosed a list of photographs with an indication of the pages they should face: "I'm sorry to be so tiresome but I must have them like that at all costs, or they lose their entire point". On 7 June 1937, de la Mare asked Auden to return the proofs of his photographs (which had not been included in the proof copies of the book): "Our intention was to arrange the illustrations as nearly as possible to face the pages that you wanted them to face, and I hope you will find that this has been successfully accomplished." Auden apparently now asked that some of the captions be moved from above the photographs to the foot of the page, but de la Mare replied on 10 June that the photographs at the foot of the page had been made to "bleed off at the foot of the page", and if the captions were to be moved they would be at risk of being trimmed by the binder. (In the present edition, the captions appear beneath the illustrations.)

Probably late in June the printer produced sheets for the finished book, and on 7 July 1937 the New York office of Curtis Brown delivered a proof copy and a set of finished sheets to Random House with a cover note: "The copy bound in green [wrappers] is *not* setting copy. This is important as it contains libel which has been omitted from the sewn set of sheets, which *is* setting copy. Faber published July seventh." Two weeks later the New York office of Curtis Brown told Random House that Faber had postponed publication until 6 August 1937.

Meanwhile, on 8 July 1937, Faber sent to Auden four hundred copies of the first gathering of the printed book for Auden to sign on the front flyleaf so that they could be bound into copies distributed by the Book Society. On 29 July 1937 a letter from Faber urgently asked for the signed gatherings, which were needed by the first week of August. Auden eventually returned the gatherings, and the Book Society supplied its members with signed copies.

The authorship of the separate chapters of the book is partly indicated in the table of contents (p. 176), partly by initials at the ends of some chapters. Chapter II, "Journey to Iceland", is Auden's work, except for the questions supplied by Isherwood. Chapter IV, "For Tourists", is Auden's except for parenthetical comments initialled by MacNeice. Chapter VI, "Sheaves from Sagaland", was almost certainly compiled by Auden. Chapter XII, "Hetty to Nancy", although obviously MacNeice's work, was not attributed to him in the first Faber edition. A note sent on 26 August 1937 from Faber to the printer asks that MacNeice's initials be added in brackets after the title of this chapter in the table of contents in future editions; this instruction was forgotten when the second Faber edition was published in 1967, but a misunderstanding of a similar instruction led to the addition of Mac-Neice's bracketed initials at the end of the text of the chapter in the first Random House edition. Chapter XIV, listed in the table of contents as "W. H. Auden to William Coldstream, Esq.", concludes with a poem signed by MacNeice. In Chapter XVII some lines are initialled by Auden, some by MacNeice, some by both; further details on authorship are noted in §3 below.

A review of the book by Geoffrey Gorer, in *Time and Tide*, 7 August 1937, written in the form of a letter to Auden, began: "Dear Mr Auden,—(I suppose in a way I ought to include Mr MacNeice too, for his name is on the frontispiece; but he's not really written much of the book, and, except for a couple of nice short poems, his portions are very much subdued by the general tenor; and light verse is not his *forte*). . . ." Auden replied in a letter to the editor, published on 21 August 1937:

> SIR,—With reference to Mr Geoffrey Gorer's review of *Letters from Iceland*, I should like to point out that, out of a total of 240 pages of writing, 81 are by Mr Louis MacNeice.
>
> I am, etc.
> W. H. Auden

Auden's arithmetic apparently includes, in addition to sixty-four pages of chapters and complete poems signed by MacNeice, about seven pages of passages in the "Last Will and Testament" initialled by MacNeice and seven pages initialled by both authors but written by MacNeice.

Auden's manuscripts and typescripts for *Letters from Iceland* are almost entirely lost. The manuscript of "Journey to Iceland" that he sent Michael Roberts for inclusion in *Poetry*, January 1937, is now in the Berg Collection; it is the only surviving English text that has the original reading "the poets have names for the sea" (see p. 186). (The Icelandic translation by Magnús Ásgeirsson published in the annual literary magazine *Rauðir Pennar*, 1936, was evidently based on a manuscript with the same original reading.) A manuscript of "O who can ever praise enough", evidently sent to Roberts for the same number of *Poetry*, is in the Poetry Collection at the State University of New York at Buffalo. Drafts and notes for MacNeice's contributions to the book are in a notebook in the same collection; this notebook includes drafts of "Letter to Graham and Anne Shepard", "Eclogue

from Iceland", and "Epilogue"; notes for "Hetty to Nancy"; and a draft list of re-
cipients and bequests for "Auden and MacNeice: Their Last Will and Testament".

Faber advertised the book for publication on 8 July 1937, but delayed its ap-
pearance until 6 August 1937. The reset Random House edition was published on
23 November 1937.

MacNeice died in 1963. Auden revisited Iceland for a week in April 1964, at the
invitation of the British ambassador, Basil Boothby, whom he had met in Hankow
in 1938 when Boothby was the British vice consul. In 1965 Auden prepared a
partly reset second edition of the book, which Faber published in paperback on
7 December 1967. Random House published a clothbound edition of the same
setting on 14 April 1969.

Auden printed some of the poems in the book in magazines, and republished
most of them in his later collected and selected editions, as well as in the second
edition of *Letters from Iceland*. Variant readings will be noted in the volumes of
Poems in this edition. In the list below, *1945* signifies *The Collected Poetry of W. H.
Auden* (and the corresponding 1950 British volume, *Collected Shorter Poems, 1930–
1944*); *1966* signifies *Collected Shorter Poems, 1927–1957*. Titles introduced in later
editions are noted in parentheses:

"Letter to Lord Byron": reprinted in *Collected Longer Poems* (1968), with the cuts
Auden made for the second edition of *Letters from Iceland;* this abridged text
had already appeared in the 1966 Penguin anthology *Longer Contemporary
Poems*.

"Journey to Iceland": *The Listener,* 7 October 1936; *Poetry,* January 1937. Revised
in *1945*; further revised in *Iceland Review,* [Autumn] 1964 (with essentially
the same text used in the second edition of *Letters from Iceland*); separately
revised in *1966*.

"Detective Story": *1966*.

"O who can ever praise enough": *Poetry,* January 1937; *1945*; *1966* ("The
Price").

"'O who can ever gaze his fill'": *The New Statesman and Nation,* 16 January 1937;
Auden's *Selected Poems* (1938); *1945* ("The Dead Echo"); the 1958 Penguin
selection of Auden's poems (also published 1959 in the Modern Library as
The Selected Poetry of W. H. Auden); *1966* ("Death's Echo").

§2 The Text of the First Edition

The text that Auden and MacNeice delivered to their publisher incorporated so
many errors of spelling, transcription, and fact that any effort to correct them all
would create a different and more antiseptic book. This edition corrects a few
obvious errors that Faber's editors missed, and attempts to correct nonsensical
readings that probably resulted from a typist's misreading of Auden's hand, but I
have not altered Auden's errors in copying from his sources, his inconsistent and
erroneous spelling of proper names in English and Icelandic, and his errors in
Icelandic vocabulary. For example, Auden spells the family name of George Steu-
art Mackenzie variously as MacKenzie, McKenzie, and Mackenzie, and I have let all
his variants stand. His more serious errors are mentioned in the notes below.

In the handwritten letters Auden posted from Iceland he used the Icelandic "ð", but the text in *Letters from Iceland* substitutes the roman "d" (sometimes "th"), and instead of the Icelandic "þ" prints "th". The decision to use roman characters seems to have been made by the authors, or by an editor at Faber with the consent of the authors. Neither of the Icelandic characters was available in 1937 in the Monotype typeface used for the book, Bodoni Series 135, but the printers R. MacLehose and Company, the University Press, Glasgow, routinely arranged for special characters to be drawn and cut by the Monotype Corporation. The Icelandic characters could easily have been supplied had the authors or publisher wanted them, but these Gothic letterforms were known to be unsettling to the popular audience for which the book was intended.

The notes below use the Icelandic characters in corrections of Auden's misspellings, but straightforward substitutions by Auden of "d" or "th" for these characters are not noted. Also not noted are inverted accents (Njàl for Njál), the wholesale and inconsistent omission of accents and diareses, and the use of "ae" for "æ". Some broken punctuation marks in the first edition have been corrected by reference to the proof copy.

The Random House edition was reset from sewn sheets of the Faber edition. It incorporated some minor corrections of the Faber text, which are included in this edition and noted below, and also introduced some minor typographic errors, not noted here.

Auden's alterations for the second edition are noted in §4.

Page 172.

Frontispiece. Hraensnef in the caption is an error for Hraunsnef; the error also occurs in the list of illustrations and throughout the text.

Page 175.

Preface. These are the correct forms of the most erroneously spelled names in the second paragraph: Eirikur Benedikz (corrected in the second edition), Ragnar Jóhannesson, Arni Pálsson, Kristinn Andrésson (miscorrected in the second edition to Kristjan Andresson), Dr [Jonas] Kristjánsson, Gerry Pálsson, and Steingrimur. Because "n" and "u" are generally indistinguishable in Auden's hand, the typist probably misread Saudakrókur (Auden's version of Sauðárkrókur) as Sandakrókur, the reading in the printed text; I have restored the spelling that Auden probably used.

Page 179.

Letter to Lord Byron, Part I. Notes on the text of the five parts of this poem are followed by brief annotations of local and private allusions. The typist probably miscopied Musgrove as Musgrave (p. 181), but Hvitavatn is probably Auden's error for Hvítárvatn and Auden Skökull should be Auðun Skökull (p. 184). In the first stanza, Father Charles Coughlin's right-wing religious broadcasts had a huge audience in America; the milder Richard Sheppard, canon of St Paul's, had a comparable British audience. The second stanza alludes to Frederic Prokosch, who introduced himself to Auden by sending a nude photograph of himself. In the stanza that begins "Ottava Rima" (p. 183), the English bishop who wrote on the quantum theory was Bishop Barnes of Birmingham (see note to p. 360 below). In the stanza that begins "Parnassus after all" (p. 183), the first two poets named are E. E. Bradford (1860–1944), author of *The Romance of Youth* (1920), *Ralph Rawdon: A Story in Verse* (1922), *Boyhood* (1930), and other books of verse on similar subjects, and S. E. Cottam (b. 1863), author of *Cameos of Boyhood and Other Poems* (1930). The stanza that begins "The Haig Thomases" (p. 184) refers to the Arctic explorer David Haig Thomas.

Page 185.

Journey to Iceland. D. R. Cowling, Richard de la Mare's secretary, asked Auden on 7 May 1937, "should there be a semi colon after 'everywhere'" in the second stanza, line 2. Replying in a postcard to de la Mare, Auden wrote: "Miss Cowling asks about colon after *everywhere* in Chap II. Answer No." But the semicolon remained in the text, and, although the poem seems more logical without it, Auden clearly intended the strong punctuation. In the manuscript in the Berg Collection and the printed text in *Poetry*, January 1937, based on this manuscript, Auden ended a sentence with a period after "everywhere", and began a new sentence with the following word. In the *Listener*, 7 October 1936, and in the proof copy of *Letters from Iceland*, "The" is capitalized immediately after the semicolon. For notes on manuscript versions see above (p. 772).

The arbitrarily arranged sequence of questions and answers that follows the poem is a spoof on a similar sequence in a chapter on statistics in John Barrow's *Visit to Iceland* (1835). The comic paper named in the answer to question 9 should be *Speigillinn*.

Page 195.

For Tourists. The worst-misspelled names in this section include Ausserstraeti for Austurstræti (p. 197), Olli Maggadon for Óli Maggadon (like Oddur Sigurgeirsson, a famous lunatic tramp), Pállson for Pálsson, Isafjördardjup for Ísafarðardjúp (all p. 198), Hallorastadur for Hallormsstaður (pp. 198 and 206), Skargafjördur for Skagafjörður (p. 198), the mutton dish Hángikyrl for Hángikjöt (p. 202), Markaflot for Markarfljót (p. 205), Borgafirth for Borgarfjarðar and Grimsstadur for Grímsstaðir (p. 206).

In the bibliography, "Icelandic Year-Book, *Iceland*, 1930", is probably a cross between *The Iceland Year-Book 1926* (and *1927*), edited by Snæbjörn Jónsson, and *Iceland 1930: A Handbook Published on the Fortieth Anniversary of Landsbanki Islands*. Zoëga is G. T. Zoëga. Dame Philpot is Bertha S. Phillpotts (see p. 742). W. G. Craigie should be W. A. Craigie. G. V. Gordon should be E. V. Gordon (his correct initials appear in the preface), but he was not the author of *Romance in Iceland*, which was written by Margaret Schlauch. The title of F. L. Lucas's book is *The Decline and Fall of the Romantic Ideal* (not *Romantic Tradition*).

Page 208.

Letter to Lord Byron, Part II. In the stanza that begins "Don Juan was a mixer" (p. 211), the title *Ulysses* was printed in roman in the proof copy, and the italicization was probably added by the publisher. In the stanza that begins "One day, which day" (p. 214), the dash after "ogre" in line 3 is an editorial addition; the line is unpunctuated in versions printed in Auden's lifetime. The fourth stanza

alludes to the contemporary moral debate over whether girls should ride motor-
cycles pillion or astride. In the stanza that begins "Yes, in the smart set" (p. 211),
Ely Culbertson was the dominant figure in the game of bridge; in the following
stanza, C. B. Cochran's "Young Ladies" were the leading revue chorus. In the
stanza beginning "Turn to the work" (p. 213), "The bowler hat who straphangs"
alludes to the figure created by the *Daily Express* cartoonist Sidney Strube.

Page 216.

Sheaves from Sagaland. This miscellany was almost certainly gathered by
Auden, who abridged, modified, miscopied, and misattributed many of the quo-
tations, and lightened italicization and punctuation—usually more so toward
the end of a quotation than at the beginning. The sources of most quotations
are identified more fully in the bibliography at the end of the chapter; the notes
below indicate sources that Auden neglected to list.

I have let Auden's minor transcription errors stand, and have generally cor-
rected only errors that seem to have been made by the typist who transcribed
Auden's notes; however, in a very few instances, noted below, I have restored a
word or two from the original text where the version in *Letters from Iceland* makes
no sense.

In the five sections of quotations, Auden repeatedly cites Van Troil instead
of Von Troil, McKenzie instead of Mackenzie, and W. G. Locke instead of
W. G. Lock.

Part I: The line attributed to Ketil Flatnose (p. 217) is from the *Laxdoela Saga*,
chapter 2. "A gallows of slush" (p. 217) is probably adapted from the excursus
"On the Figures and Metaphors (Kenningar) of Old Northern Poetry" in
Gudbrand Vigfusson and F. York Powell, *Corpus Poeticum Boreale* (1885); one of
the kennings for Iceland is a phrase from Egil's poem "Sonatorrek" translated as
"'the country of the elks' gallows' [ice, from the way in which elks were hunted
over water-holes]". The quotation from Hakluyt (p. 217) is a faulty recollection
rather than a copy (the original reads: "Of Iceland to write is little need, / Save
of stock-fish"), but all other quotations were evidently transcribed from the orig-
inals. Under the heading "Concerning the Scenery" (p. 217) I have restored the
original "type in nature" for Auden's or the typist's mistranscription "type of
nature". Under the heading "Concerning the Climate" (p. 218), I have let stand
"weigh out" for the original's "weigh off", although the error may have been the
typist's.

Part II: Under the heading "Concerning their hair" (p. 218) I have corrected
two probable typist's errors: "Euplokomoi" miscopied as "Euplokamo", and "fla-
vescent" miscopied as "florescent". Under the heading "Concerning their kiss-
ing" (p. 222) Auden misattributed the quotation to Howell; it is in fact from
Pliny Miles. The two passages attributed to Tremarec (pp. 219 and 222) are not
by him, and their author has not been identified. The passage headed "Bad
news for the Watch Committee" (p. 222) is from Rasmus Anderson, *Norse My-
thology* (1875), which is not listed in Auden's bibliography. Under the heading
"Plato in the North" (p. 223) Auden or his typist miscopied "Such of the clergy"
as "Some of the clergy" and "transplanted into" as "transported to".

Under the heading "A Problem for Missionaries" (p. 224) Auden or his typist miscopied "Bodvarson" as "Bodvarter". Under the heading "Tiddley om pom pom" (p. 224), the text in the printed edition, followed here, may partly have been the work of a friend of Faber's proofreader, who told Richard de la Mare on 21 May 1937: "I got a German friend to correct the paragraph on page 69. He could not make sense out of it, and corrected it until he could; but this is a quotation, and if it is intended that it be as the original, I think another comparison with the original is necessary." The original passage has "einen Typus" for Auden's "einer Typus", "verfliegt" for "verfleucht", "daherschreitet" for "einher schreitet", omits "in" before "seiner" in the last phrase, and does not capitalize the five adjectives capitalized by Auden.

The "longest word in Icelandic" (p. 224) is a joke evidently concocted by an Icelander and slightly miscopied by Auden, but it is based on a real word, *hæstaréttimálaflytningsmaður,* "a lawyer licensed to practice in the supreme court".

Part III: The passage headed "Character of a light blue" (p. 225) is not in Trollope's account of Iceland and may be by someone else. Under the heading "A French humanitarian" (p. 225) I have corrected errors, perhaps made by the typist, in which "dussé-je faire rire" was miscopied as "dusse-je faire vivre", and "n'ont jamais" as "n'ait jamais". Under the heading "A fast Victorian" (p. 227) the typist probably misread "Alice Tweedie" for "Alec Tweedie"; Auden gets the name almost right in the bibliography (p. 240), but omits the hyphen that should join the two names. The passage headed "Spread of Nazi Doctrines among the Icelandic ponies" (p. 228) is from Svend Fleuron, *The Wild Horses of Iceland* (1933), a book that Auden neglected to list in his bibliography.

In the account of the 1809 revolution, the Audenesque-sounding translation from the Latin ode (p. 232) is in fact from Mackenzie. The account of the eruption of the Öraefa Jökull (pp. 236–38) is misattributed to Mackenzie; it was in fact quoted by Henderson. Mount Flega is perhaps Auden's mistranscription of Mount Flaga (p. 236). In the paragraph beginning "After nine o'clock" (p. 236), "exudations" is probably Auden's miscopying of "exundations" (the error occurs again on p. 237), but I have corrected a probable misreading of Auden's hand in which "Lomagnupr" was miscopied as "Lounagrupr". In the paragraph beginning "On the 11th" (p. 237) I have corrected "nearly-constructed" to "newly-constructed". In the parenthesis at the end of the account (p. 238) I have corrected a typist's error by changing "Nagrus Stefansson" to "Magnus Stefansson", but have let stand Auden's erroneous correction of "Stephensen" to "Steffanson". Faber moved the names of the authors of these two long extracts from the end to the beginning of each, apparently with Auden's consent.

The extract from the Suarbar (probably Auden's mistake for Saurbar) parish register is slightly simplified and miscopied from Mackenzie.

The bibliography at the end of the section (pp. 238–41) is a chaos of misinformation, but the text printed here corrects only those errors probably made by Auden's typist. Auden took most of the titles in the first two-thirds of the list—through 1868—from the catalogue of modern travels in Iceland in Richard Burton's *Ultima Thule,* complete with Burton's errors (John Andersson for Johann Anderson, Charles Edmund for Charles Edmond) and editorial additions (the parenthetical date in the title of Dillon's book, the parenthetical addition of the real name behind the pseudonym "Umbra"). Burton's Ionr Boty is an error for Iver Boty; Auden's printed text has Jonr Boty, which probably resulted from a typist's error in transcribing Auden's notes. The German title of Horrebow's book is probably Auden's addition (Burton gives only the Danish title), although Auden quotes from the 1758 English translation, *The Natural History of Iceland*. Tremarec is Auden's error for Kerguélin-Trémarec (Burton omitted the hyphen). Auden was probably responsible for misrendering Uno Von Troil (here and throughout the book) as Van Troil; for miscopying the title of Von Troil's *Letters on Iceland* as *Letters from Iceland;* and for erroneously describing that book as written jointly with Joseph Banks (who was the captain on Von Troil's journey). Auden was presumably responsible for the extraneous uppercase "K" in Sir George MacKenzie, and for the omission of three words from the title of his *Travels in the Island of Iceland* (Auden lists the 1812 second edition, not the 1811 first edition). Auden omitted the main title of Pliny Miles's *Norðurfari, or Rambles in Iceland,* and listed C. W. Paijkull as Paykull. Auden also evidently referred to the list of books in Sabine Baring-Gould's *Iceland: Its Scenes and Sagas,* which lists Charles Forbes as Captain Forbes.

　　Among Auden's other errors, the title of Morris's *Journals of Travels in Iceland, 1871–1873* (published in 1911) is abridged; both C. W. Lock and W. G. Lock have extraneous "e"s added to their surnames; Mrs Alec-Tweedie's *A Girl's Ride in Iceland* is listed as Mrs Alec Tweedie's *A Girl's Tour in Iceland;* Paul Herrmann is listed as Paul Hermann; and *Das unbekannte Island* (1935, not 1932), attributed to Prinz, is in fact by Walther Heering, with a note on the spirit and history of the Icelandic people by Reinhard Prinz (whom Auden quotes on p. 224).

Page 241.
　　Letter to R. H. S. Crossman, Esq. Little Daimon (p. 242) is a mistranslation of Stóra Dímon (Great Dimon), the place called Rauðuskriður in the sagas; this entire stanza alludes to *Njál's Saga*. Markafljōt is Markarfljót (p. 245). The laws and regulations at the end of the letter are slightly simplified from translations in Gudbrand Vigfusson and F. York Powell's *Origines Islandicae* (1910). In the "Formula of Peace-Making" (p. 245), in the last line of paragraph 1, "ought" is a correction for the printed text's "cry'd", which is probably a typist's desperate misreading of Auden's hand. In paragraph 4, *Letters from Iceland* runs in the second line of Vigfusson and Powell's version with the first line, but begins the line with a capital letter; the error was probably the typist's, and I have restored the lineation of Vigfusson and Powell. In paragraph 5, the first edition has "As lean as men seek wolves"; "lean" is probably the typist's misreading of "far", while either Auden or the typist miscopied "seek" for "hunt" by picking up "seek" from the next line; both errors are corrected here. In the same paragraph I have let stand "heareth son" for "beareth son"; in the typeface used in Vigfusson and Powell, the "b" can easily be misread as "h", but in Auden's hand the two letters are clearly distinguished, so the error was probably made by Auden. In "The Viking Law", paragraph 13, the intrusive comma may have been added by Auden.

Page 249.
　　Letter to Lord Byron, Part III. In the stanza that begins "A poet, swimmer" (p. 249), the comma after "poetic style" is intrusive, but appears in all editions

published in Auden's lifetime. In the stanza that begins "And new plants" (p. 251), I have removed the apostrophe from "Rousseaus'", and it was also removed from *Collected Longer Poems;* Auden may have intended to write "Rousseau's" as the plural form. In the third stanza, Pritchard is a slip for the rigorously rational Oxford moral philosopher H. A. Prichard. In the stanza that begins "I'm also glad" (p. 250), Storm's was the café nearest the railway station at Keswick. In the following stanza, Milton said this in *Areopagitica,* but Auden found the phrase in W. P. Ker's *Collected Essays,* where it is quoted in Charles Whibley's introduction and in Ker's essay on Joseph Ritson. In the stanza that begins "At the Beginning" (p. 252), Heard is Gerald Heard (see note to p. 370 below). In the stanza that begins "But Savoury" (p. 254), Auden misremembered the name Savery.

Page 256.

W. H. A. to E. M. A.—No. 1. Auden's guides (p. 261) were Ólafur Briem in the south of Iceland and Ragnar Jóhannesson in the east and north. I have capitalized the first letter in some lines of Icelandic verse that were lowercased in the first edition. Hraensnef (pp. 257, 262) should be Hraunsnef. Where the typist probably misread Auden's hand I have corrected Nordara to Nordura (for Norðura, p. 262), Beula to Baula (p. 262), and Sandakrokur to Saudakrökur (Auden's version of Sauðárkrókur, pp. 263, 264, and 265). Errors that are likely to be Auden's include Vidamyri for Víðimýri (p. 264). I have emended "appendicotany" to "appendicectomy" (p. 265).

Page 277.

W. H. A. to E. M. A.—No. 2. In the sixth sentence I have hesitantly added a period after "stock". Under the heading "Friday" (p. 279), Morduradalur is the same place that Auden calls Mothrudalur in "Letter to Lord Byron" (p. 180) and that Icelanders call Möðrudalur. I have added an opening quotation mark to the paragraph that begins "Thora asked him" (p. 279). Among Auden's misspellings in this chapter are Egilsstadur for Egilsstaðir (e.g., p. 280), Laugavatn for Laugarvatn (p. 282), Hallormastadur for Hallormsstaður (p. 282), and Thérèse for Therese (Giehse, p. 286, for whom Auden wrote the cabaret sketch *Alfred,* and who performed in Erika Mann's revue *Die Pfeffermühle*). The press interview that Auden mentions at the end of the letter (p. 288) seems not to have appeared in print. In the poem "O who can ever praise enough" (p. 281) I have emended "fantasy" to "phantasy", the reading found in all other versions, including the manuscript in the Poetry Collection at the State University of New York at Buffalo; the original was probably simplified by an editor or proofreader at Faber.

Page 294.

Hetty to Nancy. Near the middle of the long opening paragraph, in the phrase that begins "I have only got a second-hand sleeping bag" (p. 297), MacNeice may have deliberately omitted the punctuation that seems to be required after the parenthesis; later in the same paragraph Hāngikýll is an error for Hángikjöt. In the August 21st paragraph, I have followed the first American edition in adding "no" to the second line of the couplet (p. 311). "La Paloma" (p. 301), or "The Dove", is the popular romantic aria. Melton Mowbray (p. 301) is a fox-hunting centre. I.F.S. (p. 302) is the Irish Free State. The horses at the Ranelagh Club (p. 303) were polo ponies. Bertram Mills (p. 309) was a circus proprietor. Italo Balbo (p. 198), Mussolini's air minister, led a squadron of twenty-four aircraft from Italy to Chicago in 1933. For Ian Hay, Peter Fleming (both p. 301), and Truby King (p. 322), see the following section (notes to pp. 362, 365, 364).

Page 326.

Letter to Lord Byron, Part IV. In the stanza that begins "My name occurs" (p. 327), "Rassenschander" is an error for *Rassenschande* (a violation of the purity of the race by intermarriage). In the stanza that begins "We all grow up" (p. 332), I have removed the umlaut from "stürm und drang", but have left the two nouns in lowercase; the quotation marks were probably added by an editor. In the stanza that begins "Father and Mother" (p. 329), Bart's is St Bartholemew's Hospital. The stanza "Surnames I must not write" (p. 330) refers to Reginald Gartside-Bagnall (see p. 770). In the stanza that begins "But indecision" (p. 332), the friend was Robert Medley (see note to p. 368 below). The stanza that begins "Three years passed" (p. 333) refers to John Layard, the anthropologist who introduced Auden to the work of Homer Lane. In the stanza that begins "The only thing" (p. 334), Rabbitarse and String is the educational employment agency Gabbitas and Thring.

Page 335.

Letter to Kristian Andreirsson, Esq. The recipient was Kristinn Andrésson (mistakenly corrected in the second edition to Kristjan Andresson), a literary historian and editor of the annual left-wing literary journal *Rauðir Pennar*, which published Magnús Ásgeirsson's translation of "Journey to Iceland" in 1936. At the end of the first paragraph (p. 336), I have corrected an obvious typist's error, "Kroil" for "Troil".

Page 344.

Letter to William Coldstream, Esq. In the opening paragraph, Hraensnef should be Hraunsnef, and Isafjördardjup should be Ísafjarðardjúp (and similarly on p. 346). I have left Auden's chaotic punctuation unchanged. The line that begins "But Landscape's so dull" (p. 344) was possibly intended to run in with "if you haven't", but the break may be authorial and is retained here. The line that begins "The Presentation of" (p. 345) may have been intended to run in with the preceding line, but the break seems worth retaining. The private jokes about Auden and Coldstream's work at the General Post Office Film Unit include allusions to his colleagues "the Chief" (John Grierson), Basil Wright, R. Q. McNaughton (not "MacNaughten"), and Stuart Legg (not "Legge"); George (p. 345) was George Noble, a freelance cameraman who worked for the unit. Further notes on the unit and its personnel appear in Elizabeth Sussex, *The Rise and Fall of British Documentary* (1975). The almost perfect quotation from the *Odyssey* is a trace of MacNeice's labors in correcting the proofs.

Page 354.

Letter to Lord Byron, Part V. In the quotation from Hölderlin that begins "Es neiget [*for* neigen]" (p. 356; quoted at length on p. 439), Auden neglected to capitalize two nouns. In the stanza that begins "The Great Utopia" (p. 356), I have restored the layout that Auden evidently intended, by moving the first dash from the end of the fifth line to the start of the sixth line; in the following stanza, I have capitalized "Players". For Truby King, in the stanza that begins "The congregation" (p. 355), see the following section (note to p. 364).

Page 357.

Auden and MacNeice: Their Last Will and Testament. The elaborate private and contemporary references in this chapter call for a separate section of notes; see below.

Page 380.

In the Faber edition the map is bound in as a foldout at the end of the book, with the roads printed in red.

§3 Notes to "Auden and MacNeice: Their Last Will and Testament"

(Annotated in collaboration with Richard Davenport-Hines)

These notes attempt to clarify the private references and the less familiar public references in the poem, many of them specific to the abdication of Edward VIII and other events of the days of its composition in mid-December 1936 (with revisions made probably in March 1937). In the sections initialled by Auden alone, and by Auden and MacNeice in collaboration, every name is either annotated or is too familiar to need annotation. In the sections initialled only by MacNeice the two unidentified legatees seem to be a fellow dog-lover from Birmingham and a drinking companion from Birmingham or London, and we have not made heroic efforts to identify them. Some bequests in the poem almost certainly refer to those in Oxford and elsewhere who opposed the appointment of Auden and MacNeice's friend E. R. Dodds as Regius Professor of Greek; together with his wife A. E. Dodds (Annie Edwards Dodds, who had been a lecturer in English at Birmingham University), Dodds arrived in Oxford to take up his professorship in the autumn of 1936. A few of Auden's legatees had earlier been named in the Last Will in *The Fronny*, in 1930 (see *Plays*, pp. 478–79). Some allusions are deliberately left unannotated because they seem self-explanatory or widely known; others may have been left unannotated merely because we failed to recognize their significance. Titles and achievements of the legatees after 1936 are mentioned only where required for identification. Most of the bequests in the published poem are substantially the same as those in the draft list in MacNeice's notebook; the notes mention a few instances where the bequest in MacNeice's draft list differs from that in the published text but helps cast light on it.

Minor misspellings on the order of Isiah (for Isaiah) Berlin, the islands of Langahans (for islets of Langerhans), and others noted below, are left unaltered in the text. In the second stanza Isafjördardjup is Ísafjarðardjúp. Book and magazine titles that were in roman type in the Faber text have not been italicized.

Further notes on MacNeice's draft list of recipients and on the authorship of specific sections of the poem follow the annotations.

Page 358.

The Jacobean tombs described here are particularly characteristic of church-yards in the Cotswolds, where Auden taught at the Downs School and not far from Birmingham.

MacNeice's father, John Frederick MacNeice, was the bishop of the Church of Ireland dioceses of Down, Connor, and Dromore. In 1935, against massive objections in Parliament and the press, he refused to allow the Union Jack to hang over the Ulster Cathedral grave of Lord Carson, who had helped design the partition of Ireland. His published sermons, which rejected all political extremes, were learned and patriotic. He married MacNeice's stepmother Georgina in 1917, three years after the death of MacNeice's mother.

Page 359.

MacNeice's former wife Mary Ezra had married her second husband in America in November 1936.

Auden's father, George Augustus Auden, was Professor of Public Health and School Medical Officer at Birmingham; a bequest of the seventh-century runic cross at Bewcastle, which was thought by some authorities to have been erected by Norsemen, would satisfy his historical, archaeological, and linguistic interests, but any more specific allusion is lost.

Auden's mother, Constance Rosalie Bicknell Auden, was an Anglo-Catholic who despised Bishop Ernest William Barnes of Birmingham for his campaign against Anglo-Catholic churches in which, in defiance of Barnes's directives, the Blessed Sacrament was given. St Aidan's Church, in the working-class suburb of Small Heath (not Smallheath), was one of the architectural glories of the Birmingham Arts and Crafts movement, and, from 1929 to 1931, was the focus of an extended legal and theological battle between Barnes and the Anglo-Catholics over Barnes's refusal to license the new incumbent unless he would agree to renounce Catholic ritual.

Auden's brother Bernard was farming in Canada, and his geologist brother John, a devoted mountaineer and founding member of the Himalayan Club, was working with the Geological Survey of India.

Page 360.

Stanley Baldwin, who had become prime minister for the third time in 1935, posed as a bluff, simple, unexcitable country squire but was in fact a passionate, subtle pessimist whose fortune came from a family metalworks; Lincoln Cathedral's imposing west front is effectively a screen over the rest of the building and not integral to it. The bequest of a school of Empire poets perhaps alludes to Baldwin's first cousin, Rudyard Kipling.

The National Government, now led by Baldwin, had been formed by Ramsay MacDonald on the basis of compromises among ministers from the three major parties. During the negotiations in 1921 that led to the creation of the Irish Free State, Churchill successfully insisted that Britain retain control over three naval bases on the Irish coast. A dry harbour is a dry dock; the nineteenth-century canal cut from Lough Corrib to Lough Mask in County Mayo, with a fine stone quay at Ballinrobe, is permanently dry, because all the water that was let in seeped immediately through the permeable local limestone to underground streams. Churchill's son Randolph, among other unappealing acts, had written in the *Daily Mail* that it was a disgrace to appoint E. R. Dodds, a noncombatant in the Great War, as a Regius Professor; the bequest of one of the "pretty little pieces" that Auden mentions elsewhere in the book (p. 326) is perhaps a teasing suggestion that the heterosexual Randolph would be less pugnacious and unhappy with a different sex life.

Sir Maurice Hankey, as secretary of the cabinet, successfully served prime ministers of all parties. George Lloyd, a fervent imperialist, had been Governor of Bombay and High Commissioner of Egypt (where he was the civilian head of the occupying forces of "invaded Egypt", p. 452); on flag days paper flags are sold in the streets for charitable or patriotic causes.

The Vickers armaments firm was a major supplier to Bolivia in its war against Paraguay over the Chaco plain; after the death of the firm's most notorious salesman, Sir Basil Zaharoff, on 27 November 1936, his transactions, many of them in the Balkans, were detailed in a series of articles in the *News Chronicle*, 1–4 December 1936. Auden and MacNeice probably invented the term "the Balkan Conscience" on the model of "the Nonconformist Conscience"; it seems to refer less to specific events of 1936 than to the proverbial unscrupulousness of Balkan political life and of those whose arms supported internecine Balkan warfare.

Hambros (not Hambro's) Bank was Iceland's largest creditor and the chief bank doing business there; the bequest of the stones of Kaldidalur (see p. 318) perhaps alludes to an incongruous object known to be stored in the vaults in the bank, but the exact reference is lost. The Port Sunlight soapworks (in a nineteenth-century model industrial village) are left to Ramsay MacDonald for soft-soaping or as an appropriate example of Victorian social idealism and antiseptic blandness; MacDonald, who had been prime minister until 1935 and was still in the cabinet, was a prolix speaker given to lofty and elaborate flights of language, although declining mental and physical health had made his recent speeches almost unintelligible.

Austen Leigh is an error for Austin Lee, a friend of Isherwood at Cambridge, who in 1932 risked his status as a naval chaplain by singing "The Red Flag" in a Maltese pub; although it appeared that he would be forced to leave the navy or the clergy, and the incident apparently received some newspaper publicity, he remained a chaplain for another year and was now Vicar of Pampisford (in a letter to the *Spectator*, 21 February 1936, part of a correspondence about *Hymns Ancient and Modern,* he described himself as "an old-fashioned country incumbent"). The bequest of the quantum theory alludes to Bishop Ernest William Barnes's *Scientific Theory and Religion* (published in 1933 and delivered as the Gifford Lectures in 1927–29), in which Barnes, a mathematician, sought to reconcile the determinism implied by modern science and the free will assumed by religion, and raised "the possibility that the Heisenberg uncertainty-relations offer a loophole through which volition can enter to modify the rigidity of the dynamics of physical systems which include a conscious being"; Auden alluded to Barnes on the quantum theory in "Letter to Lord Byron" (p. 183), and the bequest to Barnes in MacNeice's draft list reads "quantum theory & incense". Stanford's Magnificat in B-flat is among the most popular works of Anglican church music, but the tone of the bequest suggests that Auden and MacNeice had in mind the Magnificat in G, with its part for solo treble. The Chief Scout, Robert Baden-Powell, blew at World Jamborees the spiral koodoo horn that, as a young man, he had brought back from a campaign in Southern Rhodesia against the Matabele, who had supposedly used it as a war horn. The curate's bicycle is probably an allusion that we have not identified. *The Times* was reputed to have printed some time before the Great War a personal advertisement that read: "A clergyman, being in want of a second-hand portable font, will exchange for the same a portrait, in frame, of the Bishop-elect of Vermont." This limerick was commonly attributed to Ronald Knox (see the note to p. 363 below); Auden misquoted the limerick, and attributed it to Knox, in *The Oxford Book of Light Verse*.

The Gentle Shepherd hat is perhaps a play on the hymn that begins "Gentle Shepherd, thou hast stilled" (and other hymns addressed to a Loving Shepherd or similar formulae), the cloche-shaped hat conventionally worn by shepherds in pastoral paintings, and the name of a floppy tweed hat sold by the Oxford firm of Shepherd and Woodward in the 1920s and 1930s and apparently called a Shepherd hat.

Nonconformist disapproval of commercialized gift giving at Christmas was proverbial.

The Bishop of London, Dr Arthur Winnington-Ingram, campaigned against lewd plays, late opening hours, and other pleasures; he returned to Marlborough one Sunday every year, and, nearing eighty, had only recently stopped playing hockey. The spiritual emptiness and social ambition of the Group Movement founded by Frank Buchman (and later renamed Moral Rearmament) was the subject of one of Auden's essays (pp. 47–54).

Page 361.

W. R. Inge, Dean of St Paul's, and always known as "the gloomy Dean", published weekly attacks in the *Evening Standard* on popular optimism and other delusions.

Cosmo Gordon Lang, Primate of the Church of England, a celibate lover of ecclesiastical luxury, censured Edward VIII in a broadcast on 13 December 1936, soon after the abdication, for having sought happiness "within a social circle whose standard and way of life are alien to all the best instincts and traditions of his people." Pat McCormick, the genial vicar of St Martin's-in-the-Fields, broadcast a weekly nondenominational service from the BBC studios and a monthly evening service from his church, both to a prodigiously vast audience.

Lord Craigavon, first prime minister of Northern Ireland, strongly supported the Orangemen bullies of the Protestant ascendancy; on their ceremonial marches huge drums called Orange drums were beaten, partly as a threatening warning to Catholics to keep away.

Eamon De Valera, premier of the Irish Free State and a mathematician by training, was pursuing a tariff war against Britain as part of his rather unsuccessful policy of economic nationalism; his surname came from his paternal Spanish ancestors, and the allusion to the seraphim perhaps refers to his supposed wish for a more theocratic form of government in Ireland.

The Thames gives Oxford its notoriously bronchial climate, worsened by the fumes of its industrial suburb Cowley. Medicine Hat is in Alberta.

Bulldogs are the Proctors' attendants at Oxford and Cambridge whose main function is to seize drunken and otherwise malfeasant undergraduates; Jack Lovelock won the fifteen-hundred-metre race in the 1936 Olympics.

Convocation, the assembly of all Oxford Masters of Arts, is the highest legislative body of the university; the statutes enacted and repealed by Convocation were mainly published in Latin.

The Oxford Appointments Board provided information about jobs that no undergraduate wanted, in colonial towns where no one wanted to be; Calaguttis seems to be an error for Calagurris in ancient Iberia.

Sir Farquhar Buzzard, Regius Professor of Medicine, was nominated on 9 December 1936 as the Conservative candidate in the Oxford University by-election of 1937; the bequest may have a more specific point that is no longer identifiable.

Page 362.

Julian Huxley, who had examined Auden for the Natural Science Exhibition (a minor scholarship) to Christ Church that he won in his last year at school, published *Ants* in 1935; his demonstration that thyroid extract induced axolotls to develop into salamanders made headlines in 1920.

Lady Astor was a proselytizing Christian Scientist who did not believe in ill health and campaigned in Parliament and elsewhere against liquor. Basil de Sélincourt, who wrote weekly book reviews for the *Observer* and the *Manchester Guardian*, perhaps receives an unfinished Scottish reproduction of the Parthenon because it was the antithesis of the anticlassicizing argument for the evolutionary strength of the English language that he offered in his 1926 pamphlet *Pomona, or the Future of English*.

Cyril Norwood, master (i.e., headmaster) of Marlborough when MacNeice was there, was famously formal in his speech and fastidious in his person; Auden and T. C. Worsley quoted him in *Education* to illustrate a fallacy (p. 421).

The Rev. Philip ("Tubby") Clayton founded Toc H, the teetotal religious, service, and youth organization. General Eoin O'Duffy, whose blue-shirted National Guard was Ireland's closest approximation to a fascist movement, was an indefatigable orator who had grown more erratic in recent years; in November 1936 he led a contingent of volunteers to Spain to fight for Franco. "The harp that once in Tara's halls / The soul of music shed" (the opening of one of Thomas Moore's *Irish Melodies*) had been long silent.

A dramatization of Ian Hay's public school novel *Housemaster* (the dramatization was titled *The Housemaster*) had been reviewed by MacNeice in *Time and Tide*, 21 November 1936, where he noted that if "youth home for the holidays . . . are shrewd enough to see through the sentimentality it will do them some good". (Around the time that Auden and MacNeice were working on the poem, Hay offered a widely publicized self-serving toast at a Foyles literary luncheon in which, as reported in *The Times*, 16 December 1936, he said "that most of the flimsy, unsubstantial trifles such as detective stories or humorous extravaganzas [such as the ones he wrote in collaboration with P. G. Wodehouse] which they all affected to despise but all nevertheless read, cost their creators just as much labour of body, soul and spirit as it cost Milton to produce *Paradise Lost*".

Marlborough College's notoriously primitive lavatories were in an open shed. Auden describes in "The Liberal Fascist" the three broken promises he bequeaths to Gresham's School, Holt (pp. 58–59).

The BBC's Variety Department broadcast "Surprise Programmes"; the content was not revealed until the broadcast itself. J. A. Smith was an Oxford moral philosopher, famously Victorian in manner and outlook, although the bequest may allude to his unprepossessing appearance; the International Surrealist Exhibition opened in London in June 1936 (see p. 763).

The 7&5 Abstract Group (formerly the 7 and 5 Society) had become under Ben Nicholson's direction the most radical and experimental of British artists' groups. The famous collection of fossils at the Museum of Practical Geology in Jermyn Street had been moved to the new Geological Museum in South Kensington in 1935, leaving the old museum empty; Auden and MacNeice were apparently unaware that the older building had since been demolished.

Page 363.

Frederick Lindemann (later Lord Cherwell), whom Auden had known at Christ Church, was Churchill's adviser on weaponry and other scientific matters; his extreme political and cultural pessimism gave him the reputation of a warmonger.

Among the *Observer's* notably conservative reviewers, the drama critic Ivor Brown had attacked the Group Theatre's production of Auden's *The Dance of Death* and complained that Auden was "simply trotting out the most jaded nags from the Left Wing stable" in a review published on 6 October 1935 (see note to p. 364 below); the poetry critic Wilfrid Gibson had dismissed MacNeice's *Poems* in a review titled "The Awkward Squad", published on 24 November 1935; the chief drama critic St John Ervine had denounced Auden and MacNeice and their friends in a series of articles published on 29 December 1935 and 12, 19, and 26 January 1936 (see note to p. 369 below); the book reviewer Basil de Sélincourt, although he had written generously about *The Poet's Tongue* on 1 September 1935, published a broad attack on T. S. Eliot two weeks later (see note to p. 362 above); and a less frequent book reviewer, John Sparrow, had elsewhere attacked Auden as unintelligible (see note to p. 370 below). Among the *Observer's* second-string drama reviewers, however, Peter Burra and Harold Hobson had praised Auden's plays, and Hobson liked MacNeice's translation of *Agamemnon* although he shared the general distaste for the production. Beachcomber, the pseudonym used by J. B. Morton, published in his columns for the *Daily Express* both nonsense humor and satires of twentieth-century life.

The Victoria Embankment front of Shell-Mex House, built in 1931, was vast enough in scale to house all of H. G. Wells's illegitimate progeny and fascist enough in style to suit Wells's vision of a world ruled by scientists, as portrayed in his script for the 1936 film *Things to Come*.

The Fogerty School was the Central School of Speech-Training and Dramatic Art, founded by Elsie Fogerty, who trained the chorus in the first production of Eliot's *The Rock;* she famously disliked eighteenth-century formal rhetoric, and favored the rhapsodic style of Swinburne and of Gilbert Murray's translations of Greek tragedies. The Reverend Tickell is a confusion with Addison's friend Thomas Tickell; in Johnson's *Lives of the Poets* (from which Auden had quoted in his essay on Pope a few months before) the life of Tickell begins, "Thomas Tickell, the son of the reverend Richard Tickell. . . ." Johnson's first page quotes eight highly ornamented lines of Tickell's rhymed pentameter couplets. Auden found A. A. Milne's children's stories dislikably arch. Beverley Nichols, journalist, socialite, sentimental dandy, and former boy prodigy, published his memoirs in 1926 at the age of 25, and later tried to suppress any indication of his real age; his bequest followed the publication in May 1936 of *The Fool Hath Said*, his treacly defence of Christianity, written under the influence of the Group Movement, and slightly misidentifies his taste for sexual partners more rough than Peter Pan.

Lady Oxford, the widow of H. H. Asquith, often caricatured for her thin physique, had in youth been the model for the selfish, callous title character of E. F. Benson's first novel, *Dodo*. The bequest to J. L. Garvin, the imperialist high-Tory editor of the *Observer*, alludes to Garvin's widely known valuation of himself.

Rupert Doone directed Auden's and MacNeice's plays for the Group Theatre, which he had founded with Robert Medley; his arbitrary and incoherent style tried the patience of his playwrights. During preparations for his production of MacNeice's translation of *Agamemnon*, which opened in November 1936, Doone told MacNeice: "Aeschylus was static, I am dynamic, so fuck all" (E. R. Dodds, *Missing Persons* [1977], p. 132).

Daan Hubrecht (nickname of Daniel F.-M. Hubrecht), the son of a Dutch diplomat, was one year behind MacNeice at Marlborough, and a friend of Anthony Blunt; the specific point of his bequest is lost, but it may allude (via the Martello Tower in *Ulysses*) to his Irish wife or to a general interest in life near the water. (After leaving England around 1930 he worked in a sugar factory in Java and spent part of each year on Bali.) Red biddy is a mixture of cheap red wine and methylated spirits, associated with the Glasgow slums; the bequest to Hugh MacDiarmid, author of *First* (and *Second*) *Hymn to Lenin* and *A Drunk Man Looks at the Thistle*, and a connoisseur of Scotch whisky, combines allusions to his politics and his thirst (and perhaps also alludes to the multiple indiscretions listed in the divorce decree that his wife obtained early in 1932, and to the birth of his child by an unmarried woman six months later). Sir Archibald Flower was chairman of the Trustees and Guardians of Shakespeare's Birthplace and of the Council of the Shakespeare Memorial Theatre at Stratford.

The M'Gillicuddy of M'Gillicuddy is a misnomer for the McGillicuddy of the Reeks (i.e., the hills called Macgillicuddy's Reeks), Lt Col Ross McGillicuddy, a member of the Irish Senate. Norman Douglas, known for his cultivated tastes in Mediterranean food and youth, had written but not yet published an aphrodisiac cookbook, *Venus in the Kitchen*.

John Fothergill, the eccentric upper-class innkeeper who owned the Spread-eagle Inn at Thame (popular among Oxford undergraduates) when Auden and MacNeice were at Oxford, was a ferocious snob whose book *An Innkeeper's Diary* (1931) was reissued by the Right Book Club; the Lyon's Corner Houses were a chain of inexpensive restaurants that offered elaborate decor, orchestras, and other luxuries to ordinary Londoners (see p. 345).

Maurice Bowra's bequest may allude to his strikingly massive head or perhaps to his receding hairline; in MacNeice's draft list the bequest is "proscenium arch". (The bequest may also be a response to Bowra's open hostility when E. R. Dodds took up the Regius Professorship that Bowra believed should have been his; in *Adonais* the dome, which "Stains the white radiance of Eternity, / Until death tramples it to fragments", is that which is painted, false, and worldly, as opposed to that which is clear, true, and ideal.) Father Ronald Knox published, in addition to the crime novels for which he was best known, acrostics, epigrams, puzzles, and other word games.

Page 364.

The miscellaneous writer Compton Mackenzie helped found the Scottish National Party soon after he moved to Scotland; in *The Orators* Auden wrote: "In Scotland they say / That Compton Mackenzie will be king one day." James Douglas was a reviewer and editor hostile to modern literature and sexual irregularities. Roy Campbell, who dramatized himself in his poems as a larger-than-life horseman, lancer, and outdoorsman (see p. 249), was the author of *Taurine Provence* (1932), a prose book on "the philosophy, technique and religion of the bullfighter", and *Mithraic Emblems,* published in October 1936, in which the first poem was about the sacrifice of bulls.

The drama reviewers James Agate of the *Sunday Times* and Ivor Brown of the *Observer* exemplified conventional tastes; Brown had complained at length about the Group Theatre's left-wing aesthetic. Edith Sitwell, in an "Auto-Obituary" (one of a series) titled "The Late Miss Sitwell", in the *Listener,* 29 July 1936, praised her own "wider vision and more eclectic taste" and judged herself superior to her younger contemporaries; apparently alluding to *The Orators,* she wrote that "she never attempted to write a dubious scientific text-book in something which was neither prose nor verse, and label it a poem".

Auden first met Naomi Mitchison in 1929, during her feminist period; her Marxist period began in 1930, and she had recently begun her Mass-Observation period.

Sir Oswald Mosley, founder of the British Union of Fascists and the "honest Oswald" of "Letter to Lord Byron" (p. 214), led a march of three thousand of his followers toward the Jewish quarter of East London in October 1936; the ensuing street fight prompted Parliament in December 1936 to pass the Public Order Act, which prohibited the wearing of political uniforms and proscribed quasi-military organizations.

Anthony M. Ludovici earned widespread contempt for his naive accounts of Nietzsche, his whining attacks on feminism, and his self-congratulatory writings on sex; among his exhaustively detailed recommendations in *The Choice of a Mate* (1935), he repeatedly stressed the importance of relatively short legs and "large hips and buttocks" in women.

The King's Proctor intervenes on behalf of the Crown in matrimonial cases; parliamentary debate over a divorce-reform bill in 1936 publicized his office's efforts to prevent false evidence of adultery from being used in divorce cases, generally when a husband chivalrously produced false evidence of his own adultery (in a hotel room accessible with a skeleton key) so that his wife could sue him even though he had been faithful. Opponents of the bill argued that easier divorce would be a further step in the decline of the West; proponents argued that it would reduce the use of false evidence and potentially put an end to the functions of the King's Proctor. A. P. Herbert's speech in support of the bill, on 8 December 1936, was widely reported.

The cabaret performances of the female impersonator Douglas Byng were famously risqué. Geoffrey Mure was MacNeice's friend and philosophy tutor at Oxford; his two-part essay, "The Marriage of Universals", published in 1928 in the *Journal of Philosophical Studies*, took its title from a phrase in F. H. Bradley's article "Association and Thought", and referred to the attempt to join logic and psychology as means of knowledge. Sir Frederic Truby King was to middle-class families the undisputed authority on raising babies; MacNeice, who was unhappy about his wife's obedience to Truby King's dictates, alludes in "Hetty to Nancy" to the hygienic practices and strict psychological regimen that he prescribed.

Sir Bindon Blood, who led victorious campaigns in India and South Africa in the late nineteenth century, had recently been appointed chief royal engineer at the age of ninety-three.

Marie Stopes, who recommended cocoa butter as a contraceptive, claimed that her work was prompted by divine inspiration.

The most mischievous woman then alive was MacNeice's former mother-in-law, Marie Beazley, who, after first trying to discourage MacNeice's marriage to her daughter Mary, tried to restore the marriage and disrupt Mary's impending second marriage through diplomats, rabbinical curses, and miscellaneous threats, annoyances, and absurdities; see Jon Stallworthy, *Louis MacNeice* (1995).

Among the best known of Evelyn Underhill's many books on religious and mystical subjects was her *Practical Mysticism*. Osbert Lancaster delighted in Kensington Victoriana. Jimmy Nervo (James Holloway) and Teddy Knox made up one of the three teams of ribald, knockabout music-hall comedians in the Crazy Gang; the druids, bards, and other participants in the Eisteddfod conducted their celebration of Welsh national culture with pious solemnity.

Ladislas Peri is an error for the constructivist sculptor László Peri, whom Auden probably knew through Isherwood; Peri had married a sister of a member of the Mangeot Quartet (see note to p. 371 below). Bryan Guinness, an heir to the Irish brewery fortune, was a poet and novelist; his firm made stout, unlike the English bitter beer made by Bass at Burton on Trent.

Page 365.

"Camera shock" seems to be Auden and MacNeice's coinage, on the model of shell shock.

Auden alluded frequently to Henry James's exclamation on Arnold Bennett in "The New Novel": "Yes, yes—but is this *all*? These are the circumstances of the interest—we see, we see; but where is the interest itself, where and what is its centre, and how are we to measure it in relation to *that*?"

The Entertainment Tax, later repealed, was much resented by those who worked in theatre and film.

Auden recorded some of his experiences as an apprentice at John Grierson's General Post Office Film Unit in the autumn and winter of 1935–36 in his letter to William Coldstream (pp. 345–46); Grierson, who encouraged a monastic atmosphere around him, despised all films that failed to perform a public service.

During the time they worked at the Film Unit (through which they met), and afterward, Auden tried unsuccessfully to convince Benjamin Britten to overcome his emotional and sexual inhibitions. Long Meg and her daughters (misremembered here as nine daughters) is a prehistoric stone circle in Cumberland.

The low reliefs of Ben Nicholson (not Nicolson), with their motif of an open circle suitable for a loudspeaker, resembled the innovative cabinets of some of the wireless sets produced by Murphy Radio, Ltd, a firm that Nicholson and other artists admired.

I. M. Parsons, reviewing *The Dog Beneath the Skin* in the *Spectator,* called it "a shoddy affair, a half-baked little satire which gets nowhere".

On Herbert Read and Christian subjects in art, see Auden's review of Read's *In Defence of Shelley* (pp. 130–33); Read's classic past included his editing in 1924 of T. E. Hulme's antiromantic *Speculations.* Peter Fleming's books and reportage ostentatiously understated the discomforts of exotic travel (see pp. 607–11); members of public-school sports teams receive distinctively colored caps. (The *New Statesman and Nation* and *Time and Tide,* in their numbers dated 5 December 1936, reported that Fleming was to give a lantern-slide lecture in London titled "A Journey through Central Asia", in aid of the Red Cross.)

Page 366.

The martyr's stake at Abergwili (Abergwilly is an informal anglicization) is more precisely the finial of the nineteenth-century parish church; it was cut from a stone that had been taken from Carmarthen, where, at a stake reputedly affixed to the stone, the controversialist Bishop Ferrar was burned for heresy in 1555, after refusing an offer of his life if he recanted. Wyndham Lewis's distant ancestry was Welsh; his *Left Wings over Europe: or, How to Make a War about Nothing,* published in June 1936, was the most recent repetition of his argument that Britain should ally itself with Germany in its battle against Communism.

The poem's judgement of Alexander Korda, Michael Balcon, and Michael's associate and older brother Chandos Balcon is probably based on reports from Isherwood, who first worked in the film industry as a dialogue director for Berthold Viertel and, around the time *Letters from Iceland* was published, began work on a screenplay for Korda; Balcon was dislodged as director of production at the Gaumont-British Picture Corporation in early December 1936, and his bequest presumably expresses a hope that he might henceforth produce less-spurious work. The future of the British cinema was publicly debated in the first two weeks of December 1936 following publication of a report on the subject by a government committee. The supposed suicide in 1934 of the shady financier

Serge Stavisky was alleged to have been arranged by the French police in conspiracy with the premier in order to conceal corruption that involved Stavisky, politicians, police, capitalists, and the judiciary; the scandal resulted in riots, a general strike, and the resignation of two successive premiers. *Sabotage* was released in 1936.

The cottage at Piccadilly was the men's lavatory in the underground station, often used for illicit encounters; Auden mentioned "the Fairy Ring at Piccadilly" in "In Search of Dracula" (p. 77). "A certain novelist" was Charles Morgan, whose novels *The Fountain* (1932) and *Sparkenbroke* (1936) portray an aestheticized and emotionally intense pursuit of the absolute; in MacNeice's draft list of recipients, "Charles Morgan—cottage at Tottenham Court Rd" immediately precedes the entry for Lord Berners, as in the finished poem.

Lord Berners, a composer, writer, and artist famous for eccentric and malicious wit, built an enormous folly near his house in 1935 over the opposition of the local council; his wit specialized in deflating the kind of solemnity with which courtiers praised the stable married life of George VI on his accession to the throne after the abdication of Edward VIII.

Anthony Blunt, MacNeice's friend since their time at Marlborough, his companion on a journey to Spain earlier in 1936, and at this time the art critic for the *Spectator*, had begun to espouse Marxism in 1934. The bequest of a copy of "Love Locked Out" is an elaborate art-historical and sexual joke. The painting of a naked child trying to open a locked door was by Anna Lea Merritt, not Holman Hunt, but it quotes extensively from Hunt's "The Light of the World", which portrays a clothed adult Christ knocking at a door. Merritt's painting, which became widely popular (see p. 592), was misinterpreted by sophisticated viewers like MacNeice as an allegory of forbidden love.

Archie Burton was MacNeice's first cousin once removed on his father's side, and the brother of Oonagh Burton (see below); despite the severe damage that MacNeice's Austin 10 suffered when he dozed at the wheel in King's Heath, a suburb of Birmingham, and was struck by a car that had the right of way (an accident for which he was prosecuted), MacNeice thought Archie Burton would be safer in it than he was in the three-wheeled Baby Austin that Burton drove when visiting MacNeice from Coventry.

Graham Shepard, MacNeice's close friend since their days at Marlborough, was now working as a journalist; he and Ann Shepard (who indifferently spelled her name Anne or Ann) were the recipients of one of the letters in the book.

Mrs Norton reared dogs and probably sold one to MacNeice; the Selly Hill district where she and her husband, Stanley P. Norton, lived was about a mile from Birmingham University and close to MacNeice's cottage in the Selly Oak district. *Our Dogs* was published weekly. The polymath scientist Victor Rothschild, whom MacNeice met through Anthony Blunt, was among other things an expert on fertilization.

E. L. Stahl, a South African–born lecturer in German at Birmingham University, was a fellow tenant with MacNeice of the Sargant Florences and had played golf with MacNeice almost daily during a Cotswold holiday.

Page 367.
     Stahl and his sister Vera, Professor and Mrs Dodds, and MacNeice made an

expedition to Twickenham to watch a rugby match between Ireland and England in 1935.

Mrs Dodds bred Sealyham terriers.

Littleton Powys was MacNeice's headmaster at Sherborne preparatory school (and brother of the writers Theodore, John Cowper, and Llewellyn Powys); his religion, MacNeice wrote, was natural history.

Wilfrid (not Wilfred) Blunt, Anthony's elder brother and like him an art historian, had been at Marlborough with MacNeice and was now working as a schoolmaster at Haileybury College. John R. Hilton, MacNeice's friend from Marlborough, had recently set up as an architect, and retained an active interest in philosophy.

Willaim McCance, a painter and sculptor, lived with his wife Agnes Miller Parker, a painter and wood-engraver, in an Oxfordshire house filled with cats; MacNeice probably met them through Anthony Blunt, who held the post of art critic for the *Spectator* that McCance had held in the 1920s. Moore Crosthwaite, later a diplomat, shared lodgings with MacNeice at Oxford, and was impressively knowledgeable about modern architecture.

George Morrell (not Morell) was a notably hearty man who had been an undergraduate at Birmingham University and was one of MacNeice's drinking companions; "the dogs" was the working-class entertainment of greyhound racing. Tom Robinson worked as a gardener for Lella Sargant Florence, MacNeice's landlady at Birmingham; in *The Strings Are False* MacNeice mentions Robinson's interest in pigeon racing (a homer is a homing pigeon) and the worn-out blue-check pigeon that he encouraged MacNeice to keep.

Denis Binyon, who was two years ahead of MacNeice at Merton College, preferred Greek to his other languages (he had since become a lecturer in Latin at the University of Leeds); it was in character for him to remonstrate gently against the noise of those around him.

John Waterhouse (who in 1937 married Elspeth Duxbury; see below) was a lecturer in English at Birmingham who was friendly with both MacNeice and Auden; in a copy of *Letters from Iceland* (now in the possession of Samuel Hynes) that he gave his parents he signed himself "their fat son". "The Isle of Capri" was a hit song, first heard in 1934.

Page 368.

Gordon Herickx (not Herrickx), a close Birmingham friend of MacNeice and a causal friend of Auden, worked as a stonemason by day to earn a living, and worked at night carving abstract sculptures.

Robert Medley, the painter friend who first suggested that Auden write poetry, designed productions for the Group Theatre; his bequest alludes to the cellophane masks worn by the chorus in the Group's production of MacNeice's translation of *Agamemnon* in November 1936, and to his gouache, "Jokers", which had been shown at the International Surrealist Exhibition in 1936. Geoffrey Tandy, a curator at the Natural History Museum and broadcaster, was a close friend of T. S. Eliot.

Humphrey Thackrah, a man of refined tastes, was MacNeice's friend and solicitor, who specialized in society divorce cases and arranged MacNeice's divorce (which so dismayed him that he never handled another, and, after World War

II, entered a monastery where he later became the abbot); Chanel No 5 was commonly called Numero Cinq. Isaiah (not Isiah) Berlin received in MacNeice's draft list of bequests a "doctorate in gossip".

Lella Sargant (not Sargent) Florence was the wife of Professor P. Sargant Florence, subject of a bequest later in the poem; MacNeice and his wife had lived in a cottage on the grounds of the Sargant Florences' house near Birmingham. Oonagh Burton was MacNeice's highly glamorous first cousin once removed on his father's side, and sister of Archie Burton (see above); she worked for a time as a representative in America for an English cosmetics firm.

John Melville, a painter, and his poet brother Robert (later an art critic), both working as clerks in Birmingham, were staunch surrealists in a climate generally hostile to their faith. Guy Morgan (E. G. T. Morgan), later a story editor for a film company and a short-story writer, was a year behind MacNeice at Merton College and was now working as a journalist.

Guy Burgess, whom MacNeice met through Anthony Blunt, was at this time a producer in the BBC Talks Department. Ben Bonas, now in charge of his family's jewellery firm, had been at Marlborough and Oxford. Hector MacIver, later the dedicatee of MacNeice's *I Crossed the Minch*, was working as a journalist and as a producer and broadcaster for the BBC in Edinburgh; his work for the BBC brought him into contact with MacNeice. Robert F. Dunnett was working as a producer for the BBC in Glasgow, and perhaps met MacNeice either through his work there or through Hector MacIver. The poet Norman Cameron, another Scot and MacNeice's contemporary at Oxford, was a well-known figure in Bloomsbury pubs. The spelling *whiskey* presumably reflects MacNeice's preference for Irish whiskey over the Scotch whisky intended for the bequest (and confirmed by the rhyme of deceiver with MacIver).

Adrian Green-Armytage (not Green-Armitage), MacNeice's closest friend at Oxford, became a stockbroker in 1932 when the depression made it impossible for him to get the job he hoped for at the British Museum.

Helen Cooke, a school friend of MacNeice's former wife Mary, had visited the MacNeices in Birmingham.

Elspeth Duxbury (who in 1937 married John Waterhouse; see above) acted with the Birmingham Repertory Theatre.

Ivan Roe (not Rowe) was a young journalist who had written an immensely long novel that was never published, although he later published fiction, literary criticism, and (under the pseudonym Richard Savage) mystery novels; the Stephens firm made the ink most used in schools.

The novelist and journalist Walter Allen had been an undergraduate at Birmingham University, where he became friendly with MacNeice; the Midland Regional service of the BBC broadcast from Birmingham.

Edith Marcuse was a young leftist German refugee living in Birmingham. The actress Coral Brown (later spelled Browne) arrived in England from Australia in 1934; she perhaps engaged in one of the flirtations that MacNeice, in *The Strings Are False*, mentions as a feature of his first months in London in 1936.

Page 369.

Theaden Hancock was married to William Keith Hancock, professor of history at Birmingham University; both were Australians. Helen Cicely Russell (later an educator) and R. D. Smith (Reggie Smith, later a broadcaster), who were then living together, had recently been undergraduates at Birmingham; Smith, who was studying for his certificate in higher education, had become a close friend of MacNeice while an undergraduate.

The poet Bernard Spencer had been at Marlborough and Oxford with MacNeice, and worked during the 1930s as a schoolmaster and with the British Council; he was married to Norah (not Nora) Gibbs. John Bowle, a strikingly epicene contemporary of MacNeice at Marlborough and Oxford and later a popular historian, was a schoolmaster at Westminster.

Diana Sanger, not otherwise identified, was evidently part of MacNeice's circle of dog-lovers in Birmingham. The poet Ruthven Todd, who treasured his Scottish heritage, was friendly with Auden and MacNeice in London.

Curigwen Lewis acted with the Birmingham Repertory Theatre. John W. Chase, an American Rhodes Scholar, was at Merton College with MacNeice and was now a freelance writer.

The Reverend Clifford B. Canning, headmaster of Canford School, had been a friendly patron to MacNeice and his friends when he was a master at Marlborough. Christopher Holme, a poet and MacNeice's friend from Oxford, was working as a foreign correspondent in Spain.

David Gretton worked for the Midland Region of the BBC in Birmingham. May Lawrence has not been identified.

Francis Curtis, a painter friend of MacNeice from Marlborough, preferred to be called Capel or Capell while at Oxford; no other details of his history there have been recorded.

The bequest to John Betjeman (who was known to be hostile to hearties) includes the bright pink tie of the Leander rowing club; most of his other bequests refer to his taste for Victorian Gothic and ecclesiastical curiosa. Betjeman, the addressee of the "Sheaves from Sagaland" earlier in the book, was friendly with Auden but disliked MacNeice.

Harold Acton had lived in China since 1932. In the early 1930s Heinz Neddermeyer (not Nedermeyer) evaded German military service while travelling through Europe with Christopher Isherwood in search of a place to settle. John Andrews was a dancer with the Ballet Rambert who became one of Isherwood's lovers early in 1937; in March he travelled with Isherwood and Auden to the Lake Country via the L. M. S. (London Midland & Scottish) Railway, and perhaps neglected to leave some of the railway's towels in the train. (The lines about Andrews must have been written after the rest of the poem was complete; they perhaps replace lines about Auden and MacNeice's novelist friend John Hampson, who in MacNeice's draft list of recipients receives "a year of towel".)

The blustering and reactionary St John Ervine, drama critic for the *Observer*, printed a series of four attacks against Auden and Day Lewis ("renegade poets . . . who are hunting with the Bolshy-minded planners"), with sideswipes at MacNeice, in December 1935 and January 1936 (see note to p. 363 above).

Page 370.

J. W. Dunne's *An Experiment with Time* provided Auden with phrases that he used in his poem "It was Easter as I walked in the public gardens"; he had earlier become famous as an inventor and engineer. (On 7 May 1937 D. R. Cowling, Richard de la Mare's secretary, asked if "Robert Dunne" in the proof should not be "J. W. Dunne"; Auden apparently accepted the correction.) The geologist Andrew V. Corry, an American Rhodes Scholar, was one year behind MacNeice at Merton College; belemnites, easily found on the Dorset beaches where MacNeice hunted fossils as a boy, are usually only a few inches long. The bequest to Noël Coward combines his phrase "out in the midday sun" with a wish that the sun would set on the British Empire.

The bequest to Dylan Thomas (whose *Twenty-five Poems* appeared in September 1936) gives him the national emblem of Wales in the form of a handout from the wealthy patrons whose charity he noisily cultivated. Auden privately described himself as "a great admirer of and believer in" Charles Madge, poet, sociologist, and, in 1937, cofounder of Mass Observation (see p. 704).

MacNeice wrote in *The Strings Are False:* "The *New Statesman and Nation,* our leading Leftist weekly, lived upon prophecies of disaster—and was never disappointed".

John Sparrow's *Sense and Poetry* (1934) singled out Auden's work as "a monument to the misguided aims that prevail among contemporary poets" and denounced the critics who had praised it.

Roy Harrod (who had been Auden's tutor in his first year at Oxford) and Maynard Keynes (whom Auden met in November 1936) were unlikely to pull together (i.e., revive) the falling birthrate by pulling together (i.e., performing mutual masturbation). Auden tried to convince Brian Howard, who spent much of the 1930s travelling through Europe in search of a safe haven for his German boyfriend, that he could fulfil his literary ambitions only by working to a schedule; the "painted buoy" is apparently not a plausible reference to Howard's friend, and any specific reference has probably been lost.

Father Martin d'Arcy, the Roman Catholic apologist, had befriended MacNeice at Oxford, and apparently knew Auden there (he visited the Downs School around 1933); at some point he received an unnumbered (and therefore probably late) copy of Auden's 1928 *Poems.* The bequest to Auden's Oxford tutor Nevill (not Neville) Coghill alludes flatteringly to a line in Hölderlin's poem "Sokrates und Alcibiades" ("He who has pondered the deepest things loves what is most alive"), a poem Auden quoted twice earlier in 1936; the bequest also expresses Auden's long-held hope that Coghill might achieve a satisfying sexual love.

R. M. Dawkins, Professor of Byzantine and Modern Greek at Oxford, who introduced Auden to the poems of Cavafy, wrote a review-essay on string figures in *Annals of Archaeology and Anthropology* in 1931; Auden, whose poems began to allude to string figures in 1933, apparently got his information about them from Kathleen Haddon's *Cat's Cradles from Many Lands,* in which the description of "The Fighting Lions" figure ends: "While doing this say 'Oo-ah' (= the lions roaring)"—a sound that resembled Dawkins's notoriously loud laughter.

Richard Best was two years behind Auden at Christ Church; a speckled boater is a boater hat with a speckled ribbon. Geoffrey Grigson's *New Verse* printed many poems by Auden and MacNeice among Grigson's slashing reviews of every poet other than Auden; MacNeice was subletting Grigson's flat in London.

Gerald Heard, whose conversation and books on science and religion had provided Auden with much of the material in his poems after 1932, had recently taken up yoga after a visit to India; the *New Statesman and Nation*, 12 December 1936, reported that he was to speak on that day at the Peace Pledge Bookshop. Maurice Feild, arts master at the Downs School, was Auden's close friend.

Geoffrey Hoyland was headmaster at the Downs School. John Davenport drifted among scriptwriting, criticism, and the production of talks for the BBC, but had inherited enough money to avoid a permanent job.

Tom Garland (disguised as "Wreath" in "The Liberal Fascist", p. 57) and his wife Peggy, a sculptor, remained friendly with Auden through the 1930s; around December 1936, Tom, now a physician, obtained at Auden's request a supply of morphia for Auden to give to wounded soldiers when he went to Spain in January 1937.

Page 371.

Nancy Coldstream was married to William Coldstream, and became Mac-Neice's lover shortly after this poem was written. John Layard, the anthropologist and disciple of Homer Lane whom Auden befriended in Berlin in 1928 (see p. 333), had once suffered a hysterical paralysis that left him unable to walk; the "quick ones" were probably sexual rather than alcoholic. Olive Mangeot, to whom Auden dedicated the poem "Easily, my dear, you move, easily your head", was the wife of André Mangeot, who in 1925 hired Isherwood as part-time secretary to his string quartet.

The Morris-Cowley was among the least expensive of automobiles. Peter Roger, a former pupil at the Downs School, worked at the school as a gardener and lived with Auden on the grounds in a house that Auden called "Lawrence Cottage". Robert Moody, then studying pediatric medicine, was a close friend of Auden; his brother John Moody acted with the Group Theatre (see *Plays*, p. 479).

Robert Graves and Laura Riding had returned to England in August 1936 from the Spanish island of Majorca after it had been taken over by Nationalist forces; the allusion to "an Italian island" may be a slip, but it presumably refers to the Italian military presence that supported the Nationalists.

Residents of the Channel Islands paid income tax at an exceptionally low rate; residents of Sark paid none. The most notorious beneficiary of the Channel Islands' exemption from mainland taxes and death duties was the self-publicizing anti-Soviet xenophobe Dame Fanny Houston, who in 1926 had inherited millions of pounds from her Jersey-resident husband, and died on 29 December 1936.

Sean Day-Lewis, the five-year-old son of Cecil Day-Lewis, receives the world's largest waterwheel (built for the local lead mines); earlier in 1936, his bed-wetting had caused him to be taken for an examination by Auden's father, one of several physicians who failed to find a cure. Mrs Yates, Michael Yates's mother, lived with her family in Brooklands, a suburb of Manchester; Auden joined the family on its holiday on the Isle of Man in 1935.

The novelist Sapper, whose books chronicled the adventures of Bulldog Drummond and other overgrown public-school boys in the Secret Service, presumably receives the County of Surrey because its golf clubs, roadhouses, and villas for middle-class stockbrokers suited his aesthetics and politics. Hilaire Belloc, who wrote nostalgic drinking songs set in Sussex and used a horse-drawn cart to bring crates of fine wine to friends' houses, is bequeathed what he most despised, the brash, vulgar roadhouses that had sprung up to serve automobile travellers on England's noisiest and most commercialized roads.

The political ambition of Quintin (not Quinton) Hogg (later Lord Hailsham), who knew Auden at Oxford and was at this time a barrister, could find only limited satisfaction in the merely ceremonial status of the Wardenship of the Cinque Ports. St Clether's Well, in Cornwall, is double in that the water emerges first in the roofed well and then in a separate chapel; lunatics were formerly treated in Cornish holy wells by immersion.

Sebastian Sprott was the nickname of W. J. H. Sprott, a Bloomsbury figure and psychology don at the University of Nottingham; he was reputed to live in a slum among working-class friends, although his house was in fact merely a modest one. Mortimer's Hole is the cell in Nottingham Castle in which Roger Mortimer was imprisoned after the murder of Edward II. Auden described his Oxford friend Gabriel Carritt as a "snub-nosed winner" (in the poem "Between attention and attention" and elsewhere); at the Beetle and Wedge pub in Moulsford-on-Thames, near Oxford, he and Carritt spent a night in the same bed, but to Auden's disappointment not in each other's arms. T. F. Coade, headmaster of Bryanston, withdrew his offer to hire Auden in 1935 when Auden wrote a letter to an ex-pupil at the Downs, Michael Paget-Jones, with a joking request to "Put an onion in the chalice for me" (an allusion to the standard schoolboy mispronunciation of "an union" in *Hamlet*), and Paget-Jones showed it to a senior prefect who showed it to Coade.

The medieval bridge at Crowland (but not in Crowland Abbey) crosses a river that was later diverted. Richard Crossman, whom Auden knew at Oxford and who was now a member of the Oxford City Council, was the recipient of one of the letters in the book.

John Cowper Powys's *A Glastonbury Romance* was published in 1933. The White Horses are hills in the south of England with Iron Age outline figures of horses cut in the chalk; the most famous is White Horse Hill within the old county borders of Berkshire. The valley of the Evenlode River, northwest of Oxford, is notably peaceful and secluded.

Offa's Dyke, now reduced to fragmentary remains, was built by the king of the Mercians to keep the Welsh inside. The enormous limestone caves at Castleton, Derbyshire, are a few miles away from one of the sacred places of Auden's childhood, the Blue John Mine.

Page 372.

P. Sargant Florence, Professor of Commerce at Birmingham University, and MacNeice's landlord, argued for large-scale industrial amalgamations in *The Logic of Industrial Organization* (1933). The community that Leonard and Dorothy Elmhirst founded at Dartington Hall, near Totnes, Devon, in 1925, was based on such small-scale crafts as farming, horticulture, cider making, sawmilling, and textiles; Auden visited Dartington with Gerald Heard in 1932 and briefly hoped for a job there. The bequest of Dartmoor Prison to Sir Herbert Pethick Lawrence is a garbled reference to Frederick Pethick-Lawrence, the suffragist who with his wife was imprisoned and force-fed in 1912; Auden apparently muddled the name with that of Sir Herbert Lawrence, chairman of the armaments manufacturer Vickers, Ltd (the subject of a bequest on p. 360).

Rex Warner, whom Auden befriended at Oxford, bird-watched; the birds in Wicken Fen, an insect sanctuary in Norfolk, are mentioned in Auden's poem "Out on the lawn I lie in bed"; the Hillborough Dovecot, at Hillborough Manor, Temple Grafton, Warwickshire, is an imposing stone building twenty-four feet in diameter. Sidney (not Sydney) Newman, an organ scholar, was Auden's friend at Oxford; construction had begun in Westminster Abbey on a new organ intended for use in the planned coronation of Edward VIII in May 1937, and used instead at the coronation of George VI.

The Crystal Palace burned down on the night of 31 November 1936, leaving only the twin cylindrical towers at each end. ("Central Transept Collapses in Flames on Great Organ", reported the headline in the *News Chronicle*.) Boston Stump is the enormous church tower in perpendicular style at Boston, Lincolnshire.

Michael Roberts, the poet, teacher, and critic with whom Auden collaborated on the English number of *Poetry* late in 1936 (see p. 702), was a mountaineer; Snowdonia, which Roberts had not yet climbed, is the highest expanse in England and Wales. In both his personality and his music, the wild and alcoholic Constant Lambert was the antithesis of the conservative and Elgarian Three Choirs Festival. The Vale of Eden was one of the sacred landscapes of Auden's childhood; journeys to the country were among the conventional charitable offerings to the slum children of the East End.

John Masefield, like his predecessor laureate Robert Bridges, lived at Boar's Hill, near Oxford.

The Birmingham Hippodrome was the largest Birmingham theatre; it specialized in popular variety entertainments.

The first chairman of Imperial Chemical Industries after its formation in 1926 was Lord Melchett, a biography of whom was reviewed by Auden in 1933 (p. 44).

Concerned citizens and local councils organized Watch Committees to monitor sexual activity on stage and screen, as well as in parks, darkened cinemas, and other places that needed watching. The full name of the British Association is the British Association for the Advancement of Science.

Major Yogi-Brown is a spoof on Francis Yeats-Brown, whose book about India, *Lancer at Large*, published in November 1936, combined soldierly reminiscences with descriptions of yoga techniques; a review by Robert Lynd in the *News Chronicle*, 18 December 1936, quoted his recommendation of a technique called Swastikasana ("you will probably enjoy getting to know your Self"). The

Thames Conservancy Board apparently tried to prevent men from swimming naked in the river, a practice that was commonplace until the 1920s but was generally suppressed in the 1930s; an admonishing waterboard is mentioned in "Letter to Lord Byron" (p. 213).

Page 373.

"Those who cannot dig" paraphrases Luke 16.3: "Then the steward said within himself, What shall I do? for my lord taketh away from me the steward-ship: I cannot dig; to beg I am ashamed."

F. R. Leavis, reviewing *Look, Stranger!* and *The Ascent of F6* in the December 1936 number of *Scrutiny*, wrote: "He is, of course, a satirist, and we know that there is such a thing as irony."

A sermon by the Bishop of Bradford on 1 December 1936, in which he ex-pressed the wish that Edward VIII had a better sense of Christian duty, prompted the British press to bring into the open Edward's affair with Wallis Simpson, and led to Edward's abdication ten days later. Gilbert Murray was aggressively vegetarian.

Wards of Chancery remain so until they come of age.

The interlocking terza rima of the poem suggests that Auden and MacNeice wrote it together while working in the same room. In the first stage, Auden and MacNeice planned the poem while MacNeice (using a notebook now in the Po-etry Collection at the State University of New York at Buffalo) wrote out brief outlines and a draft list of recipients and bequests. Not all the names in the draft list appear in the finished poem, and not all the names in the poem are in the draft list.

In parts of MacNeice's outlines and draft list he wrote Auden's or his own first initial in the margin next to individual bequests or categories. These initials make it possible to identify the authorship of most stanzas that in the printed text are initialled by both authors, and show that some bequests initialled (and probably devised) by one author were put into verse by the other.

Auden wrote the first six stanzas (titled in MacNeice's outline "Malgraseyri—opening / European situation"). MacNeice wrote the next six (in his outline: "ancestors"). Auden wrote the stanzas from "We leave to Stanley Baldwin" through "The cock that crew" (p. 360). MacNeice wrote the stanzas from "Item, to the Bishop of London" through "And Tubby Clayton" (pp. 360–62). Auden wrote the stanzas from "We leave a mens sana" through "The Dock, in all re-spect", including the lines about Marlborough initialled by MacNeice (pp. 362–63). MacNeice probably wrote the stanza beginning "Item, to those expert" (p. 363) and certainly all stanzas from the following stanza, "To the Fogerty School", through "And to Ladislas Peri" (pp. 363–64). Auden wrote the stanzas from "Item, an antidote" through "To Lord Berners" (pp. 365–66).

MacNeice probably wrote all the stanzas from "And I to all my friends" through "D'Arcy, that dialectical disputer" (pp. 366–70), including the two sets of stanzas initialled by both Auden and MacNeice and the bequests to Heinz Nedermeyer and John Andrews initialled by Auden alone (although the lines about Andrews may replace similar lines about John Hampson; see above). Auden probably wrote all the stanzas from "To Neville Coghill" through "To Sebastian Sprott" (pp. 370–71).

MacNeice almost certainly wrote the four stanzas from "To Mayfair" through "Item, we leave to Professor Sargant Florence" (pp. 371–72). Auden wrote the four stanzas from "The twin towers" through "To the children" (p. 372). MacNeice wrote the seven stanzas from "We allot them here" through "Lastly our hearts" (pp. 372–73). Auden wrote the stanzas from "Our grit we beg" through "She add at last" (p. 373), and probably all the remaining stanzas.

§4 THE 1967 SECOND EDITION

Auden prepared the second edition of *Letters from Iceland* in 1965, although Faber did not publish the book until 7 December 1967. Faber's edition was in paperback; Random House published it in cloth on 14 April 1969. Faber apparently suggested a new edition in December 1964 or early in January 1965. Auden probably wrote his foreword for the new edition (reprinted below) in March or April 1965 (in his draft he refers to himself as fifty-eight years old), and perhaps made his revisions to the first edition around the same time; he made substantial cuts in "Letter to Lord Byron" and shorter cuts elsewhere, and revised some of the shorter poems. Back in New York, around November 1965, he discussed the new edition with his friend Peter H. Salus, a linguist who later worked with Auden and Paul B. Taylor on their translation of *The Elder Edda*. Salus offered to correct his Icelandic misspellings, but Auden said it was not worth the effort. The few corrections that found their way into the text are noted below. For reasons of economy Faber dropped all the photographs except for the postcard of the mountains of Iceland (p. 234), which is reprinted at the foot of the last page of "For Tourists". Auden told Erika Mann that he had stolen this postcard to use in the book (p. 286). The appendix was also dropped, but the foldout map was reprinted across two pages.

A draft of Auden's new foreword is in one of his notebooks in the Berg Collection. The copy of the first edition that Auden inscribed to his father and used in 1965 to mark cuts and revisions is also in the Berg Collection. Many of the stanzas deleted in this copy of "Letter to Lord Byron" were not in fact cut from the printed text.

The new foreword was inserted following the dedication and preceding the preface. In the seventh paragraph Langjökul should be Langjökull.

FOREWORD

In April 1964, I revisited Iceland. Naturally, I expected change, but the change was beyond all expectation. During the last war, the island was occupied, first by the British and then by the Americans. Military occupation, no matter by whom, is never a pleasant business for the occupied but, in the case of Iceland, it brought one benefit. Meeting one of my old guides, now a schoolmaster, I asked him what life had been like during the war. "We made money," he replied. And the prosperity begun then has increased since Iceland became an independent republic.

Reykjavik today is a very different place from the rather down-at-heels town I remembered. In many cities, modern architecture only makes one nostalgic for the old, but in Reykjavik this is not so. Concrete, steel and glass may not be one's favourite building materials but they are an improvement upon corrugated iron sheeting.

Those who wish to make strenuous treks through the wilderness can still do so, but there are now more comfortable alternatives. There are roads everywhere, good but not too good—no autobahns, thank God— and there is an air-taxi service which will transport one quickly and scenically to the most remote spots.

For the visitor, there is one loss. As I flew up to the North-West to stay for three days at a farm where I had stayed in 1936, I pictured to myself the pleasures of riding in the afternoons. But the farmer had exchanged his ponies for a Land-Rover. Sensible of him, but disappointing for me. Today, ponies are confined to tourist centres and riding, I should imagine, has become an expensive luxury.

For me personally, it was a joy to discover that, despite everything which had happened to Iceland and myself since my first visit, the feelings it aroused were the same. In my childhood dreams Iceland was holy ground; when, at the age of twenty-nine, I saw it for the first time, the reality verified my dream; at fifty-seven it was holy ground still, with the most magical light of anywhere on earth. Furthermore, modernity does not seem to have changed the character of the inhabitants. They are still the only really classless society I have ever encountered, and they have not—not yet—become vulgar.

Re-reading a book written half a lifetime ago has been an odd experience, and what readers under thirty will make of it I cannot imagine. Though writing in a "holiday" spirit, its authors were all the time conscious of a threatening horizon to their picnic—world-wide unemployment, Hitler growing every day more powerful and a world-war more inevitable. Indeed, the prologue to that war, the Spanish Civil War, broke out while we were there.

Today, Louis MacNeice who wrote half the book and my father to whom it was dedicated are dead, the schoolboys with whom we went round the Langjökul husbands and fathers, and many of the "recipients" of our Letters public figures—a Cabinet Minister, a knight, a television star, etc.

In the parts which I wrote, I have made some cuts and revisions. One chapter jointly written, *Last Will and Testament*, seems to me excessively private in its jokes, and I wondered whether I oughtn't to cut it. But

American friends to whom all the Proper Names are unknown have told me that they enjoyed it, so I have left it as it was.

As to the merits of the book, if any, I am in no position to judge. But the three months in Iceland upon which it is based stand out in my memory as among the happiest in a life which has, so far, been unusually happy, and, if something of this joy comes through the writing, I shall be content.

W. H. AUDEN, 1965

Auden made the following cuts and changes in the remainder of the book:

Page 175.

Preface. Two names are corrected in the second paragraph: Eirikur Benedikz (for Erikur Bendedictzson) and Kristjan Andresson (in the first edition Kristian Andreirsson; in fact Kristinn Andrésson). The acknowledgement in the final paragraph to Frazer Hoyland is omitted, presumably because an editor at Faber noticed that Hoyland's photographs had been dropped along with most of the other illustrations in the first edition.

Page 179.

Letter to Lord Byron, Part I. The stanza beginning "The fact is" is omitted (p. 180), and the first line of the following stanza changed from "And home" to "Now home".

Page 185.

Journey to Iceland. The poem is heavily revised, in a revision that except for trivial differences in punctuation matches the version that Auden published in *Iceland Review,* [Autumn] 1964 (but perhaps not printed until 1965). This revision probably predates the different and more extensive revision that Auden made in the poem around September 1965 when he prepared the text of his *Collected Shorter Poems, 1927–1957.*

Page 195.

For Tourists. The phrase "but you should certainly visit . . . mine of information" (p. 197) is omitted.

Page 241.

Letter to R. H. S. Crossman, Esq. In the last line of the first stanza, "The two flags" is altered to "Two flags".

Page 256.

W. H. A. to E. M. A.—No. 1. Hraensnef is corrected to Hraunsnef in the heading to the section written on 15 July (p. 257) but not in the text itself. The text of some of the Icelandic verses is also corrected. In the two-column palindrome (p. 258), "saga" in the second line is corrected to "baga", although the corresponding "Saga" in line 7 is unchanged. In the verse beginning "Yngissveinar fara" (p. 261), the second edition corrects "fara á" to "fara a", "Finna" to "Finnar", "Stúlkur" to "Stilkar", and "Ast fangnar í" to "astfangnar af", misprinted with a lower-case first letter. In the Icelandic version of the ruthless rhyme (p. 261), the second edition omits the first word ("E"), and corrects "petta" to "thetta", "Thé" to "Thá", and "kerligin" to "kerlingin".

Page 326.

Letter to Lord Byron, Part IV. The ten stanzas from "My name occurs" through the stanza that begins "So I sit down" (pp. 327–28) are omitted. The final stanza of this part is omitted, and the final stanza of Part V (p. 357) is inserted in its place.

Page 335.

Letter to Kristjan Andresson, Esq. Auden miscorrected the spelling of Kristinn Andrésson in the title and opening of the letter; in the first edition the name appeared as "Kristian Andreirsson", and that spelling was left uncorrected in the running heads of the second edition.

Page 354.

Letter to Lord Byron, Part V. Entirely omitted, except for the final stanza, which is moved to the end of Part IV. The following chapter, "Auden and MacNeice: Their Last Will and Testament", is accordingly renumbered XVI.

Essays and Reviews

1937–1938

Impressions of Valencia

Page 383.

Auden's only dispatch from his visit to Spain during the Civil War, from January through the first days of March 1937. Auden arrived in Valencia around 17 January, and left for Barcelona on his way to the Aragon front sometime after 25 January. (Further information on Auden's visit to Spain appears in Nicholas Jenkins, "Auden and Spain", *Auden Studies 1* [1990], pp. 88–93.) In the first paragraph of his dispatch Auden rendered the name of the "radio general" Queipo de Llano as "Quiepo el Llano".

Royal Poets

Page 384.

The anthology under review was compiled anonymously.

A Review of *Illusion and Reality*

Page 386.

The text is edited from the manuscript in the Poetry Collection at the State University of New York at Buffalo. This edition corrects the printed text's misreadings of Auden's transcriptions from Caudwell and corrects Auden's miscopying of "cyclothymic" as "cyclothermic", but ignores his other minor errors of transcription from the book. In the second paragraph from the end, the printed text misreads "slick" as "strict".

[From *Authors Take Sides on the Spanish War*]

Page 388.

Authors Take Sides on the Spanish War, published in December 1937, printed 148 replies to a broadside questionnaire that was drafted by Nancy Cunard in Paris in June 1937, and signed by Auden and eleven other writers, although Auden may not have seen the text before it was printed. The text of the questionnaire appears in Appendix IV above. Auden sent his reply to Cunard in an undated letter on the letterhead of the Downs School, where he was teaching from late May to late July 1937; he crossed out the address of the school and replaced it with that of his bank in Birmingham, so it is possible that he sent his reply shortly before he left or shortly afterward: "As to the question, I enclose an answer. I have my doubts as to the value of such pronouncements, but here mine is for what it's worth" (letter at the Harry Ransom Humanities Research Center). For an account of the preparation of *Authors Take Sides on the Spanish War*, see Anne Chisholm, *Nancy Cunard* (1979), pp. 239–42.

PREFACE TO THE CATALOGUE OF
OIL PAINTINGS BY PAST AND PRESENT MEMBERS OF
THE DOWNS SCHOOL, COLWALL

Page 388.

The preface was reprinted in the Downs School magazine, the *Badger*, Autumn 1937, with a prefatory note by Maurice Feild, arts master at the school, about the exhibition and its reception.

EDUCATION

Page 389.

This collaboration by W. H. Auden and T. C. Worsley was written and revised under the title *Education*, probably in October or November 1937, but not published until 2 March 1939, when it appeared under the title *Education: Today—and Tomorrow* as no. 40 in the Day to Day Pamphlets series published by the Hogarth Press. Worsley recalled that the pamphlet "was originally for the editions of *Fact*, a left-wing monthly which came out in the Thirties and devoted each number to one subject. . . . Wystan was asked to produce a number on education, and as was his practice on this sort of thing, took a collaborator—me. The result was—not unsurprisingly—far too little factual for FACT! And they turned it down flat. Then John Lehmann who was with the Hogarth . . . snapped it up for that series of theirs" (quoted in B. C. Bloomfield, *W. H. Auden: A Bibliography*, second ed. [1972], p. 37). Although Auden actively revised the typescript in 1937, he seems to have taken no part in preparing the typescript for publication in 1938 after it was accepted by the Hogarth Press, and the subtitle of the pamphlet was probably added by Lehmann or Worsley.

Worsley was a schoolmaster friend of Stephen Spender who shared a cottage with him late in 1936, and travelled with him to Spain early in 1937. Auden admired Worsley's report on refugees from the front, "The Flight from Malaga", *Left Review*, April 1937, which, as Worsley recalled, he "read as well as his *Spain* in the Albert Hall [at a public meeting held to benefit Basque refugee children, 24 June 1937] and burst into tears in the middle!" (letter to Mendelson, 13 December 1971). Of their collaboration on the pamphlet, Worsley recalled (in the same letter): "I chiefly and first worked on the first part and Wystan on the second [and third?]. Then we took each other's drafts and worked them over again, adding, subtracting or changing. So one can safely say that 80% of *Theory* was Wystan's." Probably the same percentage applies to the "Suggestion" section; Auden described the suggestions as his own work in a letter to E. R. Dodds quoted below. (The statement in *The English Auden* [1977] that "Suggestion" was Worsley's work was based on a misinterpretation of Worsley's letter, which was in reply to a question about the authorship of the "Theory" section.)

Auden and Worsley probably finished their joint draft around October 1937. They gave the draft to A. E. Dodds and E. R. Dodds, who returned it with comments in the first weeks of November. Auden and Worsley probably brought the text close to its final form during the same month. The typescript was rejected by *Fact* probably while Auden was in China in the first half of 1938. Worsley, presumably with Auden's concurrence, submitted it to John Lehmann in November 1938; Lehmann accepted it on 22 November and returned the typescript for final revisions. While Auden was in Brussels at the end of the year, Worsley signed a contract with the Hogarth Press dated 31 December 1938. The statement on page 408 that the pamphlet was set in type before the publication of "The Spens Report on Secondary Education" implies that the pamphlet was in galley proof by 30 December 1938, when the committee chaired by Will Spens released the *Report of the Consultative Committee on Secondary Education with Special Reference to Grammar Schools and Technical High Schools;* but it seems likely that the pamphlet was in fact not set in type until early in 1939.

Auden wrote to A. E. Dodds, probably on 13 November 1937: "Worsly [*sic*] has just sent me education plus your comments which I will have to think over as soon as I have a moment. Many thanks. I am sorry Nature no more intended me to write about Education than it intended Louis to review, but livings must be earned"—an allusion to Louis MacNeice who, when he was short of money in the late 1930s, reportedly took on more review assignments than he had time to complete and was rescued by friends who wrote the reviews for him (letter in the Bodleian Library). Probably at around the same time, Auden wrote to E. R. Dodds:

Thanks so much for extremely helpful criticisms, to which I herewith make rather feeble replies. . . .

11–16 [cf. 11–15, pp. 418–19]

I see I shall have to modify this. Except possibly, for the *pure* scholar, I am not convinced that a slackening of book-work will lower the standard much. At present there is an *enormous* waste of time by repetition which I believe to be due to psychological error. For the average boy the difference between what he knows at 12 and what he knows at 15 is very very small.

I didn't of course mean that manual or technical work was any more *real* than book work, only

(1) That it isn't any less real.
(2) That I think at this age most boys want something practical and useful in the Man-in-the-Street's sense of the word. i.e. I think Arts and Crafts awful.

Would you think my suggestions more sensible if I

(1) Cut down the period to 12–15.
(2) Split the Academics and the Technicals.
    (a) Technicals to do as previously suggested.
    (b) Academics to have academic schooling + some relatively un-
    skilled labour. I know some won't like that. I don't know how
    you legislate for *everybody*. At present the boot's all on the other
    foot. Thousands of adolescents are being forced to do book
    work which they hate and to which they are unsuited, with the
    result that they never want to touch the stuff again. I don't
    believe that only a few people are by *nature* suited to book-
    work but I know that *something* happens to most people which
    puts them off reading and thinking, which is what any democ-
    racy must get over.

       As to girls and the home. What do you suggest. The Board-
    ing School anyway is bad.

Private Schools [cf. pp. 422–23, paragraphs 2 and 4]

    I agree that ultimately it will be better to have compulsory state ele-
mentary education for all, but at present it isn't practical politics in this
country for a Labour or any other Government. Class-feeling in this
country is so strong, bourgeois parents would go to any lengths to avoid
the state school.

    On the whole agree about the B[oard] of E[ducation] recognition.
Will alter.

School Certificate [cf. p. 423, paragraph 6]

    Employers may not be able to assess marks, but they can't assess
credits either. My suggestion seems the lesser of two evils.

    What's your objection to the B of E setting it?

Teacher Training [cf. pp. 416–17]

    I know the psychologists are no great shakes, but some sort of self-
knowledge is desirable, and how is one to find the true saints? Don't
agree that only the failures would transfer, and anyway they could be
ploughed on interview. You would also get those who suddenly realised
they would like it. Personally I should approve of a kind of conscription
for teaching.

    Grants. To be given to bright pupils irrespective what they think at
       the moment they are going to do. i.e. State Scholarships for
       from 16–21.

Discipline [cf. pp. 419–20]

Of course you were a rebel at 16 because authority was continued when democracy should have begun.

Some are emotionally rebels and that force is useful.

The whole statement is a generalisation but I believe it to be true.

The text in this edition is based on the published pamphlet, which includes two long passages lacking in the carbon-copy typescript now at the Edinburgh University Library; it also differs from the typescript in other minor details. The lost top copy of the Edinburgh typescript probably served as setting copy for the printed text, and included the authors' latest revisions; I have followed the carbon-copy typescript, however, in most matters of spelling, punctuation, and the layout of tabular matter. I have also followed the typescript's somewhat chaotic capitalization, but in rare instances I have lightly emended punctuation in tabular matter and lists. The typescript and printed text are variously inconsistent in spelling out numbers; I have generally followed the printed text, which corresponds more closely to standard printed style, but have let many inconsistencies stand. The printed text, followed here, uses "per cent." where the typescript has "%".

The typescript has many additions and changes in Auden's and Worsley's hands, most of which are also present in the printed text, sometimes in slightly different versions; the few that are not in the pamphlet have been added to this edition, and are noted below. Some of these changes are based on suggestions written on the facing pages in an unknown hand (apparently not that of either A. E. Dodds or E. R. Dodds).

The main differences between the printed text and the typescript follow, together with notes on editorial emendations. Minor variations in wording, especially in passages inserted in the typescript in Worsley's hand, are not listed, nor are variations such as the typescript's occasional "educationist" for the printed text's "educationalist", the form generally used by Auden.

Page 389.

Part I. The printed text has a row of asterisks below the first paragraph of the section headed "Personal Freedom" (p. 392), a break that corresponds to an ordinary page break in the typescript. In the eighth paragraph of the same section (p. 393), the printed text reads "Of a necessity" for "Of necessity", the reading followed here. In the section headed "The Parent" the printed text has a row of asterisks below the paragraph beginning "At the most" (p. 394), where the typescript, followed here, has only additional space. In the typescript the heading "Futures" appears in place of the printed text's "Leaving Age" (p. 398). In the section headed "Organisation" the two sentences from "But these last" through "inferior social status" (p. 398) are not present in the typescript. The footnote under "Organisation" (p. 398) refers to *The Education of the Adolescent,* a report released in 1927 by a committee chaired by W. H. Hadow; the "new Act" that raised the school-leaving age was passed in 1936. In the second paragraph of the section headed "Discipline Method and Technique" (p. 401), the sentence beginning "The Provision of Meals Act" is inserted in Auden's hand in the typescript. The footnote to the "Universities" section (p. 404) is inserted in Auden's hand in the typescript, with a pencil draft of the note in an unknown hand on the facing page. In the section headed "Research and Scholarship" (p. 405) the Bedaux method was the Point System devised by Charles Bedaux, designed to encourage massive increases in industrial output for minimally increased wages. The "Summary" that concludes Part I (pp. 407–8) is not present in the type-script; the four final paragraphs about the Spens report may have been added after the rest of the summary was written.

Page 408.

Part II. In the typescript Worsley divided this section into three numbered sections and abandoned Auden's headings ("The Middle Ages", "The Renais-sance and the Reformation", etc.), but these changes did not appear in the printed text and are not followed here. In the section "Those Who Guard" (p. 409) the phrase "with modifications made by Puritanism" is inserted in Au-den's hand; the surrounding commas are editorial additions. In the section "The Renaissance and the Reformation" (p. 410) the phrase "study of Greece" in the first sentence may perhaps be a typist's error for "study of Greek". Near the end of the same section I have made Puritans plural in the sentence "The Puritans denied this"; apparently they are the antecedent of "them" in the last sentence of the section. In the section "Rousseau and Romantic Anarchism" (p. 411) I have added the second comma in the opening sentence. The entire passage from the heading "The Victorian Era" through the paragraph begin-ning "Liberal education also implies" (pp. 411–13) is not present in the type-script; instead the typescript has a line indicating a break between "Comments" (p. 411) and the paragraph beginning "The practical success" (p. 413). In the first sentence of that paragraph the typescript has "Rousseau methods" where the printed text, followed here, has "Rousseau's methods". In the paragraph beginning "This is not to say" (p. 413), the semicolons in the sentence "The State school imitates" are editorial emendations for commas, and the comma after "the public school" is lacking in the printed text. In the paragraph beginning "Many of Lawrence's observations" (p. 414) the typescript has a comma after "instead of the reverse".

Page 415.

Part III. In the paragraph beginning "The training colleges" (p. 416) the typescript has "MacDougall", which the printed text bafflingly replaces with "M'Dougall"; Auden had in mind the psychologist William McDougall. The heading "11–15" (p. 418) was originally "11–16" in the typescript, but was al-tered in Worsley's hand; Auden proposed the change in his letter to E. R. Dodds quoted above. This change may have implied a revision from "16" to "15" at the end of the first paragraph under the heading, but I have not incorporated it in the text. In the first sentence under "11–15", "practices" is an emendation for "practice". In section (2) under the same heading, the printed text combines the typescript's two paragraphs into one. In section (8) under the same "11–15" heading, the typescript (in a sentence inserted in Auden's hand) has "16–18" where the printed text, followed here, has "15–18". The heading "15–18" (p. 419) was "16–18" in the typescript, but was altered in Worsley's hand. In the section "Discipline" (p. 419) the typescript, followed here, has "sixteen" in paragraphs (3) and (4); the printed text, which uses numerals instead of spelling out the numbers, has "16" in (3) and "15" in (4); the lower age is possibly an error, and seems to contradict Auden's remarks in his letter to Dodds. Before the heading "A Short Term Programme" (p. 422) a pencilled note in Auden's hand reads "insert—Religion", referring to a section either lost or never written.

A Good Scout

Page 424.

In the first quotation Auden miscopied "impregnable" as "impenetrable". The Chief Scout was Lord Baden-Powell.

In Defence of Gossip

Page 425.

This talk was a weekday broadcast in the BBC National Programme, on 13 December 1937 from 1:30 to 1:45 P.M. The text is that of the "as-broadcast" typescript made by the BBC, probably from Auden's lost manuscript, and now in the BBC Written Archives Centre. The typescript was also the basis of the text in the *Listener*, in which Auden's grammar was slightly regularized. The two paragraphs from "Then there are other kinds of bores" to "inside of an elephant's foot" (p. 426) are crossed out in the typescript, and omitted from the *Listener*, but they were perhaps omitted merely to save time. The typescript occasionally capitalizes "gossip", but Auden's hand sometimes left uncertain whether he intended to capitalize words beginning with "g".

In the sentence immediately following the two omitted paragraphs, "But you and I, I hope, are not bores" (p. 426), the last two words are corrected in Auden's hand from "neither", which may have been a typist's misreading. (The *Listener* text misreads the correction as "not bored".) At the end of the paragraph beginning "Well, is it really" (p. 427), the sentence "You know the kind of thing" is added in Auden's hand. The paragraph beginning "But there's no reason" (p. 427) is printed in the *Listener* as part of the preceding paragraph. I have omitted some underlines pencilled in the typescript as cues for Auden's use during the broadcast; possibly the typed underlining that emphasizes "apologetic" on p. 429 should also be omitted.

In the first paragraph Auden misremembered the title of a 1931 selection, *The Scandal and Credulities of John Aubrey*.

Introduction to *The Oxford Book of Light Verse*

Page 430.

For the history of this anthology see Appendix I above. The Clarendon Press, an imprint of Oxford University Press, published the book in October 1938.

Auden probably wrote the introduction in December 1937; in an undated let-
ter, probably at the end of the month, he told John Mulgan at the press that
"The selection is made, copyrights applied for (but not paid) and a rough pref-
ace written". The text of this edition is from the printed book, with the omission
of the list of copyright holders printed in small type at the end of the acknowl-
edgements. This list begins: "My thanks are also due to those who have so kindly
given me permission to include certain copyright poems: . . ." The introduction
is signed "W. H. Auden"; the editorial note and acknowledgements are signed
"W. H. A."

Auden's rough typescript of the introduction, now in the files of Oxford Uni-
versity Press, is similar to the printed text, but lacks some passages probably
added in proof or in a lost intermediate typescript. The typescript has correc-
tions and changes by Auden and by A. E. Dodds, who did much of the work of
preparing the book for the press while Auden and Isherwood were travelling in
China in the first half of 1938.

The typescript is more lightly punctuated than the printed text, and has
dozens of minor variations in wording. The typescript lacks the list of three
kinds of poetry included in the volume, and the sentence that precedes and the
one that follows it (p. 431); the next sentence begins "Light verse has come".

In the paragraph beginning "Wordsworth's case" (p. 434) I have followed
what appears to be Auden's marking in the typescript by replacing the period
after "imaginary worlds" with a dash. In that same list of "imaginary worlds" I
have restored the phrase about the Pre-Raphaelites, the omission of which evi-
dently resulted from the chaos of Auden's typescript. The phrase "Keats and
Mallarmé" in the typescript follows the set-off quotation from Baudelaire in-
stead of appearing within the text above it; that phrase is then followed by a
parenthesis containing the sentences that in the printed text appear as the foot-
note on Spender's essay on Keats, and this parenthesis is then followed by "the
Pre-Raphaelites to the Middle Ages". I have placed this last phrase after the
quotation, although it is possible that A. E. Dodds or the press moved the phrase
about Keats and Mallarmé before the quotation in order to make the quotation
appear at the end of the list. The paragraph about Browning in the footnote is
not present in the typescript. In the printed text the asterisk follows the quota-
tion; I have restored it to its proper place.

In the paragraph beginning "The release from social pressure", the printed
text mistakenly adds an ellipsis after "Rimbaud." Auden's typescript has two
periods here, but the duplicated period is one of his common typing errors. The
footnote about Kipling (p. 436) is not present in the typescript.

The "Editorial Note and Acknowledgements" are not present in the type-
script. Instead, earlier versions of the second and third sentences of the first
paragraph in the editorial note appear at the end of the typescript, as a para-
graph preceded by "N.B."

A recurring source of confusion is the final sentence of the paragraph begin-
ning "In the seventeenth century" (p. 432): "Marvell and Herrick are 'tradi-
tional' in a way that these others are not, even though the former often use the
same kind of tricks." The antecedent of "the former" in this sentence is Marvell
and Herrick, while "these others" refers to Herbert, Crashaw, and Sir Thomas

Browne, who were named in the preceding sentence. In the typescript, before
A. E. Dodds wrote in the change that produced the final version, the sentence
read: "Marvell and Herrick are 'traditional' in a way that they are not, even
though the former often use the same kind of tricks."

JEHOVAH HOUSMAN AND SATAN HOUSMAN

Page 437.

The title of the review, and the title of the book under review, were added to
Auden's typescript by Geoffrey Grigson, the editor of *New Verse*. Grigson short-
ened the title of the book from the original: *A. E. H.: Some Poems, Some Letters and
a Personal Memoir by His Brother Laurence Housman.* The text in this edition is
taken from the typescript, now in the Poetry Collection at the State University of
New York at Buffalo. Among other minor pencil revisions in the typescript,
Auden expanded the final sentence from the shorter form that he had origi-
nally typed, which ended: "a quality for which, it will be remembered, Jehovah
Housman had little use."

The typescript consistently uses the misspelled form "Houseman", which is
corrected here, and slightly misquotes Housman's verse. In the first paragraph
New Verse adds a comma after "in love with the first", at which point Auden had
deleted "world", and adds a question mark at the end of the paragraph. I have
followed *New Verse* in correcting Auden's ungrammatically misremembered
quotation from Hölderlin's "Sokrates und Alcibiades". Auden's version reads:

> Wer am tiefsten gedacht, liebt Das Lebendigste,
> Hohe Tugend versteht, wer im Welt geblickt
> Und oft am Ende
> Es neiget Die Weisen zu schönem sich.

Recent editions of Hölderlin have "Jugend" where Auden and *New Verse*, follow-
ing earlier editions, have "Tugend".

CHINESE DIARY

Page 439.

The five parts of this article are compiled from three separate but overlapping
publications, and were evidently written as a "series of newspaper articles"
(p. 574). The second through fifth parts were printed under the title "Chinese
Diary" in the *New Republic*, 1 June 1938; this was signed by Auden and Isher-
wood. The first and second parts were printed under the title "The War in
China" in the *New Statesman and Nation*, 25 June 1938, and the third was printed
under the title "The Lung-Hai Railway in War-Time" in the *New Statesman and
Nation*, 16 July 1938; all the parts printed in the *New Statesman and Nation* were
signed by Isherwood alone. The numbering of the last three parts has been
added for this edition. As in the two pieces that follow, although the contents are
based in part on Auden's manuscripts, the published texts are almost certainly

Isherwood's work. For details on the composition of this and the two following pieces, see the notes to *Journey to a War* below.

The four-part "Chinese Diary" printed in the liberal weekly the *New Republic* was the first prose piece that Auden or Isherwood submitted directly to an American publication. On the date it appeared, 1 June 1938, Auden and Isherwood were still in China. The editors of the *New Republic* probably received but dropped the opening part, "Hankow", and probably rearranged the next two, so that the part about the Lung-Hai Railway preceded the part about the front line. The *New Republic* omitted the paragraph that described the front line itself, and so the name under which this part appeared there, "A Visit to the Front", was probably provided by the editors in place of the *New Statesman and Nation* title, "The Front Line". As noted below, the *New Republic* made many cuts in the text, and the two final parts, which were not published elsewhere, were probably considerably longer in the original typescript.

In the *New Statesman and Nation,* the first and second parts were preceded by this editorial note: "The following are the first two impressions of Mr. Isherwood, who is now in China with Mr W. H. Auden. We hope to publish further articles by Mr Isherwood." (In fact Auden and Isherwood had left China shortly before this.) Only one further article, the third part of the series, appeared in the *New Statesman and Nation.*

The diary describes briefly some incidents described in more detail in *Journey to a War.* "Hankow" corresponds roughly to pp. 512–26. "The Front Line" corresponds to pp. 545–53. "The Lung-Hai Railway in War-Time", which records the events of 30 March through 2 April 1938, corresponds to pp. 553–59 in the book, where the romanization of place-names is altered (e.g., Hsiuchiou to Süchow); a few sentences of the magazine article were moved to p. 540. "Missionaries in the War Area" corresponds to parts of pp. 543–44. Bits of "What Is Going to Happen?" are scattered through the diary (e.g., pp. 503, 518, 524, 569).

The *New Republic* omits many passages present in the *New Statesman and Nation.* In "II.—The Front Line" (titled in the *New Republic* "A Visit to the Front"), the *New Republic* omits from the second paragraph the sentences from "The blossom was just" to the end; from the third paragraph, the phrase from "in a village" to the end; the entire paragraph beginning "Next morning we visited"; from the paragraph beginning "It is difficult", the words "suggestions and"; and the entire final paragraph. In "III.—The Lung-Hai Railway in War-Time", the *New Republic* omits the four paragraphs from "To-day we are in luck" to the end of the paragraph that begins "Towards evening". The *New Republic* also reduces punctuation and capitalization, alters some romanizations, and Americanizes some of the vocabulary (e.g., "trucks" for "lorries").

MEETING THE JAPANESE

Page 448.

See the notes to "Chinese Diary" above. This was the second of Auden and Isherwood's dispatches for an American periodical, and it appeared in *New*

Masses, a New York weekly that held to the Communist Party line. The magazine added a subtitle: "Two English Writers Report". Auden and Isherwood probably submitted the piece while passing through New York on their way back to England in July 1938. Some passages reappear in *Journey to a War* (e.g., pp. 609, 613, 627, 628–30).

ESCALES

Page 451.

See the notes to "Chinese Diary" above. This was the third of Auden and Isherwood's dispatches for an American periodical, and it appeared in the New York edition of the fashion magazine *Harper's Bazaar,* October 1938. Auden and Isherwood may have offered it to their friend George Davis, the magazine's fiction [i.e., literary] editor, when they visited New York in July. The piece was reprinted in the London edition of the magazine, in December 1938, under the title "Ports of Call". This edition preserves the American spellings of the New York *Harper's Bazaar;* the editors of the London version restored British spellings, but preserved such American usages as "gasoline station" (p. 453). One slip in the London version is "emery-paper mountain" for "emery-paper mountains" (p. 452).

Auden and Isherwood kept a travel diary on the voyage to China, with each writing entries for a day or two before turning it over to the other. The diary is in a notebook now in a private collection. Most of the sections of "Escales" are compressed and highly rewritten extracts from Isherwood's entries, although the second sentence of the piece, "Miles from land", is lightly altered from a sentence by Auden, and some phrases about the Sphinx are based on Auden's early draft of his poem "The Sphinx". The two paragraphs on Colombo (pp. 453–54) are heavily rewritten from Auden's journal entry about the city, as are the first two paragraphs about Hong Kong harbor at the end of the piece.

THE SPORTSMEN: A PARABLE

Page 455.

Written for the special "Commitments" number of *New Verse*, which was first mentioned in the March 1938 issue under a slightly different rubric that Auden probably had in mind when he wrote his piece: "We announce for September a special 'New Verse' examining Poetry and Society since 1918". The same rubric was named again in the summer 1938 number: "The next 'New Verse' will be a double number on Poetry and Society in the last twenty years." Auden perhaps wrote the piece shortly after his return from China in late July, or in August. His typescript, now in the Harry Ransom Humanities Research Center, was originally untitled; the title and subtitle were written in by Geoffrey Grigson. I have followed the typescript, but have added a comma in the second paragraph after "in their opinion", and have followed *New Verse* in adding a comma in the fourth paragraph in "were now, most of them".

[MESSAGE TO THE CHINESE PEOPLE]

Page 458.

This message was probably Isherwood's work, and was written perhaps around October 1938, not long after the Munich crisis mentioned in the opening sentence. It appeared in 1939 in the *Far Eastern Magazine*, published in New York by the Chinese Student Patriotic Association of America, among similar pieces by other contributors under the heading "Sympathetic Messages from British Cultural Leaders". The others were H. G. Wells, A. A. Milne, Hugh Walpole, Valentine Ackland, Sylvia Townsend Warner, Narada Thera, and Eileen Power. An editor's note explained that "these messages were brought back to China by Professor Shelley Wang, noted Chinese scholar, who returned from London to Chungking, China in February, 1939."

MEN OF THOUGHT AND ACTION

Page 458.

This was the first of six book reviews that Auden wrote for the *Town Crier* in the autumn of 1938. He wrote for the paper over a series of seven weeks, but no piece by him appeared in one of the seven numbers. Philip Toynbee wrote in *Friends Apart* (1954):

> The *Birmingham Town Crier* was the only Labour newspaper in that Tory city, a weekly which had existed for many years with an undeviating sale of two thousand copies. Frank Pakenham [later the Earl of Longford] bought it, appointed me as its editor and determined that through this organ Birmingham should be won for Labour. It is true that I hired distinguished contributors—W. H. Auden to review books, R. H. S. Crossman to write on foreign affairs—but the only result of this was that the loyal readers of the earlier paper gave up their subscriptions and few new readers were won. (P. 139)

Toynbee edited the paper from August 1938 until his departure from Birmingham early in January 1939.

The title of Auden's review derives from a sentence in Mann's *The Coming Victory of Democracy:* "The French philosopher Bergson sent to a philosophical congress which recently met in Paris a message in which he formulated this imperative: 'Act as men of thought, think as men of action'" (p. 33); Auden quotes the imperative in his next review for the paper. In the first sentence of the third paragraph I have not attempted to alter the printed text in order to identify Mann as the antecedent of "he". In his long quotation from Mann, Auden made trivial changes that made the excerpts read as complete thoughts (e.g., he altered Mann's "But in him nature" to "In man nature"), and Auden or the compositor slightly altered Mann's punctuation; all these changes are retained here. The review was originally followed by a brief list of other titles, probably written by Philip Toynbee to fill out the column:

Other Books by These Authors

Thomas Mann: *Mario the Magician*. A story of a hypnotist which is also a
  parable of dictatorship.
André Malraux: *Storm over Shanghai*. A novel about revolution and
  counter-revolution in Shanghai in 1927.

IRONWORKS AND UNIVERSITY

Page 460.

The text here corrects obvious misprints and emends some misreadings of
Auden's hand by the compositor. At the end of the quotation from Forster, the
printed text has an exclamation mark that was probably a misreading of Au-
den's quotation mark. In the paragraph beginning "Mr Mumford, with the aid"
(p. 462), "cohetam" is emended to "Coketown"; "as when a balanced" to "and
where a balanced"; and "has to plan" to "needs to plan". Later in the same
paragraph, this edition places dashes instead of commas around the phrase
"cheap electrical power has largely overcome that". I have let stand Auden's
minor cuts and transcription errors in quotations.

DEMOCRACY'S REPLY TO THE CHALLENGE OF DICTATORS

Page 463.

This speech was delivered at the final meeting of a conference, "The Schools
and the State", held at High Leigh, Hoddesdon, by the English Section of the
New Education Fellowship, 22–23 October 1938. The New Education Fellow-
ship was an organization of teachers and others interested in politically and psy-
chologically progressive education. The title printed above the text of Auden's
speech in the *New Era in Home and School*, the organ of the fellowship, was the
general title of the session for which he wrote it. The text appears to have been
printed from Auden's manuscript; an editorial note following the text states:
"This version of Mr Auden's speech has had to be published without his consent
and—more serious—without his corrections." A brief report of the speech, with
quotations evidently from the same manuscript, appeared under the title
"When Democracy Is a 'Sham'", *Birmingham Post,* 24 October 1938.

NONSENSE POETRY

Page 467.

In the paragraph beginning "The logic of our conscious" I have emended "of
the limerick" to "or the limerick", and have printed "laissez-faire" in roman
instead of italics. In the paragraph beginning "Both came from", "seems to
them in inhabit" is emended to "seems to them to inhabit". In the paragraph
beginning "Psychologists, of course" (p. 468), "make and are still making" is
emended to "made and are still making". Minor errors of transcription are
ignored.

INTRODUCTION TO *Poems of Freedom*

Page 469.

John Mulgan, who was shepherding *The Oxford Book of Light Verse* through the press, compiled this anthology for publication by Victor Gollancz, and in August 1938 asked Auden for an introduction. Auden replied from Brussels on 30 August: "Of course I shall be very pleased to write an introduction to your Gollancz anthology, though I am getting hard up for something new to say. I must of course see the text so that I write something which is relevant. When do you want it by?" (Letter in the possession of R. G. Mulgan.)

Gollancz failed to send Auden the proofs until sometime in October. Auden sent the introduction to Mulgan from Birmingham on 27 October, with this cover note: "I hope this preface is the kind of thing you want. I am rather annoyed with G[ollancz] for giving me such short notice as he could easily have sent me proofs earlier." Gollancz published the book on 12 December 1938.

Mulgan asked Gollancz to pay Auden a fee for his introduction, but Gollancz refused, arguing that "the economics of the book" did not allow it (letter from Dorothy Horsman, a director at Gollancz's firm, to Mulgan, 3 November 1938). Mulgan instead paid Auden out of his own pocket. Auden (who a few years earlier had not received payment from Gollancz for his contribution to *An Outline for Boys and Girls and Their Parents*) wrote to Mulgan from Brussels on 12 December 1938: "God, what a shit Gollancz is. It's the very last time I have anything to do with him. Give me a capitalist and a gentleman like Humphrey Milford"—publisher of the Oxford University Press. (For more of this letter, see Appendix I, pp. 710–11.) A brief account of the anthology appears in P. W. Day, *John Mulgan* (1968), pp. 77–78.

The printed text indicates the sources in the anthology of the first two quotations: the phrase "Timon's speech" is followed by "(no. 22)," and the lines from Milton by "(26)". The slight misquotation of *Timon of Athens* ("head" for "heads") occurs also in the text in the anthology.

FOREWORD TO *Poet Venturers*

Page 471.

The printer of this pamphlet, Purnell and Sons, Ltd, of Paulton and London, has no records that indicate the identity of those who prepared and published it. In place of an imprint, the title page has the words "The Proceeds from the Sale of these Poems will go to the Fund for Chinese Medical Aid". The date and place at the foot of the foreword were presumably at the head of Auden's manuscript.

"THE NOBLE SAVAGE"

Page 471.

The quotation marks around the headline are present in the original. I have retained Auden's misquotation from Tennyson; in the paragraph beginning

"The first is a culture", I have removed a comma after "military virtues"; and in the final paragraph I have emended "Mr Tom Harrison as the Mass observer" to "Mr Tom Harrisson and the Mass Observers".

A NEW SHORT STORY WRITER

Page 473.

The title "A New Short Story Writer" was set as an "eyebrow head", above and to the left of the main headline, *Something Wrong*, the title of Stern's book. At the end of the paragraph beginning "'Travellers' Tears'" (p. 474), I have tentatively emended "by the action or as they would have to be" by replacing "or" with a comma. Auden's long quotation from Stern silently omits phrases and slightly alters wording and punctuation; I have corrected the family name from "Moor" to "Moon", an error that was probably a compositor's misreading.

THE TEACHING OF ENGLISH

Page 475.

In the first paragraph "widest sense" is an emendation for "wildest sense". The paragraph beginning "They may learn a lot more words" (p. 476) seems not to fit the general argument, but I have not attempted to emend it. In the first item in the list of books, the printed text has "Captain Short" for "Captain Ahab", perhaps representing the attempt of an impatient compositor to make sense of Auden's hand. The error "Macnaughten" for "Macnaghten" is copied from the anthology. Auden misremembered the title of the second of the two books by R. O. Swann, which was *Simple Tests in English*, not *Junior Tests in English*. The reference to "R. O. Swann" instead of to "Robert Swann", which is the form that appears on his title pages, suggests that Auden had corresponded with him and remembered the signature on his letters. Auden misstates the publisher of Hardress O'Grady's *Matter, Form, and Style*; it was John Murray, not George Bell (who had published Auden's own anthology, *The Poet's Tongue*).

MORALITY IN AN AGE OF CHANGE

Page 477.

This essay was commissioned by the American liberal weekly the *Nation* and the New York publishers Simon & Schuster, as one of a series of "Living Philosophies". It was probably written around November 1938. Auden's essay was the seventh in the series to be printed in the *Nation,* whose editors probably supplied the title and almost certainly made extensive cuts in the text. Together with the rest of the series and some additional essays, Auden's full text was printed, without a title and with an epigraph that did not appear in the *Nation*, in *I Believe: The Personal Philosophies of Certain Eminent Men and Women of Our Time*, edited by Clifton Fadiman. This book was published by Simon & Schuster on 15 August 1939; the editor's preface was dated 14 April 1939. The book was the successor to a volume of *Living Philosophies*, published by the same press in 1931. The first essay in the new volume was E. M. Forster's "What I Believe".

The text in the *Nation* and the text in *I Believe* probably derive from the same typescript, but the *Nation's* version seems to be the product of extensive cuts and other editorial changes made to Auden's original. Among the differences between the two versions, the only one that seems to be the work of Auden's revising hand is the addition in *I Believe* of the epigraph from Blake, perhaps when the book was in proof in 1939. Auden frequently quoted Blake's phrase after arriving in America in 1939, and it was unlikely that he could have applied the epigraph to the essay when he first wrote it in 1938, because it has virtually no relation to the tone and content of the whole. The differences between the final sentence of the essay in the *Nation* (see below) and the longer version of that sentence in *I Believe* may conceivably have resulted from authorial revision, but it is more likely that the *Nation's* resulted from changes made to the original by the editors.

Except for the title and a few minor emendations, some taken from the *Nation*, this edition follows *I Believe*. The two texts differ in the following points. (Minor variants in which the *Nation* normalizes Auden's characteristic punctuation and expands his characteristic abbreviations are not noted.) In the *Nation* the only numbered or lettered paragraphs are the four sections on pp. 482–83 from "Lack of material goods" through "Lack of suitable psychological conditions"; in the *Nation* these have numbers, not the letters used in *I Believe*. The *Nation* text is divided not by roman numerals but by additional spacing.

Part I. In the first paragraph, the *Nation*, perhaps following Auden's original, has a comma in place of the dash. In the second paragraph, I have followed the *Nation's* "this happens once for each species; the change" instead of what appears to be a botched attempt at clarification in *I Believe:* "this happens at once; for each species the change". In the same paragraph, the *Nation* twice replaces "townee" with "town dweller", and lacks the sentences from "We are right to condemn him" through the end of the paragraph. In the paragraph beginning "(3)The history of life" (p. 478), the *Nation* omits "and freedom within" and the sentence that begins "Organisms may either", and runs in the next paragraph, "Below the human level". In the paragraph beginning "Below the human level", the *Nation* has "the mutations" for "the luck of mutations" (which is an emendation in this edition for *I Believe's* "the lack of mutations"). The *Nation* lacks the paragraphs numbered (5) through (11) on pp. 479–80. In paragraph (10), "genetic characters" may be Auden's slip for "genetic characteristics". In paragraph (12), the *Nation* lacks "the" before "industrialised countries"; the *Nation* also runs in the next paragraph with paragraph (12) and, in that next paragraph, lacks the final sentence.

Part II. The *Nation* treats as a single paragraph the opening phrase and items (*a*) and (*b*) and the two sentences that follow. In paragraph (3) (p. 481), the *Nation* has "a view" for "our view", and treats items (*a*) and (*b*) as part of the paragraph. I have emended both texts by starting a new paragraph with "If we take the extremely pessimistic". In the paragraph beginning "If we take the extremely pessimistic", the *Nation* has dashes where *I Believe* has parentheses; both are probably attempts to rationalize Auden's original punctuation, which may have consisted of commas. The *Nation* lacks paragraph (4). In the paragraph beginning "Lack of occupations" (p. 482), the *Nation* has "think that carpentry is" for "think carpentry", and "stockbrokerage is" for "stockbroking". In the same paragraph, the *Nation,* perhaps following Auden's original, has "farmer" for "a farmer". And in the same paragraph, the *Nation* has "But we must never forget" for "The most one can say is that we must never forget", and lacks the final sentence. In the paragraph beginning "Lack of suitable psychological", the *Nation* lacks the phrases from "and people with as divergent" to the end of the paragraph.

Part III. In paragraph (2) (p. 484), the *Nation* has only the first sentence, which it runs in with the preceding paragraph. Near the end of the paragraph that begins "(4) Legislation is", the *Nation* has "making one another bad" for "making each other bad against their will", and "Thus we would all" for "Thus we all". In the paragraph beginning "But there are other" (p. 485), the *Nation* has "the temperature of my bath" for "the temperature at which I take my bath"; and later in that sentence, perhaps following Auden's original, has "contact, and if the legislator" for "contact. If the legislator". At the end of that paragraph, the *Nation* lacks the sentence "Nearly all legislation". In the paragraph that begins "(5) In theory", the *Nation* lacks the sentence beginning "As the different sectional", and runs in the following paragraph. In the paragraph beginning "I do not see", the *Nation* lacks the sentences from "Thus I cannot see" to the end, and runs in the next paragraph ("Intolerance is an evil"). In that next paragraph (p. 486), the *Nation,* perhaps following Auden's original, has "foresee and which" for "foresee and for which"; the *Nation* also lacks the two sentences from "We must be as tolerant" through "every one of us", and begins the next paragraph with "We have the misfortune". The *Nation* treats everything from "We have the misfortune" to the end as a single paragraph, but lacks "to remember that while an idea can be absolutely bad, a person can never be", and reads "if necessary, at the cost of our lives" for "perhaps even at the cost of our lives and those of others". These variations in the final sentence may perhaps have resulted from revisions made in proof for *I Believe,* although the text in the *Nation* more probably resulted from a heightening of Auden's rhetoric by the editors of the magazine.

George Gordon Byron

Page 487.

This was written for the anonymous anthology *Fifteen Poets,* published by Oxford University Press on 9 February 1941, and evidently prepared by John Mulgan. Auden agreed to write the piece in a letter received by the press on 3 October 1938. On 12 December 1938, he sent it to Mulgan as the enclosure to a letter otherwise concerned with *The Oxford Book of Light Verse* and *Poems of Freedom:* "Enclosed is Byron. Hope O.K." (See Appendix I above, and the notes to Auden's introduction to *Poems of Freedom* above.) The manuscript may perhaps have been titled "Byron". In the anthology the essay is preceded by a long biographical note whose style is identical to the notes preceding the essays on the other poets in the book; these notes were probably written by Mulgan.

CHINA

Page 489.

This was a talk broadcast in the "January Number" of the BBC Midland Home Service's *Midland Magazine,* 16 January 1939, from 8:30 to 9 P.M., and printed in the *Listener* (without the first three paragraphs) under the title "What the Chinese War Is Like". The title and text are from a typed copy of the as-broadcast typescript, supplied in the 1970s by a bookseller who declined to identify his source. (No copy of the typescript can now be located at the BBC Written Archives Centre.) I have made slight emendations based on the *Listener* text.

Journey to a War

Auden and Isherwood wrote much of this book during their journey to China in the first half of 1938, and finished it in Brussels late in the year. It was published by Faber & Faber on 16 March 1939. Faber published a second edition, with revised versions of Auden's poems and new introductory comments by both authors, on 2 July 1973.

The book was commissioned, probably in late June or early July 1937, by Random House, the American publisher of Auden's poems and Auden and Isherwood's plays. Random House asked for a travel book about the East; the outbreak of hostilities between China and Japan in July prompted them to decide to make their subject the Sino-Japanese War. Late in July, Auden was already telling acquaintances that he was leaving for China in January 1938. (The chronology in the foreword to the book is slightly incorrect.)

At Auden's request, T. S. Eliot had a letter of introduction drawn up on 6 January 1938, although he had Sir Geoffrey Faber sign it: "This is to certify that Mr W. H. Auden and Mr Christopher Isherwood are leaving England for a journey of indefinite extent, for the purpose of travel in preparation for a non-political book on the Far East, which this firm has commissioned them to write."

Auden and Isherwood left England on 19 January 1938. They sailed from Marseilles on 21 January and arrived at Port Said on 27 January. On 16 February they reached Hong Kong, and left there on 28 February for Canton and Hankow. The Travel-Diary in *Journey to a War* describes their travels until their departure from Shanghai on 12 June, when they left for Japan. They sailed from Yokohama on 18 June, and arrived at Vancouver on 28 June. After travelling across Canada by train they spent about two weeks in New York, and were back in London on 17 July.

Probably in October 1938 they worked their separate diaries into a single travel diary and planned the shape of the book. On 22 October Auden wrote to Richard de la Mare at Faber to report that they wanted the photographs in a single section in the middle of the book, that they wanted to use a color poster as a frontispiece, and that they had decided to call the book *Journey to a War*. Their earlier working title was *A Journey to a War;* this working title appeared in the galley proofs of Faber's announcement catalogue for spring 1939, with the subtitle "A Visit to the Chinese War", which was probably the work of the writer of the catalogue copy, not the authors of the book. De la Mare later asked Isherwood if he and Auden still wanted this subtitle, but Isherwood replied on 13 December that they wanted no subtitle at all. The final title, with no subtitle, appeared in the spring 1939 catalogue that Faber distributed to the book trade.

Isherwood delivered an incomplete typescript to Faber on 2 December 1938. In his cover letter he wrote: "Still to come is a dialogue, entitled HONGKONG-MACAO", which was intended to follow the poems in the sequence "London to Hongkong".

(At this point only the first four sonnets in this sequence were to be included.) On 4 December Auden sent a list of photographs. On 13 December Isherwood wrote from Brussels in response to some questions from de la Mare: "We hope to have the Hongkong-Macao dialogue ready by the end of this week. The travel-diary section should simply be called 'Travel-Diary. February–June. 1938.'" On 17 December Isherwood, in a letter with which he also sent the foreword to the book, told de la Mare: "After a great deal of consideration, Auden and I decided against the two proposed dialogues called 'Hongkong-Macao'. They are not the right kind of thing, we feel, for this book. Instead Auden has written these two sonnets ['Macao' and 'Hongkong']." It is unclear whether one or two dialogues had been planned from the beginning.

On 25 December Isherwood returned proofs of the photographs. On 4 January 1939 Auden returned galley proofs of his poems. In his cover note he wrote: "I must say I am a little surprised at the anxiety of your reader to rewrite some of them, but as he seems to be interested in prosody, you might tell him from me that beats and feet are not the same thing." (The printer had altered Auden's text; de la Mare apologized and promised that it would not happen again.) Isherwood returned galleys of the Travel-Diary probably around 9 January 1939.

Faber asked for suggestions for the dust-jacket illustration, and Auden proposed a photograph of the military pass that Isherwood had used in China. Faber borrowed the pass, but used instead the cartoon from the frontispiece. The caption of the frontispiece was literally translated for Faber as "Terror Bequeathed", although Faber reported to Isherwood that the phrase could "equally well be translated 'We shall Remember' or 'Living for Revenge'". Isherwood preferred "Terror Bequeathed".

Auden and Isherwood left for New York on 18 January 1939, and had already agreed to have Faber make any necessary corrections in the page proofs without consulting them. Isherwood told Faber that Peter Fleming had offered to read the page proofs, and de la Mare asked Fleming for help on 24 January 1939. Fleming returned the page proofs on 2 February, with some minor corrections to the spelling of proper names as well as some more-extensive changes:

> I also made two or three alterations in passages relating to myself. None of these is of the slightest importance and I only put them in the light of my own memory (which is as likely as not at fault) of what had been said or done. None of them, I think, changes the author's meaning or lessens the effectiveness of his narrative; but please regard them as apologetic and completely unimportant suggestions rather than as changes about which I feel strongly.
>
> I enclosed a note with the proofs recommending that the name of T. C. Liu should be altered throughout. He was the correspondent of the official Chinese news agency in Tokyo, and if he saw the book, would undoubtedly be hurt by the feeling that he was losing face among his foreign friends. You could call him T. C. Ma or T. C. Ping or practically any other Chinese name.

Faber apparently accepted all of the changes Fleming asked for in passages about himself and about incidents at which he was present, but did not tell Auden or Isherwood that the changes had been made. Faber also accepted Fleming's suggestion that the name of T. C. Liu be replaced, and changed it throughout to A. W. Kao.

This edition restores the text of the page proofs, although it incorporates Fleming's spelling corrections.

Faber published its edition on 16 March 1939. Random House followed with a photo-offset edition on 11 August 1939. The Faber and Random House editions are identical, except that the running head in the Travel-Diary reads "Hongkong–Macao" in the Faber text and this obvious error was corrected to "Hongkong–Shanghai" in the Random House version.

All the poems in the book are by Auden. The Travel-Diary, although written as a first-person narrative by Isherwood, includes passages reworked by Isherwood from diary entries, articles printed in magazines, and travel narratives that he and Auden wrote during and after their journey. In addition to the articles published under the names of both Auden and Isherwood, which are reprinted in this edition, Isherwood published a summary account of the journey, "China in Wartime", in the *Listener*, 10 November 1938; this article was illustrated by five of Auden's photographs, all of them reprinted in the book.

Two of the notebooks that the authors used as diaries survive (both in a private collection). One notebook includes drafts of Auden's first four poems in the "London to Hongkong" sequence and other verse drafts, together with diary entries written alternately by Isherwood and Auden on the voyage from Egypt to Hong Kong, from 21 January 1938 to 16 February 1938. Isherwood later reshaped these entries as the magazine article "Escales" (p. 451). The other notebook includes Isherwood's account of their travels from 15 May to 3 June 1938, followed by Auden's notes dated 13 June; both these accounts were reworked into chapter 9 (from "Soon after midnight", p. 616) and chapter 10 (pp. 625–34) of the published Travel-Diary. Isherwood's notes dated 14 June follow; these he later adapted as part of "Meeting the Japanese" (p. 448).

Probably during their journey, Auden wrote out a two-part manuscript, "Hankow" (now in the British Library). This became the basis of part of the Travel-Diary. Chapter 2 (pp. 512–26) is based ultimately on "Hankow. Part I, The City"; the last part of chapter 6 (from "April 21", p. 574) and the first part of chapter 7 (to "That night Hankow celebrated its greatest aerial victory", p. 587) are based ultimately on "Hankow. Part II, Extract from a Journal".

The "series of newspaper articles" that Isherwood mentions in his Travel-Diary entry for 21 April 1938 (p. 574) probably became the "Chinese Diary" published partially over the names of both Auden and Isherwood in the *New Republic*, 1 June 1938, and partially over Isherwood's name only in the *New Statesman and Nation*, 25 June and 16 July 1938 (see p. 812).

After returning to England, Isherwood combined and rewrote the two parts of "Hankow" as a single typescript, "Hankow—Winter and Spring, 1938", which he signed by Auden and himself (now in the University of Tulsa Library). Isherwood prepared another typescript, "From Hankow to Shanghai, Through the Back Door" (also at Tulsa); in the published Travel-Diary this was heavily reworked in chapter 8 (from "May 7", p. 596) and chapter 9 (pp. 607–24), and some brief passages were used in other chapters.

The romanization of Chinese names altered from one typescript to another, and was largely regularized in the final typescript, thanks to the help of "Mr

Hughes of Oxford" (p. 495), presumably E. R. Hughes, Reader in Chinese Religion and Philosophy. No further regularization has been attempted here.

Auden's typescript of an early version of the "In Time of War" sonnets is in the Berg Collection. The partial setting copy for the book, formerly in the possession of E. R. Dodds, is in the University of Tulsa Library. It consists of the foreword, the six poems in "London to Hongkong", a partial typescript of the Travel-Diary (up to the middle of the entry for 10 May in chapter 8, p. 603), "In Time of War: A Sonnet Sequence", and "Commentary". The prose was typed by Isherwood, the poems probably by Auden, with the exception of sonnet XIV in "In Time of War", which is a revised version typed by Isherwood.

Auden printed some of the poems in the book in magazines, and republished most of them in his later collected and selected editions, as well as in the second edition of *Journey to a War*. Variant readings will be noted in the volumes of *Poems* in this complete edition. In the list below, *1945* signifies *The Collected Poetry of W. H. Auden* (and the corresponding 1950 British volume, *Collected Shorter Poems, 1930–1944*); *1966* signifies *Collected Shorter Poems, 1927–1957*. Titles introduced in later editions are noted in parentheses:

"To E. M. Forster": *1945*; revised in *1966* (as the last of the sequence "Sonnets from China").

"The Voyage": *1945*; revised in *1966* ("Whither?").

"The Sphinx": *1945*; the 1958 Penguin selection of Auden's poems (also published in 1959 in the Modern Library as *The Selected Poetry of W. H. Auden*); *1966*.

"The Ship": *The Listener*, 18 August 1938; *The New Republic*, 7 December 1938 (one of "Five Sonnets from China"); *1945*; revised in *1966*.

"The Traveller": *The New Statesman and Nation*, 27 August 1938; *1945*.

"Macao": *1945*; the 1958 Penguin selection of Auden's poems (also published in 1959 in the Modern Library as *The Selected Poetry of W. H. Auden*); *1966*.

"Hongkong": slightly revised in *1945* and *1966*.

"In Time of War": the entire sequence was reprinted in *1945*; sonnets VII ("The Bard"), XI ("Ganymede"), XII ("A New Age"), XVII ("Surgical Ward"), and XIX ("Embassy") were reprinted in the 1958 Penguin selection of Auden's poems (also published in 1959 in the Modern Library as *The Selected Poetry of W. H. Auden*); the sequence was severely revised and reduced to twenty-one "Sonnets from China" in *1966* (with sonnet XXV printed as a separate poem, "A Major Port").

Some of the sonnets were published separately: XI was reprinted in *Common Sense*, April 1939 ("Ganymede"); XII is revised from a version in *New Verse*, June–July 1936 ("The Economic Man"); XIII and XIV are based partly on sonnets printed in *The New Republic*, 7 December 1938 ("Press Conference" and "Air Raid", two of "Five Sonnets from China"); XVIII was printed in a facsimile of Auden's manuscript in the Hangkow newspaper *Ta Kung Pao*, 22 April 1938 (see p. 579), and reprinted in *The New Statesman and Nation*, 2 July 1938 ("Chinese Soldier"), *The Living Age*, September 1938, *China Weekly Review*, 29 October 1938, and (as one of "Five Sonnets from China") in *The New Republic,* 7 December 1938; XXI is revised from a version in *New Writing,* Autumn 1938 ("Exiles"), also printed in *The New Republic,* 7 December 1938 (as one of "Five Sonnets from China"); and XXVII is revised from a version in *The Listener,* 3 November 1938 ("Sonnet").

"Commentary": revised in *1945.* (Auden had earlier, perhaps around 1940, marked some slightly different revisions to this poem in a copy of *Journey to a War* that belonged to Caroline Newton and is now in the Berg Collection.)

§2 THE TEXT OF THE FIRST EDITION

Thanks to Isherwood's care, the text of the book is remarkably clean. The changes made to the page proofs by Peter Fleming after Auden and Isherwood left for America in January 1939 were of two kinds: corrections of the spelling of proper names, and revisions designed to protect the sensibilities of persons described in the Travel-Diary—including Fleming himself. The text in this edition is based on the page proofs, but incorporates Fleming's corrected spellings because Auden and Isherwood presumably hoped that he would provide these when they accepted his offer to read the proofs; the text also incorporates minor corrections to the punctuation of the page proofs evidently made by the publisher. The text excludes Fleming's other revisions, which the authors evidently did not ask for and almost certainly never discovered. All of Fleming's corrections and changes are noted below, whether or not incorporated in this edition.

Auden's alterations for the second edition are noted in §3.

Page 495.

Foreword. In the fourth paragraph, "MacFadyen" (here and in the travel diary) is the reading in the published text for "MacFayden" in the proofs; the correction may have been made by Fleming.

Page 499.

Travel-Diary. In the typescript that Isherwood delivered to Faber, this section was titled "*Journey to a War* (travel-diary section)". When de la Mare asked for a more specific title, Isherwood offered "Travel-Diary. February–June. 1938." The dates may have been dropped in proof.

In chapter 1, in the paragraph beginning "We had been invited to lunch" (p. 505), "Teh-chen" is probably Fleming's correction for the page proofs' "Ti-chen". Sir Victor Sassoon (p. 499) was an entrepreneur active in China and the Middle East. The U.S. gunboat *Panay* (p. 500) was sunk in 1937 by Japanese bombers while it was carrying Chinese refugees down the Yangtze.

In chapter 2, the typescript has a break before the paragraph that begins "Perhaps she is nearer" (p. 513). Nansen passports (p. 512) were issued by the Norwegian diplomat Fridjtof Nansen during his relief work in Russia in the 1920s. Mikhail Borodin (p. 516), the Soviet adviser in China, was forced out after Chiang Kai-shek's coup against the Communists in 1927.

In chapter 3, in the paragraph beginning "At half-past three" (p. 533), Fleming presumably altered "The Anglo-American Tobacco Company" to "The

British-American Tobacco Company"; the reading of the page proofs is retained here.

In chapter 5, in the paragraph beginning "Beyond 'Democracy'" (p. 554) the published text replaces "one-wheel" with "two-wheel". In the paragraph beginning "Mr Smith was something" (p. 561) and elsewhere in the Travel-Diary, "Shen-si" is probably Fleming's correction for "Shen-Si".

In chapter 6, in the paragraph beginning "Without our even asking" (p. 569), "Tiwha" is probably Fleming's correction for "Ty Hua". In the paragraph beginning "The Admiral" (p. 575) the published text omits "absurd". In the paragraph beginning "The party was" (p. 576), Fleming, who had been present at the scene described here, presumably caused the second sentence to be cut from the published text. The extract from "today's News Bulletin" immediately below this is printed as ordinary text, within quotation marks, in the Faber edition, but Isherwood's typescript makes clear that it should be set as an extract, with reduced spacing. The extract is from a mimeographed China Information Committee News Release, now in the University of Tulsa Library. On 12 December 1936 (p. 568) Chiang Kai-shek was kidnapped by General Chiang Hsüeh-liang in an attempt to force him to declare war on Japan.

In chapter 7, in the paragraph beginning "'Good morning, sir'" (p. 588), I have retained the comma after "sir", which was dropped in the published text but is characteristic of Isherwood's style.

In chapter 8, in the paragraph beginning "We returned" (p. 595) the published text changes "most unpleasant" to "very voluble" and "blasphemous" to "irritating". In the following paragraph "Hsiung" is presumably Fleming's correction for "Chang". In the paragraph beginning "Never forgetting" (pp. 595–96), I have not incorporated the change from the page proofs' "Do either of you" to the published text's "Does either of you"; the change was presumably made by the publisher. In the paragraph beginning "This morning Auden" (p. 596), I have retained the comma after "thumb", which was dropped in the published text. In the paragraph beginning "At Lanchi" (p. 601), the corrections "Tsin-pu" for "Tsing-pu" and "Fu-kien" for "Fu-Kien" were presumably made by Fleming. In the paragraph beginning "About half an hour" (p. 603), Fleming presumably corrected "Dr Lin" in the proofs to "Dr Robert Lim" in the published text; I have incorporated the corrected spelling, but have not added the first name. Two paragraphs below this, "Mr T. C. Liu, of the *Central News*," is altered in the published text to "Mr A. W. Kao, a newspaper man," at Fleming's suggestion, and T. C. Liu is changed to A. W. Kao in the remainder of the diary.

In chapter 9, in the first paragraph (p. 607), Fleming evidently caused the phrase "first-aid outfit" (and the preceding comma) to be omitted from the published text. In the paragraph beginning "In a building" (p. 609) Fleming evidently changed "a cavalry colonel" to "a transport officer". In the paragraph beginning "Near Yü-tsien", "Hsaio Shen" is probably Fleming's correction for "Shaio Shen". In the paragraph beginning "On this front" (p. 610), Fleming evidently caused the phrase "in the tone of one" to be replaced with "politely assuming the tone of one". In the paragraph beginning "The way up the pass" (p. 611), Fleming evidently caused "my rook-rifle" and "bolsheviks" to be replaced with "a rook-rifle" and "ideologists". In the paragraph beginning "We waited" (p. 616), Fleming evidently caused a phrase to be added (after a comma) at the end of the paragraph, after "sleep": "while soldiers installed a field-telephone in case headquarters had to warn us of an emergency." (This addition removed the additional line of space after the paragraph.) And in the next paragraph, Fleming caused "three soldiers" to be replaced with "three of these soldiers". In the paragraph beginning "T. C. had now become" (p. 618), Faber neglected to alter "Mr Liu" to "Mr Kao", although "T. C." was changed elsewhere in the paragraph to "A. W." In the paragraph beginning "At the temple" (p. 619), T. C. Liu's identity is masked in the published text by the replacement of "from the *Central News*" with "from his own paper".

Page 635.

Picture Commentary. The arrangement of headings in this section attempts to reconstruct the arrangement that the authors asked for but did not entirely receive. Isherwood specified the correct location of the headings when he returned the first set of proofs of the photographs on 25 December 1938. As specified in his letter, the proof copies (corrected from the first set of proofs of the photographs) and this edition print the four main headings, "United Front", "Soldiers and Civilians", "Foreigners", and "War Zone", at the head of each section. (In the proof copies, "Soldiers and Civilians" is wrongly placed at the head of the third page of photographs instead of the fourth.) In the published book the headings are printed as running heads at the top of every page (and the heading "Foreigners" is omitted entirely, with the running head "Soldiers and Civilians" continuing in its place).

When Isherwood returned the second proofs of the photographs around 9 January 1939, he wrote: "Please note that the titles on two pages 'Death' and 'Destruction' are to be removed, leaving only the sub-titles." The title "Death" had been printed below the photographs "The Innocent" and "The Guilty" (p. 656), and "Destruction" had been printed below "Dynamited Railway Bridge" and "Houses (Chapei in Shanghai)"; "Dynamited" is not present in the page proofs and was evidently added when the titles were deleted.

Some names that appear incorrectly in the proof copies are corrected in the published book and in this edition: Feng Yu-hsien is corrected to Feng Yü-hsiang (p. 636), Chang-chen to Chang Tschen (p. 639), and Clark-Kerr to Clark Kerr (p. 646). The published book also omits the names of T. C. Liu and T. Y. Liu from the page titled "Reporters" (p. 644), evidently for the same reason that T. C. Liu's name was altered in the text to A. W. Kao.

Five of the photographs illustrated Isherwood's article "China in Wartime", in the *Listener*, 30 November 1938, where they were credited to Auden. The five were captioned "General and Madame Chiang Kai-shek" (the lefthand photograph on p. 635); "Chapei, after bombardment by the Japanese" (the lower photograph on p. 657); "Refugee Camp" (the upper photograph on p. 660); "Rickshaw coolies" (the righthand photograph on p. 645); and "Refugees on the Lunghai railway: they travel anyhow—on the roof, and even on the couplings between the carriages" (the upper photograph on p. 659).

Page 667.

In Time of War. In sonnet XII (p. 672), Faber's proofreader, followed here, corrected "kobbold's", the reading of the typescripts and proof copies, to "kobold's". In sonnet XVII (p. 675), Faber or the compositor was probably responsible for inserting an apostrophe in "boist'rous"; I have restored "boistrous" (a standard early form of the word) from the typescripts. In sonnet XVI (p. 674), Nanking was the site of notorious Japanese atrocities when it was taken in 1937, and Dachau became the site of the first Nazi concentration camp in 1933.

In the setting copy of the typescript (now at the University of Tulsa Library), Auden deleted a stanza from "Commentary". It immediately followed the stanza that begins "And, if we care to listen" (p. 686):

> *And man can be self-ruined; he is out of nature;*
> *His love is limitless and all his own;*
> *Only his living, not his birth, can make him good.*

The published text of "Commentary" has "*The Prince*" (p. 685) in roman, not italics as in the proof copy, probably as a result of a redundant instruction to italicize it. The setting copy of the typescript does not indicate italics for any names or titles, and these may have been italicized by the publisher on Auden's instructions; perhaps Fahrenheit and Celsius (p. 685) were not italicized because the editor did not know they were names of persons. The Laufen Ice Retreat (p. 682) ended a supposed glaciation after the last ice age. The Zulu king Chaka (p. 685) is now commonly spelled Shaka, and Shang-tzu is an error for Hsün-tzu.

Page 689.

The foldout map at the end of the book was drawn by the firm of Stanford. On 30 November 1938 Faber sent Stanford a list of provinces, place-names, railways, and so forth that "the author" (probably Auden) wanted included, and told Stanford that the author wanted the map to be based on that in *The Times Atlas*, that it should include Sinkiang and western China but not Manchuria, that it should be as simple as possible, and that "only the three rivers mentioned need be shown" (presumably the three rivers in eastern China).

§3 THE 1973 SECOND EDITION

Faber published a second edition as a paperback on 2 July 1973; the new edition was never published in America. Isherwood made no changes in the Travel-Diary, but Auden replaced the original versions of his poems with the revised versions he had prepared in 1965 for *Collected Shorter Poems, 1927–1957*. The frontispiece, photographs, and map were dropped to reduce costs.

Immediately after the original foreword (from which the two paragraphs about the frontispiece and the stills from *Fight to the Last* were dropped), both authors appended brief comments:

SECOND THOUGHTS

1. *Literary*

When, after an interval of many years, I first re-read the sonnets in this book, I was very shocked to discover how carelessly I had written them. At the same time, their substance seemed to me to be worth salvaging, so I set to work. I have never revised earlier work quite so extensively as I have revised these poems, and I hope I shall never have to again.

The verse *Commentary* is, I know, far too "preachy" in manner and, were I to preach the same sermon to-day, I should do it very differently. I have always believed, however, that, among the many functions of the poet, preaching is one.

2. *Political*

Though for obvious reasons it is not overtly stated in our book, already in 1938 Isherwood and I had the hunch that the future of China lay with Mao and the Communists, not with Chiang Kai-shek and the Kuomintang. We were fools, of course, to swallow the propaganda, so zealously spread by certain Western journalists, that Chinese communism would be different and innocuous, a sort of non-totalitarian rural democracy, but our hunch proved correct, and, if only after 1945, the American State Department had felt it too, the contemporary political climate might be more pleasant. It is, surely, the first maxim of *realpolitik* that, whatever one's ideological preferences, one must never back a certain loser.

W.H.A.

Journey to a War was well received, on the whole, when it first appeared: but there were two or three critics, I seem to remember, who objected to Isherwood's narrative tone of voice. Isherwood is indeed all too conscious of being Little Me in China; his new riding-boots and his beret and his turtleneck sweater are symptoms of an amateur's stage-fright. So is his excessive use of similes. Disregarding these, however, one can pick up a surprisingly varied assortment of information from him about the country and the period. I therefore make no apology for the republication of his part of this book.

1973   C.I.

Auden's revised versions of the poems altered the text, titles, and arrangement of the first edition. Full details of variant readings will be noted in the volume of *Poems* in this complete edition.

Page 496.

    London to Hongkong. Although this part title is retained, the original sequence is replaced by the revised version of the sequence titled "A Voyage" in *Collected*

Shorter Poems, 1927–1957, and the heading "A Voyage" appears above the first poem. The six poems, all revised from the 1938 versions, appear in this order:

"I. Whither?" (originally titled "The Voyage")
"II. The Ship"
"III. The Sphinx"
"IV. Hong Kong"
"V. Macao"
"VI. A Major Port" (revised from sonnet XXV in the 1938 text of "In Time of War")

"The Traveller", one of the poems in the sequence in 1938, is dropped.

Page 667.

In Time of War. The original title is retained, but the sonnet sequence is replaced with the massively revised version that had been printed in *Collected Shorter Poems, 1927–1957*, where it was titled "Sonnets from China". In the *Collected Shorter Poems* version, however, the revised version of the dedicatory sonnet to E. M. Forster is placed as the final sonnet (XXI), while in the second edition of *Journey to a War* the revised version retains its original position at the front of the book. Of the original twenty-seven sonnets, the following are dropped: IX, X, XIV, XV, XX, XXV, and XXVI; the original XVII and XVIII are in reverse order; and the last four of the twenty sonnets in the second edition of *Journey to a War* correspond to those numbered in the first edition XXII, XXVII, XXIII, and XXIV.

Auden had already cut and revised the "Commentary" for his 1945 *Collected Poetry*, and dropped it entirely when preparing *Collected Shorter Poems, 1927– 1957*. For the second edition of *Journey to a War* he made new changes, without reference to those published in 1945. He deleted the stanzas that begin "The State is real", "Your Ignorance keep" (both p. 684), and "Only a whole" (p. 687), and changed "The voice of Man" (p. 687) to "The human cry". In laying out the stanzas that remained after Auden's cuts, Faber mistakenly inverted the two stanzas that begin "*Barrack and bivouac*" and "By wire and wireless" (p. 684).

INDEX OF TITLES, FIRST LINES,
AND BOOKS REVIEWED

This index includes titles of each of the works printed or described in this edition, the first lines of Auden's poems, and the titles and authors of the books Auden reviewed.

Titles of Auden's works that were originally published as separate books or pamphlets are printed in Large and Small Capitals. Titles of books that Auden edited or reviewed are in *italics*. Titles of Auden's essays, reviews, and poems, and the first lines of his poems, are all printed in roman type, as are the names of the authors of books reviewed and the names of persons who were the subjects of essays.